THE WHITEHALL COMPANION 1992

THE WHITEHALL COMPANION 1992

Foreword by Sir Robin Butler GCB CVO
Secretary of the Cabinet and Head of the Home Civil Service

Copyright © Dod's Publishing and Research Limited 1992

Editor: Hilary Muggridge

Editorial Adviser: William Plowden

Assistant Editors: Polly Kelly, Sally Wilson

Production Editor: Isobel Smythe-Wood

Editorial: Carley Brown, Diana Lecore, Philippa Muggridge, Valerie Passmore, Peter Rea, Kate Truman

Design: Angela Marsh

Published by Dod's Publishing and Research Limited
60 Chandos Place
London WC2N 4HG England
Chairman: Lord Holme of Cheltenham

First published in 1992

ISBN 1 872110 85 1

Typeset by Method Limited, Epping, Essex

Printed in the United Kingdom by Redwood Press Ltd

CONTENTS

Next Steps Executive Agencies 761
A complete alphabetical list of agencies will be found at the beginning of this section

Regulatory Organisations and Public Bodies 857
A complete alphabetical list of organisations will be found at the beginning of this section

FOREWORD

Dod's Parliamentary Companion has long been a familiar friend on the desks of Whitehall, and the European Companion will be of great and growing value as the work of the British government becomes more and more closely meshed with the European Community. I feel that it is a matter of some shame that the Whitehall Companion is the last into the field. The circumstances which make such a venture valuable to the public have not recently come into being; and I hope that the era in which it was thought that the administrative machinery of Whitehall was best shrouded from public knowledge is long since past. Nothing is more infuriating for someone who has business to do with a government department than not to know where to start and to be passed from place to place, travelling hopefully but repeatedly disappointed in hopes of arriving at the right destination.

Now The Whitehall Companion, compiled with the help of departments and of the individuals who feature in it, is available to help you find your way round the bureaucratic jungle and also to tell you something about the senior residents of it. Its publication fits the tone of these times in which it is recognised that service to the public includes giving an identity for those on the other end of the line to deal with. It is consistent with the mood of open government – welcome, I believe, inside government as well as outside – which is less timid about telling the public how government departments work and how to set about approaching and dealing with them.

The Whitehall Companion, produced to the same high standard as its stablemates, will give pleasure as well as utility to its readers. I am glad to have played a part in arranging for its compilers the access necessary for its preparation and I hope it has the success and popularity which I think it deserves.

Robin Butler

Sir Robin Butler GCB CVO
Secretary of the Cabinet and
Head of the Home Civil Service

Acknowledgements

We are grateful for the support and encouragement of Sir Robin Butler, Secretary of the Cabinet Office and Head of the Home Civil Service, and Sir David Gillmore, Head of the Diplomatic Service, for this project. They opened many Whitehall doors and to them both our thanks are due.

But the Whitehall Companion could certainly not have been published in such a comprehensive way without the help and advice of many patient and long-suffering civil servants and officials in the parliamentary offices, government departments, next steps agencies and other bodies which go to make up this directory. To two of those in particular we should like to extend our gratitude: Alastair Howie and Elaine McNaughton of the Machinery of Government Division in the Cabinet Office. They have been involved from the beginning in helping us through what Sir Robin describes in his Foreword as "the bureaucratic jungle", and their help and advice has been invaluable.

Our thanks also to all those who agreed to appear in the biographies section of the book.

Finally our thanks to the unflagging and hardworking editorial team listed earlier, and to our indefatigable typesetters.

ABOUT THIS BOOK

This is the first edition of *The Whitehall Companion*, published by Dod's Publishing and Research, the first time that a single volume has brought together the biographies of senior civil servants and other top people in Whitehall and its environs, with the structure and functions of government departments, next steps agencies and various regulatory and public bodies.

Readers should note that some departments, particularly the Ministry of Defence and the Department of Trade and Industry, have recently undergone, or are experiencing, substantial change. *The Whitehall Companion* has provided as much information about these departments as was available at the time of going to press.

Last minute changes are included in the Addenda.

Biographies

The biographical section runs first and each entry contains some or all of the following information:
– Name, present job and grade (where known/if applicable) printed in bold type at the beginning of each entry
– Career details and information on any current non-Whitehall positions
– Some personal details: education, professional qualifications, honours and decorations, name of spouse, children and recreations
– Office addresses and fax numbers

There are biographies of:
– Top civil servants in government departments
– Chief executives and other senior staff in the government's "next steps" executive agencies
– Senior people in a selection of regulatory organisations and other public bodies
– Ministers' advisers
– Staff in the No 10 Policy Unit

Civil servants included in this section are mainly grades 1–4 but, occasionally, grades 5–6 where the person concerned runs a next steps executive agency.

We have not included the biographies of ministers which can be found in the current edition of Dod's Parliamentary Companion.

Institutions

Parliamentary Offices

This section covers alphabetically the parliamentary offices which are organised as follows:

Introduction
– Where relevant, when the office was founded
– Status
– Organisation
– Responsibilities

Officials
– Addresses, telephone and, where relevant, fax numbers
– Listing of senior officials

Overview
– A brief overview of the work of the office, which indicates visually the management structure which links senior officials with other staff

Officials and their Offices
– Visual presentation of all the different sections within the offices showing the management structure, including top officials, senior staff, the departments with which they deal, and the work they do

Government Departments

This section covers government departments. The entries are organised alphabetically as follows:

Introduction
– Date founded
– Number and level of ministers
– To which minister responsible if a non-ministerial department
– Responsibilities
– Names and numbers of executive agencies sponsored by that department (full details of the executive agencies carried in the next section below)

Ministers
– Main address, telephone and fax numbers of departments
– Ministers, their special advisers, parliamentary private secretaries and private secretaries
– House of Lords spokesmen

Ministers' Responsibilities
– Detailed list of each minister's responsibilities

Departmental Overview
– A brief overview of the department's work which indicates visually the management structure which links ministers to civil servants to divisions within each department.

Civil Servants and Department
– Visual presentation of all the different sections within a department showing the management structure including top officials, senior staff (grades 1/2 down to grades 5/6), the divisions with which they deal and the work those divisions do.

Addresses/telephone/fax numbers
– Details of the department's subsidiary addresses

'Next Steps' Agencies

Details of the government's 75 'next steps' executive agencies in alphabetical order of agency. At the beginning of the section is a listing of all the agencies, plus the 26 candidates being considered for agency status
    Each entry consists of:
– Name, address, telephone and fax numbers
– Senior staff
– Responsibilities
– Sponsoring department
– Date launched

Regulatory Organisations and Public Bodies

A selection of about 80 regulatory and public bodies including for example, OFTEL, the Office of Telecommunications, the Monopolies and Mergers Commission, the Parliamentary Ombudsmen and the Independent Television Commission. At the beginning of each section is a complete list of all the organisations included. The alphabetical entries are organised as follows:
— Name, address, telephone and fax numbers
— Senior officials/staff
— Responsibilities
— Date founded

Abbreviations

A complete list of abbreviations of honours and decorations, academic and professional qualifications, parliamentary offices, government departments, next steps agencies and other organisations.
This list should be used in conjunction with the complete name index (see below).

Indexes

— A name index of every person mentioned and where in the Companion they can be located. (The biographical section only includes grades 1–4). This index should be used in conjunction with the Abbreviations Section (see above).
— A general purpose index which includes the names of all the departments and organisations covered in the Companion.

Civil Service Grading

Home Civil Service

Details of the grading within the Home Civil Service is set out below.

0	Head of the Home Civil Service	
1	Permanent Secretary	Permanent head of a government department or (Grade 1A) head of
1A	2nd Permanent Secretary	distinct and major areas of policy within departments
2	Deputy Secretary	Heads of small departments or large executive agencies*. Heads of professions or substantial areas of policy within departments
3	Under Secretary	Comparable to board members in major companies. Most common level for holders of non-executive directorships
4		Generally senior professional civil servants
5	Assistant Secretary	Heads of discrete areas of policy

6	Senior Principal	In major executive areas** may command large regions with up to 30 local offices

7	Principal	In headquarters offices heads of smallest units of command reporting to grade 5

In executive areas heads of larger local offices

Higher Executive Officer (Development (HEOD)

Administration Trainee (AT)

Fast stream entry points to civil service for graduates or serving civil servants with two years service

Senior Executive Officer (SEO)

In headquarters offices may be either heads of smaller branches or deputise for grade 7s heads of larger branches.

In executive areas heads of small local offices or second tier of management in large offices. SEOs often manage over 100 staff

Higher Executive Officer HEO

In headquarters offices HEOs often work directly to grade 7s, helping formulate and amend policy, prepare briefings, and represent their branches at meetings

In executive areas HEOs have substantial management reponsibilities or deal with complex casework or a mixture of the two

Executive Officer (EO)

A major recruitment grade. In headquarters offices EOs help formulate and amend policy, prepare first drafts of briefings, gather and analyse information, and manage support staff. They normally work to an HEO

In executive areas, EOs manage large of clerical staff (AOs and AAs) where these are the working grades, or carry out relatively complex casework

Administrative Officer (AO)

Administrative Assistant (AA)

These grades carry out the more routine casework, data processing and provide clerical support to more senior staff

* Executive Agencies are headed up at levels appropriate to the size and responsibilities of the agency

** Executive areas of government, which include Next Steps agencies, are responsible for providing public services, such as paying sickness benefits and pensions, collecting taxes and national insurance contributions, running employment services, and providing services to industry and agriculture.

Note: Staff in the above grades represent 66% of the non-industrial civil service. The remaining 34% comprises professional staff and other grades, eg scientists, lawyers, prison officers etc

Diplomatic Service

The Diplomatic Service operates a different system of grading, details of which are given below.

PUS	No grade 1s in FCO
Senior grades 1 – 5	*Specialist/support staff:* Chief Economic Adviser
4	Conference Interpreter; Legal Counsellor *Specialist/support staff:* Senior Economic Adviser
5S	Senior Principal; Research Officer; Senior Assistant Legal Officer *Specialist/support staff:* Accountant
5	Principal; Research Officer; Assistant Legal Officer *Specialist/support staff:* Senior Investigating Officer; Economic Adviser; Accountant
6	*Specialist/support staff:* includes librarians, translators, information and field investigating officers and senior professional and technology officers
7D	Senior Research Officer *Specialist/support staff:* Senior Economic Assistant
7M	*Specialist/support staff:* includes librarians, translators, lecturers, information and field investigating officers and higher professional and technology officers, mapping and charting officers
8	Research Officer *Specialist/support staff:* Economic Assistant
9 S1	junior executive staff; senior secretarial staff
10 S2	clerks; personal secretaries
S3C	secretarial staff

Below is an abbreviated guide to the equivalent Home Civil Service and Diplomatic Service grades

Home Civil Service	Diplomatic Service
1	Permanent Under Secretary
2 – 4	Senior grades 1 – 5
5	DS 4

6	DS 5S
7	DS 5
SEO	DS 6
HEO(D)	DS 7D
HEO	DS 7M
AT	DS 8
EO	DS 9/S1
AO	DS 10/S2
AA	—
Clerical	DS S3C

ADDENDA

Cabinet Office/Office of Public Service and Science

Richard Mottram (previously Deputy Secretary, Defence Staff, Defence Policy, Ministry of Defence) has moved to the Cabinet Office/Office of Public Service and Science as Head of the OPSS and Chief Accounting Officer to replace **Sir Peter Kemp** who retired on 14 September 1992. At the time of going to press Mr Mottram's replacement at MoD had not been named.

Richard Bird (previously Head of Road and Vehicle Safety Directorate, Department of Transport) is now Under Secretary, Home and Social Affairs and Legislation Secretariat, Cabinet Office, replacing **A M Russell** who returns to the Scottish Office. **Mr Bird** is replaced by **Miss Sophia Lambert.**

Education

Sir Geoffrey Holland KCB (currently Permanent Secretary at the Employment Department Group) is to be Permanent Secretary at the Department of Education from 13 January 1993, replacing **Sir John Caines KCB** who is retiring.

Roger Dawe (previously Director of Training Enterprise and Education at the Employment Department Group), moved to be Head of the Higher and Further Education Division at Education on 10 August. He replaces

John Vereker who moved to be Head of the Schools Division at Education on that same date. Mr Vereker replaces **Nick Stuart** who has moved to Employment.

Employment

Nicholas Monck CB (presently Second Permanent Secretary, Public Expenditure Group, HM Treasury) will replace **Sir Geoffrey Holland** as Permanent Secretary, Employment Department Group on 13 January 1993.

Nick Stuart (previously Head of the Schools Division, Department for Education), moved to be Director of Resources, Employment Department Group on 10 August 1992, replacing

Ian Johnston who became Head of the Training and Enterprise Division at Employment on that date, replacing

Roger Dawe who has moved to Education.

Home Office

Carolyn Sinclair is now Assistant Under Secretary, Police Department, replacing **Stephen Boys Smith** who has moved to the Treasury.

Scottish Office

A M Russell (previously Under Secretary, Home and Social Affairs and Legislation Secretariat, Cabinet Office) is now Under Secretary, Housing Division, Environment Department Scottish Office.

HM Treasury

Andrew Turnbull CB (currently Deputy Secretary, Finance, Public Finance, HM Treasury) will replace Nicholas Monck as Second Permanent Secretary, Public Expenditure Group, HM Treasury on 13 January 1993. At the time of going to press Mr Turnbull's replacement had not been named.

Stephen Boys Smith (previously Assistant Under Secretary, Police Department in the Home Office) is now Under Secretary, Civil Service Management and Pay, HM Treasury. He is replaced at the Home Office by Miss Carolyn Sinclair.

Trade and Industry

R M Rumbelow (previously Head of Services Management, Establishment and Finance Divison, at Trade and Industry) is now Head of Electronics and Electrical Engineering, and Mechanical Engineering in the Industry 2 Division, DTI)

John Cammell (previously Head of Electronics and Electrical Engineering and Mechanical Engineering in the Industry 2 Division, Department of Trade and Industry) will continue to advise the Deputy Secretary, Alastair Macdonald, Head of Industry 2 Division.

Transport

Miss Sophia Lambert has replaced Richard Bird as Head of Road and Vehicle Safety Directorate. Mr Bird has moved to the Cabinet Office.

Highlands and Islands Enterprise

Sir Robert Cowan retired as Chairman of Highlands and Islands Enterprise on 1 September. He was replaced by Fraser Morrison, Chairman and Managing Director of Morrison Construction Group.

DOD'S
REPORT

WESTMINSTER · WHITEHALL · BRUSSELS

The authoritative guide to developments in Parliament and politics

Published ten times a year, The Dod's Report
provides its subscribers with a comprehensive and
well-informed overview and update of activity in
Parliament at Westminster, in Whitehall and the
Civil Service and in the European Community.

Published by
Dod's Publishing and Research Ltd
60 Chandos Place, London, WC2N 4HG

Telephone *Editorial:* 071-240 3902   *Subscriptions:* 081-863 5995

Biographies

A-Z

A

ABBOTT, Rear Admiral PETER CHARLES   Assistant Chief of Naval Staff, Ministry of Defence

Career: RN service 1964-: flag officer Flotilla Two 1989-91; assistant chief of naval staff, Ministry of Defence 1991-

Date of birth: 12 February 1942 *Education/professional qualifications:* Queen's College, Cambridge; Royal College of Defence Studies 1985

Rear Admiral Peter C Abbott, Assistant Chief of Defence Staff, Ministry of Defence, Whitehall, London SW1A 2HB *Telephone:* 071-218 9000

ADAMS, GORDON DUDLEY   Secretary of the Commission for Local Administration in England (Local Government Ombudsman)

Career: hospital secretary various London hospitals 1962-68; deputy house governor Hammersmith hospital 1968-74; district administrator North Hammersmith health district 1974-76; Bromley health authority 1976-87: area administrator 1976-82, district administrator 1982-86, director of planning 1986-87; secretary of Commission for Local Administration in England 1987-

Date of birth: 28 July 1934 *Education/professional qualifications:* Grammar School, Bristol; King's College, London, classics (BA 1956) *Marital status:* divorced; 1 daughter *Recreations:* music, photography, DIY

Gordon D Adams Esq, Secretary of the Commission for Local Administration in England, 21 Queen Anne's Gate, London SW1H 9BU *Telephone:* 071-222 5622 *Fax:* 071-233 0396

ADAMS, KEITH   Special Adviser to Minister for Agriculture, Fisheries and Food

Career: political secretary John Selwyn Gummer; research assistant Michael Marshall MP; special adviser to Mr Gummer, Minister for Agriculture, Fisheries and Food

Keith Adams Esq, Special Adviser, Ministry of Agriculture, Fisheries and Food, Whitehall Place, London SW1A 2HH *Telephone:* 071-270 3000

ADDISON, MARK ERIC   Director, Finance and Resource Management, Employment Department Group   Grade: 3

Career: British Airways 1973-74; Department of Employment (DEmp), Health and Safety Executive and Manpower Services Commission 1978-82; DEmp 1982-85; private secretary (PS) parliamentary under secretary 1982-83, principal training policy 1983-85; PS to prime minister 1985-88; DEmp 1989-: London, regional director Training Agency (later Training, Enterprise and Education Directorate) 1988-91; under secretary, director finance and resource management, resources and strategy directorate 1991-

Date of birth: 22 January 1951 *Education/professional qualifications:* Marlborough College; St John's College, Cambridge, engineering (BA, MA 1972); City University, management science (MSc 1973); Imperial College, London, industrial sociology (PhD, DIC 1979) *Marital status:* married Lucy Booth 1987

Dr Mark E Addison, Director, Finance and Resource Management, Employment Department Group, Caxton House, Tothill Street, London, SW1H 9NF *Telephone:* 071-273 5789 *Fax:* 071-273 6059

AINSCOW, ROBERT MORRISON   Deputy Secretary, Overseas Development Administration   Grade: 2

Career: Ministry of Overseas Development 1968-: head South Asia department 1976-79, under secretary 1979-86, deputy secretary 1986-

Date of birth: 3 June 1936   *Education/professional qualifications:* Liverpool University, economics (BA)

Robert M Ainscow Esq CB, Deputy Secretary, Overseas Development Administration, Eland House, Stag Place, London SW1E 5DH   *Telephone:* 071-273 3000

ALCOCK, Air Marshal ROBERT JAMES MICHAEL   Chief of Logistic Support, RAF, Ministry of Defence

Career: RAF service 1959-: air officer engineering HQ Strike Command 1988-91; chief of logistics support RAF, Ministry of Defence 1991-

Date of birth: 11 July 1936   *Education/professional qualifications:* Victoria College, Jersey; Royal Aircraft Establishment (CEng; FIMechE)

Air Marshal Robert J M Alcock CB, Chief of Logistic Support, RAF, Ministry of Defence, Whitehall, London SW1A 2HB   *Telephone:* 071-218 9000

ALDERSON, MATTI   Director-General, Advertising Standards Authority

Career: legal executive Scottish law practices 1970-72; assistant to director Poster Bureau 1972-74, Royds Advertising 1974-75; Advertising Standards Authority 1975-: executive and secretary health and nutrition committee 1975-80, manager advertising practice committee 1980-89, deputy director 1989-90, deputy director-general 1990, director-general 1990-   *Current non-Whitehall posts:* secretary Committee of Advertising Practice 1990-; governor Communications, Advertising and Marketing Foundation 1990-; vice-chairman European Advertising Standards Alliance 1991-

Date of birth: 20 December 1951   *Education/professional qualifications:* Bearsden Academy, Strathclyde; Open University   *Marital status:* married Alan 1970   *Recreations:* study, travel, reading, driving

Mrs Matti Alderson, Director-General, Advertising Standards Authority, Brook House, 2-16 Torrington Place, London WC1E 7HN   *Telephone:* 071-580 5555   *Fax:* 071-631 3051

ALDRIDGE, DENNIS STANLEY   South West Regional Controller, Inland Revenue   Grade: 4

Career: Inland Revenue 1952-: tax officer (higher grade) 1952-62; tax inspector (TI) 1962-64; TI (higher grade) 1964-71; Senior TI 1971-76; principal TI 1976-81; senior principal TI 1981-: regional controller south west 1991-   *Current non-Whitehall posts:* evangelist Reorganised Church of Jesus Christ of Latter Day Saints 1991-; chairman Camp Quality UK 1987-

Date of birth: 26 May 1934   *Education/professional qualifications:* Belle Vue Grammar School, Bradford   *Marital status:* married Jean Elizabeth 1955; 1 son, 2 daughters   *Recreations:* church work, voluntary work

Dennis S Aldridge Esq, Regional Controller, Inland Revenue, Finance House, Barnfield Road, Exeter EX1 1QX   *Telephone:* 0392 77801   *Fax:* 0392 216803

ALDRIDGE, TREVOR MARTIN   Commissioner, Law Commission   Grade: 2

Career: partner Bower Cotton and Bower (solicitors) 1962-84; law commissioner 1984-

Date of birth: 22 December 1933 *Education/professional qualifications:* Frensham Heights School, Rowledge, Farnham; Sorbonne, Paris, French civilisation (degree 1952); St John's College, Cambridge, law (BA 1955, MA) *Marital status:* married Joanna 1966; 1 son, 1 daughter *Publications:* numerous *Clubs:* United Oxford and Cambridge University

Trevor M Aldridge Esq, Commissioner, Law Commission, Conquest House, 37-38 John Street, London WC1N 2BQ *Telephone:* 071-411 1219 *Fax:* 071-411 1295

ALLAN, ALEXANDER CLAUD STUART   Principal Private Secretary to Prime Minister   Grade: 3

Career: HM Customs and Excise 1973-76; HM Treasury 1976-: principal private secretary to Chancellor of Exchequer 1986-89; under secretary: international finance 1989-90, general expenditure policy 1990-92; principal private secretary to Prime Minister 1992-

Date of birth: 9 February 1951 *Education/professional qualifications:* Harrow; Clare College, Cambridge, mathematics (BA 1972); University College, London, statistics (MSc 1973) *Marital status:* married Katie Clemson 1978 *Clubs:* Royal Ocean Racing *Recreations:* Grateful Dead music, sailing, computers, bridge

Alexander C S Allan Esq, Principal Private Secretary to the Prime Minister, 10 Downing Street, London SW1A 2AA *Telephone:* 071-930 4433

ALLAN, RICHARD ANDREW   Director of Personnel, Department of Transport   Grade: 3

Career: assistant principal/principal Department of [Trade and] Industry 1970-79; civil aviation and shipping first secretary Washington embassy 1980-84; Department of Transport 1984-: assistant secretary 1984-88: principal private secretary to secretaries of state 1985-87, under secretary 1988-: seconded to British Rail 1988-90, director of personnel 1990-

Date of birth: 28 February 1948 *Education/professional qualifications:* Bolton School; Balliol College, Oxford, modern history (BA 1969, MA) *Marital status:* married Katharine Mary Tait 1975; 1 daughter, 1 son *Recreations:* choral singing, walking, theatre

Richard A Allan Esq, Director of Personnel, Department of Transport, Lambeth Bridge House, Albert Embankment, London SE1 7SB *Telephone:* 071-238 4449 *Fax:* 071-238 5215

ALLEN, (PHILIP) RICHARD HERNAMAN   Commissioner and Director, Organisation, HM Customs and Excise   Grade: 3

Career: HM Customs and Excise (C&E) 1970-73; assistant private secretary (APS) to paymaster general HM Treasury 1973-74; APS to chancellor of Duchy of Lancaster, Cabinet Office 1974-75; C & E 1975-: principal 1975-84, assistant secretary 1984-90, commissioner and director internal taxes directorate 1990-91, commissioner and director organisation 1991-

Date of birth: 26 January 1949 *Education/professional qualifications:* Loughborough Grammar School; Merton College, Oxford, modern history (BA 1970) *Marital status:* married Vanessa Lampard 1970; 2 daughters *Recreations:* music, badminton, gardening, beer spotting

P Richard H Allen Esq, Commissioner, HM Customs and Excise, New King's Beam House, 22 Upper Ground, London SE1 9PJ *Telephone:* 071-620 1313

Parliamentary Offices
see page 275

ALLEN, RICHARD IAN GORDON   Under Secretary and Head of Local Government Group, HM Treasury   Grade: 3

Career: HM Treasury 1978-: under secretary overseas finance, European Communities group 1988-90; under secretary and head of local government group 1990-

Date of birth: 13 December 1944   *Education/professional qualifications:* Edinburgh University (MA)

Richard I G Allen Esq, Under Secretary, HM Treasury, Parliament Street, London SW1P 3AG *Telephone:* 071-270 3000

ALLIN, GEORGE   Director-General Ship Refitting, Ministry of Defence   Grade: 3

Career: Royal Navy 1957-; principal director ship refitting Ministry of Defence (MoD) 1986-87; seconded to Brown and Root as director of Aldermaston projects 1987-89; director-general, ship refitting MoD 1989-

Date of birth: 21 June 1933   *Education/professional qualifications:* Devonport Dockyard Technical College; Royal Naval Engineering College Manadon; Royal Naval College Greenwich; BSc

George Allin Esq, Director-General, Ship Refitting, Ministry of Defence, Carpenter House, Bath *Telephone:* 0225-472285

ALLISON, RODERICK STUART   Director, Special Hazards Division, Health and Safety Executive   Grade: 3

Career: Health and Safety Executive 1989-: under secretary Department of Employment 1971-89; director special hazards division 1989-

Date of birth: 28 November 1936   *Education/professional qualifications:* Balliol College, Oxford

Roderick S Allison Esq, Director, Special Hazards Division, Health and Safety Executive, Baynards House, 1 Chepstow Place, Westbourne Grove, London W2 4TF   *Telephone:* 071-243 6630

ALLNUTT, DENIS EDWIN   Head of Analytical Services Branch, Department for Education   Grade: 4

Career: statistician and assistant statistician Ministry of Housing and Local Government, Department of Environment, (DoE), Department of Transport 1967-82; chief statistician (CS) (employment) Department of Employment 1982-88; CS (housing) DoE 1988-90; head of analytical services branch (economic, operational research and statistical work) Department of Education [and Science] 1990-

Date of birth: 17 May 1946   *Education/professional qualifications:* Hampton School, Middlesex; Birmingham University, mathematical statistics (BSc 1967)

Denis E Allnutt Esq, Head of Analytical Services Branch, Department for Education, Sanctuary Buildings, Great Smith Street, London, SW1P 3BT   *Telephone:* 071-925 5400   *Fax:* 071-925 6000

AMOS, VALERIE   Chief Executive, Equal Opportunities Commission

Career: Hackney Borough Council 1985-89; chief executive Equal Opportunities Commission 1989-

Date of birth: 13 March 1954   *Education/professional qualifications:* University of Warwick, sociology (BA); University of Birmingham, cultural studies (MA); University of East Anglia

Ms Valerie Amos, Chief Executive, Equal Opportunities Commission, Overseas House, Quay Street, Manchester M3 3HN   *Telephone:* 061-833 9244

ANDERSON, GAVIN ALAN   Deputy Chief Executive, NHS in Scotland, Scottish Home and Health Department, Scottish Office   Grade: 4

Career: research architect Edinburgh University 1966-73; Scottish Development Department 1973-85: architect 1973-76, principal architect 1976-85; Scottish Office Home and Health Department 1985-: assistant secretary 1985-90, director of strategic management (strategic planning and performance review, estates, central services), deputy chief executive NHS in Scotland 1990-

Date of birth: 5 July 1939   *Education/professional qualifications:* Edinburgh College of Art, architecture (Dip Arch 1965); Edinburgh University, architecture (M Phil 1977)   *Marital status:* married Margaret Clarke 1965; 1 son, 1 daughter   *Recreations:* music, art, reading, walking

Gavin A Anderson Esq, Deputy Chief Executive, NHS in Scotland, Scottish Office Home and Health Department, St Andrew's House, Edinburgh EH1 3DE   *Telephone:* 031-244 2137

ANDREWS, Sir DEREK HENRY   Permanent Secretary, Ministry of Agriculture, Fisheries and Food   Grade: 1

Career: Ministry of Agriculture, Fisheries and Food (MAFF) 1957-66: assistant private secretary (PS) to minister 1960-61; principal 1961-68: PS to prime minister 1966-70; assistant secretary 1968-73; Kennedy School Harvard University, USA 1970-71; MAFF 1971-: under secretary 1973-81, deputy secretary 1981-87, permanent secretary 1987-

Date of birth: 17 February 1933   *Education/professional qualifications:* London School of Economics, geography and geology (BA 1955)   *Honours, decorations:* CBE 1970, CB 1984, KCB 1991   *Marital status:* married Catharine May Childe 1956 (died 1982); 2 sons, 1 daughter   *Clubs:* Reform

Sir Derek Andrews KCB CBE, Permanent Secretary, Ministry of Agriculture, Fisheries and Food, Whitehall Place, London SW1A 7HH   *Telephone:* 071-270 8701   *Fax:* 071-270 8845

APPLEYARD, LEONARD VINCENT   Deputy Under Secretary, Policy Planning Europe, Foreign and Commonwealth Office

Career: HM Diplomatic Service 1962-: head of economic relations department Foreign and Commonwealth Office (FCO) 1982-84; principal private secretary to secretary of state for foreign and commonwealth affairs 1984-1986; ambassador to Hungary 1986-89; deputy secretary Cabinet Office (on secondment) 1989-92; deputy under secretary policy planning Europe, FCO 1992-

Date of birth: 2 September 1938   *Education/professional qualifications:* Queens' College Cambridge (MA)   *Honours, decorations:* CMG 1986

Leonard V Appleyard CMG, Cabinet Office, 70 Whitehall, London SW1A 2AS   *Telephone:* 071-270 3000

ASHENHURST, Maj Gen (FRANCIS) FRANK ERNEST   Director, Defence Dental Services, Ministry of Defence

Career: officer commanding Rhine area dental unit 1964-66; chief instructor depot and training establishment Royal Army Dental College (RADC) 1967-71; commanding officer (CO) army dental centres, Hong Kong 1971-73; CO 6 Dental Group UK Land Forces 1973-76; assistant director army dental service (ADS) 1977-78; CO 1 Dental Group BAOR 1978-81; deputy director ADS 1981-84;

commandant HQ and central group RADC 1984; deputy commander medical (dentistry) BAOR 1984-86; command HQ and technical services RADC BAOR 1986-88; director ADS 1989-, director defence dental services (for all armed services) 1990-

Date of birth: 1 April 1933 *Education/professional qualifications:* Methodist College, Belfast; Queen's University, Belfast, dentistry (BDS 1955); London Hospital Medical School, dental public health (MSc 1977) *Honours, decorations:* O St J 1974; QHDS 1989 *Recreations:* music, sport, cooking, gardening, nature studies

Major General Frank E Ashenhurst, Director of Defence Dental Services, Ministry of Defence, First Avenue House, High Holborn, London WC1V 6HE *Telephone:* 071-430 5733 *Fax:* 071-430 5332

ASHKEN, KENNETH RICHARD   Director, Policy and Communications Group, Crown Prosecution Service

Career: Office of Director of Public Prosecutions Crown Prosecution Service 1972-: head of policy and information division 1986-90; director policy and communications group 1990-

Date of birth: 13 June 1945 *Education/professional qualifications:* London University, law (LLB); Cambridge Institute of Criminology (dipl)

Kenneth R Ashken Esq, Director, Policy and Communications Group, Crown Prosecution Service, 4-12 Queen Anne's Gate, London SW1H 9AZ *Telephone:* 071-273 8124

ASSCHER, Professor Sir (ADOLF) WILLIAM   Chairman, Committee on Safety of Medicines, Medicines Control Agency

Career: medical: London Hospital 1957-64; senior lecturer and honorary consultant physician, later reader and professor of medicine University of Wales College of Medicine and Cardiff Royal Infirmary 1964-87; professor of medicine and honorary consultant physician St George's Hospital London 1988-. Department of Health 1976-: member Clinical Trials Sub-committee Committee on Safety of Medicines (CSM) 1976-80; member Medicines Commission 1980-84, Committee on Review of Medicines: vice-chairman 1984-85, chairman 1985-87; CSM 1985-: member 1985, chairman 1987- *Current non-Whitehall posts:* dean St George's Hospital Medical School, London University 1988-; non-executive director Wandsworth District Health Authority 1990-

Date of birth: 20 March 1931 *Education/professional qualifications:* Maerlant Lyceum, The Hague, Netherlands; London Hospital Medical College, London University, medicine (BSc 1954, MB BS 1957, MD 1963, MRCP 1959, FRCP 1970) *Honours, decorations:* Kt 1992 *Marital status:* married Dr Jennifer Lloyd MB, MFCM 1962; 2 daughters *Publications:* Urinary Tract Infections (OUP 1973); The Challenge of Urinary Tract Infections (Academic Press 1980); Nephrology Illustrated (Gower Medical Press 1982); Nephro-Urology (Heinemann Medical 1983); Medicines and Risk Benefit Decisions (MTP Press 1985); Clinical Atlas of the Kidney (Gower Medical Press 1991) *Clubs:* Reform *Recreations:* golf, visual arts

Professor Sir William Asscher, Chairman, Committee on Safety of Medicines, c/o Dean's Office, St George's Hospital Medical School, Cranmer Terrace, London SW17 0RE *Telephone:* 081-672 3122 *Fax:* 081-672 6940

Government Departments
see page 300

 **ATTRIDGE, ELIZABETH ANN JOHNSTON** Under Secretary, Horticulture, Plant Protection and Agricultural Resources, Ministry of Agriculture, Fisheries and Food Grade: 3

Career: assistant principal (AP) department of education Northern Ireland 1955-56; Ministry of Agriculture, Fisheries and Food 1956-: AP 1956-59, 1961-63; principal: plant health 1963-66, finance 1966-69, external relations 1969-72; assistant secretary: animal health 1972-75, marketing policy and potatoes 1975-78, tropical foods 1978-83; under secretary: EC 1983-85, emergencies, food safety and pesticide control 1985-89, animal health and veterinary group 1989-91, horticulture, plant protection and agricultural resources, directorate of agricultural commodities, trade and food protection 1991-

Date of birth: 26 January 1934 *Education/professional qualifications:* Richmond Lodge School, Belfast; St Andrew's University, British constitutional and colonial history (MA 1954), political economy and geography (MA 1955) *Marital status:* married John 1956; 1 son *Clubs:* Overseas League *Recreations:* handicrafts, opera

Mrs Elizabeth A J Attridge, Under Secretary, Ministry of Agriculture, Fisheries and Food, Whitehall Place, London SW1A 2HH *Telephone:* 071-270 3000

ATWOOD, BARRY THOMAS Principal Assistant Solicitor, Ministry of Agriculture, Fisheries and Food Grade: 3

Career: solicitor 1961-66; Ministry of Agriculture, Fisheries and Food 1966-: solicitor 1966-82: conveyancing 1966-70, food legislation 1970-77, Common Agricultural Policy 1977-82; assistant solicitor 1982-89: European Court of Justice legislation 1982-86, commodities and food safety bill 1986-89; principal assistant solicitor (under secretary) legal division B (domestic and EC litigation and commercial work) 1989-

Date of birth: 25 February 1940 *Education/professional qualifications:* Bristol Grammar School; Bristol University, law (LLB 1960); Law Society (solicitor of Supreme Court 1965) *Marital status:* married Jennifer Ann Burgess 1965; 2 sons *Recreations:* family, music, swimming, walking, France

Barry T Atwood Esq, Principal Assistant Solicitor, Ministry of Agriculture, Fisheries and Food Legal Department, 55 Whitehall, London SW1H 2AE *Telephone:* 071-270 8339 *Fax:* 071-270 8096

AUSTIN, Air Marshal Sir ROGER MARK Deputy Chief of Defence Staff (Systems), Ministry of Defence

Career: pilot 1960-72; Army Staff College 1973; officer commanding (OC) 233 (Harrier) operational conversion unit 1974-77; Ministry of Defence (MoD) staff post 1977; personal staff officer to air officer commanding-in-chief Strike Command 1978-80; OC RAF Chivenor 1980-82; group captain operations HQ Strike Command 1982-84; director of operational requirements (air) 2 MoD 1984-85; Royal College of Defence Studies 1986; air officer in charge central tactics and trials organisation 1987; director general aircraft 1 MoD Procurement Executive 1987-89; air officer commanding and commandant RAF College Cranwell 1989-92; deputy chief of defence staff (systems) MoD (operational requirements and military research programme aims) 1992-

Date of birth: 9 March 1940 *Education/professional qualifications:* King Alfred's Grammar School, Wantage *Honours, decorations:* AFC 1973; FRAcS 1991; KCB 1992 *Recreations:* walking, transport systems

Air Marshal Sir Roger M Austin KCB AFC, Deputy Chief of Defence Staff (Systems), Ministry of Defence, Whitehall, London SW1A 2HB *Telephone:* 071-218 3835

AVERY, JOHN ERNEST   Deputy Parliamentary Commissioner for Administration (Ombudsman)   Grade: 3

Career: Department of Trade and Industry 1980-89: assistant secretary: chemicals, textiles and paper division 1980-85, telecommunications division 1985-89; Office of Parliamentary Commissioner for Administration 1989-: director of investigations 1989-90, deputy parliamentary commissioner (investigation of alleged government maladministration) 1990-

Date of birth: 18 April 1940   *Education/professional qualifications:* Plymouth College; Leeds University, gas engineering (BSc 1962); Grays Inn (barrister 1971)   *Marital status:* married Anna Beatrice 1966; 2 daughters   *Recreations:* squash, theatre

John E Avery Esq, Deputy Parliamentary Commissioner, Office of the Parliamentary Commissioner for Administration, Church House, Great Smith Street, London SW1P 3BW   *Telephone:* 071-276 2119   *Fax:* 071-276 2104

B

BACON, (JENNIFER) JENNY HELEN   Deputy Director-General, Policy, Health and Safety Executive   Grade: 2

Career: assistant principal Ministry of Labour/Department of Employment (DEmp) 1967-71; DEmp 1971-78: private secretary, secretary of state 1971-72; principal: health and safety law 1972-74, industrial relations law 1974-76, management review 1976-77; secretary of state's principal private secretary 1977-78; assistant secretary: training services Manpower Services Commission (MSC) 1978-80, machinery of government Civil Service Department 1981-82; under secretary, adult training director MSC 1982-86; school curriculum and assessment Department of Education and Science 1986-89; DEmp 1989-: principal finance officer 1989-91; director of resources and strategy (finance, personnel, business and economic services) 1991-92; deputy director-general, policy, Health and Safety Executive 1992- *Current non-Whitehall posts:* visiting fellow Nuffield College, Oxford 1989-

Date of birth: 16 April 1945 *Education/professional qualifications:* Bedales, Petersfield; New Hall, Cambridge, archaeology and anthropology part 1, history part 2 (BA 1967) *Marital status:* single *Recreations:* walking, travel, classical music – especially opera

Miss Jenny Bacon, Deputy Director-General, Policy, Health and Safety Executive, Baynards House, 1 Chepstow Place, London W2 4TF *Telephone:* 071-243 6630 *Fax:* 071-727 2254

BAKER, Air Vice-Marshal CHRISTOPHER PAUL   Director-General Support Management, Royal Air Force, Ministry of Defence

Career: RAF 1958-; Ministry of Defence 1986-: (director supply policy and logistics plans 1988-89, director general support management RAF 1989-

Date of birth: 14 June 1938 *Education/professional qualifications:* RAF Staff College; Royal College of Defence Studies *Honours, decorations:* CB 1991

Air Vice-Marshal Christopher P Baker, CB, Director-General Support Management, Royal Air Force, Ministry of Defence, Whitehall, London, SW1A 2HB *Telephone:* 071-218 9000

BAKER, MARTYN MURRAY   Under Secretary, Overseas Trade, Department of Trade and Industry   Grade: 3

Career: Ministry of Aviation (MAv) 1965-67; assistant private secretary (PS) to minister of state Ministry of Technology (MTech) 1968-69; PS to parliamentary under secretaries MTech, MAv and Department of Trade [and Industry] (DTI) 1969-71; DT[I] 1971-78: principal 1971-78: principal PS to secretary of state for trade 1977-78, assistant secretary 1978-86; civil aviation and shipping counsellor Washington DC embassy 1978-82; DTI 1982-: air division 1982-85, projects and export policy division 1985-86, under secretary (US) 1986-: north west regional director 1986-88, director enterprise and deregulation unit 1988-90, US overseas trade division 1990-

Date of birth: 10 March 1944 *Education/professional qualifications:* Dulwich College, London; Pembroke College, Oxford, modern history (BA, MA 1965) *Marital status:* married Rosemary Caroline 1970

Martyn M Baker Esq, Under Secretary, Department of Trade and Industry, 66-74 Victoria Street, London SW1E 6SW *Telephone:* 071-215 5345 *Fax:* 071-931 0397

BALDWIN, PETER ALAN CHARLES   Chief Executive, Radio Authority

Career: army service 1942-80; Independent Broadcasting Authority 1979-90: deputy director of radio 1979-87, director of radio 1987-90; chief executive Radio Authority 1991-

Date of birth: 19 February 1927 *Education/professional qualifications:* King Edward VI Grammar School, Chelmsford; Staff College, Camberley (psc 1960); Joint Services Staff College (jssc 1964); NATO Defence College (ndc 1972) *Marital status:* married Gail Roberts 1982; 2 stepsons *Clubs:* MCC, Army and Navy *Recreations:* cricket, music, theatre

Peter A C Baldwin Esq, Chief Executive, Radio Authority, Holbrook House, Great Queen Street, Holborn, London WC2B 5DP

BALLANTINE, (DAVID) GRANT   Directing Actuary, Pension Directorate, Government Actuary's Department   Grade: 3

Career: assistant vice-president American Insurance Group 1968-73; Government Actuary's Department 1973-: actuary 1973-82, chief actuary 1983-90, directing actuary pension directorate (public sector pensions) 1991-

Date of birth: 24 March 1941 *Education/professional qualifications:* Daniel Stewart's College, Edinburgh; Edinburgh University, mathematics (BSc 1963); FFA 1968 *Marital status:* married Marjorie Campbell Brown 1969; 1 daughter, 1 son *Recreations:* hill-walking, politics

D Grant Ballantine Esq, Directing Actuary, Government Actuary's Department, 22 Kingsway, London WC2B 6LE *Telephone:* 071-242 6828 *Fax:* 071-831 6653

BALLARD, JOHN FREDERICK   Director, Housing Associations and the Private Sector, Department of the Environment   Grade: 3

Career: Department of the Environment (DoE) 1979-: under secretary DoE and Department of Transport and regional director Yorkshire and Humberside region 1986-90, director housing associations and the private sector 1990-

Date of birth: 8 August 1943 *Education/professional qualifications:* Southampton University (BA); Exeter University (CertEd)

John F Ballard Esq, Director, Housing Associations and the Private Sector, Department of the Environment, 2 Marsham Street, London SW1P 3EB *Telephone:* 071-276 3000

BARDWELL, GEORGE   Social Security Benefits Agency (Executive Agency)   Grade: 4

Career: Ministry of Pensions and National Insurance 1962-64; Ministry/Department of Social Security 1964-87: project manager operational strategy 1984-87; personnel manager Department of Health 1987-90; personnel director Social Security Benefits Agency 1990-

Date of birth: 18 August 1945 *Education/professional qualifications:* Hertford Grammar School; Lancaster University, computer studies (BA 1973)

George Bardwell Esq, Personnel Director, Benefits Agency, Euston Tower, 286 Euston Road, London NW1 3DN *Telephone:* 071-388 1188

BARNES, CHRISTOPHER JOHN ANDREW   Under Secretary Arable Crops and Horticulture, Ministry of Agriculture, Fisheries and Food   Grade: 3

Career: Ministry of Agriculture, Fisheries and Food 1962-: head of personnel and research and development requirements divisions 1983-90; under secretary arable crops and horticulture 1990-

Date of birth: 11 October 1944 *Education/professional qualifications:* London School of Economics (BScEcon)

Christopher J A Barnes Esq, Under Secretary, Ministry of Agriculture, Fisheries and Food, Whitehall Place, London SW1A 2HH *Telephone:* 071-270 8139

BARNES, JACK HENRY   Under Secretary, NHS Management Executive, Department of Health   Grade: 3

Career: under secretary services development division, health care directorate, NHS Management Executive, Department of Health 1991-

Date of birth: 11 December 1943 *Education/professional qualifications:* Hatfield School, Hertfordshire; Sussex University, history (BA 1966); London School of Economics, social administration (MSc 1968) *Marital status:* married Nicola 1966; 2 daughters

Jack H Barnes Esq, Under Secretary, Department of Health, 79 Whitehall, London SW1A 2NS *Telephone:* 071-210 3000

BARNES, MERVYN   Managing Director (Surveying) PSA Projects, Department of the Environment   Grade: 4

Career: private and commercial practice 1956-72; Department of the Environment 1972-: senior surveyor Property Services Agency (PSA) Manchester 1972-76; regional surveyor Manchester 1976-78; SPATS 1978-80; PSA 1980-: principal, regional surveyor, regional maintenance manager Leeds 1980-86; specialist services 1986-: assistant director, director building and quantity surveying services directorate 1986-91; managing director surveying, PSA Specialist Services, PSA Projects, 1991-

Date of birth: 14 December 1939 *Education/professional qualifications:* Liverpool Collegiate School; FRICS *Marital status:* married Jean 1980; 1 son, 1 daughter from previous marriage *Recreations:* walking, reading, countryside issues

Mervyn Barnes Esq, Managing Director (Surveying), PSA Services, Apollo House, 36 Wellesley Road, Croydon, Surrey CR9 3RR *Telephone:* 081-760 8516 *Fax:* 081-760 8157

BARNES, MICHAEL CECIL JOHN   Legal Services Ombudsman   Grade: 3

Career: advertising and marketing 1957-66; MP for Brentford and Chiswick 1966-74; member National Consumer Council 1975-80; chairman Electricity Consumers' Council 1977-83; member Advertising Standards Authority 1979-85; director United Kingdom Immigrants Advisory Service 1984-90; lay member investigation committee Solicitors' Complaints Bureau 1987-90; legal services ombudsman (investigation of complaints against solicitors, barristers and licensed conveyors and their professional bodies) 1991-

Date of birth: 22 September 1932 *Education/professional qualifications:* Malvern College; Corpus Christi College, Oxford, classical mods and greats (BA, MA 1957) *Marital status:* married Anne Mason 1962; 1 son, 1 daughter *Recreations:* walking, swimming, dogs

Michael C J Barnes Esq, Legal Services Ombudsman, 22 Oxford Court, Manchester M2 3WQ *Telephone:* 061-236 9532 *Fax:* 061-236 2651

BARRELL, ANTHONY CHARLES   Chief Executive, North Sea Safety, Health and Safety Executive   Grade: 3

Career: Health and Safety Executive 1978-: director of technology 1985-90; chief executive North Sea safety 1990-

Date of birth: 4 June 1933 *Education/professional qualifications:* Birmingham University; Imperial College, London, chemical engineering (BSc)

Anthony C Barrell Esq, Chief Executive, North Sea Safety, Health and Safety Executive, Baynards House, 1 Chepstow Place, Westbourne Grove, London W2 4TF *Telephone:* 071-243 6000

BARRON, (JAMES) JIMMY WALTER   Keeper of the Registers of Scotland (Executive Agency)   Grade: 4

Career: Admiralty 1951-56: national service 1953-55; Department of Registers of Scotland (RS) 1956-73: assistant examiner 1956-65, examiner 1965-73; clerk Lands Tribunal for Scotland 1973-76; senior examiner RS 1976-85; Scottish Office 1976-: principal 1976-85, assistant secretary 1985-90; keeper of the registers of Scotland (chief executive: land transactions and personal registers; deputy keeper of the Great Seal) 1990- *Current non-Whitehall posts:* assistant secretary Edinburgh University Open Studies Association 1974-

Date of birth: 22 August 1934 *Education/professional qualifications:* Broughton Secondary School, Edinburgh *Marital status:* married Elizabeth Mary Coutts 1954; 2 daughters *Recreations:* music, reading, rugby, informal further education

Jimmy Barron Esq, Keeper, Registers of Scotland, Meadowbank House, 153 London Road, Edinburgh EH8 7AU *Telephone:* 031-659 6111 *Fax:* 031-459 1221

BARRON, Major-General RICHARD EDWARD   Director, Royal Armoured Corps, Ministry of Defence

Career: army service 1962-: Quartermaster General's staff 1988-89; director Royal Armoured Corps 1989-

Date of birth: 22 November 1940 *Education/professional qualifications:* Oundle School; Royal Military Academy, Sandhurst

Major-General Richard E Barron, Director Royal Armoured Corps, Bovington Camp, Wareham, Dorset BH20 6JA

BATES, JOHN GERALD HIGGS   Principal Assistant Solicitor, Under Secretary, Inland Revenue   Grade: 3

Career: solicitor's office Inland Revenue 1966-: principal assistant solicitor and under secretary 1990-

Date of birth: 28 July 1936 *Education/professional qualifications:* St Catharine's College, Cambridge (MA); Harvard Law School (LLM); barrister (Middle Temple)

John G H Bates Esq, Principal Assistant Solicitor and Under Secretary, Solicitor's Office, Inland Revenue, Somerset House, London WC2R 1LB *Telephone:* 071-438 6622

BATHURST, Admiral Sir (DAVID) BENJAMIN   Vice-Chief of the Defence Staff, (and from February 1993 Chief of Naval Staff and First Sea Lord) Ministry of Defence

Career: Royal Navy 1953-: commander in chief (C-in-C) Fleet, allied C-in-C Channel, C-in-C Eastern Atlantic Area 1989-91; vice-chief of the defence staff 1991-93; chief of naval staff and first sea lord 1993-

Date of birth: 27 May 1936

Admiral Sir Benjamin Bathurst GCB, Vice-Chief of the Defence Staff, Ministry of Defence, Main Building, Whitehall, London SW1A 2HB *Telephone:* 071-218 7657

BATTISHILL, Sir ANTHONY MICHAEL WILLIAM   Chairman, Inland Revenue   Grade: 1

Career: assistant principal (AP) stamps and taxes division Inland Revenue (IR) 1960-63; AP, private secretary (PS) to financial secretary HM Treasury (HMT) 1963-65; IR 1965-76; principal, stamps and taxes division 1965-70, assistant secretary (AS) personal taxation division 1970-76; AS Central Policy Review Staff Cabinet Office 1976-77; HMT 1977-82: AS, principal PS to chancellor of exchequer 1977-80, under secretary (US) fiscal policy group 1980-82; US business taxation division IR 1982-83; US central unit HMT 1983-85; IR 1985-: deputy chairman 1985-86, chairman 1986- *Current non-Whitehall posts:* member London School of Economics court of governors 1987-

Date of birth: 5 July 1937 *Education/professional qualifications:* Taunton School; Hele's School, Exeter; London School of Economics (BSc Econ 1958) *Honours, decorations:* KCB 1989 *Marital status:* married Heather Frances Lawes 1961; 1 daughter *Recreations:* gardening, old maps

Sir Anthony Battishill KCB, Chairman, Inland Revenue, Somerset House, London WC2R 1LB *Telephone:* 071-438 7711 *Fax:* 071-438 6494

BATTLE, DENNIS FRANK ORLANDO   Commissioner and Director of Personnel, HM Customs and Excise   Grade: 3

Career: commissioner and director of personnel HM Customs and Excise 1990-

Date of birth: 17 December 1942 *Education/professional qualifications:* Bedford Modern School *Marital status:* married Sandra 1965; 1 son, 1 daughter

Dennis F Battle Esq, Commissioner and Director of Personnel, HM Customs and Excise, New King's Beam House, 22 Upper Ground, London SE1 9PJ *Telephone:* 071-620 1313

BAUGH, JOHN TREVOR   Director-General Supplies and Transport (Naval), Ministry of Defence

Career: Ministry of Defence 1970-: assistant under secretary 1985-: director-general of supplies and transport (naval) 1986-

Date of birth: 24 September 1932 *Education/professional qualifications:* Queen Elizabeth's Hospital, Bristol; MCIT 1956

John T Baugh Esq, Director-General Supplies and Transport (Naval), Ministry of Defence, Ensleigh, Bath BA1 5AB *Telephone:* 0225 467707

BAYLISS, VALERIE JUNE   Under Secretary, Director of Education Programmes, Employment Department Group   Grade: 3

Career: Department of Employment 1968-: director of resources and personnel 1987-90; under secretary, director of education programmes 1991-

Date of birth: 10 June 1944 *Education/professional qualifications:* University of Wales, history (BA 1965, MA 1967)

Ms Valerie J Bayliss, Director of Education Programmes, Employment Department Group, Moorfoot, Sheffield, S1 4PQ *Telephone:* 0742 594573

BEALE, Lieutenant-General Sir PETER JOHN   Surgeon General and Director General, Army Medical Services, Ministry of Defence

Career: Army 1960-; director general, army medical services, Ministry of Defence 1990-

Date of birth: 18 March 1934 *Education/professional qualifications:* Gonville and Caius College, Cambridge (BA)

Lieutenant-General Sir Peter Beale KBE QHP, Director General, Army Medical Services, Ministry of Defence, First Avenue House, High Holborn, London, WC1V 6HE *Telephone:* 071-430 5775

BEAMISH, ADRIAN   Assistant Under Secretary, The Americas, Foreign and Commonwealth Office   Grade: 3

Career: HM Diplomatic Service 1963-: diplomatic posts Tehran, New Delhi, Bonn, ambassador Lima; various posts Foreign and Commonwealth Office, London: assistant under secretary for the Americas 1989-

Date of birth: 21 January 1939 *Education/professional qualifications:* Prior Park College, Bath; Christ's College, Cambridge, English (BA 1962) *Honours, decorations:* CMG 1988 *Marital status:* divorced; 2 daughters *Clubs:* United Oxford and Cambridge University *Recreations:* books, plants

Adrian Beamish Esq CMG, Assistant Under Secretary, Foreign and Commonwealth Office, London SW1A 2AH *Telephone:* 071-270 2217

BEASTALL, JOHN SALE   Treasury Officer of Accounts, HM Treasury   Grade: 3

Career: HM Treasury (HMT) 1963-68: assistant principal 1963-67, principal 1967-68; principal: Civil Service Department (CSD) 1968-71, HMT 1971-75; assistant secretary: HMT 1975-79, CSD 1979-81, HMT 1981-85, Department of Education and Science 1985-87; under secretary, Treasury Officer of Accounts HMT (government-parliament financial relations; government departments' and public bodies' financial transactions) 1987-

Date of birth: 2 July 1941 *Education/professional qualifications:* St Paul's School, London; Balliol College, Oxford, literae humaniores (BA 1963) *Clubs:* United Oxford and Cambridge University *Recreations:* Christian youth work

John S Beastall Esq, Under Secretary, HM Treasury, Parliament Street, London SW1P 3AG *Telephone:* 071-270 4490 *Fax:* 071-270 4311

BEATSON, JACK   Commissioner, Law Commission

Career: law lecturer Bristol University 1972-73; fellow and law tutor Merton College, Oxford 1973-; visiting law professor: Osgoode Hall law school, Toronto, Canada 1979, Virginia University, USA

1980, 1983; senior teaching fellow Singapore University 1987; commissioner (responsible for law reform) Law Commission for England and Wales 1989-

Date of birth: 3 November 1948 *Education/professional qualifications:* Whittinghame College, Brighton; Brasenose College, Oxford, law (BCL 1972, MA 1973); Inner Temple (barrister 1972) *Marital status:* married Charlotte H Christie-Miller 1973; 1 son, 1 daughter *Publications:* Administrative Law: Cases and Materials (OUP 1983, 89); ed Chitty on Contract (Sweet and Maxwell 26 ed 1989); The Use and Abuse of Unjust Enrichment (OUP 1991) *Clubs:* United Oxford and Cambridge University *Recreations:* travel, gardening

Jack Beatson Esq, Commissioner, Law Commission for England and Wales, Conquest House, 37-38 John Street, London WC1N 2BQ *Telephone:* 071-411 1216 *Fax:* 071-411 1297

BEATTIE, ANTHONY   Director and Chief Executive, Natural Resources Institute (Executive Agency)   Grade: 3

Career: economic planning division Malawi government 1966-69; Overseas Development Administration 1969-; director and chief executive Natural Resources Institute 1990-

Date of birth: 17 April 1944 *Education/professional qualifications:* Stationers' Company's School, London; Trinity College, Cambridge, economics (BA 1966, MA) *Marital status:* married Janet Frances 1973; 1 son

Anthony Beattie Esq, Director and Chief Executive, Natural Resources Institute, Central Avenue, Chatham Maritime, Kent ME4 4TB *Telephone:* 0634 880088 *Fax:* 0634 880066

BEAUMONT, N   Assistant Under Secretary (Quartermaster), Ministry of Defence   Grade: 3

N Beaumont Esq, Assistant Under Secretary (Quartermaster), Ministry of Defence, Main Building, Whitehall, London SW1A 2HB *Telephone:* 071-218 9000

BEETHAM, GEOFFREY HOWARD   Principal Assistant Treasury Solicitor, Treasury Solicitor's Department   Grade: 3

Career: assistant solicitor Battersea metropolitan borough council 1960-65, London borough of Wandsworth 1965-70; Department of Environment 1970-80: senior legal assistant 1970-76, assistant solicitor 1976-83: serving Department of Transport (DTp) 1977-83; principal assistant treasury solicitor, legal adviser to DTp, Treasury Solicitor's Department 1983-

Date of birth: 9 January 1933 *Education/professional qualifications:* City of London School; St John's College, Oxford, law (BA 1956, MA); solicitor 1960 *Marital status:* married; 3 daughters, 2 stepsons *Recreations:* music, pottery, walking

Geoffrey H Beetham Esq, Principal Assistant Treasury Solicitor, Transport Advisory Branch, Treasury Solicitor's Branch, 2 Marsham Street, London SW1P 3EB *Telephone:* 071-276 5700 *Fax:* 071-276 0818

BEETON, DAVID CHRISTOPHER   Chief Executive, Historic Royal Palaces (Executive Agency)   Grade: 3

Career: chief executive Bath City Council 1973-85; secretary National Trust 1985-89; chief executive Historic Royal Palaces executive agency (Hampton Court Palace, Tower of London, Banqueting House, Kensington Palace, Kew Palace) 1989-

Date of birth: 25 August 1939 *Education/professional qualifications:* Ipswich School; King's College, London, law (LLB 1961) *Marital status:* married Elizabeth Brenda 1968; 2 sons *Recreations:* classical music and opera, theatre, traditional cookery

David C Beeton Esq, Chief Executive, Historic Royal Palaces Executive Agency, Hampton Court Palace, East Molesey, Surrey KT8 9AU *Telephone:* 081-977 7222 *Fax:* 081-977 9714

BEIGHTON, LEONARD JOHN HOBHOUSE   Director-General, Inland Revenue   Grade: 2

Career: Inland Revenue 1957-: seconded HM Treasury 1968-69 (private secretary to Chief Secretary) and 1977-79; director-general Board of Inland Revenue 1988-

Date of birth: 20 May 1934 *Education/professional qualifications:* Tonbridge School; Corpus Christi College Oxford, politics philosophy and economics (MA) *Marital status:* married Judith Valerie 1962 (died); 1 son, 1 daughter

Leonard J H Beighton Esq CB, Director General, Board of Inland Revenue, Somerset House, Strand, London WC2R 1LB *Telephone:* 071-438 6543 *Fax:* 071-438 6937

BELFALL, D J   Under Secretary, Health Policy and Public Health Directorate, Home and Health Department, Scottish Office   Grade: 3

D J Belfall Esq, Under Secretary, Health Policy and Public Health Directorate, Home and Health Department, Scottish Office, St Andrews House, Edinburgh, EH1 3DE *Telephone:* 031-556 8400

BELL, ALEXANDER GILMOUR   Chief Reporter, Inquiry Reporters Unit, Scottish Office Environment Department   Grade: 3

Career: banker, Far East 1956-64; solicitor 1965-67; Scottish Office 1967-: senior legal officer 1967-73, Environment Department Inquiry Reporters unit (administration of planning appeals) 1973-: deputy chief reporter 1973-79, chief reporter 1979-

Date of birth: 11 March 1933 *Education/professional qualifications:* Hutchesons' Grammar School, Glasgow; Glasgow University, law (BL 1954) *Honours, decorations:* CB 1991 *Marital status:* married Mary Chisholm 1966; 4 sons *Publications:* contributor to Laws of Scotland, Stair Memorial Encyclopaedia (Butterworth 1991)

Alexander G Bell Esq CB, Chief Reporter, Inquiry Reporters, Scottish Office Environment Department, 2 Greenside Lane, Edinburgh EH1 3AG *Telephone:* 031-244 5644 *Fax:* 041-244 5680

BELL, Dr CATHERINE ELISABETH   Head of Competition Policy and Deregulation Unit, Department of Trade and Industry   Grade: 3

Career: Department of Trade and Industry 1975-: head of competition policy 1990- and of deregulation unit 1992-

Date of birth: 26 April 1951 *Education/professional qualifications:* Girton College, Cambridge; University of Kent

Dr Catherine E Bell, Head of Competition Policy and Deregulation Unit, Department of Trade and Industry, Ashdown House, 123 Victoria Street, London SW1E 6RB *Telephone:* 071-215 5000

BELL, MICHAEL JOHN VINCENT   Deputy Under Secretary Finance, Ministry of Defence   Grade: 2

Career: research associate Institute for Strategic Studies 1964-65; Ministry of Defence (MoD) 1965-86: assistant principal 1965-69, principal 1969-75, assistant secretary 1975-82 (seconded to HM Treasury 1977-79), assistant under secretary (resources and programmes) 1982-84, director general of management audit 1984-86, assistant secretary general for defence planning and policy NATO 1966-88; deputy under secretary (finance: principal finance officer) 1988-

Date of birth: 9 September 1941 *Education/professional qualifications:* Winchester College; Magdalen College, Oxford, literae humaniores (BA 1963) *Recreations:* motorcycling, military history

Michael J V Bell Esq, Deputy Under Secretary, Ministry of Defence, Whitehall, London SW1A 2HB *Telephone:* 071-218 6182

BENDER, BRIAN GEOFFREY   Under Secretary, Cabinet Office   Grade: 3

Career: industry and energy counsellor, office of UK permanent representative to EC, Brussels (UK Perm Rep) 1985-89; principal minerals and metals division Department of Trade and Industry 1982-84; first secretary trade policy (UK Perm Rep) 1977-82; under secretary Cabinet Office (co-ordination of UK EC policy) 1990-

Date of birth: 25 February 1949 *Education/professional qualifications:* Greenford County Grammar School, Middlesex; Imperial College, London, physics (BSc 1970, PhD 1973) *Marital status:* married Penelope Clark 1974; 1 daughter, 1 son *Recreations:* family, theatre

Brian G Bender Esq, Under Secretary, Cabinet Office, 70 Whitehall, London SW1A 2AS *Telephone:* 071-270 0177

BENNETT, ANDREW JOHN   Chief Natural Resources Adviser, Overseas Development Administration, Foreign and Commonwealth Office   Grade: 3

Career: VSO agricultural science lecturer, Kenya 1965-66; agricultural research officer, St Vincent government 1967-69; maize agronomist, Malawi government 1971-75; chief research officer, Sudan government 1976-80; Foreign and Commonwealth Overseas Development Administration 1980-: agricultural adviser 1980-83, natural resources adviser SE Asia development division, head of British development division in Pacific 1985-87, under secretary and chief natural resources adviser 1987- *Current non-Whitehall posts:* council member Royal Agricultural Society of England 1988-

Date of birth: 25 April 1942 *Education/professional qualifications:* St Edward's School, Oxford; University of Wales, agricultural chemistry (BSc 1965); University of West Indies, tropical agriculture (diploma 1967); Reading University, hop protection (MSc 1969) *Recreations:* walking, gardening

Andrew J Bennett Esq, Chief Natural Resources Adviser, Overseas Development Administration, 94 Victoria Street, London SW1 *Telephone:* 071-917 0513 *Fax:* 071-917 0425

BENNETT, Dr SETON JOHN   Chief Executive, National Weights and Measures Laboratory (Executive Agency)   Grade: 5

Career: research and development National Physical Laboratory 1967-85; National Weights and Measures Laboratory 1985-: deputy director 1985-90, chief executive 1990- *Current non-Whitehall posts:* chairman Western European Legal Metrology Co-operation 1990-

Date of birth: 10 July 1945 *Education/professional qualifications:* Queen Elizabeth Grammar School, Barnet; Oriel College, Oxford, physics (BA 1967, MA); Imperial College, London, applied optics (PhD 1973) *Marital status:* married Lesley Joan 1966; 2 sons *Recreations:* reading, theatre, travel

Dr Seton J Bennett, Chief Executive, National Weights and Measures Laboratory, Teddington, Middlesex, TW11 0SZ *Telephone:* 081-943 7211 *Fax:* 081-943 7270

BENTLEY, DAVID JEFFREY   Principal Assistant Legal Adviser, Home Office   Grade: 3

Career: legal adviser's branch Home Office 1979-: principal assistant legal adviser 1988-

Date of birth: 5 July 1935   *Education/professional qualifications:* New College, Oxford (BCL, MA); barrister (Lincoln's Inn)

David J Bentley Esq, Principal Assistant Legal Adviser, Home Office, Queen Anne's Gate, London SW1H 9AT   *Telephone:* 071-273 3000

BENWELL, PETER   Chief Architect, Department for Education   Grade: 4

Career: architect Southampton borough council 1958-60; senior architect Hampshire County Council (CC) 1960-62; group architect Kent CC 1962-67; principal architect Second Consortium of Local Authorities 1967-76; county architect Durham CC 1976-87; chief architect Department of Education and Science 1987-

Date of birth: 8 May 1933   *Education/professional qualifications:* Royal Masonic School, Bushey; Portsmouth School of Architecture (ARIBA 1955)   *Marital status:* married Sheila Margaret Anne 1958; 1 daughter, 3 sons   *Recreations:* Methodist Church local preacher; jogging, swimming, cycling, gardening, cooking, singing, 'DIY"

Peter Benwell Esq, Chief Architect, Department for Education, Sanctuary Buildings, Great Smith Street, London SW1P 3BT   *Telephone:* 071-925 5000   *Fax:* 071-925 6000

BERMAN, FRANKLIN DELOW   Legal Adviser, Foreign and Commonwealth Office   Senior grade

Career: HM Diplomatic Service 1965-: assistant legal adviser (LA) Foreign and Commonwealth Office (FCO) 1965-71; LA British military government Berlin 1971-72; LA Bonn embassy 1972-74; legal counsellor (LC), London 1974-82; LA UK mission to UN, New York 1982-85; FCO 1985-: LC 1985-88; deputy LA 1988-91, LA (advice on international law) 1991-

Date of birth: 23 December 1939   *Education/professional qualifications:* Rondebosch Boys' High School, Cape Town, South Africa (SA); Cape Town University, SA, mathematics (BA 1959), statistics (BSc 1960); Wadham College, Oxford, (BA 1963, MA); Wadham and Nuffield Colleges, Oxford, public international law; Middle Temple (barrister 1967)   *Honours, decorations:* CMG 1988   *Marital status:* married Christine Mary Lawler 1964; 2 sons, triplet daughters   *Clubs:* United Oxford and Cambridge University   *Recreations:* reading, walking, choral singing, gardening

Franklin D Berman Esq CMG, Legal Adviser, Foreign and Commonwealth Office, King Charles Street, London SW1A 2AH   *Telephone:* 071-270 3000   *Fax:* 071-270 2767

BEVAN, NICOLAS   Under Secretary, Cabinet Office   Grade: 3

Career: Ministry of Defence 1964-: assistant principal 1964, principal 1969, private secretary to chief of the air staff 1970-73; Cabinet Office (CO) 1973-75; assistant secretary 1976; Royal College of Defence Studies 1981; assistant under secretary 1985- 92: general finance; defence staff; CO 1992-

Date of birth: 8 March 1942   *Education/professional qualifications:* Westminster School; Corpus Christi College, Oxford, litterae humaniores (BA 1964, MA)   *Honours, decorations:* CB 1991   *Marital status:* married (Helen) Christine Berry 1982   *Clubs:* National Liberal   *Recreations:* gardening

Nicolas Bevan Esq CB, Under Secretary, Cabinet Office, 70 Whitehall, London SW1A 2AS   *Telephone:* 071-270 0050

'Next Steps' Executive Agencies
see page 761

BEVERLEY, Lieutenant-General Sir HENRY YORK LA ROCHE   Commandant General, Royal Marines, Ministry of Defence

Career: Royal Marines, Ministry of Defence: major-general training and reserve forces 1986-88; chief of staff to commandant general (CG) 1988-90; CG 1990-

Date of birth: 25 October 1935 *Education/professional qualifications:* Wellington College

Lt-Gen Sir Henry Beverley KCB OBE, Commandant General Royal Marines, Ministry of Defence, Main Building, Whitehall, London SW1A 2HB *Telephone:* 071-218 9000

BICHARD, MICHAEL G   Chief Executive, Social Security Benefits Agency (Executive Agency)   Grade: 2

Career: chief executive Brent 1980-86, Gloucestershire [1986-90] county councils; chief executive Social Security Benefits Agency 1990- *Current non-Whitehall posts:* member Economic and Social Research Council; trustee Public Management Federation

Date of birth: 31 January 1947 *Education/professional qualifications:* Manchester University, law (LLB); solicitor 1971 *Marital status:* married *Recreations:* music, food, walking, sport

Michael G Bichard Esq, Chief Executive, Benefits Agency, Quarry House, Quarry Hill, Leeds LS2 7UA *Telephone:* 0532 32400

BICKHAM, EDWARD SIDNEY CÔVER   Special Adviser to Foreign Secretary

Career: Macmillan Publishers 1977-80; European desk officer Conservative Research Department 1980-83; special adviser to James Prior and Douglas Hurd, secretaries of state for Northern Ireland 1983-85, to Douglas Hurd, Home Secretary, 1985-88; executive director British Satellite Broadcasting 1988-90; special adviser to Douglas Hurd, Foreign Secretary 1991-

Date of birth: 10 August 1956 *Education/professional qualifications:* Brockenhurst Grammar School, Hampshire; St John's College, Oxford, law (BA 1977, MA) *Honours, decorations:* Robert Schuman silver medal for services to European unity 1984 *Marital status:* single *Publications:* Raising Kane?: Media Ownership in a Free Society (1989) *Clubs:* Carlton *Recreations:* tennis, cinema

Edward S C Bickham Esq, Special Adviser, Foreign and Commonwealth Office, King Charles' Street, London SW1 *Telephone:* 071-270 2112 *Fax:* 071-270 2111

BILLINGTON, (BRIAN JOHN) BILL   Director, Network Management and Maintenance, Department of Transport   Grade: 3

Career: statistician, Ministry of Power/Department of Energy 1969-74; Department of Transport 1974-: chief statistician 1974-81, assistant secretary 1981-91; under secretary, director network management and maintenance (motorways and trunk roads) 1991-

Date of birth: 25 February 1939 *Education/professional qualifications:* Slough Grammar School; Regent Street Polytechnic, London, statistics (BSc Econ 1966); London School of Economics, statistics (MSc 1968) *Marital status:* married Gillian Elizabeth Annis 1965; 2 daughters

Bill Billington Esq, Under Secretary, Department of Transport, 2 Monck Street, London, SW1 2BQ *Telephone:* 071-276 2830 *Fax:* 071-276 2760

BIRCH, ROBIN ARTHUR   Deputy Secretary, Head of Social Security Policy Group, Department of Social Security   Grade: 2

Career: assistant principal Ministry of Health (MoH) 1961-66; principal MoH, Department [of Health] and Social Security (D[H]SS), Home Office 1966-72; assistant secretary DHSS, Privy Council Office 1973-82: principal private secretary to leader of House of Commons 1980-81; under secretary DHSS, National Audit Office (NAO), DSS 1982-90: assistant auditor general NAO 1984-86, director regional organisation DSS 1988-90; deputy secretary, head of social security policy group DSS 1990- *Current non-Whitehall posts:* honorary secretary Friends of Christ Church Cathedral, Oxford 1978-

Date of birth: 12 October 1939 *Education/professional qualifications:* King Henry VIII School, Coventry; Christ Church, Oxford, literae humaniores (BA, MA 1964) *Marital status:* married Jane Marion Irvine Sturdy 1962; 2 sons *Recreations:* eccentricities

Robin A Birch Esq, Deputy Secretary, Department of Social Security, Richmond House, 79 Whitehall, London SW1A 2NS
Telephone: 071-210 5459

BIRD, RICHARD   Head of Road and Vehicle Safety Directorate, Department of Transport   Grade: 3 *(see Addenda)*

Career: Department of Environment 1971-75: assistant private secretary (PS) to minister for planning and local government 1974-75; Department of Transport 1976-: principal 1976-78; seconded to Foreign Office as first secretary UK permanent representation to EC, Brussels 1978-82; principal (PS) to Secretary of State 1982-83; assistant secretary 1983-90: Driver and Vehicle Licensing Authority 1983-88; under secretary, head of road and vehicle safety directorate 1990- *Current non-Whitehall posts:* chairman Road Safety Committee, Permanent International Association of Road Congresses 1991-

Date of birth: 12 February 1950 *Education/professional qualifications:* King's School, Canterbury; Magdalen College, Oxford, history (BA 1971) *Marital status:* married Penelope Anne Frudd 1973; 1 son, 1 daughter *Recreations:* choral singing, summer sports

Richard Bird Esq, Under Secretary, Department of Transport, 2 Marsham Street, London SW1P 3EB
Telephone: 071-276 3000

BLACKER, Lieutenant General (ANTHONY STEPHEN) JEREMY   Master General of the Ordnance, Procurement Executive, Ministry of Defence

Career: army service 1957-; military assistant to vice-chief of general staff Ministry of Defence (MoD) army department 1976-79; commanding officer 1st Royal Tank Regiment 1979-81; military director of studies Royal Military College of Science (RMCS) 1981-82; commander 11th Armoured Brigade 1982-84; principal staff officer to chief of defence staff MoD 1985-87; commandant RMCS 1985-87; MoD 1987-: assistant chief of defence staff operational requirements (land systems) 1987-89, master general of ordnance Procurement Executive, land systems controllerate (land service equipment for all services; all army equipment) 1991- *Current non-Whitehall posts:* colonel commandant Royal Electrical and Mechanical Engineers 1987-, Royal Tank Regiment 1988-

Date of birth: 6 May 1939 *Education/professional qualifications:* Sherborne School; Corpus Christi College, Cambridge, mechanical engineering (BA 1964) *Honours, decorations:* OBE 1979, CBE 1987 *Recreations:* skiing, tennis

Lieutenant General A S Jeremy Blacker CBE, Master General of the Ordnance, Procurement Executive, Ministry of Defence, Whitehall, London SW1A 2HB *Telephone:* 071-218 7306
Fax: 071-218 2660

BLYTHE, MARK ANDREW   Principal Assistant Solicitor, Central Advisory Division, Treasury Solicitor's Department   Grade: 3

Career: Treasury Solicitor's Department 1981-: assistant solicitor European division 1986-89; principal assistant solicitor central advisory division 1989

Date of birth: 4 September 1943 *Education/professional qualifications:* University College, Oxford (BCL, MA); barrister (Inner Temple 1966)

Mark A Blythe Esq, Principal Assistant Solicitor, Treasury Solicitor's Department, Queen Anne's Chambers, 28 Broadway, London, SW1H 9JS *Telephone:* 071-210 3000

BOE, NORMAN WALLACE   Deputy Solicitor to Secretary of State, Scottish Office   Grade: 3

Career: Legal Assistant, Menzies and White 1967-70; Scottish Office 1970- : deputy solicitor 1987-

Date of birth: 30 August 1943 *Education/professional qualifications:* Edinburgh University (LLB Hons 1965)

Norman W Boe Esq, Deputy Solicitor, Solicitor's Office, Scottish Office, New St Andrew's House, Edinburgh EH1 3TE *Telephone:* 031-244 4884

BOND, Dr KEVIN PATRICK   Director of Operations, National Rivers Authority   Grade: 3

Career: police service 1972-90; National Rivers Authority 1990-: Anglian regional general manager 1990-91, director of operations 1991-

Date of birth: 17 August 1950 *Education/professional qualifications:* Cardinal Newman Secondary Modern School, Birmingham; Liverpool University, politics, philosophy, history (BA 1972); Michigan State University, USA, criminal justice management (MSc 1980); Aston Business School, business studies/cybernetics (PhD 1989) *Marital status:* married Susan 1972; 2 sons, 1 daughter *Recreations:* jogging, cycling

Dr Kevin P Bond, Director of Operations, National Rivers Authority, Rivers House, Waterside Drive, Aztec West, Almondsbury, Bristol BS12 4UD *Telephone:* 0454 624407 *Fax:* 0454 202547

BONE, ROGER BRIDGLAND   Assistant Under Secretary, Foreign and Commonwealth Office

Career: HM Diplomatic Service 1966-: head of chancery, Washington 1987-89; assistant under secretary, Foreign and Commonwealth Office 1989-

Date of birth: 29 July 1944 *Education/professional qualifications:* St Peter's College, Oxford (MA)

Roger B Bone Esq, Assistant Under Secretary, Foreign and Commonwealth Office, Whitehall, London SW1A 2AP *Telephone:* 071-270 2685

BOOKER, G ALAN   Deputy Director-General, Office of Water Services   Grade: 3

Career: chief executive East Worcestershire Water Company 1980-90. managing director: Biwater Supply Ltd, Bournemouth and West Hampshire Water Company 1989-90, deputy director-general Office of Water Services (economic regulation of the water industry in England and Wales) 1990-
Education/professional qualifications: FIWEM

G Alan Booker Esq, Deputy Director-General, Office of Water Services, 7 Hill Street, Birmingham B5 4UA *Telephone:* 021-625 1300 *Fax:* 021-625 1348

BORRETT, NEIL EDGAR   Director, Property Holdings, Department of the Environment   Grade: 3

Career: director, managing director, partner commercial property companies 1963-90; director Property Holdings, Department of Environment (management of government office estate) 1990-

Date of birth: 10 March 1940 *Education/professional qualifications:* Grammar School, Dartford; College of Estate Management, property (RICS 1968) *Marital status:* married Jane 1965; 2 daughters *Recreations:* golf, boating

Neil E Borrett Esq, Director, Property Holdings, Department of the Environment, St Christopher House, Southwark Street, London SE1 0TE *Telephone:* 071-928 3666

BOSTOCK, DAVID JOHN   Under Secretary and Head of European Community Group, HM Treasury   Grade: 3

Career: financial and economic counsellor, Office of the UK Permanent Representative to the EC 1985-90; under secretary and head of European Community Group HM Treasury 1990-

Date of birth: 11 April 1948 *Education/professional qualifications:* Balliol College, Oxford, modern history (BA1969); University College, London, economics of public policy (MSc 1978)

David J Bostock Esq, Under Secretary and Head of European Community Group, HM Treasury, Parliament Street, London SW1P 3AG *Telephone:* 071-270 3000

BOULTON, Sir CLIFFORD JOHN   Clerk of the House of Commons   Grade: 1

Career: Clerk in House of Commons 1953-: Clerk (procedures and constitutional matters, chairman management board and accounting officer) 1991- *Current non-Whitehall posts:* trustee Industry and Parliament Trust 1991-

Date of birth: 25 July 1930 *Education/professional qualifications:* Newcastle-under-Lyme School, Staffordshire; St John's College, Oxford, modern history (BA, MA 1953) *Honours, decorations:* CB 1985, KCB 1990 *Marital status:* married Anne Raven 1955; 1 son, 1 daughter *Publications:* Erskine May's Parliamentary Practice 21st edition (Butterworth 1989)

Sir Clifford Boulton KCB, Clerk of the House of Commons, House of Commons, London SW1A 0AA *Telephone:* 071-219 3300 *Fax:* 071 219 5568

BOURDILLON, Dr PETER JOHN   Head of Medical Manpower and Education, NHS Management Executive, Department of Health   Grade: 3

Career: London hospital medical posts 1969-; head of medical manpower and education division, senior principal medical officer, health care directorate NHS Management Executive, Department of Health 1991- *Current non-Whitehall posts:* consultant clinical physiologist Hammersmith and Queen Charlotte's Special Health Authority 1975-; honorary senior lecturer Royal Postgraduate Medical School 1979-

Date of birth: 10 July 1941 *Education/professional qualifications:* Rugby School; Middlesex Hospital Medical School (MB, BS 1965); FRCP 1983 *Marital status:* married Catriona 1964; 2 daughters, 1 son *Recreations:* golf, skiing, computer programming

Dr Peter J Bourdillon, Senior Principal Medical Officer, NHS Management Executive, 160 Great Portland Street, London W1N 5TB *Telephone:* 071-972 8259 *Fax:* 071-323 0420

BOURN, Sir JOHN BRYANT   Comptroller and Auditor General, National Audit Office

Career: Air Ministry 1956-63; HM Treasury 1963-64; private secretary to permanent under secretary Ministry of Defence (MoD) 1964-69; assistant secretary (AS), director of programmes Civil Service College 1969-72; AS MoD 1972-74; assistant under secretary Northern Ireland Office (NIO) 1974-77, MoD 1977-82; deputy under secretary NIO 1982-85, MoD defence procurement 1985-88; comptroller and auditor general National Audit Office (examination of the accounts of government departments, certain public bodies and international organisations) 1988- *Current non-Whitehall posts:* visiting professor London School of Economics 1983-

Date of birth: 21 February 1934 *Education/professional qualifications:* Southgate County Grammar School; London School of Economics (BSc Econ 1954, PhD 1958) *Honours, decorations:* CB 1986, KCB 1991 *Marital status:* married Ardita 1959; 1 daughter, 1 son *Publications:* Management in Central and Local Government (Pitman 1979) *Recreations:* swimming, squash

Sir John Bourn KCB, Comptroller and Auditor General, National Audit Office, 157-159 Buckingham Palace Road, London SW1W 9SP *Telephone:* 071-798 7000 *Fax:* 071-828 3774

BOVEY, PHILIP HENRY   Under Secretary and Head of Solicitor's Division D, Department of Trade and Industry   Grade: 3

Date of birth: 11 July 1948 *Education/professional qualifications:* Peterhouse College, Cambridge

Philip H Bovey Esq, Under Secretary and Head of Solicitors Division D, Department of Trade and Industry, 10-18 Victoria Street, London SW1H 0NN *Telephone:* 071-215 5000

BOWMAN, (EDWIN) GEOFFREY   Parliamentary Counsel, Parliamentary Counsel Office   Grade: 2

Career: Parliamentary Counsel Office 1971-: deputy parliamentary counsel 1981-84; parliamentary counsel 1984-

Date of birth: 27 January 1946 *Education/professional qualifications:* Trinity College, Cambridge, law (MA); barrister, Lincoln's Inn

Geoffrey Bowman Esq CB, Parliamentary Counsel, Parliamentary Counsel Office, 36 Whitehall, London SW1A 2AY *Telephone:* 071-210 6629

BOWTELL, ANN ELIZABETH   Deputy Secretary, Department of Health   Grade: 2

Career: assistant principal National Assistance Board (NAB) 1960-64; principal: NAB 1964-67, Department of Health and Social Security (DHSS) 1967-73; DHSS 1973-86: assistant secretary 1973-80, under secretary 1980-86; deputy secretary Department of Social Security 1986-90; deputy secretary Department of Health (departmental management; provision of finance for local authority services; supply of staff, office and management services) 1990- *Current non-Whitehall posts:* council member Policy Studies Institute; advisory committee member Social Policy Research Unit, York

Date of birth: 25 April 1938 *Education/professional qualifications:* Kendrick Girls' School, Reading; Girton College, Cambridge, economics (BA 1960) *Honours, decorations:* CB 1989 *Marital status:* married Michael John 1961; 2 daughters, 2 sons

Mrs Ann E Bowtell CB, Deputy Secretary, Department of Health, Richmond House, 79 Whitehall, London SW1A 2NS *Telephone:* 071-210 5449 *Fax:* 071-210 5438

BOYD-CARPENTER, Major General The Hon THOMAS PATRICK JOHN   Assistant Chief of Defence Staff (Programmes), Ministry of Defence

Career: commander 24 Infantry Brigade 1983-85; director of defence policy Ministry of Defence (MoD) 1985-87; chief of staff British Army of the Rhine 1988-89; assistant chief of defence staff (programmes) MoD 1989-

Date of birth: 16 June 1938 *Education/professional qualifications:* Stowe School *Honours, decorations:* MBE 1973 *Publications:* Conventional Deterrence: into the 1990s (Macmillan 1989)

Major General The Hon Thomas P J Boyd-Carpenter MBE, Assistant Chief of Defence Staff (Programmes), Ministry of Defence, Whitehall, London SW1A 2HB *Telephone:* 071-218 9000

BOYS, PENELOPE ANN   Deputy Director-General, Office of Electricity Regulation   Grade: 3

Career: assistant principal Ministry of Power 1969-71; private secretary to minister without portfolio 1972-73; Department of Energy (DEn) 1973-85: principal 1973-81, seconded to British National Oil Corporation 1978-80, head of international unit 1981-85; head of social services and territorial (group 2) HM Treasury 1985-87; director of personnel DEn 1987-89; deputy director-general Office of Electricity Regulation 1989-

Date of birth: 11 June 1947 *Education/professional qualifications:* Guildford County School *Marital status:* married David Charles Henshaw Wright 1977 *Recreations:* music, theatre, cooking, horse-racing

Miss Penelope A Boys, Deputy Director-General, Office of Electricity Regulation, Hagley House, Hagley Road, Birmingham B16 8QE *Telephone:* 021-456 6207 *Fax:* 021-456 6365

BOYS SMITH, STEPHEN WYNN   Assistant Under Secretary, Police Department, Home Office   Grade: 3 *(see Addenda)*

Career: Home Office (HO) 1968-73; Northern Ireland Office 1981-83; HO 1984-: assistant under secretary Police Department 1989-

Date of birth: 4 May 1946 *Education/professional qualifications:* St John's College, Cambridge (MA); University of British Columbia (MA)

Stephen W Boys Smith Esq, Assistant Under Secretary, Home Office, Queen Anne's Gate, London SW1H 9AT *Telephone:* 071-273 2746

BRACK, TERENCE JOHN   Assistant Under Secretary, General Finance, Ministry of Defence   Grade: 3

Career: Air Ministry 1961-64; Ministry of Defence (MoD) 1964-68; HM Treasury 1968-72; MoD 1972-: head of finance and secretariat for naval procurement 1975-78, of secretariat for major defence equipments and operational requirements 1978-81, Royal College of Defence Studies 1982, head of finance and secretariat for air guided weapons procurement 1983-85, assistant under secretary: naval personnel 1985-89, general finance 1989-

Date of birth: 17 April 1938 *Education/professional qualifications:* Bradfield College, Reading; Gonville and Caius College, Cambridge, history (BA 1961, MA) *Recreations:* travel, walking, family history

Terence J Brack Esq, Assistant Under Secretary, Ministry of Defence, Whitehall, London SW1A 2HB *Telephone:* 071-218 7525

BRADLEY, ROGER THUBRON   Under Secretary, Head of the Forestry Authority, Forestry Commission   Grade: 3

Career: Forestry Commission 1960-: assistant district officer 1960; mensuration officer 1961-63; planning and economics division 1963-67; working plans officer 1967-70; forest district officer West Scotland Conservancy 1970-74; assistant conservator South Wales 1974-77; director and senior officer Wales 1981-83; director harvesting and marketing 1983-85; under secretary and commissioner private forestry and development 1985-, head of the Forestry Authority, part of the FC, 1992- *Current non-Whitehall posts:* director Central Scotland Woodlands Company

Date of birth: 5 July 1936 *Education/professional qualifications:* Lancaster Royal Grammar School; St Peter's College, Oxford, geology, botany, zoology (honour moderations 1957) and forestry (BA 1959, MA) *Marital status:* married Ailsa Mary 1959; 1 daughter, 1 son *Publications:* co-author Forest Planning (Faber & Faber 1967); Forest Management Tables (Forestry Commission [FC] 1966); Thinning Control (FC 1966) *Clubs:* Commonwealth Trust, Royal Overseas League *Recreations:* sailing, gardening

Roger T Bradley Esq, Head of the Forestry Authority, Forestry Commission, 231 Corstorphine Road, Edinburgh EH12 7AT *Telephone:* 031-334 0303 *Fax:* 031-316 4891

BRAITHWAITE, Sir RODRIC   Foreign Policy Adviser to the Prime Minister

Career: HM Diplomatic Service 1955-: deputy under secretary of state Foreign and Commonwealth Office 1984-88, ambassador to Moscow 1988-92; foreign policy adviser to the Prime Minister 1992- *Education/professional qualifications:* Christ's College, Cambridge

Sir Rodric Braithwaite, Foreign Policy Adviser, Prime Minister's Office, 10 Downing Street, London SW1A 2AA *Telephone:* 071-270 3000

BRANNIGAN, FRANK   Controller, Special Compliance Office, Inland Revenue   Grade: 4

Career: Inland Revenue: regional controller south east 1990-92, controller special compliance office 1992-

Date of birth: 29 January 1942 *Education/professional qualifications:* St Malachy's College, Belfast; Queen's University, Belfast (BSc Econ 1965); Central London Polytechnic, management studies (diploma 1966) *Marital status:* married Geraldine 1969; 3 daughters *Recreations:* sport, reading, DIY

Frank Brannigan Esq, Controller, Special Compliance Office, NW Wing, Bush House, Aldwych, London WC2B 4PP *Telephone:* 071-438 7649

Regulatory Organisations and Public Bodies
see page 857

BREARLEY, CHRISTOPHER JOHN   Deputy Secretary, Local Government, Department of the Environment   Grade: 2

Career: assistant principal Ministry of Transport 1966-70: private secretary (PS) to permanent secretary 1969-70; principal Department of Environment (DoE) 1970-73; secretary Review of Development Control 1973-74; PS to Cabinet Secretary, Cabinet Office (CO) 1974-76; DoE 1977-83: assistant secretary 1977-81, director Scottish services, Property Services Agency 1981-83; under secretary CO 1983-85; DoE 1985-: director of local government finance 1985-88, of planning and development control 1988-90, deputy secretary local government group 1990-

Date of birth: 25 May 1943 *Education/professional qualifications:* King Edward VII School, Sheffield; Trinity College, Oxford, philosophy, politics and economics (BA 1964, MA); philosophy (BPhil 1966) *Marital status:* married Rosemary Stockbridge 1971; 2 sons *Clubs:* New, Edinburgh *Recreations:* crosswords, walking

Christopher J S Brearley Esq, Deputy Secretary, Department of the Environment, 2 Marsham Street, London, SW1P 3EB
Telephone: 071-276 3479

BRERETON, DONALD   Head of Prime Minister's Efficiency Unit, Cabinet Office   Grade: 3

Career: VSO service 1963-64; Ministry of Health/Department of Health and Social Security 1968-89: assistant principal 1968-70; assistant private secretary (PS) to secretary of state (SoS) 1971-72; PS to permanent secretary 1972-73; principal, health services planning and policy 1973-79; PS to SoS for social services 1979-82; head of policy strategy unit 1982-84; secretary to housing benefit review team 1984-85; assistant secretary, housing benefit 1985-89; under secretary, head of Prime Minister's Efficiency Unit 1989-

Date of birth: 18 July 1945 *Education/professional qualifications:* Plymouth College; Plymouth Technical College; Newcastle University, politics and social administration (BA 1968) *Marital status:* married Mary Frances Turley 1969; 2 daughters, 1 son *Recreations:* squash, holidays, books, bridge

Donald Brereton Esq, Head of Prime Minister's Efficiency Unit, Cabinet Office, 70 Whitehall, London SW1A 2AS *Telephone:* 071-270 0257
Fax: 071-270 0099

BRIDGEMAN, JUNE   Deputy Chair, Equal Opportunities Commission

Career: assistant principal, principal, assistant secretary Board of Trade, Department of Economic Affairs, Prices and Income Board 1954-75; under secretary 1975-90: regional and land use planning Department of Environment 1975-77, central policy review staff Cabinet Office 1977-79, Department of Transport 1979-90: London regional director 1979-86, director road and vehicle safety 1987-90; deputy chair Equal Opportunities Commission 1991-

Date of birth: 26 June 1932 *Education/professional qualifications:* Aberdeen High School for Girls; Bromley High School; Westfield College, London University, English language and literature (BA 1954) *Honours, decorations:*

CB 1990 *Marital status:* married John Michael 1958; 4 daughters, 1 son *Recreations:* opera, local history, painting, sketching, gardening

Mrs June Bridgeman CB, Deputy Chair, Equal Opportunities Commission, Overseas House, Quay Street, Manchester M3 3HN *Telephone:* 061-833 9244 *Fax:* 061-835 1657

BRIDGES, BRIAN   Under Secretary, Family Health Services, Department of Health Grade: 3

Career: joined civil service 1961: principal 1967; assistant secretary 1975; Department of Health and Social Security 1985-1988: under secretary 1985, director of establishments and personnel 1985-88; under secretary family health services division 2 (NHS dental, ophthalmic and pharmaceutical services; pharmaceutical price regulation; NHS low-income scheme) Department of Health 1988-

Date of birth: 30 June 1937 *Education/professional qualifications:* Harrow Weald County Grammar School; Keele University, history and political institutions (BA 1961) *Marital status:* married Jennifer 1970 *Recreations:* walking dog, local history, photography

Brian Bridges Esq, Under Secretary, Department of Health, 158-176 Great Portland Street, London W1N 5TB *Telephone:* 071-972 8319

BRINDLEY, JOHN   Head of Court Service Business Group, Lord Chancellor's Department   Grade: 4

Career: Lord Chancellor's Department: court business officer, Birmingham 1971-72; head of HQ personnel branch 1976-81; courts administrator, Exeter 1981-87; head of Court Service Business Group (administration of courts; IT) 1987-

Date of birth: 25 September 1937 *Education/professional qualifications:* Leek Grammar School, Staffordshire *Marital status:* married Judith 1960; 1 daughter *Recreations:* hockey, amateur dramatics

John Brindley Esq, Head of Court Service Business Group, Lord Chancellor's Department, Trevelyan House, Great Peter Street, London SW1P 2BY *Telephone:* 071-210 8500

BRITTON, JOHN WILLIAM   Assistant Chief Scientific Adviser (Projects), Ministry of Defence   Grade: 3

Career: Royal Aircraft Establishment 1959-83; Ministry of Defence 1985-: seconded to Cabinet Office 1987; director general Aircraft 3 1987-90; assistant chief scientific advisor (Projects and Research) 1990-

Date of birth: 13 December 1936 *Education/professional qualifications:* Bristol University (BScEng)

John W Britton Esq, Assistant Chief Scientific Adviser, Ministry of Defence, Main Building, Whitehall, London SW1A 2HB *Telephone:* 071-218 9000

BRODIE, ROBERT   Solicitor to Secretary of State for Scotland   Grade: 2

Career: Scottish Office (SO) 1965-74: legal assistant (LA) 1965-70, senior LA 1970-74; deputy director Scottish Courts Administration 1975-82; SO 1982-: assistant solicitor 1982-84, deputy solicitor 1984-87, solicitor to secretary of state 1987-

Date of birth: 9 April 1938 *Education/professional qualifications:* Morgan Academy, Dundee; St Andrew's University, arts (MA 1959), law (LLB 1962) *Honours, decorations:* CB 1990 *Marital status:* married Jean Margaret McDonald 1970; 2 daughter, 2 sons *Recreations:* hill walking, music

Robert Brodie Esq CB, Solicitor to Secretary of State, Solicitor's Office, Scottish Office, New St Andrew's House, Edinburgh EHI 3TE *Telephone:* 031-244 5247 *Fax:* 031-244 4782

BROOK, Air Vice Marshal J M   Director General Medical Services (RAF), Ministry of Defence

Air Vice Marshal J M Brook QHS, Director General Medical Services (RAF), Ministry of Defence, First Avenue House, High Holborn, London WC1V 6HE *Telephone:* 071-430 5775

BROOMFIELD, NIGEL HUGH ROBERT ALLEN   Deputy Under Secretary, Defence and Security, Foreign and Commonwealth Office   Senior grade

Career: military service 1959-68; HM Diplomatic Service 1969-: first secretary Bonn 1970-72; Moscow embassy 1972-74; European Communities Department, Foreign and Commonwealth Office (FCO) 1975-77; Royal College of Defence Studies 1978; political adviser and head of chancery British Military Government, Berlin 1979-81; head of Eastern European and Soviet Department FCO 1981-83, of Soviet Department 1983-85; deputy high commissioner and minister New Delhi 1985-88; ambassador to German Democratic Republic 1988-90; deputy under secretary of state for defence and security FCO 1990-

Date of birth: 19 March 1937 *Education/professional qualifications:* Haileybury College; Trinity College, Cambridge, English literature (BA) *Honours, decorations:* CMG 1986 *Marital status:* married Valerie 1963; 2 sons *Clubs:* Royal Automobile; MCC; Hawks, Cambridge *Recreations:* tennis, squash, cricket, gardening, reading, music

Nigel Broomfield Esq CMG, Foreign and Commonwealth Office, King Charles Street, London SW1A 2AH *Telephone:* 071-270 3194

BROWN, ALAN WINTHROP   Director, Resources and Planning Division, Health and Safety Executive   Grade: 3

Date of birth: 14 March 1934 *Education/professional qualifications:* Pembroke College, Cambridge; Cornell University, USA

Alan W Brown Esq, Director, Resources and Planning Division, Health and Safety Executive, Baynards House, 1 Chepstow Place, Westbourne Grove, London W2 4TF *Telephone:* 071-243 6000

BROWN, (AUSTEN) PATRICK   Permanent Secretary, Department of Transport   Grade: 1

Career: executive Carreras Ltd 1961-69; management consultant Urwick Orr and Partners 1961-69; civil servant 1972-: Department of the Environment Property Services Agency; Department of Transport: permanent secretary 1991-

Date of birth: 14 April 1940 *Education/professional qualifications:* Royal Grammar School, Newcastle-upon-Tyne; School of Slavonic and East European Studies, London University, Russian (BA 1961) *Marital status:* married Mary 1966; 1 daughter

A Patrick Brown Esq, Permanent Secretary, Department of Transport, 2 Marsham Street, London SW1P 3EB *Telephone:* 071-276 0830 *Fax:* 071-276 0818

BROWN, (HAROLD) VIVIAN BIGLEY   Head of Investigations Division, Department of Trade and Industry   Grade: 3

Career: trainee Ministry of Technology/Department of Trade and Industry (DTI) 1970-72; DTI 1972-86: private secretary to permanent secretary 1972-74, principal 1974-80 (commercial first secretary Jedda embassy 1975-79), assistant secretary 1980-86; head of science and technology assessment office Cabinet Office 1986-89; DTI 1989-: head of competition policy division 1989-91, of investigations (into commercial and financial malpractice) division 1991-

Date of birth: 20 August 1945 *Education/professional qualifications:* Leeds

Grammar School; St John's College, Oxford, oriental studies (BA 1967); St Cross College, Oxford, Islamic philosophy (BPhil 1969) *Marital status:* married Jean Josephine Bowyer 1970; 2 sons *Publications:* Islamic philosophy and the classical tradition (1972) *Recreations:* piano, cycling

H Vivian B Brown Esq, Head of Investigations Division, Department of Trade and Industry, Ashdown House, 123 Victoria Street, London SW1E 6RB *Telephone:* 071-215 6426 *Fax:* 071-215 6894

BROWN, Dr PETER MORGAN   Deputy Medical Adviser, Occupational Health Service (Executive Agency)   Grade: 4

Career: medical and public health posts 1960-67; regional medical officer National Dock Labour Board 1967-72; Department of Employment Health and Safety Executive 1972-88: employment medical adviser 1972-78, senior employment medical adviser 1978-88; senior occupational physician Merseyside police 1988-90; Civil Service Occupational Health Service 1990-: senior medical officer 1990-91, deputy medical adviser 1991-

Date of birth: 15 April 1938 *Education/professional qualifications:* Jones' West Monmouth School, Pontypool; University of Wales Welsh National School of Medicine, medicine and public health (MB, BCh 1960, DPH 1964, DIH 1970); Manchester University, occupational medicine (FFOM 1985); RCP 1985 *Marital status:* married Gwyneth Eileen Davies 1960; 2 sons *Recreations:* philately, choral singing, watching rugby

Dr Peter M Brown, Deputy Medical Adviser, Civil Service Occupational Health Service, 18-20 Hill Street, Edinburgh EH2 3NB *Telephone:* 031-220 4177 *Fax:* 031-220 4183

BROWN, (ROBERT) BOB BURNETT   Under Secretary, Corporate Management Division, Department of Social Security   Grade: 3

Career: Department of Health and Social Security (DHSS) 1967-83: principal 1971-79, assistant secretary 1979-83; assistant secretary Cabinet Office/Treasury 1983-87; DHSS/Department of Social Security (DSS) 1987-: under secretary corporate management division (planning, liaison with DSS agencies, secretariat to DSS board) 1989-

Date of birth: 10 August 1942 *Education/professional qualifications:* Kirkcaldy High School; Edinburgh University, chemistry (BSc 1963) *Marital status:* married Anne 1971 *Publications:* Government Purchasing (HMSO 1984) *Recreations:* football, jazz, Greece

Bob B Brown Esq, Under Secretary, Department of Social Security, Adelphi, 1-11 John Adam Street, London WC2N 6HT *Telephone:* 071-962 8180

BROWN, SARAH ELIZABETH   Head of Small Firms and Enterprise Initiative Divisions, Department of Trade and Industry   Grade: 3

Career: assistant principal Board of Trade 1965-70; principal Department of Trade and Industry (DTI) 1970-78; secretary Crown Agents Tribunal 1978-82; DTI 1982-: assistant secretary personnel management division 1982-84, financial services division 1985-86, under secretary and head of companies division 1986-91, head of enterprise initiative division (consultancy initiatives; managing into the '90s programme; Market Opportunities Task Force) 1991-92, of small firms division 1992, of small firms and enterprise initiative divisions 1992-

Date of birth: 30 December 1943 *Education/professional qualifications:* St Paul's Girls' School, London; Newnham College, Cambridge, natural sciences (BA 1962) *Marital status:* married Philip Anthony Russell 1976 *Recreations:* gardening, walking, travel

Mrs Sarah E Brown, Head of Small Firms and Enterprise Iniative Divisions, Department of Trade and Industry, Kingsgate House, 66-74 Victoria Street, London SW1E 6SW *Telephone:* 071-215 2780

BRYAN, Commodore RICHARD GALE   Director-General, Strategic Weapon Systems, Ministry of Defence   Grade: 4

Career: Ministry of Defence 1986-: project manager of tactical weapon systems 1986-88, of torpedoes 1988-91, director-general strategic weapon systems 1991-

Date of birth: 7 April 1947   *Education/professional qualifications:* Torquay Grammar School; Royal Naval College, Dartmouth (commission 1966); Christ's College, Cambridge, engineering (BA, MA 1969); FCIS 1985, FIEE, CEng 1986   *Recreations:* jogging, economics, membership Bath Abbey

Commodore Richard G Bryan, Director-General, Strategic Weapon Systems, Ministry of Defence, Whitehall, London SW1A 2HB

BUCK, MARCUS   Chief Executive, Queen Elizabeth II Conference Centre (Executive Agency)   Grade: 5

Marcus Buck Esq, Chief Executive, Queen Elizabeth II Conference Centre, Broad Sanctuary, London SW1P 3EE   *Telephone:* 071-798 4010

BUCKLEY, Dr TREVOR   Assistant Chief Scientific Adviser (Research), Ministry of Defence   Grade: 3

Career: Royal Signals and Research Establishment 1962-76: scientific officer (SO) 1962-67, senior SO 1967-71, principal SO 1971-72, divisional superintendent (DS) 1972-76; DS Admiralty Research Establishment Ministry of Defence (MoD) 1976-80; director underwater projects MoD Procurement Executive (PE) 1980-83; Royal College of Defence Studies 1983-84; MoD 1984-: director, general air weapons and electronic systems, PE 1984-86, deputy controller research 1986-91, assistant chief scientific adviser (research) 1991-

Date of birth: 4 February 1938   *Education/professional qualifications:* Barmouth County Grammar School, N Wales; University College of North Wales, electronic engineering (BSc 1959, PhD 1963)

Dr Trevor Buckley, Assistant Chief Scientific Adviser, Ministry of Defence, Whitehall, London SW1A 2HB   *Telephone:* 071-218 3642   *Fax:* 071-218 6481

BUDD, ALAN PETER   Chief Economic Adviser and Head of Government Economic Service, HM Treasury   Grade: 1A

Career: economics lecturer Southampton University 1966-70; HM Treasury (HMT) 1970-74: economic adviser, senior economic adviser 1970-74; London Business School 1974-88: senior research fellow 1974-80, economics professor and director Centre for Economic Forecasting 1980-88; economic adviser Barclays Bank 1988-91; chief economic adviser and head of government economic service HMT 1991-

Date of birth: 16 November 1937   *Education/professional qualifications:* Oundle; London School of Economics, economics (BScEcon 1963), Churchill College, Cambridge, economics (PhD 1970)   *Marital status:* married Susan 1964; 3 sons   *Publications:* The Politics of Economic Planning (Fontana 1978)   *Clubs:* Reform   *Recreations:* music, gardening, reading

Alan P Budd Esq, Chief Economic Adviser, HM Treasury, Parliament Street, London SW1P 3AG   *Telephone:* 071-270 5203

Complete Name Index
see page 955

BUNYAN, PETER JOHN   Chief Scientific Adviser, Ministry of Agriculture, Fisheries and Food   Grade: 2

Career: research associate: King's College, London 1960-62, University College, London 1962-63; Ministry of Agriculture, Fisheries and Food 1963-: senior scientific officer (SO) infestation control laboratory 1963-69, principal SO pest infestation control laboratory 1969-73, senior principal SO pest control chemistry department 1973-80, assistant secretary, head of food science division 1980-84, under secretary, head of agricultural science service Agricultural Development and Advisory Service (ADAS) 1984-87, director ADAS research and development service 1987-90; director-general ADAS 1990-91, chief scientific adviser 1991-

Date of birth: 13 January 1936 *Education/professional qualifications:* Raynes Park County Grammar School, Merton; University College, Durham, chemistry (BSc 1957); King's College, London, organic chemistry (PhD 1960); University College, Durham, ecotoxicology (DSc 1982) *Marital status:* married June Rose Child 1961; 2 sons *Clubs:* Farmers' *Recreations:* gardening, jogging, music

Dr Peter J Bunyan, Chief Scientific Adviser, Ministry of Agriculture, Fisheries and Food, Nobel House, 17 Smith Square, London SW1P 3JR *Telephone:* 071-238 4948 *Fax:* 071-238 6591

BURKE, (DAVID THOMAS) TOM   Special Adviser to Secretary of State for the Environment

Career: non-executive director Earth Resources Research 1975-88; executive director Friends of the Earth 1975-79; member Waste Management Advisory Council 1976-80; policy adviser European Environmental Bureau (EEB) 1978-88; director Green Alliance 1982-91; honorary visiting fellow Manchester Business School 1984-86; Chairman Planning and Environment Group, National Council of Voluntary Organisations 1984-89; director Sustainability Ltd 1987-89; member executive committee EEB 1988-91; special adviser to Michael Heseltine and Michael Howard, Secretaries of State for the Environment 1991- *Current non-Whitehall posts:* visiting fellow Cranfield School of Management 1991-; council member Royal Society of Arts 1990-; member executive board World Energy Council Commission 1990-; member Co-operative Insurance Services Environ Trust Advisory Committee 1990-

Date of birth: 5 January 1947 *Education/professional qualifications:* St Boniface's College, Plymouth; Liverpool University, philosophy (BA 1969) *Marital status:* single *Publications:* co-author Ethics, Environment and the Company (IBE 1990); Green Pages (RKP 1988); The Green Capitalists (Gollancz 1987) *Clubs:* Reform *Recreations:* bird-watching, photography, walking

Tom Burke Esq, Special Adviser, Department of the Environment, 2 Marsham Street, London SW1P 3EB *Telephone:* 071-276 4299 *Fax:* 071-276 3269

BURNS, IAN MORGAN   Head of Police Department, Home Office   Grade: 2

Career: estate duty office Inland Revenue 1960-65; Home Office (HO) 1965-72: assistant principal 1965-69-, principal 1969-72; Northern Ireland Office (NIO) 1972-76: principal 1972-74, assistant secretary (AS) 1974-76; AS HO 1977-79; assistant under secretary (US) NIO 1979-84; US Department of Health and Social Security 1985-86; deputy US NIO 1987-90; deputy US, head of police department, HO 1990-

Date of birth: 3 June 1939 *Education/professional qualifications:* Bootham School, York; King's College, London, law (LLB 1963, LLM 1965) *Honours, decorations:* CB 1990 *Marital status:* married Susan Rebecca Wheeler 1965; 2 daughters *Clubs:* Royal Commonwealth Society *Recreations:* adventurous gardening

Ian M Burns Esq CB, Deputy Under Secretary, Home Office, 50 Queen Anne's Gate, London SW1H 9AT *Telephone:* 071-273 3000

BURNS, (ROBERT) ANDREW   Assistant Under Secretary (Asia), Foreign and Commonwealth Office Senior grade

Career: HM Diplomatic Service 1965-: third secretary UK mission to UN 1965, School of Oriental and African Studies 1966-67; second secretary New Delhi 1967-71; first secretary (FS) Foreign and Commonwealth Office (FCO) and UK delegation to Conference on Security and Co-operation in Europe 1971-75; FS and head of chancery Bucharest 1976-78; private secretary to permanent under secretary FCO 1979-82; fellow Centre for International Affairs. Harvard University, USA 1982-83; and head of British Information Service, New York 1983-86; FCO 1986-: head of South Asian department 1986-88, of news department 1988-90, assistant under secretary Asia (S and SE Asia, Far East, S Pacific, Hong Kong) 1990- *Current non-Whitehall posts:* information counsellor Washington

Date of birth: 21 July 1943 *Education/professional qualifications:* Highgate School, London; Trinity College, Cambridge, classics (BA 1965, MA) *Honours, decorations:* CMG 1992 *Marital status:* married Sarah Cadogan 1973; 2 sons, 1 stepdaughter *Publications:* Diplomacy, War and Parliamentary Democracy (University Press of America 1985) *Clubs:* Garrick, Royal Automobile *Recreations:* music, theatre, country pursuits

R Andrew Burns Esq, Assistant Under Secretary, Foreign and Commonwealth Office, King Charles Street, London SW1A 2AH *Telephone:* 071-270 3000

BURNS, Sir TERENCE   Permanent Secretary, HM Treasury Grade: 1

Career: London Business School (LBS) 1970-79: economics lecturer 1970-74, senior lecturer 1974-79: director LBS centre for economic forecasting 1976-79; economics professor 1979; HM Treasury 1980-: chief economic adviser and head of government economic service 1980-91, permanent secretary 1991-

Date of birth: 13 March 1944 *Education/professional qualifications:* Houghton-le-Spring Grammar School; Manchester University, economics (BA 1965) *Honours, decorations:* Kt 1983 *Marital status:* married Anne Elizabeth 1969; 1 son, 2 daughters *Clubs:* Reform, Ealing Golf *Recreations:* music, golf, soccer spectator

Sir Terence Burns, Permanent Secretary, HM Treasury, Parliament Street, London SW1P 3AG *Telephone:* 071-270 4360 *Fax:* 071-270 5653

BURR, DAVID JOHN   Deputy Secretary and Principal Establishment and Finance Officer, Department of the Environment Grade: 2

Career: Department of the Environment 1971-: under secretary 1978-85; deputy secretary 1985-; principal establishment and finance officer 1991-

Date of birth: 10 March 1935 *Education/professional qualifications:* Oxford University

David J Burr Esq, Deputy Secretary and Principal Establishment and Finance Officer, Department of the Environment, 2 Marsham Street, London SW1P 3EB *Telephone:* 071-276 3000

BURR, T J   Under Secretary, Economic Secretariat, Cabinet Office Grade: 3

Date of birth: 31 March 1950 *Education/professional qualifications:* Dulwich College

T J Burr Esq, Under Secretary, Cabinet Office, 70 Whitehall, London SW1A 2AS *Telephone:* 071-270 3000

BUSH, GEOFFREY HUBERT   Director of Information Technology, Inland Revenue
Grade: 3

Career: Inland Revenue 1973-: district tax inspector (DIT) 1973-75; personal assistant to director-general 1975-78; DIT 1978-81; technical specialist 1981-84; policy adviser 1984-86; operations manager 1986-88; director central division 1988-90; under secretary, director information technology 1990-

Date of birth: 5 April 1942 *Education/professional qualifications:* Cotham Grammar School, Bristol *Marital status:* married Sylvia Mary Squibb 1965; 1 daughter, 1 son *Clubs:* Knowle Lawn Tennis, Topsham Sailing *Recreations:* tennis, swimming, golf, country pursuits

Geoffrey H Bush Esq, Under Secretary, Inland Revenue, Somerset House, Strand, London WC2R 1LB *Telephone:* 071-438 6120 *Fax:* 071-438 7966

BUTLER, ANTHONY JOHN   Director of Personnel and Finance, Prison Service, Home Office   Grade: 3

Career: Home Office 1969-: assistant principal 1969-74: police and criminal departments 1969-72, private secretary (PS) to minister of state 1972-74; principal 1974-80: general department, sex discrimination and race relations legislation units and broadcasting department 1974-79; PS to secretary of state 1979-80; assistant secretary, broadcasting, finance and prisons department 1980-88; assistant under secretary, seconded to Department of Environment as director Inner Cities 1988; principal finance officer 1990; director of personnel and finance HM Prison Service 1990-

Date of birth: 30 January 1945 *Education/professional qualifications:* Maidstone Boys' Grammar School; University College, Oxford, history (BA, MA); Institute of Criminology, Cambridge (Dip Crim) *Marital status:* married Margaret Ann Randon 1967; 1 daughter, 1 son

Anthony J Butler Esq, Director of Personnel and Finance, Prison Service, Cleland House, Page Street, London SW1P 4LN *Telephone:* 071-217 5234

BUTLER, (CHRISTOPHER) DAVID   Director, Department for National Savings   Grade: 2

Career: HM Treasury (HMT) 1964-70; Committee to Review National Savings 1970-72; HMT 1978-82; Central Computer and Telecoms Agency 1982-85; HMT 1985-89; director Department for National Savings 1989-

Date of birth: 27 May 1942 *Education/professional qualifications:* Jesus College, Oxford

C David Butler Esq, Director, Department for National Savings, Charles House, 375 Kensington High St, London W14 8SD *Telephone:* 071-605 9300

BUTLER, Sir (FREDERICK EDWARD) ROBIN   Secretary of the Cabinet and Head of the Home Civil Service   Grade: 0

Career: HM Treasury (HMT) 1964-70: private secretary (PS) to financial secretary 1964-65, staff secretary budgets committee 1965-70; member Central Policy Review Staff, Cabinet Office 1971-72; PS to prime minister (PM) 1972-75; HMT 1975-82: head of financial information systems team 1975-77, of general expenditure policy group 1977-80, principal establishment officer 1980-82; principal PS to PM 1982-85; second permanent secretary, public expenditure HMT 1985-87; secretary of the Cabinet and head of home civil service 1988-

Date of birth: 3 January 1938 *Education/professional qualifications:* Harrow School; University College, Oxford, mods and greats (BA 1961) *Honours, decorations:* CVO 1986, KCB 1988; GCB 1992 *Marital status:* married Gillian Lois Galley 1962; 2 daughters, 1 son *Clubs:* Anglo-Belgian, Athenaeum, Brooks's, United Oxford and Cambridge University *Recreations:* competitive games, opera

Sir Robin Butler GCB CVO, Secretary of the Cabinet and Head of the Home Civil Service, Cabinet Office, 70 Whitehall, London SW1A 2AS *Telephone:* 071-270 3000

BUTLER, ROSEMARY   Director of Statistics, Department of Health   Grade: 3

Career: Central Statistical Office 1967-73; senior assistant statistician/statistician Unit for Manpower Studies 1973-77; statistician Department of Employment 1977-80; Ministry of Defence 1980-85: statistician 1980-83, chief statistician (CS) 1983-85; CS HM Treasury 1985-89; assistant secretary Department of Social Security 1989-91; under secretary, director of statistics Department of Health 1991-

Date of birth: 15 July 1946 *Education/professional qualifications:* Maynard School, Exeter; London School of Economics, computational methods (BScEcon 1967) *Marital status:* married Anthony David 1971 *Recreations:* theatre, music, birdwatching

Mrs Rosemary Butler, Director of Statistics, Department of Health, Hannibal House, Elephant and Castle, London SE1 6TE *Telephone:* 071-972 2318 *Fax:* 071-972 2320

BUTT, GEOFFREY FRANK   Under Secretary of State (Legal), HM Customs and Excise   Grade: 3

Career: HM Customs and Excise 1971-: legal assistant 1971-74, senior legal assistant 1974-82, assistant solicitor 1982-86, under secretary (legal: civil litigation, VAT appeals) 1986-

Date of birth: 5 May 1943 *Education/professional qualifications:* Royal Masonic School, Bushey, Hertfordshire; Reading University, English literature (BA 1965); law (solicitor 1970) *Marital status:* married Lee Anne 1972; 2 sons, 1 daughter *Recreations:* classical music and art, reading, gardening

Geoffrey F Butt Esq, Under Secretary, Solicitor's Office, HM Customs and Excise, New King's Beam House, 22 Upper Ground, London SE1 9PJ *Telephone:* 071-865 5124 *Fax:* 071-865 5022

BUXTON, RICHARD JOSEPH   Commissioner, Law Commission   Grade: 2 equivalent

Career: fellow Exeter College, Oxford 1964-73; barrister 1972-88; law commissioner 1989- *Current non-Whitehall posts:* recorder Crown Court 1987-

Date of birth: 13 July 1938 *Education/professional qualifications:* Brighton College; Exeter College, Oxford, jurisprudence (1st School of Jurisprudence 1961, BCL 1962) *Honours, decorations:* QC 1983 *Marital status:* married Mary Tyerman 1987 *Publications:* Local Government (Penguin 1973) *Clubs:* United Oxford and Cambridge University, Hornsey Squash *Recreations:* walking, squash

Richard J Buxton Esq QC, Commissioner, Law Commission, 31 John Street, London WC1 *Telephone:* 071-411 1231

BYATT, IAN   Director-General Office of Water Services

Career: economics lecturer Durham University 1955-62; economic consultant HM Treasury (HMT) 1962-64; economics lecturer London School of Economics 1964-67; senior economic adviser Department of Education and Science 1967-69; director of economics and statistics Ministry of Housing and Local Government 1970-72; director of economics Department of Environment 1970-78; HM Treasury 1972-89: director of public sector economic unit 1972-78, deputy chief economic adviser 1978-89; director-general Office of Water Services (economic regulation of the water industry in England and Wales) 1989-

Date of birth: 11 March 1932 *Education/professional qualifications:* Kirkham Grammar School, Lancashire; St Edmund Hall, Oxford, philosophy, politics and economics (BA 1955); Nuffield College, Oxford, economic history (D Phil 1962); Harvard University, USA, economics *Marital status:* married Antonia Susan Drabble 1959 (divorced); 1 daughter, 1 son (deceased) *Publications:* British Electrical Industry 1875-1914 (OUP 1979) *Clubs:* United Oxford and Cambridge University *Recreations:* painting

Ian Byatt Esq, Director-General, Office of Water Services, 7 Hill Street, Birmingham B5 4UA *Telephone:* 021-625 1350 *Fax:* 021-625 1348

C

CAINES, ERIC   Director of Personnel, National Health Service Management Executive, Department of Health

Career: Home Office 1984-87; Department of [Health] Social Security 1987-90; director of personnel national health service management executive, Department of Health 1990-

Date of birth: 27 February 1936   *Education/professional qualifications:* Leeds University (LLB Hons); London University, history of art (diploma)

Eric Caines Esq, Director of Personnel, National Health Service Management Executive, Department of Health, Richmond House, 79 Whitehall, London SW1A 2NS   *Telephone:* 071-210 3000

CAINES, Sir JOHN   Permanent Secretary, Department for Education   Grade: 1 *(see Addenda)*

Career: assistant principal Ministry of Supply 1957; Ministry of Aviation 1960-66: assistant private secretary 1960-61, principal 1961-64, civil air attaché Middle East 1964-66; assistant secretary Board of Trade 1968; secretary Commission on Third London Airport 1968-71; Department of Trade and Industry (DTI) 1971-80: assistant secretary 1971-72, private secretary to Secretary of State 1972-74, under secretary 1974-77, secretary 1977-80; chief executive National Enterprise Board 1979-80; British Overseas Trade Board 1980-83; deputy secretary Cabinet Office 1983, DTI 1983-87; permanent secretary Overseas Development Administration, Foreign and Commonwealth Office 1987-89; permanent secretary Department of Education and Science 1989- *Current non-Whitehall posts:* director Business in the Community 1991-

Date of birth: 13 January 1933   *Education/professional qualifications:* Westminster; Christ Church, Oxford, modern languages (MA) *Honours, decorations:* CB 1983, KCB 1990 *Marital status:* married Mary Large 1963; 1 son, 2 daughters *Recreations:* travel, music, gardening, theatre

Sir John Caines KCB, Permanent Secretary, Department for Education, Sanctuary Buildings, Great Smith Street, London SW1P 3BT *Telephone:* 071-925 6234

CALDER, JULIAN RICHARD   Director of Statistics, Inland Revenue   Grade: 3

Career: Statistician Central Statistical Office 1973-81; Inland Revenue 1981-: statistician 1981-85, director of statistics (direct taxes analysis and forecasts) 1985-

Date of birth: 6 December 1941   *Education/professional qualifications:* Dulwich College, London; Brasenose College, Oxford, mathematics (BA 1962); Newcastle University, mathematics (MSc 1963); Birkbeck College, London University, statistics (MSc 1972) *Marital status:* married Avril 1965; 2 sons *Recreations:* cycling, listening to music

Julian R Calder Esq, Director of Statistics, Inland Revenue, Somerset House, London WC2R 1LB *Telephone:* 071-438 6609 *Fax:* 071-438 7582

CALDWELL, EDWARD GEORGE   Parliamentary Counsel, Office of the Parliamentary Counsel   Grade: 2

Career: solicitor; Law Commission (LC) 1967-69; Office of the Parliamentary Counsel (OPC) 1969- Seconded to LC 1975-77, 1986-88; parliamentary counsel (drafting government bills) OPC 1981-

Date of birth: 21 August 1941 *Education/professional qualifications:* Clifton College, Bristol; Worcester College, Oxford, law (BA 1963) *Honours, decorations:* CB 1990 *Marital status:* married Bronwen Crockett 1965; 2 daughters

Edward G Caldwell Esq CB, Parliamentary Counsel, Office of the Parliamentary Counsel, 36 Whitehall, London SW1A 2AY *Telephone:* 071-210 6633

CALMAN, Dr KENNETH CHARLES   Chief Medical Officer, **Department of Health**   Grade: 1A

Career: Glasgow University 1968-88: surgery lecturer 1968-74, oncology professor 1974-84, postgraduate dean 1984-88; chief medical officer (CMO) Scottish Office 1989-91; CMO Department of Health (advice to government on public health safeguards) 1991-

Date of birth: 25 December 1941 *Education/professional qualifications:* Allan Glen's School, Glasgow; Glasgow University, biochemistry (BSc 1964), medicine (MB ChB 1967, MD 1973, PhD 1971) *Marital status:* married Ann Wilkie 1967; 1 son, 2 daughters *Publications:* Healthy Respect (Faber & Faber 1987) *Clubs:* New, Edinburgh *Recreations:* golf, gardening

Dr Kenneth C Calman, Chief Medical Officer, Department of Health, Richmond House, 79 Whitehall, London SW1A 2NS *Telephone:* 071-210 5150 *Fax:* 071-210 5407

CAMERON, JAMES   Industrial Director, Welsh Office   Grade: 4

Career: private industry 1962-91: manufacturing director Langley Insulation Ltd 1980-84; managing director Rexel Engineering Ltd 1984-91; industrial director Welsh Office (stimulating regional industrial growth) 1991-

Date of birth: 14 March 1949 *Education/professional qualifications:* Dumfries Academy; Dumfries Technical College, mechanical engineering (HNC 1972); Strathclyde University, mechanical engineering (BSc 1974); CEng 1976; FIMechE 1988 *Marital status:* married Carolyn 1970; 1 daughter, 1 son *Clubs:* Cardiff Golf, Austin Counties Car, Rover Sports Register *Recreations:* golf, classic cars

James Cameron Esq, Industrial Director, Welsh Office, Cathays Park, Cardiff CF1 3NQ *Telephone:* 0222 825685 *Fax:* 0222 823204

CAMMELL, JOHN ERNEST   Head of Electronics and Electrical **Engineering, Mechanical Engineering, Industry 2 Division, Department of Trade and Industry**   Grade: 3 *(see Addenda)*

Career: assistant and deputy victualling officer Admiralty 1951-63; training officer Department of Scientific and Industrial Research 1963-65; principal, machine tools and automation, Ministry of Technology 1965-70; Department of Trade and Industry (DTI) 1970-81: director industrial development DTI Office for Wales 1970-74, head of small firms division 1974-76, vehicles division 1976-81; National Maritime Institute 1981-84; director 1981-82, managing director NMI Ltd on secondment 1982-84; DTI 1984-: head of regional policy division 1984-1985, head of mechanical engineering division, materials and manufacturing division, manufacturing technology and IT division 1985-90, of manufacturing technology division 1990-92, of electronics and electrical engineering and mechanical engineering, industry 2 division 1992-

Date of birth: 14 November 1932 *Education/professional qualifications:* Highfield College, Leigh-on-Sea *Marital status:* divorced *Recreations:* amateur theatre, all spectator sports, golf

John E Cammell Esq, Under Secretary Industry 2 Division, Ashdown House, 123 Victoria Street, London SW1E 6RB *Telephone:* 071-215 5000

CAMPBELL, Air Vice Marshal D G   Chief Executive, RAF Support Command Maintenance Group (Executive Agency)

Air Vice Marshal D G Campbell, Chief Executive,, RAF Support Command Maintenance Group, RAF Brampton, Huntingdon, Cambridge PE18 8QL

CAMPBELL, NIALL GORDON   Under Secretary, Social Work Services Group, Home and Health Department, Scottish Office   Grade: 3

Career: Scottish Office 1964-: assistant secretary 1978; under secretary social work services group, Home and Health Department 1989-

Date of birth: 9 November 1941 *Education/professional qualifications:* Merton College, Oxford (BA)

Niall G Campbell Esq, Under Secretary, Social Work Services Group, Home and Health Department, Scottish Office, 43 Jeffrey Street, Edinburgh EH1 1DN *Telephone:* 031-556 8400

CAPEY, MONTAGUE MARTIN   Under Secretary and Director of Establishments and Organisation, Department for Education   Grade: 3

Career: Department of Education [and Science] 1971-: assistant secretary 1976-88; under secretary and director of establishments and organisation 1988-

Date of birth: 16 July 1933 *Education/professional qualifications:* Didsbury College, University of Bristol (BA); Clare College, Cambridge (MA)

Montague M Capey Esq, Director of Establishments and Organisation, Department for Education, Sanctuary Buildings, Great Smith Street, London SW1P 3BT *Telephone:* 071-925 5000

CAPSTICK, CHARLES WILLIAM   Deputy Secretary, Food Safety Directorate, Ministry of Agriculture, Fisheries and Food   Grade: 2

Career: Ministry of Agriculture, Fisheries and Food 1961-: agriculture economist (AE) 1961-68; senior AE 1968-76; assistant secretary milk division 1976-77; director of economics and statistics 1977-89; deputy secretary food safety directorate (food safety, pesticides and emergencies, food science, animal health and veterinary) 1989-

Date of birth: 18 December 1934 *Education/professional qualifications:* Clitheroe Royal Grammar School; King's College, Durham University, agriculture (BSc 1958); Kentucky University, USA, economics (MS 1961) *Honours, decorations:* CMG 1972 *Marital status:* married Joyce Alma Dodsworth 1962; 2 sons

Charles W Capstick Esq CMG, Deputy Secretary, Ministry of Agriculture, Fisheries and Food, Whitehall Place, London SW1A 2HH *Telephone:* 071-270 8120

CARDEN, RICHARD JOHN DEREK Under Secretary, Fisheries Department, Ministry of Agriculture, Fisheries and Food Grade: 3

Career: Ministry of Agriculture, Fisheries and Food (MAFF) 1970-77; HM Treasury 1977-79; MAFF 1979-: chief regional officer, western and midlands region 1983-86, under secretary European Community and external trade policy 1987-91, fisheries secretary 1991-

Date of birth: 12 June 1943 *Education/professional qualifications:* Merchant Taylors' School, Northwood; St John's College, Oxford, literae humaniores (BA, MA 1969, D Phil 1970); Freie Universität, Berlin, Germany 1969-70 *Marital status:* married Pamela Haughton 1971; 1 daughter, 1 son *Publications:* The Papyrus Fragments of Sophocles (De Gruyter 1974)

Richard J D Carden Esq, Under Secretary, Ministry of Agriculture, Fisheries and Food, Nobel House, 17 Smith Square, London SW1P 3HX *Telephone:* 071-238 5796

CARLISLE, MARK (The Rt Hon Lord CARLISLE OF BUCKLOW) Chairman, Criminal Injuries Compensation Board

Career: member Home Office advisory council on penal system 1966-70; Conservative MP for Runcorn 1964-83, for Warrington 1983-87: front bench spokesman on home affairs 1969-70, parliamentary under secretary Home Office (HO) 1970-72, minister of state HO 1972-74, secretary of state for education and science 1979-81; chairman Conservative Home Affairs committee 1983-87; Crown Court recorder 1976-79; chairman Parole Review Committee 1987-88, Criminal Injuries Compensation Board 1989- *Current non-Whitehall posts:* Crown Court recorder 1981-; Courts of Appeal judge, Jersey and Guernsey 1990-; PM's Advisory Committee on Business Appointments of Crown Servants 1988-

Date of birth: 7 July 1991 *Education/professional qualifications:* Radley College; Manchester University, law (LLB 1953); Gray's Inn (barrister 1953, bencher 1980) *Honours, decorations:* DL, QC 1971, PC 1979 *Marital status:* married Sandra Joyce Des Yoeux 1959; 1 daughter *Clubs:* Garrick

The Rt Hon Lord Carlisle of Bucklow QC, DL, Chairman, Criminal Injuries Compensation Board, Whittington House, 19 Alfred Place, London WC1E 7LG *Telephone:* 071-636 9501

CARPENTER, MICHAEL CHARLES Assistant Legal Secretary to the Law Officers Grade: 4

Career: EC Commission 1973-81: administrator directorate-general for competition 1973-79, principal administrator: environment and consumer protection service 1979-80, legal service 1980-81; Lord Chancellor's Department 1981-89: senior legal assistant: administration of justice branch 1981-83, private and international law division (PILD) 1983-85, head of PILD 1985-88, head of civil policy division 1988-89; assistant legal secretary to law officers (finance and establishment officer; civil law support to law officers) 1989-

Date of birth: 16 March 1949 *Education/professional qualifications:* Hampton Grammar School, Middlesex; Keble College, Oxford, jurisprudence (BA 1970, MA); Inner Temple (barrister 1971) *Marital status:* married Susie Valerie 1970; 1 son, 3 daughters *Publications:* co-author Copyright Law in the United Kingdom (Legal Book Pty 1986); Private International Litigation (Longmans 1988) *Recreations:* history, sailing, vintage cars

Michael C L Carpenter Esq, Assistant Legal Secretary to the Law Officers, Attorney General's Chambers, 9 Buckingham Gate, London SW1E 6JP *Telephone:* 071-828 0496 *Fax:* 071-828 0593

CARR, (EDWARD ARTHUR) JOHN   Chief Executive, Welsh Historic Monuments (Executive Agency)   Grade: 5

Career: journalist Thomson Regional Newspapers 1960-65, Financial Times 1965-67; production editor The Sunday Times 1967-70; Times Newspapers Ltd 1970-81: project manager 1970-75, assistant general manager 1975-81; chief executive Waterlow and Sons 1981-82; director Neath Development Partnership 1982-85; Welsh Historic Monuments Executive Agency, Welsh Office (preservation and conservation of built heritage of Wales) 1985-: chief executive 1991-

Date of birth: 31 August 1938 *Education/professional qualifications:* The Leys School, Cambridge; Christ's College, Cambridge, archaeology and anthropology part 1, English part 1 (BA 1960, MA 1963) *Marital status:* married Verity Martin (dissolved 1980); Patrice Metro 1980; 3 daughters (2d previous marriage), 1 son *Clubs:* Civil Service *Recreations:* gardening, newspapers, historic structures

E A John Carr Esq, Chief Executive, Welsh Historic Monuments Executive Agency, 2 Fitzalan Road, Cardiff CF2 1UY *Telephone:* 0222 465511 *Fax:* 0222 465511

CARSBERG, Professor SIR BRYAN VICTOR   Director-General, Office of Fair Trading

Career: chartered accountant 1962-64; accountancy lecturer London School of Economics (LSE) 1964-68; visiting lecturer Graduate School of Business, Chicago University, USA 1968-69; accounting professor Manchester University 1969-81; business administration visiting professor California University, USA; member Institute of Chartered Accountants (ICA) council 1975-79; dean economics and social studies faculty Manchester University 1977-78; assistant director research and technical activities Financial Accounting Standards Board, USA 1978-81; professor of accounting LSE 1981-87; research director ICA 1981-87; visiting professor of accounting LSE 1988-89; director-general Office of Telecommunications (OFTEL) 1984-92; director-general Office of Fair Trading 1992- *Current non-Whitehall posts:* non-executive director Philip Allan Publishers 1982-; Accounting Standards Board 1990-: deputy chairman 1990-92, member 1992-

Date of birth: 3 January 1939 *Education/professional qualifications:* Berkhamsted; London School of Economics, accounting (CA 1960, MScEcon 1967) *Honours, decorations:* Kt 1989 *Marital status:* married Margaret Linda Graham 1960; 2 daughters *Publications:* Current Issues in Accountancy, 2nd ed (1984); Topics in Management Accounting (1980); The Evaluation of Financial Performance in the Water Industry (1983); Current Cost Accounting (1984); Small Company Financial Reporting (1985) *Recreations:* road running, theatre, music, opera

Professor Sir Bryan Carsberg, Director-General, Office of Fair Trading, Field House, Bream's Buildings, London EC4A 1PR *Telephone:* 071-242 2858 *Fax:* 071-269 8800

CARTER, Dr (JOHN) TIMOTHY   Director, Health Policy and Medical Services, Health and Safety Executive   Grade: 3

Career: medical officer British Petroleum 1974-78; senior medical officer BP Chemicals 1978-83; Health and Safety Executive 1983-: director of Medical Services 1983, and of health policy 1989- *Current non-Whitehall posts:* member Medical Research Council 1983-

Date of birth: 12 February 1944 *Education/professional qualifications:* Dulwich College; Corpus Christi College, Cambridge (MB, MA); University College Hospital London (FFOM 1984, FRCP 1987); London School of Hygiene (MSc 1974)

Dr J Timothy Carter FRCP FFOM, Director, Health and Medical Services, Health and Safety Executive, Baynards House, 1 Chepstow Place, London W2 4TF *Telephone:* 071-243 6608

CASE, ANTHEA FIENDLEY   Under Secretary, Pay Group, HM Treasury   Grade: 3

Career: HM Treasury 1966-: assistant principal 1966-74; principal 1974-78; assistant secretary 1978-88: public enterprises division 1978-82, deputy establishment officer 1982-83, aid and export finance division 1988; under secretary 1988-: home, education and transport group 1988-90, pay group (civil service management and pay) 1990-

Date of birth: 7 February 1945 *Education/professional qualifications:* Christ's Hospital, Hertford; St Anne's College, Oxford, history (BA 1966) *Marital status:* married David Charles 1967; 2 daughters

Mrs Anthea F Case, Under Secretary, HM Treasury, Parliament Street, London SW1P 2AG *Telephone:* 071-270 4400 *Fax:* 071-270 4312

CASTALDI, Dr PETER   Chief Medical Adviser and Director of Medical Services, Social Security Benefits Agency (Executive Agency)   Grade: 3

Career: hospital clinical and general practice posts 1966-79; medical officer (MO) Wales and South West Regional Office 1979-82; MO North Fylde Central Office 1982-84; senior MO HQ 1984-85; North Fylde Central Office 1985-92: senior MO 1985-86, principal MO 1986-92; chief medical adviser and director of medical services (medical advice on social security benefits and war pensions) Social Security Benefits Agency 1992-

Date of birth: 13 January 1942 *Education/professional qualifications:* Neath Grammar School for Boys; Welsh National School of Medicine (MB BCh 1966) *Honours, decorations:* OstJ 1977 *Marital status:* married Joan 1967; 1 daughter, 1 son *Clubs:* Lytham St Anne's Lawn Tennis and Squash; Fylde Rugby Football *Recreations:* squash, swimming, birdwatching, watching rugby

Dr Peter Castaldi, Chief Medical Adviser and Director of Medical Services, Social Security Benefits Agency, Friars House, 157-168 Blackfriars Road, London SE1 8EU *Telephone:* 071-972 2000 *Fax:* 071-972 3544

CATLIN, JOHN ANTHONY   Deputy Solicitor, Local Government Finance and Town and Country Planning Directorate, Department of the Environment   Grade: 3

Career: Treasury Solicitor's Department 1975-84; Department of the Environment 1984-: assistant solicitor 1984-89; deputy solicitor local government finance and town and country planning directorate 1989-

Date of birth: 25 November 1947 *Education/professional qualifications:* Birmingham University (LLB 1969)

John A Catlin Esq, Deputy Solicitor, Department of the Environment, 2 Marsham Street, London SW1P 3EB *Telephone:* 071-276 3000

To subscribe to The European Companion
Telephone: 071-240 3902

CAYLEY, MICHAEL FORDE   Director, Capital and Valuation Division, Inland Revenue   Grade: 3

Career: administration trainee Inland Revenue (IR) 1971-73; private secretary to chairman Price Commission 1973-75; IR 1975-: principal 1975-82, assistant secretary 1982-91, under secretary and director capital and valuation division (advising ministers on policy on, and administration of, capital gains and inheritance tax) 1991-

Date of birth: 26 February 1950 *Education/professional qualifications:* Brighton College; St John's College, Oxford, English (MA 1971) *Marital status:* married Jennifer Athalie 1987; 1 stepdaughter, 2 stepsons *Publications:* Moorings [poems] (Carcanet Press 1971); The Spider's Touch [poems] (Carcanet Press 1973) *Recreations:* classical music, piano-playing, choral singing, poetry, walking, old churches and prehistoric sites

Michael Cayley Esq, Director Capital and Valuation Division, Inland Revenue, Somerset House, Strand, London WC2R 1LB
Telephone: 071-438 7290 *Fax:* 071-438 7488

CHALFONT, ALUN ARTHUR GWYN JONES (The Rt Hon The Lord Chalfont)   Chairman Radio Authority

Career: military service 1940-61; journalist 1961-64; minister of state Foreign and Commonwealth Office 1964-70; director various companies; deputy chairman Independent Broadcasting Authority 1989-90; chairman Radio Authority 1991- *Current non-Whitehall posts:* director Lazard Bros and Co Ltd 1983-; chairman VSEL Consortium 1987-; chairman House of Lords All Party Defence Group;

Date of birth: 5 December 1919 *Education/professional qualifications:* West Monmouth School *Honours, decorations:* MC 1957; OBE 1961; PC 1964; life peer 1964 *Marital status:* married Dr Mona Mitchell 1948; 1 daughter (deceased) *Publications:* several books including The Great Commanders (1973); Montgomery of Alamein (1976) *Clubs:* MCC, Garrick, City Livery *Recreations:* music, theatre

The Rt Hon The Lord Chalfont OBE MC, Chairman, The Radio Authority, 3rd Floor, 70 Brampton Road, London SW3 1EY *Telephone:* 071-581 2888

CHANT, (ELIZABETH) ANN   Chief Executive, Social Security Contributions Agency (Executive Agency)   Grade: 4

Career: National Assistance Board 1963-70; Department of [Health and] Social Security 1970-: principal 1982-87: principal private secretary to permanent secretary 1985-87; head of contributions branch 1987-89; head of contributions unit implementation 1989-90, of contributions unit 1990-91; chief executive Social Security Contributions Agency (national insurance collection in GB) 1991-

Date of birth: 16 August 1945 *Education/professional qualifications:* Collegiate Grammar School for Girls, Blackpool *Recreations:* classical music and jazz, reading, seroptomy, victim support

Miss Ann Chant, Chief Executive, Social Security Contributions Agency, DSS Longbenton, Newcastle upon Tyne, NE98 1YX
Telephone: 091-225 7665 *Fax:* 091-225 4198

CHATAWAY, The Rt Hon CHRISTOPHER JOHN   Chairman, Civil Aviation Authority

Career: Olympic Games athlete 1952, 1956, 5,000-metre world record holder; Arthur Guinness & Sons Ltd 1953-55; newscaster Independent Television News 1955; current affairs commentator BBC tv 1956-59; co-founder World Refugee Year 1959; MP 1959-74: joint parliamentary under secretary

Department of Education and Science 1962-64, overseas development opposition spokesman 1964-66, minister for posts and telecommunications 1970-72, for industrial development 1972-74; commerce and industry 1974-88: managing director and vice-chairman Orion Royal Bank Ltd; non-executive chairman British Telecommunications Systems Ltd, United Medical Enterprises; several non-executive directorships; ActionAid 1975-: chairman 1986-; chairman Groundwork Foundation 1985-90, Civil Aviation Authority 1991- *Current non-Whitehall posts:* chairman ActionAid 1986-, Crown Communications Group 1988-, Alcohol Education and Research Council 1991-; non-executive director BET plc, Credito Italiano International Ltd

Date of birth: 31 January 1931 *Education/professional qualifications:* Sherborne School, Dorset; Magdalen College, Oxford, philosophy, politics and economics (BA, MA) *Honours, decorations:* PC 1970 *Marital status:* married Carola 1976; 1 daughter, 3 sons, 1 stepson

The Rt Hon Christopher Chataway, Chairman, Civil Aviation Authority, CAA House, 45-49 Kingsway, London WC2B 6TE *Telephone:* 071-379 7311

CHIPPERFIELD, Sir GEOFFREY HOWES   Permanent Secretary and Chief Executive, PSA Services, Department of the Environment   Grade: 1

Career: Ministry of Housing and Local Government 1956-70; Harkness Fellow 1962-63; principal private secretary Minister of Housing 1968-70; Secretary Greater London Development Plan Inquiry 1970-73; Department of the Environment (DoE) 1976-87: under secretary 1976, deputy secretary 1982-87; Department of Energy 1987-91: deputy secretary 1987-89, permanent secretary 1989-91; DoE: permanent secretary and chief executive Property Services Agency Services 1991-

Date of birth: 20 April 1931 *Education/professional qualifications:* Cranleigh School; New College, Oxford, jurisprudence *Honours, decorations:* CB 1986; KCB 1992 *Marital status:* married Gillian James 1959; 2 sons *Clubs:* United Oxford and Cambridge University *Recreations:* music, reading, gardening

Sir Geoffrey H Chipperfield KCB, Permanent Secretary and Chief Executive PSA Services, Department of the Environment, 2 Marsham Street, London SW1P 3EB *Telephone:* 071-276 3629

CHISHOLM, JOHN ALEXANDER RAYMOND   Chief Executive, Defence Research Agency (Executive Agency)   Grade: 2

Career: Various executive posts in industry 1964-91; chief executive Defence Research Agency 1991-

Date of birth: 27 August 1946 *Education/professional qualifications:* University of Cambridge (MA)

John A R Chisholm Esq, Chief Executive, Defence Research Agency, Meudon Avenue, Farnborough, Hampshire GU14 7TU *Telephone:* 0252-373434

CHIVERS, (CHRISTOPHER) KIT J.A.   Head of Specialist Support Group, HM Treasury   Grade: 4

Career: head of industry division HM Treasury (HMT) 1981-84; member efficiency unit Prime Minister's Office 1984-86; HMT 1986-: head of pay 2 division 1986-90, head of specialist support group (accountancy, operational research, management consultancy) 1990-

Date of birth: 8 March 1945 *Education/professional qualifications:* Glasgow High School; Glasgow University, classics (MA 1966); Trinity College, Oxford, greats (BA, MA 1968) *Marital status:* married Geertje Bouwes 1969; 1 daughter, 1 son

Kit J.A. Chivers Esq, Head of Specialist Support Group, HM Treasury, Parliament Street, London SW1P 3AG *Telephone:* 071-270 4544 *Fax:* 071-270 5653

CHRISTOPHERSON, ROMOLA CAROL ANDREA   Director of Information, Department of Health   Grade: 4

Career: Department of Scientific and Industrial Research, Ministry of Technology 1962-70; Department of Environment 1970-78; Ministry of Agriculture, Fisheries and Food 1978-81; Northern Ireland Office 1981-83; press secretary to prime minister 1983-84; head of information Department of Energy 1984-86; director of information Department of Health [and Social Security] 1986-

Date of birth: 10 January 1939 *Education/professional qualifications:* Collegiate School for Girls, Leicester; St Hugh's College, Oxford, English (BA) *Marital status:* single *Recreations:* amateur dramatics, antiques

Miss Romola C A Christopherson, Director of Information, Department of Health, Richmond House, Whitehall, London SW1A 2NS *Telephone:* 071-210 5440 *Fax:* 071-210 5433

CHURCH, IAN   Editor, Hansard, House of Commons   Grade: 4

Career: reporter Press Association 1964-66, Scotsman 1966-68, The Times 1968-72; House of Commons Official Report (Hansard) 1972-: reporter and sub-editor 1972-88, deputy editor 1988-89, editor and head of the Department of the Official Report 1989-

Date of birth: 18 October 1941 *Education/professional qualifications:* Roan School, London *Marital status:* married Christine 1964; 1 daughter *Recreations:* photography, writing fiction

Ian Church Esq, Editor, Official Report, House of Commons, London SW1A 0AA *Telephone:* 071-219 3000

CLAPHAM, Dr PETER   Director and Chief Executive, National Physical Laboratory (Executive Agency)   Grade: 3

Career: research National Physical Laboratory (NPL) 1960-81; assistant secretary research and technology policy division Department of Trade and Industry 1981-82; division head NPL 1982-85; chief executive National Weights and Measures Laboratory 1985-90; chief executive NPL (national measurement standards) 1990-

Date of birth: 3 November 1940 *Education/professional qualifications:* Ashville College, Harrogate; University College, London, physics (BSc 1960); Imperial College, London, physics (PhD 1969) *Marital status:* married Jean 1965; 2 sons

Dr Peter Clapham, Director and Chief Executive, National Physical Laboratory, Teddington, Middlesex TW11 0LW *Telephone:* 081-943 6015 *Fax:* 081-943 2155

Parliamentary Offices
see page 275

CLARK, (CHARLES) ANTHONY   Under Secretary, Higher Education, Department for Education   Grade: 3

Career: Department of Education and Science: under secretary (US) teacher supply and international relations 1982-87; principal finance officer 1987-89; US further and higher education 1 (higher education policy and funding) 1989-

Date of birth: 13 June 1940 *Education/professional qualifications:* King's College School, Wimbledon; Pembroke College, Oxford, physics (BA, MA 1961) *Marital status:* married Penelope Margaret Brett 1978; 2 daughters, 1 son *Recreations:* reading, gardening, golf

C Anthony Clark Esq, Under Secretary, Department for Education, Sanctuary Buildings, Great Smith Street, London SW1P 3PT *Telephone:* 071-934 9912

CLARK, DAVID JOHN   Under Secretary, Department of Social Security   Grade: 3

Career: Department of [Health and] Social Security 1969-; assistant principal 1969, principal 1973, assistant secretary 1983, under secretary and head social security division C (all pension and national insurance contributions policy) 1990-

Date of birth: 20 September 1947 *Education/professional qualifications:* University of Kent (MA) *Marital status:* married Caroline 1970; 2 sons, 3 daughters (1 foster)

David J Clark Esq, Under Secretary, Department of Social Security, Adelphi, 1-11 John Adam Street, London WC2N 6HT *Telephone:* 071-962 8451 *Fax:* 071-962 8766

CLARK, GREGOR MUNRO   Assistant Legal Secretary and Scottish Parliamentary Counsel, Lord Advocate's Department   Grade: 3

Career: advocate 1972-; law practice 1972-74; Lord Advocate's Department 1974-: assistant, later deputy parliamentary draftsman 1974-79, assistant legal secretary and Scottish parliamentary counsel (assisting Scottish law officers on Scottish matters, drafting bills relating to Scotland and Scottish adaptations of bills) 1979-

Date of birth: 18 April 1946 *Education/professional qualifications:* Queen's Park Senior Secondary School, Glasgow; St Andrew's University, law (LLB 1970) *Marital status:* married Jane Maralyn 1974; 1 son, 2 daughters *Recreations:* music, Scandinavian languages and literature

Gregor M Clark Esq, Assistant Legal Secretary and Scottish Parliamentary Counsel, Lord Advocate's Department, Fielden House, 10 Great College Street, London SW1P 3SL *Telephone:* 071-276 6817 *Fax:* 071-276 6834

CLARKE, HENRY BENWELL   Deputy Chief Executive, Crown Estate   Grade: 3

Career: British Rail Property Board (BRPB) 1972-88: management S, NW and E regions 1972-85; property consultant Transmark Worldwide Ltd 1982-; BRPB: regional estate surveyor and manager Midland region 1985-86, chief estate surveyor 1986-87, national development manager 1987-88; Crown Estate 1988-: deputy chief executive (direction and stewardship of the Crown's commercial and residential estates) 1988- (acting chief executive and accounting officer 1989) *Current non-Whitehall posts:* general council member British Property Federation 1989-; non-executive director Youth With A Mission (England) 1990-

Date of birth: 30 January 1950 *Education/professional qualifications:* St John's School, Leatherhead; South Bank Polytechnic estate management (BSc 1972); Imperial College, London University, management science (MSc 1977, DIC 1977); FRICS; ACIArb; MBIM *Marital status:* married Verena Angela Lodge 1973; 1 daughter, 3 sons *Clubs:* National *Recreations:* reading, walking, architecture, Church

Henry B Clarke Esq, Deputy Chief Executive, The Crown Estate, 16 Carlton House Terrace, London SW1Y 5AH *Telephone:* 071-210 4390 *Fax:* 071-930 1295

CLARKE, OWEN J Controller, Inland Revenue, Scotland Grade: 4

Career: Inland Revenue 1970-: district inspector 1970-73; Edinburgh 1973-80: enquiry branch 1973-76, in charge of special office 1976-80; group controller Merseyside 1980-81, Scotland 1981-88; controller north of England 1988-90, Scotland 1990-

Date of birth: 15 March 1937 *Education/professional qualifications:* Portobello Secondary School, Edinburgh *Marital status:* married Elizabeth 1964; 2 sons, 1 daughter *Clubs:* Scottish Judo Federation; Tantallon Golf, North Berwick *Recreations:* sport, primarily judo

Owen J Clarke Esq, Controller, Inland Revenue, Scotland, Lauriston House, 80 Lauriston Place, Edinburgh EH3 9SL *Telephone:* 031-229 9344 *Fax:* 031-229 0394

CLARKE, PETER JAMES Secretary to the Commissioners, Forestry Commission Grade: 4

Career: War Office 1952-67; Forestry Commission (FC) 1967-75: principal 1972-75; principal Department of Energy 1975-76; secretary to commissioners, FC (services and advice to the Forestry Commissioners) 1976-

Date of birth: 16 January 1934 *Education/professional qualifications:* Enfield Grammar School, Middlesex; St John's College, Cambridge, law (BA 1960, MA) *Marital status:* married Roberta Anne 1966; 1 daughter, 1 son *Clubs:* Commonwealth *Recreations:* gardening, walking, sailing

Peter J Clarke Esq, Secretary to the Commissioners, Forestry Commission, 231 Corstorphine Road, Edinburgh EH12 7AT *Telephone:* 031-334 0303 *Fax:* 031-316 4891

CLARKE, ROGER ERIC Under Secretary, Shipping Policy, Emergencies and Security, Department of Transport Grade: 3

Career: principal, civil aviation posts Ministry of Aviation, Board of Trade, Department of Trade and Industry 1964-72; seconded to Fiji government as air traffic rights adviser 1972-74; Department of Trade 1974-83: insurance division 1974-79: principal 1974-75, assistant secretary (AS) 1975-79; AS commercial relations and exports 1979-80, civil aviation policy 1980-83; Department of Transport 1983-: AS civil aviation policy 1983-85, under secretary 1985-: head of civil aviation policy 1985-89, of public transport 1989-91, of shipping policy, emergencies and security (UK shipping industry policy; international aspects of shipping policy; crisis and wartime use of merchant fleet; civil emergency transport; transport security) 1991-

Date of birth: 13 June 1939 *Education/professional qualifications:* University College School, London; Corpus Christi College, Cambridge, classics (BA, MA 1960) *Marital status:* married Elizabeth Pingstone 1983; 1 daughter *Clubs:* Reform *Recreations:* family, friends, church, garden, walking, theatre, music, languages, travel

Roger E Clarke Esq, Under Secretary, Department of Transport, 2 Marsham Street, London SW1P 3EB *Telephone:* 071-276 5910 *Fax:* 071-276 0818

CLARKE, Dr ROGER HOWARD   Director, National Radiological Protection Board   Grade: 3

Career: research officer Central Electricity Generating Board 1965-77; National Radiological Protection Board 1978-: head of nuclear power assessments 1978-82, board secretary 1983-87, director 1987- *Current non-Whitehall posts:* member International Commission on Radiological Protection 1989-; chairman Nuclear Energy Agency Committee on Radiation Protection and Public Health 1987-; alternate delegate UN Scientific Committee on Effects of Atomic Radiation 1987

Date of birth: 22 August 1943 *Education/professional qualifications:* King Edward VI School, Stourbridge; Birmingham University, physics (BSc 1964), reactor physics and technology (MSc 1965); Central London Polytechnic, physical aspects of nuclear reactors in public and working environment (PhD 1973) *Marital status:* married Sandra Ann Buckley 1966; 1 son, 1 daughter *Publications:* co-author Carcinogenesis and Radiation Risk: A Biomathematical Reconnaissance (BIR 1977)

Dr Roger H Clarke, Director, National Radiological Protection Board, Chilton, Didcot, Oxfordshire OX11 0RQ *Telephone:* 0235 831600 *Fax:* 0235 833891

CLAYTON, MARGARET ANN   Under Secretary, Police Department, Home Office   Grade: 3

Career: Home Office (HO) 1960-71; principal, European Communities bill, Cabinet Office 1972; principal to assistant secretary HO 1973-83; resident chairman Civil Service Selection Board 1983; under secretary 1983-: HO 1983-: establishment officer 1983-86, director of prison department services 1986-90; seconded to Department of Employment 1990; police department 1990-

Date of birth: 7 May 1941 *Education/professional qualifications:* Christ's Hospital, Hertford; Birkbeck College, London, English (BA 1964), organisational behaviour (MSc 1988) *Marital status:* single *Clubs:* Reform *Recreations:* gardening, riding, reading, theatre

Miss Margaret A Clayton, Under Secretary, Home Office, 50 Queen Anne's Gate, London SW1H 9AT *Telephone:* 071-273 3000

CLEAVE, BRIAN E   Solicitor of Inland Revenue, Board of Inland Revenue   Grade: 2

Career: Office of Solicitor of Inland Revenue 1967-: principal assistant solicitor 1986-90; solicitor 1990-

Date of birth: 3 September 1939 *Education/professional qualifications:* Exeter University

Brian E Cleave Esq, Solicitor of Inland Revenue, Board of Inland Revenue, Somerset House, London WC2R 1LB *Telephone:* 071-438 6622

CLEMITS, JOHN HENRY   Managing Director, PSA Projects Cardiff, Department of the Environment   Grade: 4

Career: Property Services Agency (PSA) Department of Environment 1973-: director of army works 1979-85, director for Wales 1985-90, managing director PSA Projects Cardiff 1990-

Date of birth: 16 February 1934 *Education/professional qualifications:* Plymouth College of Art, Architecture (ARIBA)

John H Clemits, Managing Director, PSA Projects, Government Buildings, St Agnes Road, Gabalfa, Cardiff CF4 4YF *Telephone:* 0222 586760

CLIVE, ERIC MCCREDIE   Commissioner, Scottish Law Commission

Career: law faculty Edinburgh University 1962-80: lecturer, senior lecturer, reader, professor of Scots law; Scottish law commissioner 1981-

Date of birth: 24 July 1938 *Education/professional qualifications:* Stranraer High School; Edinburgh University, arts (MA 1958), law (LLB 1960); Michigan University, USA, law (LLM 1962); Virginia University, law (SJD 1968) *Marital status:* married Kay 1962; 3 daughters, 1 son *Publications:* Scots Law for Journalists (W Green and Son 1988); Law of Husband and Wife in Scotland (W Green and Son 1982) *Recreations:* hill walking, chess

Eric M Clive Esq, Commissioner, Scottish Law Commission, 140 Causewayside, Edinburgh EH9 1PR *Telephone:* 031-668 2131 *Fax:* 031-662 4900

CLOTHIER, Sir CECIL MONTACUTE   Chairman, Council on Tribunals

Career: military service 1939-46; law practice 1950-65, QC, recorder, deputy high court judge 1965-78; parliamentary Commissioner for Administration man] 1979-84; chairman Police Complaints Authority 1985-89; chairman Council on Tribunals, vice-chairman Interception of Communications Tribunal 1989-

Date of birth: 28 August 1919 *Education/professional qualifications:* Stonyhurst College; Lincoln College, Oxford, law (BCL 1948, MA) *Honours, decorations:* QC 1965, KCB 1982 *Marital status:* married Mary Elizabeth Bush 1943 (died 1984); 1 son, 2 daughters *Clubs:* Athenaeum

Sir Cecil Clothier KCB QC, Chairman, Council on Tribunals, 22 Kingsway, London WC2B 6LE *Telephone:* 071-936 7040 *Fax:* 071-936 7044

COATES, DAVID R   Economics and Statistics, Establishment and Finance Division, Department of Trade and Industry   Grade: 3

Career: research assistant University of Manchester, Manchester Business School 1966-68; economic adviser Ministry of Technology and Department of Trade and Industry (DTI) 1968-74; DTI 1974-: senior economic adviser 1974-82, assistant secretary 1982-89, under secretary 1989, economics, market intelligence and statistics, establishment and finance division 1990-

Date of birth: 22 March 1942 *Education/professional qualifications:* Leeds Grammar School; Queen's College, Oxford; London School of Economics *Recreations:* family, gardening, travel, music

David R Coates Esq, Establishment and Finance Division, Department of Trade and Industry, Ashdown House, 123 Victoria Street, London, SW1E 6RB *Telephone:* 071-215 5000

COATES, DUDLEY JAMES   Director, Regional Services, Ministry of Agriculture, Fisheries and Food   Grade: 3

Career: assistant principal Ministry of Agriculture, Fisheries and Food (MAFF) 1968-70; second secretary UK permanent delegation to EC, Brussels 1970-72; principal MAFF 1973-78; lecturer Civil Service College 1978-81; MAFF 1981-: head of animal welfare division 1981-83, of financial management team 1983-87, director-general Intervention Board corporate service 1987-89, director regional services 1989-

Date of birth: 15 September 1946 *Education/professional qualifications:* Westcliff High School for Boys, Essex; Sussex University, politics (BA 1968) *Marital status:* married Dr Jean Margaret Walsingham 1969; 2 daughters *Publications:* contributor to Policies into Practice (Heineman 1984) *Recreations:* Christian activities, singing, cycling

Dudley J Coates Esq, Director of Regional Services, Ministry of Agriculture, Fisheries and Food, Nobel House, 17 Smith Square, London SW1P 3JR *Telephone:* 071-238 6717 *Fax:* 071-238 6709

COATES, (JAMES) JIM RICHARD   Under Secretary, Urban and General Department of Transport   Grade: 3

Career: assistant principal/principal Ministry of Transport 1959-71; Department of Environment 1971-83: assistant secretary (AS) urban transport policy 1971-75; Property Services Agency 1975-83: directorate of civil accommodation 1975-79: AS 1975-77, under secretary (US) 1977-79, director London region 1979-83; Department of Transport 1983-: US highways policy 1983-85, railway 1985-91, urban and general (provincial local public transport; parking and traffic management, environmental aspects; inter-modal considerations) 1991-

Date of birth: 18 October 1935 *Education/professional qualifications:* Nottingham High School; Clare College, Cambridge, modern languages (BA, MA 1959) *Honours, decorations:* CB 1992 *Marital status:* married (Helen) Rosamund 1969; 1 son, 1 daughter *Recreations:* listening to music, looking at buildings

Jim R Coates Esq CB, Under Secretary, Department of Transport, 2 Marsham Street, London SW1P 3EB *Telephone:* 071-276 4919

COBBOLD, Rear Admiral RICHARD FRANCIS   Assistant Chief of Defence Staff, Operational Requirements (Sea Systems) Ministry of Defence

Career: commanding officer (CO) HMS Mohawk 1977-79; Ministry of Defence (MoD) 1979-83: directorate of naval plans 1979-81, assistant director (AD) navy defence operational requirements 1981-82, AD defence concepts 1982-83; member Royal College of Defence Studies 1984; CO HMS Brazen 1985-86; director defence concepts MoD 1987-88; captain 2nd frigate squadron 1989-90; assistant chief of defence staff, operational requirements (sea systems) MoD 1991-

Date of birth: 25 June 1942 *Education/professional qualifications:* Bryanston School, Dorset *Recreations:* sport, natural history, gardening

Rear Admiral Richard F Cobbold, Assistant Chief of Defence Staff, Ministry of Defence, Whitehall, London SW1A 2HB *Telephone:* 071-218 9000

COCHLIN, M J A   Head of Economic and Regional Policy Group, Welsh Office   Grade: 3

M J A Cochlin Esq, Head of Economic and Regional Policy Group, Welsh Office, Cathays Park, Cardiff CF1 3NQ *Telephone:* 0222 825111

COLES, Sir (ARTHUR) JOHN   Deputy Under Secretary, Foreign and Commonwealth Office   Senior grade

Career: HM Diplomatic Service 1960:- Middle East Centre for Arab Studies 1960-62; third Secretary Khartoum 1962-64; Foreign and Commonwealth Office (FCO) UN Department 1964-68; assistant political agent Trucial States, Dubai 1968-71; Cabinet Office 1971-72; FCO, private secretary to ministers of state 1972-75, head of chancery Cairo 1975-77, developing countries counsellor UK Permanent Representation to EC, Brussels 1977-80, FCO, head of S Asian department 1980-81, private secretary (foreign affairs and defence) to prime minister 1981-84, ambassador to Jordan 1984-88, high commissioner to Australia 1988-91, FCO deputy under secretary for Asia and the Americas 1991-

Date of birth: 13 November 1937 *Education/professional qualifications:* Magdalen College School, Brackley; Magdalen College, Oxford, history (BA 1960) *Honours, decorations:* CMG 1984, KCMG 1989 *Marital status:* married Anne Mary Sutherland Graham 1965; 2 sons, 1 daughter *Clubs:* United Oxford and Cambridge University *Recreations:* walking, birdwatching, reading, music

Sir John Coles KCMG, Deputy Under Secretary, Foreign and Commonwealth Office, King Charles Street, London SW1A 2AH *Telephone:* 071-270 3000

COLLON, MICHAEL HYDE   Secretary of Law Commission   Grade: 4

Career: barrister 1970-75; Lord Chancellor's Department 1975-: private secretary to Lord Chancellor 1980-82, secretary of Law Commission (staffing, funding and organisation) 1987-

Date of birth: 11 May 1944 *Education/professional qualifications:* Eton College; Trinity College, Cambridge, natural sciences (BA, MA 1965) *Marital status:* married Josephine Ann 1971; 3 daughters, 1 son *Recreations:* music

Michael H Collon Esq, Secretary, Law Commission, 37-38 John Street, Theobalds Road, London WC1N 2BQ *Telephone:* 071-411 1250 *Fax:* 071-411 1297

COLVILLE OF CULROSS, (JOHN) MARK ALEXANDER (The Viscount Colville of Culross)   Chairman, Parole Board of England and Wales

Career: barrister 1960-; minister of state Home Office 1972-74; leader UK delegation to UN Human Rights Commission 1980-83; chairman Mental Health Act Commission 1983-86; chairman Alcohol Education and Research Council 1984-90; chairman Parole Board for England and Wales (advising Home Secretary on prisoners' release) 1988- *Current non-Whitehall posts:* director Securities and Futures Authority 1986-; governor BUPA 1990-

Date of birth: 19 July 1933 *Education/professional qualifications:* Rugby School; New College, Oxford, classics, law (BA, MA 1961) *Honours, decorations:* QC 1978 *Marital status:* married Margaret Birgitta Norton 1974; 5 sons (4 by previous marriage)

The Viscount Colville of Culross QC, Chairman, Parole Board of England and Wales, 1 Serjeant's Inn, London EC4Y 1NH *Telephone:* 071-583 1355

COOK, Major-General ROBERT FRANCIS LEONARD   Signal Officer-in-Chief (Army); Director-General Command, Control Communications and Information Systems (Army), Ministry of Defence

Career: secretary NATO military committee, Brussels 1986-89; Ministry of Defence 1989-: signal officer-in-chief (army) 1989-; director-general command, control, communications and information systems (army) 1990-

Date of birth: 18 June 1939 *Education/professional qualifications:* University College of Wales; Welbeck College; Royal Military Academy, Sandhurst; Royal Military College of Science; Staff College; NATO Defence College

Major-General Robert F L Cook, Signal Officer-in-Chief (Army), Ministry of Defence, Northumberland House, Northumberland Avenue, London WC2N 5BP *Telephone:* 071-218 9000

COOKE, BRIAN   Circuit Administrator, South Eastern Circuit, Lord Chancellor's Department   Grade: 3

Career: Lord Chancellor's Department 1971-: head of judicial appointments group 1987-88; circuit administrator south eastern circuit 1989-

Date of birth: 16 January 1935 *Education/professional qualifications:* University College, London (LLB); barrister (Lincoln's Inn)

Brian Cooke Esq JP, Lord Chancellor's Department, Circuit Office, New Cavendish House, 18 Maltravers Street, London WC2R 3EU *Telephone:* 071-936 6000

COOKE, DAVID THOMAS   Deputy Chief Accountancy Adviser, HM Treasury   Grade: 4

Career: private practice accountancy training 1957-62; accountancy posts in various book publishers 1962-69; financial accountant/company secretary commercial companies 1969-74; senior accountant Her Majesty's Stationery Office 1974-78; chief accountant Ministry of Defence procurement executive 1978-80; Monopolies and Mergers Commission 1980-89: senior principal 1980-83, assistant secretary 1983-89; deputy chief accountancy adviser to HM Treasury, director government accountancy management unit 1989-

Date of birth: 27 March 1938 *Education/professional qualifications:* Harrow Weald County Grammar School; Open University, social sciences (BA 1976); FCA 1964 *Marital status:* married Hazel 1963; 2 sons *Clubs:* Civil Service *Recreations:* singing, inland cruising

David T Cooke Esq, Deputy Chief Accountancy Adviser, HM Treasury, Parliament Street, London SW1P 3AG *Telephone:* 071-270 5282 *Fax:* 071-270 5653

COOKE, JOHN ARTHUR   Under Secretary, International Trade Policy, Trade Policy and Export Promotion Division, Department of Trade and Industry   Grade: 3

Career: assistant principal Board of Trade 1966; second/first secretary (FS) UK delegation to EC 1969-73; principal Department of Trade and Industry (DTI) 1973-76; FS UK permanent representation to EC 1976-77; DT[I] 1977-: principal 1977-80, assistant secretary (AS) 1980-84, seconded as assistant director to Morgan Grenfell and Co Ltd 1984-85, AS 1985-87, under secretary: head of central unit 1989- and director of deregulation unit (reduction of businesses' burdens) 1990-92; and international trade policy, trade policy and export promotion division 1992- *Current non-Whitehall posts:* non-executive director RTZ Pillar 1990-

Date of birth: 13 April 1943 *Education/professional qualifications:* Dragon School and Magdalen College School, Oxford; Heidelberg, Germany, German; King's College, Cambridge, history (BA 1964, MA); London School of Economics, history research *Marital status:* married Tania Frances 1970; 1 son, 2 daughters *Recreations:* reading, travel, looking at buildings

John A Cooke Esq, Under Secretary, Trade Policy and Export Promotion Division, Department of Trade and Industry, Ashdown House, 123 Victoria Street, London SW1E 6RB *Telephone:* 071-215 5000 *Fax:* 071-215 6471

COOKSEY, DAVID JAMES SCOTT   Chairman, Audit Commission

Career: director of various companies; chairman Audit Commission (external audit of local authorities and NHS in England and Wales) 1986- *Current non-Whitehall posts:* chairman and chief executive Advent Ltd 1981-; member Department of Trade and Industry Innovation Advisory Board 1989-

Date of birth: 14 May 1940 *Education/professional qualifications:* Westminster School; St Edmund Hall, Oxford, metallurgy (BA, MA 1963) *Marital status:* married Janet 1973; 1 daughter, 1 son, 1 stepdaughter *Clubs:* Royal Thames Yacht; New, Edinburgh *Recreations:* sailing, performing arts

David J S Cooksey Esq, Chairman, Audit Commission, 1 Vincent Square, London SW1P 2PN *Telephone:* 071-828 1212

COOPER, JOHN WALTER   Director of Field Systems, Employment Service (Executive Agency)   Grade: 4

Career: Department of Employment: director of field systems Employment Service (new systems for local job placement and unemployment benefit payment offices) 1987-

Date of birth: 16 March 1933 *Education/professional qualifications:* Woking Grammar School; University College, London, modern history (BA 1954) *Honours, decorations:* CBE 1990 *Marital status:* widowed 1983; married Joy 1987; 2 sons, 3 daughters *Clubs:* Army and Navy *Recreations:* fell-walking, travel, music

John W Cooper Esq CBE, Director of Field Systems, Employment Service, St Vincent House, 30 Orange Street, London WC2H 7HT *Telephone:* 071-389 1502 *Fax:* 071-389 1520

CORLETT, CLIVE WILLIAM   Commissioner, Inland Revenue   Grade: 2

Career: Inland Revenue (IR) 1960-; seconded to Civil Service Selection Board 1970; seconded as private secretary to chancellor of exchequer 1972-74, as head of HM Treasury direct tax division 1979-81; director IR 1985-91, deputy secretary, commissioner 1992-

Date of birth: 14 June 1938 *Education/professional qualifications:* Birkenhead School; Brasenose College, Oxford, politics, philosophy and economics (BA 1960) *Marital status:* married Margaret Catherine Jones 1964; 1 son *Recreations:* walking

Clive W Corlett Esq, Commissioner, Inland Revenue, Somerset House, Strand, London WC2R 1LB *Telephone:* 071-438 7586

CORLEY, PETER MAURICE SINCLAIR   Under Secretary, Regional Development and Inward Investment, Regional and Small Firms Division, Department of Trade and Industry   Grade: 3

Career: Ministry of Power 1957-61; Ministry of Transport 1961-65; Board of Trade 1965-69; Brussels embassy 1969-71; assistant secretary Department of Trade and Industry (D[T])I) 1972-75; director-general Economic Co-operation Office, Riyadh 1976-78; DI 1978-81; under secretary investment, development and accountancy services division (regional policy, inward investment promotion, EC structural funds) 1988-92, of regional development and inward investment, regional and small firms division 1992-

Date of birth: 15 June 1933 *Education/professional qualifications:* Marlborough College; King's College, Cambridge, economics (BA, MA 1957) *Marital status:* married Dr Marjorie Constance Doddridge 1961; 2 daughters *Clubs:* United Oxford and Cambridge University *Recreations:* bookbinding

Peter M S Corley Esq, Under Secretary, Regional and Small Firms Division, Department of Trade and Industry, Kingsgate House, 66-74 Victoria Street, London SW1E 6SW *Telephone:* 071-215 5000

CORMACK, Dr DOUGLAS   Chief Executive, Warren Spring Laboratory (Executive Agency)   Grade: 3

Career: research-associate Woods Hole Oceanographic Institution, USA 1964-67; Warren Spring Laboratory (WSL) 1967-79: senior scientific officer 1967-74, head of marine pollution division 1974-79; chief scientific adviser/spillage response co-ordinator Marine Pollution Control Unit Departments of Trade and Industry/Transport 1979-86; WSL 1986-: deputy director environment 1986-89, research/business manager 1989-92, director and chief executive 1992-

Date of birth: 10 January 1939 *Education/professional qualifications:* Greenock High School; Glasgow University, physical chemistry (BSc 1961), surface chemistry (PhD 1964) *Marital status:* married Barbara Ann 1966; 2 sons *Publications:* Response to Oil and Chemical Marine Pollution (Elsevier 1983) *Recreations:* sailing, country pursuits, reading philosophy and history

Dr Douglas Cormack, Chief Executive, Warren Spring Laboratory, Gunnels Wood Road, Stevenage, Hertfordshire SG1 2BX
Telephone: 0438 741122 *Fax:* 0438 360858

COTTRELL, Dr ELIZABETH   Special Adviser to Secretary of State for Employment

Career: consultant Charles Barker Lyons; special adviser to Richard Luce and David Mellor, ministers for arts and libraries, and then to Gillian Shephard secretary of state for employment 1992-

Dr Elizabeth Cottrell, Special Adviser, Employment Department Group, Caxton House, Tothill Street, London SW1H 9NE *Telephone:* 071-273 3000

COURTNEY, ROGER GRAHAM   Chief Executive, Building Research Establishment (Executive Agency)   Grade: 3

Career: technical director Department of Energy energy efficiency office 1984-86; Building Research Establishment 1986-: deputy director 1986-88, director 1988-

Date of birth: 11 July 1946 *Education/professional qualifications:* Trinity College, Cambridge (BA, MA); Bristol University (MSc); Brunel University

Roger G Courtney Esq, Chief Executive, Building Research Establishment, Garston, Watford WD2 7JR *Telephone:* 0923 894040

COUSINS, BRIAN HARRY   Principal Establishment and Finance Officer, Lord Chancellor's Department   Grade: 3

Career: under secretary (US) fleet support Ministry of Defence (MoD) 1981-85; permanent chairman civil service selection board 1985-86; US general finance MoD 1986-89; principal establishment and finance officer Lord Chancellor's Department 1989-

Date of birth: 18 July 1933 *Education/professional qualifications:* Devonport High School, Plymouth *Honours, decorations:* CBE 1981 *Marital status:* married Margaret 1957; 2 sons *Recreations:* theatre, tennis, gardening

Brian Harry Cousins Esq CBE, Principal Establishment and Finance Officer, Lord Chancellor's Department, Trevelyan House, Great Peter Street, London SW1 *Telephone:* 071-210 8519 *Fax:* 071-210 8549

COWAN, Sir Robert   Chairman, Highlands and Islands Enterprise (see Addenda)

Career: consultant P A management consultants 1964-82: Hong Kong 1976-82; non-executive chairman Highlands and Islands Development Board/Enterprise 1982- Current non-Whitehall posts: chairman Made in Scotland Ltd 1991-; member Scottish Post Office Board 1990-

Date of birth: 27 July 1932 Education/professional qualifications: Edinburgh Academy; Edinburgh University, economics and history (MA 1954) Honours, decorations: KB 1988 Marital status: married Margaret Morton 1959; 2 daughters Clubs: New, Highland, Hong Kong Recreations: indoor and outdoor pottering, fishing

Sir Robert Cowan KB, Chairman, Highlands and Islands Enterprise, Bridge House, 20 Bridge Street, Inverness IV1 1QR Telephone: 0463 234171 Fax: 0463 244469

COWAN, Major-General S   Assistant Chief of the Defence Staff, Operational Requirements (Land Systems), Ministry of Defence

Major-General S Cowan CBE, Assistant Chief of the Defence Staff, Ministry of Defence, Main Building, Whitehall, London SW1A 2HB Telephone: 071-218 9000

COWARD, Vice-Admiral SIR JOHN FRANCIS   Commandant, Royal College of Defence Studies, Ministry of Defence

Career: Royal Navy 1954-: commander HMS Oracle 1966-68, HMS Valiant 1976-78, HMS Brilliant 1980-82; Ministry of Defence (MoD)-1978-88: naval assistant First Sea Lord 1978-80. director naval operational requirements 1985-88; flag officer Flotilla One 1988-89, sea training 1987-88, submarines 1989-91; commandant Royal College of Defence Studies 1992-

Date of birth: 11 October 1937 Education/professional qualifications: Downside School, Bath; Royal Naval College, Dartmouth Honours, decorations: DSO 1982, KCB 1990 Recreations: golf, gardening, sailing

Vice-Admiral Sir John F Coward KCB DSO, Commandant, Royal College of Defence Studies, 37 Belgrave Square, London SW1X 8NS Telephone: 071-235 1091

CRAGG, ANTHONY JOHN   Director-General, Management Audit, Ministry of Defence   Grade: 3

Career: Ministry of Defence 1966-: chief officer sovereign base area, Cyprus 1983-85; Royal College of Defence Studies 1988; director-general management audit 1991-

Date of birth: 16 May 1943 Education/professional qualifications: Lincoln College, Oxford (BA); Royal College of Defence Studies

Anthony J Craig Esq, Director-General Management Audit, Ministry of Defence, Northumberland House, Northumberland Avenue, London WC2N 5BP Telephone: 071-218 9000

CRAIG, GEORGE CHARLES GRAHAM   Principal Establishment Officer, Welsh Office   Grade: 3

Career: Ministry of Transport 1967-78; Welsh Office 1978-: private secretary to minister of state 1978-80, assistant secretary 1980-86, under secretary/principal establishment officer 1986-

Date of birth: 8 May 1946 *Education/professional qualifications:* Brockley County Grammar School; Nottingham University *Marital status:* married Marian 1968; 2 sons, 1 daughter

George C G Craig Esq, Principal Establishment Officer, Welsh Office, Cathays Park, Cardiff CF1 3NQ *Telephone:* 0222 825111

CRAIG, JOHN FRAZER   Deputy Secretary, Economic Affairs, Welsh Office   Grade: 2

Career: HM Customs and Excise 1961-69; National Board for Prices and Incomes 1969-70; Welsh Office 1970-: private secretary (PS) to permanent secretary 1972-74, PS to secretary of state 1980-82, industry department 1982-87: assistant secretary 1982-85, under secretary 1985-87, principal finance officer 1987-90, deputy secretary economic affairs 1990-

Date of birth: 8 November 1943 *Education/professional qualifications:* Robert Richardson Grammar School, Sunderland *Marital status:* married Janet Elizabeth 1973

John F Craig Esq, Deputy Secretary, Welsh Office, Cathays Park, Cardiff CF1 3NQ *Telephone:* 0222 823579

CRAIG, Major General R PETER   Director Army Surgery and Consultant Surgeon Ministry of Defence

Career: director army surgery and consultant surgeon Ministry of Defence 1992-

Major General R Peter Craig, Director Army Surgery and Consultant Surgeon, Ministry of Defence, Room 609, First Avenue House, High Holborn, London WC1 6HE *Telephone:* 071-430 5555

CRAWFORD, IAIN   Director, Veterinary Field Services, Ministry of Agriculture, Fisheries and Food   Grade: 3

Career: Ministry of Agriculture, Fisheries and Food 1968-: assistant chief veterinary officer 1986-88, director veterinary field services 1988-

Date of birth: 8 April 1938 *Education/professional qualifications:* Glasgow University (BVMS); MRCVS 1961

Iain Crawford Esq, Director, Veterinary Field Services, Ministry of Agriculture, Fisheries and Food, Government Buildings, Hook Rise South, Tolworth, Surbiton, Surrey KT6 7NF *Telephone:* 081-330 8038

CRAWFORD, Dr ROBERT MACKAY   Director, Locate in Scotland, Scottish Office   Grade: 4

Career: director North America Locate in Scotland (LIS) 1989-91; director LIS, Scottish Office Industry Department 1991-

Education/professional qualifications: St Michael's Academy, Kilwinning, Ayrshire; Strathclyde University, politics (BA 1973); Harvard University, USA, politics and economics JF Kennedy scholar 1974); Glasgow University, politics (PhD 1982) *Marital status:* married Linda 1975; 1 son, 1 daughter *Recreations:* jogging, reading, hill-walking, swimming

Dr Robert M Crawford, Director Locate in Scotland, Scottish Office Industry Department, 120 Bothwell Street, Glasgow G2 7JP *Telephone:* 041-248 2700

CRAWLEY, JOHN MAURICE   Principal Finance Officer and Director of Manpower and Support Services, Inland Revenue   Grade: 3

Career: Inland Revenue 1959-: assistant principal 1959-63; principal, policy posts 1963-69; assistant secretary 1969-79: revenue personnel/organisation and policy posts, seconded to Cabinet Office

Central Policy Review Staff (CPRS) 1973-76; under secretary 1979-: seconded to CPRS 1979-81, director policy division (oil and interest) 1981-85, principal finance officer and director of manpower and support services 1985-

Date of birth: 27 September 1933 *Education/professional qualifications:* Rugby School; Oxford University, classical moderation and litterae humaniores (BA 1958, MA) *Honours, decorations:* CB 1992 *Marital status:* married Jane Meadows Rendel 1978; 3 sons *Recreations:* music, playing piano and viola; hill walking

John M Crawley Esq CB, Under Secretary, Inland Revenue, Somerset House, Strand, London WC2R 1LB *Telephone:* 071-438 7430

CREED, RONALD ERNEST   Senior Principal Inspector, Capital Valuation Division, Inland Revenue   Grade: 4

Career: Inland Revenue 1963-: district inspector (DI) Norwich 2 1969-72; chief inspector's secretariat 1972-75; DI Euston 1 1975-80, Soho 1 1980-82; principal inspector schedule D 1982-84, capital gains tax 1984-88; senior principal inspector partnerships 1988-89, head of technical capital gains tax advice, capital valuation division 1989-

Date of birth: 28 June 1942 *Education/professional qualifications:* Colfes Grammar School, Lewisham; London School of Economics (BSc Econ 1963) *Marital status:* married Jill 1968; 2 daughters *Recreations:* archaeology

Ronald E Creed Esq, Senior Principal Inspector, Capital Valuation Division, Inland Revenue, Somerset House, Strand, London WC2R 1LB *Telephone:* 071-438 6695

CRICKHOWELL, (ROGER) NICHOLAS (The Rt Hon The Lord Crickhowell)   Chairman National Rivers Authority

Career: commercial insurance company, latterly managing director and chairman 1957-74; MP for Pembroke 1970-87: opposition spokesman (OS) on Welsh affairs 1974, chief OS on Welsh affairs Shadow Cabinet 1975-79, secretary of state for Wales 1979-87; chairman National Rivers Authority 1989- *Current non-Whitehall posts:* director Automobile Association and Fanum Ltd 1988-, Associated British Ports Holdings, HTV Group plc 1987-, Harlech Fine Art Holdings Ltd, JS Maas and Sons Ltd, Welsh National Opera; vice-chairman Anglesey Mining plc

Date of birth: 25 February 1934 *Education/professional qualifications:* Westminster School, London; Trinity College, Cambridge, history (BA 1957, MA) *Honours, decorations:* PC 1979, baron 1987 *Marital status:* married Ankaret Healing 1963; 1 son, 2 daughters *Clubs:* Cardiff and County *Recreations:* fishing, gardening, collecting watercolours and drawings

The Rt Hon The Lord Crickhowell, Chairman, National Rivers Authority, Eastbury Plaza, 30 Albert Embankment, London SE1 7TL *Telephone:* 071-820 0101 *Fax:* 071-820 1786

Government Departments
see page 300

CROW, (HILARY) STEPHEN   Chief Executive and Chief Planning Inspector, Planning Inspectorate Agency (Executive Agency)   Grade: 3

Career: local government planning officer 1957-72; divisional planning officer East Hertfordshire 1972-74; principal assistant county planning officer Hertfordshire 1974-76; Department of Environment planning inspectorate 1976-: planning inspector (PI) 1976, assistant chief PI 1976-88, deputy chief PI 1988, chief PI 1988- and from 1992 chief executive of the Planning Inspectorate Agency

Date of birth: 2 September 1934 *Education/professional qualifications:* Leek High School, Staffordshire; William Ellis School, Highgate; St Catharine's College, Cambridge, geography (BA 1957, MA) *Marital status:* married Margaret Anderson 1958; 2 sons, 1 daughter *Recreations:* music, reading, gardening

H Stephen Crow Esq, Chief Executive and Chief Planning Inspector, Planning Inspectorate Agency, Tollgate House, Houlton Street, Bristol BS2 9DJ *Telephone:* 0272 218963 *Fax:* 0272 218408

CROWE, BRIAN LEE   Under Secretary of State, Foreign and Commonwealth Office

Career: HM Diplomatic Service 1961-: ambassador to Austria 1989-92; under secretary Foreign and Commonwealth Office 1992-

Brian L Crowe Esq, Under Secretary of State, Foreign and Commonwealth Office, King Charles Street, London SW1A 2AH *Telephone:* 071-270 2154

CRUICKSHANK, ALISTAIR RONALD   Principal Finance Officer, Ministry of Agriculture, Fisheries and Food   Grade: 3

Career: Ministry of Agriculture, Fisheries and Food 1966-: assistant principal 1966-70, principal 1970-78, assistant secretary 1978-86, under secretary animal health 1988-89, principal finance officer 1989-

Date of birth: 26 October 1944 *Education/professional qualifications:* Aberdeen Grammar School; Aberdeen University, history (MA 1966) *Marital status:* married Alexandra Mary Noble 1967; 3 daughters *Recreations:* gardening, old buildings

Alistair R Cruickshank Esq, Principal Finance Officer, Ministry of Agriculture, Fisheries and Food, 19-29 Woburn Place, London WC1H 0LU *Telephone:* 071-917 3669 *Fax:* 071-917 3715

CRUICKSHANK, DON   Chief Executive, NHS in Scotland, Home and Health Department, Scottish Office

Career: management consultant, McKinsey and Co Inc 1972-77; general manager Sunday Times 1977-80; finance director Pearson plc. 1980-84; chairman Wandsworth health authority 1986-89; managing director Virgin Group plc 1984-89; chief executive NHS in Scotland, Scottish Office Home and Health Department 1989- *Current non-Whitehall posts:* council member Manchester Business School 1986-

Date of birth: 17 September 1942 *Education/professional qualifications:* University of Aberdeen (MA); Institute of Chartered Accountants Scotland (CA); Manchester Business School (MBA) *Marital status:* married Elizabeth Buchan Taylor 1964; 1 son, 1 daughter *Recreations:* sport, golf, opera

Don Cruickshank Esq, Chief Executive, NHS in Scotland, Scottish Office Home and Health Department, St Andrew's House, Edinburgh EH1 3DE *Telephone:* 031-244 2410

CRWYS-WILLIAMS, Air Vice-Marshal DAVID OWEN   Director-General, Royal Air Force Personal Services, Ministry of Defence

Career: officer commanding (OC) RAF 230 Squadron 1975-77; Ministry of Defence (MoD) 1977-81: personnel officer 1977-79, deputy director air plans 1979-81; OC RAF Shawbury, Shropshire 1983-84; Royal College of Defence Studies 1985; MoD 1986-88: director of air support 1986-87, director of air force staff duties 1987-88; commander British forces Falkland Islands 1988-89; director-general RAF personal services MoD (policy for pay, welfare etc) 1989- *Current non-Whitehall posts:* council member Navy, Army and Air Force Institute 1989-, board member Services Sound and Vision Corporation 1989-

Date of birth: 24 December 1940 *Education/professional qualifications:* Oakham School; RAF College, Cranwell (pilot 1961); Army Staff College (graduate 1973); Royal College of Defence Studies (graduate 1985) *Honours, decorations:* CB 1990 *Recreations:* fly fishing, furniture restoration, building

Air Vice-Marshal David O Crwys-Williams CB, Director-General RAF Personal Services, Ministry of Defence, Adastral House, Theobalds Road, London WC1X 8RU *Telephone:* 071-430 7239

CUBIE, GEORGE   Clerk of the Overseas Office, House of Commons   Grade: 3

Career: House of Commons 1966-: clerk of select committees 1989-91; clerk of overseas office 1991-

Date of birth: 30 August 1943 *Education/professional qualifications:* Edinburgh University (MA)

George Cubie Esq, Clerk of the Overseas Office, House of Commons, London SW1A 0AA *Telephone:* 071-219 3000

CULHAM, MICHAEL JOHN   Assistant Under Secretary, Civilian Management (Administrators), Ministry of Defence   Grade: 3

Career: Ministry of Defence 1964-: assistant under secretary 1982-, (Adjutant-General) 1982-87, (Civilian Management [Administrators]) 1987-

Date of birth: 24 June 1933 *Education/professional qualifications:* Lincoln College, Oxford (MA)

Michael J Culham Esq, Assistant Under Secretary, (Civilian Management [Administrators]), Ministry of Defence, Lacon House, Theobolds Road, London WC1X 8RY *Telephone:* 071-218 9000

CULLEN, Sir (EDWARD) JOHN   Chairman, Health and Safety Commission

Career: senior scientific officer United Kingdom Atomic Energy Authority, Windscale 1956-58; deputy works manager ICI Billingham oil works 1958-67; Rohm and Haas 1967-: European engineering co-ordinator 1967-73, managing director UK 1973-78, European director for engineering, regulatory affairs, health and safety 1978-83; chairman Health and Safety Commission (occupational health and safety strategy) 1983- *Current non-Whitehall posts:* member Civil Service Occupational Health Committee 1988-; chairman British National Committee for International Engineering Affairs 1991-; council member Engineering Council 1990-

Date of birth: 19 October 1926 *Education/professional qualifications:* Culford School, Bury St Edmunds; Cambridge University, chemical engineering (BA, MA 1952, PhD 1956); Texas University, USA, chemical engineering (MS 1953) *Honours, decorations:* Kt 1991 *Marital status:* married Betty Hopkins 1954; 2 sons, 2 daughters *Clubs:* Institute of Directors *Recreations:* travel, reading, walking, swimming

Sir John Cullen, Chairman, Health and Safety Commission, Baynards House, 1 Chepstow Place, Westbourne Grove, London W2 4TF *Telephone:* 071-243 6610 *Fax:* 071-727 1202

CULPIN, R P   Under Secretary, Fiscal Policy Division, HM Treasury   Grade: 3

R P Culpin Esq, Under Secretary, Fiscal Policy Division, HM Treasury, Parliament Street, London SW1P 3AG *Telephone:* 071-270 3000

CURTIS, STEPHEN RUSSELL   Chief Executive, Driver and Vehicle Licensing Agency (Executive Agency)   Grade: 3

Career: Department of Trade and Industry 1970-: statistician Business Statistics Office 1970-83, chief statistician 1983-85; chief executive and registrar Companies House 1985-90; chief executive Driver and Vehicle Licensing Agency 1990-
Education/professional qualifications: Forest School, London; Exeter University, economics and statistics (BA 1970) *Marital status:* married Gillian Mary 1972; 3 sons, 1 daughter *Clubs:* Civil Service *Recreations:* family, photography, walking

Stephen R Curtis Esq, Chief Executive, Driver and Vehicle Licensing Agency, Longview Road, Morriston, Swansea SA99 6JL
Telephone: 0792 782363 *Fax:* 0792 783003

CUTLER, (TIMOTHY ROBERT) ROBIN   Director-General and Deputy Chairman, Forestry Commission   Grade: 2

Career: colonial forest service, Kenya 1958-64; New Zealand (NZ) forest service 1964-86: director of forest management 1978-86, deputy director-general 1986-88; chief executive NZ Ministry of Forestry 1988-90; director-general and deputy chairman UK Forestry Commission (policy advice, services and reporting to forestry ministers on relevant matters) 1990-

Date of birth: 24 July 1934 *Education/professional qualifications:* Banff Academy; Aberdeen University, forestry (BSc 1956) *Marital status:* married Ishbel 1958; 1 son, 1 daughter *Clubs:* New, Edinburgh; Commonwealth Trust, London *Recreations:* tennis, golf, gardening, stamps

Robin Cutler Esq, Director-general and Deputy Chairman, Forestry Commission, 231 Corstorphine Road, Edinburgh EH12 7AT
Telephone: 031-334 0303 *Fax:* 031-316 4891

D

d'ANCONA, JOHN EDWARD WILLIAM   Director-General
**Offshore Supplies Office, Energy Division, Department of Trade and
Industry**   Grade: 3

Career: teacher 1959-61; Department of Education and Science 1961-67:
assistant principal 1961-64, private secretary to minister of state 1964-65,
principal 1965-67; principal Ministry of Technology and Department of
Trade and Industry (DTI) 1967-74; Department of Energy (DEn) 1974-
(most of whose responsibilities were taken over by the DTI in 1992):
assistant secretary, Offshore Supplies Office (OSO) 1974-77, DEn
1977-81, under secretary (director-general) OSO (UK supply industries to
offshore oil and gas concerns) 1981-

Date of birth: 28 May 1935 *Education/professional qualifications:* St Edward's
College, Malta; St Cuthbert's School, Newcastle-upon-Tyne; King's
College (Newcastle) Durham University, modern history (BA 1958) and
education (DipEd 1959) *Marital status:* married Mary Helen 1958; 3 sons
Clubs: Crow's Nest Officers', St John's, Newfoundland *Recreations:* cricket,
philately, wine-bibbing

John E W d'Ancona Esq, Director-General Offshore Supplies Office,
Energy Division, Department of Trade and Industry, Alhambra House, 45
Waterloo Street, Glasgow G2 6AS *Telephone:* 041-221 8777

DAVENPORT, (JOHN) MICHAEL LAUGHARNE   Senior Principal Inspector, Taxes,
Savings and Investments Division, Inland Revenue   Grade: 4

Career: Inland Revenue 1963-: district inspector (DI) 1968-70; information technology specialist
1970-73; DI 1973-78; operations planning 1978-83; DI 1983-84; trusts, charities, individual residence
technical adviser 1984-90; senior principal inspector, taxes, savings and investments division
(abolition of composite rate tax project director) 1990-

Date of birth: 8 December 1934 *Education/professional qualifications:* Wolverhampton Grammar
School; King's College, Cambridge, classics (BA 1958) *Marital status:* married Jean 1959; 1 son, 1
daughter

J Michael L Davenport Esq, Senior Principal Inspector Taxes, Savings and Investments Division,
Inland Revenue, Somerset House, Strand, London WC2R 1LB *Telephone:* 071-438 6975
Fax: 071-438 7752

**DAVIDSON, CHARLES KEMP (The Hon Lord
Davidson)**   **Chairman, Scottish Law Commission**

Career: advocate 1956-83; dean Faculty of Advocates 1979-83; senator
College of Justice in Scotland 1983-; chairman Scottish Law Commission
1988-

Date of birth: 13 April 1929 *Education/professional qualifications:* Fettes
College, Edinburgh; Brasenose College, Oxford, literae humaniores (BA
1951, MA); Edinburgh University, law (LLB 1956) *Honours, decorations:*
QC (Scotland 1969) *Marital status:* married Mary Mactaggart 1960; 2
daughters, 1 son

The Hon Lord Davidson QC, Chairman, Scottish Law Commission, 140
Causewayside, Edinburgh EH9 1PR *Telephone:* 031-668 2131
Fax: 031-662 4900

DAVIE, (STEPHEN) REX   Principal Establishment and Finance Officer, Cabinet Office   Grade: 3

Career: Inland Revenue 1951-52; national service 1952-54; Office of Minister for Science 1962-67; National Economic Development Office 1967-70; Civil Service Department 1970-83: principal 1970-79, assistant secretary (AS) 1979-83; Cabinet Office 1983-: AS 1983-89, principal establishment and finance officer 1989-

Date of birth: 11 June 1933 *Education/professional qualifications:* Ilfracombe Grammar School *Marital status:* married Christine 1955; 1 son, 1 daughter *Clubs:* Civil Service *Recreations:* reading, gardening

S Rex Davie Esq, Principal Establishment and Finance Officer, Cabinet Office, Government Offices, Great George Street, London SW1P 3AL *Telephone:* 071-270 6030 *Fax:* 071-270 6136

DAVIES, (JOHN) MICHAEL   Clerk Assistant and Clerk of Public Bills, House of Lords   Grade: 2

Career: House of Lords 1964-: clerk 1964-71; private secretary to leader of House and government chief whip 1971-74; private secretary to chairman of committees, establishment officer, secretary of statute law committee 1974-83; principal clerk: European and overseas office 1983-85, private bills 1985-88; reading clerk and clerk of public bills 1988-90; clerk assistant and clerk of public bills (passage of legislation, including amendments rules of order; certification of Acts for publication; minutes and order papers) 1991-

Date of birth: 2 August 1940 *Education/professional qualifications:* King's School, Canterbury; Peterhouse, Cambridge, history (BA 1963) *Marital status:* married Amanda Mary Atkinson JP 1971; 1 daughter, 2 sons *Recreations:* sport, travel

J Michael Davies, Clerk Assistant and Clerk of Public Bills, House of Lords, London SW1A 0PW *Telephone:* 071-219 3171

DAVIES, PHILIP JOHN   Deputy Parliamentary Counsel, Office of the Parliamentary Counsel

Career: law lecturer Manchester University 1977-82; Office of the Parliamentary Counsel 1982-: assistant parliamentary counsel (PC) 1982-86, senior assistant PC 1986-90, deputy PC (drafting government bills) 1990-

Date of birth: 19 September 1954 *Education/professional qualifications:* St Julian's High School, Newport, Gwent; Hertford College, Oxford, jurisprudence (BA 1976, BCL 1977); Middle Temple (barrister 1981) *Marital status:* married Jacqueline Sara 1981; 1 daughter *Recreations:* family, dog

Philip J Davies Esq, Deputy Parliamentary Counsel, Office of the Parliamentary Counsel, London SW1A 2AY *Telephone:* 071-210 6630 *Fax:* 071-210 6632

'Next Steps' Executive Agencies
see page 761

DAVIS, DEREK RICHARD   Under Secretary, Head of Oil and Gas, Energy Division, Department of Trade and Industry   Grade: 3

Career: assistant principal Board of Trade 1967-70; principal Department of Trade and Industry (DTI) 1970-74; Department of Energy 1974- (most of whose responsibilities were taken over by the DTI in 1992): assistant secretary 1977-85; under secretary and head of gas division 1985-87, under secretary and head of oil and gas division (UK oil and gas policy) 1987-

Date of birth: 3 May 1945 *Education/professional qualifications:* Clifton College, Bristol; Balliol College, Oxford, litterae humaniores (BA 1967) *Marital status:* married Diana Levinson 1987; 1 daughter, 1 son

Derek R Davis Esq, Under Secretary, Energy Division, Department of Trade and Industry, 1 Palace Street, London SW1E 5HE
Telephone: 071-238 3099

DAVIS, Rear-Admiral G N   Director-General Fleet Support Policy and Services, Ministry of Defence

Rear-Admiral G N Davis ADC, Director-General Fleet Support Policy and Services, Ministry of Defence, Main Building, Whitehall, London SW1A 2HB *Telephone:* 071-218 9000

DAWE, ROGER JAMES   Director-General, Training, Enterprise and Education Directorate, Employment Department Group   Grade: 2 *(see Addenda)*

Career: Ministry of Labour 1962-64: assistant principal safety, health and welfare and industrial relations divisions 1962-64; assistant principal Department of Economic Affairs 1964-65; private secretary (PS) to Prime Minister 1966-70; Department of Employment (DEmp) 1970-: principal, pay policy 1970-72, PS to secretaries of state 1972-74, assistant secretary 1974-81: public service pay, manpower policy, head of group personnel unit, of unemployment benefit service; Manpower Services Commission 1981-85: under secretary, director of special programmes 1981-82, chief executive training division 1982-85; DEmp 1985-: deputy secretary manpower policy 1985-88, director-general (DG) Training Commission 1988, DG Training Agency, which later became Training, Enterprise and Education Directorate, 1988-

Date of birth: 26 February 1941 *Education/professional qualifications:* Hardyes School, Dorchester; Fitzwillian College, Cambridge, economics (BA 1962) *Honours, decorations:* OBE 1970, CB 1988 *Marital status:* married Ruth Day 1965; 1 son, 1 daughter *Recreations:* tennis, soccer, music, theatre

Roger J Dawe Esq CB OBE, Director-General, Training, Enterprise and Education Directorate, Department of Employment, Caxton House, Tothill Street, London SW1H 9NF *Telephone:* 071-837 2795

DAWSON, IAN DAVID   Assistant Under Secretary (Policy), Ministry of Defence   Grade: 3

Career: Ministry of Defence 1958-: assistant under secretary (AUS) resources 1988-90; seconded to Center for International Affairs, Harvard 1990-91; AUS (policy) 1991-

Date of birth: 24 November 1934 *Education/professional qualifications:* Fitzwilliam House, Cambridge (MA)

Ian D Dawson Esq CBE, Assistant Under Secretary (Policy), Ministry of Defence, Main Building, London SW1A 2HB *Telephone:* 071-218 2533

DAWSON, JOHN ANTHONY LAWRENCE   Director of Roads and Chief Road Engineer, Scottish Office   Grade: 3

Career: British Rail 1968-72; Transport and Road Research Laboratory 1972; Department of Environment 1973-76; Department of Transport (DTp) 1976-81; overseas transport consultant 1981-85; director London regional office DTp 1985-88; Scottish Office 1988-: chief road engineer 1988-, director of roads 1989-

Date of birth: 6 February 1950 *Education/professional qualifications:* Mill Hill School, London; Southampton University, civil engineering (BSc 1972): MICE 1976, FICE 1992 *Marital status:* married Frances Anne Elizabeth 1980; 2 daughters *Recreations:* touring, hard rock

John A L Dawson Esq FICE, Director of Roads and Chief Road Engineer, Scottish Office, New St Andrew's House, St James Centre, Edinburgh EH1 3DD *Telephone:* 031-556 8400

DAY, Sir MICHAEL JOHN   Chairman, Commission for Racial Equality

Career: Probation Service 1960-64: probation officer (PO) Surrey 1960-64, senior PO West Sussex 1964-67, chief PO Surrey 1968-76; West Midlands 1976-88; chairman Commission for Racial Equality 1988 *Current non-Whitehall posts:* member Grubb Institute Council 1978-

Date of birth: 4 September 1933 *Education/professional qualifications:* University College School, Hampstead; Selwyn College, Cambridge, English (BA, MA 1959) *Honours, decorations:* OBE 1981, Kt 1992 *Marital status:* married June Mackay 1960; 1 daughter, 1 son *Clubs:* Royal Society of Arts *Recreations:* gardening, countryside

Sir Michael J Day Esq OBE, Chairman, Commission for Racial Equality, Elliot House, 10-12 Allington Street, London SW1E 5EH *Telephone:* 071-828 7022 *Fax:* 071-620 7605

DAYKIN, CHRISTOPHER DAVID   Government Actuary, Government Actuary's Department

Career: actuarial officer (AO) Government Actuary's Department (GAD) 1970; VSO teacher 1971; GAD 1972-78: AO 1972-73, assistant actuary 1973-75, actuary 1976-78; principal HM Treasury 1978-80; GAD 1980-: actuary 1980-82, chief actuary 1982-84, directing actuary 1985-89 (head of actuarial profession in civil service; advice on social security, pensions, insurance, demography, consumer credit etc) 1989- *Current non-Whitehall posts:* chairman Civil Service Insurance Society 1990-

Date of birth: 18 July 1948 *Education/professional qualifications:* Merchant Taylors' School, Northwood, Middlesex; Pembroke College, Cambridge, mathematics (BA 1970, MA); FIA 1973 *Marital status:* married Kathryn Ruth Tingey 1977; 1 daughter, 2 sons *Clubs:* Actuaries, Gallio *Recreations:* travel, photography, music, languages

Christopher D Daykin Esq, Government Actuary, Government Actuary's Department, 22 Kingsway, London WC2B 6LE *Telephone:* 071-242 6828 *Fax:* 071-831 6653

DEACON, KEITH VIVIAN   Under Secretary, Director of Operations, Inland Revenue   Grade: 3

Career: Inland Revenue 1962-: director of insurance and specialist division 1988-91; director of operations 1991-

Date of birth: 19 November 1935 *Education/professional qualifications:* Bristol University, English language and literature

Keith V Deacon Esq, Director of Operations, Inland Revenue, Bush House, Strand, London WC2B 4RD *Telephone:* 071-438 6622

DEAN, PETER HENRY   Deputy Chairman, Monopolies and Mergers Commission

Career: RTZ Corporation plc 1966-85: solicitor 1966-72, secretary 1972-74, director 1974-85; deputy chairman Monopolies and Mergers Commission 1990- *Current non-Whitehall posts:* director Associated British Ports Holdings plc 1982-, Liberty Life Assurance Company Ltd 1986-

Date of birth: 24 July 1939 *Education/professional qualifications:* Rugby School; London University, law (LLB 1961); solicitor 1962 *Marital status:* married Linda Louise Keating 1965; 1 daughter *Recreations:* choral singing, skiing

Peter H Dean Esq, Deputy Chairman, Monopolies and Mergers Commission, New Court, 48 Carey Street, London WC2A 2JT *Telephone:* 071-324 1433 *Fax:* 071-324 1400

DEARING, SIR RONALD ERNEST   Chairman, Polytechnics and Colleges Funding Council; Financial Reporting Council; Universities Funding Council

Career: Ministry of Labour and National Service 1946-49; Ministry of [Fuel and] Power (MoP) 1949-62: national service 1949-51; HM Treasury 1962-64; MoP/Technology/Department of [Trade and] Industry 1964-82: under secretary, Newcastle regional director 1972-74, under secretary/deputy secretary 1974-82; Post Office [Corporation] 1980-87: deputy chairman 1980-81, chairman 1981-87; Chairman County Durham Development Corporation 1987-91, Accounting Standards Review Committee 1987-88, Polytechnics and Colleges Funding Council 1988-, Financial Reporting Council 1990-, Universities Funding Council 1991- *Current non-Whitehall posts:* director (non-executive): London Education Business Partnership 1989-, Prudential plc 1987-, IMI plc 1988-, British Coal 1988-, Erisson 1988-; member council Industrial Society 1985-;

Date of birth: 27 July 1930 *Education/professional qualifications:* Malet Lambert High School, Hull; Doncaster Grammar School; Hull University, economics (BScEcon 1954); London Business School (Sloan Fellowship 1967, Fellowship of School 1987) *Honours, decorations:* CB 1979; Kt 1984 *Marital status:* married Margaret Patricia Riley 1954; 2 daughters *Clubs:* Royal Over-Seas League *Recreations:* gardening, stamps

Sir Ronald Dearing CB, Chairman, Polytechnics and Colleges Funding Council, and Universities Funding Council, 3rd Floor, Metropolis House, Percy Street, London W1P 9FF *Telephone:* 071-637 1132 *Fax:* 071-436 4320

de DENEY, GEOFFREY IVOR   Clerk of the Council, Privy Council Office   Grade: 3

Career: Home Office 1956-84; clerk of the Council, Privy Council Office 1984-

Date of birth: 8 October 1931 *Education/professional qualifications:* St Edmund Hall, Oxford (MA, BCL)

Geoffrey I de Deney Esq CVO, Clerk of the Privy Council, Privy Council Office, Whitehall, London SW1A 2AT *Telephone:* 071-270 0495

DEMPSTER, JOHN WILLIAM SCOTT   Deputy Secretary, Highways, Safety and Traffic, Department of Transport   Grade: 2

Career: tax inspector Inland Revenue 1961-64; various posts Departments of Transport (DTp) and Environment 1964-80; principal establishment and finance officer (PEFO) Lord Chancellor's Department 1980-84; DTp 1984-: head of marine directorate 1984-89, PEFO 1989-91, deputy secretary Highways, Safety and Traffic 1991-

Date of birth: 10 May 1938 *Education/professional qualifications:* Plymouth College; Oriel College, Oxford, politics, philosophy and economics (BA, MA 1960) *Marital status:* divorced *Clubs:* Alpine, Royal Southampton Yacht *Recreations:* mountaineering, sailing

John W S Dempster Esq, Deputy Secretary, Department of Transport, 2 Marsham Street, London SW1P 3EB *Telephone:* 071-276 5240

DENHAM, PAMELA ANNE   North East Regional Director, Department of Trade and Industry   Grade: 3

Career: north east regional director Department of Trade and Industry 1990-

Pamela A Denham, Regional Director, DTI-NE, Stanegate House, 2 Groat Market, Newcastle-upon-Tyne, NE1 1YN *Telephone:* 091-235 2201 *Fax:* 091-261 7839

DENNER, Dr HOWARD   Chief Scientist (Food), Ministry of Agriculture, Fisheries and Food   Grade: 3

Career: Ministry of Agriculture, Fisheries and Food 1972-; chief scientist (food) 1992-

Dr Howard Denner, Chief Scientist (Food), Ministry of Agriculture, Fisheries and Food, Nobel House, 17 Smith Square, London SW1P 3JR *Telephone:* 071-270 3000

DENTON, GEOFFREY RICHARD   Director and Chief Executive, Wilton Park (Executive Agency)

Career: reader in economics Reading University 1967-82; economics professor College of Europe, Bruges, Belgium 1972-83; director Federal Trust, London 1976-83; Wilton Park, Foreign and Commonwealth Office 1983-: director 1983-, chief executive 1991- (running international conferences; directing Wiston House conference centre)

Date of birth: 10 June 1931 *Education/professional qualifications:* Loughborough College School; University College, Oxford, philosophy, politics and economics (BA, MA 1951) *Marital status:* married Maria 1961; 1 son, 1 daughter *Recreations:* hill-walking, gardening

Geoffrey R Denton Esq, Director and Chief Executive, Wilton Park, Wiston House, Steyning, West Sussex BN44 3DZ
Telephone: 0903 815020 *Fax:* 0903 815931

DEWAR, DAVID ALEXANDER   Assistant Auditor General, National Audit Office
Grade: 3

Career: National Audit Office 1953-: deputy secretary 1981-84; assistant auditor general 1984-

Date of birth: 28th October 1934 *Education/professional qualifications:* Leith Academy, Edinburgh

David A Dewar Esq, Assistant Auditor General National Audit Office, 157-197 Buckingham Palace Road, London SW1W 9SP *Telephone:* 071-798 7000

DICKINSON, BRIAN HENRY BARON   Under Secretary, Food Safety, Ministry of Agriculture, Fisheries and Food   Grade: 3

Career: Ministry of Agriculture, Fisheries and Food 1964-: assistant principal 1964-68: assistant private secretary to minister 1967-68; principal general agricultural policy, milk 1968-75; assistant secretary food subsidies and prices, department of prices and consumer protection 1975-78; assistant secretary food policy and finance 1978-84; under secretary finance and milk 1984-89, food safety (general responsibility for protecting public) 1989-

Date of birth: 2 May 1940 *Education/professional qualifications:* Leighton Park School, Reading; Balliol College, Oxford, mathematics, literae humaniores mathematics (BA 1962) *Marital status:* married Sheila 1971

Brian H B Dickinson Esq, Under Secretary, Ministry of Agriculture, Fisheries and Food, Ergon House, 17 Smith Square, London SW1P 3JR *Telephone:* 071-238 6429 *Fax:* 071-238 6430

DOBBIE, Dr BOB   Under Secretary, Industrial Competitiveness Division, Department of Trade and Industry   Grade: 3

Career: ICI fellow Bristol University 1967-68; chemistry lecturer Newcastle University 1968-76; chemistry tutor Open University 1975-85; Department of Trade and Industry (DTI) 1976-90: principal 1976-83, assistant secretary 1983-90; under secretary (US), director Merseyside Task Force 1990-92; US industrial competitiveness division, DTI 1992- *Current non-Whitehall posts:* non-executive director Vickers Marine Engineering Division 1988-

Date of birth: 16 January 1942 *Education/professional qualifications:* Dollar Academy; Edinburgh University, chemistry (BSc 1963); Fitzwilliam College, Cambridge, chemistry (PhD 1966) *Marital status:* married Elizabeth Charlotte Barbour 1964; 3 sons

Dr Bob Dobbie, Under Secretary, Industrial Competitiveness Division, Department of Trade and Industry, Ashdown House, 123 Victoria Street, London SW1E 6RB *Telephone:* 071-215 5000

DONNISON, (JOHN) RICHARD   Deputy Inspector-General and Senior Official Receiver, Insolvency Service Agency (Executive Agency)   Grade: 4

Career: Official Receiver Service 1975-: assistant official receiver London 1975-80; chief/principal examiner (PE) Insolvency HQ (Policy) (IHQP) 1980-81; deputy inspector of companies, companies investigation branch 1981-83; PE IHQP 1983-86; official receiver Birmingham 1986-89; deputy inspector general and senior official receiver, official receiver operations, Insolvency Service Agency (line manager for all official receivers in England and Wales) 1989-

Date of birth: 5 January 1933 *Honours, decorations:* Imperial Service Order 1986 *Marital status:* married Theresa Dawson 1954; 2 sons, 2 daughters

J Richard Donnison Esq ISO, Deputy Inspector General and Senior Official Receiver, Insolvency Service Agency, Bridge Place, 88-89 Eccleston Square, London SW1V 1PT *Telephone:* 071-215 0978

DRAPER, PETER SYDNEY   Group Personnel Director, Property Services Agency, Department of the Environment   Grade: 3

Career: Government Communications Headquarters 1953-56; Department of Transport 1956-71: principal 1969-71; Property Services Agency, Department of Environment (PSA) 1971-81: principal 1971-74, head of staff resources 1975-78, assistant director home regional services 1978-81; Royal College of Defence Studies 1981; Rayner Study of district work offices 1982; PSA 1982-: director of eastern region 1982-85, under secretary, director of defence services II 1985-87, principal establishments officer then group personnel director 1987-

Date of birth: 18 May 1935 *Education/professional qualifications:* Haberdashers' Aske's School, London; Regent Polytechnic, London, management studies (diploma 1966) *Marital status:* married Elizabeth Ann French 1959; 3 sons *Clubs:* Saffron Walden Golf *Recreations:* golf, gardening, walking

Peter S Draper Esq, Under Secretary, Property Services Agency, Department of the Environment, 2 Marsham Street, London SW1P 3EB *Telephone:* 071-276 3520 *Fax:* 071-276 4960

DREW, PHILIPPA   Director of Custody, HM Prison Service, Home Office   Grade: 3

Career: Home Office 1975-: seconded to Save the Children Fund, Nepal 1985-87; director of Custody HM prison service 1992-
Education/professional qualifications: Oxford University; Pennsylvania University

Miss Philippa Drew, Director of Custody, HM Prison Service, Home Office, Cleland House, Page Street, London SW1P 4LN *Telephone:* 071-270 3000

DUDDING, RICHARD SCARBOROUGH   Under Secretary, Central Finance, Department of the Environment   Grade: 3

Career: Department of Environment (DoE) 1972-75; Privy Council Office 1976-78; Cabinet Office 1978; DoE 1978-: seconded to Overseas Containers Ltd 1983-85, secretary to committee of enquiry into local government 1985-86, under secretary 1990-: finance central (public expenditure, estimates, financial management, accounts, internal audit) 1991-

Date of birth: 29 November 1950 *Education/professional qualifications:* Cheltenham College; Jesus College, Cambridge, history (BA 1972, MA) *Marital status:* married Priscilla Diana 1987; 2 sons *Recreations:* gardening, golf, walking

Richard S Dudding Esq, Under Secretary, Department of the Environment, 2 Marsham Street, London SW1P 3EB *Telephone:* 071-276 3000

DUFF, GRAHAM   Field Director, Operations, Crown Prosecution Service   Grade: 3

Career: Crown Prosecution Service 1986-: chief crown prosecutor Northumbria and Durham 1987-90, field director (operations) 1990-

Date of birth: 7 January 1947 *Education/professional qualifications:* University of Durham, law (BA Hons); University of Newcastle upon Tyne (Graduate Certificate of Education); Lincoln's Inn (barrister 1976)

Graham Duff Esq, Field Director (Operations), Crown Prosecution Service, 4-12 Queen Anne's Gate, London SW1H 9AZ *Telephone:* 071-273 8146

DUFFELL, Lieutenant-General Sir PETER ROYSTON   Inspector General of Doctrine and Training (Army), Ministry of Defence

Career: commanding officer 1st battalion 2nd Gurkha Rifles 1978-81; military operations Ministry of Defence (MoD) 1981-83; commander Gurkha Field Force 1984-85; chief of staff HQ 1 British Corps 1986-87; student Royal College of Defence Studies 1988; Cabinet Office efficiency unit 1989; commander British forces Hong Kong 1989-92; inspector general of Army doctrine and training MoD 1992-

Date of birth: 19 June 1939 *Education/professional qualifications:* Dulwich College; Army Staff College (psc 1971); Royal College of Defence Studies (RCDS 1988) *Honours, decorations:* MC 1966; OBE 1981; CBE 1988; KCB 1992 *Recreations:* travel, reading, golf, tennis, picture collecting, photography

Lieutenant-General Sir Peter R Duffell KCB CBE MC, Inspector General of Doctrine and Training (Army), Erskine Barracks, Wilton, Salisbury, Wiltshire SP2 0AG *Telephone:* 0722 433390

DUNBAR, IAN   Director of Inmate Administration, Prison Service, Home Office   Grade: 3

Career: HM Prison Service, Home Office 1972-: Usk borstal and detention centre 1972-74; HQ 1974-78, Feltham borstal 1978-79; Wakefield prison 1979-83; Wormwood Scrubs prison 1983-85; director south-west region 1985-90; director of inmate administration 1990-

Date of birth: 6 January 1934 *Education/professional qualifications:* Buckhurst Hill County High School, Chigwell; Keele University, politics and economics (BA 1959), social studies (diploma 1959); Reed College, Portland, USA, American political and economic systems; London School of Economics, applied social studies (diploma 1964) *Marital status:* married Sally Ann 1966; 1 daughter, 2 sons *Recreations:* bee-keeping, gardening, photography, walking

Ian Dunbar Esq, Director of Inmate Administration, HM Prison Service, Cleland House, Page Street, London SW1P 4LN *Telephone:* 071-217 6393

DUNN, ERIC   Chief Mechanical Engineer, Road and Vehicle Safety Directorate, Department of Transport   Grade: 4

Career: engineer in industry 1955-68; Department of Transport 1968-: NW traffic area mechanical engineer 1968-72; HQ branch head 1976-83; head of vehicle and component approval division 1983-87; chief mechanical engineer road and vehicle safety directorate 1987-

Date of birth: 2 September 1932 *Education/professional qualifications:* Chippenham Grammar School; Birmingham University, mechanical engineering (BSc 1955) *Marital status:* married Judith Diane 1961; 2 sons *Recreations:* walking on Dartmoor, gardening, 'DIY"

Eric Dunn Esq, Chief Mechanical Engineer, Road and Vehicle Safety Directorate, Department of Transport, 2 Marsham Street, London SW1P 3EB *Telephone:* 071-276 6260 *Fax:* 071-276 6419

Regulatory Organisations and Public Bodies
see page 857

DUNSTAN, TESSA JANE   Head of Legal Services, Investigations Division, Department of Trade and Industry   Grade: 4

Career: Board of Trade/Department of Trade and Industry (DTI) 1968-84: legal assistant (LA) prosecutions, Solicitor's Office (SO) 1968-73, senior LA SO 1973-84; legal adviser Office of Telecommunications 1984-87; DTI 1987-: adviser on insolvency and insider dealing SO 1987-89, head of investigations division legal services (companies, insider dealing, insolvency offences) 1989-

Date of birth: 18 July 1944 *Education/professional qualifications:* Convent of the Sacred Heart, Woldingham, Surrey; Lady Margaret Hall, Oxford, modern history (BA 1966, MA); Middle Temple (barrister 1967) *Marital status:* married Richard James Rowley 1973; 2 daughters, 2 sons *Recreations:* opera, gardening

Mrs Tessa J Dunstan, Head of Legal Services, Investigations Division, Department of Trade and Industry, Ashdown House, 123 Victoria Street, London, SW1E 6RB *Telephone:* 071-215 6406 *Fax:* 071-215 6894

DURHAM, DAVID EDWARD   Chief Executive and Registrar of Companies, England and Wales (Executive Agency)   Grade: 4

Career: army 1956-82; director of housing, environmental health, public works Rochester city council 1982-86; unit general manager Parkside Health Authority 1986-90; chief executive and registrar of companies, England and Wales, Companies House (registers companies and collects statutory returns) 1990-

Date of birth: 8 August 1936 *Education/professional qualifications:* Magdalen College School, Oxford; Medway College, civil engineering (diploma 1959); RMCS Staff College (graduate 1969); Open University, science and technology (BA 1971); South West London College, (ACIS 1982) *Marital status:* married Valerie Susan 1960; 1 daughter, 1 son *Recreations:* squash, golf, DIY

David E Durham Esq, Chief Executive and Registrar of Companies, Companies House, Crown Way, Cardiff CF4 3UZ *Telephone:* 0222 380400 *Fax:* 0222 380617

DUTTON, Major-General BRYAN HAWKINS   Director of Infantry, Ministry of Defence

Career: military service 1963-: planning staff N Ireland Office 1979-81; staff college instructor 1981-82; military assistant to adjutant general Ministry of Defence (MoD) 1982-84; commanding 1st battalion Devonshire and Dorset regiment 1984-87; deputy assistant chief of staff G3 operations (NATO/rest of world) 1987; commander 39 infantry brigade 1987-89; MoD 1990-: director army public relations 1990-92, director of infantry 1992-

Date of birth: 1 March 1943 *Education/professional qualifications:* Lord Weymouth School, Warminster; Royal Military Academy, Sandhurst (commission 1963); Royal Military College of Science; Staff College, Camberley *Honours, decorations:* MBE 1978, mention in despatches 1979, OBE 1984, CBE 1990 *Recreations:* history, sailing, natural history, fishing

Major-General Bryan H Dutton CBE, Director of Infantry, Ministry of Defence, Warminster, Wiltshire BA12 0DJ *Telephone:* 0985-214000

Complete Name Index
see page 955

DYMOND, MICHAEL JOHN   Director-General, Directorate General of Defence Accounts
(Executive Agency)   Grade: 4

Career: chartered accountant, auditor 1960-66; British Railways 1966-70: auditing 1966-69, passenger fares officer 1969-70; group financial controller Metals Research Ltd 1970-73; Ministry of Defence (MoD) 1973-76; senior auditor 1973-74, assistant director audit 1974-76; careers officer for accountants Department of Trade and Industry government accountancy service 1976-81; MoD 1981-: deputy director-general management audit 1981-87, director-general Directorate General of Defence Accounts 1989-

Date of birth: 11 August 1936 *Education/professional qualifications:* Colston's School, Bristol; Merton College, Oxford, jurisprudence (BA 1960, MA); accountancy (ACA 1963, FCA 1973) *Recreations:* singing, music, cricket

Michael J Dymond Esq, Director-General, Directorate General of Defence Accounts, Ministry of Defence, Warminster Road, Bath BA1 5AA *Telephone:* 0225 828106 *Fax:* 0225 828176

E

EATON, Vice-Admiral Sir KENNETH JOHN   **Controller of the Navy, Procurement Executive, Ministry of Defence**

Career: Admiralty Surface Weapons Establishment (ASWE) 1961-65; HMSs Eagle, Collingwood and Bristol 1965-71; Defence Communications Network 1971-72; ASWE 1972-76; HMS Ark Royal 1976-78; Ministry of Defence (MoD) 1978-81; ASWE 1981-83; director torpedoes 1983-85; director-general underwater weapons (navy) 1985-87; flag officer and commander Portsmouth naval base 1987-89; controller of the Navy Procurement Executive MoD (all new RN equipment) 1989-

Date of birth: 12 August 1934 *Education/professional qualifications:* Borden Grammar School; Fitzwilliam College, Cambridge (BA); C Eng; FIEE *Honours, decorations:* KCB 1990 *Recreations:* countryside, theatre, opera, classical music

Vice-Admiral Sir Kenneth Eaton KCB, Controller of the Navy, Procurement Executive, Old Admiralty Building, Spring Gardens, London SW1A 2BE *Telephone:* 071-218 3765

ECCLESTONE, BARRY JAMES   Solicitor, Health and Safety Commission and Executive   Grade: 4

Career: solicitor 1968-71; assistant parliamentary counsel 1972-80; Treasury Solicitor's Department energy branch 1980-89: senior legal assistant 1980-83, assistant solicitor 1983-89; solicitor, Solicitor's Office, Health and Safety Commission and Health and Safety Executive 1990-

Date of birth: 18 April 1944 *Education/professional qualifications:* King Edward's School, Birmingham; Bristol University, law (LLB 1965); Birmingham University, law (LLM 1972) *Marital status:* married Mary Penelope Susan Quicke 1973; 3 daughters *Recreations:* sailing, woodwork

Barry J Ecclestone Esq, Solicitor, Solicitor's Office, Health and Safety Executive, Baynards House, 1 Chepstow Place, Westbourne Grove, London W2 4TF *Telephone:* 071-243 6650 *Fax:* 071-221 8875

EDGAR, WILLIAM   Chief Executive, National Engineering Laboratory (Executive Agency)   Grade: 3

Career: principal engineer British Aircraft Corporation 1963-67; manufacturing general manager Weir Pumps 1967-73; director/chief executive Seaforth Maritime/Engineering 1973-86; director Vickers Marine 1986-88; executive chairman Cochrane Shipbuilders 1988-90; chief executive National Engineering Laboratory (preparing agency for privatisation) 1990-

Date of birth: 16 January 1938 *Education/professional qualifications:* St John's Grammar School, Hamilton; Strathclyde University, mechanical engineering (ARCST 1961); Birmingham University, mechanical engineering (MSc 1962) *Marital status:* married June Gilmour 1961; 2 sons *Clubs:* Sloane *Recreations:* reading, golf, music, soccer

William Edgar Esq, Chief Executive, National Engineering Laboratory, East Kilbride, Glasgow, G75 0QU *Telephone:* 03552 20222 *Fax:* 03552 36930

EDWARDS, ANDREW JOHN CUMMING   Deputy Secretary, Public Services, HM Treasury   Grade: 2

Career: HM Treasury (HMT) 1963-75: assistant principal 1963-67, private secretary to joint permanent secretary 1966-67, principal 1967-75; Harkness Fellow, Harvard University, USA

1971-73; assistant secretary (AS) HMT 1975-83; Royal College of Defence Studies 1979; AS Department of Education and Science 1983-85; HMT 1985-: under secretary 1985-89, deputy secretary public services (public expenditure) 1990- *Current non-Whitehall posts:* secretary Royal Opera House board 1988-

Date of birth: 3 November 1940 *Education/professional qualifications:* Fettes College, Edinburgh; St John's College, Oxford, literae humaniores (BA, MA 1962); Harvard University, USA, public administration (master's 1972), economics (master's 1973) *Marital status:* divorced; 2 daughters, 1 son *Publications:* Nuclear Weapons, The Balance of Power, The Quest for Peace (Macmillan 1985) *Recreations:* music, writing, reading, walking

Andrew J C Edwards Esq, Deputy Secretary, HM Treasury, Parliament Street, London SW1P 3AG *Telephone:* 071-270 4870

EDWARDS, PATRICIA ANNE   Principal Assistant Legal Adviser, Home Office   Grade: 3

Career: Home Office 1977-: assistant legal adviser 1980-88; principal assistant legal adviser 1988-

Date of birth: 29 May 1944 *Education/professional qualifications:* Kings College, London (LLB); barrister (Middle Temple 1967)

Ms Patricia A Edwards, Principal Assistant Legal Adviser, Home Office, 50 Queen Anne's Gate, London SW1H 9AT *Telephone:* 071-273 3000

ELLIS, Dr ADRIAN FOSS   Under Secretary, Technology and Health Sciences Division, Health and Safety Executive   Grade: 3

Career: Health and Safety Executive 1985-: head of major hazards assessment unit 1985-86; deputy chief inspector (chemicals) 1986-90; field operations regional director 1990; director of hazardous installations policy and of technology 1990-91; under secretary, head of renamed technology and health sciences division (combining hazardous installations and technology) 1991-

Date of birth: 15 February 1944 *Education/professional qualifications:* Dean Close School, Cheltenham; Battersea College, London University, chemical engineering (BSc 1966); Loughborough University, chemical engineering (PhD 1969), FICE 1977, FIE 1977 *Marital status:* married Hilary Jean 1973; 2 daughters, 1 son *Recreations:* bridge, Swindon Town Football Club

Dr Adrian F Ellis, Under Secretary, Health and Safety Executive, St Anne's House, Stanley Precinct, Bootle, Merseyside L20 3MF *Telephone:* 051-951 4574 *Fax:* 051-951 4232

ELLIS, (ARTHUR) JOHN   Chairman, Intervention Board for Agricultural Produce (Executive Agency)

Career: Fyffes Group Ltd 1965-: financial director 1965-69, managing director and chief executive officer (CEO) 1969-85, chairman and CEO 1985-; member economic development committee for agricultural industry 1978-85; part-time chairman national seed development organisation 1982-87; chairman Intervention Board for Agricultural Produce, executive agency (implements market support measures of the EEC's common agricultural policy) 1989-

Date of birth: 22 August 1932 *Education/professional qualifications:* South West Essex Technical College and School of Art; City of London College; FCIS 1956; FCAA 1958; FICMA 1959; MBCS 1960 *Honours, decorations:*

CBE 1986 *Marital status:* married Rita Patricia 1956; 2 sons, 1 daughter
Clubs: Reform, Farmers' *Recreations:* golf, fishing, reading

A John Ellis Esq CBE, Chairman, Intervention Board for Agricultural
Produce, c/o 12 York Gate, Regent's Park, London NW1 4QJ
Telephone: 071-487 4472 *Fax:* 071-487 3645

**ELLIS, BRYAN JAMES   Under Secretary, Income Support and
Housing Benefit Policy, Department of Social Security**   Grade: 3

Career: Department of Health and Social Security and predecessors
1958-86; chairman Civil Service Selection Board 1986-87; deputy director
Office of Population Censuses and Surveys 1987-90; under secretary
policy group division D (income support and housing benefit policy)
Department of Social Security 1990-

Date of birth: 11 June 1934 *Education/professional qualifications:* Merchant
Taylors' School, Northwood; St John's College, Oxford, greats (BA 1957,
MA) *Marital status:* married Barbara Muriel 1960; 1 daughter, 1 son
Publications: Pensions in Britain: 1955-75 (HMSO 1989) *Clubs:* MCC
Recreations: bridge, cricket, politics

Bryan J Ellis Esq, Under Secretary, Department of Social Security, The
Adelphi, John Adam Street, London WC2N 6HT
Telephone: 071-962 8338 *Fax:* 071-962 8359

**ELTIS, Dr WALTER ALFRED   Director-General, National Economic
Development Office**   Grade: 1A

Career: fellow and economics tutor Exeter College, Oxford 1963-86;
visiting economics professor Toronto University, Canada 1976-77; visiting
economics professor European University, Florence, Italy 1979; National
Economic Development Office 1986-: economic director 1986-88,
director-general 1988- *Current non-Whitehall posts:* emeritus fellow Exeter
College, Oxford 1988-

Date of birth: 23 May 1933 *Education/professional qualifications:* Wycliffe
College, Stonehouse, Gloucestershire; Emmanuel College, Cambridge,
economics (BA 1956); Oxford University, economics (MA 1960, DLitt
1990) *Marital status:* married Shelagh Mary Owen 1959; 1 son, 2
daughters *Publications:* Growth and Distribution (Macmillan 1973);
co-author Britain's Economic Problem): Too Few Producers (Macmillan
1976); The Classical Theory of Economic Growth (Macmillan 1984) *Clubs:*
Reform, Royal Automobile *Recreations:* chess, music

Dr Walter A Eltis, Director-General, National Economic Development
Office, Millbank Tower, London SW1P 4QX *Telephone:* 071-217 4049
Fax: 071-976 5736

**EMES, BRIAN ARTHUR   Director of Inmate Programmes, HM Prison Service, Home
Office**   Grade: 3

Career: Home Office HM Prison Service 1957-: director of Inmate programmes 1988-

Date of birth: 31 January 1933 *Education/professional qualifications:* London School of Economics

Brian A Emes Esq, Director of Inmate Programmes, HM Prison Service, Home Office, Cleland House,
Page Street, London SW1P 4LN *Telephone:* 071-270 3000

EMMOTT, MICHAEL   Director of Business Development, Employment Service (Executive Agency)   Grade: 4

Career: Ministry of Labour/Department of Employment/Employment Department Group 1965-: assistant principal 1965-68; private secretary (PS) 1968-70; principal incomes policy 1970-73; seconded to Australia Department of Labour 1973-75; PS 1975-77; assistant secretary: industrial relations 1977-81, employment policy 1981-84; seconded to enterprise and deregulation unit unit 1984-86; director of enterprise and special measures Manpower Services Commission 1986-87; director of programmes/business development 1987-

Date of birth: 2 February 1943 *Education/professional qualifications:* Keighley Boys' Grammar School; Gonville and Caius College, Cambridge, law (BA 1965, MA) *Marital status:* married Janet Anita 1964; 2 sons *Recreations:* running, reading

Michael Emmott Esq, Director of Business Development, Employment Service, Rockingham House, 123 West Street, Sheffield S1 4ER *Telephone:* 0742 596250 *Fax:* 0742 724528

EMMS, PETER FAWCETT   Eastern Regional Director, Departments of the Environment and Transport   Grade: 3

Career: modern languages teacher, UK and USA 1959-67; principal Department of the Environment (DoE) 1974-79; assistant secretary DoE, Departments of Education and Science and of Transport (DTp) 1979-89; eastern regional director DoE, DTp 1989-

Date of birth: 25 April 1935 *Education/professional qualifications:* Derby School; Magdalen College, Oxford, modern languages (BA, MA 1959) *Marital status:* married Carola 1960; 3 daughters *Publications:* Social Housing: A European Dilemma? (Bristol University 1990) *Recreations:* music, theatre, travel

Peter F Emms Esq, Regional Director, Departments of the Environment and Transport, Heron House, 49-51 Goldington Road, Bedford MK40 3LL *Telephone:* 0234 276109 *Fax:* 0234 276272

ENGLEFIELD, DERMOT JOHN TRYAL   Librarian, House of Commons   Grade: 3

Career: St Marylebone reference library 1952-54; House of Commons Library 1954-: assistant librarian parliamentary division 1967-76, deputy librarian 1976-91, librarian 1991-

Date of birth: 27 August 1927 *Education/professional qualifications:* Mount St Mary's College, Sheffield; Trinity College, Dublin, modern history and political science (MA 1952) *Marital status:* married Dora Grahoval 1962; 1 son, 1 daughter *Publications:* The Printed Records of the Parliament of Ireland 1613-1800 (Lemon Tree Press 1978); Parliament and Information (Library Association 1981); Whitehall and Westminster (Longman 1985); Study of Parliament Group 1964-1985 (SPG 1985)

Dermot J T Englefield Esq, Librarian, House of Commons, London SW1A 0AA *Telephone:* 071-219 3635

ESSERY, DAVID JAMES   Under Secretary, Home and Health Department, Scottish Office   Grade: 3

Career: Scottish Office Departments 1956-: under secretary Agriculture and Fisheries Department 1985-91; Home and Health Department (superannuation, police, fire, home defence, emergency services) 1991-

Date of birth: 10 May 1938   *Education/professional qualifications:* Royal High School, Edinburgh

David J Essery Esq, Under Secretary, Home and Health Department, Scottish Office, St Andrew's House, Edinburgh EH1 3DE   *Telephone:* 031-556 8400

ETHERINGTON, GORDON DAVID   Field Director Resources, Crown Prosecution Service   Grade: 3

Gordon D Etherington Esq, Field Director Resources, Crown Prosecution Service, 4-12 Queen Anne's Gate, London SW1H 9AZ   *Telephone:* 071-273 8152

EVANS, HUW PRIDEAUX   Deputy Secretary, Overseas Finance, HM Treasury   Grade: 2

Career: HM Treasury 1976-: under secretary 1980-89; deputy secretary overseas finance 1989-

Date of birth: 21 August 1941   *Education/professional qualifications:* King's College, Cambridge (MA); London School of Economics (MSc)

Huw P Evans Esq, Deputy Secretary, Overseas Finance, HM Treasury, Parliament Street, London SW1P 3AG   *Telephone:* 071-270 4430

EVANS, MARGARET   Director, Chief Executive's Office, National Rivers Authority   Grade: 3

Career: principal/assistant secretary (AS) Welsh Office 1970-86: assistant private secretary to secretary of state 1972-74; AS Department of Social Security 1986-89; director chief executive's office National Rivers Authority 1989-

Date of birth: 5 November 1948   *Education/professional qualifications:* Glanafan Comprehensive School, Port Talbot; University College, London, medieval and modern history (BA 1970)   *Marital status:* married Dr W Howard Evans 1975   *Clubs:* London Welsh   *Recreations:* cooking, embroidery, Welsh literature

Mrs Margaret Evans, Director, Chief Executive's Office, National Rivers Authority, Eastbury House, Albert Embankment, London SE1 7TL   *Telephone:* 071-820 0101   *Fax:* 071-820 1603

EVANS, RUTH   Director, National Consumer Council   Grade: 4

Career: co-ordinator Maternity Alliance 1981-86; MIND (National Association for Mental Health) 1986-90: deputy director 1986-89, acting director 1989-90; general secretary War on Want 1990; management consultant for National Rubella Council and Department of Health 1990-91; director National Consumer Council (independent body for domestic consumers of publicly and privately provided goods and services) 1992-

Date of birth: 12 October 1957   *Education/professional qualifications:* Camden

School for Girls, London; Girton College, Cambridge, history (BA, MA 1980)

Ms Ruth Evans, Director, National Consumer Council, 20 Grosvenor Gardens, London SW1W 0DH *Telephone:* 071-730 3469 *Fax:* 071-730 0191

EVANS, Dr WILLIAM DAVID   Under Secretary, Science and Technology Division, Department of Trade and Industry   Grade: 3

Career: Department of Energy (most of whose responsibilities were taken over by the Department of Trade and Industry [DTI] in 1992) 1974-: assistant secretary 1984-89, chief scientist 1989-92, US environment, science and technology division DTI 1992-

Date of birth: 20 April 1949 *Education/professional qualifications:* St Catherine's College, Oxford (BA 1971, DPhil 1974)

Dr William D Evans, Under Secretary, Science and Technology Division, Department of Trade and Industry, 1 Palace Street, London SW1E 5HE *Telephone:* 071-238 3204

EVERED, Dr DAVID CHARLES   Second Secretary, Medical Research Council

Career: junior hospital posts London and Leeds 1964-70; Newcastle University 1970-74: first assistant in medicine 1970-72, Wellcome senior research fellow 1972-74; consultant physician Newcastle Royal Victoria Infirmary 1974-78; director CIBA Foundation 1978-88; second secretary (deputy chief executive) Medical Research Council 1988- *Current non-Whitehall posts:* non-executive member Hammersmith and Queen Charlotte's Special Health Authority 1990-

Date of birth: 2 January 1940 *Education/professional qualifications:* Cranleigh School, Surrey; Middlesex Hospital medical school (BSc 1961, MB BS 1964, MD 1971); MRCP 1967; FRCP 1978; FIBiol 1978 *Marital status:* married Anne Elizabeth Massey Lings 1964; 2 daughters, 1 son *Publications:* Diseases of the Thyroid (Pitman 1976); Atlas of Endocrinology (Wolfe Medical 1979/90); Collaboration in Medical Research in Europe (Pitman 1981) *Recreations:* reading, history, antiques, gardening, tennis, sailing, walking

Dr David C Evered, Second Secretary, Medical Research Council, 20 Park Crescent, London W1N 4AL *Telephone:* 071-636 5422 *Fax:* 071-580 4369

EVERETT, CHARLES WILLIAM VOGT   Head of Policy and Legal Services Group, Lord Chancellor's Department   Grade: 3

Career: Lord Chancellor's Department 1971-: assistant private secretary to Lord Chancellor 1974-76; seconded to Department of Transport 1982-84; head of legal aid bill division 1987-88; secretary to legal aid board 1988-89; head of court strategy division 1989-90, of central unit 1990-91, of policy and legal services group 1991-

Date of birth: 15 October 1949 *Education/professional qualifications:* Reading University (BA 1971) *Marital status:* married Elizabeth Vanessa 1978; 3 sons

Charles W V Everett, Head of Policy and Legal Services Group, Lord Chancellor's Department, Trevelyan House, 30 Great Peter Street, London SW1P 2BY *Telephone:* 071-210 8769

EVES, DAVID CHARLES THOMAS   Deputy Director-General, Operations, Health and Safety Executive   Grade: 2

Career: schoolteacher 1963-64; factory inspector Ministry of Labour 1964-67; Health and Safety Executive 1977-: head of planning section 1977-78, director of corporate services 1978-80, head of planning 1981-83, deputy chief inspector of factories 1983-85, chief inspector of factories 1985-88, director of resources and planning 1988-89, deputy director-general (technology and health sciences, research and field operations, railway and mines) 1989-

Date of birth: 10 January 1942 *Education/professional qualifications:* King's School, Rochester; University College, Durham University, English (BA 1963) *Marital status:* married Valerie Ann Carter 1964; 1 daughter *Clubs:* Athenaeum *Recreations:* sailing, fishing, painting, reading

David C T Eves Esq, Deputy Director-General, Operations, Health and Safety Executive, Baynards House, 1 Chepstow Place, London W2 4TF *Telephone:* 071-243 6450 *Fax:* 071-727 6828

EWINS, P D   Managing Director, Command and Maritime Systems Group, Defence Research Agency (Executive Agency)   Grade: 3

P D Ewins Esq, Managing Director, Command and Maritime Systems Group, Defence Research Agency, Portsdown, Portsmouth, Hants PO6 4AA *Telephone:* 0705 219999

F

FACER, ROGER LAWRENCE LOWE   Deputy Under Secretary, Personnel and Logistics, **Ministry of Defence**   Grade: 2

Career: War Office/Ministry of Defence (MoD) 1957-75: assistant secretary (AS) 1970-73; counsellor HM Diplomatic Service 1973-75; MoD 1975-81: AS 1975-79, assistant under secretary (AUS) 1979-81; under secretary Cabinet Office 1981-83; MoD 1984-: AUS 1984-87, deputy under secretary (armed forces' pay and conditions; information technology; defence estate and works services) 1988-

Date of birth: 28 June 1933   *Education/professional qualifications:* Rugby School; St John's College, Oxford, literae humaniores (BA, MA 1957)   *Honours, decorations:* CB 1992   *Recreations:* alpine gardening, hillwalking, opera

Roger L L Facer Esq CB, Deputy Under Secretary, Ministry of Defence, Whitehall, London SW1A 2HB   *Telephone:* 071-218 9000

FAINT, (JOHN) ANTHONY LEONARD   Under Secretary Eastern European Division, **Overseas Development Administration**   Grade: 3

Career: Ministry of Overseas Development/Overseas Development Administration (ODA) 1965-86: assistant principal 1965-68; study leave 1968-69; first secretary (aid), Blantyre, Malawi 1971-73; principal, London 1974-80; head of SE Asia development division, Bangkok 1980-83; head of finance department, London 1983-86; alternative executive director World Bank, Washington 1986-89; ODA 1989-: head East Asia department 1989-91; under secretary international division 1990-91, Eastern European division 1991-   *Current non-Whitehall posts:* UK director European Bank for Reconstruction and Development 1991-

Date of birth: 24 November 1942   *Education/professional qualifications:* Chigwell School; Magdalen College, Oxford, classics (BA 1965); Fletcher School, Massachusetts, USA, international economics (MA 1969)   *Marital status:* married Elizabeth Theresa Winter 1979   *Recreations:* music, bridge, chess, squash

J Anthony L Faint Esq, Under Secretary, Overseas Development Administration, 94 Victoria Street, London SW1E 5JL   *Telephone:* 071-917 0091

FARMER, PETER JOHN   Public Trustee and Accountant General of the Supreme Court, Lord Chancellor's Department

Career: HM Customs and Excise 1975-79; HM Treasury 1979-81; Lord Chancellor's Department 1981-: principal, legal remuneration 1981- 83; circuit principal, Leeds 1983-87; assistant secretary, management support 1987-88; assistant public trustee 1988-91, public trustee and accountant general of Supreme Court (executor, trustee and Mental Health Act receiver; protection of mentally incapable people's property and affairs) 1991-

Date of birth: 5 November 1952   *Education/professional qualifications:* King Edward VI School, Southampton; Gonville and Caius College, Cambridge, mathematics (BA 1975, MA); London University, psychology (certificate 1983)   *Marital status:* married Christine Ann 1986   *Clubs:* Royal Over-seas League   *Recreations:* English country dancing, hill walking

Peter J Farmer Esq, Public Trustee and Accountant General of the Supreme Court, Public Trust Office, 24 Kingsway, London WC2B 6JX   *Telephone:* 071-269 7000   *Fax:* 071-831 0060

FARQUHARSON, JONATHAN   Commissioner, Charity Commission   Grade: 4

Career: solicitor 1962-64; Charity Commission 1964-: legal assistant (LA) 1964-70, senior LA 1970-81, deputy commissioner 1981-85, commissioner 1985-

Date of birth: 27 December 1937 *Education/professional qualifications:* St Albans School; Manchester University, law (LLB 1959) *Marital status:* married Maureen Elsie 1963; 2 daughters *Recreations:* geography, photography, painting

Jonathan Farquharson Esq, Charity Commissioner, Charity Commission, Graeme House, Derby Square, Liverpool L2 7SB *Telephone:* 051-227 2400

FAUSET, I D   Assistant Under Secretary, Civilian Management Specialists, Ministry of Defence   Grade: 3

I D Fauset Esq, Assistant Under Secretary, Civilian Management Specialists, Ministry of Defence, Pinesgate East, Lower Bristol Road, Bath, Avon BA1 5AB *Telephone:* 0225 449256

FELLOWS, JOHN WALTER   South East Regional Director, Departments of the Environment and Transport   Grade: 3

Career: private industry civil engineer 1954-59; civil engineer county boroughs of Dudley 1959-63, Coventry 1963-66, Wolverhampton 1966-69; Department of Transport (DTp) 1969-90: civil engineer 1969-84, assistant secretary highway maintenance division 1984-88, director south east region 1988-90; south east regional director Department of Environment/DTp (regional planning, house and trunk road network) 1990-

Date of birth: 27 July 1938 *Education/professional qualifications:* Dudley Technical High School; Wolverhampton Polytechnic/Birmingham University, civil engineering and transport planning (MSc 1974); FICE 1990 *Marital status:* married Maureen 1964; 2 sons *Recreations:* boating, sailing, golf, music, theatre

John W Fellows Esq, Regional Director, Departments of the Environment and Transport, Charles House, 375 Kensington High Street, London W14 4QH *Telephone:* 071-605 9010 *Fax:* 071-605 9133

FIELD, Major General GEOFFREY WILLIAM   Director-General, Logistic Policy (Army), Ministry of Defence

Career: Royal Engineers 1961-; Ministry of Defence 1983-: director defence programmes 1989-90, director-general logistic policy (army) 1990-

Date of birth: 30 November 1941 *Education/professional qualifications:* Royal Military Academy, Sandhurst; Royal Military College of Science; Royal College of Defence Studies

Major General Geoffrey W Field OBE, Director-General Logistic Policy (Army), Ministry of Defence, Whitehall, London SW1A 2HB *Telephone:* 071-218 7531

To subscribe to The Whitehall Companion
Telephone: 071-240 3902

FIELD, JOHN LESLIE   Head of Demography and Statistics Division, Government Actuary's Department   Grade: 4

Career: private practice actuary 1959-69; Government Actuary's Department 1969-: actuary 1969-74, head of demography and statistics division (for occupational pension schemes) 1974-

Date of birth: 30 June 1931 *Education/professional qualifications:* Varndean County Grammar School, Brighton; Manchester University, mathematics (BSc 1952); FIA 1959 *Marital status:* married Margaret 1962; 3 sons *Recreations:* gardening, travel, reading

John L Field Esq, Chief Actuary, Government Actuary's Department, 22 Kingsway, London WC2B 6LE *Telephone:* 071-242 6878 *Fax:* 071-831 6653

FIGGIS, ANTHONY ST JOHN HOWARD   Assistant Under Secretary, Foreign and Commonwealth Office   Senior grade

Career: HM Diplomatic Service 1962-: Belgrade, Bahrain, Madrid, Bonn; assistant under secretary and vice-marshal diplomatic corps 1991-

Date of birth: 12 October 1940 *Education/professional qualifications:* Rugby School; King's College, Cambridge *Marital status:* married Miriam Ellen Mayella 1964; 1 daughter, 2 sons

Anthony St J H Figgis Esq, Assistant Under Secretary, Foreign and Commonwealth Office, Old Admiralty Building, Whitehall, London, SW1A 2AF *Telephone:* 071-210 6360 *Fax:* 071-210 6870

FINDLAY, ALASTAIR DONALD FRASER   Under Secretary, Industry Department, Scottish Office   Grade: 3

Career: assistant principal Department of Agriculture and Fisheries for Scotland (DAFS) 1966-70; private secretary to joint parliamentary under secretary Scottish Office (SO) 1970-71; principal SO 1971-74; on secondment to Foreign and Commonwealth Office as agriculture and food first secretary, The Hague 1975-78; assistant secretary: higher education division Scottish Education Department 1979-82, DAFS fisheries division 1982-85, DAFS livestock division 1985-88; under secretary SO Industry Department (Scottish enterprise and employment; highlands and islands tourism; energy, transport, local roads 1988-

Date of birth: 3 February 1944 *Education/professional qualifications:* Kelso High School, Roxburghshire; Edinburgh University, mental philosophy (MA 1966) *Marital status:* married Morag Cumming 1969; 1 son, 3 daughters *Clubs:* Royal Commonwealth Society *Recreations:* gardening, walking, golf, cars, rugby watching

Alastair D F Findlay Esq, Under Secretary Scottish Office Industry Department, New St Andrew's House, Edinburgh EH1 3TA *Telephone:* 031-244 4609 *Fax:* 031-244 4785

Parliamentary Offices
see page 275

FINDLAY, Dr DAVID ROBERT   Principal Medical Officer, Social Security Benefits Agency (Executive Agency)   Grade: 4

Career: army medical service 1958-75; Department of Social Security 1975-: medical officer (MO) 1975-78, senior MO 1978-87, principal MO Social Security Benefits Agency medical service (management of medical staff in disability benefit centres in south and medical reference service throughout GB) 1987-

Date of birth: 25 January 1934 *Education/professional qualifications:* Epsom College; Aberdeen University, medicine (MB, ChB 1957) *Marital status:* married Ruth; 2 sons by previous marriage *Recreations:* Anglo-German societies and twinning

Dr David R Findlay, Principal Medical Officer, Social Security Benefits Agency, Department of Social Security, Friars House, 157-168 Blackfriars Road, London SE1 8EU *Telephone:* 071-972 3289 *Fax:* 071-972 3313

FINER, Dr ELLIOT GEOFFREY   Under Secretary, Head of Chemicals and Biotechnology, Industry 2 Division, Department of Trade and Industry   Grade: 3

Career: research scientist Unilever Research 1968-75; Department of Energy 1975-: principal, assistant secretary, director-general Energy Efficiency Office 1988-90; head of management development group Cabinet Office (Office of Minister for the Civil Service) 1990-92; head of enterprise initiative division, Department of Trade and Industry 1992, of chemicals and biotechnology, industry 2 division 1992-

Date of birth: 30 March 1944 *Education/professional qualifications:* Royal Grammar School, High Wycombe; Cheadle Hulme School; East Barnet Grammar School; St Catharine's College, Cambridge (BA 1965); East Anglia University (MSc 1966, PhD 1968) *Marital status:* married Viviane Kibrit 1970; 2 sons *Recreations:* home and family, reading, 'DIY", gardening, computing, music

Dr Elliot G Finer, Head of Chemicals and Biotechnology, Industry 2 Division, Department of Trade and Industry, Ashdown House, 123 Victoria Street, London SW1E 6RB *Telephone:* 071-215 5000

IRTH, JOAN MARGARET   Deputy Director of Finance, Finance Division A, Department f Health   Grade: 3

areer: Department of [Health and] Social Security 1967-: under secretary 1981-, social security ivision C 1987-90; deputy director of finance, finance division A Department of Health 1990-

ate of birth: 25 March 1935 *Education/professional qualifications:* University of Leeds (BSc, PhD)

Irs Joan M Firth, Deputy Director of Finance, Finance Division A, Department of Health, Richmond Iouse, 79 Whitehall, London SW1A 2NS *Telephone:* 071-210 3000

ISK, Dr DAVID JOHN   Chief Scientist, Air, Climate and Toxic Substances Directorate, Iepartment of the Environment   Grade: 3

areer: Department of Environment 1976-: Building Research Establishment 1976-84: head of /stems dynamic branch 1976-79, of mechanical and electrical engineering division 1979-84; ssistant secretary: environment policy planning and co-ordination 1985-87, air noise policy 1988; eputy chief scientist 1988-89; chief scientist (science of technology) and under secretary air, climate Id toxic substances directorate 1988-

Date of birth: 9 January 1947 *Education/professional qualifications:* Stationers' Company's School, London; St John's College, Cambridge, natural sciences (BA, MA 1972); Manchester University, low temperature physics (PhD 1972); Cambridge University (ScD 1983), FCIBS 1983 *Marital status:* married Anne Thoday 1972; 1 daughter, 1 son *Publications:* Thermal Control of Buildings (Applied Science 1981) *Recreations:* theatre, opera, concerts

Dr David J Fisk, Chief Scientist, Department of the Environment, 43 Marsham Street, London SW1P 3EB *Telephone:* 071-276 3000

FLAXEN, DAVID WILLIAM   Director of Statistics, Department of Transport   Grade: 3

Career: Central Statistical Office (CSO), Department of Employment, Inland Revenue 1964-83; adviser UN Development Programme, Swaziland 1971-72; assistant director CSO 1983-89; director of statistics Department of Transport 1989-

Date of birth: 20 April 1941 *Education/professional qualifications:* Manchester Grammar School; Brasenose College, Oxford, physics (BA 1961, MA); University College, London, statistics (Dip Stat 1964) *Marital status:* married Eleanor Easton 1969; 2 daughters

David W Flaxen Esq, Director of Statistics, Department of Transport, Romney House, 43 Marsham Street, London SW1P 3PY *Telephone:* 071-276 8030 *Fax:* 071-276 8161

FLETCHER, PHILIP JOHN   Director, Planning and Development Control, Department of the Environment   Grade: 3

Career: Department of the Environment 1973-: structure plans West Midlands 1973-76; central unit and private secretary posts 1976-79; private housebuilding and mortgage finance 1980-82; local government finance 1982-85; director central finance 1986-89; director (under secretary) planning and development control 1990- *Current non-Whitehall posts:* non-executive director Northern Rock Building Society London region 1991-

Date of birth: 2 May 1946 *Education/professional qualifications:* Marlborough College; Trinity College, Oxford, history (BA, MA 1987) *Marital status:* married Margaret Anne 1977; 2 daughters (1 deceased) *Recreations:* walking; reader, Church of England

Philip J Fletcher Esq, Under Secretary, Department of the Environment, 2 Marsham Street, London SW1P 3EB *Telephone:* 071-276 3854 *Fax:* 071-276 4995

FLYNN, DESMOND JAMES   Deputy Inspector General, Insolvency Service (Executive Agency)   Grade: 4

Career: Department of Economic Affairs 1968-69; Department of Trade and Industry (DTI) Insolvency Service (IS) companies winding up 1969-71; student 1971-74; IS 1974-: Official Receiver, Birmingham 1974-78: examiner 1974-80, assistant official receiver (AOR) 1980-84; AOR companies winding up, London 1984-86, seconded to DTI trade policy division 1986-88, principal inspector of official receivers 1988-89, deputy inspector general HQ operations (finance, personnel and training; disqualification and prosecution; procurement and common services) 1989-

Date of birth: 21 March 1949 *Education/professional qualifications:* Ealing Boys' Grammar School; East Anglia University, philosophy, economic history (BA 1974) *Marital status:* married Kumari 1975; 1 daughter, 1 son *Clubs:* Royston Golf *Recreations:* golf, reading

Desmond J Flynn Esq, Deputy Inspector General, Insolvency Service, Bridge Place, 88-89 Eccleston Square, London SW1V 1PT *Telephone:* 071-215 0769

FOGDEN, MICHAEL ERNEST GEORGE   Chief Executive Employment Service (Executive Agency)   Grade: 3

Career: Department of Health and Social Security 1970-83: private secretary to Richard Crossman and Keith Joseph, secretaries of state for social services 1968-70, head of operational computer development 1981-83; Department of Employment 1983-: head of manpower policy division 1983-87, chief executive Employment Service (job centres and unemployment benefit services) 1987- *Current non-Whitehall posts:* chairman London regional council, Royal Institute of Public Administration 1988-

Date of birth: 30 May 1936 *Education/professional qualifications:* Worthing High School for Boys *Marital status:* married Ann Diamond 1957; 3 sons, 1 daughter *Recreations:* gardening, talking, music

Michael E G Fogden Esq, Chief Executive Employment Service, St Vincent House, 30 Orange Street, London WC2H 7HT *Telephone:* 071-389 1497 *Fax:* 071-389 1457

FOOT, DAVID LOVELL   Commissioner, Operations, Forestry Commission   Grade: 3

Career: Forestry Commission (FC) 1961-64; government of Malawi 1964-70; FC 1970-: commissioner, operations 1986-

Date of birth: 20 May 1939 *Education/professional qualifications:* Edinburgh University (BSc Hons 1961)

David L Foot Esq, Commissioner, Operations, Forestry Commission, 231 Corstorphine Road, Edinburgh EH12 7AT *Telephone:* 031-334 0303

FORRESTER, DAVID MICHAEL   Under Secretary and Head of Schools Branch 4, Department for Education   Grade: 3

Career: Department for Education 1967-: seconded to HM Treasury 1976-78; assistant secretary 1979-85; seconded to Department of Trade and Industry 1985-87; undersecretary and head of schools branch 4 1988-

Date of birth: 22 June 1944 *Education/professional qualifications:* King's College, Cambridge (BA, MA); Harvard University, USA

David M Forrester Esq, Under Secretary and Head of Schools Branch 4, Department for Education, Sanctuary Buildings, Great Smith Street, London SW1P 3BT *Telephone:* 071-925 5000

FORSHAW, PETER   Under Secretary, Purchasing Group, HM Treasury   Grade: 3

Career: army service 1954-90; under secretary purchasing group and director of public competition and purchasing unit HM Treasury (professional head of government purchasing) 1990- *Current non-Whitehall posts:* member Institute of Purchasing and Supply management board 1991-

Date of birth: 12 June 1936 *Education/professional qualifications:* Queen Elizabeth's Grammar School, Wimborne, Dorset; Royal Military College of Science; Staff College; Naval Postgraduate College, Monterey, USA; FBIM 1985; FInstPS 1990 *Honours, decorations:* OBE 1980, CBE 1984; *Marital status:* married Helen Patricia Talbot Cliff 1960; 2 daughters *Clubs:* Army and Navy *Recreations:* country sports, watercolours, glass engraving

Peter Forshaw Esq CBE, Under Secretary, HM Treasury, Parliament Street, London SW1P 3AG *Telephone:* 071-270 6464 *Fax:* 071-270 6473

FOSTER, ANDREW WILLIAM   Deputy Chief Executive, NHS Management Executive, Department of Health   Grade: 2

Career: social worker, London 1966-71; area social services officer 1971-75; assistant director of social services (DSS), Haringey 1975-79; DSS Greenwich 1979-82, North Yorkshire 1982-87; general manager Yorkshire regional health authority 1987-91; deputy chief executive NHS management executive Department of Health performance management directorate (director performance management; development of purchasing; district health authorities' role) 1991-

Date of birth: 29 December 1944 *Education/professional qualifications:* Abingdon School; Newcastle Polytechnic, sociology (BSc); London School of Economics, applied social studies (diploma) *Marital status:* married Christine Marquiss 1967; 1 daughter, 1 son *Recreations:* golf, squash, walking, travel, theatre, food, wine

Andrew W Foster Esq, Deputy Chief Executive, NHS Management Executive, Department of Health, Richmond House, 79 Whitehall, London SW1A 2NS *Telephone:* 071-210 5737 *Fax:* 071-210 5080

FOSTER, ANN   Director, Scottish Consumer Council

Career: lecturer College for Distributive Trades 1972-78; National Consumer Council 1978-91: consultant 1978-88, food policy adviser 1988-91; director Scottish Consumer Council 1991-

Date of birth: 28 September 1949 *Education/professional qualifications:* Hutchesons' Girls' Grammar School, Glasgow; St Andrew's University, French and medieval history (MA 1970); Reading University, education (MA Educ 1980) *Marital status:* separated *Publications:* The Retail Handbook (McGraw Hill 1979); Food Policy and the Consumer (NCC 1989) *Clubs:* Westminster Dining *Recreations:* theatre, skiing, opera, gardening

Mrs Ann Foster, Director, Scottish Consumer Council, 314 St Vincent Street, Glasgow G3 8XW *Telephone:* 041-226 5261 *Fax:* 041-221 0731

FOSTER, JOANNA   Chair, Equal Opportunities Commission

Career: journalist San Francisco Chronicle, USA 1960-61; head of press office Conservative Central Office 1961-67; management adviser Industrial Society (IS) 1967-71; director Centre Actif and press attaché INSEAD, Fontainebleau, France 1971-79; director corporate services Western Psychiatric Institute and Clinic, Pittsburgh University, USA 1981; IS 1981-88: head of youth department 1981-84, head of Pepperell department 1984-88; chair Equal Opportunities Commission (elimination of discrimination on grounds of sex and marital status) 1988- *Current non-Whitehall posts:* honorary fellow St Hilda's College, Oxford 1988-; director Welsh National Opera 1990-

Date of birth: 5 May 1939 *Education/professional qualifications:* Benenden School, Kent *Marital status:* married Jerome 1961; 1 daughter, 1 son *Recreations:* food, family, friends

Joanna Foster, Chair, Equal Opportunities Commission, Overseas House, Quay Street, Manchester M3 3HN *Telephone:* 061-833 9244 (Manchester); 071-287 3953 (London) *Fax:* 061-835 1657

Government Departments
see page 300

FOSTER, ROBERT   Deputy Head of Science and Technology Secretariat, Cabinet Office   Grade: 3

Career: electronics and telecommunications industry 1964-77; Department of Trade and Industry 1977-91: principal 1977-84, assistant secretary 1984-91; deputy head of science and technology secretariat, Cabinet Office (coordination of science and technology policy) 1992-

Date of birth: 12 May 1943 *Education/professional qualifications:* Oundle School; Corpus Christi College, Cambridge, engineering (BA, MA 1967) *Marital status:* married Judy 1967; 1 son, 1 daughter *Recreations:* squash, tennis, reading

Robert Foster Esq, Deputy Head, Science and Technology Secretariat, Cabinet Office, 70 Whitehall, London SW1A 2AS
Telephone: 071-270 0320

FOX, Dr ALAN MARTIN   Assistant Under Secretary (Ordnance), Ministry of Defence   Grade: 3

Career: private secretary to parliamentary secretary Ministry of Aviation 1965-67; aviation and defence first secretary Paris embassy 1973-75; Ministry of Defence 1975-78; Royal College of Defence Studies 1979; Ministry of Defence 1980-: assistant under secretary (ordnance) land systems controllerate 1988-

Date of birth: 5 July 1938 *Education/professional qualifications:* Bancroft's School, Woodford Green; Queen Mary College, London University, physics (BSc 1959), mathematical physics (PhD 1963) *Recreations:* chess, bridge, watching rugby, cricket

Dr Alan M Fox, Assistant Under Secretary, Ministry of Defence, Whitehall, London SW1A 2HB
Telephone: 071-218 7315

FOX, DR (ANTHONY) JOHN   Deputy Director and Chief Medical Statistician, Office of Population Censuses and Surveys   Grade: 3

Career: Office of Population Censuses and Surveys (OPCS) 1975-79; professor of social statistics, City University 1980-88; deputy director and chief medical statistician OPCS 1988-

Date of birth: 25 April 1946 *Education/professional qualifications:* University College London (BSc); Imperial College London (PhD, DIC)

Dr A John Fox, Deputy Director and Chief Medical Statistician, Office of Population Censuses and Surveys, St Catherine's House, 10 Kingsway, London WC2B 6JP *Telephone:* 071-242 0262

FOX, BRIAN MICHAEL   Principal Establishments and Finance Officer, HM Treasury   Grade: 3

Career: HM Treasury 1963-: private secretary to Financial Secretary 1967-69, seconded to 3is 1981-82, deputy establishment officer 1983-87, head of defence policy and materiel division 1987-89, principal establishment and finance officer 1989-

Date of birth: 21 September 1944 *Education/professional qualifications:* East Ham Boys' Grammar School *Marital status:* married Maureen 1966; 1 daughter *Recreations:* table tennis, badminton, soccer

Brian M Fox Esq, Principal Establishments and Finance Officer, HM Treasury, Parliament Street, London SW1P 3AG *Telephone:* 071-270 4870

FRANCE, Sir CHRISTOPHER WALTER   Permanent Secretary, Ministry of Defence
Grade: 1

Career: HM Treasury 1959-84: various posts including private secretary to chancellors of exchequer 1959-80, seconded to Electricity Council 1980-81, to Ministry of Defence (MoD) 1981-84; Department of Health [and Social Security] 1984-: deputy secretary 1984-86, second permanent secretary (PS) social security 1986-87, first PS 1987-88, PS 1988-92; PS MoD 1992-

Date of birth: 2 April 1934   *Education/professional qualifications:* East Ham Grammar School, London; New College, Oxford, philosophy, politics and economics (BA 1957) and education (Dip Ed 1958); CDipAF 1981   *Honours, decorations:* CB 1984, KCB 1989

Sir Christopher France KCB, Permanent Secretary, Department of Health, Richmond House, 79 Whitehall, London SW1A 2NS   *Telephone:* 071-210 5310   *Fax:* 071-210 5409

FRASER, ALASDAIR MacLEOD   Director of Public Prosecutions for Northern Ireland   Grade: 1A

Career: N Ireland bar 1970-; Office of Director of Public Prosecutions for Northern Ireland 1973-: court prosecutor 1973; assistant director 1974-82, senior assistant director 1982-89, deputy director 1988, director 1989-

Date of birth: 29 September 1946   *Education/professional qualifications:* Sullivan Upper School, Holywood; Trinity College, Dublin (BA, LLB); law, Queen's University, Belfast (Dip Laws)   *Honours, decorations:* QC 1989   *Marital status:* married Margaret Mary Glancy 1975; 2 sons, 1 daughter

Alasdair M Fraser Esq QC, Director of Public Prosecutions, Royal Courts of Justice, Belfast BT1 3NX *Telephone:* 0232 235111

FRASER, MAURICE   Special Adviser to Foreign Secretary

Career: Conservative Research Department 1984-89: home affairs 1984-85, political desk 1985-86, head of political section 1986-87, assistant director 1987-89; special adviser to Douglas Hurd, Foreign Secretary 1989-

Date of birth: 2 March 1960   *Education/professional qualifications:* French Lycée, London; London School of Economics, government and history (BSc Econ 1981)   *Marital status:* married Louise Nicolette Le Pelley 1989 *Recreations:* history, philosophy, fine arts, tennis

Maurice Fraser Esq, Special Adviser, Foreign and Commonwealth Office, King Charles Street, London SW1A 2AL   *Telephone:* 071-270 2117 *Fax:* 071-270 2111

FREEMAN, PAUL ILLIFE   Controller and Chief Executive, HM Stationery Office   Grade: 2

Career: Central Computer and Telecommunications Agency, HM Treasury 1983-88; controller and chief executive of HM Stationery Office 1989-
Education/professional qualifications: Victoria University of Manchester, chemistry (BSc Hons, PhD)

Paul I Freeman Esq, Controller and Chief Executive, HMSO, St Crispins, Duke Street, Norwich NR3 1DN   *Telephone:* 0603 622211   *Fax:* 0603 695582

FREEMAN, PETER   Head of International Division, Overseas Development Administration   Grade: 3

Career: Overseas Development Administration (ODA) 1970-75: assistant private secretary to minister 1973-75; office of UK executive director World Bank 1975-78; ODA 1978-80; first secretary, aid, Zimbabwe High Commission 1980-83; ODA 1984-: head of European Community department 1984-88, of central and southern Africa department 1988-90, of aid policy department 1990-91, of international division (UK relations with multi-lateral aid organisations) 1991-

Date of birth: 8 December 1947

Peter Freeman Esq, Head of International Division, Overseas Development Administration, 94 Victoria Street, London SW1

FREMANTLE, SYDNEY WALTER   Head, International Energy Unit, Energy Division, Department of Trade and Industry   Grade: 4

Career: various posts in energy divisions of Department of Trade and Industry (DTI) and its predecessors 1961-: head of international energy unit DTI 1992-

Date of birth: 5 November 1936   *Education/professional qualifications:* Sherborne School; Oriel College, Oxford, history (BA 1959, MA)   *Marital status:* married Susan Delia Aiton Bell 1961; 1 son   *Recreations:* gardening, plant-hunting, running, fencing

Sydney W Fremantle Esq, Head of International Energy Unit, Energy Division Department of Trade and Industry, 1 Palace Street, London SW1E 5HE   *Telephone:* 071-238 3501   *Fax:* 071-233 5807

FRIES, RICHARD JAMES   Chief Commissioner, Charity Commission

Career: Home Office 1965-: head of equal opportunities and general department -1991; under secretary broadcasting and miscellaneous department (broadcasting, press freedom, data protection, coroners, local legislation, animals) 1991-92; chief commissioner, Charity Commission 1992-

Date of birth: 7 July 1940

Richard J Fries Esq, Chief Commissioner, Charity Commission, 57 Haymarket, London SW1Y 4QX   *Telephone:* 071-210 4409   *Fax:* 071-930 9174

FRIZZELL, EDWARD WILLIAM   Chief Executive, Scottish Prison Service, Scottish Office Home and Health Department   Grade: 3

Career: Scottish Milk Marketing Board 1968-73; Scottish Council (development and industry) 1973-76; principal Scottish Office (SO) Department of Agriculture and Fisheries 1976-78; first secretary (fisheries) UK permanent representation to EC, Brussels 1978-82; SO 1982-: assistant secretary (AS) higher education Scottish Education Department 1982-86, AS finance division 1986-89; director Locate in Scotland, Industry department 1989-91, chief executive Scottish prison service 1991-

Date of birth: 4 May 1946   *Education/professional qualifications:* Paisley Grammar School; Glasgow University, history and political economy (MA 1968)   *Marital status:* married Moira 1969; 1 daughter, 2 sons   *Clubs:* Mortonhall Golf, Edinburgh

Edward W Frizzell Esq, Chief Executive, Scottish Prison Service, Calton House, 5 Redheughs Rigg, Edinburgh EH12 9HW   *Telephone:* 031-244 8522   *Fax:* 031-244 8774

'Next Steps' Executive Agencies
see page 761

FULLER, BRIAN LESLIE   Commandant Chief Executive, Fire Service College (Executive Agency)

Career: fire service 1960-: fireman to station officer Hertfordshire Fire Brigade (FB) 1960-66; station officer Warwickshire FB 1966-68; assistant divisional officer Nottinghamshire FB 1968-69; divisional commander, Essex FB 1969-72; deputy chief officer 1972-73 then chief fire officer (CFO) 1973-74 Glamorgan FB; CFO Mid Glamorgan FB 1974-80, Nottinghamshire FB 1980-81, West Midlands Fire Service 1981-90; commandant Fire Service College 1990-

Date of birth: 18 April 1936 *Education/professional qualifications:* St Albans County Grammar School *Honours, decorations:* FIFireE 1975; QFSM 1981; CBE 1989 *Marital status:* married Linda; 3 sons *Recreations:* cricket, squash, music, reading

Brian L Fuller CBE, Commandant Chief Executive, Fire Service College, Moreton-in-Marsh, Gloucestershire GL56 0RH *Telephone:* 0608 52153 *Fax:* 0608 51788

G

GAINSBOROUGH, MICHAEL   Assistant Under Secretary, Service Personnel, Ministry of Defence   Grade: 3

Career: Air Ministry 1959-64; Ministry of Defence (MoD) 1964-78; defence counsellor UK delegation to NATO, Brussels, Foreign and Commonwealth Office 1978-81; MoD 1981-86: director resources and programmes (strategic systems) 1981-83, assistant under secretary (AUS) naval staff 1984, programmes 1985-86; Center for International Affairs, Harvard University, USA 1986-87; MoD 1987-: AUS to adjutant general MoD (army administration and personnel) 1987-92, AUS service personnel 1992-

Date of birth: 13 March 1938 *Education/professional qualifications:* St Paul's School, London; Trinity College, Oxford (BA, MA) *Recreations:* music, gardening, walking

Michael Gainsborough Esq, Assistant Under Secretary, Ministry of Defence, Whitehall, London SW1A 2HB *Telephone:* 071-218 9000

GALLACHER, T N   HM Senior Chief Inspector of Schools, Education Department, Scottish Office   Grade: 3

T N Gallacher Esq, HM Senior Chief Inspector of Schools, Education Department, Scottish Office, New St Andrew's House, Edinburgh EH1 3S9 *Telephone:* 031-556 8400

GALLAGHER, EDWARD PATRICE   Chief Executive, National Rivers Authority

Career: Black and Decker 1978-86: director of marketing services 1978-79, of service and distribution 1979-81, of business analysis 1981-83, of market and product development 1983-86; Amersham International 1986-92: director of corporate development 1986-88, divisional chief executive 1988-90, manufacturing director 1990-92; chief executive National Rivers Authority (water resources, quality, flood defence, fisheries, recreation, conservation, navigation) 1992-

Date of birth: 4 August 1944 *Education/professional qualifications:* Dunstable Grammar School; Sheffield University, engineering (BSc 1966); CEng 1976 *Marital status:* married Helen 1969; 2 sons *Recreations:* golf, tennis, theatre, rambling, guitar

Edward P Gallagher Esq, Chief Executive, National Rivers Authority, 30-34 Albert Embankment, London SE1 7TL *Telephone:* 071-820 0101 *Fax:* 071-820 1789

GALLAGHER, (WILLIAM) BILL EDWARD   Director, South West Construction Programme, Department of Transport   Grade: 4

Career: highway engineer Warwickshire County Council (CC) 1955-70; senior engineer Durham CC 1970-74; Department of Transport 1974-: assistant chief engineer 1974-87, director south west construction programme division (major improvements to motorway and trunk road network) 1987-

Date of birth: 14 July 1932 *Education/professional qualifications:* St Mary's College, Crosby, Liverpool; Birmingham University, civil engineering (BSc 1953) *Marital status:* married Beryl 1957; 3 daughters, 2 sons

Bill E Gallagher Esq, Director, South West Construction Programme Division, Department of Transport, Tollgate House, 2 Houlton Street, Bristol BS2 9DJ *Telephone:* 0272 218534 *Fax:* 0272 218264

Regulatory Organisations and Public Bodies
see page 857

GAMMIE, GORDON EDWARD   Counsel to the Speaker, House of Commons   Grade: 3

Career: army service 1941-45; Whitehall legal departments 1949-69; principal assistant solicitor Department of Environment 1969-74; constitution unit Cabinet Office 1975-77; deputy Treasury Solicitor 1977-79; solicitor and legal adviser Ministry of Agriculture, Fisheries and Food 1979-83; Counsel to the Speaker (advising principally Commons select committees on draft EC legislation), House of Commons 1983-

Date of birth: 9 February 1922 *Education/professional qualifications:* St Paul's School, London; Queen's College, Oxford, history, law (BA, MA 1947) *Honours, decorations:* CB 1981, QC 1989 *Marital status:* married Olive Susie Joyce 1949; 2 sons *Clubs:* Athenaeum; St Andrew's Lawn Tennis, Cheam *Recreations:* tennis, dog

Gordon E Gammie Esq CB QC, Counsel to the Speaker, European Legislation Committee, House of Commons, London SW1A 0AA *Telephone:* 071-219 5561

GANDY, DAVID STEWART   Deputy Director and Chief Executive, Crown Prosecution Service   Grade: 2

Career: assistant solicitor Manchester 1956-59; chief prosecuting solicitor Manchester 1959-68, Manchester 1968-74, Greater Manchester 1974-85, Crown Prosecution Service 1985: head of field management 1985-87, deputy director and chief executive 1987-

Date of birth: 19 September 1932 *Education/professional qualifications:* Manchester Grammar School; Manchester University; solicitor 1954 *Honours, decorations:* OBE 1981, CB 1989 *Marital status:* married Mabel Sheldon 1956; 1 daughter, 1 son *Recreations:* theatre, bridge, walking

David S Gandy Esq CB, OBE, Deputy Director and Chief Executive, Crown Prosecution Service, 4-12 Queen Anne's Gate, London SW1H 9AZ *Telephone:* 071-273 8097 *Fax:* 071-222 0802

GARDEN, Air Vice-Marshal TIMOTHY   Assistant Chief of Air Staff, Ministry of Defence

Career: squadron commander RAF 50 squadron 1979-81; director of defence studies RAF 1982-85; station commander RAF Odiham, Hampshire; Ministry of Defence 1988-: director air force staff duties 1988-91, assistant chief of air staff 1991-

Date of birth: 23 April 1944 *Education/professional qualifications:* King's School, Worcester; St Catherine's College, Oxford, physics (BA 1965, MA); Magdalene College, Cambridge, international relations (MPhil 1982) *Honours, decorations:* CB 1992 *Publications:* Can Deterrence Last? (Buchan and Enright 1984); The Technology Trap (Brasseys 1989) *Recreations:* bridge, computing, reading, windsurfing

Air Vice-Marshal Timothy Garden CB, Assistant Chief of Air Staff, Ministry of Defence, Whitehall, London SW1A 2HB *Telephone:* 071-218 6316 *Fax:* 071-218 6779

To subscribe to

**The Dod's Report
The European Companion
The Whitehall Companion**

Telephone 071-240 3902

GARRETT, ANTHONY DAVID   Chief Executive, Royal Mint

Career: Procter and Gamble 1969-82: managing director UK 1969-71, president Italy 1971-72, international vice-president 1973-82; member board Post Office Corporation 1983-87; deputy master (chief executive) Royal Mint 1988- *Current non-Whitehall posts:* non-executive director National Provident Institution 1988-, Pitney Bowes plc 1989-

Date of birth: 26 August 1928 *Education/professional qualifications:* Ellesmere College; Clare College, Cambridge, history (BA, MA 1950) *Marital status:* married Monica 1952; 3 sons, 1 daughter *Clubs:* United Oxford and Cambridge University *Recreations:* sailing, golf, bridge, gardening

Anthony D Garrett Esq, Chief Executive, Royal Mint, 7 Grosvenor Gardens, London SW1W 0BH, Llantrisant, Mid Glamorgan CF7 8YT *Telephone:* 071-828 8724; 0443 222111 *Fax:* 071-630 6592; 0443 228799

GARROD, Dr DAVID JOHN   Director of Fisheries Research, Ministry of Agriculture, Fisheries and Food   Grade: 4

Career: scientific officer (SO) East African High Commission, Uganda 1955-61; Ministry of Agriculture, Fisheries and Food 1961-: senior SO 1961-66, principal SO 1966-73, head of section 1973-80, deputy director fish stock management division 1980-89, director of fisheries research 1989- *Current non-Whitehall posts:* chairman Buckland Foundation trustees 1989-; trustee Sir Alister Hardy Foundation for Ocean Science 1991-

Date of birth: 2 May 1934 *Education/professional qualifications:* Harrow Weald County Grammar School; Bristol University, zoology (BSc 1955, PhD 1978) *Marital status:* married Sally Ann 1960; 2 sons *Recreations:* gardening, especially bonsai

Dr David J Garrod, Director, Directorate of Fisheries Research, Pakefield Road, Lowestoft, Suffolk NR33 0HT *Telephone:* 0502 524262 *Fax:* 0502 524515

GEDDES, MICHAEL DAWSON   Chief Executive and Civil Service Commissioner, Recruitment and Assessment Services Agency (Executive Agency)   Grade: 3

Career: Cranfield Institute of Technology 1968-84: planning officer, development and estates officer, financial controller Royal Military College of Science; trust secretary and administration director Ashridge Management College 1984-90; chief executive and civil service commissioner Recruitment and Assessment Services Agency (for civil servants) 1990-

Date of birth: 9 March 1944 *Education/professional qualifications:* Sherborne School, Dorset; British Columbia University, Canada, English and history (BA 1965) *Marital status:* married Leslie Rose 1966; 2 sons *Publications:* Project Leadership (Gower 1990) *Recreations:* golf, bridge, gardening

Michael D Geddes Esq, Chief Executive, Recruitment and Assessment Services Agency, Alencon Link, Basingstoke, Hampshire RG21 1JB *Telephone:* 0256 846300 *Fax:* 0256 846315

GEORGE, (EDWARD) EDDIE ALAN JOHN   Deputy Governor, Bank of England

Career: Bank of England 1966-: seconded as economist to Bank of International Settlements, Basle, Switzerland 1966-69, as personal assistant to chairman of deputies International Monetary Fund committee on international monetary reform 1972-74; adviser overseas department 1974-77; deputy chief cashier banking department 1977-80, assistant director gilt-edged division 1980-82; executive director monetary policy, market operations and market supervision 1982-90; deputy governor 1990-

Date of birth: 11 September 1938 *Education/professional qualifications:* Dulwich College, London; Emmanuel College, Cambridge, economics (BA 1962, MA) *Marital status:* married (Clarice) Vanessa Williams 1962; 2 daughters, 1 son *Recreations:* family, sailing, bridge

Eddie A J George Esq, Deputy Governor, Bank of England, Threadneedle Street, London EC2R 8AH *Telephone:* 071-601 4444 *Fax:* 071-601 4771

GEORGE, KESTER WILLIAM NORTON   Director, Former Soviet Union, Control and Eastern Europe Directorate, Department of Trade and Industry Grade: 4

Career: assistant principal Ministries of Pensions and National Insurance and of Aviation 1957-62; principal: Ministry of Technology 1962-65, Cabinet Office 1965-67, Department of Trade and Industry (DTI) 1967-70; assistant secretary: DTI 1970-76, HM Treasury 1976-79, DTI 1979-91; director former Soviet Union, control and eastern Europe directorate DTI (trade promotion and commercial relations) 1991-

Date of birth: 21 July 1934 *Education/professional qualifications:* Gayhurst School, Gerrards Cross; Winchester College; New College, Oxford, modern history (BA, MA 1956); London Business School, economics (Sloan Fellow 1973) *Honours, decorations:* CBE 1991 *Marital status:* married Philippa Jane Morley 1963; 2 sons, 1 daughter *Clubs:* Athenaeum *Recreations:* chess, gardening, travel in Europe

Kester W N George Esq CBE, Director Former Soviet Union, Central and Eastern Europe Directorate, Department of Trade and Industry, Kingsgate House, 66-74 Victoria Street, London, SW1E 6SW *Telephone:* 071-215 4733 *Fax:* 071-215 5269

GERMAN, ROBERT EDWARD   Controller, South London Region, Inland Revenue Grade: 4

Career: Inland Revenue 1959-: principal inspector oil taxation office 1974-79, City of London district 1979-82; senior principal inspector 1982-88; South London regional controller 1988-

Date of birth: 28 March 1936 *Education/professional qualifications:* Royal Grammar School, Worcester; Birmingham University, economics (B Com 1959) *Marital status:* married Annette Hazel 1960; 1 daughter, 2 sons *Recreations:* music, theatre, wine

Robert E German Esq, Regional Controller, Inland Revenue, New Court, 48 Carey Street, London WC2A 2JE *Telephone:* 071-324 1255 *Fax:* 071-324 1298

Complete Name Index
see page 955

GIBSON, Air Vice-Marshal (MICHAEL) MIKE JOHN   Director-General Policy and Plans, National Air Traffic Services, Ministry of Defence

Career: RAF 1961-88; National Air Traffic Services 1988-: director of airspace policy 1988-91, director-general policy and plans 1991-

Date of birth: 2 January 1939 *Education/professional qualifications:* Monkwearmouth Grammar School, Sunderland; City and Guilds College, London, aeronautics (ACGI 1961); Imperial College, London, aeronautical engineering (BSc 1961); Selwyn College, Cambridge (fellowship 1985); FRAeS 1990 *Honours, decorations:* OBE 1979 *Recreations:* boating, organ music and singing

Air Vice-Marshal Mike J Gibson OBE, Director-General (Policy and Plans), National Air Traffic Services, Civil Aviation Authority House, 45-59 Kingsway, London WC2B 6TE *Telephone:* 071-832 5781 *Fax:* 071-832 6478

GIBSON, Hon Sir PETER LESLIE (The Hon Mr Justice Gibson)   Chairman, Law Commission

Career: chancery barrister 1960-81; chancery treasury counsel 1972-81; justice of the High Court Chancery division 1981-; chairman Law Commission 1990-

Date of birth: 10 June 1934 *Education/professional qualifications:* Malvern College; Worcester College, Oxford, literae humaniores (BA 1959); Inner Temple (barrister 1960) *Honours, decorations:* Kt 1981 *Marital status:* married Katharine Mary Beatrice Hadow 1968; 2 sons, 1 daughter

The Hon Mr Justice Gibson, Chairman, Law Commission, Conquest House, 37-38 John Street, Theobalds Road, London WC1N 2BQ *Telephone:* 071-411 1249 *Fax:* 071-411 1297

GIEVE, (EDWARD) JOHN WATSON   Under Secretary, Banking Group, HM Treasury   Grade: 3

Career: under secretary financial institutions and markets, HM Treasury 1991-

Date of birth: 20 February 1950 *Education/professional qualifications:* Charterhouse; New College, Oxford, politics, philosophy, and economics (BA). philosophy (BPhil) *Marital status:* married; 2 sons

E John W Gieve, Under Secretary, HM Treasury, Parliament Street, London SW1P 3AG *Telephone:* 071-270 4870

GILLMORE, Sir DAVID HOWE   Permanent Under Secretary and Head of Diplomatic Service, Foreign and Commonwealth Office   Senior grade

Career: Reuters 1958-60; assistant to director-general Polypapier, Paris 1960-65; teacher 1965-69; HM Diplomatic Service 1970-: Foreign and Commonwealth Office (FCO) 1970-72, first secretary Moscow 1972-75, counsellor UK delegation Vienna 1975-78, FCO 1979-: head of defence department 1979-81, assistant under secretary 1981-83, high commissioner to Malaysia 1983-86, deputy under secretary, FCO 1986-90; visiting fellow Harvard University 1990-91; FCO 1991-: permanent under secretary and head of diplomatic service

Date of birth: 16 August 1934 *Education/professional qualifications:* Trent College, Long Eaton, Nottinghamshire; King's College, Cambridge, French and Russian (BA, MA 1958) *Honours, decorations:* CMG 1982, KCMG 1990 *Marital status:* married Lucile Morin 1964; 2 sons *Publications:* A Way from Exile (Macdonalds 1967) *Recreations:* books, music, exercise

Sir David Gillmore KCMG, Permanent Under Secretary, Foreign and Commonwealth Office, King Charles Street, London SW1A 2AH *Telephone:* 071-270 2150 *Fax:* 071-270 3776

To subscribe to The Dod's Report
Telephone: 071-240 3902

GILMORE, BRIAN TERENCE   Head of Resource Management and Planning Group, Department of Social Security   Grade: 2

Career: HM Diplomatic Service 1958-68: assistant principal Commonwealth Relations Office 1958-65; first secretary Washington DC embassy 1965-68; principal Ministry of Technology/Department of Trade and Industry 1968-71; private secretary to leader of House of Lords 1971-72; assistant secretary Civil Service (CS) Department 1972-79; principal CS College 1979-82; HM Treasury 1982-88: principal establishment and finance officer 1982-84, under secretary 1984-88; deputy secretary, director of management development Office of Minister for CS, Cabinet Office, Office of the Minister for the Civil Service, 1988-92; head of resource management and planning group, principal establishment and finance officer, Department of Social Security 1992- *Current non-Whitehall posts:* governor Ashridge Management College 1989-; council member City University Business School 1990-

Date of birth: 25 May 1937 *Education/professional qualifications:* Wolverhampton Grammar School; Christ Church, Oxford, literae humaniores (MA 1958) *Honours, decorations:* CB 1992 *Marital status:* married Rosalind 1962 *Clubs:* Athenaeum *Recreations:* walking, music, Greece

Brian T Gilmore Esq CB, Head of Resource Management and Planning Group, Department of Social Security, Richmond House, 79 Whitehall, London SW1A 2NF *Telephone:* 071-210 5470 *Fax:* 071-210 5480

GILMORE, ROSALIND EDITH JEAN   Chairman, Building Societies Commission, Chief Registrar of Friendly Societies, Industrial Assurance Commissioner   Grade: 2

Career: HM Treasury (HMT) 1960-65: assistant principal 1960-62, assistant private secretary (PS) to chancellor of exchequer 1962-65; executive assistant to economics director International Bank for Reconstruction and Development 1966-67; principal HMT 1968; principal PS to Paymaster General 1973; principal PS to chancellor of duchy of Lancaster, Cabinet Office 1974; HMT 1975-82: assistant secretary 1975, head of financial institutions division 1977-80, press secretary to chancellor of exchequer and head of information 1980-82; general manager corporate planning, Dunlop Ltd 1982-83; director of marketing National Girobank 1983-86; director and consultant in various commercial companies 1986-89; deputy chairman and commissioner Building Societies Commission (BSC) 1989-91; chairman BSC, chief registrar of Friendly Societies and Industrial Assurance Commissioner 1991-

Date of birth: 23 March 1937 *Education/professional qualifications:* King Alfred School, London; University College, London, modern history (BA 1958); Newnham College, Cambridge, medieval history (BA 1960, MA); FRS 1985 *Marital status:* married Brian Terence 1962 *Recreations:* music, reading, travel, Greece

Mrs Rosalind E J Gilmore, Chairman, Building Societies Commission, 15 Great Marlborough Street, London W1V 2AX *Telephone:* 071-494 6688

Parliamentary Offices
see page 275

GLENCROSS, DAVID   Chief Executive, Independent Television Commission

Career: producer BBC 1958-70; Independent Broadcasting Authority/Television Commission 1970-: senior television programme officer 1970-76; head of programme services 1976-77; deputy director of television 1977-83; director of television 1983-90; chief executive 1990-

Date of birth: 3 March 1936   *Education/professional qualifications:* Salford Grammar School; Trinity College, Cambridge (BA 1958)   *Marital status:* married Elizabeth Louise Richardson 1965; 1 daughter   *Recreations:* music, reading, radio, walking

David Glencross Esq, Chief Executive, Independent Television Commission, 70 Brompton Road, London, SW3 1EY   *Telephone:* 071-824 7960   *Fax:* 071-823 9116

GOLDMAN, (ANTONY) TONY JOHN   Under Secretary of State, Civil Aviation Policy, Department of Transport   Grade: 3

Career: International Computers Ltd 1961-73; Department of the Environment 1973-76; Department of Transport (DTp) 1976-80: private secretary to secretary of state for transport 1976-78, assistant secretary 1977; HM Treasury 1981-83; DTp 1984-: under secretary public transport directorate 1984-89, civil aviation policy directorate 1989

Date of birth: 28 February 1940   *Education/professional qualifications:* Marlborough College; Peterhouse, Cambridge, mathematics (BA 1961) and computer science (diploma 1961)   *Marital status:* married Anne Rosemary 1964; 3 sons   *Recreations:* music, sailing

Tony J Goldman Esq, Under Secretary, Department of Transport, 2 Marsham Street, London SW1P 3EB   *Telephone:* 071-276 5379   *Fax:* 071-276 5314

GOODSON, MICHAEL JOHN   Assistant Auditor-General, National Audit Office

Career: Exchequer and Audit Department/National Audit Office (examination of the accounts of government departments, certain public bodies and international organisations) 1955-: auditor 1965-67; private secretary to comptroller and auditor general 1967-70; senior auditor 1970-73; principal, seconded to health service ombudsman 1973-76; chief auditor 1976-78; deputy director of audit 1978-81; director of audit 1981-84; assistant auditor general unit A (finance, personnel, training, corporate and audit policy) 1984-

Date of birth: 4 August 1937   *Education/professional qualifications:* King Henry VIII School, Coventry   *Marital status:* married Susan Elizabeth Higley 1958; 1 son, 1 daughter

Michael J Goodson Esq, Assistant Auditor-General, National Audit Office, 157-197 Buckingham Palace Road, London SW1W 9SP   *Telephone:* 071-798 7386   *Fax:* 071-828 3774

GORDON, J A   Director-General Aircraft 1, Ministry of Defence   Grade: 3

J A Gordon Esq, Director-General Aircraft 1, Ministry of Defence, St Giles Court, 1-13 St Giles High Street, London WC2H 8LD   *Telephone:* 071-218 9000

Government Departments
see page 300

GORE-BOOTH, Hon DAVID ALWYN   Assistant Under Secretary, Middle East, Foreign and Commonwealth Office   Senior grade

Career: H M Diplomatic Service 1964-: third secretary (TS) Baghdad 1966-67; TS/second secretary (SS) Lusaka 1967-69; SS Tripoli 1969-71; SS/first secretary (FS) Foreign and Commonwealth Office (FCO) 1971-74; FS UK permanent representation to EC, Brussels 1974-77; FS FCO 1978-79; commercial counsellor Jeddah 1980-83; counsellor and head of chancery UK mission to UN, New York 1983-86; FCO 1987-: head of policy planning staff 1987-88, assistant under secretary Middle East department 1989- *Current non-Whitehall posts:* member Committee for Middle East Trade 1989-; committee member: Royal Institute for International Affairs, Royal United Service Institute, Centre for Near and Middle East Studies, School of Oriental and African Studies

Date of birth: 15 May 1943 *Education/professional qualifications:* Eton College; Christ Church, Oxford, history (BA, MA 1964) *Honours, decorations:* CMG 1989 *Marital status:* married Mary Elizabeth Janet Muirhead 1977; 2 sons from previous marriage *Clubs:* MCC, Travellers, Hurlingham *Recreations:* current affairs, tennis playing, cricket watching, island of Hydra, Greece

The Hon David A Gore-Booth CMG, Assistant Under Secretary, Foreign and Commonwealth Office, Downing Street West, London SW1A 2AH *Telephone:* 071-270 2197 *Fax:* 071-270 3510

GOULD, DAVID JOHN   Assistant Under Secretary, Supply and Organisation (Air), Ministry of Defence   Grade: 3

Career: Ministry of Defence 1973-: naval weapons department 1973-78; principal 1978, assistant head of branch managing finance for military aircraft 1978-80, NATO Defence College 1980-81, planning RAF forward programme 1981-83, seconded to HM Diplomatic Service, UK delegation to NATO 1983-87; assistant secretary 1987, assistant under secretary supply and organisation (air) (budget manager and senior finance officer) 1991-

Date of birth: 9 April 1949 *Education/professional qualifications:* West Buckland School, Barnstaple; Sussex University, French and European Studies (BA 1971) *Recreations:* music, especially opera and lieder; fitness; watching rugby

David J Gould Esq, Assistant Under Secretary, Ministry of Defence, Whitehall, London SW1A 2HB *Telephone:* 071-218 2730

GOULDEN, (PETER) JOHN   Assistant Under Secretary, Foreign and Commonwealth Office   Senior grade

Career: HM Diplomatic Service 1962-: office of the UK permanent representative to the EC 1984-87; assistant under secretary 1988-

Date of birth: 21 February 1941 *Education/professional qualifications:* Queen's College, Oxford, history (BA 1962)

P John Goulden Esq CMG, Assistant Under Secretary, Foreign and Commonwealth Office, King Charles Street, London SW1 *Telephone:* 071-270 3000

To subscribe to

The Dod's Report
The European Companion
The Whitehall Companion

Telephone 071-240 3902

GOYDER, DANIEL GEORGE   Deputy Chairman, Monopolies and Mergers Commission

Career: private practice assistant solicitor/partner 1964-83; part-time law lecturer Essex University 1981-91; consultant private practice solicitor 1983-; Monopolies and Mergers Commission 1980-: member 1980-, deputy chairman 1991- *Current non-Whitehall posts:* consultant Birkett Westhorp and Long (solicitors) 1989-; visiting professor King's College, London 1991, Essex University 1991-

Date of birth: 26 August 1938 *Education/professional qualifications:* Rugby School; Trinity College, Cambridge, law (BA 1959, LLB 1960); Harvard Law School, USA (LLM 1963) *Marital status:* married Jean Mary Dohoo 1962; 2 daughters, 2 sons *Clubs:* Law Society; Royal Society of Arts; Ipswich and Suffolk *Recreations:* choral singing, tennis

Daniel G Goyder Esq, Deputy Chairman, Monopolies and Mergers Commission, New Court, 48 Carey Street, London WC2A 2JT *Telephone:* 071-324 1440 *Fax:* 071-324 1400

GRAHAM, PETER   First Parliamentary Counsel, Parliamentary Counsel Office   Grade: 1

Career: barrister 1958-; assistant counsel Parliamentary Counsel Office (PCO) 1959-66, Law Commission (LC) 1966-67; PCO 1967-79: senior assistant counsel 1967-70, deputy counsel 1970-72, parliamentary counsel 1972-79; parliamentary counsel LC 1979-81; PCO 1981-: parliamentary counsel 1981-86, second parliamentary counsel 1987-91, first parliamentary counsel (drafting and advisory services, advice on parliamentary and constitutional matters) 1991-

Date of birth: 7 January 1934 *Education/professional qualifications:* St Bees School, Cumbria; St John's College, Cambridge, law (BA 1957, MA, LLM 1958); Gray's Inn (barrister 1958) *Honours, decorations:* CB 1982, QC 1990 *Marital status:* married Anne Silvia Garcia 1980; 2 sons from previous marriage *Clubs:* The Sette of Odd Volumes *Recreations:* playing church organs, gardening, silviculture, bridge

Peter Graham Esq CB QC, First Parliamentary Counsel, Parliamentary Counsel Office, 36 Whitehall, London SW1A 2AY *Fax:* 071-210 6632

GRANTHAM, CLIFF(ORD) MARTIN   Special Adviser to Secretary of State for Education

Career: reporter BBC radio news 1984-85; political consultant/partner political consultancy firms 1985-91; political assistant to seven Conservative MPs 1988-91; special adviser to ministers of state Home Office 1991-91, to John Patten, Secretary of State for Education 1992-

Date of birth: 30 June 1961 *Education/professional qualifications:* Royal Hospital School, Ipswich; Hull University, politics and sociology (BA 1984) *Marital status:* single

Clifford M Grantham Esq, Special Adviser, Department for Education, Sanctuary Buildings, Great Smith Street, London SW1P 3ET *Telephone:* 071-925 5000 *Fax:* 071-925 6000

GRAY, JAMES   Special Adviser, Department of the Environment

Career: special adviser to ministers of state Department of the Environment 1992-

James Gray Esq, Special Adviser, Department of the Environment, 2 Marsham Street, London SW1P 3EB *Telephone:* 071-276 3000

GRAY, PAUL RICHARD CHARLES   Under Secretary, Monetary Group, HM
Treasury   Grade: 3

Career: HM Treasury 1979-: economic affairs private secretary to the Prime Minister 1988-90; under
secretary monetary group 1990-

Date of birth: 2 August 1948   *Education/professional qualifications:* London School of Economics,
economics (BSc 1969)

Paul R C Gray Esq, Under Secretary, Monetary Group, HM Treasury, Parliament Street, London
SW1P 3AG   *Telephone:* 071-270 3000

GREEN, DAMIAN   Member of Prime Minister's Policy Unit

Career: industrial editor 'Business Daily', Channel 4; member Prime Minister's Policy Unit 1992-

Damian Green, Prime Minister's Policy Unit, 10 Downing Street, London SW1A 2AA
Telephone: 071-270 3000

GREEN, (JOHN TERENCE) TERRY   Territorial Director, Dales and
**Central England, Social Security Benefits Agency (Executive
Agency)**   Grade: 4

Career: National Assistance Board/Ministry of Social Services/Department
of [Health and] Social Security 1960-: head of methods of paying social
security benefit section 1979-82; head of branch 1980-82; regional
controller 1982-89, territorial director Wales and Central England, Benefits
Agency 1991-

Date of birth: 10 June 1936   *Education/professional qualifications:* King James'
Grammar School, Huddersfield   *Marital status:* married Doreen 1958; 1
son, 1 daughter   *Recreations:* walking, photography

Terry Green Esq, Territorial Director, Social Security Benefits Agency,
Fiveways Tower, Frederick Road, Edgbaston, Birmingham B15 1ST
Telephone: 021-626 3115   *Fax:* 021-626 3000

GREEN, (ROBERT) BOB JAMES   Under Secretary, Local Government, Department of the
Environment   Grade: 3

Career: Board of Trade 1957-63; assistant principal, principal Ministry of Housing and Local
Government 1963-71; secretary Water Resources Board 1971-74; assistant secretary Department of
Environment (DoE) 1974-82; under secretary 1982-: Yorkshire and Humberside regional director
DoE and Department of Transport 1982-86; DoE 1988-: director rural affairs 1988-91, local
government (general policy except finance) 1991-

Date of birth: 27 January 1937   *Education/professional qualifications:* Kent College, Canterbury   *Marital
status:* married Jill Marianne Small 1960; 1 daughter, 1 son deceased   *Recreations:* theatre, amateur
dramatics

Bob J Green Esq, Under Secretary, Department of the Environment, 2 Marsham Street, London SW1P
3EB   *Telephone:* 071-276 4070

GREENSHIELDS, GORDON   Director of Finance and Corporate Information, NHS
Management Executive, Department of Health   Grade: 2

Education/professional qualifications: Heriot Watt University, Edinburgh

Gordon Greenshields Esq, Director of Finance and Corporate Information, NHS Management
Executive, Department of Health, Richmond House, 79 Whitehall, London SW1A 2NS
Telephone: 071-210 3000

GREENSTOCK, JEREMY QUENTIN   Assistant Under Secretary, West and South Europe, Foreign and Commonwealth Office   Senior grade

Career: teacher 1966-69; Foreign and Commonwealth Office 1969-: second secretary (SS) London 1969-70; language student Middle East Centre for Arab Studies 1970-72; SS and first secretary (FS) Dubai 1972-74; private secretary to ambassador Washington 1974-78; FS planning, personnel and Near East departments, London 1978-83; commercial counsellor Jedoa, Riyadh 1983-86; head of chancery Paris 1987-90; assistant under secretary (W and S Europe and Ireland, deputy political director, UK permanent representative West European Union council) 1990-

Date of birth: 27 July 1943   *Education/professional qualifications:* Harrow School; Worcester College, Oxford, classics (BA 1966)   *Honours, decorations:* CMG 1991   *Marital status:* married Anne Hodges 1969; 2 daughters, 1 son   *Clubs:* Combined Oxford and Cambridge University   *Recreations:* travel, golf, skiing, music

Jeremy Q Greenstock Esq CMG, Assistant Under Secretary, Foreign and Commonwealth Office, Whitehall, London SW1A 2AP   *Telephone:* 071-270 3000

GREGORY, PETER ROLAND   Under Secretary, Transport, Planning and Environment Group, Welsh Office   Grade: 3

Career: Welsh Office 1971-: assistant secretary 1982-; under secretary transport, planning and environment group 1990-

Date of birth: 7 October 1946   *Education/professional qualifications:* University College, Swansea (BA 1968); Manchester University (PhD 1972)

Peter R Gregory Esq, Under Secretary, Transport, Planning and Environment Group, Welsh Office, Cathays Park, Cardiff CF1 3NQ   *Telephone:* 0222-825111

GREGSON, Sir PETER LEWIS   Permanent Secretary, Department of Trade and Industry   Grade: 1

Career: various posts Board of Trade 1961-68; private secretary to prime minister 1968-72; assistant secretary, secretary Industrial Development Advisory Board, Department of Trade and Industry (DTI) 1972-74; secretary National Enterprise Board 1975-77; Department of Trade 1977-81: under secretary (US) 1977-80, deputy secretary (DS) 1980-81; DS Cabinet Office 1981-85; permanent US Department of Energy 1985-89; permanent secretary DTI 1989-   *Current non-Whitehall posts:* council member Industrial Society 1990-

Date of birth: 28 June 1936   *Education/professional qualifications:* Nottingham High School; Balliol College, Oxford, classical moderations and greats (BA1959, MA)   *Honours, decorations:* CB 1983, KCB 1988   *Marital status:* single   *Recreations:* gardening, listening to music

Sir Peter Gregson KCB, Permanent Secretary, Department of Trade and Industry, Ashdown House, 123 Victoria Street, London SW1E 6RB   *Telephone:* 071-215 4439

'Next Steps' Executive Agencies
see page 761

GRIBBON, (EDWARD) JOHN   Director, Business Profits Division, Inland Revenue   Grade: 3

Career: private practice accountant 1960-66; Inland Revenue 1966-: tax inspector (TI) 1966-81; principal TI 1981-89; deputy director of operations, compliance; under secretary, director business profits division 1991-

Date of birth: 10 July 1943   *Education/professional qualifications:* Coleraine Academical Institution; Institute of Chartered Accountants in Ireland (CA 1965); London University, law (LLB 1980)   *Marital status:* married Margaret 1968; 2 daughters, 1 son   *Recreations:* family, photography, local church

E John Gribbon Esq, Director, Business Profits Division, Inland Revenue, Somerset House, Strand, London WC2R 1LB   *Telephone:* 071-438 6774   *Fax:* 071-438 6494

GRIFFITHS, DAVID HUBERT   Director of Establishments, Ministry of Agriculture, Fisheries and Food   Grade: 3

Career: Ministry of Agriculture, Fisheries and Food 1963-: head of food, drink and marketing policy 1987-90, director of establishments 1990-

Date of birth: 24 December 1940   *Education/professional qualifications:* St Catharine's College, Cambridge (BA, MA)

David H Griffiths Esq, Director of Establishments, Ministry of Agriculture, Fisheries and Food, Whitehall Place, London SW1A 2HH   *Telephone:* 071-270 8659

GRIMSEY, COLIN ROBERT   Under Secretary, Director of Finance, Department of Transport   Grade: 3

Career: assistant principal Department of Transport (DT) 1968-72; principal Department of Environment 1972-79; DT 1979-: assistant secretary 1979-89, under secretary (US) seconded to London Transport 1989-91-, US director of finance 1991-

Date of birth: 24 December 1943   *Education/professional qualifications:* Dartford Grammar School, Kent; King's College, London, physics (BSc 1964)   *Marital status:* married Elizabeth 1976; 1 daughter, 1 son   *Recreations:* family, opera, choral singing

Colin R Grimsey Esq, Under Secretary, Department of Transport, 2 Marsham Street, London SW1P 3EB   *Telephone:* 071-276 3000   *Fax:* 071-276 0818

GRIST, Major-General ROBIN DIGBY   Director-General, Adjutant General's Corps, Ministry of Defence

Career: Ministry of Defence (MoD) 1973-79; commanding officer 1 Glosters 1979-82; military director of studies Royal Military College of Science 1982-84; commander 6 Airmobile Brigade 1984-87; Royal College of Defence Studies 1987; military attache and commander British army staff, Washington 1988-89; director Army Air Corps 1989-92; director-general Adjutant General's Corps MoD (professional administrative services for army) 1992-   *Current non-Whitehall posts:* colonel The Gloucestershire Regiment 1991-

Date of birth: 21 October 1940   *Education/professional qualifications:* Radley College, Abingdon; Royal Military Academy, Sandhurst (commissioned 1960)   *Honours, decorations:* MBE 1975, OBE 1979   *Clubs:* Army and Navy   *Recreations:* flyfishing

Major-General Robin D Grist OBE, Director-General, Adjutant General's Corps, Ministry of Defence, Whitehall, London SW1A 2HB   *Telephone:* 071-218 9000

GROVER, DEREK JAMES LANGLAND   Under Secretary, Director of Training Strategy and Standards, Employment Department Group   Grade: 3

Career: Department of Employment 1971-78: principal 1976-78; principal Cabinet Office 1978-80; Manpower Services Commission 1980-89: principal 1980-84; Employment Department 1989-: director of youth training 1989, of training strategy and standards 1989-   *Current non-Whitehall posts:* director UK Skills Ltd 1991-

Date of birth: 26 January 1949   *Education/professional qualifications:* Hove County Grammar School; Clare College, Cambridge, English literature (BA 1971, MA)   *Marital status:* married Mary Katherine 1972; 1 son   *Recreations:* music, reading, walking

Derek J L Grover Esq, Director of Group Training Strategy and Standards, Employment Department, Moorfoot, Sheffield S1 4PQ   *Telephone:* 0742 593948   *Fax:* 0742 593677

GRUNDY, DAVID STANLEY   Policy and Resources Commissioner, Forestry Commission   Grade: 3

Career: assistant principal Ministry of Power 1967-70; assistant private secretary to Minister of Technology 1970-71; principal Department of Trade and Industry 1971-76; economic adviser Foreign and Commonwealth Office 1976-78, Department of Environment 1978-79; chief economic adviser to Vanuatu government 1979-81; Forestry Commission 1982-: chief economist 1982-90, commissioner administration and finance 1990-92; commissioner policy and resources 1992-

Date of birth: 10 April 1943   *Education/professional qualifications:* De la Salle College, Manchester; Jesus College, Cambridge (BA, MA 1965); Jesus College, Oxford (MPhil 1974)   *Marital status:* married Elizabeth Jenny 1965; 1 son   *Clubs:* Royal Commonwealth, London; Dean Tennis, Edinburgh   *Recreations:* angling, bird-watching, gardening, tennis

David S Grundy Esq, Commissioner, Forestry Commission, 231 Corstorphine Road, Edinburgh EH12 7AT   *Telephone:* 031-334 0303   *Fax:* 031-316 4891

GULVIN, J A   Assistant Under Secretary (International and Domestic Procurement), Ministry of Defence   Grade: 3

J A Gulvin Esq, Assistant Under Secretary (International and Domestic Procurement), Ministry of Defence, Main Building, Whitehall, London SW1A 2HB   *Telephone:* 071-218 9000

GUNN, JOHN ANGUS LIVINGSTON   Head of Heritage and Tourism Group, Department of National Heritage   Grade: 3

Career: Department of the Environment 1976-92: water directorate 1981-87, water privatisation directorate 1987-90, director heritage and royal estate directorate 1990-92; head of heritage and tourism group Department of National Heritage 1992-

Date of birth: 20 November 1934   *Education/professional qualifications:* Fettes College, Edinburgh; Christ Church, Oxford (MA)

John A L Gunn Esq, Head of Heritage and Tourism Group, Department of National Heritage, Horseguards Road, London SW1P 3AL   *Telephone:* 071-270 3000

H

HADDON, MARTIN THOMAS   Under Secretary, Animal Health and Veterinary Group, Ministry of Agriculture, Fisheries and Food   Grade: 3

Career: Ministry of Agriculture, Fisheries and Food (MAFF) 1966-74: assistant principal 1966-71; Cabinet Office 1974-76; MAFF 1976-: under secretary, management services 1990-91, animal health and veterinary group 1991-

Date of birth: 8 December 1944   *Education/professional qualifications:* Beaumont College, Old Windsor; Worcester College, Oxford, literae humaniores (BA 1966)   *Marital status:* married Helen Parry 1977; 2 daughters, 1 son

Martin T Haddon Esq, Under Secretary, Ministry of Agriculture, Fisheries and Food, 10 Whitehall Place, London SW1A 2HH   *Telephone:* 071-270 8059   *Fax:* 071-270 8786

HADLEY, DAVID ALLEN   Deputy Secretary, European Community Affairs, Cabinet Office   Grade: 2

Career: Ministry of Agriculture, Fisheries and Food (MAFF) 1959-78: assistant principal 1959-64, principal 1964-71, assistant secretary (AS) 1971-75; AS HM Treasury 1975-78; MAFF 1979-89: AS 1979-81, under secretary 1981-87, deputy secretary (DS) 1987-89; DS EC affairs Cabinet Office 1989-

Date of birth: 18 February 1936   *Education/professional qualifications:* Wyggeston Grammar School, Leicester; Merton College, Oxford (BA, MA 1959)   *Honours, decorations:* CB 1991   *Marital status:* married Veronica Ann Hopkins 1965; 1 son

David A Hadley Esq CB, Deputy Secretary, Cabinet Office, 70 Whitehall, London SW1A 2AS   *Telephone:* 071-270 0044

HAGARD, SPENCER   Chief Executive, Health Education Authority

Career: various hospital appointments 1971-87; chief executive Health Education Authority 1987-

Date of birth: 22 October 1942   *Education/professional qualifications:* University of St Andrews (MB ChB 1968); University of Glasgow (PhD 1977)

Dr Spencer Hagard, Chief Executive, Health Education Authority, Hamilton House, Mabledon Place, London WC1H 9TX   *Telephone:* 071-383 3833

HAGGER, DAVID OSBORNE   Business Manager, Medicines Control Agency (Executive Agency)   Grade: 4

Career: air force national service 1954-56; National Assistance Board/Department of Health and Social Security (DHSS) 1958-69; course director Civil Service College 1969-70; Civil Service Department 1970-76; DHSS 1976-84: social research manager 1976-77, principal unemployment benefit branch 1977-83, personnel manager 1980-83, assistant secretary (AS) national insurance contributions branch 1983-84; Department of Health 1984-: AS medicines division 1984-90, business manager, abridged licensing business, Medicines Control Agency (post-marketing surveillance of medicines) 1990-

Date of birth: 2 May 1935 *Education/professional qualifications:* Crypt Grammar School, Gloucester *Marital status:* married Mary 1962; 3 daughters *Recreations:* walking, cycling, theatre, school government

David O Hagger Esq, Business Manager, Medicines Control Agency, Market Towers, 1 Nine Elms Lane, London SW8 5NQ *Telephone:* 071 273 0300 *Fax:* 071 627 2185

HALE, NORMAN MORGAN   Under Secretary, Health Promotion Division, Department of Health   Grade: 3

Career: Department of [Health and] Social Security 1966-70; seconded to Cabinet Office 1970-72; Department of Health 1972-; under secretary health promotion division 1975-

Date of birth: 28 June 1933 *Education/professional qualifications:* St John's College, Oxford (MA)

Norman M Hale Esq, Under Secretary, Department of Health, Alexander Fleming House, Elephant and Castle, London SE1 6BY *Telephone:* 071-972 2000

HALL, DAVID   Head of Projects and Export Policy Division, Department of Trade and Industry   Grade: 3

David Hall Esq, Head of Projects and Export Policy Division, Department of Trade and Industry, Ashdown House, 123 Victoria Street, London SW1E 6RB *Telephone:* 071-215 4933

HALLIDAY, JOHN FREDERICK   Deputy Under Secretary, Criminal, Research and Statistics, Home Office   Grade: 2

Career: Home Office (HO) 1966-: seconded to Department of [Health and] Social Security 1987-90; deputy under secretary 1990-

Date of birth: 19 September 1942 *Education/professional qualifications:* St John's College, Cambridge (MA)

John F Halliday Esq, Deputy Under Secretary, Home Office, 50 Queen Anne's Gate, London SW1H 9AT *Telephone:* 071-273 3000

HALLIDAY, Dr NORMAN PRYDE   Senior Medical Officer, Department of Health

Career: NHS nursing posts 1950-64; NHS medical posts 1964-70; medical under secretary, senior principal medical officer (supra regional clinical services policy, organ transplants, renal disease, accidents) 1977-92 when he retired from that post and is now a senior medical officer

Date of birth: 28 March 1932 *Education/professional qualifications:* Woodside School, Glasgow; King's College Hospital, London (MB BS 1964); Warwick University, business management *Honours, decorations:* QHP 1990 *Marital status:* married Eleanor Smith 1953; 4 sons, 2 daughters *Recreations:* photography, reading, crossbow shooting, sub-aqua

Dr Norman P Halliday QHP, Senior Medical Officer, Department of Health, Eileen House, 8-94 Newington Causeway, London, SE1 6EF *Telephone:* 071-972 2829 *Fax:* 071-972 2844 Until October 1992 and then The Solicitor, Department of Trade and Industry, 10/18 Victoria Street, London SW1H 0NN, *Telephone:* 071-215 3039 *Fax:* 071-215 3141

HAMILL, J   Secretary, Home and Health Department, Scottish Office   Grade: 2

J Hamill Esq, Secretary, Home and Health Department, Scottish Office, St Andrew's House, Edinburgh, EH1 3DE *Telephone:* 031-556 8400

HAMMOND, ANTHONY HILGROVE   Legal Adviser to Home Office and Northern Ireland Office until October 1992 and then Solicitor to the Department of Trade and Industry   Grade: 2

Career: solicitor Greater London Council 1965-68; Home Office (HO) 1968-: legal assistant (LA) 1968-70, senior LA 1970-74, assistant legal adviser (ALA) 1974-80; HO and Northern Ireland Office 1980-: principal ALA 1980-88; deputy under secretary, legal adviser 1988-92; solicitor Department of Trade and Industry 1992-

Date of birth: 27 July 1940 *Education/professional qualifications:* Malvern College; Emmanuel College, Cambridge, classics and law (BA 1962), public law (LLB 1963); solicitor 1965 *Honours, decorations:* CB 1992 *Marital status:* married Avril Collinson 1988 *Clubs:* Athenaeum *Recreations:* bridge, listening to music, birdwatching

Anthony H Hammond Esq CB, Legal Adviser, Home Office, 50 Queen Anne's Gate, London, SW1H 9AT *Telephone:* 071-273 2681 until October 1992 and then The Solicitor, Department of Trade and Industry, 10/18 Victoria Street, London SW1H 0NN, *Telephone:* 071-215 3039   *Fax:* 071-215 3141

HANCOCK, GRAHAM ERIC   Director, North West Construction Programme, Department of Transport   Grade: 4

Career: senior engineering partner commercial consultancy 1959-67; deputy surveyor Carlton Urban District Council 1967-70; Department of Transport 1970-: East Midlands regional office 1970-78: area engineer 1970-74, principal engineer (PE) 1974-78; PE Yorkshire and Humberside regional office 1978-81; north west region 1981-: superintending engineer 1981-84, deputy director 1984-90, director construction programme division (building of and improvements to major trunk roads including motorways) 1990-

Date of birth: 22 October 1932 *Education/professional qualifications:* Chesterfield Grammar School; Chesterfield Technical College, civil engineering (MICE 1954) *Marital status:* married Judith Ann 1959; 1 daughter, 1 son *Clubs:* National Liberal *Recreations:* golf, field sports

Graham E Hancock Esq, Director, North West Construction Programme Division, Department of Transport, Sunley Towers, Piccadilly Plaza, Manchester *Telephone:* 061-832 9111

HARBISON, Dr SAMUEL ALEXANDER   HM Chief Inspector of Nuclear Installations, Director of Nuclear Safety, Health and Safety Executive   Grade: 3

Career: reactor physicist United Kingdom Atomic Energy Authority, Windscale 1962-64; teaching, research assistant California University, USA 1964-66; research student London University 1969; senior lecturer Royal Naval College Greenwich nuclear science and technology department 1969-74; Health and Safety Executive HM Nuclear Inspectorate 1974-: chief inspector and director of nuclear safety 1991-

Date of birth: 9 May 1941 *Education/professional qualifications:* Ballymena Academy, Co Antrim; Queen's University, Belfast, physics (BSc 1962); California University, USA, nuclear physics (MS 1966); Westfield College, London University, nuclear physics (PhD 1969) *Marital status:* married

Margaret Gail 1991; 3 daughters from previous marriage *Publications:* An Introduction to Radiation Protection (Chapman and Hall 1986)

Dr Samuel A Harbison, HM Chief Inspector of Nuclear Installations, Health and Safety Executive, Baynards House, 1 Chepstow Place, Westbourne Grove, London W2 4TF *Telephone:* 071-243 6850 *Fax:* 071-727 4116

HARDCASTLE, Sir ALAN JOHN   Chief Accountancy Adviser, Head of Government Accountancy Service, HM Treasury

Career: accountant 1956-; chief accountancy adviser and head of government accountancy service HM Treasury 1989-

Date of birth: 10 August 1933 *Education/professional qualifications:* Haileybury College; qualified as a solicitor 1956

Sir Alan J Hardcastle, Chief Accountancy Adviser, Head of Government Accountancy Service, HM Treasury, 1 Parliament Street, London SW1P 3AG *Telephone:* 071-270 3000

HARDING, Air Chief Marshal Sir PETER (ROBIN)   Chief of the Air Staff, (and from January 1993 Chief of the Defence Staff) Ministry of Defence

Career: RAF pilot, flying instructor 1954-60; Ministry of Defence (MoD) 1960-62; officer commanding 18 squadron 1962-66; MoD 1966-71: director air staff briefing 1971; station commander RAF Bruggen 1971-74; director defence policy MoD 1974-76; assistant chief of staff Supreme Headquarters Allied Powers Europe 1976-78; air officer commanding HQ No 11 group 1978-81; MoD 1981-85: vice chief of the air staff 1981-82, of defence staff 1982-85; air officer commanding-in-chief HQ Strike Command and Commander in Chief UK air forces 1985-88; MoD 1988-: chief of the air staff; 1988-92, chief of the defence staff 1993-

Date of birth: 2 December 1933 *Education/professional qualifications:* Chingford High School *Honours, decorations:* CB 1980, FRAes 1983, KCB 1983, GCB 1988, Air ADC to the Queen 1988, DSc 1990, CBIM *Recreations:* birdwatching, walking, piano, tennis, shooting

Air Chief Marshal Sir Peter Harding GCB, Chief of the Air Staff, Ministry of Defence, Whitehall, London SW1A 2HB *Telephone:* 071-218 6313 *Fax:* 071-218 3834

HARLEY, Major-General ALEXANDER GEORGE HAMILTON   Assistant Chief of Defence Staff (Overseas), Ministry of Defence

Career: Army 1962-: assistant chief of staff (Ops), Northern Army Group 1988-90; assistant chief of defence staff (Overseas) Ministry of Defence 1990-

Date of birth: 3 May 1941 *Education/professional qualifications:* RMA Sandhurst

Major-General Alexander Harley CB OBE, Assistant Chief of Defence Staff (Overseas), Ministry of Defence, Main Building, Whitehall, London SW1 *Telephone:* 071-218 9000

Regulatory Organisations and Public Bodies
see page 857

HARRIS, CHRISTOPHER JOHN   Director, Marine Emergency Operations, Department of Transport   Grade: 4

Career: marine engineer officer Royal Navy 1957-74; Department of Transport 1974-: director marine emergency operations (marine pollution control unit and HM Coastguard) 1992- *Current non-Whitehall posts:* non-executive director Oil Spill Response Ltd 1992-

Date of birth: 19 May 1937 *Education/professional qualifications:* Roundhay School, Leeds; Royal Naval College, Dartmouth; Royal Naval Engineering College, Manadon (BSc Eng 1962); Royal Naval College, Greenwich (advanced marine engineering qualification); CEng; MIMechE, MIMarE *Honours, decorations:* MBE 1974

Christopher J Harris, MBE, Director Marine Emergency Operations, Department of Transport, 6-9 Sunley House, 90-93 High Holborn, London WC1V 6LP *Telephone:* 071-404 6911

HARRIS, LEONARD JOHN   Director Internal Taxes Directorate, HM Customs and Excise   Grade: 3

Career: HM Customs and Excise (C & E) 1964-70: assistant principal 1964-69, principal 1969-70; principal: Civil Service Selection Board 1970-71, C & E 1971, Cabinet secretariat (CS) 1971-74; UK permanent representation to EC, Brussels 1974-77: first secretary 1974-76, counsellor 1976-77; assistant secretary: C & E 1977-80, CS 1980-83; commissioner C & E 1983-87; under secretary, head of personnel policy group 1987-91; director internal taxes C&E 1991-

Date of birth: 4 July 1941 *Education/professional qualifications:* Westminster City School, London; St John's College, Cambridge, English (BA 1964, MA) *Marital status:* married Jennifer Dilys 1986; 2 daughters, 1 son from previous marriage, 1 stepson, 1 stepdaughter

Leonard J Harris Esq, Director, Internal Taxes Directorate, HM Customs and Excise, New Kings Beam House, 22 Upper Ground, London SE1 9PJ *Telephone:* 071-620 1313

HARRIS, PETER MICHAEL   Northern Circuit Administrator, Lord Chancellor's Department   Grade: 3

Career: Royal Navy 1953-72; private practice barrister 1972-74; Lord Chancellor's Department 1974-: circuit administrator northern circuit 1986-

Date of birth: 13 April 1937 *Education/professional qualifications:* Dursley Grammar School, Gloucestershire; Cirencester Grammar School; Royal Naval College, Dartmouth (commission 1958) *Marital status:* married Bridget Burke 1963; 2 daughters, 1 son *Publications:* The Children Act 1989: A Procedural Handbook (Butterworths 1991) *Recreations:* walking, gardening, reading, theatre

Peter M Harris Esq, Circuit Administrator, Northern Circuit, Lord Chancellor's Department, Aldine House, New Bailey Street, Salford, M5 3EU *Telephone:* 061-832 9571

To subscribe to

The Dod's Report
The European Companion
The Whitehall Companion
Telephone 071-240 3902

HARRISON, MICHAEL MILLER   Managing Director, PSA Building Management (Manchester), Department of the Environment   Grade: 4

Career: architect War Department, Singapore 1962-67; Property Services Agency (PSA) 1967-: government projects overseas 1967-75: head of overseas design 1967-73, head of design organisation Germany 1973-75, superintendent architect design standard office 1975-79, SE regional design manager 1979-83, Manchester regional works officer 1983-85, managing director PSA Building Management Manchester (serving public and private sectors) 1985-

Date of birth: 5 January 1938 *Education/professional qualifications:* St Michael's College, Leeds; Leeds School of Architecture (DiplArch 1961); RIBA *Marital status:* married Patricia Sawyer 1962; 2 daughters *Clubs:* Naval, Civil Service *Recreations:* walking, tennis, classical music

Michael M Harrison Esq, Managing Director, PSA Building Management, Ashburner House, Seymour Grove, Old Trafford, Manchester M16 0JL *Telephone:* 061-954 6249 *Fax:* 061-872 0348

HART, GRAHAM ALLAN   Permanent Secretary, Department of Health   Grade: 1

Career: Ministry of Health 1962-69: assistant principal 1962-67, principal 1967-69; assistant registrar General Medical Council 1969-71; Department of Health and Social Security 1972-82: principal private secretary to secretary of state for social services 1972-74; assistant secretary 1974; under secretary 1979; under secretary Central Policy Review Staff 1982-83; deputy secretary Department of Health (DH) 1984-89; seconded as secretary Home and Health Department, Scottish Office 1990-92; permanent secretary DH 1992-

Date of birth: 13 March 1940 *Education/professional qualifications:* Brentwood School; Pembroke College, Oxford, literae humaniores (BA 1962) *Honours, decorations:* CB 1987 *Marital status:* married Margaret Aline Powell 1964; 2 sons

Graham A Hart Esq CB, Permanent Secretary, Department of Health, Richmond House, 79 Whitehall, London SW1A 2NS *Telephone:* 071-210 5310

HARTE, Dr MICHAEL JOHN   Under Secretary, Resources, Ministry of Defence   Grade: 3

Career: principal Ministry of Defence (MoD) 1967-73; assistant secretary (AS) Central Policy Review Staff 1973-75; AS MoD 1975-77; budget and infrastructure UK delegation to NATO 1977-81; chairman budget committees NATO 1981-83; MoD 1983-: AS 1983-85, assistant under secretary dockyard planning team 1985-87, personnel (air) 1987-90, under secretary resources (financial co-ordination of defence programme and budget) 1990-

Date of birth: 15 August 1936 *Education/professional qualifications:* Charterhouse; Trinity College, Cambridge, natural sciences (BA 1959); University College, London, biochemical engineering (PhD 1964) *Recreations:* vegetable growing, wine drinking

Dr Michael J Harte, Under Secretary, Ministry of Defence, Whitehall, London SW1A 2HB *Telephone:* 071-218 2318

Complete Name Index
see page 955

HARTLEY, BRYAN HOLROYD   Chief Pharmaceutical Officer, Department of Health; Business Head, Inspection and Enforcement, Medicines Control Agency (Executive Agency)   Grade: 4

Career: pharmaceutical development pharmacist Wellcome 1962-64; community pharmacy manager 1964-65; process development and quality assurance pharmacist Winthrop Laboratories 1965-68; process development manager Wyeth Laboratories 1968-71; Department of Health [and Social Security] 1971-: medicines division 1971-79: medicines inspectorate 1971-76, principal, Medicines Act advertising policy 1976-79; principal, pharmaceutical division 1979-82; deputy chief pharmaceutical officer 1982-85; chief medicines inspector 1985-90; chief pharmaceutical officer 1990-, and business head, inspection and enforcement Medicines Control Agency 1990-

Date of birth: 27 April 1939 *Education/professional qualifications:* Municipal Grammar School, Wolverhampton; London University, pharmacy (BPharm 1962); FRPharmS 1986 *Marital status:* married Wendy Barbara 1963; 2 daughters *Clubs:* Civil Service *Recreations:* trekking

Bryan H Hartley Esq, Business Head, Medicines Control Agency, Market Towers, 1 Nine Elms Lane, London SW8 5NG *Telephone:* 071-273 0500 *Fax:* 071-273 0676

HARTNACK, PAUL RICHARD SAMUEL   Comptroller General and Chief Executive, Patent Office (Executive Agency)   Grade: 3

Career: Board of Trade 1961-67; assistant secretary (AS) committee of enquiry into civil air transport 1967-68; second secretary Paris embassy 1969-72; export promotion Department of Trade and Industry (DTI) 1973-78; AS National Enterprise Board 1979-80; secretary British Technology Group 1980-85; AS finance and resource management division DTI 1985-89; comptroller general and chief executive Patent Office 1989-

Date of birth: 17 November 1942 *Education/professional qualifications:* Hastings Grammar School *Marital status:* married Marion 1966; 2 sons *Recreations:* gardening, watching rugby

Paul R S Hartnack Esq, Comptroller General and Chief Executive, Patent Office, Concept House, Cardiff Road, Newport, Gwent NP9 1RH *Telephone:* 0633 814500 *Fax:* 0633 814505

HARVEY, DEREK WILLIAM   Chief Executive, Vehicle Certification Agency (Executive Agency)   Grade: 5

Career: project engineer: Science and Research Council 1973-75, Forestry Commission 1975-78; Department of Transport (DTp) 1978-: vehicle and component approvals (VCA) 1978-85, director operations vehicle inspectorate 1985-87, head of division VCA 1987-90; chief executive DTp Vehicle Certification executive agency (testing and approval of new road vehicles and their components) 1990-

Date of birth: 2 January 1948 *Education/professional qualifications:* Royal Grammar School, Worcester; University College of Wales, Swansea, mechanical engineering (BSc 1968); CEng 1976; MIMeche 1976 *Marital status:* married Veronica 1973; 1 daughter *Clubs:* Rotary *Recreations:* motoring, camping, angling, DIY

Derek W Harvey Esq, Chief Executive, Vehicle Certification Agency, 1 Eastgate Office Centre, Eastgate Road, Bristol BS5 6XX *Telephone:* 0272-524100 *Fax:* 0272-524103

HASTINGS, A J   Clerk of the Journals, House of Commons   Grade: 3

Career: clerk's department House of Commons 1960-

A J Hastings Esq, Clerk of the Journals, House of Commons, Westminster, London SW1A 0AA
Telephone: 071-219 3000

HAWKINS, Professor ANTHONY DONALD   Director of Fisheries Research for Scotland, Agriculture and Fisheries Department, Scottish Office   Grade: 4

Career: Department of Agriculture and Fisheries for Scotland (DAFS) 1965-72: scientific officer (SO) 1965-69, senior SO 1969-72; consultant UN Food and Agriculture Organisation 1972, DAFS 1972-87: principal SO 1972-78, senior principal SO 1978-83, deputy chief SO 1983-87; chief SO, director of fisheries research for Scotland, Scottish Office Agriculture and Fisheries Department 1987- *Current non-Whitehall posts:* honorary research professor Aberdeen University 1987-; honorary lecturer St Andrews University 1983-

Date of birth: 25 March 1942 *Education/professional qualifications:* Poole Grammar School, Dorset; Bristol University, zoology (BSc 1963) and physiology (PhD 1968) *Honours, decorations:* AB Wood Medal and Prize, Institute of Acoustics 1978; FRSE 1989 *Marital status:* married Susan Mary Fulker 1966; 1 son *Publications:* Sound Reception in Fish (Elsevier 1976); Aquarian Systems (Academic Press 1981) *Recreations:* whippet racing, salmon fishing, walking

Professor Anthony D Hawkins, Director of Fisheries Research for Scotland, Marine Laboratory, PO Box 101, Victoria Road, Torry, Aberdeen
Telephone: 0224 876544 *Fax:* 0224 879156

HAWKINS, Air Vice-Marshal DAVID RICHARD   Commandant-General, Royal Air Force Regiment; Director-General of Security (RAF), Ministry of Defence

Career: RAF Regiment 1959-: director RAF personal services 1 Ministry of Defence 1989-90; director RAF Regiment 1990-91, commandant general 1991-; director-general RAF security 1991-

Date of birth: 5 April 1937 *Education/professional qualifications:* Downside School; Royal Military Academy, Sandhurst

Air Vice-Marshal David R Hawkins MBE, Director-General of Security (RAF), Ministry of Defence, Metropole Building, Northumberland Avenue, London WC2N 5BL *Telephone:* 071-218 9000

HAWTIN, BRIAN RICHARD   Assistant Under Secretary of State (Material/Naval), Procurement Executive, Ministry of Defence   Grade: 3

Career: Ministry of Defence 1967-: assistant secretary 1981-89; private secretary to secretary of state for defence 1987-89; assistant under secretary (material/naval) 1989-

Date of birth: 31 May 1946 *Education/professional qualifications:* Christ Church, Oxford (MA)

Brian R Hawtin Esq, Assistant Under Secretary (Material/Naval), Procurement Executive, Ministry of Defence, Main Building, Whitehall, London SW1A 2HB *Telephone:* 071-218 9000

To subscribe to The European Companion
Telephone: 071-240 3902

HAWTIN, MICHAEL VICTOR   Director, Underwriting Group, Export Credit Guarantee Department   Grade: 3

Career: HM Treasury (HMT) 1964-83: assistant principal 1964-69, principal 1969-77: seconded to Barclays Bank 1969-71, assistant secretary 1977-83; under secretary (US) principal finance officer Property Services Agency, Department of Environment 1983-86; US HMT 1986-88; director resource management group and principal establishment and finance officer Export Credit Guarantee Department 1988-89, director underwriting group 1991-

Date of birth: 7 September 1942 *Education/professional qualifications:* Bournemouth School; St John's College, Cambridge, economics (BA, MA 1963); California University, Berkeley, USA, economics (MA 1964) *Marital status:* married Judith Mary Eeley 1966; 1 son, 1 daughter *Clubs:* Overseas Bankers' *Recreations:* music, travel

Michael V Hawtin Esq, Director Underwriting Group, Export Credit Guarantee Department, 2 Exchange Tower, Harbour Exchange Square, London E14 9GS *Telephone:* 071-512 7008 *Fax:* 071-512 7400

HAYMAN-JOYCE, Major-General ROBERT JOHN   Director, Royal Armoured Corps, Ministry of Defence

Career: Army 1963-: director-general land fighting systems Procurement Executive, Ministry of Defence 1989-92, director Royal Armoured Corps 1992-

Date of birth: 16 October 1940 *Education/professional qualifications:* Magdalene College, Cambridge (MA)

Major-General R J Hayman-Joyce CBE, Director-General Royal Armoured Corps, Royal Artillery Barracks, Woolwich, London SE18 4BH *Telephone:* 081-854 2242

HAYR, Air Marshal Sir KENNETH WILLIAM   Deputy Chief of Defence Staff (Commitments), Ministry of Defence

Career: fighter pilot 1959-76; inspector flight safety Ministry of Defence (MoD) 1976-79; Royal College of Defence Studies 1980; assistant chief of air staff (operations) MoD 1980-82; air officer commanding Number 11 Group 1982-85; commander British forces Cyprus 1985-88; deputy commander-in-chief HQ Strike Command 1988-90; deputy chief of defence staff (commitments) MoD 1990-

Date of birth: 13 April 1935 *Education/professional qualifications:* Auckland Grammar School, New Zealand *Honours, decorations:* AFC 1963, Bar to AFC 1972, CBE 1976, CB 1982, KCB 1988, KBE 1991 *Recreations:* hang gliding, para gliding, skydiving, windsurfing, skiing, tennis

Air Marshal Sir Kenneth Hayr KCB KBE AFC, Deputy Chief of Defence Staff, Ministry of Defence, Whitehall, London SW1A 2HB *Telephone:* 071-218 6762 *Fax:* 071-218 7503

HAYTER, PAUL DAVID GRENVILLE   Reading Clerk and Principal Finance Officer, House of Lords   Grade: 3

Career: House of Lords 1964-: clerk parliament office 1964-74; private secretary to leader of house and chief government whip 1974-77; clerk of committees 1977-85; principal clerk of committees 1985-90; reading clerk (ceremonial duties) and principal finance officer 1991-

Date of birth: 4 November 1942 *Education/professional qualifications:* Eton; Christ Church, Oxford, history (BA, MA 1964) *Marital status:* married Deborah Gervaise Maude 1973; 2 sons, 1 daughter *Recreations:* music, gardening, botany, archery, painting

Paul D G Hayter Esq, Reading Clerk and Principal Finance Officer, House of Lords, London SW1A 0PW *Telephone:* 071-219 3151

HAYZELDEN, JOHN EASTCOTT   Chief Executive, United Kingdom Passport Agency (Executive Agency)   Grade: 5

Career: army national service 1956-57; Home Office 1966-: principal 1966-73, assistant secretary 1973-88, head of passport department 1988-91; chief executive United Kingdom Passport Agency 1991-

Date of birth: 20 June 1936 *Education/professional qualifications:* Merchant Taylors' School, Northwood; St John's College, Oxford, litterae humaniores (BA, MA 1960) *Marital status:* married Susan Clare 1963; 2 daughters *Recreations:* golf

John E Hayzelden Esq, Chief Executive, United Kingdom Passport Agency, Queen Anne's Gate, London SW1H 9AT *Telephone:* 071-271 8500

HEAD, MICHAEL EDWARD   Under Secretary, Equal Opportunities and General Department, Home Office   Grade: 3

Career: Home Office 1960-: assistant principal immigration and general departments, private secretary to permanent under secretary 1960-66; principal fire, general department 1966-72: secretary Erroll Committee on Liquor Licensing 1970-72; assistant secretary probation and aftercare, community programmes, equal opportunities and criminal departments 1972-84; assistant under secretary: general 1984-86, criminal justice and constitutional 1986-91, broadcasting and miscellaneous 1991, equal opportunities and general departments (ethnic minority; voluntary sector policy, charity law; national, local and European elections; gambling; deregulation; cults) 1991-

Date of birth: 17 March 1936 *Education/professional qualifications:* Kingston Grammar School; Woking Grammar School; University College, London, history (BA 1957); Pittsburgh University, USA, history (BA 1957); Pittsburgh University, USA, history, English (MA 1958) *Honours, decorations:* CVO 1991 *Marital status:* married Wendy Elizabeth Davies 1963; 2 sons, 2 daughters *Clubs:* Reform *Recreations:* reading, theatre, golf

Michael E Head Esq CVO, Under Secretary, Home Office, 50 Queen Anne's Gate, London SW1H 9AT *Telephone:* 071-273 3383 *Fax:* 071-273 4198

HEAD, PHILIP JOHN   Chief Executive, Welsh Development Agency

Career: senior commercial surveyor Milton Keynes Development Corporation 1973-78; Welsh Development Agency 1978-: principal estates surveyor 1978-81, development and funding manager 1981-84, commercial director 1984-86, executive director property and regional services 1986-90, chief executive 1991- *Current non-Whitehall posts:* director Institute of Welsh Affairs 1991-; member Confederation of British Industry Council for Wales

Date of birth: 24 November 1951 *Education/professional qualifications:* Surbiton County Grammar School; Hereford Technical College; Reading University, estate management (BSc 1973); ARICS 1975; FRICS 1986 *Marital status:* married Barbara 1974; 2 sons *Clubs:* Llantrisant Round Table *Recreations:* charity fundraising, badminton, gardening, swimming, family

Philip J Head Esq, Chief Executive, Welsh Development Agency, Pearl House, Greyfriars Road, Cardiff CF1 3XX *Telephone:* 0222 222666

Parliamentary Offices
see page 275

HEATH, Major-General (MICHAEL) MIKE STUART   Director-General Equipment Support, Ministry of Defence

Career: commissioned into army 1961-; Royal Military College of Science 1961-63; army staff course 1971-73; directing staff Armour School, Bovington 1974-75; commander 7 Armoured Workshop BAOR 1976-77; National Defence College 1978; assistant adjutant and quartermaster general Berlin field force 1978-80; commander maintenance 2 Armoured Division BAOR/York 1981-82; colonel (Weapons) Master General of Ordnance 3 Ministry of Defence (MoD) 1982-85; Royal College of Defence Studies 1986; director support planning (army) MoD 1987-89; commander maintenance HQ BAOR 1990-91; director-general equipment support (army), logistic executive MoD (head of Royal Electrical and Mechanical Engineers; army equipment engineering, testing, repair and recovery) 1991-

Date of birth: 7 September 1940 *Education/professional qualifications:* St Alban's School; Welbeck College; Royal Military College of Science (BSc Eng 1966) *Honours, decorations:* CBE 1991 *Recreations:* walking, music, photography, restoring antique furniture

Major-General Mike S Heath CBE, Director-General Equipment Support, Logistic Executive (Army), Monxton Road, Andover, Hampshire SP11 8HT *Telephone:* 0264 382431 *Fax:* 0264 382439

HEATHCOTE, Dr (FREDERIC) ROGER   Under Secretary, Services Management, Establishment and Finance Division, Department of Trade and Industry   Grade: 3

Career: research associate Birmingham University 1969-70; Ministry of Technology/Department of Trade and Industry (DTI) 1970-73: private secetary to secretary for industrial development 1973; Department of Energy 1974- (most of whose responsibilities were taken over by the DTI in 1992): private secretary to permanent under secretary 1974, Offshore Technology Unit 1975-81, petroleum engineering division 1981-82, gas division 1982-84, electricity division 1984-87, establishment and finance division (EFD) 1987-89; head of finance branch 1987-88, director of resource management 1988-89, head of coal division 1989-91; principal establishment and finance officer EFD 1991-92; under secretary services management, establishment and finance divison 1992- *Current non-Whitehall posts:* non-executive director Trafalgar House Property Ltd 1988-

Date of birth: 19 March 1944 *Education/professional qualifications:* Bromsgrove School, Worcestershire, Birmingham University, physics (BSc 1966) and high-energy nuclear physics (PhD 1969) *Marital status:* married Mary Campbell Syme 1986; 1 step-daughter, 1 son *Recreations:* reading, gardening, painting

Dr F Roger Heathcote, Under Secretary, Establishment and Finance Division, Kingsgate House, 56-74 Victoria Street, London SW1E 6SW *Telephone:* 071-215 5000

HEDGER, JOHN CLIVE   Under Secretary, Schools, Department for Education   Grade: 3

Career: Department of Education [and Science] 1969-: assistant private secretary 1969-70; principal 1970-77; secretary to Committee of Enquiry into the Education of the Handicapped 1974-76; assistant secretary schools and further and higher education branches 1977-88; under secretary, schools 1988-

Date of birth: 17 December 1942 *Education/professional qualifications:* Quirister School; Winchester College; Victoria College, Jersey; Sussex University, English (BA 1965, MA 1966) *Marital status:* married Jean

Felstead 1966; 2 sons, 1 daughter *Clubs:* Odney (Cookham) *Recreations:* coarse acting, coarse sailing, walking, growing things

John C Hedger Esq, Under Secretary, Department for Education,, Sanctuary Buildings, Great Smith Street, London SW1P 3BT
Telephone: 071-925 5650

HENDERSON, CHARLES EDWARD   Deputy Secretary, Corporate and Consumer Affairs Division, Department of Trade and Industry   Grade: 2

Career: investment manager 1960-70; principal: Export Credit Guarantee Department 1971-73, Departments of Trade and Industry (DTI) and of Energy (DoEn) 1973-75; DoEn 1976-88: under secretary, head of atomic energy division 1982-84, head of oil division 1984-85, principal finance and establishment officer 1985-88; deputy secretary, head of Office of Arts and Libraries 1989-92; deputy secretary, corporate and consumer affairs division 1992-

Date of birth: 19 September 1939 *Education/professional qualifications:* Charterhouse; Pembroke College, Cambridge, mathematics (BA, MA 1960); FIA 1966 *Marital status:* married Rachel 1966; 1 daughter, 1 son *Recreations:* music, golf, mountain walking, reading

Charles E Henderson Esq, Deputy Secretary, Department of Trade and Industry, Ashdown House, 123 Victoria Street, London SW1E 6RB *Telephone:* 071-215 3483 *Fax:* 071-215 3466

HENES, JOHN DEREK   Director, International Transport, Department of Transport Grade: 3

Career: Department of Trade and Industry 1971-83: assistant secretary 1975-83; Department of Transport 1983-: director of international transport 1989-

Date of birth: 8 June 1937 *Education/professional qualifications:* Christ's Hospital; Gonville and Caius College, Cambridge (MA)

John D Henes Esq, Director of International Transport, Department of Transport, 2 Marsham Street, London SW1P 3EB *Telephone:* 071-276 3000

HENRY, JOHN   Yorkshire and Humberside Regional Director, Departments of the Environment and Transport   Grade: 3

Career: psychologist Transport and Road Research Laboratory 1968-72; Department of Environment (DoE) 1972-89: principal 1977-83, assistant secretary 1983-89; under secretary, regional director Yorkshire and Humberside regional office, DoE and Transport (regional planning, housing, highway network, inner city and EC regional policy) 1990- *Current non-Whitehall posts:* non-executive director Cunard Line Ltd 1991-

Date of birth: 8 October 1946 *Education/professional qualifications:* Cheltenham College; Queen's College, Oxford, politics, philosophy and economics (BA, MA 1968) *Marital status:* single *Recreations:* walking, reading, art

John Henry Esq, Regional Director, Yorkshire and Humberside Regional Office, Departments of the Environment and Transport, City House, Leeds *Telephone:* 0532 438232 *Fax:* 0532 429954

Government Departments
see page 300

HEPBURN, JOHN WILLIAM   Under Secretary, Food, Drink and Marketing Policy, Ministry of Agriculture, Fisheries and Food   Grade: 3

Career: Ministry of Agriculture, Fisheries and Food 1961-: assistant secretary 1973-81, under secretary food, drink and marketing 1982-

Date of birth: 8 September 1938   *Education/professional qualifications:* Glasgow University (MA); Brasenose College, Oxford

John W Hepburn Esq, Under Secretary, Ministry of Agriculture, Fisheries and Food, Whitehall Place, London SW1A 2HH   *Telephone:* 071-270 8515

HEPPELL, (THOMAS) STRACHAN   Deputy Secretary, Department of Health   Grade: 2

Career: Department of [Health and] Social Security 1958-: under secretary 1974-83; deputy secretary health and social services group 1983-

Date of birth: 15 August 1935   *Education/professional qualifications:* The Queen's College, Oxford

Strachan Heppell Esq CB, Deputy Secretary, Department of Health, Richmond House, 79 Whitehall, London SW1A 2NS   *Telephone:* 071-210 3000

HEPPLEWHITE, ROSALIND MARY JOY   Chief Executive, Social Security Child Support Agency (Executive Agency April 1993)   Grade: 4

Career: unit administrator Hammersmith and Fulham health authority (HA) 1983-84; Brighton HA 1985-89: unit general manager 1985-88, director of corporate development 1988-89; national director MIND 1989-91; chief executive Social Security Child Support Agency 1992- (comes fully into effect in April 1993)

Date of birth: 20 December 1952   *Education/professional qualifications:* Portsmouth Northern Grammar School; University College, London, classics (BA 1974)   *Marital status:* married Julian; 2   *Recreations:* home and family

Mrs Rosalind M J Hepplewhite, Chief Executive, Social Security Child Support Agency, Department of Social Security, Millbank Tower, Millbank, London SW1 4QU   *Telephone:* 071-217 4789   *Fax:* 071-217 4824

HEWITSON, (THOMAS) WILLIAM   Chief Actuary, Life Insurance Division, Government Actuary's Department   Grade: 4

Career: private practice actuarial training 1977-82; Government Actuary's Department 1982-: actuary, insurance division 1982-84; senior actuary, pensions division 1984-89; chief actuary, life insurance division 1989-

Date of birth: 31 December 1956   *Education/professional qualifications:* George Watson's College, Edinburgh; Edinburgh University, mathematics (BSc 1977); FFA 1981   *Marital status:* single   *Recreations:* reading, music, travel

T William Hewitson Esq, Chief Actuary, Government Actuary's Department, 22 Kingsway, London WC2B 6LE   *Telephone:* 071-242 6828   *Fax:* 071-831 6653

HEWLETT, RICHARD DEREK   Secretary, Broadcasting Complaints Commission

Career: colonial service, Northern Rhodesia 1954-57; publications officer Royal Institute of Public Administration 1957-59; BBC 1959-87: secretariat 1959-64, African service 1964-65, head of reference and registry services department 1969-80, general manager BBC Data 1980-87; secretary Broadcasting Complaints Commission 1987-

Date of birth: 7 September 1931   *Education/professional qualifications:* Plymouth College; Magdalen College, Cambridge, modern languages (BA 1953)   *Marital status:* married Joan Lesley 1958; 2 daughters, 1 son   *Clubs:* Royal Society of Arts   *Recreations:* reading, walking

Richard D Hewlett Esq, Secretary, Broadcasting Complaints Commission, Grosvenor Gardens House, 35-37 Grosvenor Gardens, London SW1W 0BS   *Telephone:* 071-630 1966   *Fax:* 071-828 7316

HEYHOE, DAVID CHARLES ROSS   Assistant Under Secretary (Fleet Support) Ministry of Defence   Grade: 3

Career: Ministry of Defence 1967-: private secretary to Leader of the House of Commons 1981-84; assistant under secretary (AUS) and director general of management audit 1986-91; AUS fleet support 1991-

Date of birth: 29 June 1938   *Education/professional qualifications:* Worcester College, Oxford (MA)

David C R Heyhoe Esq, Under Secretary (Fleet Support), Ministry of Defence, Main Building, Whitehall, London SW1A 2HB   *Telephone:* 071-218 9000

HEYWOOD, BARRY KEITH   Regional Procurator Fiscal, (Tayside Central and Fife) Crown Office   Grade: 4

Career: Procurator Fiscal Service, Crown Office 1971-: depute procurator fiscal (PE) Ayr 1971-76, Glasgow 1976-77; PF Wick 1978-83; assistant PF Glasgow 1983-86; PF Inverness 1986-91; regional PF Tayside Central and Fife (public prosecution; sudden death and fire investigation, 1991-

Date of birth: 24 July 1946   *Education/professional qualifications:* Kirkcaldy High School; Edinburgh University, law (MA 1967, LLB 1969)   *Marital status:* married Mary 1970; 1 daughter, 1 son   *Recreations:* Roman and Byzantine history; walking

Barry K Heywood Esq, Regional Procurator Fiscal, 15 West Bell Street, Dundee   *Telephone:* 0382 27535   *Fax:* 0382 202719

HICKS, Dr COLIN PETER   Under Secretary Research and Technology Policy, Department of Trade and Industry   Grade: 3

Career: chemistry lecturer University of West Indies 1970-73; ICI research fellow Exeter University 1973-75; researcher National Physical Laboratory 1975-80; Department of Trade and Industry (DTI) 1980-84: research policy 1980-83, seconded as technical adviser to Barclays Bank 1983-84; deputy director Laboratory of Government Chemist 1984-87; DTI 1988-: secretary Industrial Development Advisory Board 1988-90, under secretary research and technology division (policy and budgets for innovation) 1990-

Date of birth: 1 May 1946   *Education/professional qualifications:* Rutlish Grammar School, Merton;

Bristol University, chemistry (BSc 1967, PhD 1970) *Marital status:* married Elizabeth Joan Payne 1967; 2 daughters *Recreations:* computing

Dr Colin P Hicks, Under Secretary, Department of Trade and Industry, 151 Buckingham Palace Road, London SW1W 9SS *Telephone:* 071-215 1659 *Fax:* 071-215 1590

HIGGINS, Sir EOIN JOHN PATRICK BASIL (The Hon Mr Justice HIGGINS)   Deputy Chairman, Northern Ireland Boundary Commission

Career: barrister 1948-; county court judge 1971-84; recorder of Belfast 1982-84; high court judge 1984-; deputy chairman Northern Ireland Boundary Commission 1989- *Current non-Whitehall posts:* Northern Ireland high court judge 1984-

Date of birth: 14 June 1927 *Education/professional qualifications:* St Columb's College, Derry; Queen's University, Belfast, law (LLB 1947) *Honours, decorations:* Kt 1988 *Marital status:* married Bridget O'Neill 1960; 3 daughters, 2 sons

Sir Eoin Higgins, Deputy Chairman, Boundary Commission for Northern Ireland, c/o Northern Ireland Office, Whitehall, London SW1A 2AZ *Telephone:* 071-210 6569 *Fax:* 071-210 6549

HIGGINS, JOHN ANDREW   Assistant Auditor General, National Audit Office
Grade: 3 equivalent

Career: Exchequer and Audit Department 1958-84: audit manager 1978-81, deputy director 1981-84: seconded officer Office of Auditor General, Canada 1983-84; National Audit Office (examination of the accounts of government departments, certain public bodies and international organisations) 1984-: director 1984-88, assistant auditor general 1988-

Date of birth: 19 February 1940 *Education/professional qualifications:* Hendon Grammar School; Hastings Grammar School; organ playing, Royal College of Organists (associateship 1988) *Marital status:* married Susan Jennifer 1965; 1 son *Clubs:* Ifield Golf and Country *Recreations:* classical organ, bridge, golf, supporting Crystal Palace ·

John A Higgins Esq, Assistant Auditor General, National Audit Office, 157-197 Buckingham Palace Road, London SW1W 9SP *Telephone:* 071-798 7380 *Fax:* 071-828 3774

HILL, JONATHAN HOPKIN   Political Secretary to the Prime Minister

Career: special adviser to Kenneth Clarke, secretary of state Department of Health; Lowe Bell Communications; member Prime Minister's (PM) Policy Unit (transport, housing and inner cities) 1991-92; political secretary to the PM 1992-

Date of birth: 24 July 1960 *Education/professional qualifications:* Highgate School, London; Trinity College, Cambridge, history (BA, MA 1982) *Marital status:* Alexandra Jane Nettelfield; 1 daughter

Jonathan H Hill Esq, Political Secretary to the Prime Minister, 10 Downing Street, London SW1A 2AA *Telephone:* 071-930 4433

HILL, Vice-Admiral Sir ROBERT CHARLES FINCH   Director-General Submarines, Deputy Controller of Navy, Ministry of Defence

Career: Royal Navy 1964-: chief staff officer (engineering) to commander-in-chief fleet 1987-89; Ministry of Defence 1971-74, 1980-84, 1989-: deputy controller of navy and chief abovewater systems executive MoD 1989-

Date of birth: 1 May 1937 *Education/professional qualifications:* Royal Naval Engineering College, Manadon (BSc Eng)

Vice-Admiral Sir Robert C F Hill KBE, Deputy Controller of the Navy, Ministry of Defence, Foxhill, Bath BA1 5AB *Telephone:* 0225 884884

HILLHOUSE, Sir (ROBERT) RUSSELL   Permanent Under Secretary, Scottish Office   Grade: 1

Career: Scottish Education Department (SED) 1962-71: assistant principal 1962-66, principal 1966-71; principal HM Treasury 1971-74; assistant secretary: Scottish Office (SO) 1974-77, Scottish Home and Health Department 1977-80; under secretary (US), principal finance officer SO 1980-85; SED 1985-88: US 1985-87, secretary 1987-88; permanent under secretary SO 1988- *Current non-Whitehall posts:* director Scottish Business in the Community 1990-

Date of birth: 23 April 1938   *Education/professional qualifications:* Hutchesons' Grammar School, Glasgow; Glasgow University, mathematics and physics (MA 1960)   *Honours, decorations:* KCB 1991   *Marital status:* married Alison Janet Fraser 1966; 2 daughters   *Recreations:* making music; countryside

Sir Russell Hillhouse KCB, Permanent Under Secretary, Scottish Office, St Andrew's House, Regent Road, Edinburgh EH1 3DG
Telephone: 031-244 4026   *Fax:* 031-244 2756

HILLIER, RICHARD   Director of Industrial Relations, Division 2, Employment Department Group   Grade: 3

Richard Hillier Esq, Director of Industrial Relations, Division 2, Employment Department Group, Caxton House, Tothill Street, London SW1H 9NF   *Telephone:* 071-273 3000

HINTON, PETER HUGH   Chief Actuary, General Insurance, Government Actuary's Department

Career: Government Actuary's Department 1971-: chief actuary, general insurance division (advice to Department of Trade and Industry on supervision of general insurance business and some life insurance) 1987-

Date of birth: 26 May 1946   *Education/professional qualifications:* Peterhouse, Cambridge, mathematics (BA 1968); FIA 1975   *Marital status:* married; four

Peter H Hinton Esq, Chief Actuary, Government Actuary's Department, 22 Kingsway, London, WC2B 6LE   *Telephone:* 071-242 6828   *Fax:* 071-831 6653

HOBSON, JOHN   Director, Pollution Control and Wastes, Department of the Environment   Grade: 3

Career: assistant principal Ministry of Transport 1967-72; principal: Department of the Environment (DoE) 1972-74, Civil Service Department 1974-78, DoE 1978-79; assistant secretary (AS) Department of Transport 1979-80; DoE 1980-: AS 1980-86, under secretary 1986-: director pollution control and wastes directorate 1988-

Date of birth: 30 March 1946   *Education/professional qualifications:* Northampton Grammar School; Manchester Grammar School; King's College, Cambridge, mathematics (BA, MA 1971)   *Marital status:* married Jeanne Gerrish 1970; 1 son, 1 daughter   *Recreations:* gardening, reading, walking

John Hobson Esq, Under Secretary, Department of the Environment, 2 Marsham Street, London SW1P 3BU   *Telephone:* 071-276 3000

HODDINOTT, (DAVID) MICHAEL   Chief Executive and Director, Accounts Services Agency (Executive Agency)   Grade: 5

Career: audit and investigations, Price Waterhouse & Co 1965-69; financial controller First National Development Ltd 1969-71; Department of Trade and Industry 1971-: chief executive and director Accounts Services Agency 1991-

Date of birth: 1 August 1943   *Education/professional qualifications:* Bloxham School, Banbury; FCA 1965   *Marital status:* married Heather Clare Stuart 1970; 1 son   *Recreations:* beagling, fellwalking, opera

D Michael Hoddinott Esq, Chief Executive and Director, Accounts Services Agency, Government Buildings, Cardiff Road, Newport, Gwent   *Telephone:* 0633 812332   *Fax:* 0633 812807

HODGKINS, DAVID JOHN   Director of Safety and General Policy, Health and Safety Executive   Grade: 3

Career: assistant principal/principal Ministry of Labour 1956-65; principal HM Treasury 1965-68; Department of Employment 1970-84: assistant secretary 1970-76, under secretary 1976-84; director of safety and general policy Health and Safety Executive 1984-

Date of birth: 13 March 1934   *Education/professional qualifications:* Buxton College; Peterhouse, Cambridge, history (BA, MA 1956)   *Marital status:* married Sheila Lacey 1963; 2 sons   *Clubs:* Royal Commonwealth Society

David J Hodgkins Esq, Director of Safety and General Policy, Health and Safety Executive, Baynards House, Chepstow Place, London W2 4TF   *Telephone:* 071-243 6370

HODGSON, MARTIN JOHN   Regional Controller, Inland Revenue   Grade: 4

Career: Inland Revenue 1967-: inspector of taxes 1967-73; training centre tutor 1973-76; district inspector 1976-77; inspector (senior principal) head office 1977-81; district inspector Holborn 1981-82; principal inspector in charge of Centre 1 Scotland 1982-85; district inspector City 24 1985-87; assistant director head office 1987-90; regional controller for eastern counties region 1990-

Date of birth: 1 May 1943   *Education/professional qualifications:* Bradford Grammar School; St Andrew's University, Latin and Greek (MA 1965)   *Marital status:* married Doreen 1968; 1 son, 1 daughter   *Recreations:* music, walking, gardening, swimming

Martin J Hodgson Esq, Regional Controller, Inland Revenue, Midgate House, Peterborough PE1 1TD   *Telephone:* 0733 63241   *Fax:* 0733 313426

HOGG, DAVID ALAN   Head of Litigation Division, Treasury Solicitor's Department   Grade: 3

Career: private practice solicitor 1969-78; Treasury Solicitor's Department (TSD) 1978-89: senior legal assistant 1978-85, assistant treasury solicitor (ATS) 1985-89; ATS Department of Energy 1989-90; principal assistant solicitor, head of litigation division (civil litigation in England and Wales for most government departments) 1990-

Date of birth: 8 October 1946   *Education/professional qualifications:* Brighton

College; College of Law, Guildford (solicitor 1969) *Marital status:* married Pauline Pamela 1981; 3 sons, 1 daughter *Recreations:* theatre, canal boating

David A Hogg Esq, Head of Litigation Division, Treasury Solicitor's Department, Queen Anne's Chambers, 28 Broadway, London SW1H 9JS *Telephone:* 071-210 3090 *Fax:* 071-222 6006

HOGG, SARAH ELIZABETH MARY   Head of Prime Minister's Policy Unit   Grade: 1A

Career: The Economist: various posts, economics editor 1967-81; economics editor Sunday Times 1981-82; presenter Channel 4 news 1982-83; economics editor The Times 1984-86; business and finance editor The Independent 1986-89; economics editor Daily and Sunday Telegraph 1989-90; second permanent secretary, head of Prime Minister's Policy Unit 1990-

Date of birth: 14 May 1946 *Education/professional qualifications:* St Mary's School, Ascot; Lady Margaret Hall, Oxford, philosophy, politics and economics (BA 1967) *Marital status:* married Douglas 1968; 1 daughter, 1 son *Recreations:* skiing, theatre

Mrs Sarah E M Hogg, Head of Prime Minister's Policy Unit, 10 Downing Street, London SW1A 2AA *Telephone:* 071-930 4433

HOGGETT, Professor BRENDA MARJORIE   Commissioner, Law Commission Grade: 2 equivalent

Career: Manchester University law faculty 1966-89: assistant lecturer 1966-68, lecturer 1968-76, senior lecturer 1976-81, reader 1981-86, professor 1986-89; private practice barrister 1969-72; legal member NW mental health review tribunal 1979-80; member Council on Tribunals 1980-84; professor of English law London University 1989-90; law commissioner (law reform proposals) 1984- *Current non-Whitehall posts:* managing trustee Nuffield Foundation 1987-; chairman National Family Conciliation Council 1989-; recorder, deputy high court judge 1989-; governor Centre for Policy on Ageing 1990-; visiting professor King's College, London University 1990-; member Human Fertilisation and Embryology Authority 1990-

Date of birth: 31 January 1945 *Education/professional qualifications:* High School for Girls, Richmond, Yorkshire; Girton College, Cambridge, law (BA 1966, MA); Gray's Inn (barrister 1969) *Honours, decorations:* QC 1989 *Marital status:* married A J C Hoggett 1968; 1 daughter *Publications:* co-author Women and the Law (Blackwell 1984); Parents and Children (Sweet and Maxwell 1987); Mental Health Law (Sweet and Maxwell 1990); co-author The Family, Law and Society (Butterworth 1991) *Recreations:* bridge, drama, domesticity

Professor Brenda M Hoggett QC, Commissioner, Law Commission, Conquest House, 37-38 John Street, London WC1N 2BQ *Telephone:* 071-411 1240 *Fax:* 071-411 1297

HOLDEN, His Hon Judge DEREK   President, Independent Tribunal Service

Career: senior partner private practice solicitors; resident judge Isleworth Crown Court 1988-89; president Independent Tribunal Service (social security, medical, disability and vaccine damage appeals in Great Britain) 1990-

Date of birth: 7 July 1935 *Education/professional qualifications:* Staines Grammar School, Egham, Surrey *Marital status:* married Dorien Elizabeth 1960; 2 sons *Clubs:* Leander, Royal Solent Yacht *Recreations:* sailing, music, skiing, photography

His Hon Judge Derek Holden, President, Independent Tribunal Service, Clements House, Gresham Street, London EC2V 7DN *Telephone:* 071-606 2106

 **HOLLAND, (DAVID ANTHONY) TONY   Director, Highway Programme Support Services, Department of Transport**   Grade: 4

Career: Department of Transport 1969-: director highway programme support services (design, construction, land acquisition, impact assessment) 1987- *Current non-Whitehall posts:* council member Steel Construction Institute 1988-

Date of birth: 15 October 1939 *Education/professional qualifications:* Highgate School, London; Pembroke College, Cambridge, mechanical sciences (BA 1962); MICE 1966 *Marital status:* married Susan Elizabeth 1962; 1 daughter, 2 sons *Recreations:* gardening, walking, woodwork, bridge

Tony Holland Esq, Director, Highway Programme Support Services, Department of Transport, 2 Marsham Street, London SW1P 3EB *Telephone:* 071-276 4847 *Fax:* 071-276 4864

HOLLAND, Sir GEOFFREY   Permanent Secretary, Employment Department Group   Grade: 1 *(see Addenda)*

Career: Ministry of Labour/Department of Employment/Employment Department Group 1961: Manpower Services Commission 1973-86: assistant secretary 1973-81: head of planning 1973-77, director of special programmes 1977-81, deputy secretary, director 1981-86; second permanent secretary 1986-88, permanent secretary 1988-

Date of birth: 9 May 1938 *Education/professional qualifications:* Merchant Taylors' School, Northwood; St John's College, Oxford (BA, MA) *Honours, decorations:* CB 1984, KCB 1989

Sir Geoffrey Holland KCB, Permanent Secretary, Employment Department Group, Caxton House, Tothill Street, London SW1H 9NF *Telephone:* 071-273 3000

HOLLIS, G A   Under Secretary and Head of Meat Group, Ministry of Agriculture, Fisheries and Food   Grade: 3

G A Hollis Esq, Under Secretary and Head of Meat Group, Ministry of Agriculture, Fisheries and Food, Whitehall Place, London SW1A 2HH *Telephone:* 071-270 8111

HOLMES, ROBIN EDMOND KENDALL   Head of Judicial Appointments, Lord Chancellor's Department   Grade: 3

Career: Wolverhampton County Borough Council 1961-64; assistant principal/principal Ministry of Housing and Local Government 1965-73; assistant colonial secretary Hong Kong government 1973-75; assistant secretary (AS): Department of the Environment 1976-78, Property Services Agency 1978-82; Lord Chancellor's Department 1982-: AS 1982-83, under secretary 1983-: Midland and Oxford circuit administrator 1983-92, head of judicial appointments 1992-

Date of birth: 14 July 1938 *Education/professional qualifications:* Wolverhampton Grammar School; Clare College, Cambridge, law (BA 1961); Birmingham University, law (LLM 1963); Law Society (solicitor 1964) *Marital status:* married Karin Kutter 1964; 2 sons *Recreations:* travel

Robin E K Holmes Esq, Head of Judicial Appointments Group, Lord Chancellor's Department, House of Lords, London SW1A 0PW *Telephone:* 071-219 8500

'Next Steps' Executive Agencies
see page 761

HOLROYD, JOHN HEPWORTH   First Civil Service Commissioner, Cabinet Office   Grade: 2

Career: assistant principal to under secretary Ministry of Agriculture, Fisheries and Food 1959-85; Cabinet Office 1985-: deputy head of European secretariat 1985-89; first civil service commissioner (recruitment and fast-stream entry to Grade 7 and above, advice on recruitment of junior grades) 1985- *Current non-Whitehall posts:* treasurer to governors Kingswood School, Bath 1985-

Date of birth: 10 April 1935 *Education/professional qualifications:* Kingswood School, Bath, Worcester College, Oxford, history (BA 1959, MA) *Marital status:* married Judith 1963; 1 son, 1 daughter *Clubs:* United Oxford and Cambridge University *Recreations:* choral singing, travel, joinery, bee-keeping

John H Holroyd Esq, First Civil Service Commissioner, Cabinet Office, Horse Guards Road, London SW1P 3AL *Telephone:* 071-270 5960 *Fax:* 071-270 0132

HOLT, Dr ANDREW ANTHONY   Director, Information Systems, Department of Health   Grade: 4

Career: operations research (OR) consultant HM Treasury 1974-78; head of OR Inland Revenue 1978-87; Department of Health [and Social Security] 1987-: director OR services 1987-90; director information services directorate 1990-

Date of birth: 4 January 1944 *Education/professional qualifications:* Latymer Upper School, Hammersmith; University College, London, mathematics (BSc 1965, PhD 1969) *Marital status:* married Janet Margery 1969; 3 sons *Recreations:* soccer

Dr Andrew A Holt, Director Information Systems, Department of Health, State House, High Holborn, London WC1R 4SX *Telephone:* 071-972 1676

HOPE, (TERENCE) TERRY LIONEL   Controller, Greater Manchester Executive Office, Inland Revenue   Grade: 4

Career: Inland Revenue 1967-: district inspector Buxton 1967-69; investigator Manchester 1969-75; officer in charge of special office Manchester 1975-81; Manchester 4 district inspector 1981-84; Sheffield regional office group controller 1984-90; controller Greater Manchester executive office 1990-

Date of birth: 14 May 1936 *Education/professional qualifications:* Barnstaple Grammar School *Marital status:* married Rosemarie Jennifer 1960; 2 sons *Clubs:* Hale Golf *Recreations:* golf, reading

Terry L Hope Esq, Controller, Greater Manchester Executive Office, Inland Revenue, Apsley House, Wellington Road North, Stockport, Lancashire SK4 1EY *Telephone:* 061-480 6009 *Fax:* 061-480 1031

HOPKINS, ELIZABETH A   Regional Director (South West) Departments of Environment and Transport   Grade: 3

Date of birth: 25 September 1941

Miss Elizabeth A Hopkins, Regional Director (South West), Departments of Environment and Transport, Tollgate House, Houlton Street, Briston BS2 9DJ *Telephone:* 0272-218490

HOPSON, CHRIS IAN   Special Adviser to Secretary of State for National Heritage

Career: Social Democratic Party 1985-89: constituency organiser 1985-87, director of elections and campaigns 1987-89, national secretary 1989; consultant Corporate Communications Strategy 1989-91; special adviser to secretary of state for national heritage 1992-

Date of birth: 9 April 1963 *Education/professional qualifications:* Marlborough College; Sussex University, politics (BA 1985); Cranfield School of Management, business administration (MBA 1992)

Chris Hopson Esq, Special Adviser to Secretary of State, Department of National Heritage, Horseguards Road, London SW1P 3AL
Telephone: 071-270 5920 *Fax:* 071-270 6026

HORNE, ROBERT DRAKE   Under Secretary, Teachers' Pay and General, Department for Education   Grade: 3

Career: Department of Education [and Science] 1968-: under secretary teachers' pay and general branch (school teachers' and further and higher education lecturers' pay; sport and recreation) 1988-

Date of birth: 23 April 1945 *Education/professional qualifications:* Mill Hill School, London; Oriel College, Oxford, classics (BA 1967) *Marital status:* married Jennifer Mary Gill 1972; 3 daughters *Recreations:* entertaining Australians, running

Robert D Horne Esq, Under Secretary, Department for Education, Sanctuary Buildings, Great Smith Street, London SW1P 3BT *Telephone:* 071-925 6134 *Fax:* 071-925 6073

HORSMAN, (MICHAEL) MIKE JOHN   Regional Director, London and South East, Employment Service (Executive Agency)   Grade: 4

Career: Department of Employment/Employment Department Group 1974-: regional director London and south east, Employment Service (unemployment benefit assessment, job placement) 1989-

Date of birth: 3 March 1949 *Education/professional qualifications:* Dollar Academy, Glasgow; Glasgow University, history and politics (MA 1971); Balliol College, Oxford (scholar, exhibitioner) *Marital status:* married Dr Anne Margaret 1977; 3 sons *Recreations:* golf, cycling, history, literature

Mike J Horsman Esq, Regional Director, Employment Service, London and South East Region, 236 Gray's Inn Road, London WC1K 8HL *Telephone:* 071-278 0363 *Fax:* 071-278 3309

HOSKER, GERALD ALBERY   Solicitor, Department of Trade and Industry (until October 1992 and then Procurator General and Treasury Solicitor, Treasury Solicitor's Department)   Grade: 2

Career: Treasury Solicitor's Department (TSD) 1960-: deputy treasury solicitor 1984-87; solicitor Department of Trade and Industry 1987-92; Procurator General and Treasury Solicitor TSD 1992-

Date of birth: 28 July 1933 *Education/professional qualifications:* Berkhamsted School, Hertfordshire; Law Society's School of Law (solicitor 1956); AFSA 1964 *Honours, decorations:* CB 1987 *Marital status:* married Rachel Victoria Beatrice Middleton 1956; 1 daughter, 1 son *Clubs:* Royal Commonwealth

Gerald A Hosker Esq CB, 10-18 Victoria Street, London SW1H 0NN *Telephone:* 071-215 3039 *Fax:* 071-215 3141 until October 1992, then Procurator General and Treasury Solicitor, Treasury Solicitor's Department, Queen Anne's Chambers, 28 Broadway, London SW1H 9JS, *Telephone:* 071-2100 3000

HOWARD, DAVID JOHN   Deputy Director, Department for National Savings   Grade: 3

Career: Exchequer and Audit Department 1960-69; HM Customs and Excise (C & E) 1969-72: assistant principal 1969, principal 1969-72; private secretary to chief secretary to the Treasury 1972-74; C & E 1974-91: assistant secretary 1976-84, director of VAT control 1985-87, of personnel 1987-90, of organisation 1990-91; deputy director of savings, principal establishment and finance officer Department for National Savings 1991-

Date of birth: 1 June 1941 *Education/professional qualifications:* Whitgift School, Croydon *Marital status:* married Anne; 2 sons, 2 daughters

David J Howard Esq, Deputy Director, Department for National Savings, Charles House, 375 Kensington High Street, London W14 8SD *Telephone:* 071-605 9462

HOWE, ERIC JAMES   Registrar, Data Protection Register Grade: 2 equivalent

Career: National Coal Board, British Cotton Industry Research Association, English Electric Computer Company 1954-66; National Computing Centre 1966-84: board director, deputy director; chairman National Computer Users' Forum; registrar, Data Protection Register (implementing and enforcing the Data Protection Act 1984) 1984-

Date of birth: 4 October 1931 *Education/professional qualifications:* Stretford Grammar School; Liverpool University, economics (BA 1954); FIDPM; FBCS *Honours, decorations:* CBE 1990 *Marital status:* married Patricia Schollick 1957; 2 daughters *Clubs:* Reform *Recreations:* family, gardening, local community work

Eric J Howe Esq CBE, Data Protection Registrar, Wycliffe House, Water Lane, Wilmslow, Cheshire SK9 5AZ *Telephone:* 0625 535711 *Fax:* 0625 524510

HOWE, (JOHN DORIAN) DON   Circuit Administrator, Wales and Chester, Lord Chancellor's Department   Grade: 4

Career: HM Customs and Excise 1958-80; Lord Chancellor's Department 1980-: courts administrator Stafford 1980-83, central criminal court 1984-86; deputy south eastern circuit administrator 1986-88; circuit administrator, Wales and Chester (management of area's crown and county courts' business) 1988-

Date of birth: 15 October 1936 *Education/professional qualifications:* St Cuthbert's Grammar School, Newcastle-upon-Tyne; London University, law (LLB 1972); Middle Temple (barrister 1980) *Marital status:* married Noreen 1959; 2 daughters, 1 son

J Don Howe Esq, Circuit Administrator,, Wales and Chester Circuit Office, Churchill House, Churchill Way, Cardiff CF1 4HH *Telephone:* 0222 396925 *Fax:* 0222 373882

HOWE, JOHN FRANCIS   Deputy Under Secretary (Civilian Management), Ministry of Defence   Grade: 2

Career: Ministry of Defence 1967-: assistant under secretary (personnel and logistics) 1988-91; deputy under secretary (Civilian Management) 1991-

Date of birth: 29 January 1944 *Education/professional qualifications:* Balliol College, Oxford (MA)

John F Howe Esq OBE, Deputy Under Secretary, (Civilian Management), Ministry of Defence, Main Building, Whitehall London SW1A 2HB *Telephone:* 071-218 9000

HOWE, MARTIN   Director, Competition Policy Division, Office of Fair Trading   Grade: 3

Career: Office of Fair Trading 1977-: assistant secretary 1980-84; director, competition policy division 1984-

Date of birth: 9 December 1936 *Education/professional qualifications:* Leeds University (PhD)

Martin Howe Esq, Director, Competition Policy Division, Office of Fair Trading, Field House, Breams Buildings, London EC4A 1PR *Telephone:* 071-242 2858

HOWES, CHRISTOPHER KINGSTON   Second Commissioner and Chief Executive, Crown Estate   Grade: 2

Career: planning and valuation assistant Greater London Council 1965-67; private practice 1967-79; Department of the Environment 1979-89: deputy director land economy 1979-81, chief estates officer 1981-85, director land and property division 1985-89; chief executive and second commissioner Crown Estate (direction and stewardship of the Crown's commercial and residential estates) 1989- *Current non-Whitehall posts:* visiting professor Bartlett School of Architecture and Planning, University College, London 1984-; member Prince of Wales's Council 1990-

Date of birth: 30 January 1942 *Education/professional qualifications:* Gresham's School, Holt, Norfolk; London University College of Estate Management (BSc 1965); Reading University, land values research (MPhil 1976); ARICS 1967 *Marital status:* married Clare Cunliffe 1967; 2 daughters (1 deceased), 2 sons *Publications:* Value Maps: aspects of land and property values (Geoabstracts 1979) *Clubs:* Athenaeum, Aldeburgh Yacht, Royal Household Golf *Recreations:* music, sailing, painting

Christopher K Howes Esq, Chief Executive, Crown Estate, 16 Carlton House Terrace, London SW1Y 5AH *Telephone:* 071-210 4231

HUDSON, (NORMAN) BARRIE   Under Secretary, Africa Division, Overseas Development Administration   Grade: 3

Career: economist Tube Investments Ltd 1960-62, Economic Intelligence Unit 1962-63; statistics technical assistance adviser to Jordan government 1963-65; Overseas Development Ministry/Administration 1966-: statistician 1966-67, economic adviser British Middle East development division 1967-72, senior economic adviser 1973-74, head SE Asia development division 1974-76, assistant secretary 1977-80, under secretary (US) principal establishment officer 1981-85, US Africa division (Africa and Middle East) 1986-

Date of birth: 21 June 1937 *Education/professional qualifications:* King Henry VIII School, Coventry; Sheffield University, economics and French (BA 1958); University College, London, economics (MSc Econ 1960) *Marital status:* married Hazel 1963; 2 sons, 1 daughter *Recreations:* reading, theatre, walking, football, cricket

N Barrie Hudson Esq, Under Secretary, Overseas Development Administration, 94 Victoria Street, London SW1 *Telephone:* 071-917 0549

Regulatory Organisations and Public Bodies
see page 857

HUEBNER, MICHAEL DENIS   Deputy Secretary, Law and Policy, Lord Chancellor's Department   Grade: 2

Career: Lord Chancellor's Department 1966-: seconded to Law Officers' Department 1968-70; assistant solicitor 1978-85; under secretary 1985-89: NE circuit administrator 1985-88, principal establishment and finance officer 1988-89; deputy secretary 1989-: appointments and legislation 1989-91, head of law and policy groups 1991-

Date of birth: 3 September 1941 *Education/professional qualifications:* Rugby School; St John's College, Oxford, modern history (BA 1963); Gray's Inn (barrister 1965) *Marital status:* married Wendy Crosthwaite 1965; 1 son, 1 daughter

Michael D Huebner Esq, Deputy Secretary, Lord Chancellor's Department, Trevelyan House, Great Peter Street, London SW1P 2BY *Telephone:* 071-210 8734

HUGHES, Dr (ANTHONY) DAVID   Director of Research and Development, ADAS (Executive Agency)   Grade: 4

Career: Ministry of Agriculture, Fisheries and Food 1970-: soil scientist National Agricultural Advisory Service/Agricultural Development and Advisory Service (ADAS) 1970-84; administrative principal 1984-86; regional agricultural scientist ADAS/science adviser to Welsh Office 1986-88, ADAS 1988-: director field research and development (R&D) 1988-91, director of R&D 1991-

Date of birth: 22 September 1943 *Education/professional qualifications:* Dialstone Secondary Modern School, Stockport; Stockport School; Newcastle University, soil science (BSc 1967); Leeds University, soil science (PhD 1970) *Marital status:* married Janet Christine 1970; 1 daughter, 1 son *Publications:* contributor The Agricultural Notebook *Clubs:* Civil Service *Recreations:* gardening, swimming

Dr A David Hughes, Director of Research and Development, ADAS, Building A, Spires Business Park, Langley Lane, Kidlington, Oxford OX5 NZ

HUGHES, KATHERINE   Director, Welsh Consumer Council

Career: research associate University of Wales Institute of Science and Technology 1973-75; assistant planning officer mid-Glamorgan County Council 1975-77; Welsh Consumer Council 1977-: senior research officer 1977-78, director 1978-

Date of birth: 24 July 1949 *Education/professional qualifications:* Woodhouse Grammar School, London; Bethesda Chevy Chase High School, USA; East Anglia University, economics (BA 1971); University of Wales Institute of Science and Technology, town planning (MSc 1973); MRTPI 1983 *Marital status:* single *Recreations:* swimming, gardening, crafts

Miss Katherine Hughes, Director, Welsh Consumer Council, Castle Building, Womanby Street, Cardiff CF4 3BR *Telephone:* 0222 396056 *Fax:* 0222 238360

Complete Name Index
see page 955

HUGHES, (LEWIS) LEW HARRY   Assistant Auditor General, National Audit Office

Career: National Audit Office (examination of accounts of government departments, certain public bodies and international organisations) 1979-: audit manager, deputy director 1979-85; director of health audit 1985-88, of defence audit 1988-90; assistant auditor general 1991- *Current non-Whitehall posts:* board member Auditing Practices Board 1991-

Date of birth: 6 March 1945 *Education/professional qualifications:* Devenport High School, Plymouth; City of London College, accountancy audit and law (internal public sector qualification 1966) *Marital status:* married Irene 1975; 1 son *Clubs:* Tavistock Golf *Recreations:* golf, violin and piano-playing, vintage cars

Lew H Hughes Esq, Assistant Auditor General, National Audit Office, Buckingham Palace Road, London SW1W 9SP *Telephone:* 071-798 7678 *Fax:* 071-233 6163

HUMPHREYS, PETER JOHN   Director of Personnel, National Rivers Authority   Grade: 3

Career: personnel officer (PO) GEC Hotpoint 1970-72; PO William Press & Son 1972-75; PE group industrial relations manager British Steel 1975-83; personnel director Stanton plc 1983-89; director of personnel National Rivers Authority 1989-

Date of birth: 19 September 1947 *Education/professional qualifications:* St Ambrose College, Hale Barns, Cheshire; Newcastle Polytechnic, sociology (BSc 1969); Salford University, management (diploma 1970); corporate membership Institute of Personnel Management 1974 *Marital status:* married Glynis Megan 1971; 1 daughter, 1 son *Recreations:* swimming, squash

Peter J Humphreys Esq, Director of Personnel, National Rivers Authority, Rivers House, Waterside Drive, Aztec West, Almondsbury, Bristol BS12 4UD *Telephone:* 0454 624400 *Fax:* 0454 624479

HURLEY, Professor Dame ROSALINDE   Chairman, Medicines Commission

Career: consultant microbiologist Queen Charlotte's Hospital, London 1963-; chair Medicines Commission (regulation of medicines) 1982- *Current non-Whitehall posts:* professor Royal Postgraduate Medical School's Institute of Obstetrics and Gynaecology 1975-

Date of birth: 29 December 1929 *Education/professional qualifications:* Academy of the Assumption, Wellesley Hills, Massachusetts, USA; Queen's College, London; Charing Cross Hospital Medical School (MB, BS, LRCP, MRCS 1955); London University (MD 1962); Royal College of Pathologists (member 1964, fellow 1976); London University, law (LLB 1958); Inns of Court (barrister); D Univ (Surrey) 1984 *Honours, decorations:* DBE 1988 *Marital status:* married Peter Gortvai 1964 *Publications:* Candida albicans (Churchill 1964); Viral hepatitis (SOGsrl, Italy 1983) *Clubs:* Royal Society of Medicine *Recreations:* gardening, reading

Professor Dame Rosalinde Hurley DBE, Chairman, Medicines Commission, c/o Department of Microbiology, Queen Charlotte's and Chelsea Hospital, Goldhawk Road, London W6 0XG *Telephone:* 081-740 3923 *Fax:* 081-741 1948

To subscribe to The Whitehall Companion
Telephone: 071-240 3902

HUTCHESON, JAMES FORBES   Chief Agricultural Officer, Agriculture and Fisheries Department, Scottish Office   Grade: 4

Career: Scottish Office Agriculture and Fisheries Department 1958-: inspector 1971-79; senior/principal inspector 1979-81; assistant chief agricultural officer (AO) 1981-85; deputy chief AO 1985-87; chief AO 1987-

Date of birth: 1 May 1934 *Education/professional qualifications:* George Watson's Boys' College, Edinburgh; Edinburgh University, agriculture (BSc Agric 1955) *Marital status:* married Irene May Taylor 1964; 1 daughter, 2 sons *Clubs:* Watsonian, Mortonhall Golf, Nairn Golf *Recreations:* golf, music, gardening

James F Hutcheson Esq, Chief Agricultural Officer, Scottish Office Agriculture and Fisheries Department, Pentland House, 47 Robb's Loan, Edinburgh EH14 1TW *Telephone:* 031-244 6029 *Fax:* 031-244 6001

HUTTON, ANTHONY CHARLES   Principal Establishment and Finance Officer, Department of Trade and Industry   Grade: 2

Career: tax inspector Inland Revenue 1962-64; Board of Trade/Department of Trade [and Industry] 1964-: assistant principal 1964-68, principal 1968-77: principal private secretary to secretary of state for trade 1974-77, assistant secretary 1977-84, under secretary 1984-91, deputy secretary, principal establishment and finance officer 1991-

Date of birth: 4 April 1941 *Education/professional qualifications:* Brentwood School, Essex; Trinity College, Oxford, modern history (BA, MA 1962) *Marital status:* married Sara Flemming 1963; 2 sons, 1 daughter *Clubs:* Athenaeum *Recreations:* music, reading, odd-jobbing, walking

Anthony C Hutton Esq, Principal Establishment and Finance Officer, Department of Trade and Industry, Ashdown House, 123 Victoria Street, London, SW1E 6RB *Telephone:* 071-215 6911 *Fax:* 071-215 6917

I

INGE, General Sir PETER   Chief of General Staff, Ministry of Defence

Career: army service 1956-; Staff College student 1966; Ministry of Defence (MoD) 1967-69; Joint Services Staff College student 1971; Staff College instructor 1973-74; commandant Junior Division, Staff College 1977-79; director general logistic policy MoD (Army) 1986-87; chief of general staff, army, MoD 1992- *Current non-Whitehall posts:* colonel, The Green Howards 1982-; colonel commandant Royal Military Police 1987-; colonel commandant Army Physical Training Corps 1988-

Date of birth: 5 August 1935 *Education/professional qualifications:* Summer Fields School; Wrekin College *Honours, decorations:* KCB 1988, ADCGen 1991, GCB 1992 *Recreations:* military history, tennis

General Sir Peter Inge GCB ADCGen, Chief of General Staff, Ministry of Defence, Whitehall, London SW1A 2HB *Telephone:* 071-218 7873

INGLESE, ANTHONY MICHAEL CHRISTOPHER   Legal Director, Office of Fair Trading   Grade: 3

Career: Home Office 1975-91: senior legal assistant 1980-86; seconded to legal secretariat to law officers 1986-88; legal adviser's branch 1988-91; legal director Office of Fair Trading (advising on consumer and competition law) 1991-

Date of birth: 19 December 1951 *Education/professional qualifications:* Salvatorian College, Harrow Weald; Fitzwilliam College, Cambridge, law (BA 1974, LLB 1975) *Marital status:* married Jane Elizabeth Kerry Bailes 1974; 1 son, 1 daughter

Anthony M C Inglese Esq, Legal Director, Office of Fair Trading, Field House, 15-25 Breams Buildings, London EC4A 1PR *Telephone:* 071-269 8892

INNES, WILLIAM JAMES ALEXANDER   Head of Fire and Emergency Planning Department, Home Office   Grade: 3

Career: Home Office 1972-: seconded to Northern Ireland Office 1985-88; director of operational policy, prison department 1988-90; head of fire and emergency planning department 1991-

Date of birth: 11 October 1934 *Education/professional qualifications:* Aberdeen University (MA)

William J A Innes Esq, Head of Fire and Emergency Planning Department, Home Office, 50 Queen Anne's Gate, London SW1H 9AT *Telephone:* 071-273 3000

IRETON, BARRIE ROWLAND   Under Secretary Aid Policy Department, Principal Finance Officer, Overseas Development Administration   Grade: 3

Career: Overseas Development Administration 1973-: under secretary aid policy department and principal finance officer (joint ECO/ODA department) 1988-

Date of birth: 15 January 1944 *Education/professional qualifications:* Trinity College, Cambridge (MA); London School of Economics (MSc 1970)

Barrie R Ireton Esq, Under Secretary Aid Policy Department and Principal Finance Officer, Overseas Development Administration, Eland House, Stag Place, London SW1E 5DH *Telephone:* 071-273 0439

J

JACKLING, ROGER TUSTIN   Deputy Under Secretary (Resources and Programmes) Ministry of Defence   Grade: 2

Career: Ministry of Defence 1972-: assistant under secretary (programmes) 1989-91; deputy under secretary (resources and programmes) 1991-

Date of birth: 23 November 1943   *Education/professional qualifications:* New York University (BA); Jesus College, Oxford

Roger T Jackling Esq CBE, Deputy Under Secretary (Resources and Programmes), Ministry of Defence, Whitehall, London SW1A 2HB   *Telephone:* 071-218 9000

JACKSON, Air Chief Marshal Sir BRENDAN JAMES   Air Member for Supply and Organisation, Ministry of Defence

Career: RAF 1956-: chief of staff and deputy commander-in-chief RAF Strike Command 1986-88; air member for supply and organisation Ministry of Defence 1988-

Date of birth: 23 August 1935   *Education/professional qualifications:* London University, modern Japanese (BA)

Air Chief Marshal Sir Brendan J Jackson GCB, Air Member for Supply and Organisation, Ministry of Defence, Whitehall, London SW1A 2HB   *Telephone:* 071-218 9000

JACKSON, Major-General M D   Director-General of Personal Services (Army) Ministry of Defence

Major-General M D Jackson MBE, Director-General of Personal Services, Ministry of Defence, Main Building, Whitehall, London SW1A 2HB   *Telephone:* 071-218 9000

JAMES, Commodore REGINALD FREDERICK   Director-General Marine Engineering, Procurement Executive, Ministry of Defence

Career: engineer officer HMS Juno 1969-71; staff officer Royal Naval Engineering College (RNEC) 1971-74; senior engineer HMY Britannia 1974-75; project officer T22 frigate Ministry of Defence Procurement Executive, Sea Systems Controllerate (MoD[PE]/SSC) 1976-79; squadron marine engineer officer 1st frigate squadron 1979-81; director naval engineering RNEC 1981-83; assistant director MoD(PE)/SSC 1984-87; captain fleet maintenance Rosyth naval base 1987-88; MoD(PE)/SSC 1988-: director mechanical engineering 1988-89, director-general marine engineering 1989-

Date of birth: 6 September 1940   *Education/professional qualifications:* Pangbourne College; Royal Naval College, Dartmouth; Royal Naval Engineering College, Manadon   *Honours, decorations:* ADC 1990

Commodore Reginald F James ADC, Director-General Marine Engineering, Procurement Executive, Ministry of Defence, Foxhill, Bath BA1 5AB   *Telephone:* 0225 883935

JAMES, ROY LEWIS   Chief Inspector of Schools, Welsh Office   Grade: 4

Career: mathematics teacher/head of department, Surrey and Wales 1959-70; Welsh Office 1970-: schools inspector 1970-84: seconded as secretary to Schools Council committee for Wales 1975-77, staff inspector 1984-90, chief schools inspector 1990-

Date of birth: 9 February 1937   *Education/professional qualifications:* Llandysul Grammar School;

University College of Wales, Aberystwyth, mathematics (BSc 1959); education (postgraduate diploma 1959) *Marital status:* married Mary 1962; 1 daughter *Recreations:* travel, walking, reading

Roy L James Esq, Chief Inspector of Schools Welsh Office, Cathays Park, Cardiff CF1 3NQ *Telephone:* 0222 823431 *Fax:* 0222 823204

JAMES, STEVEN WYNNE LLOYD   Circuit Administrator, North-Eastern Circuit, Lord Chancellor's Department   Grade: 3

Career: Lord Chancellor's Department 1971-: deputy circuit administrator 1976-82; under secretary 1982; circuit administrator 1982-88; circuit administrator, north-eastern circuit 1988-

Date of birth: 9 June 1934 *Education/professional qualifications:* London School of Economics (LLB)

Steven W L James Esq, Circuit Administrator, North-Eastern Circuit Office, West Riding House, Albion Street, Leeds LS1 5AA *Telephone:* 0532-441841

JARMAN, ROGER WHITNEY   Under Secretary Housing, Health and Social Services Policy, Welsh Office   Grade: 3

Career: motor manufacturing company 1960-64; assistant secretary to appointments board Bristol University 1964-68; principal Civil Service Commission 1968-72; Welsh Office 1972-: principal European division 1972-74, assistant secretary (AS) devolution division 1974-78, AS permanent secretary's division 1978-80, under secretary (US) land use and planning group 1980-83, US transport planning, water and environmental group 1983-89, US housing, health and social services policy group 1988-

Date of birth: 16 February 1935 *Education/professional qualifications:* Cathays High School, Cardiff; Birmingham University, economics, politics and sociology (BSocSc 1957), teaching (PGCE 1960) *Marital status:* married Patricia Dorothy 1959; 1 son *Clubs:* Civil Service

Roger W Jarman Esq, Under Secretary, Welsh Office, Cathays Park, Cardiff CF1 3NQ *Telephone:* 0222 825257

JAY, MICHAEL HASTINGS   Assistant Under Secretary, EC Affairs, Foreign and Commonwealth Office

Career: Ministry of Overseas Development (ODM) 1969-73; UK delegation to International Monetary Fund/World Bank, Washington DC 1973-75; ODM 1976-78; first secretary New Delhi high commission 1978-81; Foreign and Commonwealth Office (FCO), London 1981-85; seconded as counsellor to Cabinet Office 1985-87; financial and commercial counsellor Paris embassy 1987-90; assistant under secretary for EC FCO 1990-

Date of birth: 19 June 1946 *Education/professional qualifications:* Winchester College; Magdalen College, Oxford (BA, MA); School of Oriental and African Studies, London (MSc 1969) *Marital status:* married Sylvia Mylroie 1975

Michael H Jay Esq, Assistant Under Secretary, Foreign and Commonwealth Office, Downing Street East, London SW1A 2AL *Telephone:* 071-270 3000

JEFFERSON, (JOHN) BRYAN   Chairman, PSA Projects, Department of the Environment   Grade: 2

Career: architect 1957-84: president Royal Institute of British Architects 1979-81; Department of the Environent (DoE) 1984-: director general of design, Property Services Agency (PSA) 1984-, chairman PSA projects (pre-design advice, quality control project management for major construction works) 1984-, chief architectural adviser secretary of state, DoE 1984-

Date of birth: 26 April 1928 *Education/professional qualifications:* Lady Manners School, Bakewell; Sheffield University (Dipl Arch 1952) *Honours, decorations:* CBE 1983, CB 1989 *Marital status:* divorced *Clubs:* Royal Western Yacht *Recreations:* sailing

J Bryan Jefferson Esq CB CBE, Chairman, PSA Projects, Department of the Environment, 2 Marsham Street, London SW1P 3EB
Telephone: 071-276 3625 *Fax:* 071-276 4902

JEFFERSON SMITH, PETER   Deputy Chairman and Principal Establishments and Finance Officer, HM Customs and Excise   Grade: 2

Career: HM Customs and Excise (C & E) 1960-68: assistant principal 1961-65, principal 1965-68; principal HM Treasury 1968-71; C & E 1971-: principal (1971-73; assistant secretary 1973-80; commissioner 1980-88: director of organisation 1980-83, of internal taxes 1983-88; deputy chairman (DC) internal taxes and customs group 1988-89; DC and principal establishments and finance officer corporate services and outfield group 1989-

Date of birth: 14 July 1939 *Education/professional qualifications:* Cranleigh School, Surrey; Trinity College, Cambridge, history (BA 1960) *Honours, decorations:* CB 1992 *Marital status:* married Anna Willett 1964; 2 daughters

Peter Jefferson Smith Esq CB, Deputy Chairman, HM Customs and Excise, 22 Upper Ground, London SE1 9PJ *Telephone:* 071-865 5010

JEFFREY, BILL   Assistant Under Secretary (Operations and Resources) and Chief Inspector Immigration and Nationality Department, Home Office   Grade: 3

Career: Home Office 1971-: under secretary (operations and resources) and chief inspector immigration and nationality department 1991-
Education/professional qualifications: Glasgow University

Bill Jeffrey Esq, Under Secretary, (Operations and Resources), and Chief Inspector Immigration and Nationality Department, Home Office, Lunar House, 40 Wellesley Road, Croydon CR9 2BY
Telephone: 071-273 3000

JEFFREYS, Dr DAVID BARRINGTON   Business Manager, European and New Drugs Licensing, Medicines Control Agency (Executive Agency)   Grade: 4

Career: medical posts Guy's and St Thomas hospitals, London 1976-83; locum consultant physician Tunbridge Wells 1983-84; Medicines Control Agency 1984-: business manager of European and new drug licensing 1986- *Current non-Whitehall posts:* alternate delegate to Committee on Proprietary Medicinal Products (CPMG); chairman CPMG operations working party, Pharmaceutical Evaluation Report Scheme

Date of birth: 1 August 1952 *Education/professional qualifications:* St Dunstan's College, London; London University (BSc 1973, MD 1983); Guy's Hospital (MB BS 1976); MRCP 1978; FRCP 1989; FFPM 1990 *Marital status:* married Ann-Marie 1985; 1 daughter, 1 son *Clubs:* Surrey County Cricket *Recreations:* sport, theatre, music, photography, art

Dr David B Jeffreys, Business Manager, European and New Drugs Licensing, Medicines Control Agency, 1 Nine Elms Lane, London SW8 5NP *Telephone:* 071-720 2188

JENKINS, GARTH JOHN   Legal Adviser, Ministry of Agriculture, Fisheries and Food   Grade: 2

Career: Birmingham Corporation 1954-64; Southshields Corporation 1964-67; Land Commission 1967-71; Ministry of Agriculture, Fisheries and Food 1971-: under secretary 1981-, legal adviser 1983-

Date of birth: 7 December 1933 *Education/professional qualifications:* Birmingham Royal Institute for the Blind; Royal National College for the Blind; Birmingham University, law (LLB) *Marital status:* married Patricia Margaret Lindsay 1965; 1 daughter *Recreations:* literature, theatre, music, chess, food, drink, conversation

Garth J Jenkins Esq, Legal Adviser, Ministry of Agriculture, Fisheries and Food, 55 Whitehall, London SW1A 2EY *Telephone:* 071-270 8379 *Fax:* 071-270 8096

JENKINS, (JAMES) CHRISTOPHER   Second Parliamentary Counsel, Parliamentary Counsel Office   Grade: 2

Career: Parliamentary Counsel Office 1967-: seconded to Law Commission 1970-72, 1983-86; parliamentary counsel 1978-91; second parliamentary counsel 1991-

Date of birth: 20 May 1939 *Education/professional qualifications:* Magdalen College, Oxford

Christopher Jenkins Esq, Second Parliamentary Counsel, Parliamentary Counsel Office, 36 Whitehall, London SW1A 2AY *Telephone:* 071-210 6633

JOHNS, MICHAEL ALAN   Director, Central Division, Inland Revenue   Grade: 3

Career: Inland Revenue (IR) 1967-79: principal 1971-79; adviser to Cabinet Office Central Policy Review Staff 1979-80; IR 1980-: assistant secretary (AS) 1980-84, seconded to Orion Royal Bank 1985, AS 1986-87, director policy division 1987-88, director oil and financial division 1988-91, director central division (corporate planning, budget and finance bill advice co-ordination; economic advice on direct taxation) 1992-

Date of birth: 20 July 1946 *Education/professional qualifications:* Judd School, Tonbridge; Queen's College, Cambridge, history (BA 1967, MA) *Marital status:* single *Recreations:* skiing, teaching adults, moral philosophy

Michael A Johns Esq, Director, Central Division, Inland Revenue, Somerset House, Strand, London WC2R 1LB *Telephone:* 071-438 7739 *Fax:* 071-438 6148

Parliamentary Offices
see page 275

JOHNSON, ALBERT GEORGE   Director of Finance and Resources, Employment Service, (Executive Agency)   Grade: 4

Career: head of branch, Commission on Industrial Relations 1972-74, Advisory, Conciliation and Arbitration Service 1974-79; Department of Employment (DEm) 1979-: head of careers service 1979-83, of employment policy 1983-85, of industrial relations 1985-90; director of finance and resources DEmp Employment Service executive agency 1990-

Date of birth: 28 May 1937 *Education/professional qualifications:* Bancroft's School, Woodford; St Peter's College, Oxford, history (BA, MA 1960); Birkbeck College, London, psychology (BSc 1971) *Marital status:* married Laura Edith 1967; 2 sons, 1 daughter

Albert G Johnson Esq, Director of Finance and Resources, Employment Service Agency, St Vincent House, 30 Orange Street, London WC2H 7HT *Telephone:* 071-389 1538 *Fax:* 071-389 1457

JOHNSTON, ANDREW IAN   Chief Actuary, Public Service Pensions, Government Actuary's Department

Career: chief actuary, public services pensions, Government Actuary's Department 1991-

Date of birth: 10 January 1956 *Education/professional qualifications:* Harrogate Grammar School; St Edmund Hall, Oxford, mathematics (BA 1978); FIA 1984 *Marital status:* married Sara; 1 daughter

Andrew I Johnston Esq, Chief Actuary, Government Actuary's Department, 22 Kingsway, London WC2B 6LE *Telephone:* 071-242 6828 *Fax:* 071-831 6653

JOHNSTON, Dr IAN ALISTAIR   Director, Resources and Strategy, Employment Department Group   Grade: 2

Career: assistant principal Department of Employment (DEmp) 1969-75; labour attache Brussels embassy 1975-77; director Advisory Conciliation Arbitration Service 1978-82; DEmp 1984-: deputy director-general training education enterprise directorate 1984-92, director resources and strategy 1992-

Date of birth: 2 May 1944 *Education/professional qualifications:* High Wycombe Grammar School; Birmingham University, metallurgy (BSc 1966, PhD 1969) *Marital status:* married Mary Bridget Lube 1973; 1 daughter, 1 son *Publications:* 'Changing Environment' chapter in Gower Handbook of Training and Development (Gower 1991)

Dr Ian A Johnston, Director, Resources and Strategy Directorate, Employment Department Group, Moorfoot, Sheffield S1 4PQ *Telephone:* 0742 594108 *Fax:* 0742 593295

JOHNSTON, Maj-Gen JAMES FREDERICK JUNOR   Director-General, Army Manning and Recruitment, Ministry of Defence

Career: army service 1959-: deputy chief of staff 4 Armoured Division 1981-84; assistant chief of staff HQ BAOR 1986-89; director-general army manning and recruiting Ministry of Defence 1990-
Current non-Whitehall posts: chairman Army Sport Control Board 1990-

Date of birth: 5 August 1939 *Education/professional qualifications:* George Watson's College, Edinburgh; Welbeck College, Worksop; Royal Military Academy, Sandhurst; Royal Military College of Science, engineering (BSc Eng 1962); CEng, Eur Ing, FIMechE, FBIM *Honours, decorations:* CBE 1984 *Recreations:* travel, photography, postal history

Major-General James F J Johnston CBE, Director-General, Army Manning and Recruiting, Ministry of Defence, Whitehall, London SW1A 2HB *Telephone:* 071-218 7536 *Fax:* 071-218 3561

JOHNSTON, (ROBERT) GORDON SCOTT   Managing Director, Property Services Agency International   Grade: 3

Career: army national service 1955-57; Air Ministry 1957-64: assistant principal 1957-59, private secretary (PS) to parliamentary under secretary 1959-62, principal overseas works secretariat 1962-64; secretary building regulation advisory committee Ministry of Public Building and Works (MPBW) 1964-68: 1964-65; principal PS to Ministers of PBW 1965-68; seconded as financial adviser to Shell International Chemical Co 1968-70; assistant director of home estate Property Services Agency (PSA). Department of the Environment 1970-73; seconded to Cabinet Office 1973-75; railways directorate Department of Transport 1975-79; Price Commission 1979; PSA 1979-: director of civil accommodation 1979-88, of defence services 1988-90, managing director PSA International (building and maintenance in overseas territories) 1990-

Date of birth: 27 August 1933 *Education/professional qualifications:* Clifton College, Bristol; Clare College, Cambridge, classics (BA 1955, MA) *Marital status:* married Jill Maureen Campbell 1960; 1 son, 1 daughter

R Gordon S Johnston Esq, Managing Director, PSA International, Whitgift Centre, Wellesley Road, Croydon CR9 3LY *Telephone:* 081-760 3671 *Fax:* 081-760 3654

JOHNSTONE, (JOHN) RAYMOND   Chairman, Forestry Commission

Career: investment analyst for merchant bankers 1955-60; investment management partner, chartered accountants firm 1960-68; managing director investment managers firm 1968-89; chairman Forestry Commission 1989- *Current non-Whitehall posts:* director Scottish Amicable Life Assurance 1971-; chairman Dominion Insurance Co 1978-, Murray Johnstone Ltd 1984-; honorary president Scottish Opera 1986-; director Glasgow Cultural Enterprise 1988-

Date of birth: 27 October 1929 *Education/professional qualifications:* Eton; Trinity College, Cambridge, mathematics (BA 1951); CA *Honours, decorations:* CBE 1988 *Marital status:* married Sara 1979; 2 stepdaughters, 5 stepsons *Clubs:* Western, Glasgow *Recreations:* fishing, shooting, opera

J Raymond Johnstone Esq CBE, Chairman Forestry Commission, 231 Corstorphine Road, Edinburgh EH12 7AT *Telephone:* 031-334 0303 *Fax:* 031-316 4891

Government Departments
see page 300

JONES, GLYNN   Circuit Administrator, Western Circuit, Lord Chancellor's Department   Grade: 4

Career: Local Government Service 1950-71; Lord Chancellor's Department 1971-: circuit administrator, western circuit 1987-

Date of birth: 5 March 1933   *Education/professional qualifications:* Pontllanfraith Grammar Technical School

Glynn Jones Esq, Circuit Administrator, Western Circuit Office, Bridge House, Clifton Down, Bristol BS8 4BN   *Telephone:* 0272-745763

JONES, (JAMES) ROGER   Deputy Parliamentary Counsel, Parliamentary Counsel Office

Career: barrister 1975-83; Parliamentary Counsel Office 1983-: assistant parliamentary counsel (APC) 1983-88, senior APC with Law Commission 1988-91, deputy PC (drafting of parliamentary bills) 1991-

Date of birth: 30 May 1952   *Education/professional qualifications:* Shrewsbury School; St Catharine's College, Cambridge, history and law (BA 1973, MA)   *Clubs:* Travellers   *Recreations:* walking dog

J Roger Jones Esq, Deputy Parliamentary Counsel, Office of the Parliamentary Counsel, 36 Whitehall, London SW1A 2AY   *Telephone:* 071-210 6612   *Fax:* 071-210 6632

JONES, Dr KEITH HOWARD   Chief Executive, Medicines Control Agency (Executive Agency)   Grade: 3

Date of birth: 14 October 1937

Dr Keith H Jones, Chief Executive, Medicines Control Agency, Market Towers, 1 Nine Elms Lane, London SW8 5NQ   *Telephone:* 071-720 2188

JONES, Dr (MIAH GWYNFOR) GWYN   Chairman, Welsh Development Agency

Career: British Steel Corporation; ICL; chairman Corporate Technology Group plc 1981-87; chairman Welsh Development Agency (economy and environment) 1988-   *Current non-Whitehall posts:* director ACT Group plc 1990-, Welsh Water Enterprises Ltd 1990-

Date of birth: 2 December 1948   *Education/professional qualifications:* Eifionydd School, Porthmadog; Manchester University, computer science (BSc 1970); Essex University, computer networks (PhD 1977)   *Marital status:* married Maria Johnson 1976; 2 daughters   *Recreations:* golf, skiing, tennis

Dr M Gwyn Jones, Chairman, Welsh Development Agency, Pearl House, Greyfriars Road, Cardiff CF1 3XX   *Telephone:* 0222 222666   *Fax:* 0222 237166

JONES, PETER BENJAMIN GURNER   Director of Personnel, Inland Revenue   Grade: 3

Career: Inland Revenue 1957-: tax inspector (TI) 1957-63; higher grade TI 1963-69; Senior TI 1969-78; principal TI: head office, PAYE 1975-78, City 3 1978-80; senior principal TI head office technical division 1980-81; under secretary 1981-: director of data processing 1981-84, of personnel 1984-

Date of birth: 25 December 1932   *Education/professional qualifications:* Bancroft's School, Woodford

Green, Essex; St Catherine's Society, Oxford, English language and literature (BA 1956) *Honours, decorations:* CB 1991 *Marital status:* married Diana Margaret Henley 1962; 1 daughter, 1 son

Peter B G Jones Esq CB, Director of Personnel, Inland Revenue, Bush House, Aldwych, London WC2B 4PP *Telephone:* 071-438 6780 *Fax:* 071-438 7186

JONES, (RICHARD) DICK ADRIAN JEREMY   East London Regional Controller, Inland Revenue   Grade: 4

Career: Inland Revenue 1956-: East London regional controller 1988-

Date of birth: 9 October 1936 *Education/professional qualifications:* Bideford Grammar School *Marital status:* married Ida Elizabeth 1961; 1 son *Publications:* contributor to One Day for Life (Bantam 1987); The Tree (David and Charles 1990) *Clubs:* Royal Photographic Society *Recreations:* photography, tennis, walking, reading

Dick Jones Esq, Controller, East London Region, Inland Revenue, New Court, 48 Carey Street, London WC2A 2JE *Telephone:* 071-324 1232 *Fax:* 071-324 1298

JOYCE, PETER ROBERT   Inspector General and Chief Executive, Insolvency Service (Executive Agency)   Grade: 3

Career: Department of Trade and Industry 1960-: Insolvency Service (IS) 1960-79; consumer affairs 1979-81; IS 1981-: chief examiner 1981-82, official receiver 1982-84, principal examiner 1984-85, deputy inspector general 1985-89, inspector general and chief executive IS executive agency (administration and investigation of bankruptcies) 1989-

Date of birth: 14 January 1942 *Education/professional qualifications:* Westwood's Grammar School, Northleach, Gloucestershire; FCCA 1970 *Marital status:* married Marian 1988

Peter R Joyce Esq, Chief Executive, Insolvency Service, Bridge Place, 88-89 Ecclestone Square, London SW1V 1PT *Telephone:* 071-215 0770 *Fax:* 071-215 0764

K

KEEMER, PETER JOHN CHARLES   Assistant Auditor General, National Audit Office

Career: Exchequer and Audit Department (EAD) 1952-65: private secretary to comptroller and auditor general 1962-65; Office of Parliamentary Commissioner for Administration (Ombudsman) 1966-70; EAD/National Audit Office 1970-: chief auditor 1970-73, deputy director 1973-77, director 1978-89: seconded to EC Court of Auditors as director 1978-86, assistant auditor general (for Departments of Health, Employment and Social Security) 1989-

Date of birth: 27 January 1932 *Education/professional qualifications:* Price's School, Fareham; Bath University (MPhil 1986) *Marital status:* married Yvonne Griffin 1954; 1 daughter, 1 son *Clubs:* Anglo-Belgian

Peter J C Keemer Esq, Assistant Auditor General, National Audit Office, Buckingham Palace Road, London SW1W 9SP *Telephone:* 071-798 7390 *Fax:* 071-233 6163

KEITH, MICHAEL ALAN   Assistant Director, Financial Institutions Division, Inland Revenue   Grade: 4

Career: Inland Revenue 1954-: assistant director financial institutions division (taxation of building societies, unit and investment trusts, securities markets, foreign exchange, financial instruments) 1989-

Date of birth: 23 March 1935 *Education/professional qualifications:* Heles School, Exeter

Michael A Keith Esq, Assistant Director, Inland Revenue, Somerset House, Strand, London WC2R 1LB *Telephone:* 071-438 6262 *Fax:* 071-438 7752

KELLY, CHRISTOPHER WILLIAM   Under Secretary, Social Services and Territorial Group, HM Treasury   Grade: 3

Career: HMT Treasury 1970-: private secretary to financial secretary 1971-73; secretary to Wilson Committee of Inquiry into Financial Institutions 1978-80; under secretary social services and territorial group 1987-

Date of birth: 18 August 1946 *Education/professional qualifications:* Beaumont School, Windsor; Trinity College, Cambridge, economics (BA 1968); Manchester University, sociology (MA Econ 1970) *Marital status:* married Alison Durant 1970; 2 sons, 1 daughter *Recreations:* narrow boating

Christopher W Kelly Esq, Under Secretary, HM Treasury, Parliament Street, London SW1P 3AG *Telephone:* 071-270 4500 *Fax:* 071-270 5671

KENDELL, Dr ROBERT EVAN   Chief Medical Officer, Home and Health Department, Scottish Office

Career: visiting professor Vermont University College of Medicine, USA 1969-70; reader in psychiatry Institute of Psychiatry, London University 1970-74; member Medical Research Council 1984-88; psychiatry professor Edinburgh University 1986-90; chief medical officer Scottish Office Home and Health Department 1991- *Current non-Whitehall posts:* member World Health Organisation expert advisory panel on mental health 1979-

Date of birth: 28 March 1935 *Education/professional qualifications:* Mill Hill School, London ; Peterhouse, Cambridge (BA 1956, MB, BChir, MA 1959, MD 1967) *Honours, decorations:* Gaskell Gold Medal of Royal College of Psychiatrists 1967, Paul Hoch Medal of American Psychopathological Association 1988 *Marital status:* married Dr Ann Whitfield 1961; 2 daughters, 2 sons *Publications:* The Classification of Depressive Illnesses (OUP 1968); Psychiatric Diagnosis in New York and London (OUP 1972); The Role of Diagnosis in Psychiatry (Blackwell Scientific 1975) *Clubs:* Climbers' *Recreations:* overeating, hill walking

Dr Robert E Kendell, Chief Medical Officer, Scottish Office Home and Health Department, St Andrew's House, Edinburgh EH1 3DD *Telephone:* 031-244 2264 *Fax:* 031-244 2683

KENT, BRIAN DUNCAN   Controller, Capital Taxes Office, Inland Revenue   Grade: 4

Career: Inland Revenue 1957-: estate duty/capital taxes office (CTO) 1957-74: examiner 1962-69, senior examiner 1969-75, chief examiner 1975-81, manpower and organisation division 1974-77, international division 1977-81, CTO 1981-: deputy controller 1981-90, controller (inheritance tax, tax on unquoted shares, both ex-Scotland) 1990-

Date of birth: 7 April 1939 *Education/professional qualifications:* Hove Grammar School; King's College, London, law (LLB 1961) *Marital status:* married Jill Rosemary 1961; 1 son, 1 daughter *Recreations:* walking, skiing, cricket, crosswords, reading

Brian D Kent Esq, Controller, Capital Taxes Office, Minford House, Rockley Road, London W14 0DF *Telephone:* 071-603 4622 *Fax:* 071-603 4622

KENWORTHY, (FREDERICK) JOHN   Chief Executive, Social Security Information Technology Services Agency (Executive Agency)   Grade: 3

Career: assistant principal: Ministry of Defence (MoD) Navy 1966-68, HM Treasury Centre for administrative studies 1968-69, seconded to British Steel Corporation 1969-72; principal: MoD defence sales 1972-74, Royal Commission on the Press secretariat 1974-79; MoD 1979-86: assistant secretary, director weapons resources and programmes 1979-83; head of resources and programmes Royal Navy size and shape policy 1983-86; director of operations Disablement Services Authority 1986-88; Department of Social Security 1989-: under secretary, director information services directorate 1989-90; chief executive Social Security Information Technology Services Agency (computing and communication systems for DSS and agencies) 1990-

Date of birth: 6 December 1943 *Education/professional qualifications:* William Hulme's Grammar School, Manchester; Manchester University, politics (BA Econ) *Marital status:* married Diana Flintham 1968; 1 daughter *Clubs:* Lansdown Lawn Tennis and Squash Racquets, Bath *Recreations:* music, sport, photography

F John Kenworthy Esq, Chief Executive, Social Security Information Technology Services, Euston Tower, 286 Euston Road, London NW1 3DN *Telephone:* 071-383 3884 *Fax:* 071-387 6826

KERBY, JOHN VYVYAN   Principal Establishment Officer and Under Secretary, Overseas Manpower Division, Overseas Development Administration   Grade: 3

Career: assistant principal Colonial Office 1965-67; Ministry of Overseas Development 1967-70; private secretary to parliamentary under secretary Foreign and Commonwealth Office 1970-71; principal: Overseas Development Administration (ODA) 1971-74, Civil Service Selection Board 1974-75; ODA 1975-: principal 1975-77, head of British development division in Southern Africa 1983-86, principal establishment officer and under secretary overseas manpower division 1986- *Current non-Whitehall posts:* governor Centre for International Briefing 1986-

Date of birth: 14 December 1942 *Education/professional qualifications:* Eton; Christ Church, Oxford, classics (BA 1965, MA) *Marital status:* married Shirley Elizabeth 1977; 1 stepson, 1 stepdaughter *Recreations:* gardening, cricket, entomology

John V Kerby Esq, Principal Establishment Officer and Under Secretary of State, Overseas Development Administration, 94 Victoria Street, London SW1E 5JL *Telephone:* 071-917 0380 *Fax:* 071-917 0686

KERRIGAN, GREER SANDRA   Head of Legal Division, Department of Social Security   Grade: 3

Career: under secretary, solicitor's office Department of Social Security 1991-

Date of birth: 7 August 1948 *Education/professional qualifications:* Bishop Anstey High School, Port of Spain, Trinidad; Council of Legal Education, law (barrister 1971) *Marital status:* married Donal Brian 1974; 1 son, 1 daughter *Recreations:* reading, bridge, squash

Mrs Greer S Kerrigan, Under Secretary, Department of Social Security, New Court, 48 Carey Street, London WC2A 2LS *Telephone:* 071-412 1341 *Fax:* 071-412 1583

KERSE, CHRISTOPHER STEPHEN   Under Secretary, Head of Consumer Affairs Division, Department of Trade and Industry   Grade: 3

Career: Office of Fair Trading 1976-81; Department of Trade and Industry 1981-; under secretary 1988-, head of consumer affairs division 1991-

Date of birth: 12 December 1946 *Education/professional qualifications:* University of Hull (LLB); solicitor 1972

Christopher S Kerse Esq, Under Secretary, Head of Consumer Affairs Division, Department of Trade and Industry, 10-18 Victoria Street, London SW1H 0NN *Telephone:* 071-215 5000

KESWICK, (ANNABEL THERESE) TESSA   Special Adviser to Home Secretary   Grade: 3

Career: founder member Cluff Oil plc 1971; London editor Business and Energy International 1974-79; London borough councillor 1982-86; director Cluff Investments and Trading 1983-; special adviser to Kenneth Clarke secretary of state education and science 1989-92, Home Secretary 1992-

Date of birth: 15 October 1942 *Education/professional qualifications:* Convent of the Sacred Heart, Woldingham, Surrey *Marital status:* married Henry 1985; 2 sons, 1 daughter by former marriage *Recreations:* riding and horse breeding; collecting books and pictures

Mrs Tessa Keswick, Special Adviser, Home Office, 50 Queen Anne's Gate, London SW1H 9AT *Telephone:* 071-273 2713 *Fax:* 071-273 3596

KIDGELL, JOHN EARLE   Head of Division 3, Central Statistical Office   Grade: 3

Career: Central Statistical Office (CSO) and Treasury 1970-79; Department of the Environment and Property Services Agency 1979-88; CSO 1988-: head of division 3 1991-

Date of birth: 18 November 1943 *Education/professional qualifications:* University of St Andrews (MA); London School of Economics (MSc)

John E Kidgell Esq, Head of Division 3, Central Statistical Office, Great George St, London SW1
Telephone: 071-270 6040

KIRK, MALCOLM WINDSOR   Controller, Inland Revenue, Wales   Grade: 4

Career: Inland Revenue 1972-: district inspector Newport, Gwent 1972-74; claims branch advisory division 1974-80; district inspector Soho 1980-81; management division personnel 1981-; group controller Wales 1981-83; head of Llanishen tax complex 1983-87; district inspector Bristol 1987-89; controller Wales 1989-

Date of birth: 9 July 1943 *Education/professional qualifications:* Canton High School for Boys, Cardiff; Leicester University, geography and industrial location (BA 1966) *Marital status:* married Glenys 1965; 1 daughter *Recreations:* bonsai trees, averting gaze from rugby field

Malcolm W Kirk Esq, Controller, Inland Revenue Wales, Tŷ Rhodfa Tŷ Glas Avenue, Llanishen, Cardiff CF4 5TS *Telephone:* 0222 755789
Fax: 0222 755730

KNAPP, TREVOR FREDERICK WILLIAM BERESFORD   Assistant Under Secretary, Infrastructure and Logistics, Ministry of Defence   Grade: 3

Career: Ministry of Aviation 1961; secretary Downey Committee 1965-66; secretary British Defence Research and Supply Staff, Canberra 1968-72; assistant secretary Ministry of Defence (MoD) 1974; GEC Turbine Generators Ltd 1976; Central Policy Review Staff, Cabinet Office 1977-79; MoD 1983-: director-general marketing 1983-88, assistant under secretary (AUS) (supply and organisation, air) 1988-92, AUS (infrastructure and logistics) 1992-

Date of birth: 26 May 1937 *Education/professional qualifications:* Christ's Hospital; King's College, London University (BSc 1958); ARIC 1960

Trevor F W B Knapp Esq, Assistant Under Secretary, Ministry of Defence, Whitehall, London SW1A 2HB *Telephone:* 071-218 9000

KNILL, Professor JOHN LAWRENCE   Chairman, Natural Environment Research Council   Grade: 2

Career: academic posts, Imperial College 1957-: professor of engineering geology 1973- (on leave of absence); dean Royal School of Mines 1980-83; chairman Natural Environment Research Council 1988- *Current non-Whitehall posts:* chairman Radioactive Waste Management Committee 1987-; member Joint Nature Conservation Committee 1990-

Date of birth: 22 November 1934 *Education/professional qualifications:* Whitgift School, Croydon; Imperial College, London, geology (BSc 1955, PhD 1957, DSc 1981); FICE 1981; FIGeol 1985; FEng 1991 *Marital status:* married Diane Constance Judge 1957; 1 daughter, 1 son *Clubs:* Athenaeum, Chaps *Recreations:* viticulture

Professor John L Knill, Chairman, Natural Environment Research Council, Polaris House, North Star Avenue, Swindon SN2 1EU
Telephone: 0793 411653 *Fax:* 0793 411691

KNORPEL, HENRY   Counsel to the Speaker, House of Commons   Grade: 3

Career: barrister 1947-52; Ministry of [Pensions and] National Insurance 1952-65: legal assistant (LA) 1952-58, senior LA 1958-65; senior LA: Law Commision 1965-67, Ministry of Social Security 1967-68; Department of Health and Social Security (DHSS) 1968-78: assistant solicitor (AS) 1968-71, principal AS 1971-78; solicitor DHSS, Office of Population Censuses and Surveys, General Register Office 1978-85; counsel to the Speaker, House of Commons (legal advice to speaker, MPs, committees etc) 1985-   *Current non-Whitehall posts:* bencher Inner Temple 1990-

Date of birth: 18 August 1924   *Education/professional qualifications:* City of London School; Magdalen College, Oxford, jurisprudence (BA 1945, BCL 1946, MA); Inner Temple (barrister 1947)   *Honours, decorations:* CB 1982, QC 1988   *Marital status:* married Brenda Sterling 1953; 2 daughters   *Recreations:* relaxing

Henry Knorpel Esq CB QC, Counsel to the Speaker, House of Commons, London SW1A 0AA   *Telephone:* 071-219 3776   *Fax:* 071-219 5568

KNOWLES, PETER FRANCIS ARNOLD   Parliamentary Counsel, Parliamentary Counsel Office   Grade: 2

Career: Parliamentary Counsel Office 1975-: seconded to Law Commission 1979-81; parliamentary counsel 1991-

Date of birth: 10 July 1949   *Education/professional qualifications:* University College, Oxford (MA)

Peter F A Knowles Esq, Parliamentary Counsel, Parliamentary Counsel Office, 36 Whitehall, London SW1A 2AY   *Telephone:* 071-210 6633

KNOX, JOHN ANDREW   Deputy Director, Serious Fraud Office   Grade: 2

Career: Serious Fraud Office 1987-: chief accountant 1987-90; deputy director 1990-

Date of birth: 22 July 1937   *Education/professional qualifications:* Merton College, Oxford (MA)

John A Knox Esq, Deputy Director, Serious Fraud Office, Elm House, Elm Street, London WC1X 0BJ   *Telephone:* 071-239 7272

KOWALSKI, GREGOR   Assistant Legal Secretary and Scottish Parliamentary Counsel, Lord Advocate's Department   Grade: 3

Career: Lord Advocate's Department 1978-: assistant legal secretary to the Lord Advocate 1978-, Scottish parliamentary counsel 1987-

Date of birth: 7 October 1949   *Education/professional qualifications:* Strathclyde University, law (1972)

Gregor Kowalski Esq, Assistant Legal Secretary and Scottish Parliamentary Counsel, Lord Advocate's Department, Fielden House, 10 Great College Street, London SW1P 3SL   *Telephone:* 071-276 3000

L

LAING, ELEANOR Special Adviser to Secretary of State for Transport

Career: solicitor 1983-88; special adviser to John MacGregor, secretary of state for education and science 1989-90, lord president of the council and leader of the House of Commons 1990-92, secretary of state for transport 1992-

Date of birth: 1 February 1958 *Education/professional qualifications:* St Columba's School, Kilmacolm, Renfrewshire; Edinburgh University, history and economics (BA 1980), law (LLB 1982) *Marital status:* married Alan 1983 *Recreations:* theatre, music, golf

Mrs Eleanor Laing, Special Adviser, Department of Transport, 2 Marsham Street, London SW1P 3EB *Telephone:* 071-276 5090 *Fax:* 071-276 5139

LAING, JAMES FINDLAY Under Secretary, Environment Department, Scottish Office Grade: 3

Career: assistant principal/principal Scottish Office (SO) 1957-68; principal HM Treasury 1969-71; SO 1972-: assistant secretary 1972-79, under secretary (US) Industry Department 1979-88, US environment protection and rural affairs Environment Department 1988-

Date of birth: 7 November 1933 *Education/professional qualifications:* Nairn Academy; Edinburgh University, history (MA 1955) *Marital status:* married Christine Joy Canaway 1969; 1 son *Recreations:* squash, chess

James F Laing Esq, Under Secretary, Scottish Office Environment Department, New St Andrew's House, Edinburgh EH1 3SZ *Telephone:* 031-244 4052 *Fax:* 031-244 4785

LAMBERT, DAVID GEORGE Solicitor and Legal Adviser, Welsh Office Grade: 3

Career: solicitor 1964-; Welsh Office 1966-: lawyer 1966-74, assistant legal adviser 1974-91, solicitor and legal adviser 1991- *Current non-Whitehall posts:* diocesan registrar Llandaff diocese, Church in Wales 1986-; tutor University College of Wales, Cardiff 1972-

Date of birth: 7 August 1940 *Education/professional qualifications:* Boys' Grammar School, Barry; University of Wales, Aberystwyth, law (LLB 1961); Law Society (solicitor 1964) *Marital status:* married Diana Mary 1966; 1 son, 1 daughter *Recreations:* ecclesiastical law, classical music

David G Lambert Esq, Solicitor and Legal Adviser, Welsh Office, Cathays Park, Cardiff CF1 3NQ *Telephone:* 0222 823510

LAMBERT, JOHN Director of Operations (North and West), Training, Enterprise and Education Directorate, Employment Department Group Grade: 3

Career: Department of Employment 1970-; private secretary to permanent secretary 1973-74; on secondment to Marconi Space and Defence Systems 1977-78; deputy chief conciliation officer ACAS 1982-83; head of European Communities branch 1983-85; director of field operations Manpower Services Commission 1987-90; director of operations (north and west) training enterprise and education directorate 1990-

Date of birth: 8 April 1948 *Education/professional qualifications:* Denstone College, Uttoxeter; Selwyn College, Cambridge, natural sciences (BA, MA 1970) *Marital status:* married Ann 1971; 2 sons

John Lambert Esq, Director of Operations, Employment Department, Moorfoot, Sheffield, S1 4PQ *Telephone:* 0742 593979 *Fax:* 0742 594821

LAMING, (WILLIAM) HERBERT   Chief Inspector, Social Services Inspectorate, Department of Health

Career: Nottinghamshire probation department/Nottingham city and county combined probation and aftercare department 1961-71; Hertfordshire County Council social services 1971-91: deputy director 1971-75, director 1975-91; chief social services inspector Department of Health 1991-

Date of birth: 19 July 1936 *Education/professional qualifications:* Durham University, social administration (degree 1960); probation training 1961; London School of Economics, mental health course 1966 *Honours, decorations:* CBE 1985 *Marital status:* married Aileen Margaret 1962

W Herbert Laming Esq CBE, Chief Inspector, Social Services Inspectorate, Department of Health, Richmond House, 79 Whitehall, London SW1A 2NS *Telephone:* 071-210 5561 *Fax:* 071-321 0942

LAMMIMAN, Surgeon Rear Admiral DAVID ASKEY   Medical Director-General (Naval) and Deputy Surgeon General, Ministry of Defence

Career: Royal Navy 1959-: HMS Eagle 1967-69; Royal Naval Hospital (RNH) Malta 1969-71; consultant anaesthetist RNH Haslar 1971-73; RNH Gibraltar 1973-75; RNH Plymouth 1975-76; HM Yacht Britannia 1976-78; RNH Haslar 1978-82; director medical personnel, medical directorate general (naval) Ministry of Defence (MoD) 1982-84; medical officer in charge of RNH Plymouth 1984-86, of RNH Haslar 1986-89; MoD 1989-: surgeon rear admiral support medical services 1989-90; medical director-general (naval) 1990-, deputy surgeon general (operation and plans) 1991-

Date of birth: 30 June 1932 *Education/professional qualifications:* Wyggeston School, Leicester; St Bartholomew's Hospital (MB BS 1957, DA 1962, DObst RCOG 1962, FFARCS 1969) *Honours, decorations:* LVO 1979, QHS 1987 *Recreations:* fly fishing, golf, tennis

Surgeon Rear Admiral David A Lammiman LVO, QHS, Medical Director-General (Naval) and Deputy Surgeon General, Ministry of Defence, Room 623, First Avenue House, High Holborn, London WC1V 6HE *Telephone:* 071-430 5890 *Fax:* 071-430 6348

LANE, ANTHONY JOHN   Deputy Secretary, Industry 1 Division, Department of Trade and Industry   Grade: 2

Career: Department of Trade and Industry (DTI) and predecessors 1965-87; deputy director-general Office of Fair Trading 1987-91; deputy secretary, industrial policy DTI 1991-92, and industry 1 division (textiles, retailing, telecommunications and posts and various executive agencies) 1992-

Date of birth: 30 May 1939 *Education/professional qualifications:* Caterham School, Surrey; Balliol College, Oxford, philosophy, politics and economics (BA, MA 1961) *Honours, decorations:* CB 1990 *Marital status:* married Judith Sheila Dodson 1967; 2 sons, 1 daughter *Recreations:* travel, music, gardening

Anthony J Lane Esq CB, Deputy Secretary, Industry 1 Division, Department of Trade and Industry, 151 Buckingham Palace Road, London SW1W 9SS *Telephone:* 071-215 5000

LANGDON, ANTHONY JAMES   Deputy Under Secretary, Home Office   Grade: 2

Career: HM Treasury 1967-69; Cabinet-Office 1985-89; deputy under secretary (broadcasting, equal opportunities, immigration and nationality) Home Office 1989-

Date of birth: 5 June 1935   *Education/professional qualifications:* Christ's College, Cambridge

Anthony J Langdon Esq, Deputy Under Secretary, Home Office, 50 Queen Anne's Gate, London SW1H 9AT   *Telephone:* 071-273 3000

LANGFORD, (ANTHONY) JOHN   Deputy Chief Executive, Valuation Office (Executive Agency)   Grade: 3

Career: Inland Revenue Valuation Office (valuation of land and buildings for taxation) 1957-: superintending valuer northern region 1981-83; chief valuer's office 1983-91: assistant chief valuer 1983-88, deputy chief valuer 1988-91; deputy chief executive (personnel, training, management planning, operational services) 1988-

Date of birth: 25 June 1936   *Education/professional qualifications:* Soham Grammar School   *Marital status:* married Joan Barber 1958; 1 son, 1 daughter

A John Langford Esq, Deputy Chief Executive, Valuation Office, New Court, Carey Street, London WC2A 2JE   *Telephone:* 071-324 1154   *Fax:* 071-324 1185

LANKESTER, TIM(OTHY) PATRICK   Permanent Secretary, Overseas Development Administration   Grade: 1A

Career: VSO, Belize 1960-61; Fereday Fellow St John's College, Oxford 1965-66; economist World Bank (IBRD) 1966-73: Washington DC 1966-69, New Delhi 1970-73; HM Treasury (HMT) 1973-78: principal 1973-77, assistant secretary 1977-78; private secretary to prime ministers James Callaghan 1978-79, Margaret Thatcher 1979-81; under secretary HMT, seconded to SG Warburg & Co Ltd 1983-85; economic minister Washington DC and executive International Monetary Fund and IBRD 1985-88; deputy secretary HMT 1988-89; permanent secretary Overseas Development Administration 1989-

Date of birth: 15 April 1942   *Education/professional qualifications:* Monkton Combe School, Somerset; St John's College, Cambridge (BA); Henry fellow Yale University, USA (MA)   *Marital status:* married Patricia Cockcroft 1968; 3 daughters   *Recreations:* tennis, music, sailing

Tim P Lankester Esq, Permanent Secretary, Overseas Development Administration, 94 Victoria Street, London SW1E 5JL   *Telephone:* 071-917 0500   *Fax:* 071-917 0634

LAURANCE, (ANTHONY) TONY   Scotland and North East Territorial Director, Social Security Benefits Agency (Executive Agency)   Grade: 4

Career: Department of [Health and] Social Security 1982-: finance policy division 1982-85; principal private secretary to Secretary of State for Social Services 1985-87; head of central management services establishment office 1987-89; controller Newcastle central office 1989-90; Scotland and North East territorial director Social Security Benefits Agency 1990-

Date of birth: 11 November 1950 *Education/professional qualifications:* Bryanston School; Clare College, Cambridge, economics and philosophy (BA 1972) *Marital status:* married Judith 1981; 2 daughters

Tony Laurance Esq, Territorial Director, Social Security Benefits Agency, Sandyford House, Archhold Terrace, Jesmond, Newcastle upon Tyne *Telephone:* 091-225 6249 *Fax:* 091-225 6384

LAWS, STEPHEN CHARLES   Parliamentary Counsel, Office of the Parliamentary Counsel   Grade: 2

Career: assistant lecturer Bristol University 1972-73; pupil barrister 1973-75; legal assistant Home Office 1975-76; Parliamentary Counsel Office 1976-: parliamentary counsel (drafting government bills) 1991-

Date of birth: 28 January 1950 *Education/professional qualifications:* St Dunstan's College, London; Bristol University, law (LLB 1972) *Marital status:* married Angela Mary Deardon 1972; 3 daughters, 2 sons

Stephen C Laws Esq, Parliamentary Counsel, Office of the Parliamentary Counsel, 36 Whitehall, London SW1A 2AY *Telephone:* 071-210 6639

LAYDEN, PATRICK JOHN   Assistant Legal Secretary and Scottish Parliamentary Counsel, Lord Advocate's Department   Grade: 3

Career: practising advocate 1973-77; Lord Advocate's Department 1977-: deputy Scottish parliamentary counsel and assistant legal secretary 1977-87, assistant legal secretary and Scottish parliamentary counsel (drafting legislation for Scotland, assisting Scottish law officers; legal advice to government departments) 1987-

Date of birth: 27 June 1949 *Education/professional qualifications:* Holy Cross Academy, Edinburgh; Edinburgh University, law (LLB 1971) *Honours, decorations:* TD 1981 *Marital status:* married Patricia Mary 1984; 1 daughter, 2 sons *Recreations:* reading, walking

Patrick J Layden Esq TD, Assistant Legal Secretary and Scottish Parliamentary Counsel, Lord Advocate's Department, 10 Great College Street, London SW1P 3SL *Telephone:* 071-276 6811 *Fax:* 071-276 6834

LEARMONT, General Sir JOHN HARTLEY   Quartermaster General, Ministry of Defence

Career: joined Army 1954-; military secretary Ministry of Defence (MoD) 1989-91; quarter master general MoD 1991-

Date of birth: 10 March 1934 *Education/professional qualifications:* RMA Sandhurst

General Sir John Learmont KCB, CBE, Quartermaster General, Ministry of Defence, Main Building, Whitehall, London SW1A 2HB *Telephone:* 071-218 9000

LEES, ROBERT FERGUSON   Regional Procurator Fiscal, (Lothian and Borders), Crown Office   Grade: 3

Career: Crown Office Procurator Fiscal Service (public prosecution; sudden death and fire investigations) 1972-: procurator fiscal (PF) depute Paisley 1972-75, Glasgow 1975-78; senior depute PF Glasgow 1978-81; assistant PF Dundee 1982-88; regional PF North Strathclyde 1989-91, Lothian and Borders 1991-

Date of birth: 15 September 1938 *Education/professional qualifications:* Bellshill Academy; Strathclyde

University, law (LLB 1970) *Marital status:* married Elsie 1966 *Publications:* co-author Criminal Procedure (Butterworths 1990) *Recreations:* music, photography, travel

Robert F Lees Esq, Regional Procurator Fiscal for Lothian and Borders, Procurator Fiscal's Office, 3 Queensferry Street, Edinburgh EH2 4RG *Telephone:* 031-226 4962

LEGG, (THOMAS) TOM STUART   Permanent Secretary and Clerk of the Crown in Chancery, Lord Chancellor's Department   Grade: 1

Career: Lord Chancellor's Department 1962-: private secretary to Lord Chancellor 1965-68; assistant solicitor 1975; under secretary 1977-82: SE circuit administrator 1980-82; deputy secretary 1982-89: deputy clerk of Crown in Chancery 1986-89; secretary of commissions 1989; permanent secretary and clerk of the Crown in Chancery 1989- *Current non-Whitehall posts:* Master of the Bench 1984-

Date of birth: 13 August 1935 *Education/professional qualifications:* Horace Mann-Lincoln School, New York, USA; Frensham Heights School, Surrey; St John's College, history and law (MA 1958), law (LLM 1959); barrister 1960 *Honours, decorations:* CB 1985, QC 1990 *Marital status:* married Marie-Louise Clarke 1983; 2 daughters by previous marriage *Clubs:* Garrick

Tom S Legg Esq CB QC, Permanent Secretary, Lord Chancellor's Department, House of Lords, London SW1A 0PW *Telephone:* 071-219 3246 *Fax:* 071-219 4711

LEIGH-PEMBERTON, The Rt Hon (ROBERT) ROBIN   Governor, Bank of England

Career: private practice barrister 1954-60; director Birmid Qualcast 1966-83: chairman 1975-77, University Life Assurance Society 1967-78, Redland Ltd 1972-83, National Westminster Bank 1972-83: chairman 1977-83, Equitable Life Assurance Society 1979-83: vice-president 1982-83; governor Bank of England 1983- *Current non-Whitehall posts:* director Bank for International Settlements 1983-

Date of birth: 5 January 1927 *Education/professional qualifications:* Eton; Trinity College, Oxford (MA) *Honours, decorations:* DL Kent 1970;, FRSA 1977; FBIM 1977; Lord Lieutenant of Kent 1982; Kent KStJ 1983; PC 1987 *Marital status:* married Rosemary Davina Forbes 1953; 5 sons *Clubs:* Brooks's, Cavalry and Guards *Recreations:* country life

The Rt Hon Robin Leigh-Pemberton, Governor, Bank of England, Threadneedle Street, London EC2R 8AH *Telephone:* 071-601 4444

LE MARECHAL, ROBERT NORFORD   Deputy Comptroller and Auditor General, National Audit Office   Grade: 2

Career: army national service 1958-60; Exchequer and Audit Department 1961-83: housing, local government, finance, environment, trade and industry, energy, Foreign Office, Overseas Development Administration, UK Atomic Energy Authority, Civil Aviation Authority, nationalised industries; National Audit Office 1984-: policy and planning director 1984-86, assistant auditor general 1986-89, deputy comptroller and auditor general 1989-

Date of birth: 29 May 1939 *Education/professional qualifications:* Tauton's School, Southampton *Marital status:* married Linda Mary Williams 1963; 2 daughters *Recreations:* reading, gardening

Robert N Le Marechal Esq, Deputy Comptroller and Auditor General, National Audit Office, 157-197 Buckingham Palace Road, London SW1W 9SP *Telephone:* 071-798 7381 *Fax:* 071-233 6163

LEVENE, Sir PETER KEITH   Prime Minister's Adviser on Efficiency and Effectiveness

Career: United Scientific Holdings plc 1963-85: managing director 1968-85, chairman 1982-85; Ministry of Defence: personal adviser to secretary of state (PASS) 1984-, chief of defence procurement 1985-91; PASS Department of Environment 1991-92; prime minister's adviser on efficiency and effectiveness (in public service management) 1992- *Current non-Whitehall posts:* deputy chairman and managing director Wasserstein Perella & Co Ltd 1991-; chairman Docklands Light Railway Ltd 1991-

Date of birth: 8 December 1941 *Education/professional qualifications:* City of London School; Manchester University, economics and politics (BAEcon 1963) *Honours, decorations:* KBE 1989 *Marital status:* married Wendy Fraiman 1966; 2 sons, 1 daughter *Clubs:* City Livery, Guildhall, Royal Automobile *Recreations:* skiing, watching football

Sir Peter Levene KBE, Prime Minister's Adviser on Efficiency and Effectiveness, 70 Whitehall, London SW1A 2AS *Telephone:* 071-270 0273 *Fax:* 071-270 0099

LEWIS, Dr GWYNETH HELEN   Principal Medical Officer, AIDS and Communicable Disease Unit, Department of Health   Grade: 4

Career: medical posts 1973-81; lecturer Cambridge University 1976-77; hospital medical director, Newfoundland, Canada 1978-79; civil servant 1981-: principal medical officer, medical head of AIDS and communicable diseases unit Department of Health 1989-

Date of birth: 4 October 1951 *Education/professional qualifications:* Oxford High School for Girls; University College Hospital, London (MB BS 1975); Royal College of General Practitioners (MRCGP 1980); London University, public health (MSc 1989) *Marital status:* married Dr Colin Sanderson 1990; 1 son *Recreations:* choral music

Dr Gwyneth H Lewis, Principal Medical Officer, AIDS Unit, Department of Health, 167 Blackfriars Road, London SE1 *Telephone:* 071-972 3355 *Fax:* 071-972 3031

LEWIS, LEIGH WARREN   Director, International Division, Employment Department Group   Grade: 3

Career: Department of Employment 1973-: private secretary (PS) to parliamentary under secretary 1975-76; manager department personnel unit 1976-78; principal, head of section, incomes division 1978-79; team manager departmental efficiency unit 1979-81; head of section, industrial relations policy division: member Employment Act 1982 and Trade Union Act 1984 legislation teams 1981-84; principal PS to Lord Young 1984-86; assistant secretary, head of EC branch 1986-87; director of operations Unemployment Benefit Service 1987-88; seconded as group personnel director to Cable and Wireless plc 1988-91; under secretary, director international and tourism division (EC, ILO, OECD and Council of Europe employment issues; international relations; tourism policy) international and industrial relations directorate 1991-

Date of birth: 17 March 1951 *Education/professional qualifications:* Harrow County Grammar School for Boys; Liverpool University, Hispanic studies (BA 1973) *Marital status:* married Susan Evelyn 1973; 2 sons *Recreations:* tennis, phone card collecting, Watford Football Club

Leigh W Lewis Esq, Director International Division, Employment Department Group, Caxton House, Tothill Street, London SW1H 9NF *Telephone:* 071-273 4735

LEWIS, PETER   Director, Company Tax Division, Inland Revenue   Grade: 3

Career: Inland Revenue 1960-: tax inspector (TI) 1960-66; higher grade TI 1966-69; principal 1969-74; assistant secretary 1974-86; under secretary, director company tax division (company and oil taxation) 1986-

Date of birth: 24 June 1937 *Education/professional qualifications:* Ealing Grammar School; St Peter's Hall, Oxford, modern history (BA 1960) *Marital status:* married Ursula Brigitte 1962; 1 son, 1 daughter

Peter Lewis Esq, Director, Company Tax Division, Inland Revenue, Somerset House, Strand, London WC2R 1LB *Telephone:* 071-438 6371 *Fax:* 071-438 6106

LIBBY, DONALD GERALD   Secretary, Advisory Board for the Research Councils, Office of Public Service and Science, Cabinet Office   Grade: 3

Career: Department of Education and Science 1967-: under secretary further and higher education Branch 2 1986-91; secretary Advisory Board for the Research Councils 1991-

Date of birth: 2 July 1934 *Education/professional qualifications:* RMA Sandhurst; London University, physics (BSc, PhD); CEng; MIEE

Donald G Libby Esq, Secretary, Advisory Board for the Research Councils, Cabinet Office, 70 Whitehall, London SW1A 2AS *Telephone:* 071-270 3000

LILLYWHITE, MICHAEL GEORGE   Principal Establishment Officer, Department Management Division, Department of Health   Grade: 3

Date of birth: 29 November 1937 *Education/professional qualifications:* University of London

Michael G Lillywhite Esq, Principal Establishment Officer, Department Management Division, Department of Health, Richmond House, 79 Whitehall, London SW1A 2NS *Telephone:* 071-210 3000

LIMON, DONALD WILLIAM   Clerk Assistant, House of Commons   Grade: 2

Career: clerk's department House of Commons (HoC) 1956-: assistant clerk 1956-60; senior clerk 1960-73; deputy principal clerk 1973-81; secretary HoC commission 1979-81; clerk of financial committees 1981-84; principal clerk Table Office 1985-89; clerk of committees 1989-90; clerk assistant (deputy clerk of the House; head of night at Table; departmental establishment officer; adviser to the chairman of Ways and Means Committee) 1990-

Date of birth: 29 October 1932 *Education/professional qualifications:* Durham Cathedral Chorister School; Durham School; Lincoln College, Oxford, politics, philosophy and economics (BA 1956, MA) *Marital status:* married Joyce Beatrice Clifton 1987; 1 stepson, 1 stepdaughter *Recreations:* cricket, golf, singing

Donald W Limon Esq, Clerk Assistant, House of Commons, London SW1A 0AA *Telephone:* 071-219 3311

'Next Steps' Executive Agencies
see page 761

LING, JEFFREY   Assistant Under Secretary and Director of Information Systems Division, Foreign and Commonwealth Office

Career: HM Diplomatic Service 1966-: assistant under secretary and director of information systems 1989-

Date of birth: 9 September 1939 *Education/professional qualifications:* Bristol University (BSc)

Jeffrey Ling Esq CMG, Director of Information Systems, Foreign and Commonwealth Office, King Charles Street, London SW1A 2AH *Telephone:* 071-270 3000

LINSTEAD, STEPHEN GUY   Director, West Midlands Regional Office, Department of Trade and Industry   Grade: 3

Career: Board of Trade 1964-76: assistant principal 1964-67, private secretary to minister of state 1967-69, principal 1969-76; assistant secretary Department of Prices and Consumer Protection 1976-82; seconded to Office of Fair Trading 1982-90; under secretary, director West Midlands regional office Department of Trade and Industry (briefing and intelligence, export services, regional selective assistance, support for innovation and technology transfer) 1990-

Date of birth: 23 June 1941 *Education/professional qualifications:* King Edward VII School, Sheffield; Corpus Christi College, Oxford, modern history (BA, MA) and public and social administration (diploma); Carleton University, Canada, political science (MA) *Marital status:* married Rachael Marian Feldman 1982; 2 sons by previous marriage, 2 daughters *Publications:* The Law of Crown Privilege in Canada and Elsewhere (Ottawa Law Review 1968) *Clubs:* Royal Over-seas League *Recreations:* Biblical criticism, swimming, travel, entertainment

Stephen G Linstead Esq, Director, West Midlands Regional Office, Department of Trade and Industry, 77 Paradise Circus, Queensway, Birmingham B12 DT *Telephone:* 021-212 5206 *Fax:* 021-212 1010

LIPWORTH, Sir (MAURICE) SYDNEY   Chairman, Monopolies and Mergers Commission

Career: practising barrister, Johannesburg 1956-64; non-executive director South African insurance company 1957-64; director private trading companies 1964-67; director Abbey Life Assurance Group 1968-70; Allied Dunbar (AD) 1970-88: director, managing director, chairman AD Assurance plc 1970-88, chairman AD Unit Trusts plc 1982-88; non-executive director J Rothschild Holdings plc 1985-87; director BAT Industries plc 1985-88; Monopolies and Mergers Commission 1981-: member 1981, chairman 1988-

Date of birth: 13 May 1931 *Education/professional qualifications:* King Edward VII School, Johannesburg, South Africa (SA); Witwatersrand University, SA (B Com 1951), law (LLB 1954) *Honours, decorations:* Kt 1990 *Marital status:* married Rosa 1957; 2 sons *Clubs:* Reform, Queen's *Recreations:* tennis, music, theatre

Sir Sydney Lipworth, Chairman, Monopolies and Mergers Commission, New Court, 48 Carey Street, London WC2A 2JT *Telephone:* 071-324 1428 *Fax:* 071-324 1400

LITTLE, Dr (THOMAS WILLIAM ANTHONY) TONY   Director and Chief Executive,
Central Veterinary Laboratory (Executive Agency)   Grade: 3

Career: private practice veterinary surgeon 1963-66; Ministry of Agriculture, Fisheries and Food
1966-: Central Veterinary Laboratory (CVL) 1966-82: research officer (RO) 1966-72, senior RO
1972-82; Tolworth 1982-86: deputy regional veterinary officer 1982-85, veterinary head of section
1985-86; CVL 1986-: deputy director 1986-90, director and chief executive 1990-

Date of birth: 27 June 1940 *Education/professional qualifications:* Dame Allan's School,
Newcastle-upon-Tyne; Edinburgh University, veterinary medicine (BVMS 1963); London University,
veterinary micro-biology (DipBact 1968, PhD 1973); MRCVS 1963 *Marital status:* married Sally
Anne 1985; 1 daughter, 3 sons (1 from previous marriage) *Recreations:* sailing, walking

Dr T W Tony Little, Director and Chief Executive, Central Veterinary Laboratory, New Haw,
Weybridge, Surrey KT15 3NB *Telephone:* 09323 41111 *Fax:* 09323 47046

LITTLECHILD, Professor STEPHEN CHARLES   Director General,
Office of Electricity Regulation   Grade: 2

Career: professor of commerce and head of industrial economics and
business studies department Birmingham University 1975-; on leave of
absence as director-general Office of Electricity Regulation 1989-

Date of birth: 27 August 1943 *Education/professional qualifications:* Wisbech
Grammar School; Birmingham University (B Com 1964); Texas University
(PhD 1969) *Marital status:* married Kate Crombie 1974 (died 1982); 1
daughter, 2 sons *Publications:* Operational Research for Managers (1977);
The Fallacy of the Mixed Economy (1978, 1986); Elements of
Telecommunications Economics (1979); Energy Strategies for the UK
(1982) *Recreations:* football, genealogy

Professor Stephen C Littlechild, Director-General, Office of Electricity
Regulation, Hagley House, Hagley Road, Edgbaston, Birmingham B16
8QG *Telephone:* 021-456 2100 *Fax:* 021-456 6365

LITTMODEN, CHRIS(TOPHER)   Special Adviser, Market Testing, Ministry of Defence

Career: general manager BOC 1968-72; audit manager Ernst & Whinney 1972-74; Marks and Spencer
plc 1974-: textiles financial controller, PA to chairman, foods buying executive, company financial
controller, finance divisional director, finance director 1991-; special adviser (competition
programme) Ministry of Defence 1992-

Date of birth: 28 September 1943 *Education/professional qualifications:* Brentwood School, Essex; FCA
1965 *Recreations:* music, opera, history, reading, squash, soccer

Chris Littmoden Esq, Marks and Spencer plc, 47 Baker Street, London W1A 1DN
Telephone: 071-268 7445 *Fax:* 071-268 2713

LIVESAY, Vice-Admiral Sir MICHAEL   Second Sea Lord and Chief of Naval Personnel,
Ministry of Defence

Career: Royal Navy 1952-: direction officer HMS Hermes, HMS Aisne, Fighter Direction School and
893 squadron 1959-66; in command HMS Hubberston 1966-68, HMS Plymouth 1970-72; captain
fishery protection, mine counter-measures 1975-77; commanding officer HMS Invincible 1979-82;
director of naval warfare Ministry of Defence (MoD) 1982-84; flag officer (FO) sea training 1984-85;

assistant chief of naval staff MoD 1986-88; FO Scotland and Northern Ireland 1989-91; Second Sea Lord and chief of naval personnel MoD (recruitment, training and deployment) 1991-

Date of birth: 5 April 1936 *Education/professional qualifications:* Acklam Hall Grammar School, Middlesborough; Royal Naval College, Dartmouth *Honours, decorations:* KCB 1989 *Recreations:* sailing, skiing, golf, fishing, gardening

Vice-Admiral Sir Michael Livesay KCB, Second Sea Lord, Ministry of Defence, Whitehall, London SW1A 2HB *Telephone:* 071-218 9000

LLOYD, JOHN WILSON   Deputy Secretary, Social Policy, Welsh Office   Grade: 2

Career: assistant principal HM Treasury (HMT) 1962-67: private secretary (PS) to financial secretary 1965-67; principal HMT, Civil Service Department, Welsh Office (WO) 1967-75: PS to secretary of state 1974-75; WO 1975-: assistant secretary 1975-82, under secretary 1982-88: principal establishment officer 1982-86, head of housing, health and social services policy group 1986-88, deputy secretary social policy (health and social services policy, education, transport planning, environment) 1988-

Date of birth: 24 December 1940 *Education/professional qualifications:* Swansea Grammar School; Clifton College, Bristol; Christ's College, Cambridge, biochemistry (BA 1962, MA) *Honours, decorations:* CB 1992 *Marital status:* married Buddug Roberts 1967; 1 daughter, 2 sons *Recreations:* golf, swimming, squash

John W Lloyd Esq, Deputh Secretary, Welsh Office, Cathays Park, Cardiff CF1 3NQ *Telephone:* 0222 825706 *Fax:* 0222 823036

LLOYD JONES, Sir RICHARD ANTHONY   Permanent Secretary, Welsh Office   Grade: 1

Career: Admiralty 1957-64; Ministry of Defence 1964-74; Welsh Office 1974-: under secretary 1974-78, deputy secretary 1978-85, permanent secretary 1985- *Current non-Whitehall posts:* chairman Civil Service Benevolent Fund 1987-

Date of birth: 1 August 1933 *Education/professional qualifications:* Long Dene School, Kent; Nottingham High School; Balliol College, Oxford, English language and literature (BA, MA 1959) *Honours, decorations:* KCB 1988 *Marital status:* married Patricia 1955; 2 daughters *Clubs:* United Oxford and Cambridge University

Sir Richard Lloyd Jones KCB, Permanent Secretary, Welsh Office, Cathays Park, Cardiff CF1 3NQ *Telephone:* 0222 823455

LOADES, DAVID HENRY   Under Secretary and Directing Actuary, Social Security and Research Division, Government Actuary's Department   Grade: 3

Career: Government Actuary's Department 1956-: directing actuary and under secretary 1983-, social security and research division 1991-

Date of birth: 16 October 1937 *Education/professional qualifications:* Beckenham and Penge County Grammar School for Boys

David H Loades, Under Secretary and Directing Actuary, Social Security and Research Division, Government Actuary's Department, 22 Kingsway, London WC2B 6LE *Telephone:* 071-242 6828

LOCKE, JOHN CHRISTOPHER   Chief Executive, NHS Estates (Executive Agency)
Grade: 3

Career: Prudential Assurance Co Ltd 1964-88: surveyor 1964-88, estate management director 1987-88; estate management divisional director Prudential Portfolio Managers Ltd 1989-91; Southbank Technopark Ltd 1985-90: director 1985-91, chairman 1989-90; chairman Briggait Co Ltd 1987-90; surveyor to Watling Street Properties 1989-90; chief executive NHS Estates (property advice and consultancy) 1991-

Date of birth: 4 March 1947 *Education/professional qualifications:* Nautical College, Pangbourne; Regent Street Polytechnic, Brixton School of Building, Northern Polytechnic, surveying (ARICS 1971, FRICS 1984) *Marital status:* married Jacqueline Mercer Pamment (divorced), 2 sons; Maria Patricia Rogers 1990 *Recreations:* opera, music, theatre, the arts, travel, wife, sons

John C Locke Esq, Chief Executive, NHS Estates, Euston Tower, 286 Euston Road, London NW1 3DN *Telephone:* 071-388 1188 *Fax:* 071-387 3222

LOMAX, (JANIS) RACHEL   Deputy Secretary, Financial Institutions and Markets   Grade: 2

Career: HM Treasury 1968-: principal private secretary to chancellor of exchequer 1985-86; under secretary 1986-90; deputy secretary, deputy chief economic adviser 1990-92; deputy secretary (financial institutions and markets, financial services)

Date of birth: 15 July 1945 *Education/professional qualifications:* Cheltenham Ladies' College; Girton College, Cambridge, history (BA, MA 1966); London School of Economics (BSc Econ 1968) *Marital status:* divorced; 2 sons

Mrs J Rachel Lomax, Deputy Secretary, HM Treasury, Parliament Street, London SW1P 3AG *Telephone:* 071-270 4409 *Fax:* 071-270 5735

LOVE, Professor PHILIP NOEL   Commissioner, Scottish Law Commission   Grade: 2

Career: partner in firm of solicitors 1963-74, consultant 1974-; Aberdeen University 1974-: professor of conveyancing and professional practice of law 1974-, dean of law faculty 1991-; chairman Scottish conveyancing and executry services board, Scottish Office Home and Health Department 1986-; Commissioner Scottish Law Commission, Scottish Courts Administration (reviewing Scottish law) 1986- *Current non-Whitehall posts:* professor of law 1974- and dean of the faculty of law 1991- Aberdeen University

Date of birth: 25 December 1939 *Education/professional qualifications:* Aberdeen Grammar School; Aberdeen University, arts (MA 1961) and law (LLB 1963) *Honours, decorations:* CBE 1983 *Marital status:* married Isabel Leah Mearns 1963; 3 sons *Clubs:* New, Edinburgh; Royal Aberdeen Golf *Recreations:* keep fit, rugby, golf

Professor Philip N Love CBE, Faculty of Law, Taylor Building, Aberdeen University, Old Aberdeen AB9 2UB *Telephone:* 0224 272414 *Fax:* 0224 272442

LOVEMAN, STEPHEN CHARLES GARDNER   Under Secretary, Youth and Adult Training, Employment Department Group   Grade: 3

Career: Department of Employment (DEmp) 1967-: cabinet office 1988-89; under secretary, director of youth and adult training (training and enterprise division) 1989-

Date of birth: 26 December 1943 *Education/professional qualifications:* Emmanuel College, Cambridge (BA)

Stephen C G Loveman Esq, Under Secretary, Employment Department Group, Porter Brook House, Sheffield, S1 4PQ *Telephone:* 0742 597673

LOWE, (JOHN) DUNCAN   Crown Agent, Crown Office, Scotland   Grade: 2

Career: Procurator Fiscal (PF) Service 1974-: regional PF Lothian and Borders 1988-91; crown agent (criminal prosecution in Scotland) 1991-

Date of birth: 18 May 1948 *Education/professional qualifications:* Hamilton Academy; Glasgow University, law (MA 1969, LLB 1971) *Honours, decorations:* CBE *Marital status:* married Jacqueline 1971; 2 sons

J Duncan Lowe Esq CBE, Crown Agent, Crown Office, Regent Road, Edinburgh EH7 5BL *Telephone:* 031-557 3800 *Fax:* 031-556 0154

LUCE, THOMAS RICHARD HARMAN   Under Secretary, Community Services Division, Department of Health   Grade: 3

Career: Department of Health (DH) 1972-: seconded to HM Treasury 1987-90, under secretary community services division DH 1990-

Date of birth: 11 July 1939 *Education/professional qualifications:* Christ's College, Cambridge (BA Hons); Indiana University, USA

Thomas R H Luce Esq, Under Secretary, Community Services Division, Department of Health, Richmond House, 79 Whitehall, London SW1A 2NS *Telephone:* 071-210 3000

LYNESS, DAVID   Under Secretary, Highways Policy and Resources, Department of Transport   Grade: 3

Career: Ministry of Transport 1961-: under secretary shipping policy 1988-90, freight and road haulage 1990-91, highways policy and resources 1991-

Date of birth: 27 October 1935 *Education/professional qualifications:* Brasenose College, Oxford, philosophy, politics and economics (BA 1959) *Marital status:* married Susan 1961; 3 sons

David Lyness Esq, Under Secretary, Department of Transport, 2 Marsham Street, London, SW1P 3EB *Telephone:* 071-276 5710

LYNN, (MICHAEL) MIKE DAVID   Deputy Chief Executive, Her Majesty's Stationery Office   Grade: 4

Career: Her Majesty's Stationery Office 1980-: director of publications distribution 1980-83, of finance 1983-84, of print procurement 1984-86; director general of information technology and supply 1986-87, of corporate services 1987-89; deputy chief executive (trading operations) 1989-

Date of birth: 18 July 1942 *Education/professional qualifications:* Lincoln School *Marital status:* married Hilary 1965; 1 daughter, 1 son *Recreations:* swimming, chess, rough gardening

Mike Lynn Esq, Deputy Chief Executive, Her Majesty's Stationery Office, St Crispins, Duke Street, Norwich NR3 1PD *Telephone:* 0603 694200 *Fax:* 0602 695045

M

MABBERLEY, J C Director-General, Avionics, Weapons and Information Systems, Ministry of Defence Grade: 3

J C Mabberley Esq, Director-General of Avionics, Weapons and Information Systems, Ministry of Defence, Turnstile House, 98 High Holborn, London WC1V 6LL *Telephone:* 071-430 5226

McCLUSKIE, JOHN CAMERON Legal Secretary to Lord Advocate and First Scottish Parliamentary Counsel, Lord Advocate's Department Grade: 2

Career: apprentice solicitor in private practice 1967-69; assistant town clerk Cumbernauld Burgh Council 1969-70; private practice 1970; solicitor South of Scotland Electricity Board 1970-72; Lord Advocate's Department (LAD) 1972-: junior/senior assistant legal secretary and parliamentary draftsman 1972-89, legal secretary to Lord Advocate and first Scottish parliamentary counsel (head of LAD, responsible for assisting Scottish law officers; drafting legislation relating to Scotland) 1989-

Date of birth: 1 February 1946 *Education/professional qualifications:* Hyndland School, Glasgow; Glasgow University, law (LLB 1967); Law Society of Scotland (solicitor 1970); Faculty of Advocates (advocate 1974) *Honours, decorations:* QC (Scotland) 1989 *Marital status:* married Janis Mary Helen McArthur 1970; 1 daughter, 1 son *Recreations:* vegetable growing

John C McCluskie Esq QC, Legal Secretary to Lord Advocate and First Scottish Parliamentary Counsel, Lord Advocate's Chambers, 10 Great College Street, London SW1P 3SL *Telephone:* 071-276 6831 *Fax:* 071-276 6834

MACDONALD, ALASTAIR JOHN PETER Deputy Secretary, Industry 2 Division, Department of Trade and Industry Grade: 2

Career: journalist 1962-68; Civil Service 1968-: deputy secretary, (DS) Department of Trade and Industry (DTI) 1985-90; deputy under secretary (procurement executive) Ministry of Defence 1990-92, DS industry 2 division DTI 1992-

Date of birth: 11 August 1940 *Education/professional qualifications:* Trinity College, Oxford

Alastair Macdonald Esq CB, Industry 2 Division, Department of Trade and Industry, Ashdown House, 123 Victoria Street, London SW1E 6RB *Telephone:* 071-215 5000

McDONALD, DAVID ARTHUR Director of Information, Department of the Environment Grade: 3

Career: Ministry of Housing and Local Government/Department of Environment 1970-: under secretary, construction industry and sport and recreation directorates 1987-90; director of information 1990-

Date of birth: 16 January 1940 *Education/professional qualifications:* Trinity College, Dublin, classics (BA)

David A McDonald Esq, Director of Information, Department of the Environment, 2 Marsham Street, London SW1P 3EB

MACDONALD, Major General JOHN DONALD Director-General of Transport and Movements (Army), Ministry of Defence

Career: commissioned into King's Own Scottish Borderers 1958; deputy assistant quartermaster general (DAQMG) organisation HQ1 (BR) Corps 1972-74; student National Defence College 1976; DAQMG plans G4 HQ Landsoutheast 1977-78; commanding officer 4 Armoured Division Transport Regiment 1978-80; instructor/senior instructor Australian Staff College 1980-82;

Commandant School of Transportation 1983; deputy chief of staff 3 Armoured Brigade 1983-86; colonel personnel branch 1st British Corps 1987-88; commander transport HQ1 (BR) Corps 1988-91; director-general of transport and movements, logistic executive (army) 1991-

Date of birth: 5 April 1938 *Education/professional qualifications:* George Watson's Boys' College, Edinburgh; Royal Military Academy Sandhurst (commission 1958); Indian Defence Services Staff College; National Defence College *Honours, decorations:* OBE 1981, CBE 1986 *Recreations:* rugby, skiing, golf, travel, collecting

Major-General John D MacDonald CBE, Director-General of Transport and Movements, Ministry of Defence, Portway, Monxton Road, Andover, Hants SP11 8HT

McDONALD, MAVIS   Under Secretary, Director of Public Housing, Management and Resources, Department of the Environment   Grade: 3

Career: Department of the Environment 1966-: under secretary directorate of administration resources 1988-90, directorate of personnel management 1990-92, director of public housing management and resources 1992-

Date of birth: 23 October 1944 *Education/professional qualifications:* London School of Economics, economics (BSc)

Mrs Mavis McDonald, Under Secretary, Director of Public Housing Management and Resources, Department of the Environment, 2 Marsham Street, London SW1P 3EB *Telephone:* 071-276 3000

MACE, BRIAN ANTHONY   Director, Savings and Investment Division, Inland Revenue   Grade: 3

Career: Inland Revenue (IR) 1971-73; secretary inflation accounting committee 1974-75; IR 1975-: director savings and investment division (tax on savings; stamp duty; charities' taxation) 1990-

Date of birth: 9 September 1948 *Education/professional qualifications:* Maidstone Boys' Grammar School; Gonville and Caius College, Cambridge, mathematics (BA 1971, MA) *Marital status:* married Anne Margaret 1973 *Recreations:* opera, cricket, new plays

Brian A Mace Esq, Under Secretary, Inland Revenue, Somerset House, Strand, London WC2R 1LB *Telephone:* 071-438 6622

McGIVERN, EUGENE   Director, Personal Tax Division, Inland Revenue   Grade: 3

Career: Inland Revenue (IR) 1955-: under secretary (US) business taxation division 1986-91, director personal tax division 1991-

Date of birth: 15 September 1938 *Education/professional qualifications:* St Mary's Grammar School, Belfast

Eugene McGivern Esq, Under Secretary, Inland Revenue, Somerset House, Strand, London WC2R 1LB *Telephone:* 071-438 6622

Regulatory Organisations and Public Bodies
see page 857

McGREGOR, OLIVER ROSS (Lord McGregor of Durris)   Chairman, Press Complaints Commission

Career: economic history lecturer Hull University 1945-47; lecturer Bedford College, London 1947-60; reader London University 1960-64; head sociology department Bedford College 1964-77; social institutions professor London University 1964-85; director Centre for Socio-legal studies, fellow Wolfson College, Oxford 1972-75; chairman Royal Commission on Press 1975-77, Advertising Standards Authority 1980-90, Press Complaints Commission 1991-

Date of birth: 25 August 1921 *Education/professional qualifications:* Worksop College; Aberdeen University; London School of Economics *Marital status:* married Nellie Weate 1944; 3 sons *Publications:* Divorce in England (1957); co-author Separated Spouses (1970); Social History and Law Reform (1981)

Lord McGregor of Durris, Chairman, Press Complaints Commission, 1 Salisbury Square, London EC4Y 8AE *Telephone:* 071-353 1248

McINTOSH, Dr MALCOLM KENNETH   Chief of Defence Procurement, Ministry of Defence   Grade: 1

Career: Australia 1970-90: research scientist Weapons Research Establishment 1970-72; army service 1972-74; Economic Ministries 1974-82; Department of Defence 1982-90: chief of defence production 1987, deputy secretary acquisitions and logistics 1988; secretary Department of Industry, Technology and Commerce 1990; chief of defence procurement Procurement Executive Ministry of Defence 1991-

Date of birth: 14 December 1945 *Education/professional qualifications:* Telopea Park High School, Canberra, Australia; Australian National University, science (BSc), physics (PhD)

Dr Malcolm K McIntosh, Chief of Defence Procurement, Ministry of Defence, Whitehall, London SW1A 2HB *Telephone:* 071-218 6304 *Fax:* 071-218 2483

MACINTYRE, WILLIAM IAN   Under Secretary Coal, Energy Division, Department of Trade and Industry   Grade: 3

Career: BP Co Ltd 1965-72; principal: Export Credits Guarantee Department 1972-73, oil division Department of Trade and Industry 1973-74, oil division Department of Energy (DEn 1974-77; controller Industrial and Commercial Finance Corporation on secondment 1977-79; DEn) 1979-: assistant secretary gas division 1979-83, director-general energy efficiency office 1983-87, under secretary: electricity division 1987-91, coal division 1991-

Date of birth: 20 July 1943 *Education/professional qualifications:* Merchiston Castle School, Edinburgh; St Andrews University, history and political economy (MA 1965) *Honours, decorations:* CB 1992 *Marital status:* married Jennifer Mary 1967; 2 daughters, 1 son

William I MacIntyre Esq CB, Under Secretary, Energy Division, Department of Trade and Industry, 1 Palace Street, London SW1E 5HE *Telephone:* 071-238 3000

Complete Name Index
see page 955

McIVOR, (FRANCES) JILL   Northern Ireland Parliamentary Commissioner for Administration [Ombudsman]; Deputy Chairman, Radio Authority

Career: law tutor Queen's University, Belfast 1965-74; NI Legal Quarterly 1966-76; member lay panel Juvenile Court 1976-77; librarian director of public prosecutions department 1977-79; NI member Independent Broadcasting Authority 1980-86; member Fair Employment Agency/Commission 1984-91; deputy chairman Radio Authority 1990-; Northern Ireland ombudsman 1991- *Current non-Whitehall posts:* member Queen's University, Belfast Board of Visitors 1988-

Date of birth: 10 August 1930 *Education/professional qualifications:* Methodist College, Belfast; Lurgan College, County Armagh; Queen's University, Belfast, law (LLB 1951); barrister 1980 *Marital status:* married Rt Hon William Basil 1953; 2 sons, 1 daughter *Publications:* contributor and consultant Manual of Law Librarianship (1976); editor Elegentia Juris: selected writings of FH Newark (1973); Chart of the English Reports (1982) *Clubs:* Royal Over-Seas League *Recreations:* gardening

Mrs F Jill McIvor, Ombudsman, Office of the Ombudsman, Progressive House, 33 Wellington Place, Belfast BT1 6HN *Telephone:* 0232 233821 *Fax:* 0232 234912

MACKAY, EILEEN ALISON   Under Secretary, Central Services, Scottish Office   Grade: 3

Career: research officer Department of Employment 1965-72; principal: Scottish Office (SO) 1972-78, HM Treasury 1978-80; policy adviser Central Policy Review Staff, Cabinet Office 1980-83; SO 1983-: assistant secretary 1983-88, under secretary housing group 1988-92, central services 1992- *Current non-Whitehall posts:* non-executive director Moray Firth Maltings plc 1988-

Date of birth: 7 July 1943 *Education/professional qualifications:* Dingwall Academy, Ross-shire; Edinburgh University, geography (MA 1965) *Marital status:* married (Alasdair) Muir Russell 1983

Miss Eileen A Mackay, Under Secretary, Central Services, Scottish Office, St Andrew's House, Edinburgh EH1 3DE *Telephone:* 031-244 4049 *Fax:* 031-244 2683

McKAY, GREGOR   Special Adviser to Secretary of State for Scotland

Career: special adviser to secretary of state for Scotland 1992- *Education/professional qualifications:* St Andrew's University

Gregor McKay Esq, Special Adviser, Scottish Office, St Andrew's House, Edinburgh EH1 3DE *Telephone:* 031-556 8400

MACKAY, H M   Clerk of Public Bills, House of Commons   Grade: 3

H M MacKay Esq, Clerk of Public Bills, House of Commons, Westminster, London SW1A 0AA *Telephone:* 071-219 3000

MACKAY, PETER   Secretary, Industry Department, Scottish Office   Grade: 2

Career: Scottish Office (SO) 1963-78; Nuffield travelling fellowship 1978-79; director for Scotland, Manpower Services Commission 1982-85; under secretary: Department of Employment 1985-87, Scottish Education Department 1987-89; principal establishment officer SO 1989-90; secretary SO Industry Department 1990-

Date of birth: 6 July 1940 *Education/professional qualifications:* High School, Glasgow; St Andrew's University, political economy (MA 1962) *Marital status:* married Sarah Holdich 1964; 2 daughters, 1 son *Clubs:* Clyde Canoe, Scottish Arctic *Recreations:* dinghy sailing, sea canoeing, rock climbing, Alps, Arctic

Peter MacKay Esq, Secretary, Scottish Office Industry Department, New St Andrew's House, Edinburgh EH1 3TA *Telephone:* 031-244 4602 *Fax:* 031-244 4599

MACKENZIE, KENNETH JOHN   Secretary, Agriculture and Fisheries Department, Scottish Office   Grade: 2

Career: Scottish Home and Health Department (SHHD) 1965-70: assistant principal 1965-69, private secretary (PS) to joint parliamentary under secretary (US) 1969-70; principal: General Register Office 1970, Scottish Office (SO) regional development division 1970-73; civil service fellow (CSF) Downing College, Cambridge 1972; principal Scottish Education Department 1973-77; CSF department of politics Glasgow University 1974-75; principal PS to secretary of state for Scotland 1977-79; assistant secretary: Scottish economic planning department 1979-83, SO finance division 1983-85; principal finance officer SO 1985-88; US SHHD 1988-91; Secretary, Head of Department and Accounting Officer SO Agriculture and Fisheries Department 1991-

Date of birth: 1 May 1943 *Education/professional qualifications:* Birkenhead School, Cheshire; Pembroke College, Oxford, modern history (BA 1964, MA); Stanford University, USA: history (AM) *Marital status:* married Irene Mary Hogarth 1975; 1 son, 1 daughter *Clubs:* National Liberal *Recreations:* Congregational Church convenor, amateur dramatics

Kenneth J MacKenzie Esq, Secretary, Scottish Office Agriculture and Fisheries Department, Pentland House, 47 Robb's Loan, Edinburgh EH14 1TW *Telephone:* 031-244 6032 *Fax:* 031-244 6001

McLAUCHLAN, DEREK JOHN   Chief Executive, National Air Traffic Services, Civil Aviation Authority

Career: engineer British Aircraft Corporation 1954-66; project manager European Space Technology Centre, Netherlands 1966-70; space general manager Marconi Space and Defence Systems 1970-76; engineering director ICL 1976-88; managing director Renishaw Research Ltd 1988-89; National Air Traffic Services, Civil Aviation Authority 1989-: director-general projects and engineering 1989-91, chief executive 1991-

Date of birth: 5 May 1933 *Education/professional qualifications:* Queen Elizabeth's Hospital School, Bristol; Bristol University, physics (BSc 1954);

CEng 1988; FIEE 1988 *Marital status:* married Sylvia June 1963; 2 daughters *Recreations:* music, theatre, badminton

Derek J McLauchlan Esq, Chief Executive, National Air Traffic Services, 45-49 Kingsway, London WC2B 6TE *Telephone:* 071-832 5772 *Fax:* 071-832 6368

McLENNAN, WILLIAM   Director and Head of Government Statistical Service, Central Statistical Office (Executive Agency)   Grade: 1A

William McLennan Esq, Director and Head of Government Statistical Service, Central Statistical Office, Great George Street, London SW1P 3AG *Telephone:* 071-270 3000

MACLEOD, ANDREW KENNETH   Chief Executive, Scottish Fisheries Protection Agency (Executive Agency)   Grade: 5

Career: National Economic Development Office 1974-78; economic adviser (EA) Manpower Services Commission 1978-83; Industry Department for Scotland 1983-90: EA 1983-87, principal 1987-90; assistant secretary Department of Agriculture and Fisheries for Scotland 1990-91; chief executive Scottish Fisheries Protection Agency 1991-

Date of birth: 28 March 1950 *Education/professional qualifications:* Larchfield School, Helensburgh; Fettes College, Edinburgh; St John's College, Oxford, politics, philosophy and economics (BA); Nuffield College, Oxford, labour economics *Marital status:* married Sheila Janet 1980; 2 daughters

Andrew K Macleod Esq, Chief Executive, Scottish Fisheries Protection Agency, Pentland House, 47 Robb's Loan, Edinburgh EH14 1TW *Telephone:* 031-244 6059 *Fax:* 031-244 6001

MACPHAIL, SHERIFF IAIN DUNCAN   Commissioner, Scottish Law Commission

Career: advocate 1963-73; sheriff at Glasgow 1973-81, at Dunfermline and Alloa 1981-82, at Linlithgow 1982-88, at Edinburgh 1988-90; Scottish law commissioner (criminal law, evidence and civil procedure) 1990-

Date of birth: 24 January 1938 *Education/professional qualifications:* George Watson's College, Edinburgh; Edinburgh University, history (MA 1959); Glasgow University, law (LLB 1962) *Honours, decorations:* QC Scotland 1989 *Marital status:* married Rosslyn Graham Lillias Hewitt 1970; 1 son, 1 daughter *Publications:* Evidence (Law Society of Scotland 1987); Sheriff Court Practice (W Green and Son 1988) *Clubs:* New, Edinburgh *Recreations:* music, theatre, reading, writing

Sheriff Iain D Macphail QC, Commissioner, Scottish Law Commission, 140 Causewayside, Edinburgh EH9 1PR *Telephone:* 031-668 2131 *Fax:* 031-662 4900

McQUAID, Dr JAMES   Research Director, Health and Safety Executive   Grade: 3

Career: engineer 1961-; research director Health and Safety Executive 1985-

Date of birth: 5 November 1939 *Education/professional qualifications:* University College, Dublin (BEng); Jesus College, Cambridge (PhD)

Dr James McQuaid, Research Director, Health and Safety Executive, Broad Lane, Sheffield S3 7HQ *Telephone:* 0742-768141

McQUAIL, PAUL CHRISTOPHER   Deputy Secretary, Planning, Rural Affairs and Heritage, Department of the Environment   Grade: 2

Career: Ministry of Housing and Local Government, Department of the Environment 1957-: under secretary 1977-88, on secondment as chief executive Hounslow Borough Council 1983-85, deputy secretary planning rural affairs and heritage 1988-

Date of birth: 22 April 1934   *Education/professional qualifications:* Sidney Sussex College, Cambridge

Paul C McQuail Esq, Deputy Secretary, Department of the Environment, 2 Marsham Street, London SW1P 3EB   *Telephone:* 071-276 3000

MADDEN, MICHAEL   Under Secretary, Flood Defence, Plant Protection and Agricultural Resources, Ministry of Agriculture, Fisheries and Food   Grade: 3

Career: Ministry of Agriculture, Fisheries and Food 1963-: head management services group 1985-90, flood defence, plant protection and agricultural resources 1990-

Date of birth: 12 February 1936   *Education/professional qualifications:* King Edward VII School, Sheffield

Michael Madden Esq, Under Secretary, Ministry of Agriculture, Fisheries and Food, 3 Whitehall Place, London SW1A 2HH   *Telephone:* 071-270 3000

MAGEE, IAN B V   Territorial Director, Social Security Benefits Agency (Executive Agency)   Grade: 4

Career: Department of Social Security (DSS) 1976-84: private secretary to minister for social security 1976-78, various policy and management posts 1978-84; member Enterprise Unit, Cabinet Office 1984-86; DSS/Department of Health and Social Security 1986-: deputy to director of personnel 1986-89, DSS regional controller 1989-90, director southern territory, Social Security Benefits Agency 1990-   *Current non-Whitehall posts:* non-executive director Laing Management Contracting 1989-

Date of birth: 9 July 1946   *Education/professional qualifications:* St Michael's College, Leeds; Leeds University, history (BA 1968)   *Clubs:* MCC, Verulam Golf   *Recreations:* cricket, golf, reading

Ian B V Magee Esq, Director Southern Territory Benefits Agency, Cannon Building, Olympic Way, Wembley, Middlesex   *Telephone:* 081-902 8822

MAINES, (JAMES) DENNIS   Director-General Guided Weapons and Electronic Systems (Land), Procurement Executive, Ministry of Defence   Grade: 3

Career: Procurement Executive Ministry of Defence 1981-: head of guided weapons optics and electronics group 1981-83, of microwave and electro-optics group 1983-84, of sensors, electronic warfare and guided weapons 1984-86; deputy director weapons Royal Aerospace Establishment, Farnborough 1986-88; director general guided weapons and electronic systems (land) directorate 1988-

Date of birth: 26 July 1937   *Education/professional qualifications:* Leigh Grammar School; City University, London, applied physics (BSc 1960)   *Publications:* contributor to Surface Wave Filters (1977)

J Dennis Maines Esq, Director-General, Guided Weapons and Electronic Systems (Land), Procurement Executive, Ministry of Defence, Whitehall, London SW1A 2HB   *Telephone:* 071-218 9000

MAKEHAM, PETER DEREK JAMES   Director, Business Services Division, Employment Department Group   Grade: 4

Career: Department of Employment (DEmp) 1971-83: economist 1971-82, on secondment as economic adviser to Unilever 1982-83; speechwriter for chancellor of exchequer and chief secretary HM Treasury 1983-84; economist cabinet office enterprise unit 1984-85; DEmp 1985-: enterprise and deregulation unit 1985-86, employment policy branch 1986-87, central unit 1987-90, manager financial services branch 1990-91, director business services division (management and corporate services, estates management, IT) 1991-

Date of birth: 15 March 1948   *Education/professional qualifications:* Chichester High School for Boys; Nottingham University, economics and economic history (BA 1970); Leeds University, labour economics (MA 1971)   *Marital status:* married Carolyne Rosemary 1972; 1 son, 3 daughters

Peter D J Makeham Esq, Director, Business Services Division, Employment Department Group, Caxton House, Tothill Street, London SW1H 9NF   *Telephone:* 081-273 5383   *Fax:* 081-273 5384

MALONE-LEE, MICHAEL CHARLES   Deputy Secretary, Director of Operations, Department of Health   Grade: 2

Career: principal finance officer Home Office 1987-90; deputy secretary director of operations Department of Health 1990-

Date of birth: 4 March 1941   *Education/professional qualifications:* Campion Hall, Oxford (MA)

Michael C Malone-Lee Esq, Deputy Secretary, Director of Operations, Department of Health, Whitehall, London SW1   *Telephone:* 071-210 3000

MANNING, R G M   Head of Asia and the Oceans Division, Overseas Development Administration   Grade: 3

R G M Manning Esq, Head of Asia and the Oceans Division, Overseas Development Administration, 94 Victoria Street, London SW1E 5JL   *Telephone:* 071-917 7000

MANSFIELD, (EDWARD) JOHN   Principal Director of Patents, Procurement Executive, Ministry of Defence   Grade: 4

Career: patent officer (PO): Ministry of Supply 1956-59, Ministry of Aviation (MA) 1959-63; senior PO (SPO) MA 1963; SPO Royal Radar Establishment 1963-72: MA 1963-67, Ministry of Technology 1967-71, Ministry of Defence (MoD) 1971-72; MoD Procurement Executive 1972-: assistant director of patents (DP) 1972-81, DP 1981-85, principal DP advising the MoD and other departments on all aspects of intellectual property rights) 1985-

Date of birth: 14 April 1933   *Education/professional qualifications:* Silcoates School, Wakefield, Yorkshire; Manchester University, mathematics (BSc 1954); CPA 1962; European Patent Attorney 1977   *Recreations:* music

E John Mansfield Esq, Principal Director of Patents, Ministry of Defence Procurement Executive, Empress State Building, Lillie Road, London SW6 1TR   *Telephone:* 071-385 1244   *Fax:* 071-385 1244 ext 2318

MANTHORPE, JOHN   Chief Registrar and Chief Executive, HM Land Registry (Executive Agency)   Grade: 2

Career: HM Land Registry 1974-: head of plans and survey branch 1974-78; controller of registration 1978-85; principal finance officer 1985-90 and chief executive 1985-; chief registrar (management and delivery of land registration services in England and Wales) 1991-

Date of birth: 16 June 1936 *Education/professional qualifications:* Beckenham and Penge Grammar School *Marital status:* married Kathleen Mary 1967; 1 daughter, 3 sons *Recreations:* Sussex and Ashdown Forest

John Manthorpe Esq, Chief Registrar, Land Registry, Lincoln's Inn Fields, London WC2A 3PH *Telephone:* 071-405 3488 *Fax:* 071-242 0825

MARSH, RICHARD   Special Adviser to Secretary of State for Health

Career: Conservative Research Department; special adviser to secretaries of state for health: William Waldegrave 1991-92, Virginia Bottomley 1992-

Richard Marsh Esq, Special Adviser, Department of Health, Richmond House, 79 Whitehall, London SW1A 2NS *Telephone:* 071-210 3000

MARSON, ANTHONY   Group Finance Director, Property Services Agency Services, Department of the Environment   Grade: 3

Career: finance director pharmaceutical division Beecham Group plc 1968-90; group finance director Property Services Agency Services, Department of the Environment 1990-

Date of birth: 12 January 1938 *Education/professional qualifications:* St Marylebone Grammar School, London; Bristol University, modern languages (BA 1962) *Marital status:* married Margaret Joy 1963; 3 sons *Recreations:* walking, music, travel

Anthony Marson Esq, Group Finance Director, Property Services Agency Services, Department of the Environment, 2 Marsham Street, London SW1P 3EB *Telephone:* 071-276 3669 *Fax:* 071-276 3495

MARTIN, FRANK   Principal Establishment and Finance Officer, Central Statistical Office   Grade: 4

Career: Central Office of Information 1969-75; Department of Trade and Industry 1975-76; HM Treasury 1976-89; deputy director central unit on purchasing 1987-89; principal establishment and finance officer Central Statistical Office 1989-

Date of birth: 1 April 1946 *Education/professional qualifications:* Allsop High School for Boys, Liverpool; Sidney Sussex College, Cambridge, history (BA 1968); London School of Economics, international relations (MSc 1969) *Marital status:* married Jean; 1 son, 1 daughter

Frank Martin Esq, Principal Establishment and Finance Officer, Central Statistical Office, Great George Street, London SW1P 3AQ *Telephone:* 071-270 6496 *Fax:* 071-270 6085

MARTIN, JOHN SHARP BUCHANAN   Under Secretary, School Education, Education Department, Scottish Office   Grade: 3

Career: Scottish Office 1968-: assistant principal Education Department (ED) 1968-73; principal ED and Home and Health Department 1973-80; Industry and Environment Departments 1980-92; under secretary schools education ED 1992-

Date of birth: 7 July 1946 *Education/professional qualifications:* Bell Baxter High School, Cupar, Fife; St Andrews University, chemistry (BSc 1968) *Marital status:* married Catriona Meldrum 1971; 1 daughter, 1 son *Clubs:* Colinton Lawn Tennis, Woodcutters Cricket *Recreations:* tennis, cricket, philately

John S B Martin Esq, Under Secretary, Scottish Office Education Department, New St Andrews House, Edinburgh EH1 3SY *Telephone:* 031-244 4413 *Fax:* 031-244 4785

MASON, Dr PAUL JAMES   Director of Research, Meteorological Office (Executive Agency)   Grade: 4

Career: Meteorological Office 1967-: scientific officer (SO) 1967-71; senior SO 1971-74; principal SO 1974-82; assistant director boundary layer research 1982-89; deputy director physical processes 1989-91; director of research 1991-

Date of birth: 16 March 1946 *Education/professional qualifications:* Whitchurch Grammar School, Cardiff; Nottingham University, physics (BSc 1967), geophysics (PhD 1972) *Marital status:* married Elizabeth Mary 1968; 1 daughter, 1 son *Recreations:* walking

Dr Paul J Mason, Director of Research, Meteorological Office, London Road, Bracknell, Berkshire RG12 2SZ *Telephone:* 0344 854604 *Fax:* 0344 856909

MATHESON, (STEPHEN) STEVE CHARLES TAYLOR   Commissioner and Director-General, Inland Revenue   Grade: 2

Career: Inland Revenue 1961-: tax inspector 1961-70; principal 1970-75; private secretary to paymaster general 1975-76, to chancellor of exchequer 1976-77; assistant secretary, manager computerisation of PAYE project 1977-84; under secretary, director of information technology 1984-89; deputy secretary, commissioner, director-general, principal establishment officer 1989- *Current non-Whitehall posts:* president British Computer Society 1991-

Date of birth: 27 June 1939 *Education/professional qualifications:* Aberdeen Grammar School; Aberdeen University, English language and literature (MA 1961) *Marital status:* married Marna Rutherford Burnett 1960; 2 sons *Publications:* Maurice Walsh, Storyteller (Brandon 1985) *Recreations:* reading, cooking, cardplaying

Steve C T Matheson Esq, Director General, Inland Revenue, Somerset House, Strand, London WC2R 1LB *Telephone:* 071-438 6789 *Fax:* 071-438 7444

MAYHEW, JEREMY PAUL   Special Adviser to Secretary of State for Social Security

Career: assistant producer BBC tv 1980-84; producer/director Channel 4 tv 1984-87; management consultant 1989-90; special adviser to Peter Lilley, secretary of state for trade and industry 1990-92, secretary of state for social security 1992-

Date of birth: February 1959 *Education/professional qualifications:* Clifton College, Bristol; Balliol College, Oxford, philosophy, politics and economics (BA, MA, 1980); Harvard Business School, USA (MBA 1989) *Marital status:* single   *Clubs:* Harvard, Boston, USA

Jeremy P Mayhew Esq, Special Adviser, Department of Social Security, Richmond House, 79 Whitehall, London SW1 2NS   *Telephone:* 071-210 5101   *Fax:* 071-839 1285

MEADOWS, PAMELA   **Chief Economic Adviser, Employment Department Group** Grade: 3

Career: chief economic adviser, head of economics, research and evaluation division Employment Department Group 1992-
Education/professional qualifications: Kenya High School, Nairobi; Penrhos College, Colwyn Bay, Durham University, economics (BA 1970), Birkbeck College, London, economics (MSc 1978)
Marital status: married; 1 son

Ms Pamela Meadows, Chief Economic Adviser, Employment Department Group, Caxton House, Tothill Street, London SW1H 9NF   *Telephone:* 071-273 3000

MEADWAY, RICHARD JOHN   **Under Secretary, Overseas Trade Division 2, Department of Trade and Industry**   Grade: 3

Career: assistant principal Ministry of Technology 1970-73; private secretary: to Minister for Trade and Consumer Affairs Department of Trade and Industry (DTI) 1973-74, to Secretary of State for Prices and Consumer Protection 1974-76, to Prime Minister 1976-78; assistant secretary: Department of Trade 1979-83, DTI 1983-89; under secretary, overseas trade division 2 (N America and E and SE Asia) DTI 1989-

Date of birth: 30 December 1944   *Education/professional qualifications:* Collyer's School, Horsham; natural sciences, Peterhouse, Cambridge (BA 1965, MA); Edinburgh University, molecular biology, (PhD 1969), Oxford University, molecular biology (MA 1969)   *Marital status:* married Dr Jeanette Meadway 1968; 2 daughters   *Clubs:* Reform   *Recreations:* reading, travel

Richard J Meadway Esq, Under Secretary, Department of Trade and Industry, Kingsgate House, 66-74 Victoria Street, London SW1E 6SW   *Telephone:* 071-215 5230   *Fax:* 071-931 0397

MEARS, Dr A L   **Technical and Quality Director, Defence Research Agency (Executive Agency)**   Grade: 3

Dr A L Mears, Technical and Quality Director, Defence Research Agency, Meudon Avenue, Farnborough, Hampshire GU14 7TU   *Telephone:* 0252-373434

MELDRUM, KEITH CAMERON   **Chief Veterinary Officer, Ministry of Agriculture, Fisheries and Food**   Grade: 3

Career: private veterinary practice 1961-63; Ministry of Agriculture, Fisheries and Food 1963-: veterinary officer (VO) 1963-72; divisional VO 1972-78; deputy regional VO 1978-80; regional VO 1980-83; assistant chief VO 1983-86; director veterinary field service 1986-88; chief VO animal health and veterinary group (for GB) 1988-

Date of birth: 19 April 1937   *Education/professional qualifications:* Uppingham School; Edinburgh University; veterinary studies (MRCVS 1961, BVM & S 1961, DVSM 1966)   *Marital status:* married Vivien Mary Fisher 1982; 1 daughter, 2 sons   *Clubs:* North London Rifle, Farmers'   *Recreations:* competitive target rifle shooting, outdoor activities

Keith C Meldrum Esq, Chief Veterinary Officer, Government Buildings, Hook Rise South, Tolworth, Surbiton, Surrey KT6 7NF
Telephone: 081-330 8050   *Fax:* 081-330 6872

MERIFIELD, ANTHONY JAMES   Under Secretary, Cabinet Office   Grade: 3

Career: district officer Overseas Civil Service, Kenya 1958-65; Ministry of Health/Department of Health and Social Security (DHSS) 1965-82: principal 1965-71, assistant secretary 1971-78, under secretary industries and exports division 1978-79, director of establishments (HQ) 1979-82; assistant under secretary of state Northern Ireland Office 1982-85; DHSS/Department of Health 1986-91: regional liaison director NHS management board/executive 1986-91; head of senior and public appointments group Cabinet Office 1991-

Date of birth: 5 March 1934 *Education/professional qualifications:* Chesterfield School; Shrewsbury School; Wadham College, Oxford, history (BA, MA 1957) *Marital status:* married Pamela Pratt 1980 *Clubs:* Commonwealth Trust, Achilles

Anthony J Merifield ESq, Under Secretary, Cabinet Office, Horse Guards Road, London SW1P 3AL *Telephone:* 071-270 6220 *Fax:* 071-270 5828

MICHELL, MICHAEL JOHN   Chief Executive, Radiocommunications Agency (Executive Agency)   Grade: 3

Career: HM Treasury 1977-80; DTI 1980-: head of air division 1984-88; chief executive Radiocommunications Agency 1988-

Date of birth: 12 December 1942 *Education/professional qualifications:* Corpus Christi College, Cambridge (BA)

Michael J Michell Esq, Chief Executive, Radiocommunications Agency, Department of Trade and Industry, Waterloo Bridge House, London SE1 8UA *Telephone:* 071-215 2000

MILBANK, NEIL OSCAR   Deputh Chief Executive and Director Materials Group, Building Research Establishment (Executive Agency)   Grade: 4

Career: apprentice, design engineer de Havilland 1953-60; design engineer English Electric nuclear power division 1960-63; Building Research Establishment 1963-: deputy chief executive and director materials group (materials research; energy economy advice to EC) 1991- *Current non-Whitehall posts:* director Trada QA

Date of birth: 21 December 1935 *Education/professional qualifications:* Enfield Grammar School; City University, mechanical engineering (BSc Eng 1957); MIME 1970; MCIBSE 1971; CEng 1976 *Honours, decorations:* bronze medal Chartered Institute of Building Services Engineers 1971 *Marital status:* married Sheila 1960; 2 daughters *Recreations:* bridge, golf

Neil O Milbank Esq, Deputy Chief Executive, Building Research Establishment, Garston, Watford, Herts WD2 7JR *Telephone:* 0923 664212 *Fax:* 0923 664089

Parliamentary Offices
see page 275

MILES, (RICHARD) OLIVER   Director-General, Overseas Trade Joint Directorate, Foreign and Commonwealth Office and Department of Trade and Industry   Senior grade

Career: HM diplomatic service 1960-: service in Middle and Near East 1960-83, ambassador to Libya 1984, to Luxembourg 1986-89; assistant under secretary Foreign and Commonwealth Office (FCO) 1989-91; under secretary, director FCO and Department of Trade and Industry Overseas Trade Services directorate (advises on government export promotion policy) 1991- *Current non-Whitehall posts:* non-executive director Vickers Defence Systems 1990-

Date of birth: 6 March 1936 *Education/professional qualifications:* Ampleforth College, York; Merton College, Oxford, Oriental languages (BA 1960) *Honours, decorations:* CMG 1984 *Marital status:* married Julia Weiner 1968; 3 sons, 1 daughter *Clubs:* Travellers *Recreations:* birdwatching, playing the flute

R Oliver Miles Esq CMG, Director-General, Overseas Trade Joint Directorate, Kingsgate House, 68 Victoria Street, London SW1E 6SW *Telephone:* 071-215 4249 *Fax:* 071-215 5644

MILLAR, DOUGLAS GEORGE   Principal Clerk of Select Committees, House of Commons   Grade: 3

Career: joint secretary Association of Secretaries General of Parliaments 1971-77; House of Commons Department of the Clerk 1979-: clerk of defence committee 1979-83; clerk private members' bills, public bill office 1983-87; clerk of home affairs committee 1987-89, of financial and treasury and civil service committees 1989-91; principal clerk of select committees 1991-

Date of birth: 15 February 1946 *Education/professional qualifications:* City of Norwich School; Bristol University, history (BA 1967); Reading University, politics (MA 1968) *Marital status:* married Victoria 1987; 2 daughters, 2 sons *Clubs:* Parliamentary Golfing Society *Recreations:* golf, family

Douglas G Millar Esq, Principal Clerk of Select Committees, Committee Office, House of Commons, London SW1A 0AA *Telephone:* 071-219 6257

MILLER, BARRY   Assistant Under Secretary, Director-General, Test and Evaluation Directorate, Procurement Executive, Ministry of Defence   Grade: 3

Career: Ministry of Defence (MoD) 1961-75: Royal Aircraft Establishment, Farnborough 1961-65; assistant principal 1965-69, principal 1969-75; principal Civil Service Department 1975-77; MoD 1977-: assistant secretary 1977-86, assistant secretary and director general (DG) defence quality assurance (including military adherence to Montreal Protocol for ozone layer protection) 1986-92, DG test and evaluation directorate 1992- *Current non-Whitehall posts:* chairman Civil Service Club 1990-

Date of birth: 11 May 1942 *Education/professional qualifications:* Royal Grammar School, Lancaster *Recreations:* military uniforms

Barry Miller Esq, Director-General, Test and Evaluation Directorate, Procurement Executive, Ministry of Defence, St Christopher's House, Southwark Street, London SE1 0TD *Telephone:* 071-928 3666

MILLER, PERRY   Special Adviser to Secretary of State for Defence

Career: Bank of England; Conservative Research Department; special adviser to Malcolm Rifkind, secretary of state for defence 1992-

Perry Miller Esq, Special Adviser, Ministry of Defence, Main Building, Whitehall, London SW1A 2HB *Telephone:* 071-218 9000

MILLS, BARBARA JEAN LYON   Director of Public Prosecutions, Crown Prosecutions Service   Grade: 1

Career: barrister 1967-90; director Serious Fraud Office (investigates and prosecutes cases of serious and complex fraud in England, Wales and Northern Ireland) 1990-92; Director of Public Prosecutions, Crown Prosecutions Service 1992-

Date of birth: 10 August 1940 *Education/professional qualifications:* St Helen's School, Northwood, Middlesex; Lady Margaret Hall, Oxford, jurisprudence (BA, MA 1962) *Honours, decorations:* QC 1986 *Marital status:* married John Angus Donald 1962; 3 daughters, 1 son

Mrs Barbara J L Mills QC, Director of Public Prosecutions, Crown Prosecutions Service, 4-12 Queen Anne's Gate, London SW1H 9AZ *Telephone:* 071-273 8152 *Fax:* 071-222 0392

MILLS, HAROLD   Secretary and Chief Economic Adviser, Environment Department, Scottish Office   Grade: 2

Harold Mills Esq, Secretary and Chief Economic Adviser, Environment Department, Scottish Office, St Andrews House, Edinburgh EH1 3DD *Telephone:* 031-556 8400

MILLS, Dr HAROLD HERNSHAW   Secretary, Environment Department, Scottish Office   Grade: 2

Career: cancer research scientist Roswell Park Memorial Institute, USA 1962-64; lecturer Glasgow University 1964-69; principal Scottish Home and Health Department 1970-76; assistant secretary: Scottish Office (SO) 1976-81, Privy Council Office 1981-83, Scottish Development Department (SDD) 1983-84; under secretary: SDD 1984-88, SO, principal finance officer 1988-92; secretary environment department 1992- *Current non-Whitehall posts:* director St Giles' Luckembooths Ltd 1987-

Date of birth: 2 March 1938 *Education/professional qualifications:* Greenock High School; Glasgow University, chemistry (BSc 1959) and X-ray crystallography (PhD 1962) *Marital status:* married Marion Elizabeth Beattie 1973

Dr Harold H Mills, Secretary, Environment Department, Scottish Office, New St Andrew's House, Edinburgh EH1 3DE *Telephone:* 031-244 4714

Government Departments
see page 300

MITCHELSON, IAN SYDNEY   Chief Executive, Service Children's Schools (North West Europe) (Executive Agency)

Career: teacher 1960-65; administrative assistant Worcestershire County Council (CC) local education authority 1966-69; assistant education officer (EO) North Riding CC 1969-74; North Yorkshire CC 1974-90: principal EO 1974-85, deputy county EO 1985-90; chief executive Service Children's Schools (North West Europe) 1991-

Date of birth: 10 December 1936 *Education/professional qualifications:* Morecambe Grammar School, Lancashire; Downing College, Cambridge, geography (BA 1959, MA); Cambridge University (Cert Ed 1960) *Marital status:* married Betty 1964; 2 daughters, 1 son *Recreations:* walking, gardening

Ian S Mitchelson, Chief Executive, Service Children's Schools (North West Europe), HQ BAOR, BFPO 140 *Telephone:* (010) 49 2161 4723296 *Fax:* (010) 49 2161 4723487

MONCK, NICHOLAS   Second Permanent Under Secretary, Public Expenditure, HM Treasury   Grade: 1A *(see Addenda)*

Career: assistant principal: Ministry of Power 1959-62, National Economic Development Office 1962, 65, National Board for Prices and Incomes 1965-66; senior economist Ministry of Agriculture, Tanzania 1966-69; HM Treasury 1969-: principal 1969-71, assistant secretary 1971-75, principal private secretary to chancellor 1976-77, under secretary 1977-84, deputy secretary (industry) 1984-90, second permanent secretary (public expenditure) 1990-

Date of birth: 9 March 1935 *Education/professional qualifications:* Eton College; King's College, Cambridge, classics, history (BA 1958); Pennsylvania University, USA, American civilisation; London School of Economics, economics (BSc) *Honours, decorations:* CB 1988 *Marital status:* married Elizabeth 1960; 3 sons

Nicholas Monck Esq CB, Second Permanent Under Secretary, HM Treasury, Parliament Street, London SW1P 3AG *Telephone:* 071-270 3000

MONGER, GEORGE WILLIAM   Head of Industry, Agriculture and Employment Group, HM Treasury   Grade: 3

Career: Ministry of Power 1961-68; Ministry of Technology 1968-70; Department of Trade and Industry 1970-74; Department of Energy 1974-81; HM Treasury (HMT) 1981-87; Cabinet Office 1987-90; head of industry, agriculture and employment group HMT 1990-

Date of birth: 1 April 1937 *Education/professional qualifications:* Holloway School, London; Jesus College, Cambridge, history (BA, MA, PhD) *Marital status:* single *Publications:* The End of Isolation: British Foreign Policy 1900-1907 (Nelson 1963) *Clubs:* United Oxford and Cambridge University

George W Monger Esq, Head of Industry, Agriculture and Employment Group, HM Treasury, Parliament Street, London SW1P 3AG *Telephone:* 071-270 4449 *Fax:* 071-270 4651

'Next Steps' Executive Agencies
see page 761

MONTAGU, NICHOLAS LIONEL JOHN   Deputy Secretary, Public Transport, Department of Transport   Grade: 2

Career: philosophy assistant lecturer/lecturer Reading University 1966-74; Department of [Health and] Social Security 1974-: principal 1974-81: seconded to Cabinet Office 1978-79, assistant secretary 1981-86, under secretary 1986-90, deputy secretary (DS) resource management and planning 1990-92; DS public transport, Department of Transport 1992-

Date of birth: 12 March 1944 *Education/professional qualifications:* Rugby School; New College, Oxford, literae humaniores (BA 1966, MA) *Marital status:* married Dr Jennian Ford Geddes 1974; 2 daughters *Recreations:* cooking, wild flowers, fishing

Nicholas L J Montagu Esq, Deputy Secretary, Department of Transport, 2 Marsham Street, London SW1P 3EB *Telephone:* 071-276 3000 *Fax:* 071-276 0818

MOORE, DAVID JAMES LADD   Under Secretary, Defence Policy, Manpower and Material Group, HM Treasury   Grade: 3

Career: HM Treasury (HMT) 1982-83; Inland Revenue 1983-85; under secretary HMT 1985-, public enterprises group 1985-90, defence policy manpower and material group 1990-

Date of birth: 6 June 1937 *Education/professional qualifications:* Brasenose College, Oxford (BA)

David J L Moore Esq, Under Secretary, HM Treasury, 1 Parliament Street, London SW1P 3AG *Telephone:* 071-270 3000

MORDUE, RICHARD ERIC   Under Secretary, Director, Economics and Statistics, Ministry of Agriculture, Fisheries and Food   Grade: 3

Career: Ministry of Agriculture, Fisheries and Food 1964-: head of horticulture division 1982-89, director of economics and statistics 1989-

Date of birth: 14 June 1941 *Education/professional qualifications:* King's College, University of Durham (BSc); Michigan State University, USA (MS)

Richard E Mordue Esq, Director of Economics and Statistics, Ministry of Agriculture, Fisheries and Food, 3 Whitehall Place, London SW1A 2HH *Telephone:* 071-270 8539

MORGAN, Rear-Admiral CHARLES CHRISTOPHER   Naval Secretary, Ministry of Defence

Career: Royal Navy 1957-; Ministry of Defence (MoD) 1981-83; Staff Joint Service Defence College 1987-89; Naval Secretary MoD 1990-

Date of birth: 11 March 1939 *Education/professional qualifications:* Royal Naval College, Dartmouth; National Defence College; Royal College Defence Studies

Rear-Admiral Charles C Morgan, Naval Secretary, Ministry of Defence, Old Admiralty Building, London SW1A 2BE *Telephone:* 071-218 6047

MORGAN, MARILYNNE ANN   Under Secretary, Principal Assistant Solicitor, Department of the Environment   Grade: 3

Career: Department of [Health and] Social Security 1973-91: under secretary (US), principal assistant solicitor (AS) 1985-91; US, principal AS Department of Environment 1991-

Date of birth: 22 June 1946 *Education/professional qualifications:* Bedford College, London, history (BA); Middle Temple (barrister 1972)

Ms Marilynne A Morgan, Under Secretary, Department of the Environment, 2 Marsham Street, London SW1P 3EB *Telephone:* 071-276 3000

MORRELL, DAVID WILLIAM JAMES   Scottish Legal Services Ombudsman

Career: university posts 1957-89; consultant OECD Paris 1990-91; Scottish legal services ombudsman 1991-

David W J Morrell, Scottish Legal Services Ombudsman, 2 Greenside Lane, Edinburgh EH1 3AH *Telephone:* 031-556 5574

MORRIS, NORMA FRANCES   Administrative Secretary, Medical Research Council   Grade: 3

Career: assistant lecturer Hull University 1959-60; Medical Research Council 1960-: executive office 1960-, administrative secretary 1989- *Current non-Whitehall posts:* member National Biological Standards Board 1990-

Date of birth: 17 April 1935   *Education/professional qualifications:* Ilford County High School; University College, London, English (BA 1956, MA 1960)   *Marital status:* married Samuel 1960; 2 daughters, 1 son   *Recreations:* opera, edible fungi

Mrs Norma F Morris, Administrative Secretary, Medical Research Council, 20 Park Crescent, London W1N 4AL   *Telephone:* 071-637 6036   *Fax:* 071-580 4369

MORRIS, ROBERT MATTHEW   Assistant Under Secretary, Home Office   Grade: 3

Career: Home Office 1961-: head of Crime Policy planning unit 1979-81; assistant under secretary and head of criminal justice and constitutional department 1983-

Date of birth: 11 October 1937   *Education/professional qualifications:* Christ's College, Cambridge

Robert M Morris Esq, Assistant Under Secretary, Home Office, 50 Queen Anne's Gate, London SW1H 9AP   *Telephone:* 071-273 3000

MORRISON, DENNIS JOHN   Regional Director, East Midlands, Departments of the Environment and Transport   Grade: 4

Career: planning Lancashire county 1966-70, Cardiff Welsh Office 1970-75; Department of Environment (DoE) 1975-: NW region 1975-81, NW enterprise unit regional controller 1981-84, Merseyside Task Force urban and economic affairs regional controller 1984-89, East Midlands regional director DoE/Department of Transport 1989-

Date of birth: 20 May 1942   *Education/professional qualifications:* Lymm Grammar School, Cheshire; Manchester University, geography (BA 1964), town and country planning (DipTP 1969); FRGS; MRTPI   *Marital status:* married Polly 1967; 1 daughter, 1 son   *Clubs:* Altrincham 41   *Recreations:* antiquarian horology, antiquarian book collecting, gardening, hill walking

Dennis J Morrison Esq, Regional Director, Departments of the Environment and Transport, Cranbrook House, Cranbrook Street, Nottingham NG1 1EY   *Telephone:* 0602 476121

Regulatory Organisations and Public Bodies
see page 857

MORTIMER, (JAMES) JAMIE EDWARD Under Secretary, Aid and Export Finance, HM Treasury Grade: 3

Career: HM Treasury 1971-: head of EC budget division 1983-89, of Home Office, legal departments and Department of Transport expenditure division 1989-91; under secretary aid and export finance group (overseas debt; Foreign and Commonwealth Office and Overseas Development Administration expenditure) 1991-

Date of birth: 9 November 1947 *Education/professional qualifications:* Latymer Upper School, Hammersmith; Wadham College, Oxford, politics, philosophy and economics (BA 1969, MA), economics (D Phil 1971) *Marital status:* married Lesley Patricia 1969 *Clubs:* Old Latymerians Association *Recreations:* cinema, soccer refereeing

Jamie E Mortimer Esq, Under Secretary, HM Treasury, Parliament Street, London SW1P 3AG *Telephone:* 071-270 4479 *Fax:* 071-270 5653

MOSELEY, ELWYN RHYS Local Commissioner, Local Administration in Wales (Local Government Ombudsman)

Career: assistant solicitor (AS) Newport County Borough Council (CBC) 1969-72; principal AS Cardiff CBC 1972-74; Cardiff City Council 1974-91: city solicitor 1974-91, deputy chief executive 1979-91, director administrative and legal services 1987-91; local commissioner for local administration [ombudsman] in Wales (investigation of local authority and other bodies' maladministration) 1991-

Date of birth: 6 August 1943 *Education/professional qualifications:* Caterham School, Surrey; Queen's College, Cambridge, law (BA, MA 1965); College of Law (solicitor 1969) *Marital status:* married Annick Andrée Guyomard 1968; 2 sons, 1 daughter *Recreations:* rugby, travel

Elwyn R Moseley Esq, Local Commissioner, Commission for Local Administration in Wales, Derwen House, Court Road, Bridgend CF31 1BN *Telephone:* 0656 661325 *Fax:* 0656 658317

MOSS, DAVID CHRISTOPHER Under Secretary, International Aviation, Department of Transport Grade: 3

Career: Ministry of Public Buildings and Works/Department of Environment (DoE) 1968-77; principal Department of Transport (DTp) 1977-79, HM Treasury 1979-80; assistant secretary DTp 1980-81, DoE 1981-83, DTp 1983-88; under secretary international aviation [DTp] 1988- *Current non-Whitehall posts:* president European Civil Aviation Conference 1990-; chairman Joint Aviation Authorities Board 1990-

Date of birth: 17 April 1946 *Education/professional qualifications:* King's School, Chester; Magdalene College, Cambridge, history (BA 1968) *Marital status:* married Angela Mary Wood 1971; 1 son *Clubs:* United Oxford and Cambridge University

David C Moss Esq, Under Secretary, Department of Transport, 2 Marsham Street, London SW1P 4EB *Telephone:* 071-276 5399 *Fax:* 071-276 5390

MOSS, (JOHN) MICHAEL Assistant Under Secretary, Naval Personnel, Ministry of Defence Grade: 3

Career: air force national service 1958-60; Air Ministry 1960-64: assistant principal 1960-63: private secretary (PS) to air member for supply and organisation 1962-63, principal 1963-64; Ministry of Defence (MoD) 1964-72: principal 1964-70: PS to parliamentary under secretary for RAF 1964-70, assistant secretary (AS) 1971-72; AS Cabinet Office 1972-75: establishment officer 1972-75, secretary Radcliffe Committee of Privy Counsellors on Ministerial Memoirs 1975; MoD 1976-: AS 1976-83, Royal College of Defence Studies 1983, assistant under secretary (AUS) (air) procurement executive 1984-88, fellow Center for International Affairs, Harvard University, USA 1988-89, AUS (naval personnel) 1989-

Date of birth: 21 April 1936 *Education/professional qualifications:* Accrington Grammar School, Lancashire; King's College, Cambridge, mathematics (BA 1957, MA) *Recreations:* travel, photography, choral singing

J Michael Moss Esq, Assistant Under Secretary, Ministry of Defence, Old Admiralty Buildings, Spring Gardens, London SW1A 2BE *Telephone:* 071-218 2033

MOSSOP, JAMES R   Deputy Chief Planning Inspector, Department of the Environment   Grade: 4

Career: deputy chief planning inspector Department of the Environment (public enquiries and appeals on planning, housing, highways) 1988-

Date of birth: 19 December 1932 *Education/professional qualifications:* Workington Grammar School, Cumbria; FICE 1955; FIHT *Marital status:* married Jennifer 1956; 2 sons, 1 daughter *Recreations:* campanology

James R Mossop Esq, Deputy Chief Inspector, Planning Inspectorate, Tollgate House, Houlton Street, Bristol BS2 9DJ *Telephone:* 0272 218961

MOUATT, (RICHARD) BRIAN   Chief Dental Officer, Department of Health   Grade: 3

Career: dental officer RAF 1960-65; public health dental officer Bournemouth 1965-68; chief dental officer, Zambia 1968-72; general practice 1972-74; Department of Health 1984-: dental officer (DO)/senior DO 1984-91, chief DO 1991- *Current non-Whitehall posts:* regional dental officer South East Thames Regional Health Authority

Date of birth: 4 September 1936 *Education/professional qualifications:* Blundell's School, Tiverton; Edinburgh University, dental surgery (BDS 1960); Royal College of Surgeons, dental surgery (MGDS RCS 1979) *Marital status:* married Ursula 1962; 1 son, 1 daughter *Recreations:* watercolour painting

R Brian Mouatt Esq, Chief Dental Officer, Department of Health, Richmond House, 79 Whitehall, London SW1A 2NS *Telephone:* 071-210 5247 *Fax:* 071-210 5585

MOUNTFIELD, ROBIN   Deputy Secretary, Public Expenditure: Industry, HM Treasury   Grade: 2

Career: Ministry of Power/of Technology/Department of [Trade and] Industry 1961-: assistant principal 1961-65: private secretary (PS) to permanent secretary 1965-74; principal 1965-74: petroleum division 1965-68, iron and steel division 1968-72, PS to Minister for Industry 1972-74; assistant secretary 1974-80: air division 1974-77, seconded to Stock Exchange 1977-78, industrial and commercial policy division 1978-80; under secretary, head of vehicle division 1980-84; deputy secretary 1984-: manufacturing industry 1984-87, financial services, company and competition affairs (also including insurance, consumer affairs, insolvency service, Companies House) 1987-92; head of industry, public expenditure division of HM Treasury 1992-

Date of birth: 16 October 1934   *Education/professional qualifications:* Merchant Taylors' School, Crosby, Liverpool; Magdalen College, Oxford, modern history (BA 1961)   *Honours, decorations:* CB 1988   *Marital status:* married Anne Newsham 1963; 1 daughter, 2 sons

Robin Mountfield Esq CB, Deputy Secretary, HM Treasury, Parliament Street, London SW1P 3AG   *Telephone:* 071-270 3000

MOWL, COLIN JOHN   Under Secretary, Head of Economic Analysis and Forecasting Group, HM Treasury   Grade: 3

Career: HM Treasury 1983-: senior economic adviser 1983-90; under secretary and head of economic analysis and forecasting group 1990-

Date of birth: 19 October 1947   *Education/professional qualifications:* London School of Economics, economics (BSc, MSc)

Colin J Mowl Esq, Under Secretary and Head of Economic Analysis and Forecasting Group, HM Treasury, Parliament Street, London SW1P 3AG   *Telephone:* 071-270 4459

MUIR, RICHARD JOHN SUTHERLAND   Assistant Under Secretary, Foreign and Commonwealth Office

Career: HM Diplomatic Service 1964-: Foreign [and Commonwealth] Office (F[C]O) 1964-65; Middle East Centre for Arabic Studies 1965; commercial second secretary Jedda 1967-70, Tunis 1970-73; FCO 1973-75; first secretary Washington DC 1975-81, Riyadh, later counsellor 1981-85; FCO 1985-: counsellor 1985, head of information department; assistant under secretary, principal finance officer and chief inspector 1991-

Date of birth: 25 August 1942   *Education/professional qualifications:* The Stationers' School, London; Reading University, French (BA 1963); Middle East Centre for Arabic Studies, Arabic   *Marital status:* married Caroline Simpson 1966; 1 daughter, 1 son   *Clubs:* St Stephen's Constitutional   *Recreations:* reading, opera, theatre, walking

Richard J S Muir Esq, Assistant Under Secretary, Foreign and Commonwealth Office, King Charles Street, London SW1A 2AH   *Telephone:* 071-210 8260

MUIR, TOM   Under Secretary, Textiles and Retailing, Industry 1 Division, Department of Trade and Industry   Grade: 3

Career: assistant principal, principal Board of Trade 1962-68; first secretary UK permanent delegation to Organisation for Economic Co-operation and Development 1968-71; assistant secretary (AS) Department of Trade and Industry (DTI) 1972-75; counsellor UK permanent representation to EC, Brussels 1975-79; AS: Department of Industry 1979-81, Department of Trade 1981-82; DTI 1982: under secretary insurance division 1982-87, overseas trade division 1987-89, international trade policy division 1989-92, textiles and retailing, industry 1 division 1992-

Date of birth: 15 February 1936   *Education/professional qualifications:* King Edward VI School, Stafford; Leeds University, economics (BA 1962)   *Marital status:* married Brenda Dew 1968; 1 son, 1 daughter   *Recreations:* walking, reading, tennis, swimming

Tom Muir Esq, Under Secretary, Industry 1 Division, Department of Trade and Industry, Ashdown House, 123 Victoria Street, London SW1E 6RB   *Telephone:* 071-215 5000

MUNIR, (ASHLEY) EDWARD   Under Secretary, Legal Department, Ministry of Agriculture, Fisheries and Food   Grade: 3

Career: barrister 1956-60; crown counsel 1960-64; government legal service 1964-; under secretary legal department Ministry of Agriculture, Fisheries and Food (legal advise on various subjects including constitutional, administrative and EC law matters, food, animal health protection) 1982-

Date of birth: 14 February 1934 *Education/professional qualifications:* Brentwood School, Essex; St John's College, Cambridge, law (BA 1955, MA), King's College, London, law (MPhil 1990) *Marital status:* married Sureyya 1960; 1 son *Publications:* Fisheries after Factortame (Butterworths 1991) *Clubs:* United Oxford and Cambridge University *Recreations:* walking, playing double bass, listening to music

A Edward Munir Esq, Under Secretary, Ministry of Agriculture, Fisheries and Food, 55 Whitehall, London SW1A 2EY *Telephone:* 071-270 8369 *Fax:* 071-270 8096

MUNRO, GRAEME NEIL   Chief Executive, Historic Scotland (Executive Agency)   Grade: 3

Career: assistant principal Scottish Development Department (SDD) 1968-72; principal SDD, Scottish Home and Health Department (SHHD) 1972-79; assistant secretary Department of Agriculture and Fisheries for Scotland, SHHD, Scottish Office (SO) central services 1979-90; director Historic Buildings and Monuments SO Environment Department 1990-91; chief executive Historic Scotland (conservation and presentation of Scotland's built heritage) 1991-

Date of birth: 28 August 1944 *Education/professional qualifications:* Daniel Stewart's College, Edinburgh; St Andrew's University, French (MA 1967) *Marital status:* married Nicola Susan Wells 1972; 1 daughter, 1 son *Recreations:* local history, walking, swimming

Graeme N Munro Esq, Chief Executive, Historic Scotland, 20 Brandon Street, Edinburgh EH3 5RA *Telephone:* 031-244 3068 *Fax:* 031-244 3030

MURPHY, (PATRICK) PAT WALLACE   Under Secretary, Pesticides, Veterinary Medicines, Emergencies and Biotechnology Group, Ministry of Agriculture, Fisheries and Food   Grade: 3

Career: Ministry of Agriculture, Fisheries and Food (MAFF) 1966-74: assistant principal 1966-71, principal 1971-74; first secretary Washington DC embassy 1974-78; MAFF 1978-: assistant secretary 1978-86, under secretary, pesticides, veterinary medicines, emergencies and biotechnology group 1986-

Date of birth: 16 August 1944 *Education/professional qualifications:* St Chad's College, Wolverhampton; Trinity Hall, Cambridge, history (BA 1966) *Marital status:* married Denise Lillieth 1972; 2 sons *Clubs:* Elstead Cricket, Elstead Tennis, Mandarins cricket

Pat W Murphy Esq, Under Secretary, Ministry of Agriculture, Fisheries and Food, Whitehall Place, London SW1 *Telephone:* 071-270 8189 *Fax:* 071-270 8186

MURRAY, GORDON   Director, Scottish Courts Administration   Grade: 3

Career: Scottish Office, 1970-76; director Scottish Courts Administration 1986-

Date of birth: 25 August 1935   *Education/professional qualifications:* Edinburgh University (BSc, PhD)

Gordon Murray Esq, Director Scottish Courts Administration, 26/27 Royal Terrace, Edinburgh EH7 5AH   *Telephone:* 031-556 0755

MYALL, JOHN MICHAEL   Assistant Registrar of Trade Marks, Patent Office (Executive Agency)   Grade: 4

Career: Ministry of Supply/Patent Office 1951-: assistant registrar of trade marks (administration of the Trade Marks Act) 1982-

Date of birth: 1 March 1933   *Education/professional qualifications:* St Ignatius College, London; Queen Mary College, London University, French   *Marital status:* married Margaret 1956; 3 sons, 1 daughter   *Recreations:* golf

John M Myall Esq, Assistant Registrar of Trade Marks, Patent Office, Cardiff Road, Newport, Gwent NP9 1RH   *Telephone:* 0633 814834   *Fax:* 0633 814817

MYRES, Rear-Admiral JOHN ANTONY LOVELL   Chief Executive, Hydrographic Office Defence, Support Agency (Executive Agency)

Career: Royal Navy 1954-; chief executive Hydrographic Office Ministry of Defence (charts and navigational publications for the Royal Navy and others) 1990-

Date of birth: 11 April 1936   *Education/professional qualifications:* Winchester College

Rear-Admiral John A L Myres, Hydrographer of the Navy   *Telephone:* 0823 337900   *Fax:* 0823 284077

N

NEEDHAM, PHILLIP   Director, Farm and Countryside Service/Commercial Director, Agricultural Development and Advisory Service (Executive Agency)   Grade: 3

Career: National Agricultural Advisory Service/Agricultural Development and Advisory Service, Ministry of Agriculture, Fisheries and Food 1961-: deputy director of research and development 1987-88; director farm and countryside service and commercial director 1988-

Date of birth: 21 April 1940   *Education/professional qualifications:* Birmingham University (BSc); Imperial College, London (MSc, DIC)

Phillip Needham Esq, Commercial Director, Agricultural Development and Advisory Service, Nobel House, 17 Smith Square, London SW1P 3JR   *Telephone:* 071-238 5776

NEVILLE-JONES, (LILIAN) PAULINE   Head, Overseas and Defence Secretariat, Cabinet Office   Grade: 2

Career: HM Diplomatic Service 1963-76: third later second secretaries Rhodesia, Singapore; second later first secretary Foreign and Commonwealth Office (FCO) 1968-71, Washington DC 1971-1975, FCO 1975-76; *Chef de Cabinet* to Christopher Tugendhat, EC Commissioner 1976-82; FCO 1982-91: head of policy planning staff 1982-87, minister Bonn embassy 1987-91; deputy secretary, head of overseas and defence secretariat Cabinet Office 1991-

Date of birth: 2 November 1939   *Education/professional qualifications:* Leeds Girls' High School; Lady Margaret Hall, Oxford, modern history (BA 1961)   *Honours, decorations:* CMG 1987   *Marital status:* single

Miss L Pauline Neville-Jones CMG, Deputy Secretary, Cabinet Office, 70 Whitehall, London, SW1A 2AS   *Telephone:* 071-270 0360   *Fax:* 071-930 1419

NEVILLE-ROLFE, LUCY JEANNE   Member, Prime Minister's Policy Unit   Grade: 5

Career: Ministry of Agriculture, Fisheries and Food 1977-: head of land use and tenure division 1986-89; head of food legislation division (food safety act 1990) 1989-90; head of personnel 1990-92; member Prime Minister's Policy Unit 1992-

Date of birth: 2 January 1953   *Education/professional qualifications:* St Mary's School, Cambridge; Somerville College, Oxford, philosophy, politics and economics (BA, MA, 1973)   *Marital status:* married Richard John Packer; 3 sons   *Recreations:* cricket, racing, art and architecture, theatre

Miss Lucy J Neville-Rolfe, Prime Minister's Policy Unit, 10 Downing Street, London SW1A 2AA   *Telephone:* 071-930 4433

NEVILLE-ROLFE, MARIANNE TERESA   Chief Executive, Civil Service College (Executive Agency); Director, Top Management Programme, Office of Public Service and Science, Cabinet Office   Grade: 3

Career: Confederation of British Industry 1965-73; Department of Trade and Industry 1973-: principal 1973-82, assistant secretary 1982-87, under secretary 1987-90; seconded to Cabinet Office, Office of Public Service and Science as Chief Executive Civil Service College 1990- and director top management programme

Date of birth: 9 October 1944   *Education/professional qualifications:* St Mary's Convent, Shaftesbury; Lady Margaret Hall, Oxford, politics, philosophy and economics (BA 1965)   *Marital status:* married David William John

Blake 1972 (separated) *Recreations:* travel; opera; walking; reading, especially history

Miss Marianne T Neville-Rolfe, Chief Executive, Civil Service College, Sunningdale Park, Larch Avenue, Ascot SL5 0QE *Telephone:* 0344 23444 *Fax:* 0344 842491

NEWELL, CHRISTOPHER WILLIAM PAUL   **Director of Headquarters Casework, Crown Prosecution Service**   **Grade: 3**

Career: assistant legal secretary Law Officers' Department 1987-89; director of headquarters casework Crown Prosecution Service 1989-

Date of birth: 30 November 1950 *Education/professional qualifications:* Southampton University, law; barrister, Middle Temple 1973

Christopher W P Newell Esq, Director of Headquarters Casework, Crown Prosecution Service, 4/12 Queen Anne's Gate, London SW1H 9AZ *Telephone:* 071-417 7158

NICHOL, DUNCAN KIRKBRIDE   **Chief Executive, National Health Service Management Executive, Department of Health**   **Grade: 1A**

Career: assistant group secretary and hospital secretary Manchester Royal Infirmary 1969-73; deputy group secretary and acting group secretary S Manchester University Hospital management committee 1973-74; district administrator Manchester South district 1974-77; area administrator Salford area health authority (teaching) 1977-81; Mersey regional health authority 1981-89: regional administrator 1981-84, regional general manager 1984-89; chief executive NHS management executive, Department of Health 1989-

Date of birth: 30 May 1941 *Education/professional qualifications:* Bradford Grammar School; St Andrew's University (MA 1963) *Honours, decorations:* CBE 1988 *Marital status:* married Elizabeth Elliott Mitchell Wilkinson 1972; 1 daughter, 1 son *Publications:* contributor to Healthcare in the UK (1982), Management for Clinicians (1982), Working with People (1983), Managers as Strategists (1987) *Clubs:* Athenaeum *Recreations:* golf, walking, squash

Duncan K Nichol Esq CBE, Chief Executive, NHS Management Executive, Department of Health, Richmond House, London SW1A 2NS *Telephone:* 071-210 5160 *Fax:* 071-210 5454

NICHOLLS, NIGEL HAMILTON   **Assistant Under Secretary (Systems), Ministry of Defence**   **Grade: 3**

Career: assistant principal (AP) Admiralty 1962-64; Ministry of Defence (MoD) 1964-: assistant secretary (AS) 1964-66: assistant private secretary (APS) to Minister of Defence for Royal Navy 1965-66; principal 1966-74: directing staff Royal College of Defence Studies 1971-73, APS to secretary of state 1973-74; AS 1974-84: head of defence secretariat 16 1974-77, defence counsellor UK delegation to Mutual and Balanced Force Reductions talks, Vienna 1977-80; assistant under secretary (AUS) 1984-: air staff 1984, defence staff 1984-85; under secretary Cabinet Office 1986-89; MoD 1989-: AUS systems, Office of Management and Budget (defence equipment requirements) 1989-

Date of birth: 19 February 1938 *Education/professional qualifications:* King's School, Canterbury; St

John's College, Oxford, literae humaniores (BA 1962, MA) *Honours, decorations:* CBE 1982 *Recreations:* choral singing, genealogy, mountain walking

Nigel H Nicholls Esq CBE, Assistant Under Secretary, Ministry of Defence, Whitehall, London SW1A 2HB *Telephone:* 071-218 9000

NICHOLS, DINAH ALISON   Deputy Secretary, Property Holdings, Construction and Central Support Services, Department of the Environment   Grade: 2

Career: Ministry of Transport (MoT) 1965-: assistant private secretary (PS) to ministers 1969-70, principal 1970-74, seconded to Cabinet Office 1974-77; assistant secretary Department of the Environment (DoE) 1977-80; responsible for privatisation docks industry MoT 1980-81; inner city policy DoE 1981-83; principal PS to secretaries of state Department of Transport (DT) 1983-85; director of administrative resources DoE/DTp 1985-89; DoE 1989-: head of water directorate 1989-91, deputy secretary property holding, construction and central support services (management government office property; provision of transport and security services to government departments; construction industry policy and sponsorship) 1991-

Date of birth: 28 September 1943 *Education/professional qualifications:* Wyggeston Girls' Grammar School, Leicester; Bedford College, London University, history (BA 1965) *Clubs:* Swiss Alpine, Hampstead Cricket, Royal Society of Arts *Recreations:* mountaineering and fellwalking, choral singing, music, theatre, travel

Ms Dinah A Nichols, Deputy Secretary, Department of the Environment, 2 Marsham Street, London SW1P 3EB *Telephone:* 071-276 3623 *Fax:* 071-276 3638

NICKSON, Sir DAVID WIGLEY   Chairman, Scottish Enterprise

Career: military service 1949-54; William Collins publishers 1954-85: vice-chairman and group managing director 1979-82; Scottish and Newcastle Breweries plc 1981-: chairman 1983-89. Member CBI Council for Scotland 1974-83: chairman 1979-81; member CBI Council 1977-: president 1986-88; Top Salaries Review Body 1988-: chairman 1989-; chairman Scottish Development Agency (became Scottish Enterprise 1990) (economic development and training in Scotland on behalf of the Scottish Office) 1989- *Current non-Whitehall posts:* chairman Clydesdale Bank plc 1991-; director Scottish Newcastle plc 1981-, General Accident plc 1971-, Hambro's plc 1988-, Edinburgh Investment Trust plc 1970-

Date of birth: 27 November 1929 *Education/professional qualifications:* Eton; Royal Military Academy, Sandhurst *Honours, decorations:* CBE 1981, DL 1982, KBE 1987; FRSA, FRSE, Officer of Queen's Body Guard for Scotland *Marital status:* married Helen Louise Cockcraft 1952; 3 daughters *Clubs:* Boodles; Flyfishers; MCC; Western, Glasgow *Recreations:* countryside activities, especially salmon fishing

Sir David Nickson KBE DL, Chairman, Scottish Enterprise, 120 Bothwell Street, Glasgow *Telephone:* 041-248 2700 *Fax:* 041-221 2250

Complete Name Index
see page 955

NIEDUSZYŃSKI, ANTHONY JOHN   Under Secretary, Head of
Aerospace, Industry 2 Division, Department of Trade and
Industry   Grade: 3

Career: Board of Trade 1964-72: assistant principal 1964-67, private
secretary to president 1967-68, principal 1968-72; principal private
secretary (pps) to Minister for Trade and Consumer Affairs, Department of
Trade and Industry (DTI) 1972-74; pps to Secretary of State for Trade
1974; assistant secretary: Department of Prices and Consumer Protection
1974-77, Department of Industry 1977-82, Home Office 1982-83; DTI
1983-: assistant secretary 1983-85, under secretary 1985, head of business
task force 2 (aerospace, shipbuilding and vehicles; defence industries)
1990-92, head of aerospace, industry division 2 1992-

Date of birth: 7 January 1939 *Education/professional qualifications:* St Paul's
School, London; Merton College, Oxford litterae humaniores (BA 1959,
MA 1961) *Marital status:* married Frances Oxford 1980; 1 daughter *Clubs:*
Polish Hearth *Recreations:* gardening, fell walking, riding, opera, ballet

Anthony J Nieduszyński Esq, Under Secretary, Industry 2 Division,
Department of Trade and Industry, Ashdown House, 123 Victoria Street,
London SW1E 6RB *Telephone:* 071-215 5000

NILSSON, PETER CARL   Proceedings Operational Director, Office
of the Solicitor to Departments of Health and of Social
Security   Grade: 4

Career: army 1962-64; Ministry of Pensions and National Insurance
1964-69: legal assistant 1964-70, clerk to adjudicator 1967-69; Department
of Health and Social Security 1970-83: senior legal assistant 1970-83
(principal administrator EC Commission, Brussels 1974-80), assistant
solicitor 1983-90; proceedings operational director, Office of the Solicitor
(provision of legal services and advice) Department of Social Security
1990-, Department of Health 1991-, Office of Population Censuses and
Surveys 1991-

Date of birth: 10 June 1938 *Education/professional qualifications:* East Barnet
Grammar School, Hertfordshire; King's College, London, law (LLB 1961);
Inner Temple (barrister 1962) *Marital status:* married Alish Veronica 1969
Publications: joint editor, Law Relating to Supplementary Benefits and
Family Income Supplements (HMSO 1972), editor, Law Relating to
National Insurance and Family Allowances (HMSO 1973) *Recreations:*
theatre, music, walking

Peter C Nilsson Esq, Proceedings Operational Director, Office of the
Solicitor, Department of Social Security, New Court, 48 Carey Street,
London WC2A 2LS *Telephone:* 071-412 1369 *Fax:* 071-412 1244

NIMMO SMITH, WILLIAM AUSTIN   Member, Scottish Law Commission

Career: advocate 1969-: statutory junior counsel to Department of Employment 1977-82; advocate
depute 1983-86; chairman Medical Appeal Tribunals and Vaccine Damage Tribunals 1986-91;
member Scottish Law Commission 1988-

Date of birth: 6 November 1942 *Education/professional qualifications:* Dragon School, Oxford; Eton
College; Balliol College, Oxford, litterae humaniores (BA 1965); Edinburgh University, law (LLB
1967); member Faculty of Advocates 1969 *Honours, decorations:* QC 1982 *Marital status:* married
Jennifer Main 1968; 1 daughter, 1 son *Clubs:* New, Edinburgh *Recreations:* hillwalking, music

William A Nimmo Smith Esq QC, Commissioner, Scottish Law Commission, 140 Causewayside,
Edinburgh EH9 1PR *Telephone:* 031-668 2131

NISSEN, David Edgar Joseph   Under Secretary, Solicitor's Division, Department of Trade and Industry   Grade: 3

Career: prosecuting solicitor Sussex Police Authority 1970-73; HM Customs and Excise 1973-90; assistant solicitor (AS) 1983-87, principal AS 1987-90; under secretary (legal), principal AS Department of Energy (DEn) division Treasury Solicitor's Department (legal adviser to DEn) 1990-92; solicitor's division Department of Trade and Industry 1992-

Date of birth: 27 November 1942 *Education/professional qualifications:* King's School, Chester; University College, London, law (LLB 1964) *Marital status:* married Pauline Jennifer Meaden 1969; 2 daughters *Recreations:* opera, gardening

David E J Nissen Esq, Under Secretary, Solicitor's Division, Department of Trade and Industry, 1 Palace Street, London SW1E 5HE *Telephone:* 071-238 3470 *Fax:* 071-238 3452

NORBURY, BRIAN MARTIN   Head of Schools Branch 2, Department for Education   Grade: 3

Career: War Office/Ministry of Defence (MoD) 1961-69; MoD 1973-84; Department of Education [and Science] 1984-: head of schools branch 2 (special needs, school health services, discipline, welfare, European schools, careers advice, under-fives) 1988-

Date of birth: 2 March 1938 *Education/professional qualifications:* King's College, London (BA, AKC 1959)

Brian M Norbury Esq, Under Secretary, Department for Education, Sanctuary Buildings, Great Smith Street, London SW1P 3BT *Telephone:* 071-925 5000

NORMAN, Sir RICHARD OSWALD CHANDLER   Chief Scientific Adviser, Department of Trade and Industry   Grade: 2 equivalent

Career: chemistry lecturer Oxford University 1958-65; chemistry professor York University 1965-83; chief scientific adviser Ministry of Defence 1983-88, Department of Energy 1988-92, Department of Trade and Industry 1992- *Current non-Whitehall posts:* rector Exeter College, Oxford 1987-

Date of birth: 27 April 1932 *Education/professional qualifications:* St Paul's School, London; Balliol College, Oxford, chemistry (BA 1954, DPhil 1956) *Honours, decorations:* FRS 1977, KBE 1987 *Marital status:* married Jennifer Tope 1982 *Publications:* Principles of Organic Synthesis (Chapman and Hall 1968) *Clubs:* United Oxford and Cambridge Universities *Recreations:* cricket, music, gardening

Sir Richard Norman KBE, Chief Scientific Adviser, Department of Trade and Industry, 1 Palace Street, London SW1E 5HE *Telephone:* 071-238 3489 *Fax:* 071-828 7969

NORMAND, A N   Regional Procurator Fiscal (Glasgow and Strathkelvin), Crown Office   Grade: 3

A N Normand Esq, Regional Procurator Fiscal (Glasgow and Strathkelvin), Crown Office, 10 Ballater Street, Glasgow G5 9PS *Telephone:* 041-429 5566

To subscribe to The European Companion
Telephone: 071-240 3902

NORMINGTON, DAVID JOHN   Head of Strategy and Employment Policy, Employment Department Group   Grade: 3

Career: Department of Employment 1973-: East London area training manager Manpower Services Commission 1982-84; principal private secretary to secretary of state 1984-85; head of long-term unemployment policy branch 1985-87; London and SE regional director and leader London City Action Team 1987-89; head of strategy and employment policy division 1989-

Date of birth: 18 October 1951 *Education/professional qualifications:* Bradford Grammar School; Corpus Christi College, Oxford, modern history (BA 1973, MA) *Marital status:* married Winifred Anne Charlotte Harris 1985 *Recreations:* gardening, walking, tennis, watching ballet

David J Normington Esq, Head of Strategy and Employment Policy, Employment Department Group, Caxton House, Tothill Street, London SE1H 9NF *Telephone:* 071-273 5766

NORRISS, Air Vice-Marshal PETER COULSON   Director-General Aircraft 2, Procurement Executive, Ministry of Defence

Career: flying instructor RAF College Cranwell 1969-71; pilot 1972-76; personal air secretary to under secretary of state (RAF) Ministry of Defence (MoD) 1977-79; No 16 squadron commander 1980-83; MoD 1983-85: staff officer, 1983-84 head of RAF presentation team 1984-85; RAF Marham station commander 1985-87; MoD 1988-: deputy director operational requirements (OR) (air) 1988-89, director OR (air) 1989-91, director-general aircraft 2 (all helicopters and aircraft except European fighter aircraft and Tornado for all armed forces) 1991-

Date of birth: 22 April 1944 *Education/professional qualifications:* Beverley Grammar School, Yorkshire; Magdalene College, Cambridge, modern languages (BA 1966, MA 1970); FRAeS *Honours, decorations:* AFC 1977 *Recreations:* golf, squash

Air Vice-Marshal Peter C Norriss AFC, Director-General, Directorate-General Aircraft 2, Ministry of Defence Procurement Executive, St Giles Court, 1 St Giles High Street, London WC2H 8LD *Telephone:* 071-632 6340 *Fax:* 071-632 6920

NOTLEY, Major General (CHARLES) ROLAND SYKES   President, Ordnance Board, Ministry of Defence Procurement Executive

Career: command Royal Scots Dragoon Guards 1979-82; Ministry of Defence 1986-: director operational requirements (land) 1986-89, director logistics operations (army) 1989-90, Procurement Executive Ordnance Board [all-service weapon systems using explosives] 1991-: vice-president 1991-92, president 1992-

Date of birth: 5 May 1939 *Education/professional qualifications:* Winchester College; Royal Military Academy Sandhurst; School of Tank Technology (tt 1966); Army Staff College (psc 1971) *Honours, decorations:* CBE 1991 *Recreations:* sailing, riding

Major General C Roland S Notley CBE, President, Ordnance Board, Ministry of Defence Procurement Executive, Empress State Building, Lillie Road, London SW6 1TR *Telephone:* 071-385 1244 *Fax:* 071-381 9992

NUTTALL, CHRISTOPHER PETER   Assistant Under Secretary, Director of Research and Statistics, Home Office   Grade: 3

Career: Solicitor General's Office (SGO) Ottawa, SGO Canada 1975-89; assistant under secretary, director of research and statistics Home Office 1989-

Date of birth: 20 April 1939 *Education/professional qualifications:* University of Keele (BA); University of California at Berkeley (MA)

Christopher P Nuttall Esq, Director of Research and Statistics, Home Office, 50 Queen Anne's Gate, London SW1H 9AT *Telephone:* 071-273 2616

O

OATES, LAURENCE   Circuit Administrator (Midland and Oxford), Lord Chancellor's
Department   Grade: 3

Career: barrister 1970-77; legal assistant (LA)/ senior LA Department of Employment 1977-81, Law
Officers' Department 1981-84; assistant solicitor advising Department of Transport, Treasury
Solicitor's Department 1984-89; under secretary, head of legal and law reform group Lord
Chancellor's Department 1989-92, Circuit administrator (Midland and Oxford) 1992-

Date of birth: 14 May 1946   *Education/professional qualifications:* Beckenham and Penge Grammar
School; Bristol University, law (LLB 1967); Inner Temple (barrister 1968)   *Marital status:* married
Brenda Lilian Hardwick 1968; 1 daughter, 1 son   *Recreations:* flute, golf

Laurence Oates Esq, Circuit Administrator (Midland and Oxford), Lord Chancellor's Department, 2
Newton Street, Birmingham B4 7LU   *Telephone:* 021-200 1234   *Fax:* 021-212 1359

ODDY, IAN VAUGHAN   Property Adviser, NHS Management
Executive, Department of Health

Career: private practice chartereed surveyor 1956-; member council for
Licensed Conveyancers 1986-88; property adviser to NHS management
executive Department of Health 1990-; board member NHS Estates 1991-
Current non-Whitehall posts: partner St Quintin, chartered surveyors 1967-;
member general council Royal Institution of Chartered Surveyors 1982-

Date of birth: 5 June 1938   *Education/professional qualifications:* Headstone
Secondary Modern School, Harrow; Christopher Wren Technical School,
London; Regent Street Polytechnic, London; FRICS 1961; corporate
member IRRV 1962; FCIA 1976   *Marital status:* married Lesley Mackintosh
1970; 1 son,.1 daughter   *Publications:* Bow Group pamphlets; technical
working party reports; co-author Professional Liability (HMSO 1989)
Clubs: Carlton   *Recreations:* fell-walking; Mozart, jazz and opera

Ian V Oddy Esq, Property Adviser, NHS Management Executive, St
Quinton Chartered Surveyors, 71 Queen Victoria Street, London EC4V
4QQ   *Telephone:* 071-236 4040   *Fax:* 071-236 7668

OLIVER, RONALD JAMES   Chief Executive, Vehicle Inspectorate (Executive
Agency)   Grade: 4

Career: chief executive Vehicle Inspectorate 1985-

Date of birth: 28 October 1945   *Education/professional qualifications:* Windsor Grammar School; Brunel
University, engineering (BEng 1968); CEng 1973; MIMechE 1973   *Marital status:* married

Ronald J Oliver Esq, Chief Executive, Vehicle Inspectorate, Berkeley House, Croydon Street, Bristol
BS5 0DA   *Telephone:* 0272 543210   *Fax:* 0272 543209

OMAND, DAVID BRUCE   Assistant Under Secretary (Programmes), Ministry of
Defence   Grade: 3

Career: Ministry of Defence 1970-: assistant principal 1970-75; assistant private secretary (PS) to
secretary of state (SOS) 1974-75, 1979-81; PS to SOS 1981-82; head of management services and
organisation 1982-84; defence reorganisation team 1984; on secondment as defence counsellor UK
delegation to NATO, Brussels 1985-88; assistant under secretary (AUS) management strategy
1988-91; AUS programmes (annual defence long-term planning) 1991-

Date of birth: 15 April 1947 *Education/professional qualifications:* Glasgow Academy; Corpus Christi College, Cambridge, economics (BA 1969) *Recreations:* opera, hill walking

David B Omand Esq, Assistant Under Secretary, Ministry of Defence, Whitehall, London SW1A 2HB *Telephone:* 071-218 9000

OSBORN, F DEREK A   Director-General, Environmental Protection, Department of the Environment   Grade: 2

Career: Ministry of Housing and Local Government 1965-74: assistant principal 1965, private secretary to minister of state and permanent secretary 1967; Royal Commission on Standards of Conduct in Public Life 1974; assistant secretary (AS) Department of Transport 1975-77; Department of Environment 1977-: AS 1977, under secretary: finance 1982-86, housing group 1986-87, deputy secretary local government and finance 1987-89, director-general environmental protection 1990-

Date of birth: 14 January 1941 *Education/professional qualifications:* Leys School, Cambridge; Balliol College, Oxford, mathematics (BA 1963), philosophy (PhB 1965) *Honours, decorations:* CB 1991 *Marital status:* married Caroline Niebuhr Tod 1971; 1 daughter, 1 son *Recreations:* music, reading, chess

F Derek A Osborn Esq CB, Director-General, Environmental Protection, Department of the Environment, 2 Marsham Street, London SW1P 3EB *Telephone:* 071-276 3570 *Fax:* 071-276 0590

O'SHEA, (MICHAEL) MIKE KENT   Under Secretary, Finance & Resource Management, Department of Trade and Industry   Grade: 3

Career: Department of Trade and Industry 1973-: director Inner Cities Unit 1991-92, under secretary finance and resource management 1992-

Date of birth: 12 March 1951 *Education/professional qualifications:* Bristol Grammar School; Corpus Christi College, Cambridge, history (BA 1972) *Marital status:* married Linda Szpala 1988 *Recreations:* cricket, walking, Wagner, beer and wine

Mike K O'Shea Esq, Under Secretary, Finance and Resource Management, Department of Trade and Industry, Ashdown House, 123 Victoria Street, London SW1E 6RB *Telephone:* 071-215 5000

OSMOTHERLY, EDWARD BENJAMIN CROFTON   Deputy Secretary, Principal Establishment and Finance Officer, Department of Transport   Grade: 2

Career: assistant principal Ministry of Housing and Local Government (MHLG) 1963-68; principal MHLG and Department of Environment (DoE) 1968-74; Harkness fellow (Brookings Institution Washington and UCLA) 1972-73; DoE 1976-79: assistant secretary 1976-78, seconded to British Rail (BR) 1979; head of machinery of government Civil Service Department 1980-82; Department of Transport 1962-: under secretary 1982-89, deputy secretary public transport and research (BR, London Transport, public transport; research and development) 1989-92, principal establishment and finance officer 1992-

Date of birth: 1 August 1942 *Education/professional qualifications:* East Ham Grammar School, London; Fitzwilliam College, Cambridge, economics, anthropology, history (BA, MA 1966) *Marital status:* married Valerie 1970; 1 daughter, 1 son *Clubs:* United Oxford and Cambridge University *Recreations:* squash, reading

Edward B C Osmotherly Esq, Deputy Secretary, Department of Transport, 2 Marsham Street, London SW1P 3EB *Telephone:* 071-276 3000

OSWALD, Admiral Sir (JOHN) JULIAN ROBERTSON   Chief of the Naval Staff and First Sea Lord (until February 1993), Ministry of Defence

Career: shipboard naval service 1951-62; commander HMS Yarnton 1962-63, HMS Bacchante 1971-72; Ministry of Defence (MoD) 1972-75; Royal College of Defence Studies 1976; commander HMS Newcastle 1977-79; RN Presentation Team 1979-80; captain Royal Naval College Darmouth 1980-82; MoD 1982-85: assistant chief of defence staff, programmes 1982-84, policy and nuclear 1985; flag officer Third Flotilla and commander anti-submarine warfare, striking fleet 1985-87; commander-in-chief (C-in-C) Fleet, Allied C-in-C Channel and C-in-C East Atlantic 1987-89; Chief of Naval Staff and First Sea Lord MoD 1989-

Date of birth: 11 August 1933 *Education/professional qualifications:* Beaudesert Park, Minchinhampton; Royal Naval College, Dartmouth *Honours, decorations:* KCB 1987, GCB 1989 *Recreations:* gliding, tennis, walking, stamp collecting, family

Admiral Sir Julian Oswald GCB, Chief of the Naval Staff and First Sea Lord, Ministry of Defence, Whitehall, London SW1A 2HB *Telephone:* 071-218 2214

OSWALD, RICHARD ANTHONY   Deputy Health Service Commissioner, Office of the Parliamentary Commissioner for Administration and Health Services Commissioners (Ombudsman)   Grade: 3

Career: NHS administrative posts 1961-72; hospital secretary London Hospital 1972-74; support services manager South Camden Health District (HD) 1974-77; district administrator Leeds West HD 1977-84; district general manager Leeds Western Health Authority 1985-89; deputy health service commissioner Ombudsman's Office (complaints about NHS services in GB) 1989-

Date of birth: 12 January 1941 *Education/professional qualifications:* Leys School, Cambridge; AHSM 1966 *Marital status:* married Janet Iris 1963; 3 sons, 1 daughter *Recreations:* classical music, acting, bird-watching

Richard A Oswald Esq, Deputy Health Service Commissioner, Office of the Parliamentary Commissioner for Administration and Health Services Commissioners, Church House, Great Smith Street, London SW1P 3BW *Telephone:* 071-276 2089 *Fax:* 071-276 2104

OWEN, JOHN AUBREY   Director of Personnel Management, Department of the Environment   Grade: 3

Career: assistant principal Ministry of Transport 1969-72; Department of Environment (DoE) 1972-75: assistant private secretary to minister for transport industries 1972-73, principal 1973-75; principal Department of Transport 1975-80: seconded to Cambridgeshire county council 1978-80; DoE 1980-: assistant secretary 1980-87, northern regional director 1987-91, director of personnel management 1991- *Current non-Whitehall posts:* non-executive director Tarmac housing division 1992-

Date of birth: 1 August 1945 *Education/professional qualifications:* City of London School; St Catharine's College, Cambridge, classics (BA 1967, MA) *Marital status:* married Julia Margaret Jones 1971; 1 daughter, 1 son *Recreations:* opera, gardening

John A Owen Esq, Director of Personnel Management, Department of the Environment, Lambeth Bridge House, Albert Embankment, London SE1 7SB *Telephone:* 071-238 4090

OWEN, JOHN WYN   Director, National Health Service, Wales   Grade: 3

Career: deputy hospital secretary West Wales general hospital 1966-67; hospital secretary Glantawe hospital management committee (HMC), Swansea 1967-70; staff training officer Welsh Hospital Board, Cardiff 1968-70; divisional administrator (DA) University of Wales Cardiff HMC 1970-72; assistant clerk and King's Fund fellow St Thomas' hospital 1972-74; DA St Thomas' health district teaching 1974-79; praeceptor, school of health administration, Minnesota University, USA; visiting fellow New South Wales University, Australia 1979; executive director United Medical Enterprises, London 1979-85; director NHS Wales, Welsh Office 1985- *Current non-Whitehall posts:* chairman Welsh Health Common Services Authority 1985-

Date of birth: 15 May 1942 *Education/professional qualifications:* Friar's School, Bangor; St John's College, Cambridge, geography (BA 1964, MA); Hospital Administration Staff College (MHSM, Dip HSM 1968); FRGS 1968 *Honours, decorations:* fellow University of Wales, Aberystwyth 1991 *Marital status:* married Elizabeth Ann MacFarlane 1967; 1 son, 1 daughter *Clubs:* Athenaeum *Recreations:* organ, opera, travel

John W Owen Esq, Director NHS Wales, Welsh Office, Cathays Park, Cardiff CF1 3NQ *Telephone:* 0222 823695 *Fax:* 0222 823036

OWEN, PETER FRANCIS   Deputy Secretary, Cabinet Office   Grade: 2

Career: Department of the Environment (DoE) 1975-90: assistant secretary housing policy review 1975-77, local government finance (LGF) 1977-80; regional director DoE/Department of Transport 1980-82; director rural affairs 1982-83; under secretary LGF 1984-86; deputy secretary (DS) housing and construction 1986-90; DS Cabinet Office 1990-

Date of birth: 4 September 1940 *Education/professional qualifications:* Liverpool Institute; Liverpool University, French (BA) *Honours, decorations:* CB 1990 *Marital status:* married Ann 1963; 1 son, 1 daughter *Recreations:* reading, gardening, French language and literature

Peter F Owen Esq CB, Deputy Secretary, Cabinet Office, 70 Whitehall, London SW1A 2AS *Telephone:* 071-270 3000

OXBURGH, Professor Sir ERNEST RONALD   Chief Scientific Adviser, Ministry of Defence   Grade: 1A

Career: professor of mineralogy and petrology, University of Cambridge 1978-; chief scientific adviser Ministry of Defence 1988-

Date of birth: 2 November 1934 *Education/professional qualifications:* University of Oxford (BA 1957, MA 1960); University of Princeton (PhD 1960)

Professor Sir Ernest R Oxburgh KBE, Chief Scientific Adviser, Ministry of Defence, Main Building, Whitehall, London SW1A 2HB *Telephone:* 071-218 9000

Parliamentary Offices
see page 275

P

PACKER, RICHARD JOHN   Deputy Secretary, Agricultural Commodities, Trade and Production, Ministry of Agriculture, Fisheries and Food   Grade: 2

Career: Ministry of Agriculture, Fisheries and Food (MAFF) 1967-73: assistant principal 1967-71, principal 1971-73; first secretary UK permanent representation to EC, Brussels 1973-76; MAFF 1976-: principal private secretary to minister 1976-78, assistant secretary fisheries, EC 1979-85, under secretary food, regions 1985-89, deputy secretary agricultural commodities, trade and production 1989-

Date of birth: 18 August 1944   *Education/professional qualifications:* City of London School; Manchester University, chemistry (BSc 1965) and organic chemistry (MSc 1966)   *Marital status:* married Lucy Jeanne Neville Rolfe; 5 sons (2 from previous marriage), 1 daughter (from previous marriage)   *Recreations:* sports spectator, theatre, books

Richard J Packer Esq, Deputy Secretary, Ministry of Agriculture, Fisheries and Food, Whitehall Place, London SW1A 2HH   *Telephone:* 071-270 8109   *Fax:* 071-270 8834

PAINTER, TERENCE JAMES   Deputy Chairman and Director-General, Inland Revenue   Grade: 2

Career: assistant principal Inland Revenue (IR) 1959-61; principal IR, Civil Service Selection Board 1961-68; assistant secretary IR, HM Treasury 1968-75; IR 1975-: under secretary 1975-86, deputy secretary, deputy chairman and director-general 1986-

Date of birth: 28 November 1935   *Education/professional qualifications:* City of Norwich School; Downing College, Cambridge, history (BA 1957)   *Honours, decorations:* CB 1990   *Marital status:* married Margaret Janet 1959; 2 daughters, 2 sons   *Recreations:* music, reading, hillwalking, gardening

Terence J Painter Esq CB, Deputy Chairman, Inland Revenue, Somerset House, Strand, London WC2R 1LB   *Telephone:* 071-438 6622

PALIN, Air Chief Marshal Sir ROGER HEWLETT   Air Member for Personnel, Ministry of Defence

Career: Royal Air Force 1964-; Ministry of Defence 1983-: air member for personnel 1991-
Education/professional qualifications: St John's College, Cambridge (BA 1967, MA 1979)

Air Chief Marshal Sir Roger Palin KCB CBE ADC, Air Member for Personnel, Ministry of Defence, Main Building, Whitehall, London SW1A 2HB   *Telephone:* 071-218 6000

PAREN, NIGEL DAVID   Director-General Marketing, Defence Export Services Organisation, Ministry of Defence   Grade: 3

Career: Ministry of Transport 1957-62; Ministry of Aviation/Technology 1963-70: assistant private secretary to minister 1963-64, assistant principal 1964-66, principal 1967-70; Department of Trade and Industry 1970-72; seconded to Westland Helicopters Ltd as commercial manager 1972-75; Ministry of Defence 1975-: procurement executive 1975-78, regional marketing director 1978- 83, strategic systems executive 1983-86, assistant under secretary (AUS) fleet support 1988-91, AUS, director-general marketing Defence Export Services Organisation 1991-

Date of birth: 18 July 1936   *Education/professional qualifications:* Highgate School, London   *Recreations:* walking, gardening, photography

Nigel D Paren Esq, Director-General Marketing, Defence Export Services Organisation, Ministry of Defence, Whitehall, London SW1A 2HB   *Telephone:* 071-218 6828   *Fax:* 071-218 6940

PARKER, ROBERT STEWART   Deputy Parliamentary Counsel, Office of the Parliamentary Counsel   Grade: 3

Career: classics teacher 1971-74; private practice barrister 1975-80; Parliamentary Counsel Office 1980-: assistant parliamentary counsel (PC) 1980-84, senior assistant PC 1984-87: at Law Commission 1985-87, deputy PC (drafting government bills) 1987-

Date of birth: 13 January 1949   *Education/professional qualifications:* Brentwood School, Essex; Trinity College, Oxford, classics (BA 1971, MA); Middle Temple (barrister 1975); British Institute of Management (MBIM 1984)   *Honours, decorations:* freeman City of London 1984   *Marital status:* single   *Publications:* co-author Cases and Statutes on General Principles of Law (Sweet and Maxwell 1980)   *Clubs:* Athenaeum, City Livery   *Recreations:* cricket, bridge, books, music, the livery

Robert S Parker Esq, Deputy Parliamentary Counsel, Office of the Parliamentary Counsel, 36 Whitehall, London SW1A 2AY   *Telephone:* 071-210 6611

PARTRIDGE, Sir MICHAEL JOHN ANTHONY   Permanent Secretary, Department of Social Security   Grade: 1

Career: assistant principal Ministry of Pensions and National Insurance (MPNI) 1960-64: private secretary to permanent secretary 1962-64; principal, pensions policy MPNI, Ministry of Social Security, Department of [Health and] Social Security (D[H]SS) 1964-71; D[H]SS 1971-83: assistant secretary NI contributions 1971-75, regional organisation 1975-76; under secretary supplementary benefit commission 1976-79, director social security regional organisation 1979-81; deputy secretary, administration and principal establishment officer 1981-82, social security policy 1982-83; deputy under secretary police department Home Office 1964-71; D[H]SS 1987-: second permanent secretary (health policy and NHS) 1987-88, permanent secretary 1988-   *Current non-Whitehall posts:* senior treasurer Methodist church 1980-; Liveryman Merchant Taylors' Company 1987-; trustee Harefield Trust 1991-

Date of birth: 29 September 1935   *Education/professional qualifications:* Merchant Taylors' School, London; St John's College, Oxford, greats (BA 1960, MA)   *Honours, decorations:* CB 1983, KCB 1990   *Marital status:* married Joan Elizabeth Hughes 1968; 2 sons, 1 daughter   *Clubs:* United Oxford and Cambridge University   *Recreations:* 'DIY", reading, skiing

Sir Michael Partridge KCB, Permanent Secretary, Department of Social Security, Richmond House, 79 Whitehall, London SW1A 2NS   *Telephone:* 071-210 5543   *Fax:* 071-210 5838

Government Departments
see page 300

PATON, ALASDAIR CHALMERS   Under Secretary, Chief Engineer, Environment Department, Scottish Office   Grade: 3

Career: assistant engineer: Clyde Port Authority 1967-71, Department of Agriculture and Fisheries for Scotland 1971-72; senior engineer Scottish Development Department (SDD) 1972-77; engineer Hong Kong Public Works Department 1977-80; SDD (became Scottish Office Environment Department 1991-) 1980-: senior engineer 1980-84, principal engineer 1984-87, deputy chief engineer 1987-91, chief engineer and under secretary civil engineering and water services 1991- *Current non-Whitehall posts:* council member Foundation for Water Research 1991-

Date of birth: 28 November 1944 *Education/professional qualifications:* John Neilson Institution, Paisley; Glasgow University, civil engineering (BSc Eng 1966) and management (Dip MS); MIWEM 1984; FICE 1989 *Marital status:* married Zona 1969; 1 daughter, 1 son *Recreations:* rotary, golf, sailing

Alasdair C Paton Esq BSc C Eng, Chief Engineer, Scottish Office Environment Department, 27 Perth Street, Edinburgh EH3 5RB *Telephone:* 031-244 3035 *Fax:* 031-244 2903

PAWLEY, ROBERT JOHN   Deputy Chief Executive (Technical), Valuation Office Agency (Executive Agency)   Grade: 3

Career: Valuation Office 1972-: assistant chief valuer 1987-88; deputy chief executive (technical) 1989-

Date of birth: 10 September 1939 *Education/professional qualifications:* Exeter University (BA)

Robert J Pawley Esq, Deputy Chief Executive (Technical), Valuation Office Agency, New Court, Carey Street, London WC2A 2JE *Telephone:* 071-324 1151

PAYNTER, ALAN GUY HADLEY   Head of Information Technology, HM Customs and Excise   Grade: 4

Career: Ministry of [Public Building and] Works 1960-72: assistant private secretary to minister 1968-71; HM Customs and Excise 1972-: principal general customs directorate 1978-81, seconded to Overseas Containers Ltd 1981-83; senior principal, assistant secretary computer services division 1987-89; head of information technology divisions 1989-

Date of birth: 5 November 1941 *Education/professional qualifications:* East Ham Grammar School; Central London Polytechnic, management studies (diploma 1972) *Marital status:* married Mary 1964; 2 daughters *Recreations:* theatre, books, running, swimming, tennis

Alan G H Paynter Esq, Head of Information Technology, HM Customs and Excise, Alexander House, Victoria Avenue, Southend, Essex SS99 1AA *Telephone:* 0702 367038

PEARSON, Dr GRAHAM SCOTT   Director-General, Chemical and Biological Defence Establishment, Ministry of Defence   Grade: 3

Career: Joined scientific civil service 1962; Ministry of Defence (MoD) 1973-83: assistant director scientific naval ordnance services 1973-76; technical adviser explosives, materials and safety, chief weapons systems engineer 1976-79, principal superintendent Propellant Explosives and Rocket Motor Establishment 1979-80, deputy director Royal Armament Research and Development Establishment 1980-83; director-general of research and development Royal Ordnance Factories 1983-84; director-general Chemical and Biological Defence Establishment MoD 1984-

Date of birth: 20 July 1935 *Education/professional qualifications:* Woodhouse Grove School, Bradford; St Salvator's College, St Andrew's University, chemistry (BSc 1957), physical chemistry (PhD 1960); postdoctoral fellow, University of Rochester, New York, USA 1960-62; FRSA 1989 *Honours, decorations:* CB 1990 *Publications:* contributor to Advances in Photochemistry (John Wiley 1964) and Oxidation and Combustion Reviews (Elsevier 1968, 69) *Recreations:* long-distance walking, photography, travel

Dr Graham S Pearson CB, Director-General, Chemical and Biological Defence Establishment, Porton Down, Salisbury, Wiltshire SP4 0JQ *Telephone:* 0980 613100 *Fax:* 0980 611777

PEASE, ROSAMUND DOROTHY BENSON   Under Secretary, Health Aspects of the Environment and Food Division, Department of Health   Grade: 3

Career: Ministry of Health 1958-75; Cabinet Office 1975-76; Department of Health and Social Security 1976-83; Office of Population Censuses and Surveys 1983-85; under secretary (environmental health, food safety, nutrition, NHS hotel services and transport policy) Department of Health 1985-

Date of birth: 20 March 1935 *Education/professional qualifications:* Chester School, Nova Scotia, Canada; Perse School, Cambridge; Mount School, York; Newnham College, Cambridge, classical tripos (BA 1958) *Marital status:* single; 1 son *Clubs:* University Women's *Recreations:* gardening, family

Miss Rosamund D B Pease, Under Secretary, Department of Health, Eileen House, 80-94 Newington Causeway, London SE1 *Telephone:* 071-972 2710 *Fax:* 071-972 2818

PECKHAM, Professor MICHAEL JOHN   Director, Research and Development, Department of Health

Career: civilian consultant Royal Navy 1974-86; professor Institute of Cancer Research (ICR) and Royal Marsden Hospital radiotherapy department 1974-86; dean ICR 1984-86; director British Postgraduate Medical Research 1986-90; director research and development Department of Health 1991- *Current non-Whitehall posts:* founder Bob Champion Cancer Trust 1986-; patron Jenny Wood Environmental Trust 1990-; director ECCO5 Cancer Trust 1991-

Date of birth: 2 August 1935 *Education/professional qualifications:* William Jones West Monmouthshire School, St Catharine's College, Cambridge, natural sciences (BA 1956); University College London Medical School (MB 1959) *Marital status:* married Catherine Stevenson King 1958; 3 sons *Publications:* The Management of Testicular Tumours (Edward Arnold 1981); The Biological Basis of Radiotherapy (Elsevier 1983); Conservative Management of Early Breast Cancer (Edward Arnold 1985) *Clubs:* Reform *Recreations:* painting

Professor Michael J Peckham, Director Research and Development, Department of Health, Richmond House, 79 Whitehall, London SW1A 2NS *Telephone:* 071-210 5556 *Fax:* 071-210 5868

PEEL, DAVID ALEXANDER ROBERT   Director of Administration Resources, Department of the Environment   Grade: 3

Career: assistant principal Department of Transport (DTp) 1964-67; principal Department of the Environment (DoE) 1968-71; principal/first secretary, Brussels, Foreign and Commonwealth Office 1972-74; principal private office DoE 1975-76; assistant secretary DoE, DTp and Property Services Agency 1976-89; under secretary, director of administration resources DoE (finance, management, except personnel, corporate planning) 1990-

Date of birth: 12 November 1940 *Education/professional qualifications:* St Edmund's College, Ware, Hertfordshire; University College, Oxford, classics (BA 1963) *Marital status:* married Patricia 1971; 2 sons *Recreations:* vegetable gardening, European architectural history, opera, classical music, ballet

David A R Peel Esq, Director of Administration Resources, Department of the Environment, 2 Marsham Street, London SW1P 3EB *Telephone:* 071-276 3544 *Fax:* 071-276 4124

PEIRSON, MARGARET ELLEN   Under Secretary, Department of Social Security   Grade: 3

Career: HM Treasury 1965-: seconded to Bank of England 1982-84, Department of Social Security 1990-: under secretary (1986) B Division (European policy, cross-benefit issues, unemployment and family benefits, income statistics, work incentives)

Date of birth: 28 November 1942 *Education/professional qualifications:* North London Collegiate School; Somerville College, Oxford, mathematics (BA 1942, MA) *Recreations:* choral singing, theatre

Miss Margaret E Peirson, Under Secretary, Department of Social Security, Adelphi, 1-11 John Adam Street, London WC2N 6HT *Telephone:* 071-962 8361 *Fax:* 071-962 8439

PENNICOTT, Major-General BRIAN THOMAS   Defence Services Secretary, Ministry of Defence

Career: Royal Artillery (RA) 1957-: deputy military secretary (A) Ministry of Defence (MoD) 1987-89; director RA 1989-91; defence services secretary MoD 1991-

Date of birth: 15 February 1938 *Education/professional qualifications:* Portsmouth Northern Grammar School; Royal Military Academy, Sandhurst; Royal Military College of Science; Staff College; National Defence Colleges UK and Canada

Major-General Brian T Pennicott, Defence Services Secretary, Ministry of Defence, Main Building, Whitehall, London SW1A 2HB *Telephone:* 071-218 9000

PENTREATH, Dr RICHARD JOHN   Chief Scientist, National Rivers Authority

Career: Ministry of Agriculture, Fisheries and Food 1969-89: fisheries radiobiological laboratory 1969-85, head of radioecology 1985-88, of aquatic environment protection division 1988-89; chief scientist National Rivers Authority 1989-

Date of birth: 28 December 1943 *Education/professional qualifications:* Humphry Davey Grammar School, Penzance; Queen Mary College, London University, zoology (BSc 1965); Auckland University, New Zealand, zoology (PhD 1968); London University, zoology (DSc 1980), FIBiol, FSRP *Marital status:* married Elizabeth Amanda 1965; 2 daughters *Publications:* Nuclear Power, Man and the Environment (Taylor and Francis 1980) *Recreations:* visual arts, Cornish history

Dr Richard J Pentreath, Chief Scientist, National Rivers Authority, Rivers House, Waterside Drive, Aztec West, Almondsbury, Bristol BS12 4UD *Telephone:* 0454 624400 *Fax:* 0454 624409

PERKINS, ALICE ELIZABETH   Director of Personnel, Department of Social Security   Grade: 3

Career: Department of [Health and] Social Security (D[H]SS) 1971-: private secretary to minister of state for social security 1974-75; assistant to supplementary Benefits Commission chairman 1975-77; responsible for local implementation of social security legislation in GB 1984-88; implementation of split of DHSS into DH and DSS, central resource management and planning DSS 1988-90; under secretary, director of personnel DSS 1990- *Current non-Whitehall posts:* parent governor Henry Fawcett Junior School 1988

Date of birth: 24 May 1949 *Education/professional qualifications:* North London Collegiate School; St Anne's College, Oxford, modern history (BA 1971) *Marital status:* married J W Straw 1978; 1 son, 1 daughter

Ms Alice E Perkins, Director of Personnel, Department of Social Security, Richmond House, 76 Whitehall, London SW1A 2NS *Telephone:* 071-210 5831

PERKINS, H   Director-General, Surface Ships, Ministry of Defence   Grade: 3

H Perkins Esq, Director-General Surface Ships, Ministry of Defence, Foxhill, Bath BA1 5AB *Telephone:* 0225-884884

PHILLIPS, DIANE SUSAN   Under Secretary and Principal Finance Officer, Property Holdings, Department of the Environment   Grade: 3

Career: Department of the Environment 1981-: assistant secretary local government finance 1988-90; under secretary and principal finance officer 1990-

Date of birth: 29 August 1942 *Education/professional qualifications:* University of Wales

Mrs Diane S Phillips, Under Secretary and Principal Finance Officer, Property Holding, Department of the Environment, 2 Marsham Street, London SW1P 3EB *Telephone:* 071-921 4319

PHILLIPS, (GERALD) HAYDEN   Permanent Secretary, Department of National Heritage   Grade: 1A

Career: Home Office (HO) 1967-76: assistant principal, economic adviser, principal 1967-74, assistant secretary and principal private secretary to Home Secretary 1974-76; seconded as deputy chef de cabinet to EC Commission president 1977-79; HO 1979-86: assistant secretary 1979-81, assistant under secretary police department 1981-83, head of immigration and nationality department 1983-86; deputy secretary Cabinet Office 1986-88; HM Treasury 1988-: deputy secretary public services 1988-90, civil service management and pay 1990-92; permanent secretary Department of National Heritage 1992- *Current non-Whitehall posts:* council member Institute of Management Services 1990-

Date of birth: 9 February 1943 *Education/professional qualifications:* Cambridgeshire High School; Clare College, Cambridge, history (BA, MA 1965); Yale University, USA political science and economics (MA 1967) *Honours, decorations:* CB 1989 *Marital status:* married Laura 1980; 2 sons, 3 daughters (1s, 1d by previous marriage) *Clubs:* Brooks's

G Hayden Phillips Esq CB, Permanent Secretary, Department of National Heritage, Horse Guards Road, London SW1P 3AL *Telephone:* 071-270 3000

PICKFORD, M A   Directing Actuary, Supervision of Insurance Companies and Friendly Societies Division, Government Actuary's Department   Grade: 3

Career: Government Actuary's Department 1957-

Date of birth: 22 September 1937 *Education/professional qualifications:* City of Oxford School

M A Pickford Esq, Directing Actuary, Supervision of Insurance Companies and Friendly Societies Division, Government Actuary's Department, 22 Kingsway, London WC2B 6LE *Telephone:* 071-242 6828

PICKLES, Dr HILARY   Deputy Director of Research Management,
Department of Health   Grade: 4

Career: medical posts in Bath, Oxford, Hammersmith, Hillingdon and
Northwick Park hospitals 1972-75; lecturer London School of Pharmacy
1975-78; Medical Research Council clinical pharmacology training fellow
National and St Bartholomew's hospitals 1978-82; Department of Health
1982-: medicines division 1982-86: senior medical officer 1982-84,
principal medical officer, (PMO) 1984-86, PMO AIDS unit 1986-88,
pathology section 1988-91, deputy director research management 1991-

Date of birth: 23 February 1948 Education/professional qualifications:
Sheffield High School for Girls; Newnham College, Cambridge, medical
sciences and pharmacology (BA 1969); Oxford University medical school
(MB, B Chir Cantab) 1972; London University, pharmacology (PhD 1978);
Royal College of Physicians, medicine (MRCP 1974), clinical
pharmacology and therapeutics Marital status: married Dr R S Pereira
1972; 1 daughter, 1 son Recreations: vintage boating

Dr Hilary Pickles, Deputy Director, Research Management, Department of
Health, State House, High Holborn, London WC1R 4SX
Telephone: 071-972 3899 Fax: 071-972 3920

PICKUP, DAVID FRANCIS WILLIAM   Legal Adviser, (Ministry of
Defence) Treasury Solicitor's Department   Grade: 3

Career: barrister 1976-; Treasury Solicitor's Department 1978-: legal
assistant litigation division 1978-81, senior legal assistant Department of
Energy advisory division 1981-87, litigation division 1987-88, principal
establishment, finance and security officer 1988-90, litigation division
1990-91, legal adviser Ministry of Defence advisory division 1991-

Date of birth: 28 May 1953 Education/professional qualifications: Poole
Grammar School; law, Central London Polytechnic, law (LLB 1975), Inns of
Court School of Law (bar finals 1976) Marital status: married Anne
Elizabeth 1975 Clubs: Pyrford Cricket Recreations: cricket, skiing, music,
food and wine, travel

David F W Pickup Esq, Legal Adviser, Treasury Solicitor's Department,
Neville House, Page Street, London SW1P 4LS Telephone: 071-218 0723
Fax: 071-218 0844

PILKINGTON, The Reverend Canon PETER   Chairman,
Broadcasting Complaints Commision

Career: curate, Bakewell, Derbyshire 1959-62; schoolmaster Eton College
1967-75; headmaster King's School, Canterbury 1975-86; high master St
Paul's School, London 1986-92; Chairman Broadcasting Complaints
Commission 1992-

Date of birth: 5 September 1933 Education/professional qualifications: Dame
Allan's Boys' School, Newcastle-upon-Tyne; Jesus College, Cambridge,
history (BA 1955, MA) Marital status: married Helen Wilson 1966; 2
daughters Clubs: Beefsteak, Garrick

The Reverend Canon Peter Pilkington, Chairman, Broadcasting Complaints
Commission, Grosvenor Gardens House, 35 Grosvenor Gardens, London
SW1W 0BS Telephone: 071-630 1966

PILLING, JOSEPH GRANT   Director-General, HM Prison Service, Home Office   Grade: 2

Career: Director of Personnel and Finance, HM Prison Service, Home Office (HO) 1987-90; Deputy Under Secretary Northern Ireland Office 1990-91; director-general HM Prison Service HO 1991-

Date of birth: 8 July 1945 *Education/professional qualifications:* King's College, London; Harvard, USA

Joseph G Pilling Esq, Director-General, HM Prison Service, Home Office, Cleland House, Page Street, London SW1P 4LN *Telephone:* 071-217 3000

PIRNIE, Rear Admiral IAN HUGH   Chief of Strategic Systems Executive, Procurement Executive, Ministry of Defence

Career: service on aircraft carriers, destroyers and submarines; commander Royal Naval Engineering College, Manadon 1986-88; chief strategic systems directorate Ministry of Defence Procurement Executive (management of the British naval strategic systems) 1988-

Date of birth: 17 June 1935 *Education/professional qualifications:* Christ's Hospital, Horsham; Pembroke College, Cambridge (BA, MA); Royal Military College of Science 1964-65; FIEE 1986 *Honours, decorations:* CB 1991 *Recreations:* fell-walking, bird watching, opera, classical music, topiary

Rear Admiral Ian H Pirnie CB, Chief of Strategic Systems Executive, Procurement Executive, Ministry of Defence, Whitehall, London SW1A 2HB

PITTMAN, NIGEL   Director of Resources and Services, Department of National Heritage   Grade: 4

Career: Scottish Office 1971-85: various posts in Education, Agriculture and Housing departments; head of arts branch/secretary to Museums Advisory Board 1980-85; museum administrator and secretary to the trustees National Museum of Scotland 1985-89; Office of Arts and Libraries/Department of National Heritage 1989-: head of museums and galleries division, principal finance officer 1989-92, director of resources and services 1992-

Date of birth: 3 September 1948 *Education/professional qualifications:* Epsom College; Royal Academy of Dramatic Art (diploma 1969) *Marital status:* married Dr Riitta Heino 1971; 1 daughter *Clubs:* National Liberal *Recreations:* walking, mountaineering, the arts, countryside, travel, family, friends

Nigel Pittman Esq, Director of Resources and Services, Department of National Heritage, Horseguards Road, London SW1 *Telephone:* 071-270 5850 *Fax:* 071-270 5776

PLATT, (TERENCE) TERRY   Deputy Under Secretary, Home Office   Grade: 2

Career: Home Office 1982-: assistant under secretary Prison Department regimes and services director 1982-86, Immigration and Nationality Department operations and resources 1986-92; deputy under secretary, principal establishment officer 1992-

Date of birth: 22 September 1936 *Education/professional qualifications:* St Olave's and St Saviour's Grammar School, London. *Marital status:* married Margaret Anne Cotmore 1959; 2 sons *Recreations:* rose growing, photography, butterflies

Terry Platt Esq, Deputy Under Secretary, Home Office, Queen Anne's Gate, London SW1H 9AT *Telephone:* 071-273 2143 *Fax:* 071-273 3420

POOLE, DAVID   Member of Prime Minister's Policy Unit

Career: director James Capel, and on secondment as member of Prime Minister's Policy Unit 1992-

David Poole, Prime Minister's Policy Unit, 10 Downing Street, London SW1A 2AA
Telephone: 071-270 3000

**POPE, GEOFFREY GEORGE   Deputy Chief Scientific Adviser, Ministry of
Defence   Grade: 2**

Career: Ministry of Defence 1981-: director Royal Aircraft Establishment 1984-89; deputy chief
scientific adviser 1989-

Date of birth: 17 April 1934   *Education/professional qualifications:* Imperial College, London,
engineering (MSc)

Geoffrey G Pope Esq CB, Deputy Chief Scientific Adviser, Ministry of Defence, Main Building,
Whitehall, London SW1A 2HB   *Telephone:* 071-218 9000

**POTTER, RAYMOND   Head of Court Service, Deputy Clerk of the
Crown in Chancery, Lord Chancellor's Department   Grade: 2**

Career: Lord Chancellor's Department 1950-: clerk Royal Courts of Justice
1950-62; circuit officer Leicester assize circuit 1962-71; chief clerk Bristol
crown court 1971-76; deputy circuit administrator western circuit 1976-82;
circuit administrator northern circuit 1982-86; head of court service,
deputy clerk of Crown in Chancery (administration of the superior courts
and tribunals in England and Wales) 1986-

Date of birth: 26 March 1933   *Education/professional qualifications:* Henry
Thornton School, Clapham, London; Inner Temple (barrister 1971, bencher
1989)   *Honours, decorations:* CB 1989   *Marital status:* married Jennifer Mary
Quicke 1959; 1 son   *Clubs:* Athenaeum   *Recreations:* painting

Raymond Potter Esq CB, Head of Court Service, Lord Chancellor's
Department, Trevelyan House, Great Peter Street, London SW1P 2BY
Telephone: 071-210 8719   *Fax:* 071-210 8549

POULTER, BRIAN HENRY   Secretary, Northern Ireland Audit Office   Grade: 3

Career: Commercial chartered accountancy 1959-62; Department of Health and Social Services
1962-71; Department of Commerce 1971-75; Exchequer and Audit Department 1975-87: chief
auditor 1975-81, deputy director 1981-82, director 1982-87; Northern Ireland Audit Office
(examination of the accounts of government departments and certain public bodies) 1987-: director
1987-89, secretary 1989-

Date of birth: 1 September 1941   *Education/professional qualifications:* Regent House Grammar School,
Newtownards, County Down   *Marital status:* married (Margaret) Ann Dodds 1968; twin daughters, 1
son   *Recreations:* reading, walking, cricket

Brian H Poulter Esq, Secretary, Northern Ireland Audit Office, Rosepark House, Upper Newtownards
Road, Belfast BT4 3NS   *Telephone:* 0232 484567

'Next Steps' Executive Agencies
see page 761

POWELL, ROGER HINE   Chief Executive, Buying Agency (Executive Agency)   Grade: 5

Career: apprenticeship and production management Lucas CAV Ltd 1959-69; management consultant ICFC Numas Ltd 1969-71; internal consultant on manufacturing Declon Plastics Ltd 1972-73; STC plc 1973-86, latterly in general management 1973-86; managing director UK Tools Ltd 1986-91; chief executive Buying Agency (sales to and procurement of equipment and services for public sector) 1991-

Date of birth: 31 January 1941 *Education/professional qualifications:* Bishopshalt Grammar School, Hillingdon; Brunel University, production management and technology (Bachelor of Technology 1963); CEng; MIPE; MIPS *Marital status:* married Brenda Marie 1966; 1 son, 1 daughter *Recreations:* swimming, squash, boating, windsurfing

Roger H Powell Esq, Chief Executive, Buying Agency, Royal Liver Building, Pier Head, Liverpool L3 1PE *Telephone:* 051-227 4262 *Fax:* 051-258 1249

POWNALL, JOHN HARVEY   North West Regional Director, Department of Trade and Industry

Career: scientific officer (SO) Atomic Energy Research Establishment 1955-59; SO and senior SO Warren Spring Laboratory 1959-64; principal Board of Trade, Department of Economic Affairs, Ministry of Technology, Department of Trade and Industry (DTI) 1964-74; assistant secretary DTI 1974-83; director-general Council of Mechanical and Metal Trade Associations 1983-85; head of electricity division Department of Energy 1985-87; adviser Central Electricity Generating Board 1987-88; north west regional director DTI 1988- *Current non-Whitehall posts:* member Salford University Council 1989-; vice-chairman University Estates and Building Committee 1991-

Date of birth: 24 October 1933 *Education/professional qualifications:* Tonbridge School; Imperial College, London, metallurgy (BSc Eng Met 1955) and mineral technology (ARSM 1955) *Marital status:* married Pauline Mary 1958; 1 son, 2 daughters *Clubs:* Athenaeum; St James's, Manchester

John H Pownall Esq CEng, Regional Director, Department of Trade and Industry North West, Sunley Tower, Piccadilly Plaza, Manchester M1 4BA *Telephone:* 061-838 5500 *Fax:* 061-838 5503

PRATT, TIMOTHY JEAN GEOFFREY   Deputy Treasury Solicitor, Treasury Solicitor's Department   Grade: 2

Career: barrister 1959-; Treasury Solicitor's Department (TSD) 1961-72: legal assistant 1961-67, senior legal assistant 1967-72; senior legal assistant Law Officers' Department 1972-74; assistant solicitor Department of Trade and Industry 1974-79; legal adviser Office of Fair Trading 1979-85; legal adviser Cabinet Office European Secretariat 1985-90; deputy treasury solicitor TSD 1990- *Education/professional qualifications:* Brighton College; Trinity Hall, Cambridge, law (BA, MA 1958), Middle Temple barrister (1959) *Marital status:* married Pamela Ann 1963; 2 daughters *Clubs:* United Oxford and Cambridge University

Timothy J G Pratt Esq, Deputy Treasury Solicitor, Treasury Solicitor's Department, Queen Anne's Chambers, 28 Broadway, London SW1 *Telephone:* 071-210 3129

PRESTON, JEFFREY WILLIAM   Deputy Director-General, Office of Fair Trading   Grade: 2

Career: assistant principal Ministry of Aviation 1963-66; Board of Trade 1966-70: private secretary to permanent secretary 1966-67, principal 1967-70; principal HM Treasury 1970-73; Department of Trade and Industry 1973-85: principal 1973-75, assistant secretary 1975-82, under secretary and Yorkshire and Humberside regional director 1982-85; deputy secretary industrial and economic affairs, Welsh Office 1985-90; deputy director-general Office of Fair Trading (administration of fair trading legislation) 1990-

Date of birth: 28 January 1940 *Education/professional qualifications:* Liverpool Collegiate College; Hertford College, Oxford, literae humaniores (BA 1963, MA) *Honours, decorations:* CB 1989 *Clubs:* United Oxford and Cambridge University *Recreations:* opera, swimming, motoring

Jeffrey W Preston Esq CB, Deputy Director-General, Office of Fair Trading, Field House, Bream's Building, London EC4A 1PR *Telephone:* 071-242 2858 *Fax:* 071-269 8800

PRICE, DAVID BROOKHOUSE   Director of Human Resources, Employment Service (Executive Agency)   Grade: 4

Career: Manpower Services Commission 1977-87: deputy chief executive employment services division 1977-84, director of personnel and central services 1984-87; director of personnel and business services Employment Service 1987-92, of human resources 1992-

Date of birth: 9 September 1936 *Education/professional qualifications:* Boys' Grammar School, Woking; St John's College, Cambridge, history (BA 1958, MA) *Marital status:* married Judith Anne Ebben 1967; 2 daughters, 1 son *Clubs:* Commonwealth Trust *Recreations:* walking, reading, history, piano

David B Price Esq, Director of Human Resources, Employment Service Head Office, Rockingham House, 123 West Street, Sheffield S1 4ER *Telephone:* 0742 596247 *Fax:* 0742 724528

PRIDDLE, ROBERT JOHN   Deputy Secretary, Energy Division, Department of Trade and Industry   Grade: 2

Career: Department of Energy (DoE) 1974-85; Department of Trade and Industry (DTI) 1985-89; deputy secretary (DS) DoE 1989 (most of whose responsibilities were taken over by the DTI in 1992)-1992, DS energy division DTI 1992-

Date of birth: 9 September 1938 *Education/professional qualifications:* Peterhouse College, Cambridge (MA)

Robert J Priddle Esq, Deputy Secretary, Energy Division, Department of Trade and Industry, 1 Palace Street, London SW1E 5AG *Telephone:* 071-238 3000

PROCTOR, BILL   Clerk of Domestic Committees and Secretary of the House of Commons Commission   Grade: 4

Career: research associate Manchester University 1970-72; House of Commons (HoC) 1968-: clerk of domestic committees (MPs' accommodation and services), secretary HoC Commission, 1987-

Date of birth: 1 May 1945 *Education/professional qualifications:* Bristol Cathedral School; Keele University, politics and English (BA 1968) *Marital status:* married Susan Mottram 1969; 2 sons, 1 daughter *Publications:* co-author The European Parliament: Structure, Procedure and Practice (HMSO 1973) and The Parliamentary Assembly: Procedure and Practice (Council of Europe 1990) *Recreations:* reading, music, amateur acting

Bill Proctor, Clerk of Domestic Committees and Secretary of the House of Commons Commission, Committee Office, House of Commons, London SW1A 0AA *Telephone:* 071-219 3270 *Fax:* 071-219 6864

PRYOR, Dr ARTHUR JOHN   Director-General British National Space Centre, Department of Trade and Industry   Grade: 3

Career: Board of Trade/Department of Trade [and Industry] 1966-: under secretary, West Midlands regional director 1985-88; director-general British National Space Centre 1988-

Date of birth: 7 March 1939 *Education/professional qualifications:* Downing College, Cambridge (BA, MA, PhD)

Dr Arthur J Pryor, Director-General, British National Space Centre, Dean Bradley House, 52 Horseferry Road, London SW1P 2AG *Telephone:* 071-276 2688

PURSE, HUGH ROBERT LESLIE   Principal Assistant Solicitor, Employment Department Group, Employment Division, Treasury Solicitor's Department   Grade: 3

Career: Government legal service 1979-: principal assistant solicitor Department of Employment division, Treasury Solicitor's Department 1988-

Date of birth: 22 October 1940 *Education/professional qualifications:* King's College, London (LLB); Gray's Inn (barrister)

Hugh R L Purse Esq, Legal Adviser, Employment Department Group, Caxton House, Tothill Street, London SW1H 9NF *Telephone:* 071-273 5849

R

RAMSAY, KATHARINE CELIA   Member of the Prime Minister's Policy Unit

Career: Citibank NA 1977-79; desk officer, later head of economics section Conservative Research Department 1979-83; special adviser Departments of Transport, Environment, Trade and Industry 1983-90, of Health 1990-92; member of Prime Minister's Policy Unit 1992-

Date of birth: 28 May 1955 *Education/professional qualifications:* St Paul's Girls' School, London; Girton College, Cambridge, history (BA, MA 1977) *Marital status:* married Andrew 1983; 2 daughters

Mrs Katharine C Ramsay, Prime Minister's Policy Unit, 10 Downing Street, London SW1A 2AA *Telephone:* 071-270 3000

RAMSBOTHAM, Gen Sir DAVID JOHN   Adjutant General, Ministry of Defence (Army)

Career: commanding officer Royal Green Jackets 1974-76; commander 39 Infantry Brigade 1978-80; Ministry of Defence director Public Relations (Army) 1982-84; commander 3 Armoured Division 1984-87; commander UK First Army and Inspector General TA 1987-90; adjutant general Ministry of Defence (Army) 1990-

Date of birth: 6 November 1934 *Education/professional qualifications:* Haileybury College; Corpus Christi College, Cambridge, history (BA 1957, MA) *Honours, decorations:* OBE 1974, CBE 1980, KCB 1987, ADC Gen 1991 *Publications:* Meeting the Challenge of Change (MoD 1984) *Recreations:* shooting, gardening, sailing

General Sir David Ramsbotham KCB CBE ADC Gen, Adjutant General, Ministry of Defence, Main Building, Whitehall, London SW1A 2HB *Telephone:* 071-218 9400

RAWSTHORNE, ANTHONY ROBERT   Assistant Under Secretary, Immigration and Nationality, Home Office   Grade: 3

Career: Home Office (HO) 1966-82: head of crime policy planning unit 1977-79, of division establishment department 1979-82; secretary Falkland Islands Review Committee Cabinet Office 1982; HO 1983-: principal private secretary 1983, head of division, immigration and nationality department (IND) 1983-86, head of establishment department 1986-91, of equal opportunities and general department 1991, assistant under secretary IND 1991-

Date of birth: 25 January 1943 *Education/professional qualifications:* Ampleforth College, York; Wadham College, Oxford, litterae humaniores (BA 1965) *Marital status:* married Beverley Jean Osborne 1967; 1 son, 2 daughters *Recreations:* bridge, cycling, squash

Anthony R Rawsthorne, Assistant Under Secretary, Home Office Immigration and Nationality Department, 40 Wellesley Road, Croydon CR9 2BY *Telephone:* 081-760 2733 *Fax:* 081-760 2435

Regulatory Organisations and Public Bodies
see page 857

REED, Dr JOHN LANGDALE   Senior Principal Medical Officer, Department of Health   Grade: 3

Career: consultant psychiatrist City and Hackney Health Authority 1967-86; senior lecturer St Bartholomew's Hospital medical college 1967-86; senior principal medical officer Department of Health (health care policy advice apart from maternity and child health) 1986-

Date of birth: 16 September 1931 *Education/professional qualifications:* Oundle School; St John's College, Cambridge, natural sciences (BA 1953), medicine (MB, BChir 1956); FRCP 1974; FRCPsych 1974 *Honours, decorations:* QHP 1990 *Marital status:* married Hilary 1959; 1 daughter, 1 son *Publications:* co-editor Psychiatric Services in the Community (Croom Helm 1984) *Recreations:* historical research, bridge, walking

Dr John L Reed QHP, Senior Principal Medical Officer, Department of Health, Wellington House, 133-55 Waterloo Road, London SE1 8UG *Telephone:* 071-972 4327 *Fax:* 071-972 4340

REES, Dr DAVID ALLAN   Secretary, Medical Research Council

Career: chemistry lecturer Edinburgh University 1960-70; various posts, latterly principal scientist Unilever Research 1970-82; Medical Research Council 1982-: director National Institute of Medical Research 1982-87, secretary (chief executive) 1987-

Date of birth: 28 April 1936 *Education/professional qualifications:* Hawarden Grammar School, Clwyd; University College of North Wales, chemistry (BSc 1956, PhD 1959); Edinburgh University, chemistry (DSc 1970); FRS 1981; Hon FRCP 1986 *Marital status:* married Myfanwy Owen 1959; 1 daughter, 2 sons *Publications:* Polysaccharide Shapes (Chapman & Hall 1977) *Clubs:* Royal Society of Medicine *Recreations:* reading, walking, river boats

Dr David A Rees FRS, Secretary, Medical Research Council, 20 Park Crescent, London W1N 4AL *Telephone:* 071-636 5422 *Fax:* 071-436 6179

REES, OWEN   Under Secretary, Agriculture Department, Welsh Office   Grade: 3

Career: research economist Bank of London and South America 1957-59; regional policy research Board of Trade 1959-69; principal Cabinet Office 1969-71; Welsh Office 1971-: principal, economic planning 1971-72, assistant secretary: European division 1972-75, education department 1975-77, under secretary: education department 1977-80, industry department 1980-85, economic and regional policy group 1985-90, agriculture department (policy and management responsibilities) 1990-

Date of birth: 26 December 1934 *Education/professional qualifications:* Llanelli Grammar School; Manchester University, economics and politics (BA Econ 1955) *Honours, decorations:* CB 1991 *Marital status:* married Elizabeth Gosby 1959; 2 daughters, 1 son

Owen Rees Esq CB, Under Secretary, Welsh Office, Cathays Park, Cardiff CF1 3NQ *Telephone:* 0222 823114

Complete Name Index
see page 955

REES-MOGG, WILLIAM (The Lord Rees-Mogg)   Chairman, Broadcasting Standards Council

Career: Financial Times 1952-60: chief leader writer 1952-60, assistant editor 1957-60; Sunday Times 1960-67: city editor 1960-61, political and economic editor 1961-63, deputy editor 1964-67; The Times 1967-81: editor 1967-81, director 1968-81; chairman Sidgwick and Jackson 1985-89; vice-chairman BBC board of governors 1981-86; chairman Arts Council of Great Britain 1982-89, Broadcasting Standards [violence, sex, taste and decency] Council 1988- *Current non-Whitehall posts:* chairman and proprietor Pickering and Chatto Ltd 1981-; non-executive director General Electric Co plc 1981-, M&G plc 1987-, St James's Place Capital plc 1990-

Date of birth: 14 July 1928 *Education/professional qualifications:* Charterhouse; Balliol College, Oxford *Honours, decorations:* Kt 1981; life baron 1988 *Marital status:* married Gillian Morris 1962; 2 sons, 3 daughters *Publications:* The Reigning Error: The Crisis of World Inflation (1974); An Humbler Heaven (1977); How to Buy Rare Books (1985); co-author Blood in the Streets (1988) and The Great Reckoning (1992) *Clubs:* Garrick *Recreations:* collecting

Lord Rees-Mogg, Chairman, Broadcasting Standards Council, 5-8 The Sanctuary, London SW1P 3JS *Telephone:* 071-233 0406 *Fax:* 071-233 0397

REEVES, WILLIAM DESMOND   Assistant Under Secretary, Commitments, Ministry of Defence   Grade: 3

Career: Ministry of Defence (MoD) 1964-: assistant under secretary (AUS) resources and programmes 1984-85, office of management and budget 1985-88; under secretary Cabinet Office 1989-92; AUS Commitments MoD 1992-

Date of birth: 26 May 1937 *Education/professional qualifications:* King's College, Cambridge, history (BA)

William D Reeves Esq, Assistant Under Secretary, Ministry of Defence, Main Building, Whitehall, London SW1A 2HB *Telephone:* 071-218 9000

REID, GRAHAM LIVINGSTONE   Deputy Secretary, Industrial Relations and International Directorate, Employment Department Group   Grade: 2

Career: Department of Employment 1984-: deputy secretary of manpower policy 1988-90, resources and strategy 1990, industrial relations and international directorate 1990-

Date of birth: 30 June 1937 *Education/professional qualifications:* University of St Andrews (MA); Queen's University, Kingston, Canada (MA)

Graham L Reid Esq CB, Deputy Secretary, Employment Department Group, Caxton House, Tothill Street, London SW1H 9NF *Telephone:* 071-273 3000

To subscribe to The Whitehall Companion
Telephone: 071-240 3902

REID, WILLIAM KENNEDY   Parliamentary Commissioner for Administration and Health Service Commissioner for England, for Scotland and for Wales [Ombudsman]   Grade: 1 equivalent

Career: Ministry of Education 1956-64; Cabinet Office 1964-67; Department of Education and Science 1967-78; Scottish Office central services 1978-84; Scottish Home and Health Department 1984-89; parliamentary commissioner for administration and health service for England, for Scotland and for Wales (ombudsman: investigation of complaints of maladministration and failures in service) 1990- *Current non-Whitehall posts:* ex officio member Council on Tribunals 1990-, Commission for Local Administration in England 1990-, Commission for Local Administration in Wales 1990-

Date of birth: 1931 *Education/professional qualifications:* George Watson's College, Edinburgh; Edinburgh University (MA); Trinity College, Cambridge (MA) *Honours, decorations:* CB 1981 *Marital status:* married Ann 1959; 2 sons, 1 daughter *Clubs:* New, Edinburgh; United Oxford and Cambridge University

William K Reid Esq CB, Parliamentary Commissioner for Local Administration, Church House, Great Smith Street, London SW1P 3BW *Telephone:* 071-276 3000 *Fax:* 071-276 2104

REISZ, JULIET ELIZABETH   Director of Buildings and Services, HM Prison, Home Office   Grade: 3

Career: Home Office 1968-: director of buildings and services HM Prison Service 1990-

Date of birth: 25 February 1945 *Education/professional qualifications:* University of Kent

Mrs Juliet E Reisz, Director of Buildings and Services, HM Prison Service, Home Office, Cleland House, Page Street, London SW1P 4LN *Telephone:* 071-270 3000

RENSHALL, (JAMES) MICHAEL   Deputy Chairman, Financial Reporting Review Panel

Career: Pilkington Brothers 1957-60; Institute of Chartered Accountants in England and Wales 1960-77: assistant secretary 1960-69, technical director 1969-70; partner/consultant private practice accountancy 1977-; deputy chairman Financial Reporting Review Panel (company accounts presentation standards) 1991- *Current non-Whitehall posts:* consultant KPMG Peat Marwick 1992-

Date of birth: 27 July 1930 *Education/professional qualifications:* Rydal School, Colwyn Bay; Clare College, Cambridge, English literature (BA, MA 1953) *Honours, decorations:* CBE 1991 *Marital status:* married Kathleen Valerie 1960; 1 daughter *Publications:* co-author Added Value in External Financial Reporting (Institute of Chartered Accountants in England and Wales [ICA] 1979) and Purchase of Own Shares (ICA 1983); joint editor The Companies Act Handbook 1981 (ICA 1981); general editor Butterworth's Company Law Guide *Clubs:* United Oxford and Cambridge University, City Livery

J Michael Renshall Esq CBE, Deputy Chairman, Financial Reporting Review Panel, c/o 1 Puddle Dock, Blackfriars, London EC4V 3PD *Telephone:* 071-236 8000 *Fax:* 071-832 8748

RENSHAW, DAVID CHARLES   North West Regional Director, Departments of the Environment and Transport   Grade: 3

Career: Ministry of Labour 1959-63; Department of Transport (DTp) 1964-70: assistant principal 1964-67, principal 1967-70; Department of the Environment (DoE) 1970-75: principal 1970-73, assistant secretary (AS) 1973-75; AS Civil Service Department 1975-77, DoE 1977-81; NW regional director DoE/DTp 1982-84; DoE 1984-89: director Merseyside task force 1984-88; NW regional director DoE/DTp 1989-

Date of birth: 6 September 1937 *Education/professional qualifications:* Doncaster Grammar School *Marital status:* divorced; 1 daughter, 1 son *Recreations:* music, walking, bowls

David C Renshaw Esq, Regional Director, Departments of the Environment and Transport, Sunley Tower, Piccadilly Plaza, Manchester M1 4BE *Telephone:* 061-832 9111 *Fax:* 061-838 5790

RHIND, Professor DAVID WILLIAM   Director-General and Chief Executive Ordnance Survey (Executive Agency)   Grade: 3

Career: research fellow Edinburgh University 1968-69, Royal College of Art 1969-73; reader in geography Durham University 1973-81; geography professor Birkbeck College, London 1982-91; director-general and chief executive Ordnance Survey 1992-

Date of birth: 29 November 1943 *Education/professional qualifications:* Berwick Grammar School, Berwick-upon-Tweed; Bristol University, geography (BSc 1965); Edinburgh University, geomorphology (PhD 1969); London University, geographical information systems (DSc 1991) *Marital status:* married Christine 1966; 2 daughters, 1 son *Publications:* seven books including co-editor Geographical Information Systems (Longman 1991); co-author Land Use (Methuen 1980) *Clubs:* Athenaeum *Recreations:* walking, house-painting, music

Professor David W Rhind, Director-General and Chief Executive, Ordnance Survey, Romsey Road, Maybush, Southampton SO9 4DH *Telephone:* 0703 792000 *Fax:* 0703 792888

RICHARDS, BRIAN HENRY   Chief Executive, Atomic Weapons Establishment, Ministry of Defence   Grade: 2

Career: technical director Hunting Engineering 1988-90; chief executive atomic weapons establishment, Ministry of Defence 1990-

Date of birth: 19 July 1938 *Education/professional qualifications:* St John's College, Cambridge, mechanical science (BA 1960, MA 1965)

Brian H Richards Esq, Chief Executive, Atomic Weapons Establishment, Ministry of Defence, Aldermaston, Reading, Berkshire RG7 4PR *Telephone:* 0734 814111

RICKARD, Dr JOHN   Under Secretary Economics, HM Treasury   Grade: 3

Career: economist Atomic Energy Authority 1970-72; research fellow Oxford University 1972-74; economics adviser: Department of Health 1974-76, Department of Industry 1976-78, Central Policy Review Staff, Cabinet Office 1978-82; senior economics adviser (SEA) HM Treasury (HMT) 1982-84; adviser, Bahrain 1984-87; SEA Department of Transport 1987-91; under secretary public sector economics HMT 1991-

Date of birth: 27 January 1940 *Education/professional qualifications:* County High School, Ilford; St John's College, Oxford, politics, philosophy and economics (BA, MA 1962), economics (DPhil 1976); Aston University, economics (MSc 1969) *Marital status:* married Christine 1963; 2 daughters, 1 son *Publications:* Macro-economics (Pitmans 1970) *Clubs:* Civil Service Sailing Association *Recreations:* music, sailing

Dr John Rickard, Under Secretary, HM Treasury, 1 Parliament Street, London SW1P 3AG *Telephone:* 071-270 5492

RICKETT, WILLIAM FRANCIS SEBASTIAN   Director General, Energy Efficiency Office, Department of the Environment   Grade: 3

Career: Department of Energy (DEn) 1975-81: private secretary to permanent under secretary 1977-78, principal atomic energy division 1978-81;; private secretary to Prime Minister 1981-83; seconded to corporate finance division Kleinwort Benson Ltd 1983-85; DEn 1985-: assistant secretary: oil division 1985-87, electricity division 1987-89, grade 4 electricity division 1989-90, under secretary and director general Energy Efficiency Office (now part of the Department for Environment) 1990-

Date of birth: 23 February 1953 *Education/professional qualifications:* Eton; Trinity College, Cambridge, natural sciences (BA 1974) *Marital status:* married Lucy Caroline Clark 1979; 1 son, 1 daughter *Recreations:* sport, painting, children

William F S Rickett Esq, Director General Energy Efficiency Office, Department of the Environment, 1 Palace Street, London SW1E 5HE *Telephone:* 071-238 3096

RICKETTS, (ROBERT) TRISTRAM   Chief Executive, Horserace Betting Levy Board

Career: Greater London Council 1968-74: personal assistant to leader of Council 1972-73, deputy head London transport policy 1973-74; Horserace Betting Levy Board 1974-: assistant principal officer 1974-76, deputy secretary 1976-79, chief executive 1980- *Current non-Whitehall posts:* director Racecourse Technical Services Ltd 1980-, Horseracing Forensic Laboratory Ltd 1986-

Date of birth: 17 April 1946 *Education/professional qualifications:* Winchester College; Magdalene College, Cambridge, modern languages (BA 1968, MA) *Marital status:* married Ann 1969; 1 son, 1 daughter *Clubs:* Athenaeum *Recreations:* cinema, theatre, horseracing

R Tristram Ricketts Esq, Chief Executive, Horserace Betting Levy Board, 52 Grosvenor Gardens, London SW1W 0AU *Telephone:* 071-333 0043 *Fax:* 071-333 0041

RICKS, ROBERT NEVILLE   Legal Adviser to Department for Education, Treasury Solicitor's Department   Grade: 3

Career: private practice 1965-69; Treasury Solicitor's Department 1969-: legal assistant (LA) 1969-73, senior LA 1973-81, assistant treasury solicitor (ATS) 1981-86, principal ATS 1986-: senior legal adviser and head of legal branch Department for Education 1990-

Date of birth: 29 June 1942 *Education/professional qualifications:* Highgate School, London; Worcester College, Oxford, jurisprudence (BA 1964, MA); solicitor 1967 *Marital status:* single *Clubs:* United Oxford and Cambridge University *Recreations:* collecting original cartoons, wine

Robert N Ricks Esq, Legal Adviser, Department for Education, Sanctuary Buildings, Great Smith Street, London SW1P 3BJ *Telephone:* 071-925 6174

RIDD, P L   Principal Assistant Solicitor, Board of Inland Revenue   Grade: 3

P L Ridd Esq, Principal Assistant Solicitor, Board of Inland Revenue, Somerset House, London WC2R 1LB *Telephone:* 071-438 6622

RIGGS, DAVID GEORGE   Finance Director, Social Security Benefits Agency (Executive Agency)   Grade: 3

Career: Bury County Borough Council 1958-68; Greater London Council 1968-82: finance officer 1968-74, head of public services finance 1974-76, assistant comptroller of finance 1976-82; director of finance Inner London Education Authority 1982-90; acting director of finance London borough of Hammersmith and Fulham 1990-91; finance director Social Security Benefits Agency 1991-

Date of birth: 6 May 1942 *Education/professional qualifications:* Bury Grammar School, Lancashire; Manchester University, economics (BA Econ 1968) *Children:* 2 sons, 2 daughters *Recreations:* choral singing, running

David G Riggs Esq, Finance Director, Social Security Benefits Agency, Euston Tower, 286 Euston Road, London NW1 3DN *Telephone:* 071-388 1188 *Fax:* 071-388 1188

RILEY, CHRIS(TOPHER) JOHN   Under Secretary, Medium-Term and Policy Analysis Group, HM Treasury   Grade: 3

Career: HM Treasury (HMT) 1969-77: economic assistant 1969-72, senior economic assistant 1972-74, economic adviser 1974-77; research fellow Nuffield College, Oxford 1977-78; HMT 1978-: senior economic adviser 1978-88, under secretary medium-term and policy analysis group 1988-

Date of birth: 20 January 1947 *Education/professional qualifications:* Ratcliffe College, Leicester; Wadham College, Oxford, mathematics (BA 1967; Leicester University MA 1978); East Anglia University, economics (MA 1969) *Marital status:* married Helen Marion Mynett 1982; 2 sons *Recreations:* music, especially choral singing

Chris J Riley Esq, Under Secretary, HM Treasury, 1 Parliament Street, London SW1P 3AG *Telephone:* 071-270 4439 *Fax:* 071-270 5653

RIMINGTON, JOHN DAVID   Director-General, Health and Safety Executive   Grade: 2

Career: army national service 1954-56; Board of Trade 1959-65: seconded to HM Treasury to work on decimal currency 1961-63; principal, tariff division 1963-65; economic first secretary New Delhi high commission 1965-69; mergers division Department of Trade and Industry 1969-70; Department of Employment 1970-74: assistant secretary employment policy and manpower 1972-74; social and regional policy counsellor UK permanent representation to EC, Brussels 1974-77; under secretary industrial training Manpower Services Commission 1977-81; Health and Safety Executive 1981-: director safety policy division 1981-83, deputy secretary and director-general (health and safety law enforcement, protection of workers and public from industrial hazards) 1984-

Date of birth: 27 June 1935 *Education/professional qualifications:* Nottingham High School; Jesus College, Cambridge, history (BA, MA 1959) *Honours, decorations:* CB 1987 *Marital status:* married Stella 1963; 2 daughters *Recreations:* walking, gardening, watching cricket

John D Rimington Esq CB, Director-General, Health and Safety Executive, Baynards House, Chepstow Place, London W2 4TF *Telephone:* 071-243 6000

Parliamentary Offices
see page 275

RIMINGTON, STELLA   Director-General, Security Service

Career: Security Service 1969-: director-general 1992-

Date of birth: 1935 *Education/professional qualifications:* Nottingham High School for Girls; Edinburgh University (MA 1958) *Marital status:* married John David 1963; 2 daughters

RIPPENGAL, DEREK   Counsel to Chairman of Committees, House of Lords

Career: barrister 1953-55; university posts 1955-58; adviser Treasury Solicitor's Office 1958-72; solicitor and legal adviser Department of Trade and Industry 1972-73; parliamentary counsel Law Commission 1973-77; counsel to chairman of committees (advice on private bills, statutory instruments, relevant legal aspects; counsel to Ecclesiastical Committee) House of Lords 1977-

Date of birth: 8 September 1928 *Education/professional qualifications:* Hampton Grammar School, Middlesex; St Catharine's College, Cambridge, law (BA 1952, MA); Inner Temple (barrister 1953) *Honours, decorations:* QC 1980, CB 1982 *Marital status:* married Elizabeth Melrose 1963 (deceased); 1 daughter, 1 son *Clubs:* Athenaeum *Recreations:* music, fishing

Derek Rippengal Esq CB QC, Counsel to Chairman of Committees, House of Lords, London SW1A 0PW *Telephone:* 071-219 3211 *Fax:* 071-219 6715

RITCHIE, DAVID ROBERT   West Midlands Regional Director, Departments of the Environment and Transport   Grade: 3

Career: Ministry of Transport 1970-75; Department of the Environment (DoE) 1975-: principal, planning and inner cities NW regional office 1975-79, water legislation 1979-83; NW regional housing and environment controller 1983-86; head of water legislation division 1986-88, of housing association (capital) division 1988-89; W Midlands regional director DoE and Transport 1989- *Current non-Whitehall posts:* non-executive director Blue Circle Home Products plc 1991-

Date of birth: 10 March 1948 *Education/professional qualifications:* Manchester Grammar School; St John's College, Cambridge, classics (BA 1970), theology (MA 1976) *Marital status:* married Joan Gibbons 1989 *Recreations:* fellwalking, gardening, cooking

David R Ritchie Esq, Regional Director, Departments of the Environment and Transport, Five Ways Tower, Frederick Road, Edgbaston, Birmingham B15 1SJ *Telephone:* 021-626 2570 *Fax:* 021-626 2483

RIVETT, Dr GEOFFREY CHRISTOPHER   Senior Principal Medical Officer, NHS Management Executive, Department of Health   Grade: 3

Career: medical practice 1957-72 (national service 1958-60); Department of Health 1972-: medical officer (MO) 1972-73, senior MO 1973-79, principal MO 1979-85; senior principal MO health care directorate NHS management executive (professional issues relating to primary health care) 1985-

Date of birth: 11 August 1932 *Education/professional qualifications:* Manchester Grammar School; University College Hospital, Oxford, medicine (BM, BCh, RCOG, FRCGP 1956) and animal physiology (MA 1957) *Marital status:* married Elizabeth Barbara Hartman 1976; 2 sons from previous marriage *Publications:* The Development of the London Hospital

System (King Edward's Hospital Fund 1986) *Clubs:* Wig and Pen, Royal Society of Medicine *Recreations:* house conversion

Dr Geoffrey C Rivett, Senior Principal Medical Officer, NHS Management Executive, Portland Court, 160 Great Portland Street, London W1N 5TB *Telephone:* 071-972 8089 *Fax:* 071-972 8241

ROBERTS, ALLAN DEVERELL   **Head of Division, Solicitor's Office, Departments of Health and Social Security**   Grade: 3

Career: private practice solicitor 1974-76; government legal service 1976-: head of division C, Solicitor's Office (legal services other than litigation and prosecution), Department of Health/Social Security 1989-

Date of birth: 14 July 1950 *Education/professional qualifications:* Eton; Magdalen College, Oxford, jurisprudence (BA 1971, MA) *Marital status:* married Dr Irene Anne Graham 1991 *Recreations:* walking, music, football

Allan D Roberts Esq, Head of Division C, Solicitor's Office, Department of Health, New Court, Carey Street, London WC2 2LS *Telephone:* 071-412 1465

ROBERTS, CHRISTOPHER WILLIAM   **Deputy Secretary, Trade Policy and Export Promotion, Department of Trade and Industry**   Grade: 2

Career: Cabinet Office 1966-68; private secretary to the Prime Minister 1970-73; Department of Trade and Industry 1973-: deputy secretary external trade policy, single European market and other EC matters 1991-92, trade policy and export promotion 1992-

Date of birth: 4 November 1937 *Education/professional qualifications:* Magdalen College, Oxford (MA)

Christopher W Roberts CB Esq, Deputy Secretary, Department of Trade and Industry, Ashdown House, 123 Victoria Street, London SW1E 6RB *Telephone:* 071-215 5000

ROBERTS, JOHN HERBERT   **Director, Compliance and Collection Division, Inland Revenue**   Grade: 3

Career: Inland Revenue 1957-: tax inspector 1957-81; director of operations 1981-85; director technical division 2 1985-88; director compliance and collection division 1988-

Date of birth: 18 August 1933 *Education/professional qualifications:* Canton High School, Cardiff; London School of Economics, economics (BSc 1954) *Marital status:* married Patricia 1965; 3 daughters, 1 son *Recreations:* music, walking

John H Roberts Esq, Director, Compliance and Collection Division, Inland Revenue, Somerset House, Strand, London WC2R 1LB *Telephone:* 071-438 7649 *Fax:* 071-438 6230

ROBERTSON, IAIN ALASDAIR   **Chief Executive, Highlands and Islands Enterprise**

Career: British Petroleum 1975-90, latterly director of acquisitions and divestitures BP America; chief executive Highlands and Islands Enterprise (social, economic, training and environmental development) 1990-

Date of birth: 30 October 1949 *Education/professional qualifications:* Perth Academy; Aberdeen University, law (LLB 1973) *Marital status:* married Judith Helen 1977; 2 sons, 1 daughter *Recreations:* skiing, music

Iain A Robertson Esq, Chief Executive, Highlands and Islands Enterprise, Bridge House, 20 Bridge Street, Inverness 1VI 1QR *Telephone:* 0463 234171 *Fax:* 0463 244469

ROBERTSON, Dr JAMES A S   Head of Industrial and Regional Economics, Department of Trade and Industry   Grade: 4

Career: head of industrial and regional economics, economics, market intelligence and statistics division Department of Trade and Industry 1990-

Dr James A S Robertson, Head of Industrial and Regional Economics, Department of Trade and Industry, 151 Buckingham Palace Road, London SW1W 9SS *Telephone:* 071-215 1876 *Fax:* 071-215 2909

ROBINSON, ANN   Director of Policy and Planning, Social Security Benefits Agency (Executive Agency)   Grade: 3

Career: Department of [Health and] Social Security 1969-: assistant principal and principal; seconded to Central Policy Review Staff 1974-77; nurses' and midwives' professions 1981-85; regional liaison division 1985-86; controller north London region 1986-90; director of policy and planning Social Security Benefits Agency 1990-
Education/professional qualifications: Preston Technical College *Marital status:* married Peter Crawford Robinson 1961 *Recreations:* fine wine, bridge, walking, fun tennis

Mrs Ann Robinson, Director of Policy and Planning, Benefits Agency, Quarry House, Quarry Hill, Leeds LS2 7UA *Telephone:* 0532 324000

ROBINSON, Dr BILL   Special Adviser to the Chancellor of the Exchequer   Grade: 2

Career: economics adviser HM Treasury (HMT) 1971-74; head of division EC Commission 1974-78; senior research fellow London Business School 1978-86; director Institute for Fiscal Studies 1986-91; economics columnist The Independent 1989-91; special adviser (tax and macro-economics) to Chancellor of the Exchequer 1991- *Current non-Whitehall posts:* adviser Treasury Committee 1982-; member Retail Price Advisory Committee 1988-

Date of birth: 6 January 1943 *Education/professional qualifications:* Bryanston School; St Edmund Hall, Oxford, philosophy, politics and economics (BA 1964); Sussex University, philosophy (DPhil 1969); London School of Economics, economics (1971) *Marital status:* married Heather Mary Jackson 1966; 2 sons, 1 daughter *Recreations:* bassoon, skiing, opera, sailing

Dr Bill Robinson, Special Adviser, HM Treasury, Parliament Street, London SW1P 3AG *Telephone:* 071-270 4359 *Fax:* 071-839 2029

ROBINSON, GEOFFREY   Chief Adviser on Science and Technology, Department of Trade and Industry   Grade: 2

Geoffrey Robinson Esq, Chief Adviser on Science and Technology, Department of Trade and Industry, Ashdown House, 123 Victoria Street, London SW1E 6RB *Telephone:* 071-215 5000

ROBSON, GODFREY   Fisheries Secretary, Agriculture and Fisheries Department, Scottish Office   Grade: 3

Career: Scottish Office 1970-: assistant secretary, roads and transport 1981-86, local government finance 1986-89; fisheries secretary, Agriculture and Fisheries Department 1989-

Date of birth: 5 November 1946   *Education/professional qualifications:* Edinburgh University (MA)

Godfrey Robson Esq, Fisheries Secretary, Agriculture and Fisheries Department, Scottish Office, Pentland House, 47 Robb's Loan, Edinburgh EH14 1TW   *Telephone:* 031-556 8400

ROBSON, JOHN A   Midlands Regional Controller, Inland Revenue   Grade: 4

Career: Inland Revenue 1967-: district inspector 1967-77; group controller: South London region 1977-80, West Midlands region 1980-84; regional controller North 1984-88, Midlands 1988-

Date of birth: 30 October 1934   *Education/professional qualifications:* Rutherford Grammar School, Newcastle-upon-Tyne; King's College, Durham University, economics (BA 1963)   *Marital status:* married Aline 1971; 1 daughter, 1 son   *Recreations:* sailing, reading, golf

John A Robson, Regional Controller, Inland Revenue, Chadwick House, Blenheim Court, Solihull B91 2AA   *Telephone:* 021-711 1144   *Fax:* 021-711 3623

ROBSON, STEPHEN ARTHUR   Under Secretary, Public Enterprises and Privatisation Group, HM Treasury   Grade: 3

Career: HM Treasury 1969-: undersecretary defence policy and material group 1987-89, public enterprises and privatisation group 1990-

Date of birth: 30 September 1943   *Education/professional qualifications:* St John's College, Cambridge (MA, PhD); Stanford University, USA (MA)

Stephen A Robson Esq, Under Secretary, Public Enterprises and Privatisation Group, HM Treasury, Parliament Street, London SW1P 3AG   *Telephone:* 071-270 3000

ROCHESTER, T A   Chief Highway Engineer, Engineering Policy Directorate, Department of Transport   Grade: 3

T A Rochester Esq, Chief Highway Engineer, Engineering Policy Directorate, Department of Transport, St Christopher House, Southwark Street, London SE1 0TE   *Telephone:* 071-276 3000

ROCK, PATRICK   Special Adviser to the Secretary of State for the Environment

Career: Conservative Research Department; Tricentrol; special adviser to secretaries of state for the environment: Chris Patten 1989-91, Michael Heseltine 1991-92, Michael Howard 1992-

Patrick Rock Esq, Special Adviser, Department of the Environment, 2 Marsham Street, London SW1P 3EB   *Telephone:* 071-276 3000

RODDA, JIM   Director of Finance and Administration, House of Commons   Grade: 3

Career: director of finance and administration House of Commons 1991-

Jim Rodda Esq, Director of Finance and Administration, House of Commons, London SW1A 0AA   *Telephone:* 071-219 5460   *Fax:* 071-219 4979

ROE, GEOFFREY ERIC   Director-General Defence Contracts, Procurement Executive, Ministry of Defence   Grade: 3

Career: Ministry of Aviation 1963-67; Ministry of Technology 1967-74; exports and international relations division 1969-74; Ministry of Defence 1974-: guided weapons contracts branch 1974-76, seconded to British Aerospace 1976-78, secretary rocket motor executive 1978-81, assistant director contracts (air) 1981-86, director contracts (underwater weapons) 1986-89, head of material co-ordination (navy) 1989-90, principal director navy and nuclear contracts 1990-91, director-general defence contracts 1991-

Date of birth: 20 July 1944 *Education/professional qualifications:* Tottenham Grammar School *Recreations:* skiing, fell walking, sailing, flying

Geoffrey E Roe Esq, Director-General Defence Contracts, Ministry of Defence Procurement Executive, Foxhill, Bath BA1 5AB *Telephone:* 0225 884884

ROSLING, (RICHARD) ALAN   Member, Prime Minister's Policy Unit

Career: SG Warburg and Co Ltd 1983-86; Harkness Fellow 1986; Courtaulds Textiles plc 1988-90; member Prime Minister's Policy Unit (responsible for energy, Scottish Office, science, Ministry of Defence) 1990-
Education/professional qualifications: Downing College, Cambridge, history (BA 1983); Harvard Business School, (MBA 1988) *Marital status:* married Dr Sarmila Bose

R Alan Rosling, Policy Unit, 10 Downing Street, London SW1A 2AA *Telephone:* 071-270 3000

ROUS, Lieutenant General The Hon Sir (WILLIAM) WILLIE EDWARD   Military Secretary, Ministry of Defence

Career: military assistant to Field Marshal Lord Carver, Foreign and Commonwealth Office 1977-79; commanding officer 2nd battalion Coldstream Guards 1979-81; colonel staff duties HQ BAOR 1981-82; commander 1st Infantry Brigade 1983-84; director public relations (army) Ministry of Defence (MoD) 1985-87; general officer commanding 4th Armoured Division 1988-89; commandant staff college, Camberley 1990-91; military secretary MoD (army officers' careers; honours and awards administration) 1990-

Date of birth: 22 February 1939 *Education/professional qualifications:* Harrow School; Royal Military Academy, Sandhurst *Honours, decorations:* MBE 1974, OBE 1980, KCB 1992

Lieutenant General The Hon Sir William Rous KCB OBE, Military Secretary, Ministry of Defence, Whitehall, London, SW1A 2HB *Telephone:* 071-218 7581

ROWCLIFFE, JOHN PHILIP GORDON   Managing Director, PSA Projects, Department of the Environment   Grade: 2

Career: Ministry of Housing and Local Government 1958-70; Department of Environment 1970-: private secretary to secretary of state 1970-72; assistant secretary: third London airport division 1972-74, land use policy 1974-76; Property Services Agency (PSA) 1976-78: head of defence secretariat air 1976-77, of management review team 1977-78; director of central directorate of environmental pollution (CDEP) 1978-82, of local government directorate 1982-86, of CDEP 1982-86; PSA 1987-: deputy chief executive 1987-90, managing director PSA Projects (construction management and design consultancy) 1990- *Current non-Whitehall posts:* member London and South East board Bradford and Bingley Building Society 1987-

Date of birth: 19 July 1933 *Education/professional qualifications:* Bristol Grammar School; Magdalen College, Oxford, literae humaniores (BA, MA 1956) *Marital status:* married Shirley Amelia 1958; 2 sons, 1 daughter

John P G Rowcliffe Esq, Managing Director, PSA Projects, Whitgift Centre, Wellesley Road, Croydon CR9 3LY *Telephone:* 081-760 3085 *Fax:* 081-760 3778

ROWE, Rear-Admiral PATRICK BARTON   Military Deputy, Defence Export Services, Ministry of Defence

Career: Royal Navy 1960-: student Royal College of Defence Studies 1989; military deputy, defence export services, Ministry of Defence 1989-

Date of birth: 14 April 1939 *Education/professional qualifications:* Royal Naval College, Dartmouth, army staff college; Royal College of Defence Studies *Honours, decorations:* LVO 1975; CBE 1990

Rear-Admiral Patrick B Rowe CBE LVO, Military Deputy, Defence Export Services, Ministry of Defence, Whitehall, London SW1A 2HB *Telephone:* 071-218 3060

ROWLANDS, DAVID J   Head of Railways 1 Directorate, Department of Transport
Grade: 3

Date of birth: 31 May 1947 *Education/professional qualifications:* St Edmund Hall, Oxford

David J Rowlands Esq CB, Head of Railways 1 Directorate, Department of Transport, 2 Marsham Street, London SW1P 3EB *Telephone:* 071-276 3000

RUBERY, Dr EILEEN DORIS   Head of Health Promotion (Medical) Division, Department of Health Grade: 3

Career: biochemistry research Cambridge University 1967-73; Addenbrookes Hospital, Cambridge 1973-88: radiotherapy and oncology registrar 1973-83, honorary consultant and research fellow 1983-88; Department of Health 1983-: principal medical officer (PMO) toxicology, radiation and environmental protection 1983-88, senior PMO communicable diseases 1988-91, head of health promotion (medical) division 1990-

Date of birth: 16 May 1943 *Education/professional qualifications:* Westcliffe High School for Girls, Essex; Sheffield Medical School (MB ChB 1966) *Marital status:* married 1970; 1 daughter *Publications:* Indications for Iodine Prophylaxis after a Nuclear Accident (Pergamon/WHO 1990); Medicine – A Degree Course Guide (CRAC 1974-83) *Clubs:* Royal Society of Medicine *Recreations:* music, tapestry, theatre, reading

Dr Eileen D Rubery, Head of Health Promotion (Medical) Division, Department of Health, Wellington House, 133-35 Waterloo Road, London SE1 8UG *Telephone:* 071-972 4420 *Fax:* 071-972 4319

RUCKER, ARTHUR GREY   Assistant Under Secretary, Security and Common Services, Ministry of Defence Grade: 3

Career: assistant principal Air Ministry 1961-67; principal Ministry of Defence (MoD) 1967-72; private secretary to Lord President of the Council 1972-75; MoD 1985-: various posts 1985-90, assistant under secretary security and common services 1990-

Date of birth: 2 November 1939 *Education/professional qualifications:* Radley College, Abingdon; Magdalen College, Oxford, jurisprudence (BA 1961)

Arthur G Rucker Esq, Assistant Under Secretary, Ministry of Defence, Metropole Building, Northumberland Avenue, London WC2N 5BL

RUFFLEY, DAVID   Special Adviser, Home Office

Career: special adviser to ministers of state, Home Office 1992-

David Ruffley Esq, Special Adviser, Home Office, 50 Queen Anne's Gate, London SW1H 9AT *Telephone:* 071-273 3000

RULE, BRIAN FRANCIS   Director General of Information Technology Systems, Ministry of Defence   Grade: 3

Career: director of scientific services Natural Environment Research Council 1979-85; director general of information technology systems Ministry of Defence 1985-
Education/professional qualifications: Loughborough University of Technology (MSc)

Brian F Rule Esq, Director General of Information, Technology Systems, Ministry of Defence, Northumberland House, Northumberland Avenue, London WC2N 5BP *Telephone:* 071-218 4828

RUMBELOW, (ROGER) MARTIN   Under Secretary, Services Management, Establishment and Finance Division, Department of Trade and Industry   Grade: 3 *(see Addenda)*

Career: RAF national service 1955-57; British Aircraft Corporation 1958-74: technical sales 1958-65, personal assistant to managing director and corporate planning 1966-67, deputy production contoller 1967-73, Concorde components project manager 1973-74; Department of Trade and Industry 1974-: principal 1974-78, assistant secretary 1979-86, under secretary services management division (infrastructure, information management, information technology and office services) 1987-

Date of birth: 3 June 1937 *Education/professional qualifications:* Cardiff High School; Bristol University, aeronautical engineering (BSc 1961); Cranfield Institute of Technology (MSc 1965) *Marital status:* married Marjorie Elizabeth 1965 *Recreations:* tennis, theatre, opera, singing, electronics, computing

R Martin Rumbelow Esq, Under Secretary, Establishment and Finance Division, Department of Trade and Industry, Kingsgate House, 66-74 Victoria Street, London SW1E 6SW *Telephone:* 071-215 3609 *Fax:* 071-215 8449

RUSSELL, (ALASTAIR) MUIR   Under Secretary, Cabinet Office   Grade: 3 *(see Addenda)*

Career: Scottish Office 1970-83: assistant principal 1970-74; principal 1974-81: seconded as secretary to Scottish Development Agency 1975-76; assistant secretary 1981-91: principal private secretary to secretary of state 1981-83; under secretary Cabinet Office 1990-

Date of birth: 9 January 1949 *Education/professional qualifications:* Glasgow High School; Glasgow University, natural philosophy (BSc 1970) *Marital status:* married Alison Mackay 1983 *Clubs:* Commonwealth Trust *Recreations:* music, food, wine

A Muir Russell Esq, Under Secretary, Cabinet Office, 70 Whitehall, London SW1A 2AS *Telephone:* 071-270 0189 *Fax:* 071-270 0113

RUSSELL, ALEXANDER WILLIAM   Director Customs, HM Customs and Excise   Grade: 3

Career: Scottish Office 1961-76: water, housing and industrial development 1961-72, principal private secretary to secretary of state 1972-73, head of local transport division 1973-76; Civil Service Department 1976-82: head of machinery of government division 1976-79, of efficiency group 1979-82; head of financial management unit HM Treasury and Management and Personnel Office 1982-85; HM Customs and Excise 1985-: director organisation 1985-90, director customs directorate 1990-

Date of birth: 16 October 1938   *Education/professional qualifications:* Royal High School, Edinburgh; Edinburgh University, history (MA 1960); Manitoba University, Canada political science (MA 1961)   *Marital status:* married Elspeth Rae Robertson 1962

Alexander W Russell Esq, Director, Customs Directorate, HM Customs and Excise, Dorset House, Stamford Street, London SE1 9PS
Telephone: 071-865 4141   *Fax:* 071-928 7835

RUSSELL, ARTHUR C   Under Secretary, Companies Division, Department of Trade and Industry   Grade: 3

Arthur C Russell Esq, Under Secretary, Companies Division, Department of Trade and Industry, 10-18 Victoria Street, London SW1H 0NN   *Telephone:* 071-215 5000

RUSSELL, Sir GEORGE   Chairman, Independent Television Commission

Career: senior posts in industry 1958- including ICI and Alcan; member Northern Development Board 1977-80; board member Washington Development Corporation 1978-80; board member Megaw Inquiry into Civil Service Pay 1981; council member Confederation of British Industry 1984-85; member Widdicombe Inquiry into Conduct of Local Authority Business 1985; deputy chairman Channel 4 TV 1987-88, chairman Independent Television News 1988, chairman Independent Broadcasting Authority 1989-90, chairman Independent Television Commission 1990-   *Current non-Whitehall posts:* director Northern Rock Building Society 1985-, group Chief executive Marley plc 1986-, director Alcan Aluminium Ltd, Montreal 1987-, chairman Marley plc 1989-

Date of birth: 25 October 1935   *Education/professional qualifications:* Gateshead Grammar School; King's College, Durham University, politics and economics (BA 1958)   *Honours, decorations:* CBE 1985, Kt 1992   *Marital status:* married Dorothy Brown 1959; 3 daughters   *Recreations:* theatre, opera, tennis, badminton, bird watching

Sir George Russell CBE, Chairman Independent Television Commission, 70 Brompton Road, London SW3 1EY   *Telephone:* 071-584 7011
Fax: 071-823 9116

RUTTER, JILL   Member of Prime Minister's Policy Unit

Career: fiscal policy division HM Treasury; member Prime Minister's Policy Unit 1992-

Jill Rutter, Prime Minister's Policy Unit, 10 Downing Street, London SW1A 2AA
Telephone: 071-270 3000

RUTTER, Dr J M   Chief Executive, Veterinary Medicines Directorate (Executive Agency)   Grade: 3

Dr J M Rutter, Chief Executive, Veterinary Medicines Directorate, Woodham Lane, New Haw, Weybridge, Surrey KT15 3NB   *Telephone:* 0932 336911

Government Departments
see page 300

RYDER, Dr PETER   Director of Operations and Deputy Chief Executive, Meteorological Office (Executive Agency)   Grade: 3

Career: Meteorological Office 1976-: assistant director of cloud physics research 1976-82, of systems development 1982-84; deputy director of observational services 1984-88, of forecasting services 1988-89; director of operations and deputy chief executive 1989-

Date of birth: 10 March 1942 *Education/professional qualifications:* Yorebridge Grammar School, Askrigg, Yorkshire; Leeds University, physics (BSc 1963), cosmic ray research (PhD 1966) *Marital status:* married Jacqueline Doris Sylvia 1965; 2 sons, 1 daughter *Recreations:* gardening, walking, fishing, photography, philately

Dr Peter Ryder, Director of Operations, Meteorological Office, London Road, Bracknell, Berkshire RG12 2SZ *Telephone:* 0344 854608 *Fax:* 0344 856909

S

SADLER, BRIAN   Head of Allocation (Technical), Business Profits Division, Inland Revenue   Grade: 4

Career: Inland Revenue: senior principal inspector 1983-: head of allocation (technical), business profits division 1991-

Date of birth: 5 April 1935   *Education/professional qualifications:* Whitchurch Grammar School, Cardiff   *Marital status:* married Jean Margaret Patricia 1961; 1 daughter

Brian Sadler Esq, Senior Principal Inspector, Business Profits Division, Inland Revenue, Somerset House, London WC2R 1LB   *Telephone:* 071-438 6247

SALVIDGE, PAUL   Under Secretary, Telecommunications and Posts Division, Department of Trade and Industry   Grade: 3

Career: Ministry of Power 1967-72; Department of Trade and Industry 1972- : assistant secretary 1982-89; under secretary telecommunications and posts division 1989-

Date of birth: 22 August 1946   *Education/professional qualifications:* Birmingham University (LLB)

Paul Salvidge Esq, Under Secretary, Department of Trade and Industry, 151 Buckingham Palace Road, London SW1W 9SS   *Telephone:* 071-215 5000

SANDARS, CHRISTOPHER THOMAS   Assistant Under Secretary Defence Export Services (Administration), Ministry of Defence   Grade: 3

Career: assistant private secretary (PS) to minister of state Ministry of Defence (MoD) 1967-69; Central Policy Review Staff, Cabinet Office 1971-74; MoD 1975-84: PS to minister of state 1975-77, head of defence secretariat 13 1980-84; Royal College of Defence Studies 1985; MoD 1986-: head of secretariat 9 (air) 1986-90, assistant under secretary defence export services (administration) 1990-

Date of birth: 6 March 1942   *Education/professional qualifications:* Oundle; Corpus Christi College, Cambridge, history (BA, MA 1964)   *Recreations:* tennis, squash, painting, gardening

Christopher T Sandars Esq, Assistant Under Secretary, Ministry of Defence, Whitehall, London SW1A 2HB   *Telephone:* 071-218 6748

SANDERS, NICHOLAS JOHN   Accountant General, Finance Branch, Department for Education   Grade: 3

Career: Department of Education [and Science] 1971-: accountant general 1989-

Nicholas J Sanders Esq, Accountant General, Finance Branch, Department for Education, Sanctuary Buildings, Great Smith Street, London SW1P 3ET   *Telephone:* 071-925 5000

SANDERS, Dr PETER BASIL   Chief Executive, Commission for Racial Equality   Grade: 3

Career: administrative officer Overseas Civil Service, Basutoland 1961-66; principal officer Ministry of Defence 1971-73; Race Relations Board/Commission for Racial Equality 1973-: regional principal officer 1973-75, deputy chief officer 1975-77, director 1977-88, chief executive 1988-

Date of birth: 9 June 1938   *Education/professional qualifications:* Queen Elizabeth's Grammar School, Barnet; Wadham College, Oxford, literae humaniores (BA 1960, MA), African history (DPhil 1970)   *Marital status:*

married Anita 1988; 1 daughter, 2 sons (by previous marriage) *Publications:* co-editor Lithoko: Sotho Praise Poems (Clarendon Press 1974); Moshoeshoe, Chief of the Sotho (Heinemann Educational 1975); The Simple Annals (Alan Sutton 1989) *Recreations:* walking, gardening, piano playing

Dr Peter B Sanders, Chief Executive, Commission for Racial Equality, Elliot House, 12-14 Allington Street, London SW1E 5EH
Telephone: 071-828 7022 *Fax:* 071-630 7605

SANDS, ROGER BLAKEMORE   Principal Clerk of Select Committees and Registrar of Members' Interests, House of Commons   Grade: 3

Career: Clerks' department House of Commons (HOC) 1965-: secretary of HoC Commission 1985-87; principal clerk Overseas Office 1987-91; principal clerk of select committees (overall supervision of several select committees) and registrar of members' interests 1991- *Current non-Whitehall posts:* council member Royal Institute of Public Administration 1989-; vice-chairman Study of Parliament Group 1991-

Date of birth: 6 May 1942 *Education/professional qualifications:* University College School, London; Oriel College, Oxford, literae humaniores (BA 1965, MA) *Marital status:* married Jennifer Ann Cattell 1966; 2 daughters *Recreations:* gardening, occasional golf

Roger B Sands Esq, Committee Office, House of Commons, London SW1A 0AA *Telephone:* 071-219 3277

SAUNDERS, Air Vice-Marshal DAVID JOHN   Assistant Chief of Defence Staff (Logistics), Ministry of Defence

Career: RAF 1961-: Ministry of Defence 1989-: director RAF engineering policy 1989-91, logistics assistant chief of defence staff 1991-

Date of birth: 12 June 1943 *Education/professional qualifications:* RAF College; Cranfield Institute of Technology (BSc, MSc) *Honours, decorations:* CBE 1986

Air Vice-Marshal David J Saunders CBE, Assistant Chief of Defence Staff, Ministry of Defence, Whitehall, London SW1A 2HB *Telephone:* 071-218 3634

SAUNDERS, DAVID WILLIAM   Parliamentary Counsel, Office of the Parliamentary Counsel   Grade: 2

Career: solicitor 1964-70; Office of Parliamentary Counsel 1970-: deputy parliamentary counsel (PC) 1978-80; (seconded to Law Commission 1972-74, 1986-87); deputy secretary and PC (drafting government bills) 1980-

Date of birth: 4 November 1936 *Education/professional qualifications:* Hornchurch Grammar School; Worcester College, Oxford, law (BA 1960, MA) *Honours, decorations:* CB 1989 *Marital status:* married Margaret Susan Rose 1963 *Clubs:* United Oxford and Cambridge University, Redhill Flying *Recreations:* bridge, golf, flying

David W Saunders Esq CB, Parliamentary Counsel, Office of the Parliamentary Counsel, 36 Whitehall, London SW1A 2AY
Telephone: 071-210 6646 *Fax:* 071-210 6632

SAUNDERS, MICHAEL LAWRENCE   The Solicitor, HM Customs and Excise (from October 1992 Legal Adviser to the Home Office and Northern Ireland Office)   Grade: 2

Career: third secretary Hague Conference on Private International Law 1966-72; senior legal assistant: Department of Trade and Industry 1972-73, of Energy 1973-76, Law Officers' Department (LOD) 1976-79; assistant legal adviser Cabinet Office European secretariat 1979-83; LOD 1983-89: assistant legal secretary 1983-86, legal secretary 1986-89; solicitor to HM Customs and Excise (legal advice; prosecutions) 1989-92; legal adviser Home Office and Northern Ireland Office 1992-

Date of birth: 13 April 1944 *Education/professional qualifications:* Clifton College, Bristol; Birmingham University, law (LLB 1965); Jesus College, Cambridge, international law (LLB 1966); Gray's Inn (barrister 1970) *Honours, decorations:* CB 1990 *Marital status:* married Anna 1970; 1 daughter, 1 son *Recreations:* theatre, squash, cricket

Michael L Saunders Esq CB, The Solicitor, HM Customs and Excise, New King's Beam House, 22 Upper Ground, London SE1 9PJ
Telephone: 071-865 5121
Fax: 071-865 5022 (Home Office from October 1992)

SAVILLE, CLIVE HOWARD   Under Secretary, Department for Education   Grade: 3

Career: assistant principal Department of Education and Science (DES) 1965-70: private secretary (PS) to minister for the arts 1968-70; principal 1970-77: DES 1970, University Grants Committee 1973-75, Cabinet Office 1975, principal PS to Lord President of the Council and Leader of House of Commons 1975-77; DES 1977-: assistant secretary 1977-87, under secretary (supply and training of teachers, international relations) 1987-

Date of birth: 7 July 1943 *Education/professional qualifications:* Bishop Gore Grammar School, Swansea; University College, Swansea (BA) *Marital status:* married Camille Kathleen Burke 1967

Clive H Saville Esq, Under Secretary, Department for Education, Sanctuary Buildings, Great Smith Street, London SW1P 3BT *Telephone:* 071-925 5000 *Fax:* 071-925 6000

SAWYER, TONY CHARLES   Commissioner, Outfield Directorate, HM Customs and Excise   Grade: 3

Career: HM Customs and Excise 1964-: Collector Edinburgh 1984-88; outfield directorate (regional operations and investigation division) 1988-: deputy director 1988-91, director 1991-

Date of birth: 3 August 1939 *Education/professional qualifications:* technical college, Redhill and Croydon *Marital status:* married Kathleen Josephine 1962; 1 daughter, 2 sons *Clubs:* National Liberal, Civil Service *Recreations:* sports, theatre, music

Tony C Sawyer Esq, Commissioner, HM Customs and Excise, New King's Beam House, 22 Upper Ground, London SE1 9PS
Telephone: 071-865 5017 *Fax:* 071-865 4417

'Next Steps' Executive Agencies
see page 761

SCHOFIELD, NEILL   Director, Quality Assurance, Employment Department Group   Grade: 3

Career: economist: Department of Environment 1970-78, Department of Energy 1978-82, Department of Employment (DEmp) 1982-: director business and enterprise 1990-92, quality assurance 1992-, training, enterprise and education directorate

Date of birth: 2 August 1946 *Education/professional qualifications:* Leeds University, economics (BA 1967); Queen Mary College, London University, economics (MSc 1975) *Marital status:* married Carol 1969; 2 daughters *Recreations:* walking, theatre, family

Neill Schofield Esq, Director, Quality Assurance, Employment Department Group, Moorfoot, Sheffield S1 4PQ *Telephone:* 0742 593298 *Fax:* 0742 594328

SCHOLAR, MICHAEL CHARLES   Deputy Secretary, Civil Service Management and Pay, HM Treasury   Grade: 2

Career: HM Treasury 1969-: principal; private secretary (PS) to chief secretary 1974-76; seconded to Barclays Bank International 1979-81; PS to prime minister 1981-83; under secretary 1983-87; deputy secretary public finance 1987-, civil service management and pay 1992-

Date of birth: 3 January 1942 *Education/professional qualifications:* St Olave's and St Saviour's Grammar School, Bermondsey; St John's College, Cambridge, classics and moral sciences (BA, MA 1964), philosophy (PhD 1969); California University, Berkeley and Harvard University, USA *Honours, decorations:* CB 1991 *Marital status:* married Angela Mary Sweet 1964; 3 sons (1 daughter deceased) *Recreations:* music, walking

Michael C Scholar Esq CB, Deputy Secretary, HM Treasury, Parliament Street, London SW1P 3AG *Telephone:* 071-270 4389 *Fax:* 071-270 5653

SCICLUNA, MARTIN LEONARD ANDREW   Assistant Under Secretary, Adjutant General's Department, Ministry of Defence   Grade: 3

Career: military service 1953-74; Ministry of Defence 1974-: principal 1974-80: naval personnel division 1974-76, defence secretariats 1976-80; assistant secretary 1980-91: head of air force secretariat 1980-83, deputy chief of public relations 1983-85, head of general staff secretariat 1985-88; student Royal College of Defence Studies 1989; head of resources and programmes (manpower) 1990-91, (management planning) 1991; assistant under secretary adjutant general's department 1992-

Date of birth: 16 November 1935 *Education/professional qualifications:* St Edward's College, Malta; Royal Military Academy, Sandhurst (commission 1953); Army Staff College, defence studies (psc 1965); Royal College of Defence Studies, defence and international relations (rcds 1989) *Recreations:* painting, theatre, sports spectator, other sedentary pursuits

Martin L A Scicluna Esq, Assistant Under Secretary, Ministry of Defence, Whitehall, London SW1A 2HB *Telephone:* 071-218 7545

Regulatory Organisations and Public Bodies
see page 857

SCOBLE, CHRISTOPHER LAWRENCE   Assistant Under Secretary, Establishment Department, Home Office   Grade: 3

Career: Home Office 1965-: seconded to Welsh Office 1969-70; assistant under secretary, broadcasting and miscellaneous department 1988-91, establishment department 1991-

Date of birth: 21 November 1943 *Education/professional qualifications:* Corpus Christi College, Oxford

Chrstopher L Scoble Esq, Assistant Under Secretary, Establishment Department, Home Office, Grenadier House, 99-105 Horseferry Road, London SW1P 2DD *Telephone:* 071-217 0174

SCOTT, T H   Solicitor for Scotland, Board of Inland Revenue

T H Scott Esq, Solicitor for Scotland, Board of Inland Revenue, 80 Lauriston Place, Edinburgh EH3 9SL *Telephone:* 031-229 9344

SEAMMEN, DIANA JILL   Assistant Under Secretary, Air, Procurement Executive, Ministry of Defence   Grade: 3

Career: HM Treasury 1969-89; commissioner and director VAT Control, HM Customs and Excise 1989-92; seconded to Ministry of Defence procurement executive as assistant under secretary 1992-

Date of birth: 24 March 1948 *Education/professional qualifications:* University of Sussex

Ms Diana J Seammen, Assistant Under Secretary, Air, Procurement Executive, Ministry of Defence, Main Building, Whitehall, London SW1A 2HB *Telephone:* 071-218 9000

SEDGWICK, PETER NORMAN   Under Secretary, International Finance, HM Treasury   Grade: 3

Career: HM Treasury 1969-: economic assistant 1969-71; economic adviser (EA) 1971-77; senior EA 1977-84; under secretary 1984-: head of international finance group 1990-

Date of birth: 4 December 1943 *Education/professional qualifications:* Lincoln College, Oxford, politics, philosophy and economics (BA 1967), economics (BPhil 1969) *Marital status:* married Catherine Jane Saunders 1984; 2 daughters, 2 sons *Recreations:* choral singing

Peter N Sedgwick Esq, Deputy Secretary, HM Treasury, Parliament Street, London SW1P 3AG *Telephone:* 071-270 4430 *Fax:* 071-270 6329

SELBORNE, JOHN ROUNDELL (The Earl of Selborne)   Chairman, Joint Nature Conservation Committee

Career: chairman Hops Marketing Board 1978-82; chairman Agricultural and Food Research Council 1983-89; president Royal Agricultural Society of England 1988-89; chairman Joint Nature Conservation Committee 1991- *Current non-Whitehall posts:* director Blockmans Estate Ltd 1958-, Agricultural Mortgage Corporation plc 1990-

Date of birth: 24 March 1940 *Education/professional qualifications:* Eton College; Christ Church, Oxford *Honours, decorations:* KBE 1987; FRS 1991 *Marital status:* married Joanna van Antwerp 1969; 3 sons, 1 daughter *Clubs:* Brooks's, Farmers'

The Earl of Selborne KBE DL,, Chairman, Joint Nature Conservation Committee, Monkstone House, City Road, Peterborough PE1 1JY *Telephone:* 0733 62626 *Fax:* 0733 555948

SELLERS, JOHN MARSLAND   Deputy Parliamentary Counsel, Office of the Parliamentary Counsel   Grade: 3

Career: lecturer Lincoln College, Oxford 1973-75, London School of Economics 1975-77; private practice solicitor 1977-83; Office of Parliamentary Counsel 1983-: assistant parliamentary counsel (PC) 1983-88, senior assistant PC 1988-91, deputy PC (drafting government bills) 1991-

Date of birth: 15 July 1951 *Education/professional qualifications:* Manchester Grammar School; Magdalen College, Oxford, jurisprudence (BA 1972, BCL 1973); Law Society (solicitor 1980) *Marital status:* married Patricia 1975; 2 sons *Recreations:* reading, fine wine

John M Sellers Esq, Deputy Parliamentary Counsel, Office of the Parliamentary Counsel, 36 Whitehall, London SW1A 2AY *Telephone:* 071-210 6649 *Fax:* 071-210 6632

SELWOOD, Maj Gen DAVID HENRY DEERING   Director of Army Legal Services, Ministry of Defence

Career: legal training 1952-57; national service 1957-59; solicitor 1959-61; military service 1959-: army legal service 1961-: director of army legal services Ministry of Defence 1990- *Current non-Whitehall posts:* recorder of Crown Court, Western Circuit 1985-; honorary advocate US Court of Military Appeals 1972-

Date of birth: 27 June 1934 *Education/professional qualifications:* Kelly College, Tavistock, Plymouth; University College of the South West; Law Society's School of Law (solicitor 1957) *Publications:* Criminal Law and Psychiatry (Kluwer 1987) *Recreations:* reading, gardening, sailing

Major General David H D Selwood, Director, Army Legal Services, Ministry of Defence, Empress State Building, Lillie Road, London SW6 1TR *Telephone:* 071-385 1244 *Fax:* 071-385 1244 ext 2705

SELWOOD, DEREK   Director Information Technology, Ministry of Agriculture, Fisheries and Food   Grade: 4

Career: Inland Revenue 1960-88: tax officer 1960, surtax assessor 1960-69, systems analyst, senior programmer 1969-72, computer project manager 1972-75, manager computerised personnel system 1975-78, PAYE computerisation project team management 1978-80, procurement manager 1980-84, assistant director information technology 1984-88; government liaison manager Racal Data Networks 1988-89; director of information technology Ministry of Agriculture, Fisheries and Food 1989-

Date of birth: 19 December 1942 *Education/professional qualifications:* Boys' Grammar School, Woking *Marital status:* married Margaret 1982; 1 daughter, 1 son *Recreations:* orienteering, running

Derek Selwood Esq, Director of Information Technology, Ministry of Agriculture, Fisheries and Food, Victory House, 30-34 Kingsway, London WC2B 6TV *Telephone:* 071-413 2694 *Fax:* 071-413 2692

SHACKLETON, EDWARD ARTHUR ALEXANDER (The Rt Hon Lord Shackleton)   Chairman, Political Honours Scrutiny Committee

Career: exploration expeditions 1932-35; author, lecturer, broadcaster; RAF war service 1939-45; Labour MP for Preston 1946-50, for Preston South 1950-55; minister of defence for RAF 1964-67; minister without portfolio and deputy leader House of Lords (HoL) 1967-68; paymaster general 1968; Lord Privy Seal 1968-70; leader HoL 1968-70; minister in charge Civil Service Department 1968-70; opposition leader HoL 1970-74; director John Lewis Partnership 1955-64; RTZ 1973-83: deputy chairman 1975-82; chairman Anglesey Aluminium Ltd 1981-85; Chairman Political Honours Scrutiny Committee 1976-

Date of birth: 15 July 1911 *Education/professional qualifications:* Radley College; Magdalen College, Oxford (BA, MA); FBIM *Honours, decorations:* OBE 1945; PC 1966; KG 1974; FRS 1989 *Marital status:* married Betty Homan 1938; 1 daughter *Publications:* Arctic Journeys; Nansen the Explorer; co-author Borneo Jungle *Clubs:* Brooks's

Rt Hon the Lord Shackleton KG AC OBE,, Chairman, Political Honours Scrutiny Committee, 53 Parliament Street, London SW1A 2NH *Telephone:* 071-210 5059

SHANNON, Dr DAVID WILLIAM FRANCIS   Chief Scientist, Agriculture and Horticulture, Ministry of Agriculture, Fisheries and Food   Grade: 3

Career: director Poultry Research Centre, Agriculture and Food Research Council 1978-86; chief scientist agriculture and horticulture, Ministry of Agriculture, Fisheries and Food 1986-

Date of birth: 16 August 1941 *Education/professional qualifications:* Queen's University, Belfast, agriculture (BAgr, PhD); Napier College, Edinburgh (DMS)

Dr David W F Shannon, Chief Scientist, Agriculture and Horticulture, Ministry of Agriculture, Fisheries and Food, Nobel House, 17 Smith Square, London SW1P 3HX *Telephone:* 071-238 5526

SHARP, ROBIN J A   Under Secretary and Director of Rural Affairs, Department of the Environment   Grade: 3

Date of birth: 30 July 1935 *Education/professional qualifications:* Oxford University; Cambridge University

Robin J A Sharp Esq, Under Secretary and Director of Rural Affairs, Department of the Environment, 2 Marsham Street, London SW1P 3EB *Telephone:* 071-276 3000

SHAW, COLIN DON   Director, Broadcasting Standards Council   Grade: 3

Career: BBC 1969-77: secretary 1969-71, chief secretary 1971-77; director of television Independent Broadcasting Authority 1977-83; director of programme planning secretariat Independent Television Companies Association 1983-87; freelance writer and lecturer 1987-88; director Broadcasting Standards Council 1988-

Date of birth: 2 November 1928 *Education/professional qualifications:* Merton House School, Penmaenmawr; Liverpool College; St Peter's Hall, Oxford, English literature (BA 1952, MA), Inner Temple (barrister 1960) *Marital status:* married Elizabeth Ann Bowker 1955; 2 daughters, 1 son *Clubs:* Reform *Recreations:* reading, theatre, travel

Colin D Shaw Esq, Director, Broadcasting Standards Council, 5-8 The Sanctuary, London SW1P 3JS *Telephone:* 071-233 0544 *Fax:* 071-233 0397

SHAW, ELIZABETH ANGELA   Executive Director, Charity Commission   Grade: 4

Career: Home Office 1965-67; Foreign and Commonwealth Office 1967-70; Department of [Health and] Social Security (D[H]SS) 1970-87: principal 1977-84, assistant secretary 1984-87; Civil Service College 1987-90: director of finance and planning 1987-89, acting chief executive 1989-90; head of staff development DH 1990-91; executive director Charity Commission 1991-

Date of birth: 5 June 1946 *Education/professional qualifications:* Sydenham High School, London

Marital status: divorced; 2 sons, 1 daughter *Recreations:* classical music, singing, English literature, theatre, cinema, walking, swimming

Mrs Elizabeth E Shaw, Executive Director, Charity Commission, St Alban's House, 57-60 Haymarket, London SW1Y 4QX *Telephone:* 071-210 4420

SHAW, JOHN FREDERICK   Deputy Director Performance Management, NHS Management Executive, Department of Health Grade: 3

Career: army national service 1955-57; Church Commissioners 1960-62; accountant Industrial Christian Fellowship 1962-63; head of recruitment Voluntary Service Overseas 1963-73; Department of [Health and] Social Security 1973-: principal 1973-78, assistant secretary 1978-87, under secretary, deputy director performance management NHS management executive 1987-

Date of birth: 7 December 1936 *Education/professional qualifications:* Loretto School, Musselburgh; Worcester College, Oxford, law (MA 1960) *Marital status:* married Ann Rodden 1964; 1 daughter, 2 sons *Recreations:* church activities, singing, gardening, pig keeping

John F Shaw Esq, Under Secretary, NHS Management Executive, Department of Health, Richmond House, 79 Whitehall, London SW1A 2NS *Telephone:* 071-210 5630 *Fax:* 071-210 5080

SHAW, PETER ALAN   Northern Regional Director, Departments of the Environment and Transport   Grade: 3

Career: Department of Education and Science (DES) 1979-85: private secretary to Secretary of State 1979-81, head of local government expenditure division 1982-85; head of employment division HM Treasury 1985-86; DES 1986-88: head of school teachers' pay division 1986-88, of information branch 1988-89, of grant-maintained schools division 1989-91; regional director northern regional office Departments of Environment and Transport 1991-

Date of birth: 31 May 1949 *Education/professional qualifications:* Bridlington School; Bede College, Durham University, geography (BSc 1970); Bradford University, traffic engineering and planning (MSc 1972); British Columbia University, Canada, Christian studies (MCS 1974) *Marital status:* married Frances 1975; 1 daughter, 2 sons *Recreations:* walking

Peter A Shaw Esq, Regional Director, Departments of the Environment and Transport, Wellbar House, Gallowgate, Newcastle-upon-Tyne *Telephone:* 091-232 7575

SHOTTON, KEITH CRAWFORD   Head of Information and Manufacturing Technology Division, Department of Trade and Industry   Grade: 3

Career: Department of Trade and Industry 1987-: director radio technology, radio communications division 1987-90; head of information technology division 1990-92, of information and manufacturing technology division 1992-

Education/professional qualifications: Trinity College, Cambridge (MA, PhD)

Dr Keith C Shotton, Head of Information and Manufacturing Technology Division, Department of Trade and Industry, 151 Buckingham Palace Road, London SW1W 9SS *Telephone:* 071-215 1239

SHREEVE, Dr BRIAN JOHN   Director of Research and Deputy Director, Central Veterinary Laboratory (Executive Agency)
Grade: 4

Career: veterinary practice 1960-64; research fellow Liverpool University 1964-67; senior scientific officer Moredun Research Institute, Edinburgh 1967-69; Ministry of Agriculture, Fisheries and Food, assistant veterinary investigation officer Veterinary Investigation Centre, Penrith 1969-70; Central Veterinary Laboratory 1970-: research officer (RO) 1970-72, senior RO Grade 2 1972-80, grade 1 1980-86, deputy director, director of research 1986-

Date of birth: 24 November 1936 *Education/professional qualifications:* King Edward VI School, Norwich; Liverpool University, veterinary science (BVSc 1960, PhD 1968); MRCVS *Marital status:* married Jean 1971; 1 daughter, 1 son *Recreations:* sailing, swimming, theatre

Dr Brian J Shreeve, Deputy Director, Central Veterinary Laboratory, New Haw, Weybridge, Surrey KT1S 3NB *Telephone:* 0932 341111 *Fax:* 0932 347046

SHUTLER, (RONALD) REX BARRY   Chief Executive, Valuation Office (Executive Agency)   Grade: 2

Career: commercial surveyor 1952-59; Inland Revenue Valuation Office 1959-1991: district valuer Hereford 1972-75, superintending valuer Wales 1975-85, deputy chief valuer 1985-88, chief valuer 1988-91; chief executive Valuation Office Executive Agency 1991-

Date of birth: 27 June 1933 *Education/professional qualifications:* Hardye's School, Dorchester; FRICS 1957; FAAV 1962 *Marital status:* married Patricia Elizabeth Longman 1958; 2 sons *Clubs:* Chartridge Park Golf *Recreations:* golf, country pursuits, gardening

R Rex B Shutler Esq, Chief Executive, Valuation Office, New Court, Carey Street, London WC2A 2JE *Telephone:* 071-324 1155 *Fax:* 071-324 1190

SIMMONS, Air Marshal Sir MICHAEL GEORGE   Deputy Controller Aircraft, Ministry of Defence

Career: RAF 1958-: Ministry of Defence (MoD) 1971-72, 1976-79, 1982-84, 1987-: assistant chief of air staff 1987-89; deputy controller aircraft 1989-

Date of birth: 8 May 1937 *Education/professional qualifications:* RAF College, Cranwell; Royal Naval Staff College

Air Marshal Sir Michael Simmons KCB AFC, Deputy Controller Aircraft, Ministry of Defence, Whitehall, London SW1A 2HB *Telephone:* 071-218 7880

SIMPSON, ROBIN   Under Secretary, Steel, Metals and Minerals, Industry 2 Division, Department of Trade and Industry   Grade: 3

Career: Department(s) of Trade and Industry 1962-: Patent Office 1962-73; civil aviation division 1973-76; industrial development unit 1976-79; shipping policy 1979-82; management services and manpower 1982-85; north east regional director 1986-90; head of Business Task Force Division 1 (environment unit, steel and commodities) 1990-92, under secretary steel, metals and minerals, industry 2 division 1992-

Date of birth: 14 June 1940 *Education/professional qualifications:* Perth Academy; St Andrew's University, chemistry (BSc 1962)

Robin Simpson Esq, Under Secretary, Industry 2 Division, Department of Trade and Industry, Ashdown House, 123 Victoria Street, London SW1E 6RB *Telephone:* 071-215 5000

SKINNER, ANGUS   Chief Social Work Adviser, Home and Health Department, Scottish Office   Grade: 4

Career: social work Kent County Council 1973-75; senior area divisional manager Lothian region 1975-88; deputy director of social work Borders region 1988-91; chief social work adviser to secretary of state, Scottish Office Home and Health Department social work services group 1991-

Date of birth: 4 January 1950 *Education/professional qualifications:* Daniel Stewart's College, Edinburgh; Edinburgh University, social science (BSc 1971); London University, social work (CQSW 1973); Strathclyde University, management (MBA 1988) *Marital status:* married Kate 1971; 2 daughters, 1 son *Recreations:* music, painting, poetry, walking

Angus Skinner Esq, Chief Adviser, Social Work Services Group, Scottish Office Home and Health Department, 43 Jeffres Street, Edinburgh *Telephone:* 031-244 5414

SLATER, Dr DAVID HOMFRAY   Chief Inspector, HM Inspectorate of Pollution, Department of the Environment   Grade: 3

Career: lecturer in combustion Imperial College, London 1970-75; Cremer and Warner 1975-81: senior scientist 1975-79, partner 1979-81; founding director Technica 1981-91; chief inspector HM Inspectorate of Pollution Department of Environment 1991-

Date of birth: 16 October 1940 *Education/professional qualifications:* University College of Wales, Aberystwyth (BSc 1963); Ohio State University, USA (PhD 1966) *Marital status:* married Edith Mildred 1964; 4 daughters *Publications:* numerous contributions to science journals and conferences *Recreations:* music, photography, fishing

Dr David H Slater, Chief Inspector, HM Inspectorate of Pollution, Romney House, 43 Marsham Street, London SW1P 3PY *Telephone:* 071-276 8080 *Fax:* 071-276 8800

SLATER, Admiral Sir JOCK   Vice-Chief of the Defence Staff (from January 1993) Ministry of Defence

Career: Royal Navy 1956-: chief of fleet support Ministry of Defence 1991-2; vice-chief of the defence staff 1993-

Date of birth: 27 March 1938 *Education/professional qualifications:* Edinburgh Academy

Admiral Sir Jock Slater, GCB LVO, Vice-Chief of the Defence Staff (from Jan 1993), Ministry of Defence, Main Building, Whitehall, London SW1A 2HB *Telephone:* 071-218 9000

SLEEMAN, TONY   Regional Controller, South Yorkshire, Inland Revenue   Grade: 4

Career: Inland Revenue 1966-: group controller 1981-91; regional controller South Yorkshire region 1991-

Date of birth: 3 July 1945 *Education/professional qualifications:* Lockleaze Comprehensive, Bristol; University College, Swansea, physics (BSc 1966) *Marital status:* married Pearl 1966; 3 daughters *Recreations:* golf, gardening

Tony Sleeman Esq, Regional Controller, Inland Revenue, South Yorkshire, Sovereign House, 110 Queen Street, Sheffield S1 2EN *Telephone:* 0742 739099 *Fax:* 0742 750258

SMART, KENNETH PETER ROSS   Chief Inspector of Air Accidents, Department of Transport   Grade: 4

Career: Ministry of Aviation 1967-75; Department of Transport Air Accidents Investigation Branch 1975-: inspector of accidents (IA) 1975-78, senior IA 1978-80, principal IA 1980-86, deputy chief IA 1986-90, chief IA 1990-

Date of birth: 28 April 1946 *Education/professional qualifications:* Aylesford School; Ministry of Aviation College of Electronics, aeronautical engineering (certificate); Worcester College of Technology, mechanical engineering (HNC); Open University, technology (BA) *Marital status:* divorced; 1 son, 1 daughter *Recreations:* sailing

Kenneth P R Smart Esq, Chief Inspector, Air Accidents Investigation Branch, Royal Aerospace Establishment, Farnborough, Hampshire SO5 4QQ *Telephone:* 0252 510300

SMEE, CLIVE HARROD   Under Secretary, Chief Economic Adviser, Department of Health   Grade: 3

Career: economic adviser (EA) Ministry of Overseas Development 1969-75; senior EA Department of Health and Social Security (DHSS) 1975-82; adviser Central Policy Review Staff 1982-83; senior EA HM Treasury 1983-84; chief EA DHSS 1984-89; under secretary, chief EA economic and operational research directorate Department of Health 1989-

Date of birth: 29 April 1942 *Education/professional qualifications:* Royal Grammar School, Guildford; London School of Economics (BSc Econ 1963); Indiana University, USA, business administration (MBA 1965) *Marital status:* married Denise Eileen Sell 1976; 2 daughters, 1 son *Recreations:* running, family, gardening

Clive H Smee Esq, Under Secretary, Department of Health, Millbank Tower, Millbank, London SW1P 4QU *Telephone:* 071-972 8518 *Fax:* 071-972 8509

SMITH, Sir DOUGLAS BOUCHER   Chairman, Advisory Conciliation and Arbitration Service

Career: Department of Employment 1953-: seconded to Cabinet Office 1977-79; deputy secretary 1979-87; chairman Advisory, Conciliation and Arbitration Service 1987-

Date of birth: 9 June 1932 *Education/professional qualifications:* Leeds University

Sir Douglas B Smith, Chairman, Advisory, Conciliation and Arbitration Service, 27 Wilton Street, London SW1X 7AZ *Telephone:* 071-210 3000

SMITH, GRAHAM WILLIAM   Chief Inspector of Probation, Home Office

Career: Home Office Probation Service 1965-: Durham combined probation area 1965-71: probation officer (PO) 1965-69, senior PO 1969-71; Inner London probation service 1971-92: senior PO 1971-73, assistant chief PO 1973-78, deputy chief PO 1978-80, chief PO 1981-92; HM chief inspector of probation 1992-

Date of birth: 15 August 1939 *Education/professional qualifications:* Bishop Wordsworth School, Salisbury; King's College, Durham University, social studies (DipSocSA 1964); Newcastle University, social studies (CQSW

1965) *Honours, decorations:* CBE 1990 *Marital status:* married Jeanne 1958; 1 daughter, 2 sons *Recreations:* theatre, gardening, sport

Graham W Smith Esq CBE, HM Chief Inspector of Probation, Home Office, 50 Queen Anne's Gate, London SW1H 9AT *Telephone:* 071-273 3766 *Fax:* 071-273 4078

SNELL, DAVID CHARLES   Director of Finance and Corporate Services, Royal Mint (Executive Agency)   Grade: 4

Career: Royal Mint 1976-: finance director 1976-83; marketing and finance director 1983-87; finance director 1987-88, deputy chief executive and director of finance and corporate services 1988- *Current non-Whitehall posts:* chairman Royal Mint Services Ltd 1989-; vice-chairman Enterprise Taff Ely Ogwr Partnership Ltd 1990-

Date of birth: 30 September 1940 *Education/professional qualifications:* Devonport High School, Plymouth *Marital status:* divorced; 1 son, 1 daughter *Recreations:* travel, golf

David C Snell Esq, Deputy Chief Executive, Royal Mint, Llantrisant, Pontyclun, Mid-Glamorgan CF7 8YT *Telephone:* 0443 222111 *Fax:* 0443 237039

SORRIE, Dr GEORGE STRATH   Medical Adviser, Occupational Health Service (Executive Agency)   Grade: 3

Career: Department of Employment and Health and Safety Executive 1972-87; medical adviser (on health aspects of civil servants' work) to Civil Service Director, Occupational Health Service 1987-

Date of birth: 19 May 1933 *Education/professional qualifications:* Robert Gordon's College, Aberdeen; Aberdeen University, medicine (MB ChB 1957); London University, public health (DPH 1963); Dundee University, industrial health (DIH 1976) *Marital status:* married Gabrielle Ann Baird 1959; 3 daughters *Clubs:* Athenaeum

Dr George S Sorrie, Medical Adviser, Occupational Health Service, 20 Hill Street, Edinburgh EH2 3NB *Telephone:* 031-220 4177

SOUTHWOOD, Sir (THOMAS) RICHARD EDMUND   Chairman, National Radiological Protection Board

Career: zoology professor Imperial College, London 1967-79; Linacre professor of zoology, Oxford 1979-; chairman British Museum (Natural History) trustees 1980-84; chairman, royal commission on environmental pollution 1981-86; chairman working party on bovine spongiform encephalopathy 1988-89; chairman National Radiological Protection Board 1989- *Current non-Whitehall posts:* vice-chancellor Oxford University 1989-

Date of birth: 20 July 1931 *Education/professional qualifications:* Gravesend Grammar School for Boys; Imperial College, London, zoology (BSc ARCS 1952); Rothamsted Experimental Station, London, entomology (PhD 1955); London University, zoology (DSc 1963); Merton College, Oxford: zoology (MA 1979, DSc 1987) *Honours, decorations:* FRS 1977, Kt 1984, Fellow Imperial College London 1984, Cavaliere Ufficiale della Repubblica Italiana 1991 *Marital status:* married Alison Longley 1955; 2 sons

Publications: Land and Water Bugs of the British Isles (Warne 1959); Life of the Wayside and Woodland (Warne 1963); Ecological Methods (Chapman & Hall 1966, 1979); Insects on Plants (Blackwells 1984) *Clubs:* Athenaeum, United Oxford and Cambridge University *Recreations:* reading, natural history, travel

Sir Richard Southwood, Chairman, National Radiological Protection Board, Chilton, Didcot, Oxfordshire OX11 0RQ *Telephone:* 0235 831600

SPACKMAN, MICHAEL JOHN   Chief Economic Adviser, Department of Transport   Grade: 3

Career: army national service 1955-57; physicist United Kingdom Atomic Energy Authority 1960-69; senior physicist, engineer Nuclear Power Group Ltd 1969-71; principal scientific officer then economic adviser Department of Energy 1971-77; economic adviser HM Treasury (HMT) 1977-79; director of economics and accountancy Civil Service College 1979-80; HMT 1980-91: head of public services economics division 1980-85, of public expenditure economics group 1985-91; chief economic adviser Department of Transport 1991-

Date of birth: 8 October 1936 *Education/professional qualifications:* Malvern College; Clare College, Cambridge (BA, MA 1960); Queen Mary College, London, (MSc Econ 1974) *Marital status:* married Judith Ann Leatham 1965; 2 sons, 2 daughters *Recreations:* walking, children

Michael J Spackman Esq, Chief Economic Adviser, Department of Transport, 2 Marsham Street, London SW1P 3EB *Telephone:* 071-276 5299 *Fax:* 071-276 0818

SPARROW, Sir JOHN   Chairman, Horserace Betting Levy Board

Career: chairman and director of various companies; seconded as head of Central Policy, Review Staff, Cabinet Office 1982-83; chairman Horserace Betting Levy Board 1991- *Current non-Whitehall posts:* vice-chairman London School of Economics 1984-; director ASW Holdings plc 1987-; chairman Universities' Superannuation Scheme Ltd 1988-; director National Provincial Building Society 1989-, Regalian Properties plc 1990-

Date of birth: 4 June 1933 *Education/professional qualifications:* Stationers' Company's School, London; London School of Economics, economics (BSc Econ 1954); FCA 1957 *Honours, decorations:* Kt 1984 *Marital status:* married Cynthia Naomi 1967 *Clubs:* Marylebone Cricket *Recreations:* cricket, crosswords, horseracing

Sir John Sparrow Kt, Chairman, Horserace Betting Levy Board, 52 Grosvenor Gardens, London SW1W 0AU *Telephone:* 071-333 0043 *Fax:* 071-333 0041

SPENCE, IAN RICHARD   Director, International Division, Board of Inland Revenue   Grade: 3

Date of birth: 15 October 1938 *Education/professional qualifications:* Jesus College, Cambridge

Ian R Spence Esq, Director, International Division, Board of Inland Revenue, Somerset House, London WC2R 1LB *Telephone:* 071-438 6622

Complete Name Index
see page 955

SPENCER, Dr JONATHAN PAGE   Under Secretary, Insurance, Corporate and Consumer Affairs Division, Department of Trade and Industry   Grade: 3

Career: Department of Trade, Department of [Trade and] Industry (DTI) 1974-87: principal private secretary to secretaries of state 1982-83, policy planning unit 1983-85, minerals and metals (international steel negotiations) 1985-87; machinery of government office of Cabinet Office, 1987-89; DTI 1989-: personnel management I 1989-91, under secretary insurance division 1991- *Education/professional qualifications:* Bournemouth School; Downing College, Cambridge, natural sciences (BA 1970); Oxford University, metallurgy (D Phil 1974)   *Marital status:* married Caroline 1976; 2 daughters, 1 son   *Recreations:* music, keeping house up and garden down

Dr Jonathan P Spencer, Under Secretary, Corporate and Consumer Affairs Division, Department of Trade and Industry, 10-18 Victoria Street, London SW1H 0NN   *Telephone:* 071-215 3120

SPENCER, ROSEMARY JANE   Assistant Under Secretary for the Public Departments, Foreign and Commonwealth Office   Senior grade

Career: HM Diplomatic Service 1962-: Foreign and Commonwealth Office (FCO) 1962-65; third secretary Nairobi 1965-67, second secretary (SS) FCO 1967-70; SS UK delegation to EEC 1970-71; first secretary (FS) UK permanent representation to EEC, Brussels 1972-73; FS (economic) Lagos 1974-77; FS, assistant head of Rhodesian department FCO 1977-80; Royal College of Defence Studies 1980; agriculture and economic affairs counsellor Paris 1980-84; head of EC department (external) FCO 1987-89; assistant under secretary, public departments 1989-   *Current non-Whitehall posts:* chairman governors Upper Chine School, Shanklin, Isle of Wight 1990-

Date of birth: 1 April 1941   *Education/professional qualifications:* Upper Chine School, Shanklin, Isle of Wight; St Hilda's College, Oxford, modern languages (BA 1962)   *Honours, decorations:* CMG 1991   *Clubs:* Commonwealth Trust, United Oxford and Cambridge University   *Recreations:* country walking, travel, domestic arts

Miss Rosemary J Spencer CMG, Assistant Under Secretary, Foreign and Commonwealth Office, London SW1   *Telephone:* 071-210 6349   *Fax:* 071-210 3789

SPERRING, BERNARD ARTHUR   Director, Construction Programme, South-East Region, Department of Transport   Grade: 4

Career: civil engineer Glamorgan county council 1962-72; Department of Transport 1972-: director, construction programme south-east region, highways, safety and traffic, command road programme directorate 1990-

Date of birth: 27 January 1939   *Education/professional qualifications:* Midsomer Norton Grammar School; University College, Cardiff, mining engineering (BSc 1962); MICE 1969;   *Marital status:* married Marlene Joan 1959; 2 daughters   *Recreations:* hockey, cricket, rugby; travel

Bernard A Sperring Esq, Director South-East Construction Programme, Department of Transport, Federated House, London Road, Dorking, Surrey RH4 1SZ   *Telephone:* 0306 885922   *Fax:* 0306 741676

SPIERS, DONALD MAURICE   Controller, Aircraft, Aircraft Controllerate, Procurement Executive, Ministry of Defence   Grade: 1/2

Career: military service 1952-54; development engineer de Havilland 1957-60; Ministry of Defence 1960-: principal scientific officer 1960-67, scientific adviser to Far East Air Force Singapore 1967-70, chief scientist RAF department 1970-72, assistant chief scientist (ACS) training 1972-75, ACS RAF operations 1975-78, Procurement Executive 1979-: director military aircraft projects 2 1979, director aircraft post-design services 1979-81, director-general aircraft 1 1981-84, deputy controller aircraft 1984-86, controller establishments research and nuclear 1986-89, controller aircraft (for all armed services) 1989-, air force board, member defence council and procurement management board 1986-

Date of birth: 27 January 1934 *Education/professional qualifications:* Raynes Park County Grammar School; Trinity College, Cambridge, mechanical sciences (BA, MA 1957) *Honours, decorations:* TD 1966, CB 1987 *Recreations:* flying, repairing old cars

Donald M Spiers Esq TD CB, Controller, Aircraft, Aircraft Controllerate, Procurement Executive, Ministry of Defence, Whitehall, London SW1A 2HB *Telephone:* 071-218 7813 *Fax:* 071-218 3849

STANLEY, JOHN MALLALIEU   Under Secretary (Legal), Department of Trade and Industry   Grade: 3

Career: practising solicitor 1965-75; Department of Trade and Industry 1975-: under secretary (legal) 1989-

Date of birth: 30 September 1941 *Education/professional qualifications:* Clare College, Cambridge (MA)

John M Stanley Esq, Under Secretary (Legal), Department of Trade and Industry, 10-18 Victoria St, London SW1H 0NN *Telephone:* 071-215 3470

STANLEY, Dr PETER IAN   Chief Executive, Central Science Laboratory Agency (Executive Agency)   Grade: 3

Career: Ministry of Agriculture, Fisheries and Food 1970-: director Central Science Laboratory 1988-, chief executive 1992-

Date of birth: 25 June 1946 *Education/professional qualifications:* University College, London

Dr Peter I Stanley, Chief Executive, Central Science Laboratory Agency, London Road, Slough, Berks SL3 7JH *Telephone:* 0753-534626

STANTON, DAVID   Director, Analytical Services Division, Department of Social Security   Grade: 3

Career: HM Treasury 1974-75; seconded to Hong Kong Government 1975-77; Employment Department Group 1977-92; director analytical services division Department of Social Security 1992-

Date of birth: 5 November 1942 *Education/professional qualifications:* Worcester College, Oxford (BA 1965); London School of Economics, economics (MSc 1971)

David Stanton Esq, Director, Analytical Services Division, Department of Social Security, Adelphi, 1-11 John Adam Street, London WC2N 6HT *Telephone:* 071-962 8000

STAPLE, GEORGE   Director, Serious Fraud Office   Grade: 2

Career: senior litigation partner Clifford Chance until 1992; director Serious Fraud Office 1992-

George Staple Esq, Director, Serious Fraud Office, Elm House, 10-16 Elm Street, London WC1X 0BJ *Telephone:* 071-239 7272

To subscribe to

The Dod's Report
The European Companion
The Whitehall Companion

Telephone 071-240 3902

STAPLETON, GUY   Chief Executive, Intervention Board (Executive Agency)   Grade: 3

Career: Ministry of Transport and Civil Aviation 1954-59; Ministry of Aviation 1959-65: civil aviation assistant Rome embassy 1960-63, private secretary (PS) to national air traffic control services controller 1963-65; Ministry of Agriculture, Fisheries and Food (MAFF) 1965-74: assistant principal 1965-68: PS to joint parliamentary secretary 1967-68, principal 1968-73, assistant secretary 1973-81: Department of Prices and Consumer Protection 1974-76; under secretary 1981-: deputy head European Secretariat Cabinet Office 1982-85, director of establishments MAFF 1985-86; chief executive Intervention Board for Agricultural Produce (implements market support measures of the EEC's common agricultural policy) 1986-

Date of birth: 10 November 1935 *Education/professional qualifications:* Hill Place School, Stow-on-the-Wold; Malvern College *Marital status:* single *Publications:* A Walk of Verse (Citizens Press 1961); Poets' England Series (Brentham Press); Memories of Moreton (Drinkwater 1989) *Clubs:* Civil Service, Commonwealth Trust *Recreations:* local and family history, topographical verse

Guy Stapleton Esq, Chief Executive, Intervention Board, PO Box 69, Reading RG1 7QW *Telephone:* 0734 583626 *Fax:* 0734 393817

STEADMAN, Dr JOHN HUBERT   Senior Principal Medical Officer, Head of Division of Toxicology and Environmental Health, Department of Health   Grade: 3

Career: various hospital appointments 1968-81; Department of Health 1981- : senior principal medical officer and head of toxicology and environmental health division 1988-

Date of birth: 10 August 1938 *Education/professional qualifications:* Guy's Hospital (MB, BS); University College, London (MSc)

Dr John H Steadman, Senior Principal Medical Officer, Department of Health, Hannibal House, London SE1 6TE *Telephone:* 071-972 2142

STEVENS, CLIFFORD DAVID   Director, Industry Department, Welsh Office   Grade: 3

Career: Civil Service Department (CSD) 1970-76; Cabinet Office 1976-78; CSD 1978-86; Welsh Office 1986-: director Industry Department 1987-

Date of birth: 11 June 1941 *Education/professional qualifications:* Stationer's Company's School

Clifford D Stevens Esq, Director, Industry Department, Welsh Office, Cathays Park, Cardiff CF1 3NQ *Telephone:* 0222-823325

STEVENS, HANDLEY MICHAEL GAMBRELL   Under Secretary, London Public Transport, Department of Transport   Grade: 3

Career: third/second secretary Foreign and Commonwealth Office 1964-69, assistant private secretary to Lord Privy Seal 1970-71; principal Civil Service Department 1971-73; Department of Trade and Industry 1973-83: principal 1973-75, assistant secretary 1975-83; under secretary Department of Transport 1983-: international aviation 1983-87, finance 1988-91, London public transport 1991-

Date of birth: 29 June 1941 *Education/professional qualifications:* Leys School, Cambridge; Phillips Academy, Andover, Massachusetts, USA; King's College, Cambridge, modern languages (BA 1963) *Marital status:* married Professor Anne F Ross 1966; 3 daughters *Recreations:* music, walking

Handley M G Stevens Esq, Under Secretary, Department of Transport, 2 Marsham Street, London SW1 3EB *Telephone:* 071-276 5020

STEWART, G M   Under Secretary, Criminal Justice, Licensing, Parole and Life Imprisonment, Home and Health Department, Scottish Office   Grade: 3

Mrs G M Stewart, Under Secretary, Home and Health Department, Scottish Office, St Andrew's House, Edinburgh EH1 3DE *Telephone:* 031-556 8400

STEWART, IAN ROY   Special Adviser to the Lord President of the Council and Leader of the House of Commons

Career: Conservative Research Department; Confederation of British Industry; special adviser to Antony Newton, secretary of state for social security 1990-92, lord president of the council and leader of the House of Commons 1992-

Date of birth: 26 September 1961 *Education/professional qualifications:* Marling School, Stroud, Gloucestershire; London School of Economics (BSc Econ 1984) *Marital status:* married Rosalind 1989 *Clubs:* Naval and Military

Ian R Stewart Esq, Special Adviser, Lord President of the Council, Privy Council Office, 68 Whitehall, London SW1A 2AT *Telephone:* 071-270 0479 *Fax:* 071-270 0494

STEWART, (JAMES) MORAY   Second Permanent Under Secretary, Ministry of Defence   Grade: 1a

Career: Air Ministry/Ministry of Defence 1962-75, 1977-84, 1986-: deputy under secretary personnel and logistics 1986-88, defence procurement 1988-90, second permanent under secretary office of management and budget 1990-

Date of birth: 21 June 1938 *Education/professional qualifications:* Marlborough College; Keele University, history and economics (BA)

J Moray Stewart Esq CB, Second Permanent Under Secretary, Ministry of Defence, Whitehall, London SW1A 2HB *Telephone:* 071-218 6014

STEWART, Professor WILLIAM DUNCAN PATERSON   Chief Scientific Adviser, Head of the Office of Science and Technology, Office of Public Service and Science, Cabinet Office

Career: assistant lecturer Nottingham University 1961-63; lecturer Westfield College, London University 1963-68; Dundee University 1968-87: head of biological sciences department 1968-83; vice-principal 1983-87; visiting resident worker Wisconsin University, USA 1966, 1968; visiting professor Kuwait University 1980, Otago University, NZ 1984; chief scientific adviser Office of Public Service and Science Cabinet Office (advises Prime Minister and Cabinet Office on scientific and technological matters) 1990- head of the Office of Science and Technology 1992- *Current non-Whitehall posts:* Boyd Baxter professor of biology, Dundee University 1968

Date of birth: 7 June 1935 *Education/professional qualifications:* Dunoon Grammar School; Glasgow University, biology (BSc 1958, PhD, DSc)

Honours, decorations: FRSE 1977, FRS 1977 *Marital status:* married Cat Macleod 1958; 1 son *Publications:* Nitrogen Fixation in Plants (1966), co-author The Blue-Green Algae (1973) and Algal Physiology and Biochemistry (1974) *Clubs:* Athenaeum *Recreations:* watching soccer, playing the bagpipes

Professor William D P Stewart, Chief Scientific Adviser, Office of Public Service and Science, Cabinet Office, 70 Whitehall, London SW1A 2AS *Telephone:* 071-270 0259 *Fax:* 071-270 0432

STIBBARD, PETER JACK   Director of Statistics, Employment Department Group   Grade: 3

Career: under secretary statistics division 2, Department of Trade and Industry 1985-89; director of statistics Department of Employment 1989-

Date of birth: 15 May 1936 *Education/professional qualifications:* Hull University (BSc Econ; MIS)

Peter J Stibbard Esq, Director of Statistics, Employment Department Group, Caxton House, Tothill Street, London SW1H 9NF *Telephone:* 071-273 3000

STOKES, PETER RONALD PEGRAM   Senior Principal Inspector of Taxes, Business Profits Division, Inland Revenue   Grade: 4

Career: Inland Revenue 1966-: tax inspector (TI) 1966-72; higher grade TI 1972-76; senior TI 1976-81; principal TI 1981-90; senior principal TI business profits division 1990-

Date of birth: 25 March 1943 *Education/professional qualifications:* Brighton College; Hertford College, Oxford, physics (BA 1965) and education (Dip Ed 1966) *Marital status:* married Sarah 1971; 2 daughters *Recreations:* train travel

Peter R P Stokes Esq, Senior Principal Inspector of Taxes, Business Profits Division, Inland Revenue, Somerset House, Strand, London WC2R 1LB *Telephone:* 071-438 6482

STONE, Major General ANTHONY CHARLES PETER   Director-General Land Fighting Systems, Ministry of Defence   Grade: 3

Career: directing staff Royal Military College of Science (RMCS) 1978-80; commanding officer 5th regiment Royal Artillery 1980-83; staff defence programmes staff (operational requirements) Ministry of Defence (MoD) 1983-85; military director of studies RMCS 1985-86; MoD 1986-: director of operational requirements (land) 1986-89, of light weapons projects 1989-90; director-general policy and special projects (principal technical adviser to master general of ordnance; land systems controllerate procurement policy; management of proof and experimental establishments, logistic vehicles and special projects) 1990-

Date of birth: 25 March 1939 *Education/professional qualifications:* St Joseph's College; Royal Military Academy, Sandhurst; Royal Military College of Science; Staff College, Camberley *Recreations:* shooting, country pursuits, skiing, family

Major-General Anthony C P Stone, Director-General, Land Fighting Systems, Ministry of Defence, Whitehall, London SW1A 2HB *Telephone:* 071-218 6341

STRACHAN, VALERIE PATRICIA MARIE   Deputy Chairman and Director-General, HM Customs and Excise   Grade: 2

Career: assistant principal: HM Customs and Excise (C & E) 1961-64, Department of Economic Affairs 1964-66, Home Office 1966; principal: C & E 1966-72, HM Treasury (HMT) 1972-74; C & E 1974-85: assistant secretary 1974-80, commissioner, director VAT control 1980-83, commissioner, director organisation 1983-85; head of joint management unit HMT/Cabinet Office 1985-87; C & E 1987-: deputy chairman, principal establishments and finance officer 1987-89, director-general (overall director of the VAT customs and excise work of the department) 1989- *Current non-Whitehall posts:* vice-chairman Royal Institute of Public Administration 1990-

Date of birth: 10 January 1940 *Education/professional qualifications:* Newland High School, Hull; Manchester University, politics and modern history, (BA 1961) *Honours, decorations:* CB 1991 *Marital status:* married John 1965; 1 son, 1 daughter *Clubs:* Reform

Mrs Valerie P Marie Strachan CB, Deputy Chairman and Director General, HM Customs and Excise, New King's Beam House, 22 Upper Ground, London SE1 9PJ *Telephone:* 071-865 5011

STRATHNAVER, EILEEN   Special Adviser to President of Board of Trade

Career: special adviser to Michael Heseltine, secretary of state for environment, and then President of the Board of Trade, Department of Trade and Industry 1992-

Lady Strathnaver, Special Adviser, Department of Trade and Industry, 1-19 Victoria Street, London SW1H 0ET *Telephone:* 071-215 5000

STUART, (CHARLES) MURRAY   Deputy Chairman, Audit Commission

Career: Ford Motor Company 1962-65; finance director (FD) and secretary Sheffield Twist Drill and Steel Co Ltd 1965-69; FD and assistant managing director (MD) Unicorn Industries Ltd 1969-73; FD Hepworths Ltd 1973-74; ICL plc 1974-81: FD 1974-78, deputy MD 1978-81; MB Group Ltd 1981-90: FD 1981-83, finance, planning and administration director 1983-86, MD 1986-87, chief executive 1988-89, chairman 1989-90; deputy chairman Audit Commission (external audit of local government and NHS) 1991- *Current non-Whitehall posts:* chief executive Berisford International plc 1991-; non-executive director Scottish Power plc 1990 and Hunter Saphir 1991; member W Surrey and NE Hampshire health authority 1990-

Date of birth: 28 July 1933 *Education/professional qualifications:* Glasgow Academy; Glasgow University, history and geography (MA 1954), law (LLB 1957) *Marital status:* married Netta Caroline 1963; 1 daughter, 1 son *Recreations:* sailing, tennis, theatre, ballet

C Murray Stuart Esq, Deputy Chairman, Audit Commission, c/o Berisford International plc, 1 Prescot Street, London E1 8AY *Telephone:* 071-481 9144 *Fax:* 071-481 8357

Parliamentary Offices
see page 275

STUART, MARIAN ELIZABETH   Under Secretary, Finance, **Department of Health**   Grade: 3

Career: Department of Health and Social Security 1967-88: principal anti-smoking, family planning and psychiatric services policies 1971-78; assistant secretary hospital services, family planning and abortion, medical manpower planning and local government finance 1979-88; Department of Health 1988-: deputy chief inspector of social services 1988-89, under secretary finance (family health services [part], centrally financed services, personal social services) 1989-

Date of birth: 17 July 1944 *Education/professional qualifications:* Eye Grammar School, Suffolk; Mountgrave Comprehensive School, Potters Bar; Leicester University, combined studies (BA 1965) and English and its social background (MA 1966) *Children:* 1 son, 1 daughter *Recreations:* reading, bridge, skiing

Ms Marian E Stuart, Under Secretary, Department of Health, Friars House, 157-168 Blackfriars Road, London SE1 8FU *Telephone:* 071-972 3450 *Fax:* 071-972 3584

STUART, (NICHOLAS) NICK W   Deputy Secretary, Schools Policy, Department for Education   Grade: 2 *(see Addenda)*

Career: Department of Education and Science (DES) 1964-73: assistant principal 1964-68, private secretary (PS) to Minister for Arts 1968-69, principal 1969-73; PS to head of civil service, to prime ministers 1973-76; assistant secretary DES 1976-78, member cabinet of EC Commission president 1978-81; DES 1981-: under secretary (schools) 1981-85, principal finance officer 1985-87, deputy secretary schools policy 1987-

Date of birth: 2 October 1942 *Education/professional qualifications:* Harrow School; Christ Church, Oxford, modern history (BA, MA 1963) *Honours, decorations:* CB 1990 *Marital status:* married Susan J Fletcher 1974; 2 daughters, 1 son *Recreations:* allotment, collecting antiques

Nick W Stuart Esq CB, Deputy Secretary, Department for Education, Sanctuary Buildings, Great Smith Street, London SW1P 3BT *Telephone:* 071-925 6210 *Fax:* 071-925 6000

STUART-SMITH, The Rt Hon Sir MURRAY (The Rt Hon Lord Justice Stuart-Smith)   Security Service Commissioner, Security Service Tribunal

Career: barrister 1952-; crown court recorder 1972-81; high court judge 1981-86; presiding judge western circuit 1983-87; lord justice of appeal 1988-; security service commissioner 1989-

Date of birth: 18 November 1927 *Education/professional qualifications:* Radley College; Corpus Christi College, Cambridge, law (LLM, MA); Gray's Inn (barrister 1952) *Honours, decorations:* QC 1970; Bencher 1977; Kt 1981; PC 1988 *Marital status:* married Joan Elizabeth Mary Motion 1953; 3 daughters, 3 sons *Recreations:* cello-playing, shooting, building, bridge

The Rt Hon Lord Justice Stuart-Smith, Security Service Commissioner, Security Service Tribunal, PO Box 18, London SE1 0TL *Telephone:* 071-273 4096

SUMMERS, NICHOLAS   Under Secretary, Further and Higher Education, Department for Education   Grade: 3

Career: Ministry of Education 1961-64; Department of Education and Science (DES) 1964-74; private secretary to Minister for Arts 1965-66; Cabinet Office 1974-76; DES 1976-: under secretary further and higher education branch 3 (student support, adult further education, Open University) 1986-

Date of birth: 11 July 1939 *Education/professional qualifications:* Tonbridge School; Corpus Christi College, Oxford *Marital status:* married Marian Elizabeth Ottley 1965; four sons *Recreations:* family, music

Nicholas Summers Esq, Under Secretary, Department for Education, Sanctuary Buildings, Great Smith Street, London SW1P 3ET *Telephone:* 071-925 5000

SUNDERLAND, (GODFREY) RUSSELL   Deputy Secretary, Aviation, Shipping and International, Department of Transport   Grade: 2

Career: assistant principal, principal Ministry of Aviation 1962-69; first secretary civil aviation Beirut embassy and other Middle East posts 1969-71; Board of Trade, Department of Trade [and Industry] 1971-84: principal 1971-74, assistant secretary 1974-79, under secretary commercial relations and exports 1979-84; Department of Transport 1984-: under secretary shipping policy 1984-88, deputy secretary aviation, shipping and international 1988-

Date of birth: 28 July 1936 *Education/professional qualifications:* Heath Grammar School, Halifax; Queen's College, Oxford, literae humaniores (BA 1961, MA) *Honours, decorations:* CB 1991 *Marital status:* married Greta Jones 1965; 1 daughter, 1 son *Clubs:* Royal Society of Arts

G Russell Sunderland Esq CB, Deputy Secretary, Department of Transport, 2 Marsham Street, London SW1P 3EB *Telephone:* 071-276 5310 *Fax:* 071-276 6806

SURR, JEREMY   Director Operations (South and East), Training, Education and Enterprise Division, Employment Department Group   Grade: 3

Career: Ministry of Labour/Department of Employment 1959-: assistant private secretary to secretary of state 1971-73; seconded to Australian Department of Employment and Industrial Relations 1978-80; head of rehabilitation and sheltered employment Manpower Services Commission 1980-82; established special employment measures branch 1982; director special measures 1985-86; chief executive employment and enterprise group 1986-87; director of adult programmes 1987-89, of operations and training and enterprise councils 1989-90, of operations (south and east) training, education and enterprise division 1990-

Date of birth: 23 January 1938 *Education/professional qualifications:* Rutlish School, Wimbledon; Bury Grammar School, Lancashire *Marital status:* married Gillian Mary Lapage 1965 *Clubs:* Abbeydale Golf, Sheffield *Recreations:* golf, gardening, walking, 'DIY"

Jeremy Surr Esq, Director of Operations, Employment Department Group (TEED), W419, Moorfoot, Sheffield S1 4PQ

SUTHERLAND, E R   Parliamentary Counsel, Parliamentary Counsel Office   Grade: 2

E R Sutherland Esq, Parliamentary Counsel, Parliamentary Counsel Office, 36 Whitehall, London SW1A 2AY *Telephone:* 071-210 6633

SUTHERLAND, EVAN MACRAE   Acting National Director of Supplies, NHS Supplies Authority, Department of Health   Grade: 3

Career: production buyer in private industry 1973-76; contracts negotiator Norfolk Area Health Authority (AHA) 1976-79; deputy area supplies officer Derbyshire AHA 1979-82; divisional supplies manager Trent Regional Health Authority (RHA) 1982-84; North Western RHA 1984-87: regional supplies officer 1984-86, regional supplies director 1986-87; NHS national procurement directorate 1987-91: assistant national director 1987-90, acting national director of procurement and distribution 1990-91; acting national director of supplies NHS Supplies Authority 1991-

Date of birth: 23 April 1949 *Education/professional qualifications:* Fortrose Academy, Ross-shire; Aberdeen University, statistics, psychology, sociology, economics (MA 1971); St Helen's College (diploma 1974) *Marital status:* divorced; 1 daughter, 1 son *Recreations:* sport, theatre, music

Evan M Sutherland Esq, Acting National Director, NHS Supplies Authority, 14 Russell Square, London WC1B 5EP *Telephone:* 071-636 6811 *Fax:* 071-637 8990

SUTHERLAND, VERONICA EVELYN   Assistant Under Secretary, Foreign and Commonwealth Office   Senior grade

Career: HM Diplomatic Service 1965-: second, later first secretary Copenhagen 1967-70; Foreign and Commonwealth Office (FCO) 1970-75; first secretary New Delhi 1975-78; FCO 1978-80; counsellor 1981; permanent UK delegation to UNESCO 1981-84; counsellor FCO 1984-87; ambassador to Côte d'Ivoire 1987-90; assistant under secretary of state, deputy chief clerk 1990- *Current non-Whitehall posts:* non-executive director Save and Prosper 1990-; council member Royal Institute of Public Administration 1990-

Date of birth: 25 April 1939 *Education/professional qualifications:* Royal School, Bath; Westfield College, London University, German (BA 1961), Southampton University, German (MA 1965) *Honours, decorations:* CMG 1988 *Marital status:* married Alex James 1981 *Recreations:* painting

Mrs Veronica E Sutherland MA CMG, Assistant Under Secretary, Foreign and Commonwealth Office, Downing Street, London SW1A 2AL *Telephone:* 071-270 3000

SWEETMAN, JOHN FRANCIS   Clerk of Committees, House of Commons   Grade: 2

Career: army national service 1949-51; House of Commons Department of the Clerk 1954-: clerk of select committees on nationalised industries 1962-65, on science and technology 1970; second clerk of select committees 1979-83; clerk of the overseas office 1983-87; clerk assistant 1987-90; clerk of committees (overall direction of all staff of select committees, advice on working of committee system, oversight of all administrative matters affecting committees) 1990-

Date of birth: 31 October 1930 *Education/professional qualifications:* Cardinal Vaughan School, London; St Catharine's College, Cambridge, law (BA, MA 1954) *Honours, decorations:* TD 1964, CB 1990 *Marital status:* married Celia Elizabeth Nield 1983; 1 daughter, 1 son (from previous marriage), 2 sons *Clubs:* Marylebone Cricket

John F Sweetman Esq CB TD, Clerk of Committees, House of Commons, London SW1A 0AA *Telephone:* 071-219 3313

SWINNERTON, Dr CLIVE JERRY   Technical Director National Rivers Authority

Career: senior assistant hydrologist Great Ouse River Authority 1971-74; Wessex Water 1974-88: regional hydrologist, hydrologist 1974-78, resource planning manager 1978-84, Somerset divisional manager 1984-88; regional general manager Wessex Rivers National Rivers Authority (NRA) shadow unit 1988-89; technical director (policy development for water resources, flood defence, fisheries, recreation, conservation, navigation) NRA 1989-

Date of birth: 27 February 1945 *Education/professional qualifications:* King Henry VIII Grammar School, Abergavenny; University College of Wales, Swansea, civil engineering (BSc 1967); Imperial College, London, engineering hydrology (MSc DIC 1968), water resources (PhD 1971) *Marital status:* married Janet Mary 1968; 2 daughters *Recreations:* sport, running, cycling, swimming, gym

Dr Clive J Swinnerton,, Technical Director, National Rivers Authority, Rivers House, Waterside Drive, Aztec West, Almondsbury, Bristol BS12 4UD *Telephone:* 0455 624400 *Fax:* 0455 624409

SYMONDS, Captain DAVID ERIC   Chief Executive, Naval Aircraft Repair Organisation (Executive Agency)

Career: chief executive Naval Aircraft Repair Organisation 1992-

Date of birth: 16 September 1944 *Education/professional qualifications:* King Edward VII, King's Lynn; Royal Naval Engineering College, electrical engineering (BSc 1970); Cranfield Institute of Technology, control engineering (MSc 1974) *Recreations:* skiing, sailing, fishing, golf

Captain David Eric Symonds, RV Aircraft Yard, Fleetlands, Gosport, Hampshire PO13 0AW *Telephone:* 0705 822351 *Fax:* 0329 823043

T

TAIT, MICHAEL LOGAN   Assistant Under Secretary, Foreign and Commonwealth Office

Career: HM Diplomatic Service 1961-: ambassador to United Arab Emirates 1986-89; under secretary for USSR and Eastern Europe Foreign and Commonwealth Office 1990-

Date of birth: 27 September 1936 *Education/professional qualifications:* New College, Oxford

Michael L Tait Esq CMG LVO, Assistant Under Secretary, Foreign and Commonwealth Office, London SW1A 2AH *Telephone:* 071-273 3000

TANFIELD, JENNIFER   Deputy Librarian, House of Commons   Grade: 4

Career: House of Commons Library 1963-: library clerk 1963-72; head of economic affairs section 1972-77, of statistical section 1977-87, of parliamentary division 1987-91; deputy librarian (establishment officer) 1991-
Education/professional qualifications: School of SS Mary and Anne, Abbots Bromley; London School of Economics (BSc Econ 1962) *Marital status:* single *Publications:* In Parliament 1939-50 (HMSO 1991) *Recreations:* theatre, opera, travel, squash

Miss Jennifer Tanfield, Deputy Librarian, House of Commons Library, 1 Derby Street, London SW1A 2DG *Telephone:* 071-219 6179

TAYLOR, Dr JOHN FREDERICK   Chief Medical Adviser, Department of Transport   Grade: 4

Career: medical adviser British Rail 1960-64; medical officer HM Treasury medical service 1964-66; physician Moscow embassy 1966-68; medical adviser Civil Service Department 1968-72; Department of Transport 1972-: head of medical advisory branch Driver and Vehicle Licensing Centre 1972-86, chief medical adviser road vehicle safety division (advice on medical aspects of transport policy, including air and marine) 1986-

Date of birth: 19 August 1930 *Education/professional qualifications:* Wimbledon College, Wimbledon; King's College, London and St George's Hospital (MB BS 1957) Royal Institute of Public Health and Hygiene, occupational medicine (DIH 1960); Royal College of Physicians, occupational medicine MFOM 1978, FFOM 1985 *Honours, decorations:* CBE 1991 *Marital status:* divorced; 1 son, 1 daughter *Publications:* contributor to Recent Advances in Occupational Medicine (Churchill Livingston 1987) *Clubs:* Royal Society of Medicine *Recreations:* history, historic buildings

Dr John F Taylor CBE, Chief Medical Adviser, Department of Transport, 2 Marsham Street, London SW1P 3EB *Telephone:* 071-276 4039 *Fax:* 071-276 0818

TEMPLEMAN, MICHAEL   Under Secretary, Financial Institutions, Inland Revenue   Grade: 3

Career: Inland Revenue 1965-: senior principal tax inspector and controller oil taxation office 1989-91; under secretary financial institutions 1992-

Date of birth: 6 May 1943 *Education/professional qualifications:* King Edward's School, Birmingham;

Selwyn College, Cambridge, economics (BA 1965) *Marital status:* married Jane 1970 *Recreations:* running, music, cooking

Michael Templeman Esq, Under Secretary, Inland Revenue, Somerset House, The Strand, London WC2R 1LB *Telephone:* 071-438 7739 *Fax:* 071-438 7602

TENNANT, Major General MICHAEL TRENCHARD   Director, Royal Artillery, Ministry of Defence

Career: various staff and regimental posts 1962-78; directing staff Staff College 1978-80; commanding officer 1 Royal Horse Artillery 1980-83; commander British training team, Nigeria 1983-85; commander Royal Artillery (RA) 3 armoured division 1985-87; commander RA UK 1988-90; director RA Ministry of Defence 1991-

Date of birth: 3 September 1941 *Education/professional qualifications:* Wellington College; Staff College, Camberley *Recreations:* tennis, golf, bridge

Major-General Michael T Tennant, Director Royal Artillery, Royal Artillery Barracks, Woolwich, London SE18 4BH *Telephone:* 081-781 3000

THOMAS, (JOHN) ALAN   Head of Defence Export Services, Ministry of Defence

Career: Raytheon Company 1985-: president and chief executive officer Raytheon Europe 1985-89; seconded to Ministry of Defence as head of defence export services 1989-

Date of birth: 4 January 1943 *Education/professional qualifications:* Nottingham University (BSc)

Alan Thomas Esq, Head of Defence Export Services, Ministry of Defence, Main Building, Whitehall, London SW1A 2HB *Telephone:* 071-218·3042

THOMAS, KEITH JOHN   Director of Highways, Welsh Office   Grade: 4

Career: British Transport Docks Board 1956-69; Ministry of Public Buildings and Works/Property Services Agency, Department of Environment 1969-88: civil engineer (CE) 1969-77, principal CE 1977-80, area officer: east Wales 1980-83, Colchester 1983-85, deputy director southern region 1985-88; director of highways Welsh Office 1988-

Date of birth: 26 December 1939 *Education/professional qualifications:* Cardiff High School; University College, Cardiff, civil engineering (BSc 1963); FICE 1985; FIHT 1988 *Marital status:* married Vivienne 1962; 4 sons *Clubs:* Civil Service *Recreations:* squash, windsurfing

Keith J Thomas Esq, Director of Highways, Welsh Office, Government Buildings, Ty Glas Road, Llanishen, Cardiff CF4 5PL *Telephone:* 0222 761456 *Fax:* 0222 747901

THOMAS, Admiral Sir (WILLIAM) RICHARD (SCOTT)   Gentleman Usher of the Black Rod and Serjeant at Arms, House of Lords

Career: Royal Navy 1951-; UK Military Representative to NATO 1989-92; Gentleman Usher and Serjeant at Arms, House of Lords 1992-

Date of birth: 22 March 1932 *Education/professional qualifications:* Downside School, Bath, psc 1963; jssc 1966; rcds 1979

Admiral Sir Richard Thomas KCB OBE, Usher of the Black Rod and Serjeant at Arms, House of Lords, London SW1A 0PW *Telephone:* 071-219 3000

THOMPSON, COLIN JOHN   Deputy Director of Information Technology, Inland Revenue   Grade: 4

Career: Ministry of Pensions and National Insurance 1960-63; Inland Revenue 1963-: valuer 1967-84, information technology division 1984-: assistant director 1984-89, deputy director 1989-

Date of birth: 13 April 1943   *Education/professional qualifications:* Simon Langton Grammar School, Canterbury, ARICS 1968   *Marital status:* married Margaret McIntosh 1963; 1 son, 1 daughter

Colin J Thompson Esq, Deputy Director of Information Technology, Inland Revenue, Matheson House, Grange Central Telford, Shropshire TF3 4ER   *Telephone:* 0952-294000   *Fax:* 0952-294002

THOMPSON, ERIC JOHN   Director of Statistics, Office of Population Censuses and Surveys   Grade: 3

Career: personnel selection officer scientific adviser's office Air Ministry 1956-58; statistician: International Computers and Tabulators Ltd 1958-60, Shell International Petroleum Co Ltd 1960-65; head of regional demography unit General Register Office 1965-67; Greater London Council 1967-74: head of population studies section 1967-72, assistant director of intelligence 1972-74; head of social monitoring branch Central Statistical Office 1975-80; director of statistics: Department of Transport 1980-89, Office of Population Censuses and Surveys (all non-medical statistics and publications) 1989-

Date of birth: 26 September 1934   *Education/professional qualifications:* Beverley Grammar School; London School of Economics, statistics (BSc Econ 1956)   *Marital status:* single   *Recreations:* reading and collecting books, British medieval history, English literature

Eric J Thompson Esq, Director of Statistics, Office of Population Censuses and Surveys, St Catherine's House, London WC2B 6JP   *Telephone:* 071-242 0262   *Fax:* 071-242 0262

THOMPSON, GORDON   Surveyor-General, Marine Directorate, Department of Transport   Grade: 4

Career: marine surveyor Department of Transport (DTp) and other government departments 1954-88; surveyor-general marine directorate DTp (safety UK shipping and ports; prevention of pollution by ships) 1988-

Date of birth: 14 September 1930

Gordon Thompson Esq, Surveyor-General, Marine Directorate, Department of Transport, Sunley House, 90 High Holborn, London WC1V 6LP   *Telephone:* 071-405 6911   *Fax:* 071-831 2508

To subscribe to

The Dod's Report
The European Companion
The Whitehall Companion

Telephone 071-240 3902

THOMPSON, Dr JANET   Director-General Forensic Science Service (Executive Agency)   Grade: 3

Career: director-general Forensic Science Service 1988-

Date of birth: 23 October 1941 *Education/professional qualifications:* North London Collegiate School; Brighton College of Technology, applied physics (BSc 1963); Oxford University, physics (DPhil 1968)

Dr Janet Thompson, Director-General, Forensic Science Service, Horseferry House, Dean Ryle Street, London SW1P 2AW *Telephone:* 071-217 8617 *Fax:* 071-976 5131

THOMPSON, PETER KENNETH JAMES   Solicitor to Departments of Health and Social Security   Grade: 2

Career: Lord Chancellor's Department 1978-83; Department of [Health and] Social Security 1983-: under secretary 1983-; solicitor 1989-

Date of birth: 30 July 1937 *Education/professional qualifications:* Christ's College, Cambridge (MA, LLB); Lincoln's Inn (barrister)

Peter K J Thompson Esq, Solicitor, Departments of Health and Social Security, Richmond House, 79 Whitehall, London SW1A 2NS *Telephone:* 071-210 3000

THORNTON, NEIL ROSS   Head of Europe Division, Trade Policy and Export Promotion, Department of Trade and Industry   Grade: 3

Career: Ministry of Posts and Telecommunications 1971-75; private secretary (PS) to permanent secretary Department of Industry 1975-79; principal HM Treasury 1979-84; Department of [Trade and] Industry 1984-: assistant secretary 1984-88, principal PS to secretaries of state 1988-90, head of Europe division, trade policy and export promotion 1990-

Date of birth: 11 February 1950 *Education/professional qualifications:* Sedburgh School, Cumbria; Pembroke College, Cambridge, engineering (BA 1971, MA) *Marital status:* married Christine Boyes 1977; 2 daughters

Neil R Thornton Esq, Head of Europe Division, Trade Policy and Export Promotion, Department of Trade and Industry, Ashdown House, 123 Victoria Street, London SW1H 0ET *Telephone:* 071-215 6223 *Fax:* 071-215 5226

TITCHENER, ALAN RONALD   Under Secretary, Personnel Division, Department of Trade and Industry   Grade: 3

Career: Department of Trade and Industry 1982-: under secretary: enterprise initiative division 1987-91, personnel management division 1991-92, personnel division 1992-

Date of birth: 18 June 1934 *Education/professional qualifications:* London School of Economics (BSc Econ)

Alan R Titchener Esq, Under Secretary, Personnel Division, Department of Trade and Industry, Ashdown House, 123 Victoria Street, London SW1E 6RB *Telephone:* 071-215 5000

Government Departments
see page 300

TRISTEM, Dr (CYRIL EDWARD) ROSS(ITER)   Senior Director, Health Studies, Audit Commission

Career: Atomic Weapons Research Establishment, Aldermaston 1961-66; Home Office 1966-70; operational research division Department of Health 1970-76; division head HM Treasury 1976-83; director health studies directorate Audit Commission (external audit of local government and NHS) 1983-

Date of birth: 26 August 1939 *Education/professional qualifications:* Henley Royal Grammar School; Nottingham University, metallurgy (BSc 1961); Warwick University, business studies and operational research (PhD 1970) *Marital status:* married Monika Isle Erika 1963; 2 sons *Clubs:* Henley Golf *Recreations:* cricket, golf

Dr C E Rossiter Tristem, Director, Health Studies Directorate, Audit Commission, 1 Vincent Square, London SW1P 2PN
Telephone: 071-828 1212

TROSS, JONATHAN   Under Secretary, Finance Division, Department of Social Security   Grade: 3

Career: teacher Nairobi, Kenya 1971; Department of [Health and] Social Security D[H]SS 1972-: principal 1977-84, assistant secretary (AS) 1984-87, seconded to Barclays Bank as assistant director 1987-90; AS DH 1990-91; DSS, under secretary finance division (benefit and administration spending, liaison with Treasury and National Audit Office) 1991-

Date of birth: 21 January 1949 *Education/professional qualifications:* Chislehurst and Sidcup Grammar School, Kent; University College, Oxford modern history (BA 1970) *Marital status:* married Ann 1972; 1 son, 1 daughter *Recreations:* theatre, reading, football

Jonathan Tross Esq, Under Secretary, Department of Social Security, Richmond House, 79 Whitehall, London SW1A 2NS
Telephone: 071-210 5126 *Fax:* 071-210 5219

TRUE, NICHOLAS EDWARD   Deputy Head, Prime Minister's Policy Unit

Career: member Conservative Research Department 1975-82; special adviser to secretary of state for health and social security 1982-86; director Public Policy Unit plc 1986-90; borough councillor Richmond-upon-Thames 1986-90; deputy head Prime Minister's Policy Unit 1991- *Current non-Whitehall posts:* director Orange Tree Theatre 1990-

Date of birth: 31 July 1951 *Education/professional qualifications:* Nottingham High School; Peterhouse, Cambridge, classics and history (BA 1973) *Marital status:* married Anne-Marie Hood 1979; 2 sons *Clubs:* Travellers *Recreations:* Byzantine history, music, gardening, Italy

Nicholas E True Esq, Deputy Head, Prime Minister's Policy Unit, 10 Downing Street, London SW1A 2AA *Telephone:* 071-270 3000

TUCKER, CLIVE FENEMORE   Under Secretary, Director of Industrial Relations Division 1, Employment Department Group   Grade: 3

Career: Employment Department Group 1970-: assistant secretary 1978-87, under secretary 1987-, director of industrial relations division 1 1989-

Date of birth: 13 July 1944 *Education/professional qualifications:* Balliol College, Oxford (BA)

Clive F Tucker Esq, Under Secretary, Employment Department Group, Caxton House, Tothill Street, London SW1H 9NF *Telephone:* 071-273 5777

TUMIM, STEPHEN His Honour Judge   Chief Inspector of Prisons, England and Wales, Home Office

Career: county court judge 1980-87; president Mental Health Tribunal 1983-87; chief inspector of prisons in England and Wales, Home Office 1987-

Date of birth: 15 August 1930 *Education/professional qualifications:* St Edward's School, Oxford; Worcester College, Oxford, law (degree 1953) *Marital status:* married Winifred 1962; 3 daughters *Publications:* Great Legal Disasters (Weidenfeld and Nicolson 1983); Great Legal Fiascos (Weidenfeld and Nicolson 1985) *Clubs:* Garrick, Beefsteak *Recreations:* books and pictures

His Honour Judge Stephen Tumim, Her Majesty's Chief Inspector of Prisons in England and Wales, Home Office, 50 Queen Anne's Gate, London SW1H 9AT *Telephone:* 071-273 3000

TURNBULL, ANDREW   Deputy Secretary, Public Finance, HM Treasury   Grade: 2 *(see Addenda)*

Career: economist Zambia government 1968-70; HM Treasury (HMT) 1970-76: assistant principal 1970-72, principal 1972-76; on secondment to International Monetary Fund 1976-78; assistant secretary HMT 1978-85; private secretary (PS) to Prime Minister (PM) 1983-85; head of general expenditure policy division HMT 1985-88; principal PS to PM 1988-92; deputy secretary public finance HMT 1992-

Date of birth: 21 January 1945 *Education/professional qualifications:* Enfield Grammar School; Christ's College, Cambridge, economics (BA 1967) *Marital status:* married Diane Clarke 1968; 2 sons *Recreations:* running, opera, fellwalking

Andrew Turnbull Esq, Deputy Secretary, Public Finance, HM Treasury, Parliament Street, London SW1P 3AG *Telephone:* 071-270 5939 *Fax:* 071-270 5653

TURNER, JOHN   Deputy Chief Executive, Employment Service (Executive Agency)   Grade: 3

Career: industrial policy and sponsorship Department of Trade and Industry 1961-81; Department of Employment (DEm) 1981-87: seconded to Manpower Services Commission 1981-84; DEm: assistant secretary 1985, principal private secretary to Lord Young and Norman Fowler, secretaries of state for Employment 1986-87; Central Policy Review Staff 1987-88; head of small firms and tourism division DEm 1988-89; chief executive Employment Service 1989-

Date of birth: 22 April 1941 *Education/professional qualifications:* Ramsey Abbey Grammar School; Huntingdonshire; Northwood Hills Grammar School, Middlesex *Marital status:* married Susan Georgina Cameron 1971; 1 daughter, 2 sons *Recreations:* music, motoring, outdoors

John Turner Esq, Chief Executive, Employment Service, Rockingham House, 123 West Street, Sheffield S1 4ER *Telephone:* 0742 596246 *Fax:* 0742 795994

'Next Steps' Executive Agencies
see page 761

TURTON, (EU)GENIE CHRISTINE   Deputy Secretary, Housing and Inner Cities Group, Department of the Environment   Grade: 2

Career: Department/Ministry of Transport 1970-85: assistant principal 1970-74, principal 1974-80: principal private secretary to secretary of state 1978-80, assistant secretary 1980-81, seconded to Midland Bank channel link financing group 1981-82, to Cabinet Office machinery of government 1982-85; Department of Environment 1986-: under secretary 1986-91, deputy secretary housing and inner cities group 1991- *Current non-Whitehall posts:* trustee Pilgrim Trust 1991-

Date of birth: 19 February 1946 *Education/professional qualifications:* Nottingham Girls High School; Girton College, Cambridge, classics (BA 1967, MA) *Marital status:* divorced *Recreations:* books, music, shopping

Miss Genie C Turton, Deputy Secretary, Department of the Environment, 2 Marsham Street, London SW1P 3EB *Telephone:* 071-276 3259 *Fax:* 071-276 0625

TWEEDIE, Professor DAVID PHILIP   Chairman, Accounting Standards Board

Career: private practice chartered accountancy, Glasgow 1969-72; Edinburgh University 1973-78: accounting and business methods lecturer 1973-78, director of studies 1973-75, associate dean social sciences faculty 1975-78; technical director Institute of Chartered Accountants of Scotland 1978-81; national research partner KMG Thomson McLintock 1982-87; national technical partner Peat Marwick McLintock 1987-90; chairman Accounting Standards Board 1990-

Date of birth: 7 July 1944 *Education/professional qualifications:* Grangemouth High School; Edinburgh University, business administration (BCom 1966), incomes policy (PhD 1969); CA 1972 *Marital status:* married Jan 1970; 2 sons *Publications:* co-author The Private Shareholder and the Corporate Report (ICAEW 1977); Financial Reporting Inflation – the Capital Maintenance Concept (ICRA 1979); co-author The Institutional Investor and Financial Information (ICAEW 1981) and The Debate on Inflation Accounting (CUP 1984) *Recreations:* golf, watching rugby, gardening

Professor David P Tweedie, Chairman, Accounting Standards Board, 100 Gray's Inn Road, London WC1X 8AL *Telephone:* 071-404 8818 *Fax:* 071-404 4497

TYACKE, SARAH JACQUELINE   Chief Executive and Keeper of Public Records, Public Record Office

Career: British Library 1973-92: director of special collections 1986-91; chief executive and keeper of public Records 1992-

Date of birth: 20 September 1945 *Education/professional qualifications:* Bedford College, London, history (BA)

Mrs Sarah J Tyacke, Chief Executive and Keeper of Public Records, Public Records Office, Chancery Lane, London WC2A 1LR *Telephone:* 071-876 3444

TYTE, Dr D C   Director of Operations, Defence Research Agency (Executive Agency)   Grade: 3

Dr D C Tyte, Director of Operations, Defence Research Agency, St George's Court, 14 New Oxford Street, London WC1A 1EJ *Telephone:* 071-430 5226

U

UNWIN, Sir (JAMES) BRIAN   Chairman, HM Customs and Excise   Grade: 1

Career: HM Diplomatic Service 1960-68; HM Treasury (HMT) 1968-87: private secretary to chief secretary 1970-72, assistant secretary 1972, under secretary (US) 1976; seconded to Cabinet Office 1981-83: US; HMT 1983-85: deputy secretary (DS); director European Investment Bank 1983-85; seconded to Cabinet Office 1985-87: DS; chairman of board HM Customs and Excise 1987- *Current non-Whitehall posts:* chairman Civil Service Sports Council 1988-; secretary English National Opera board of directors 1986-; member Impact Advisory Board 1989-

Date of birth: 21 September 1935 *Education/professional qualifications:* Chesterfield School, Derbyshire; New College, Oxford, literae humaniores (BA, MA 1959); Yale University, USA, politics and economics (MA 1960) *Honours, decorations:* CB 1986, KCB 1990 *Marital status:* married Diana Susan Scott 1964; 3 sons *Clubs:* Reform *Recreations:* opera, cricket, birdwatching

Sir Brian Unwin KCB, Chairman, HM Customs and Excise, New King's Beam House, Upper Ground, London SE1 9PJ *Telephone:* 071-865 5001

UPTON, PETER   Director of Operations and Information Technology, Valuation Office Agency (Executive Agency)   Grade: 4

Career: director of operations and information technology Valuation Office Agency (valuation of land and buildings for taxation) 1989-

Date of birth: 22 July 1937 *Education/professional qualifications:* ARICS 1962

Peter Upton Esq, Director of Operations and Information Technology, Valuation Office Agency, New Court, Carey Street, London WC2A 2JE *Telephone:* 071-324 1021 *Fax:* 071-324 1073

URWICK, Sir ALAN BEDFORD   Serjeant at Arms, House of Commons   Grade: 3

Career: HM Foreign (subsequently Diplomatic) Service 1952-89: Brussels 1954-56, Moscow 1958-59, Baghdad 1960-61, Amman 1965-67, Washington 1967-71, Cairo 1971-73; Central Policy Review Staff, Cabinet Office 1973-75; head of Near East and North Africa department Foreign and Commonwealth Office 1975-76; minister Madrid 1977-79; ambassador to Jordan 1979-84, to Egypt 1985-87, high commissioner to Canada 1987-89; serjeant at arms, House of Commons (responsible for order, security, ceremonial, communications, administration and upkeep in the Commons) 1989-

Date of birth: 2 May 1930 *Education/professional qualifications:* Rugby School; New College, Oxford, modern history (BA 1952, MA) *Honours, decorations:* CMG 1978, KStJ 1982, KCVO 1984 *Marital status:* married Marta Yolanda Montagne 1960; 3 sons *Recreations:* gardening, reading, antique collecting

Sir Alan Urwick KCVO CMG, Serjeant at Arms, House of Commons, London SW1A 0AA *Telephone:* 071-219 3030

V

VALLANCE WHITE, JAMES ASHTON   Principal Clerk, Judicial Office, House of Lords

Career: Department of the Clerk of the Parliaments, House of Lords 1961-: clerk of committees 1971-78; chief clerk Public Bill Office 1978-83; principal clerk judicial office and fourth clerk at the table (judicial) 1983-

Date of birth: 25 February 1938 *Education/professional qualifications:* Allhallows School; St Peter's College, Oxford, philosophy, politics and economics (BA, MA 1961) *Marital status:* married Anne Margaret O'Donnell 1987 *Clubs:* Brooks's

James A Vallance White Esq, Principal Clerk, Judicial Office, House of Lords, London SW1A 0PW *Telephone:* 071-219 3120 *Fax:* 071-219 2476

VANNET, ALFRED DOUGLAS   Deputy Crown Agent, Crown Office   Grade: 4

Career: private practice solicitor 1973-76; Crown Office (public prosecution in Scotland) 1976-: Procurator Fiscal Service 1976-84: procurator fiscal (PF) depute, Dundee 1976-77, PF depute/senior PF depute, Glasgow 1977-84; assistant solicitor 19 84-90; deputy Crown Agent 1990-

Date of birth: 31 July 1949 *Education/professional qualifications:* High School of Dundee; Dundee University, law (LLB 1973) *Marital status:* married Pauline Margaret 1979; 1 daughter, 1 son *Recreations:* music

Alfred D Vannet Esq, Deputy Crown Agent, Crown Office, Regent Road, Edinburgh EH7 5BL *Telephone:* 031-557 3800 *Fax:* 031-557 8208

VAUX, J   Principal Treasury Solicitor, European Division, Treasury Solicitor's Department   Grade: 3

J Vaux Esq, Principal Treasury Solicitor, European Division, Treasury Solicitor's Department, Queen Anne's Chambers, 28 Broadway, London SW1H 9JS *Telephone:* 071-210 3000

VENABLES, (HAROLD) DAVID SPENSER   Official Solicitor to the Supreme Court, Lord Chancellor's Department   Grade: 3

Career: air force national service 1957-58; solicitor 1959-60; Official Solicitor's Office, Lord Chancellor's Department 1960-: official solicitor to Supreme Court 1980-

Date of birth: 14 October 1932 *Education/professional qualifications:* Denstone College, Staffordshire *Marital status:* married Teresa 1964; 1 daughter, 1 son *Publications:* A Guide to the Law Affecting Mental Patients (Butterworths 1975); The Racing 1500s (TB Publications 1984) *Clubs:* Vintage Sports Car *Recreations:* vintage cars, motoring, military history

H David S Venables, Official Solicitor to the Supreme Court, 81 Chancery Lane, London WC2A 1DD *Telephone:* 071-911 7116 *Fax:* 071-911 7105

Regulatory Organisations and Public Bodies
see page 857

VENABLES, ROBERT MICHAEL COCHRANE   Head of Legal Division, Charity Commission   Grade: 3

Career: solicitor 1962-70; Treasury Solicitor's Department 1970-89: legal assistant conveyancing 1970-73, senior legal assistant conveyancing Department of Energy (DEn) 1973-80, assistant treasury solicitor: DEn 1980-83, establishments finance 1983-85, DEn 1985-87, conveyancing 1987-89; head of legal division, commissioner, Charity Commission for England and Wales 1989-

Date of birth: 8 February 1939 *Education/professional qualifications:* Portsmouth Grammar School; Law Society (solicitor 1962) *Marital status:* married Hazel Lesley 1972; 2 sons, 2 daughters *Clubs:* Civil Service, Law Society *Recreations:* opera, collecting domestic anachronisms

Robert M C Venables Esq, Head of Legal Division, Charity Commission for England and Wales, St Alban's House, 57-60 Haymarket, London SW1Y 4QX *Telephone:* 071-210 4419 *Fax:* 071-930 9174

VENNING, (ROBERT) BOB WILLIAM DAWE   Under Secretary, Health Authority Personnel, Department of Health   Grade: 3

Career: philosophy tutor Birmingham University 1968-69; logic and scientific method lecturer Lanchester Polytechnic 1969-70; Department of Health [and Social Security] 1971-: private secretary (PS) to Minister for Disabled 1974-75, principal 1975-81, PS to Minister for Health 1981-83, assistant secretary 1983-90, under secretary health authority personnel division (pay and conditions for all NHS staff; industrial relations; non-medical staff training) 1990- *Current non-Whitehall posts:* non-executive director Compel Group plc 1989-

Date of birth: 25 July 1946 *Education/professional qualifications:* Midhurst School, West Sussex; Birmingham University, mental and moral philosophy (BA 1968) *Marital status:* married Jennifer Mei-ling 1969; 1 son, 1 daughter *Recreations:* playing classical and flamenco guitar, electronics and computing

Bob Venning Esq, Under Secretary, Department of Health, Hannibal House, Elephant and Castle, London SE1 6TE *Telephone:* 071-972 2000

VEREKER, JOHN MICHAEL MEDLICOTT   Deputy Secretary, Further and Higher Education, Department for Education   Grade: 2 (see Addenda)

Career: assistant principal Overseas Development Ministry (ODM) 1967-69; World Bank, Washington 1970-72; ODM 1972-78: principal 1972-77, private secretary to ministers 1977-78; assistant secretary 1978; Prime Minister's Office 1980-83; Overseas Development Administration/Foreign and Commonwealth Office 1983-88: under secretary 1983, principal finance officer 1986-88; deputy secretary further and higher education Department of Education and Science 1988- *Current non-Whitehall posts:* chairman Student Loans Company 1989-

Date of birth: 9 August 1944 *Education/professional qualifications:* Marlborough College; Keele University (BA 1967) *Honours, decorations:* CB 1992 *Marital status:* married Judith Diane Rowen 1971; 1 daughter, 1 son

John M M Vereker Esq CB, Deputy Secretary, Department for Education, Sanctuary Buildings, Great Smith Street, London SW1P 3BT *Telephone:* 071-925 5000

VINCENT, Field Marshal SIR RICHARD FREDERICK   Chief of Defence Staff, Ministry of Defence (and from January 1993 Chairman of the Military Committee of NATO)

Career: national service Royal Artillery (RA) 1951; Germany 1951-55; gunnery staff 1959; Radar Research Establishment Malvern 1960-61; BAOR 1962; technical staff training 1963-64; Staff College 1965; Commonwealth Brigade Malaysia 1966-68; Ministry of Defence (MoD) 1968-70; commanding officer (CO) 12th Light Air Defence Regiment Germany, UK, Northern Ireland 1970-72; instructor Staff College 1972-73; military director of studies Royal Military College of Science (RMCS) 1974-75; CO 19 Airportable Brigade 1975-77; Royal College of Defence Studies 1978; deputy military secretary 1979-80; commandant RMCS 1980-83; MoD 1983-: master general of the ordnance 1983-87, vice-chief 1987-91, then Chief 1991-, of the Defence Staff (principal adviser to HMG on strategy and military operations) 1992-; Chairman military committee, NATO 1993- *Current non-Whitehall posts:* colonel commandant RA 1983-; advisory council RMCS 1983-; governor Aldenham School 1987-

Date of birth: 23 August 1931   *Education/professional qualifications:* Aldenham School, Elstree; Royal Military College of Science; FIMechE 1990; FRAeS 1990   *Honours, decorations:* DSO 1972, KCB 1984, GBE 1990   *Recreations:* sailing, model engineering

Field Marshal Sir Richard F Vincent GBE, KCB, DSO, Chief of Defence Staff, Ministry of Defence, Whitehall, London SW1A 2HB   *Telephone:* 071-218 6031   *Fax:* 071-218 6799

W

WALFORD, Dr DIANA MARION Director of Health Care and Medical Director, NHS Management Executive, Department of Health Grade: 2

Career: Department of Health 1976-: senior principal medical officer and under secretary 1983-89; director of health care and medical director 1989-

Date of birth: 26 February 1944

Dr Diana M Walford, Director of Health Care and Medical Director, NHS Management Executive, Department of Health, Richmond House, 79 Whitehall, London SW1A 2NS *Telephone:* 071-210 5593

WALKER, J G H Director General, Policy and Special Projects, Land Systems Controllerate, Procurement Executive, Ministry of Defence

J G H Walker Esq, Director General Policy and Special Projects, Land Systems Controllerate, Procurement Executive, Ministry of Defence, Main Building, Whitehall, London SW1A 2HB *Telephone:* 071-218 9000

WALKER, TIMOTHY EDWARD HANSON Head of Atomic Energy, Energy Division, Department of Trade and Industry Grade: 3

Career: strategic planner Greater London Council 1974-77, principal Department of Trade 1977-83, Sloan Fellow London Business School 1983; Department of Trade and Industry 1983-: assistant secretary 1983, administration director Alvey programme 1983-85, head of policy planning unit 1985-86, principal private secretary to secretaries of state 1986-87, under secretary 1987, director of information for engineering directorate 1987-89; head of atomic energy division Department of Energy 1989-92 and then Department of Trade and Industry 1992- *Current non-Whitehall posts:* UK government representative International Atomic Energy Agency 1989-

Date of birth: 27 July 1945 *Education/professional qualifications:* Tonbridge School; Brasenose College, Oxford, chemistry (BA 1967, MA, DPhil 1969) *Marital status:* married Judith Mann 1969 (died 1976); Anna Butterworth 1983; 3 daughters (1d previous marriage) *Publications:* contributions to scientific journals *Recreations:* cooking, gardening, collecting modern prints

Timothy E H Walker Esq, Head of Atomic Energy, Energy Division, Department of Trade and Industry, 1 Palace Street, London SW1E 5HE *Telephone:* 071-238 3000

WALLACE, HUGH GEORGE Chief Crown Prosecutor, Crown Prosecution Service (Gwent and South Wales) Grade: 4

Career: solicitor 1971-: Crown Prosecution Service 1974-: assistant prosecuting solicitor Merseyside 1974-82, deputy county prosecuting solicitor 1982-86, chief crown prosecutor (for Gwent and South Wales) 1986-

Date of birth: 22 January 1945 *Education/professional qualifications:* Stowe School, Buckinghamshire; Liverpool College of Commerce (solicitor 1971) *Marital status:* married Sarah 1972; 2 daughters *Clubs:* Cardiff Castle *Recreations:* fishing, tennis, squash

Hugh G Wallace Esq, Chief Crown Prosecuter, Crown Prosecution Service, Pearl Assurance House, Greyfriars Road, Cardiff CF1 3PL *Telephone:* 0222 382777 *Fax:* 0222 664574

WALLACE, (JAMES) FLEMING   Counsel to Scottish Law Commission   Grade: 3

Career: advocate 1957-60; Lord Advocate's Department 1960-79: parliamentary draftsman and secretary to Lord Advocate; counsel to Scottish Law Commission (law reform legislation drafting) 1979-

Date of birth: 19 March 1931 *Education/professional qualifications:* Edinburgh Academy; Edinburgh University, Latin, history and oral philosophy (MA 1951), law (LLB 1954) *Honours, decorations:* QC 1985 *Marital status:* married: Valerie Mary 1964 (died 1986); Linda Ann 1990; 2 daughters from previous marriage *Publications:* The Businessman's Lawyer [Scottish part] (Business Publications 1965); The Business and Professional Man's Lawyer [Scottish part] (Business Books 1973) *Clubs:* Royal Mid-Surrey Golf *Recreations:* hillwalking, choral singing, golf, badminton

J Fleming Wallace Esq QC, Counsel to Scottish Law Commission, 140 Causewayside, Edinburgh EH9 1PR *Telephone:* 031-668 2131

WALLACE, RICHARD ALEXANDER   Principal Finance Officer, Welsh Office

Career: Ministry of Social Security/Department of Health and Social Security 1968-1986: principal 1972-81, assistant secretary 1981-86; Welsh Office 1986-: under secretary, head of transport, planning, water and environment group 1988-90, principal finance officer 1990-

Date of birth: 24 November 1946 *Education/professional qualifications:* Clifton College, Bristol; King's College, Cambridge (BA, MA) *Marital status:* married Teresa Caroline Harington Smith 1970; 3 children (and 1 deceased)

Richard A Wallace Esq, Principal Finance Officer Welsh Office, Cathays Park, Cardiff CF1 3NQ *Telephone:* 0222 825111

WALLARD, Dr ANDREW JOHN   Deputy Director and Controller of Scientific Services, National Physical Laboratory (Executive Agency)   Grade: 4

Career: researcher National Physical Laboratory (NPL) 1968-81; Department of Trade and Industry 1981-: head of technical information section 1981-82, deputy head policy planning unit 1982-83, branch head: research and technology policy division 1983-86, electronics applications division; international affairs director information engineering directorate 1988-90; deputy director and controller of scientific services NPL (national measurement standards) 1990- *Current non-Whitehall posts:* non-executive director Rank CINTEL 1987-

Date of birth: 11 October 1945 *Education/professional qualifications:* Liverpool Institute; St Andrew's University, physics (BSc 1968, PhD 1971) *Marital status:* married Barbara Jean 1969; 2 sons *Clubs:* Papercourt Sailing *Recreations:* music, gardening, sailing, wine

Dr Andrew J Wallard, Deputy Director, National Physical Laboratory, Teddington, Middlesex TW11 0LW *Telephone:* 081-943 6013 *Fax:* 081-943 2155

Complete Name Index
see page 955

WALMSLEY, BRIAN   Under Secretary, Social Security Division A, Department of Social Security   Grade: 3

Career: Department of [Health and] Social Security 1957-: assistant Secretary 1979-85; under secretary 1985-, seconded to Cabinet Office 1988-90, social security division A 1990-

Date of birth: 22 April 1936   *Education/professional qualifications:* Prescot Grammar School

Brian Walmsley Esq, Under Secretary, Social Security Division A, Department of Social Security, Richmond House, 79 Whitehall, London SW1A 2NS   *Telephone:* 071-210 3000

WALMSLEY, Rear Admiral ROBERT   Assistant Chief of Defence Staff (Command, Control, Communications and Information Systems), Ministry of Defence

Career: HMS Ark Royal, Otus, Churchill 1962-72; Ministry of Defence (MoD) 1973-74: Ship department; HM dockyard Chatham 1975-78; MoD 1979-: Procurement Executive (PE) 1979-80, chairman naval nuclear technical safety panel 1981-83, naval staff 1984, PE 1985-86, director operational requirements (sea) 1987-89, assistant chief of defence staff (command, control, communications and information systems) 1990-

Date of birth: 1 February 1941   *Education/professional qualifications:* New Park School, St Andrew's; Fettes College, Edinburgh; Queen's College, Cambridge, mechanical sciences (BA, MA 1962); Royal Naval College, Greenwich, nuclear science and technology (MSc 1968)   *Recreations:* fly-fishing, Scotland, watching football

Rear Admiral Robert Walmsley, Assistant Chief of Defence Staff, Ministry of Defence, Whitehall, London SW1A 2HB   *Telephone:* 071-218 7445

WALSH, Dr JULIA   Chief Executive, ADAS (Executive Agency)   Grade: 2

Dr Julia Walsh, Chief Executive, ADAS, Nobel House, 17 Smith Square, London SW1P 3JR   *Telephone:* 071-238 5619

WARD, (ANTHONY) TONY JOHN   Chief Executive, Resettlement Agency (Executive Agency)   Grade: 6

Career: Department of Health and Social Security 1975-84: manager national insurance office 1980-81; manager social security offices 1981-84; consultant Cabinet Office 1984-89; chief executive Resettlement Agency (for the single homeless) 1989-

Date of birth: 3 November 1940   *Education/professional qualifications:* Devonport High School, Plymouth   *Marital status:* divorced; 1 son, 1 daughter   *Recreations:* cricket, travel

Tony J Ward Esq, Chief Executive, Resettlement Agency, Euston Tower, Euston Road, London NW1 3DN   *Telephone:* 071-388 1188   *Fax:* 071-383 7199

WARD, REGINALD GEORGE   Assistant Director, Head of Division 1, Central Statistical Office   Grade: 3

Career: HM Treasury 1978-82; Cabinet Office 1982-86; Department of Trade and Industry 1986-89; head of division 1 Central Statistical Office 1989-

Date of birth: 6 July 1942   *Education/professional qualifications:* Leicester University; Aberdeen University; Oxford University; London Business School

Reginald G Ward Esq, Assistant Director, Central Statistical Office, Millbank Tower, Millbank, London SW1P 4QP   *Telephone:* 071-270 3000

WARNER, GERALD CHIERICI   Deputy Secretary, Cabinet Office   Grade: 2

Career: HM Diplomatic Service 1954-: Foreign and Commonwealth Office 1976-90; deputy secretary Cabinet Office 1991-

Date of birth: 27 September 1931 *Education/professional qualifications:* University of Oxford (BA)

Gerald C Warner Esq, CMG, Deputy Secretary, Cabinet Office, 70 Whitehall, London SW1A 2AS *Telephone:* 071-270 3000

WARREN, Dr ROGER H   Managing Director, Military and Aeronautics Business Group, Defence Research Agency (Executive Agency)   Grade: 3

Dr Roger H Warren, Managing Director, Military and Aeronautics Business Group, Defence Research Group, Meudon Avenue, Farnborough, Hampshire GU14 7TU *Telephone:* 0252-373 434

WASSERMAN, GORDON JOSHUA   Assistant Under Secretary, Police Department, Home Office   Grade: 3

Career: Home Office 1967-: under secretary seconded to Central Policy Review Staff, Cabinet Office 1981-83; police department 1983-

Date of birth: 26 July 1938 *Education/professional qualifications:* McGill University, Canada (BA); New College, Oxford (MA)

Gordon J Wasserman Esq, Assistant Under Secretary, Police Department, Home Office, 50 Queen Anne's Gate, London SW1H 9AT *Telephone:* 071-273 3000

WATT, Dr ROBERT MACKAY   Chief Inspector, Animals (Scientific Procedures) Inspectorate, Home Office   Grade: 4

Career: physiology lecturer Edinburgh University medical school 1970-75; community medicine fellow Scottish Health Service 1975-77; Home Office 1977-: inspector (Cruelty to Animals Act 1876) 1977-84, superintending inspector 1984-87, chief inspector animals (Scientific Procedures) Inspectorate (implementing legal controls on animal use in research) 1987-

Date of birth: 5 February 1941 *Education/professional qualifications:* Aberdeen Grammar School; Manchester Grammar School; Edinburgh University, physiology (BSc 1963), medicine (MB ChB 1966), micro-chemistry (PhD 1972), community medicine (diploma 1976) *Marital status:* married Christine Wendy 1969; 2 sons *Recreations:* painting, model-making, wood carving, armchair aviation

Dr Robert M Watt, Chief Inspector, Animals (Scientific Procedures) Inspectorate, Home Office, Queen Anne's Gate, London SW1H 9AT *Telephone:* 071-273 2347 *Fax:* 071-273 2423

WATTS, LEE   Banking Group, HM Treasury   Grade: 4

Career: Post Office Savings Bank 1950-63; Colonial Office 1963-65; HM Treasury 1965-: treasury accountant, accounts division (management government funds and accounts, particularly consolidated fund; government cash flow) 1985-92, banking group 1992-

Date of birth: 29 August 1933 *Education/professional qualifications:* Royal High School, Edinburgh *Marital status:* married Barbara Louisa 1955; 1 son

Lee Watts Esq, Banking Group, HM Treasury, Parliament Street, London SW1P 3AG *Telephone:* 071-270 3000 *Fax:* 071-270 5653

WEATHERSTON, (WILLIAM) ALASTAIR (PATERSON)   Under Secretary, Education Department Scottish Office

Career: Scottish Office (SO) 1959-: seconded to Cabinet Office 1972-74; under secretary higher education Education Department SO 1989-

Date of birth: 20 November 1935 *Education/professional qualifications:* Edinburgh University, history (MA Hons)

Alastair Weatherston Esq, Under Secretary, Scottish Office Education Department, 43 Jeffrey Street, Edinburgh EH1 1DN *Telephone:* 031-244 5322

WEBBER, MICHAEL   Charity Commissioner   Grade: 4

Career: charity commissioner 1989- *Current non-Whitehall posts:* chairman and chief executive Pifco Holdings plc 1983-

Date of birth: 7 February 1946 *Education/professional qualifications:* Carmel College, Berkshire; FCA 1968 *Marital status:* single

Michael Webber Esq, Charity Commissioner, Charity Commission, St Alban's House, 57-60 Haymarket, London SW1Y 4QX *Telephone:* 071-930 9173

WEEPLE, EDWARD JOHN   Under Secretary, Industry Department, Scottish Office   Grade: 3

Career: assistant principal Ministry of Health 1968-71; Department of Health and Social Security 1971-78: private secretary to Minister of Health 1971-73, principal 1973-78; principal Scottish Office 1978-: Industry Department 1978-80; assistant secretary: Scottish Home and Health Department 1980-85, Scottish Agriculture and Fisheries Department 1985-90; under secretary (Scottish EC issues; new towns; regeneration, particularly urban) Scottish Industry Department 1990- *Current non-Whitehall posts:* chairman Wester Hailes Partnership Board 1990-; chairman Ferguslie Park Partnership Board 1990-; member Scottish Business in the Community executive council 1990-

Date of birth: 15 May 1945 *Education/professional qualifications:* St Aloysius College, Glasgow; Glasgow University, history (MA 1967) *Marital status:* married Joan Shaw 1970; 3 sons, 1 daughter

Edward J Weeple Esq, Under Secretary, Scottish Office Industry Department, New St Andrew's House, Edinburgh EH1 3TD *Telephone:* 031-244 4605 *Fax:* 031-244 4785

WEISS, JOHN ROGER   Director, Asset Management Group, Export Credits Guarantee Department   Grade: 3

Career: Inland Revenue 1961-64; Export Credits Guarantee Department 1964- : principal 1978-82; head of finance division 1982-87, of chief executive's division 1987-90; director asset management 1990-

Date of birth: 27 December 1944 *Education/professional qualifications:* St Helen's College, Thames Ditton *Marital status:* married Hazel Kay Lang 1967 *Recreations:* music, walking

John R Weiss Esq, Under Secretary, Export Credits Guarantee Department, 2 Exchange Tower, Harbour Exchange Square, London E14 9GS *Telephone:* 071-512 7376 *Fax:* 071-512 7649

WENBAN-SMITH, HUGH BOYD   Head of Marine Directorate, Department of
Transport   Grade: 3

Career: economist, Zambia government and central bank 1964-67; economic adviser (EA) Ministry of
Overseas Development 1968-71; economic first secretary New Delhi high commission 1971-74;
economic adviser Department of Trade and Industry 1975-77; senior EA Prices Commission 1977-79;
senior consultant commercial accountancy practice 1979-81; head of water finance and economics
division Department of Environment 1981-85; Department of Transport 1985-: director financial
management 1985-89, under secretary, head of marine directorate (surveyor-general's organisation;
coastguard; ports; pollution) 1989-

Date of birth: 6 November 1941   *Education/professional qualifications:* King's College, Cambridge,
economics (MA 1964); University College, London, public policy economics (MSc 1975)

Hugh B Wenban-Smith Esq, Under Secretary, Department of Transport, Sunley House, 90-93 High
Holborn, London WC1V 6LP   *Telephone:* 071-405 6911

WENTWORTH, STEPHEN   Under Secretary and Head of European Community Group,
Ministry of Agriculture, Fisheries and Food   Grade: 3

Career: Ministry of Agriculture, Fisheries and Food 1967-: European Communities division 1985;
under secretary head of livestock products group 1989-91, head of European Community group
1991-

Date of birth: 23 August 1943   *Education/professional qualifications:* Merton College, Oxford (MA MSc)

Stephen Wentworth Esq, Under Secretary and Head of European Community Group, Ministry of
Agriculture, Fisheries and Food, Whitehall Place, London SW1A 2HH   *Telephone:* 071-270 3000

WHEELER, (RICHARD) DICK JOHN   Director, Information
Technology Services, Department of Trade and Industry   Grade: 4

Career: Inland Revenue 1961-83; Ministry of Agriculture, Fisheries and
Food 1983-89: deputy head computer services 1983-85, assistant director
information technology (IT) planning 1985-89, director IT services
Department of Trade and Industry services management division 1990-

Date of birth: 5 January 1943   *Education/professional qualifications:* Glyn
Grammar School, Epsom   *Marital status:* married Carol 1979; 1 daughter, 2
sons   *Recreations:* bridge, golf, gardening

Dick Wheeler Esq, Director, Information Technology Services, Department
of Trade and Industry, Kingsgate House, 66-74 Victoria Street, London
SW1E 6SW   *Telephone:* 071-215 3630   *Fax:* 071-215 8160

WHEELER, Major-General ROGER NEIL   Assistant Chief of General Staff, Ministry of
Defence

Career: army service 1964-; director army plans Ministry of Defence (MoD) 1987-89; commander 1st
armoured division BAOR 1989-90; assistant chief of general staff MoD 1990-

Date of birth: 16 December 1941   *Education/professional qualifications:* All Hallows School, Devon
Honours, decorations: CBE 1983

Major-General Roger N Wheeler CBE, Assistant Chief of General Staff, Ministry of Defence,
Whitehall, London SW1A 2HB   *Telephone:* 071-218 7191

WHEELER-BOOTH, MICHAEL ADDISON JOHN   Clerk of the Parliaments, House of Lords   Grade: 1

Career: Parliament Office, House of Lords 1960-: seconded as private secretary to leader of house and government chief whip 1965-67, as joint secretary inter-party conference on House of Lords reform 1967-70; clerk of the journals 1970-72, chief clerk Overseas and European Office 1972-78; principal clerk 1978-83; reading clerk and clerk of the journals 1983-88; . clerk assistant of the parliaments and clerk of the journals 1988-91; clerk of the parliaments (appointment of Parliament Office staff; procedural advice; records custodian for both houses; authentication of Acts) 1991-

Date of birth: 25 February 1934 *Education/professional qualifications:* Leighton Park School, Reading; Magdalen College, Oxford, modern history (BA 1957, MA) *Marital status:* married Emily Frances Smith 1982; 2 daughters, 1 son *Clubs:* Brooks's

Michael A J Wheeler-Booth Esq, Clerk of the Parliaments, Parliament Office, House of Lords, London SW1A 0PW *Telephone:* 071-219 3181

WHELDON, JULIET LOUISE   Legal Secretary, Legal Secretariat to the Law Officers   Grade: 3

Career: legal assistant Treasury Solicitor's Department (TSD) 1976-83; senior legal assistant Law Officers' Department (LOD) 1983-84; assistant solicitor TSD 1984-86, LOD 1986-87; principal assistant solicitor in charge of Treasury advisory work TSD 1987-89; legal secretary Legal Secretariat to Law Officers (senior official in Attorney General and Solicitor General's Office; briefing law officers) 1989-

Date of birth: 26 March 1950 *Education/professional qualifications:* Sherborne School for Girls; Lady Margaret Hall, Oxford, history (BA 1971); College of Law (bar finals 1975); Gray's Inn (barrister 1975) *Marital status:* single

Miss Juliet L Wheldon, Legal Secretary, Legal Secretariat to the Law Officers, 9 Buckingham Gate, London SW1E 4JP *Telephone:* 071-828 1968

WHIPPMAN, Dr MICHAEL   Under Secretary, Home Transport and Education Group, HM Treasury   Grade: 3

Career: Pennsylvania University, USA 1963-71: post-doctoral fellow 1963-65, assistant professor 1965-71; senior research fellow Helsinki University, Finland 1971-73; Department of [Health and] Social Security 1973-88: principal 1973-80, assistant secretary 1980-88, under secretary (US) 1988-90; US home transport and education group, HM Treasury 1990-

Date of birth: 20 September 1938 *Education/professional qualifications:* King Edward VII School, Johannesburg, South Africa; Witwatersrand University, SA, theoretical physics (BSc 1960); Clare College, Cambridge, theoretical physics (PhD 1963); FAPS 1972 *Marital status:* married Constance Baskett 1967; 2 daughters *Recreations:* opera, walking

Dr Michael Whippman, Under Secretary, HM Treasury, Parliament Street, London SW1P 3AG *Telephone:* 071-270 4509 *Fax:* 071-270 5653

To subscribe to The European Companion
Telephone: 071-240 3902

WHITE, IAN   Regional Controller North West, Inland Revenue   Grade: 4

Career: Inland Revenue 1953-: Scottish districts 1953-68; Liverpool 5 tax district (TD) 1970-72; district inspector (DI) Wigan TD 1970-72; officer in charge of advisory division, claims branch 1972-77; DI Liverpool 8 TD 1977-80; group controller NW districts 1980-83; controller claims branch 1983-88; regional controller north west 1988-

Date of birth: 4 June 1932 *Education/professional qualifications:* Cumnock Academy *Marital status:* married Sarah Thomson 1959; 1 daughter *Recreations:* golf, rugby, reading

Ian White Esq, Regional Controller North West, Inland Revenue, Bradshaws Lane, Ainsdale, Southport PR8 3LG *Telephone:* 051-922 4055 *Fax:* 051-922 2573

WHITE, KEVIN CHARLES GORDON   Director Training Systems, Employment Department Group   Grade: 4

Career: Department of Employment 1976-: director training systems division, training enterprise and education directorate 1990-

Date of birth: 20 July 1950 *Education/professional qualifications:* Haberdashers' Aske's School, Elstree; East Anglia University, English and history (BA 1972); Warwick University, English (MA 1974) *Marital status:* married Louise Sarah 1977; 3 sons *Recreations:* sport, theatre, cooking

Kevin C G White Esq, Director, Training Systems Division, Employment Department Group, Moorfoot, Sheffield S1 4PQ *Telephone:* 0742 593234 *Fax:* 0742 594769

WHITFIELD, ALAN   Road Programme Director, Department of Transport   Grade: 3

Career: National Coal Board 1956-62; Northumberland County Council 1962-70; Department of Transport (DTp) 1970-: main grade engineer 1970-73; principal professional 1973-76; superintending engineer 1976-80; assistant secretary, deputy director road construction unit 1980-83; West Midlands regional office 1983-89: director of transport 1983-89, regional director DTp and Department of Environment 1989; under secretary, road programme director (major road construction outside London) 1989-

Date of birth: 19 April 1939 *Education/professional qualifications:* Consett Grammar School; Sunderland and Newcastle Colleges of Advanced Technology *Marital status:* married Sheila Carr 1964; 2 sons *Clubs:* Royal Automobile *Recreations:* golf, music, bridge

Alan Whitfield Esq, Road Programme Director, Department of Transport, Friars House, Warwick Road, Coventry CV1 2TN *Telephone:* 0203 535102 *Fax:* 0203 535330

WHITING, ALAN   Under Secretary, Securities and Investment Services Group, HM Treasury   Grade: 3

Career: HM Treasury 1968-69; economic assistant Department of Economic Affairs/Ministry of Technology 1969-70; economist European Free Trade Association, Geneva 1970-72, Confederation of British Industry 1972-74; Department of Trade and Industry 1974-: economic adviser (EA) 1974-79, Senior EA 1979-83, assistant secretary 1983-85, under secretary 1985-: economics division 1985-89, economic management and education 1989, finance and resource management 1989-92, financial services 1992-

Date of birth: 14 January 1946 *Education/professional qualifications:* Acklam Hall Grammar School, Middlesborough; East Anglia University, social studies (BA 1967); University College, London, economics (MSc Econ 1969) *Marital status:* married Annette Frances Pocknee 1968; 2 daughters, 2 sons *Publications:* co-author The Trade Effects of EFTA and the EEC 1959-1967 (EFTA 1972); editor The Economics of Industrial Subsidies (HMSO 1976) *Clubs:* Littleton Sailing *Recreations:* building, sailing, sport, gardening, photography

Alan Whiting Esq, Under Secretary, Securities and Investment Services Group, HM Treasury, c/o Department of Trade and Industry, 10-18 Victoria Street, London SW1H 0NN *Telephone:* 071-215 5000 *Fax:* 071-222 9280

WHITMORE, Sir CLIVE ANTHONY   Permanent Under Secretary, Home Office   Grade: 1

Career: War Office/Ministry of Defence (MoD) 1959-77: assistant principal 1959-64, principal 1964-71, assistant secretary 1971-75, assistant under secretary 1975-79; under secretary Cabinet Office 1977-79; principal private secretary to Prime Minister 1979-82; permanent under secretary MoD 1983-88, Home Office 1988-

Date of birth: 18 January 1935 *Education/professional qualifications:* Sutton Grammar School, Surrey; Christ's College, Cambridge, modern languages (BA 1959) *Honours, decorations:* CVO 1983, KCB 1983, GCB 1988 *Marital status:* married Jennifer Mary Thorpe 1961; 2 daughters, 1 son *Recreations:* gardening, listening to music

Sir Clive Whitmore GCB CVO, Permanent Under Secretary, Home Office, 50 Queen Anne's Gate, London SW1H 9AT *Telephone:* 071-273 2199

WHYBREW, (EDWARD) TED GRAHAM   Director of Personnel, Employment Department Group   Grade: 3

Career: economic adviser National Economic Development Office and Department of Economic Affairs 1963-69; Department of Employment 1969-; senior economic adviser 1973-77; assistant secretary employment training and industrial relations 1977-85, under secretary industrial relations 1985-89, director of personnel 1989-

Date of birth: 25 September 1938 *Education/professional qualifications:* Hertford Grammar School; Balliol College, Oxford, philosophy, politics and economics (BA, MA 1961); Nuffield College, Oxford, industrial relations research *Marital status:* married Julia Helen Bairol 1967; 2 daughters, 1 son *Recreations:* riding, gardening, watching cricket

Ted G Whybrew Esq, Director of Personnel, Employment Department Group, Caxton House, Tothill Street, London SW1H 9NF *Telephone:* 071-273 5785 *Fax:* 071-273 5787

WIBLIN, DEREK JOHN   Principal Establishment and Finance Officer, Crown Prosecution Service   Grade: 3

Career: air force national service 1954-57; Courtaulds Ltd 1957-58; Department of Scientific and Industrial Research building research station 1958-67; Civil Service Commission 1967-71; Department of Environment (DoE) 1971-79; ports division Department of Transport 1979-83; establishment division DoE 1981-83; principal establishment and finance officer (PEFO) Lord Chancellor's Department 1984-88; PEFO Crown Prosecution Service 1988-

Date of birth: 18 March 1933 *Education/professional qualifications:* Bishopshalt School, Hillingdon; Birmingham University, chemistry (BSc

1954) *Marital status:* married Pamela Jeanne Hamshere 1960; 1 daughter, 1 son *Clubs:* Royal Air Force *Recreations:* making violins

Derek J Wiblin Esq, Principal Establishment and Finance Officer, Crown Prosecution Service, 4-12 Queen Anne's Gate, London SW1H 9AZ *Telephone:* 071-273 8114 *Fax:* 071-273 0802

WICKS, Sir NIGEL LEONARD   Second Permanent Secretary, Finance, HM Treasury   Grade: 1A

Career: principal private secretary to the Prime Minister 1985-88; second permanent secretary (finance) HM Treasury 1989-

Date of birth: 16 June 1940 *Education/professional qualifications:* University of Cambridge (MA); University of London (MA)

Sir Nigel L Wicks KCB CVO CBE, Second Permanent Secretary, HM Treasury, Parliament Street, London SW1P 3AG *Telephone:* 071-270 3000

WIGGLESWORTH, (WILLIAM) BILL ROBERT BRIAN   Acting Director-General of Telecommunications, Office of Telecommunications (OFTEL)   Grade: 3

Career: general management Ranks Hovis McDougall Ltd 1961-69; principal Board of Trade/Department of Trade and Industry 1970-74; Department of Prices and Consumer Protection 1974-78: principal 1974-75, assistant secretary (AS) 1975-78; AS Department of Industry 1978-84; deputy director-general (DG) of telecommunications Office of Telecommunications 1984- and acting DG 1992-

Date of birth: 8 August 1937 *Education/professional qualifications:* Marlborough College; Magdalen College, Oxford, history (BA 1961) *Marital status:* married Susan Mary Baker 1969; 1 daughter, 1 son *Recreations:* fishing, history, gardening

Bill R B Wigglesworth Esq, Acting Director-General of Telecommunications, Office of Telecommunications, Export House, 50 Ludgate Hill, London EC4M 7JJ *Telephone:* 071-822 1604 *Fax:* 071-822 1643

WILCOCK, CHRISTOPHER CAMPLIN   Head of Electricity, Energy Division, Department of Trade and Industry   Grade: 3

Career: HM Diplomatic Service 1962-72: Foreign and Commonwealth Office (FCO) 1962-63; Middle East Centre for Arab Studies 1963-64; 3rd secretary Khartoum 1964-66, FCO 1966-68, 2nd secretary UK delegation to NATO 1968-70; hospital building division Department of Health and Social Security 1972-74; Department of Energy 1974- (most of whose responsibilities were taken over by the Department of Trade and Industry in 1992): continental shelf policy division 1974-78, electricity division 1978-81, seconded to Shell UK 1982-83, head of finance branch 1983-86, director of resource management 1986-88, head of electricity division A 1988-91, head of electricity division (relations with privatised electricity industry; monitoring Nuclear Electric plc) 1991-

Date of birth: 13 September 1939 *Education/professional qualifications:* Berkhamsted School; Ipswich School; Trinity Hall, Cambridge, modern languages (BA Tripos parts I & II 1960), oriental languages (Tripos part I 1962) *Honours, decorations:* Order of the Two Niles, Fifth Class (Sudan) 1965 *Marital status:* married Evelyn Clare Gollin 1965; 2 daughters *Recreations:* reading, cinema, travel

Christopher C Wilcock, Head of Electricity, Energy Division, Department of Trade and Industry, 1 Palace Street, London SW1E 5HE *Telephone:* 071-238 3734 *Fax:* 071-630 9570

WILCOX, JUDITH (Lady Wilcox)   Chairman National Consumer Council

Career: financial director Capstan Foods 1970-78, Channel Foods Ltd 1980-88; president directeur général Pecheries de la Morinie, France 1988-90; chair National Consumer Council (independent body for domestic consumers of publicly and privately provided goods and services) 1990- *Current non-Whitehall posts:* director Automobile Association Ltd 1991-, Fanum Ltd 1991-, Morinie et Cie, France 1990-

Date of birth: 31 October 1940 *Education/professional qualifications:* St Mary's Convent, Wantage *Marital status:* widowed; 1 son *Clubs:* Reform *Recreations:* sailing, horseracing, 14th-century calligraphy

Lady Wilcox, Chairman, National Consumer Council, 20 Grosvenor Gardens, London SW1W 0DH *Telephone:* 071-730 3469 *Fax:* 071-730 0191

WILKES, Lieutenant General Sir MICHAEL (JOHN)   Special Adviser to Secretary of State for Defence

Career: army 1960-: commander UK field army and inspector general territorial army 1990-92; special adviser to Malcolm Rifkind secretary of state for defence (Middle East and implications of the Gulf campaign) 1992-

Date of birth: 11 June 1940 *Education/professional qualifications:* RMA Sandhurst

Lt Gen Sir Michael Wilkes, Special Adviser, Ministry of Defence, Main Building, Whitehall, London SW1A 2HB *Telephone:* 071-218 9000

WILKINSON, DAVID ANTHONY   Office of Science and Technology, Office Public Service and Science, Cabinet Office   Grade: 3

Career: Department of Education and Science 1974-92: non-university higher education policy 1979-81; north-west England schools territorial officer 1981-83; school teachers' pay and conditions negotiations 1984-86; head of information branch, chief press officer to secretary of state, Kenneth Baker 1986-88. deputy principal establishment officer 1988-89; head of science branch (civil scientific research funding and management) 1989-92; Office of Science and Technology, Office of Public Service and Science, Cabinet Office 1992-

Date of birth: 27 November 1947 *Education/professional qualifications:* Boteler Grammar School, Warrington; Wigan and District Mining and Technical College; Bedford College, London University, history (BA 1970); London School of Economics and Moscow State University, Russian economic history *Marital status:* married Meryl Pugh 1973; 3 daughters

Clubs: Wimbledon Squash and Badminton

David A Wilkinson Esq, Office of Science and Technology, Office of Public Service and Science, Cabinet Office, 70 Whitehall, London SW1A 2AS *Telephone:* 071-270 3000

WILLIAMS, JENNY   Director, Privatisation and Strategy Directorate, PSA Services, Department of the Environment   Grade: 3

Career: director privatisation and strategy directorate PSA Services, Department of Environment 1990-

Date of birth: 26 September 1948 *Marital status:* married; 3 sons

Mrs Jenny Williams, Director, Privatisation and Strategy Directorate, PSA Services, Department of the Environment, 2 Marsham Street, London SW1P 3EB *Telephone:* 071-276 3476 *Fax:* 071-276 4548

WILLIAMS, ROY   Deputy Secretary, Regional and Small Firms Division, Department of Trade and Industry   Grade: 2

Career: principal private secretary (PPS) to Minister of Power/Industry 1969-70; Department of [Trade and] Industry 1971-: assistant secretary 1971-74, PPS to secretary of state 1974-76, under secretary 1976-84, deputy secretary regional policy, enterprise, small firms 1984-

Date of birth: 31 December 1934 *Education/professional qualifications:* Evered Avenue School, Liverpool; Liverpool University, economics (BA 1956); Harkness scholarship Chicago and Berkeley Universities, USA 1963-64 *Marital status:* married Shirley Warwick 1959; 1 daughter, 1 son

Roy Williams Esq, CB, Deputy Secretary, Regional and Small Firms Division, Department of Trade and Industry, 66-74 Victoria Street, London SW1E 6SW *Telephone:* 071-215 8358 *Fax:* 071-215 8545

WILLIS, Air Vice-Marshal JOHN FREDERICK   Director-General of Training (RAF), Ministry of Defence

Career: RAF pilot 1958-77; policy division air force department Ministry of Defence (MoD) 1977-82; officer commanding RAF Akrotiri, Cyprus 1982-84; chief of air staff's staff MoD 1984-85; Supreme Headquarters Allied Powers Europe, Belgium 1985-89; MoD 1989-: assistant chief of defence staff (policy and nuclear) 1989-91; director-general of RAF training 1991-

Date of birth: 27 October 1937 *Education/professional qualifications:* Dulwich College; RAF College, Cranwell *Honours, decorations:* CBE 1988, CB 1991 *Recreations:* walking, model making

Air Vice-Marshal John F Willis CB CBE, Director-General of Training (RAF), Ministry of Defence, Adastral House, Theobalds Road, London WC1X 8RU *Telephone:* 071-430 7290

WILLOTT, (WILLIAM) BRIAN   Chief Executive, Export Credits Guarantee Department   Grade: 2

Career: research associate Maryland University, USA 1965-67; Board of Trade 1967-73: assistant principal 1967-69, principal, shipping policy division 1969-73; Department of [Trade and] Industry 1975-92: assistant secretary 1975-80: industrial and commercial policy 1975-78, industrial development unit 1978-80; under secretary 1980-92: seconded to National Enterprise Board/British Technology Board 1980-84: secretary 1980, chief executive 1981-84, information technology 1984-87, financial services 1987-92; chief executive Export Credits Guarantee Department 1992-

Date of birth: 14 May 1940 *Education/professional qualifications:* Solihull School; Queen Elizabeth Grammar School, Wakefield; Trinity College, Cambridge, natural sciences (BA 1961, MA), physics (PhD 1965) *Marital status:* married Alison Leyland Pyke-Lees 1970; 2 daughters, 2 sons *Recreations:* reading, music, walking, cycling, gardening

W Brian Willot Esq, Chief Executive, Export Credits Guarantee Department, 2 Exchange Tower, Harbour Exchange Square, London E14 9GS *Telephone:* 071-512 7004 *Fax:* 071-512 7146

WILLOUGHBY, ROGER JAMES   Clerk of Private Bills, House of Commons   Grade: 3

Career: Department of the Clerk, House of Commons 1962-: clerk of private bills (conduct of private business in committee and the chamber; examiner of petitions for private bills) 1988-

Date of birth: 30 September 1939 *Education/professional qualifications:* Shrewsbury School; Balliol College, Oxford (BA 1962) *Marital status:* married Veronica Lepper 1970 *Recreations:* literature, cricket, walking

Roger J Willoughby Esq, Clerk of Private Bills, House of Commons, London SW1A 0AA *Telephone:* 071-219 3269

WILSON, ALEC   Deputy Registrar, Registry of Friendly Societies   Grade: 4

Career: national service 1950-52; colonial police, Uganda 1955-63; law student 1963-68; solicitor 1968-71; legal assistant Registry of Friendly Societies (RFS) 1971-75; acting principal Department of Prices and Consumer Protection 1976-79; RFS 1979-: senior legal assistant 1979-80, deputy registrar (registration and supervision of friendly societies and credit unions) 1980-; on attachment to HM Treasury bill team preparing new friendly society legislation 1989-91

Date of birth: 25 September 1932 *Education/professional qualifications:* Mill Hill School, London; London College of Law (solicitor 1968) *Marital status:* married Judith Cook 1962; 1 daughter, 1 son *Publications:* Encyclopedia of Forms and Precedents, 5th ed (Butterworths): Friendly Societies 1989, Industrial Assurance; Industrial and Provident Societies 1990; contributor to Halsbury's Laws of England (Butterworths 1991) *Clubs:* Law Society *Recreations:* music, fell-walking

Alec Wilson Esq, Deputy Registrar, Registry of Friendly Societies, 15 Great Marlborough Street, London W1V 2AX *Telephone:* 071-494 6681 *Fax:* 071-287 6102

WILSON, AUSTIN PETER   Head of Criminal Policy Department, Home Office   Grade: 3

Career: Home Office 1961-: seconded to Northern Ireland Office (NIO) 1977-80; assistant under secretary 1981-; NIO 1988-92; head of criminal policy department 1992-

Date of birth: 31 March 1938 *Education/professional qualifications:* St Edmund Hall, Oxford (BA)

Austin P Wilson Esq, Head of Criminal Policy Department, Home Office, 50 Queen Anne's Gate, London SW1A 9AT *Telephone:* 071-273 3000

WILSON, Vice-Admiral Sir BARRY (NIGEL)   Deputy Chief of Defence Staff, Programmes and Personnel, Ministry of Defence

Career: Royal Navy 1973-; deputy chief of defence staff, programmes and personnel Ministry of Defence 1989-

Date of birth: 5 June 1936 *Education/professional qualifications:* Britannia Royal Naval College

Vice-Admiral Sir Barry N Wilson KCB, Deputy Chief of Defence Staff (Programmes and Personnel), Ministry of Defence, Old Admiralty Building, Whitehall, London SW1 *Telephone:* 071-218 9000

WILSON, CLIVE HEBDEN   Under Secretary, Priority Health Services Division, Department of Health   Grade: 3

Career: Department of Health (DoH) 1962-77; Cabinet Office 1977-79; DoH 1979-: under secretary Priority Health Services Division 1990-

Date of birth: 1 February 1940 *Education/professional qualifications:* Corpus Christi College, Oxford

Clive H Wilson Esq, Under Secretary, Department of Health, Richmond House, 79 Whitehall, SW1A 2NS *Telephone:* 071-210 3000

WILSON, GERALD ROBERTSON   Secretary, Central Services, Scottish Office   Grade: 2

Career: Scottish Office (SO) 1961-72: assistant principal 1961-66 and principal Home and Health Department 1966-72; private secretary to Lord Privy Seal 1972-74; assistant secretary (AS) SO 1974-77; counsellor UK Permanent Representation to the EC, Brussels 1977-82; SO 1982-: AS 1982-84, under secretary Industry Department 1984-88, deputy secretary (DS) and secretary of Education Department 1988-, DS Central Services Department 1991-

Date of birth: 7 September 1939 *Education/professional qualifications:* Holy Cross Academy, Edinburgh; Edinburgh University, history (MA 1961) *Honours, decorations:* CB 1991 *Marital status:* married Margaret 1963; 1 daughter, 1 son *Clubs:* New, Edinburgh; Royal Commonwealth Trust *Recreations:* music

Gerald R Wilson Esq CB, Secretary, Central Services, Scottish Office, New St Andrew's House, Edinburgh EH1 3SY *Telephone:* 031-244 4409

WILSON, I P   Director, CCTA Government Centre for Information Systems, HM Treasury   Grade: 3

Date of birth: 24 August 1941

I P Wilson Esq, Director, CCTA, HM Treasury, Riverwalk House, 157-161 Millbank, London SW1P 4RT *Telephone:* 071-217 3000

WILSON, (JAMES) BRIAN   Chief Planning Adviser, Department of the Environment   Grade: 4

Career: architect/planner various private practices 1966-70, Edinburgh town planning department 1970-71, Richmond London borough 1971-73; private practice project director 1973-75; Department of Environment 1975-: principal planning officer (PO) historic areas and conservation 1975-78; superintending PO south-east region 1978-82; Yorkshire and Humberside regional controller 1982-88; chief planning adviser 1988-

Date of birth: 19 May 1940 *Education/professional qualifications:* Daniel Stewart's College, Edinburgh; Heriot Watt University, architecture (DA 1965), town planning (Dip TP 1967) *Marital status:* married Irenee Elizabeth 1972; 2 sons *Recreations:* history, francophilia, old buildings

J Brian Wilson Esq, Chief Planning Adviser, Department of the Environment, 2 Marsham Street, London SW1P 3EB *Telephone:* 071-276 3939

WILSON, RICHARD THOMAS JAMES   **Permanent Secretary, Department of the Environment**   Grade: 1

Career: Department of Energy 1974-86; deputy secretary 1987-92, Cabinet Office 1986-90, HM Treasury 1990-92; permanent secretary Department of the Environment 1992-

Date of birth: 11 October 1942 *Education/professional qualifications:* Clare College, Cambridge (BA, 1964, law, 1965); Middle Temple (barrister 1965)

Richard T J Wilson CB, Permanent Secretary, Department of the Environment, 2 Marsham Street, London SW1P 3EB *Telephone:* 071-276 3000

WILSON, ROBERT WILLIAM GORDON   **Principal Clerk of Financial Committees, House of Commons**   Grade: 4

Career: House of Commons Department of the Clerk 1967-: senior clerk 1972-81: secretary to UK delegation to parliamentary assemblies of Council of Europe, Western European Union and North Atlantic Assembly 1974-77, deputy principal clerk 1981-91: clerk of European legislation 1981-86, environment 1986-87 and foreign affairs 1987-91 committees; principal clerk of financial committees (clerk of treasury and civil service committee; secretary to and supervisor staff of public accounts committee) 1991-

Date of birth: 8 July 1946 *Education/professional qualifications:* Lancing College; Christ Church, Oxford, modern history (BA, MA 1967) *Clubs:* Travellers *Recreations:* theatre, opera, travel, architectural conservation

Robert W G Wilson Esq, Principal Clerk, Committee Office, House of Commons, London SW1A 0AA *Telephone:* 071-219 3285

WINNIFRITH, CHARLES BONIFACE   **Principal Clerk, Table Office, House of Commons**   Grade: 3

Career: army national service 1958-60; Department of Clerk of House of Commons 1960-: assistant clerk 1960-64; senior clerk 1964-72; deputy principal clerk 1972-83; select committees 1983-89: second clerk 1983-87, clerk 1987-89; principal clerk Table Office (advice to speaker and MPs on parliamentary questions and early day motions; preparation of order paper, notice paper and order book) 1989-

Date of birth: 12 May 1936 *Education/professional qualifications:* Tonbridge School; Christ Church, Oxford, literae humaniores (BA, MA 1961) *Marital status:* married Josephine Poile 'MBE" 1962 (deceased); 1 son, 2 daughters *Clubs:* MCC *Recreations:* cricket, American soap opera

Charles B Winnifrith Esq, Principal Clerk, Table Office, House of Commons, London SW1A 0AA *Telephone:* 071-219 3312

WISEMAN, ALFRED R   Deputy Ranger, Windsor Estate, The Crown Estate   Grade: 4

Alfred R Wiseman Esq, Deputy Ranger, Windsor Estate, The Crown Estate Office, The Great Park, Windsor, Berks SL4 2HT   *Telephone:* 07538-60222

WOOD, PHILIP   Under Secretary and Head of Railways 2 Directorate, Department of Transport   Grade: 3

Career: Department of Transport 1979-: under secretary and head of railways 2 directorate 1986-

Date of birth: 30 June 1946   *Education/professional qualifications:* Queen's College, Oxford

Philip Wood Esq OBE, Under Secretary and Head of Railways 2 Directorate, Department of Transport, 2 Marsham Street, London SW1P 3EB   *Telephone:* 071-276 3000

WOOD, Major-General ROY   Director-General, Military Survey, Ministry of Defence; Chief Executive, Military Survey, (Executive Agency)

Career: troop commander army mapping surveys, Sarawak 1965-66; leader Overseas Development Administration mapping surveys, Sierra Leone and Sabah 1967-70; senior instructor School of Military Survey 1972-75; staff officer (SO) Ministry of Defence (MoD) 1975-77; squadron commander, Germany 1977-79; commander production group, UK 1979-81; head defence mapping liaison, USA 1981-83; SO MoD 1984; commander Survey Group, UK 1985-87; MoD 1987-: director military survey operations 1987-89, director military survey plans 1989-90, director-general military survey and chief executive Military Survey Defence Support Agency 1990-   *Current non-Whitehall posts:* vice-president Photogrammetric Society 1987-; member Nottingham University Institute of Space Geodesy and Engineering Surveying advisory board 1991-

Date of birth: 14 May 1940   *Education/professional qualifications:* Farnham Grammar School; Welbeck College; Royal Military Academy, Sandhurst (commission 1960); Fitzwilliam College, Cambridge, mechanical sciences (BA 1963, MA); University College, London, photogrammetry (MSc 1971); FRICS; FBIM

Major-General Roy Wood, Director-General, Military Survey, Elmwood Avenue, Feltham, Middlesex TW13 7AH   *Telephone:* 081-890 3622

WOOD, Dr SUSAN MARION   Head of Pharmacovigilance Unit, Medicines Control Agency   Grade: 4

Career: medical posts St Bartholomew's Hospital 1979-80; research and clinical posts Hammersmith Hospital and Royal Postgraduate Medical School 1980-83; medicines division Department of Health 1983-90: senior medical officer 1983-84, head of review of medicines, principal medical officer 1988; head of adverse drug reactions unit 1988-90; head of pharmacovigilance unit Medicines Control Agency (post-marketing surveillance of medicines) 1990-

Date of birth: 20 July 1952   *Education/professional qualifications:* Tormead School; County School for Girls; King's College, London, pharmacology (BSc 1973); St Bartholomew's Hospital Medical School (MB, BS 1977); Royal Postgraduate Medical School, London (MD 1985)   *Marital status:* married John 1978   *Recreations:* walking, gardening, oriental cuisine, travel, primitive tribal cultures

Dr Susan M Wood, Head of Pharmacovigilance Unit, Medicines Control Agency, Market Towers, 1 Nine Elms Lane, London SW8 5NQ   *Telephone:* 071-720 2188   *Fax:* 071-498 1954

WOODCOCK, Sir JOHN   HM Chief Inspector of Constabulary, Home Office

Career: Lancashire Constabulary (LC) 1947-50; army national service 1950-52; constable-chief inspector LC 1952-67; superintendent/chief superintendent Bedfordshire and Luton Constabulary 1967-68; assistant chief constable (CC)- deputy CC Gwent Constabulary 1968-74; deputy CC Devon and Cornwall Constabulary 1977-78; CC North Yorkshire Police 1978-79, South Wales Constabulary 1979-83; HM Inspector of Constabulary Wales and Midlands 1983-89; HM Chief Inspector of Constabulary 1989-

Date of birth: 14 January 1932 *Honours, decorations:* Queen's Police Medal 1976; CBE 1983, KSG 1984, Kt 1989 *Marital status:* married Kathleen Margaret 1953; 2 sons, 1 daughter *Recreations:* golf, walking

Sir John Woodcock CBE QPM, HM Chief Inspector of Constabulary, Home Office, Queen Anne's Gate, London SW1H 9AT
Telephone: 071-273 3084 *Fax:* 071-273 4031

WOODMAN, Dr CHRISTOPHER MERVYN   Chief Executive, Driving Standards Agency (Executive Agency)   Grade: 5

Career: research fellow National Research Council, Canada 1967-69; Ministry of Defence 1970-75; Department of Industry 1976-79; Department of Trade 1979-83; Department of Transport 1984-: head of international transport 1984-85, of Channel fixed link 1985-87, of driver testing and training 1988-90; chief executive Driving Standards Agency (driving test administration) 1990-

Date of birth: 12 April 1944 *Education/professional qualifications:* Birkenhead School; Jesus College, Cambridge, natural sciences (BA 1964); East Anglia University, spectroscopy (1967) *Marital status:* married Mary Elizabeth Fairhead; 1 daughter, 1 son

Dr Christopher M Woodman, Chief Executive, Driving Standards Agency, Stanley House, 56 Talbot Street, Nottingham NG5 1GU
Telephone: 0602 485631 *Fax:* 0602 485734

WOODS, (ELISABETH) LIS ANN   Director VAT Control, HM Customs and Excise
Grade: 3

Career: assistant principal Ministry of Pensions and National Insurance and successors 1963-69; principal Department of [Health and] Social Security (D[H]SS) 1970-80: principal 1970-76, assistant secretary (AS) 1976-80; AS HM Treasury 1980-82; AS DHSS 1976-88; under secretary, head of finance DSS 1988-91; director VAT control HM Customs and Excise 1991-

Date of birth: 27 October 1940 *Education/professional qualifications:* South Hampstead High School for Girls, London; Girton College, Cambridge, modern languages (BA 1963) *Marital status:* married James Maurice 1976 *Recreations:* cycling, cooking, reading

Mrs Lis A Woods, Director VAT Control, HM Customs and Excise, Wilberforce House, 25 The Strand, Liverpool L2 7QA *Telephone:* 051-707 1234

Parliamentary Offices
see page 275

WOOL, Dr ROSEMARY JANE   Director of Health Care, Prison Service, Home Office   Grade: 3

Career: doctor in general practice 1963-74; Home Office Prison Service 1974-: medical officer (MO), senior MO, principal MO prison medicine service 1974-89; director prison medical services 1989- the title of which changed to director health care 1992-

Date of birth: 19 July 1935   *Education/professional qualifications:* High School, March, Cambridgeshire; Charing Cross Hospital, London (MB BS 1960, D Obst RCOG 1965, DPM 1972, MRC Psych 1974, FRC Psych 1988) *Recreations:* walking, piano playing, music

Dr Rosemary J Wool, Director of Health Care, HM Prison Service, Cleland House, Page Street, London SW1P 4LN   *Telephone:* 071-217 6419 *Fax:* 071-217 6635

WOOLER, STEPHEN JOHN   Assistant Legal Secretary to the Law Officers   Grade: 4

Career: private practice barrister 1969-73; Director of Public Prosecutions (DPP) Office 1973-87: legal assistant (LA) 1973-76, senior LA 1976-82, assistant DPP 1982-83, seconded as legal adviser to law officers 1983-87; chief crown prosecutor London north 1987-89; assistant legal secretary to law officers 1989-

Date of birth: 16 March 1948   *Education/professional qualifications:* Bedford Modern School; University College, London, law (LLB 1969); Gray's Inn (barrister 1969)   *Marital status:* married Jonquil Elizabeth 1974; 1 son, 1 daughter   *Recreations:* rugby, walking, gardening, reading

Stephen J Wooler Esq, Assistant Legal Secretary to the Law Officers, Attorney General's Chambers, 9 Buckingham Gate, London SW1E 6JP *Telephone:* 071-828 1721

WOOLMAN, ROGER   Under Secretary, Solicitor's Office, Department of Trade and Industry   Grade: 3

Career: legal assistant (LA) Office of Fair Trading (OFT) 1976-78; Department of Trade and Industry (DTI) 1978-88: Senior LA 1978-81; assistant solicitor 1981-84, under secretary (US) 1985-88; legal director OFT 1988-91; US DTI Solicitor's Office division B (legal advice on company law, financial services, insurance, insolvency) 1988-

Date of birth: 13 February 1937   *Education/professional qualifications:* Perse School, Cambridge; Trinity Hall, Cambridge, law (BA 1960, MA)   *Marital status:* married Elizabeth Ingham 1973; 1 daughter, 1 son   *Clubs:* Reform, Hampstead Golf

Roger Woolman Esq, Under Secretary, Department of Trade and Industry, 10-18 Victoria Street, London SW1E 6RB   *Telephone:* 071-215 3500

Government Departments
see page 300

WOOTTON, HAROLD JOHN   Chief Executive, Transport and
Road Research Laboratory (Executive Agency)   Grade: 3

Career: civil engineering lecturer Leeds University 1959-62; technical
director Freeman, Fox, Wilbur Smith and Associates 1963-67; director SIA
Ltd 1967-71; chairman Wootton Jeffreys Consultants Ltd 1971-91; chief
executive Transport and Road Research Laboratory Department of
Transport 1991-

Date of birth: 17 November 1936 Education/professional qualifications:
Queen Mary's Grammar School, Walsall; Queen Mary College, London,
civil engineering (BSc Eng 1958); California University, Berkeley, USA,
transport engineering (MEng 1963) Marital status: married Patricia Ann
1960; 2 sons Recreations: cricket, golf, rotary, photography

Harold J Wootton Esq, Chief Executive, Transport and Road Research
Laboratory, Crowthorne, Berkshire RG11 6AU Telephone: 0344 770001
Fax: 0344 770761

WORMALD, PETER JOHN   Director and Registrar General for
England and Wales, Office of Population Censuses and
Surveys   Grade: 2

Career: Ministry of Health (MoH) 1958-65: assistant principal 1958-63,
principal 1963-65; principal: HM Treasury 1965-67, MoH 1967-70;
Department of Health and Social Security 1970-87: assistant secretary
1970-78, under secretary 1978-87; director of personnel NHS management
board/executive 1987-90; director and registrar general for England and
Wales Office of Population Censuses and Surveys 1990-

Date of birth: 10 March 1936 Education/professional qualifications: Doncaster
Grammar School; Queen's College, Oxford, jurisprudence (BA 1958, MA)
Honours, decorations: CB 1990 Marital status: married Elizabeth North
1962; 3 sons Clubs: United Oxford and Cambridge University, Home Park
Golf Recreations: music, golf, bridge

Peter J Wormald Esq CB, Director and Registrar General for England and
Wales, Office of Population Censuses and Surveys, St Catherine's House,
10 Kingsway, London WC2B 6JP Telephone: 071-242 0262
Fax: 071-242 0262

WORSWICK, Dr RICHARD DAVID   Chief Executive and
Government Chemist, Laboratory of the Government Chemist
(Executive Agency)   Grade: 3

Career: Science Research Council research assistant department of inorganic
chemistry, Oxford 1972-73; research product manager Boots Company plc
1973-76; Harwell Laboratory, United Kingdom Atomic Energy Authority
1976-90: marketing and planning 1976-85, head of research planning
1985-88, of environmental and medical sciences division 1988-90; director
process technology and instrumentation division Atomic Energy
Authority industrial technology 1990-91; chief executive and government
chemist Laboratory of Government Chemist 1991-

Date of birth: 22 July 1946 Education/professional qualifications: Magdalen
College School, Oxford; New College, Oxford, chemistry (BA 1969);
Department of Inorganic Chemistry, Oxford (DPhil 1972); FRIC 1991

Marital status: married Jacqueline 1970; 3 daughters *Recreations:* violin playing

Dr Richard D Worswick, Chief Executive and Government Chemist, Laboratory of the Government Chemist, Queen's Road, Teddington, Middlesex TW11 0LY *Telephone:* 081-943 7300

WRIGHT, ERIC   Regional Director, Yorkshire and Humberside, Department of Trade and Industry   Grade: 3

Career: assistant principal/principal Ministry of Fuel and Power 1957-65; principal Civil Service Commission 1965-67; assistant secretary Ministry of Technology 1968-70; Sloan fellow London Business School 1970-71; Department of Trade [and Industry] (DTI) 1971-: principal private secretary to secretary of state 1971-72, assistant secretary (AS) 1972-77; D[T]I 1977-: AS 1977-79, under secretary 1983-: regional director Yorkshire and Humberside 1985-

Date of birth: 17 November 1933 *Education/professional qualifications:* Woolstanton County Grammar School, Newcastle-under-Lyme; Keble College, Oxford, history (BA 1955) *Marital status:* married Pauline 1955; 3 sons *Recreations:* music, tennis

Eric Wright Esq, Regional Director, Department of Trade and Industry, 25 Queen Street, Leeds LS1 2TW *Telephone:* 0532 338200

WROE, DAVID CHARLES LYNN   Director of National Accounts and Deputy Director, Central Statistical Office

Career: Department of the Environment 1982-91: under secretary (US) regional policy 1982-86, director of statistics 1982-91, US housing monitoring and analysis 1986-91; director of national accounts and deputy director Central Statistical Office 1991-

Date of birth: 20 February 1942 *Education/professional qualifications:* Trinity College, Cambridge (BA, MA); Trinity College, Oxford, statistics; Birkbeck College, London (MSc)

David C L Wroe Esq, Deputy Director, Central Statistical Office, Great George Street, London SW1P 3AQ *Telephone:* 071-270 3000

WYLIE, ROBERT D S   Principal Assistant Solicitor, HM Customs and Excise   Grade: 3

Robert D S Wylie Esq, Principal Assistant Solicitor, HM Customs and Excise, New King's Beam House, 22 Upper Ground, London SE1 9PJ *Telephone:* 071-620 1313

Y

YARDLEY, Dr DAVID CHARLES MILLER   Chairman, Commission for Local Administration in England (Local Government Ombudsman)   Grade: 1

Career: jurisprudence fellow and tutor St Edmund Hall, university law lecturer, Oxford 1953-74; law professor Birmingham University 1974-78; head of law, politics and economics department Oxford Polytechnic 1978-80; Rank Foundation law professor, dean of law school Buckingham University 1980-82; chairman, Commission for Local Administration in England 1982-   *Current non-Whitehall posts:* chairman Oxford Preservation Trust 1989-

Date of birth: 4 June 1929   *Education/professional qualifications:* Old Hall School, Wellington; Ellesmere College, Shropshire; Birmingham University, law (LLB 1949, LLD 1983); Lincoln College, Oxford, law (DPhil 1953); St Edmund Hall, Oxford, law (MA 1954); Gray's Inn (barrister 1952)   *Marital status:* married Patricia Anne Tempest Olver 1954; 2 daughters, 2 sons   *Publications:* several, including Introduction to British Constitutional Law (Butterworths 1960, 7th edition 1990); Principles of Administrative Law (Butterworths 1981, 2nd edition 1986); The Protection of Liberty (Blackwells 1982); Introduction to English Law (OUP, 10th edition 1991)   *Clubs:* Royal Air Force   *Recreations:* tennis, squash, opera, cats

Dr David C M Yardley, Chairman, Commission for Local Administration in England, 21 Queen Anne's Gate, London SW1H 9BU
Telephone: 071-222 5622 *Fax:* 071-233 0396

YEO, DIANE HELEN   Commissioner, Charity Commission   Grade: 4

Career: production BBC radio 1968-74; clearing house director Africa Educational Trust 1974-79; head of fundraising Girl Guides Association 1979-82; director of fundraising and public relations Young Women's Christian Association 1982-85; director Institute of Charity Fundraising Managers 1985-88; Charity Commissioner 1989-   *Current non-Whitehall posts:* consultant London School of Economics Centre for Voluntary Organisation 1988-; director Charity Appointments 1985-

Date of birth: 22 July 1945   *Education/professional qualifications:* Blackheath High School, London; Birkbeck College, London University, psychology (BSc 1970)   *Marital status:* married Timothy Stephen Kenneth 1970; 1 daughter, 1 son   *Recreations:* photography, tennis, swimming

Mrs Diane H Yeo, Commissioner, Charity Commission, St Albans House, 57-60 Haymarket, London SW1Y 4QX   *Telephone:* 071-210 3000

YOUNG, ALAN   Special Adviser to the Secretary of State for Scotland

Career: special adviser to secretary of state for Scotland 1990-

Alan Young Esq, Special Adviser, Scottish Office, St Andrew's House, Edinburgh EH1 3DE
Telephone: 031-556 8400

YOUNG, Dr ANDREW BUCHANAN   Deputy Chief Medical Officer, Home and Health Department, Scottish Office   Grade: 3

Career: Home and Health Department Scottish Office 1975-: principal medical officer 1985-89; deputy chief medical officer 1989-

Date of birth: 11 August 1937   *Education/professional qualifications:* Edinburgh University (MB, ChB)

Dr Andrew B Young Esq, Deputy Chief Medical Officer, Scottish Office Home and Health Department, St Andrew's House, Edinburgh EH1 3DE   *Telephone:* 031-244 2292

THE
EUROPEAN
COMPANION
1992

The authoritative and comprehensive guide to Europe. The European Companion contains over 1500 biographical entries with photographs of all the politicians and officials who work at senior level in the Community and also details the structure of all the Community's institutions and how legislation is passed. 800 pages.

Published by
Dod's Publishing and Research Ltd
60 Chandos Place, London, WC2N 4HG

Telephone *Editorial:* 071-240 3902   *Subscriptions:* 081-863 5995

Institutions

Parliamentary Offices

House of Commons   HC
House of Lords   HL
National Audit Office   NAO
Northern Ireland Audit Office   NIAO

Government Departments

Agriculture, Fisheries and Food   MAFF
Cabinet Office/Office of Public Service and Science   CO/OPSS
Crown Estate   CEst
Crown Office (Scotland)   CrO(S)
Crown Prosecution Service   CPS
Crown Solicitor's Office (NI)   CSolO(NI)
Her Majesty's Customs and Excise   C&E
Defence   MoD
Director of Public Prosecutions for Northern Ireland   DPP(NI)
Education   DfE
Employment Department Group   EDG
Environment   DoE
Export Credits Guarantee Department   ECGD
Foreign and Commonwealth Office   FCO
Forestry Commission   FC
Government Actuary's Department   GAD
Health   DoH
Home Office   HO
Inland Revenue   IR
Law Officers' Department   LOD
Lord Advocate's Department   LAD
Lord Chancellor's Department   LCD
National Heritage   DNH
National Savings   DNS
Northern Ireland Court Service   NICS
Northern Ireland Office   NIO
Northern Ireland Departments   NID
Office of Population, Censuses and Surveys   OPCS
Office of Public Service and Science *see* Cabinet Office
Overseas Development Administration   ODA
Parliamentary Counsel   PC
Prime Minister's Office   PMO
Privy Council Office   PCO
PSA Services   PSA

Registry of Friendly Societies   RFS
Scottish Courts Administration   SCA
Scottish Office   SO
Serious Fraud Office   SFO
Social Security   DSS
Trade and Industry   DTI
Transport   DTp
HM Treasury   HMT
Treasury Solicitor's Department   TSD
Welsh Office   WO

House of Commons

Organisation The House of Commons Service is the
permanent service of the House although its
staff are not civil servants of the Crown. The
work of this permanent staff revolves around
the activity of the House of Commons and its
committees.

Responsibilities chamber
committees
Hansard
library
private bills
public bills (Government and private
    members)
public information
research

House of Commons

Westminster, London SW1A 0AA
Tel 071-219 3000
*All staff are based at the House of Commons unless otherwise indicated.
For other addresses and telephone numbers see the end of this section.*

Principal Officers and Officials

Speaker's Office

The Speaker
The Rt Hon Betty Boothroyd MP

|

Speaker's Secretary
Sir Peter Kitcatt CB (5)
071-219 4111

|

Speaker's Counsel
H Knorpel CB QC (3)
G E Gammie CB QC (3)

|

Speaker's Chaplain
The Rev Canon Donald Gray TD

*Office of the Chairman of Ways
and Means*

Chairman of Ways and Means
The Rt Hon Michael Morris MP

|

*First Deputy Chairman of Ways and
Means*
Geoffrey Lofthouse MP

|

|

*Second Deputy Chairman of Ways
and Means*
Dame Janet Fookes MP

|

Chairman's Secretary
Ms P Helme (7)
071-219 3771

House of Commons Commission

Members of the Commission
The Rt Hon Betty Boothroyd MP (Chairman)
Alan Beith MP
Jack Cunningham MP
The Rt Hon Antony Newton MP
Rt Hon Peter Shore MP

|

Secretary
R W G Wilson (4)
071-219 3270

Overview

Principal Officers and Officials				Department
Grade 1	*Grade 2*	*Grade 3*	*Grade 4*	

Clerk of the House

Sir Clifford Boulton	D W Limon	W R McKay	Dr M R Jack	Public Bill Office
		A J Hastings		Journal Office
		C B Winnifrith		Table Office
		G Cubie		Overseas Office
		R J Willoughby		Private Bill Office
	J F Sweetman	B Sands		Committee Office
		D G Millar		
			R W G Wilson	
			W A Proctor	

Serjeant at Arms

		Sir Alan Urwick		Serjeant at Arms

Library

		D J T Englefield	Miss J B Tanfield	Library

Official Report

			I D Church (5)	Official Report

Refreshment

			Mrs S Harrison (5)	Refreshment

Finance and Administration

		J Rodda		Finance and Administration

Principal Officers and Officials

Department of the Clerk of the House
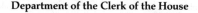

Clerk of the House of Commons
Sir Clifford Boulton KCB (1)

|

Secretary to the Clerk of the House
Mrs G Sclater
071-219 3758

|

Clerk Assistant
D W Limon (2)
071-219 3311

|

Clerk of Public Bills	*Clerk of the Journals*	*Principal Clerk*
W R McKay (3)	**A J Hastings (3)**	**C B Winnifrith (3)**
071-219 3255	071-219 3315	071-219 3312

|

Clerk of Standing Committees
Dr M R Jack (4)
071-219 3257

Public Bill Office

Government and private members'
  bills
Public legislation
Standing committees on:
  bills, statutory instruments,
  European Community
  documents, Scottish and Welsh
  Grand Committees

Journal Office

Minutes of the House
Procedural records and indices
Procedure and privilege

Table Office

Preparation of Order and Notice
  Papers (including Questions and
  Motions)

Clerk of the Overseas	*Clerk of Private Bills*
Office	*Taxing Officer and Examiner*
	of Petitions for Private Bills
G Cubie (3)	**R J Willoughby (3)**
071-219 3314	071-219 3269

| | |

Overseas Office

Commonwealth and foreign
   parliament contact
Information on rules and practice of
   Westminster Parliament

Private Bill Office

Bills promoted by outside
   individuals and bodies
Select Committees on private bills

Clerk of Committees
J F Sweetman CB TD (2)
071-219 3313

*Clerk of Select
Committees,
Registrar of Members'
Interests*
R B Sands (3)
071-219 3277

*Second Clerk of Select
Committees*

D G Millar (3)
071-219 6257

Committee Office

Provides clerks and support staff
   for Select Committees
   (see below)

*Clerk of Financial
Committees*
W A Proctor (4)
071-219 3285
(see Treasury and Public
Accounts Committees below)

*Clerk of Domestic
Committees*
R W G Wilson (4)
071-219 3270
(see below)

Clerks of Select Committees (Departmentally-related)

Agriculture	*Defence*	*Education*
D W Robson	**D L Natzler**	**A Sandall**
071-219 3263	071-219 3280	071-219 6243

Employment	*Environment*	*Foreign Affairs*
R I S Phillips	**S J Priestley**	**Ms H E Irwin**
071-219 3268	071-219 3289	071-219 3278

Health	*Home Affairs*	*National Heritage*
P A Evans	**E P Silk**	**Mrs Sharpe**
071-219 6244	071-219 3260	

Science and Technology	*Scottish Affairs*	*Social Security*
Ms Samson	**A H Doharty**	**D R Lloyd**
		071-219 5831

Trade and Industry	*Transport*	*Treasury and Civil Service*
D J Gerhold	**D W N Doig**	**W A Proctor (4)**
071-219 5469	071-219 6242	071-219 3285

Welsh Affairs
B M Hutton
071-219 3261

Clerks of Select Committees (Scrutiny Committees, etc)

Consolidation etc, Bills (Joint Committee)	*European Legislation*	*Parliamentary Commissioner for Administration*
M D Hamlyn	**Dr C R M Ward**	**A Y A Azad**
071-219 3256	071-219 5467	071-219 3310

Public Accounts	*Statutory Instruments*
Dr J S Benger	**N P Walker**
071-219 3273	071-219 3281

Clerks of Select Committees (Domestic)

Accommodation and Works	Administration	Broadcasting
K J Brown	K J Brown	D W N Doig
071-219 3275	071-219 3275	071-219 4268

Catering	Finance and Services	Information
P Moon	R W G Wilson (4)	P Moon
071-219 2420	071-219 3270	071-219 2420

Liaison	Members' Interests	Privileges
J F Sweetman CB (2)	R B Sands (3)	A J Hastings (3)
071-219 3311	071-219 6257	071-219 3315

Procedure	Selection
A Kennon	C Shore
071-219 3316	071-219 3250

Department of the Serjeant at Arms

Serjeant at Arms
Sir Alan Urwick KCVO CMG (3)
071-219 3030

|

Deputy Serjeant at Arms
R N W Jennings (5)
071-219 3040

|

Director of Works
H Webber (4)
071-219 3920
(1 Canon Row)

|

Serjeant at Arms

Order, security and ceremonial
Housekeeping
Works and accommodation

Department of the Library

Librarian
D J T Englefield (3)
071-219 3635

|

Deputy Librarian
Miss J B Tanfield (4)
071-219 6179
(Derby Gate)

|

| *Head of Division*
Miss P J Baines (5)
071-219 5781
(Derby Gate) | *Head of Division*
S Z Young (5)
071-219 3622
(Derby Gate) | *Deliverer of the Vote*
G R Russell (5)
071-219 4220 |

Parliamentary Division

Computer etc services
International affairs and defence
Members' library
Public information office

Research Division

Economic affairs
Education and social services
Home affairs
Science and environment
Statistics

Vote Office

Supply and distribution of Order
Papers and other documents

Department of the Official Report

Editor
I D Church
071-219 3388

|

Official Report

Produces verbatim report (Hansard)
of sittings of House and its
Standing Committees

Refreshment Department

Director of Catering Services
Mrs S Harrison (5)
071-219 3686

Refreshment

Catering and refreshment service
for Members, staff and guests

Finance and Administration Department

Head of Department
J Rodda (3)
071-219 5460

Accountant and Head of Fees Office	*Head of Finance Office*	*Head of Office*
A J Lewis (5)	**N J Barram (5)**	**B A Wilson (5)**
071-219 4292	071-219 2443	071-219 3692

Fees Office	**Finance Office**	**Establishments Office**
Payment of salaries and allowances for Members and their staff	Bids for financial resources	Personnel matters
Parliamentary Pension Fund	Payment of staff of House	Staff management
	Select Committee expenses	Staff pensions
		Trade unions

Computer Officer	*Internal Auditor*
R S Morgan (5)	**A A Cameron (7)**
071-219 5501	071-219 6460

Computer Office	**Internal Audit**
Coordination and advice to departments of House	

House of Commons Addresses

1 Cannon Row
London SW1A 2JN
Tel 071-219 3920

1 Derby Gate
Westminster
London SW1A 2DG
Tel 071-219 3000

House of Lords

Organisation The departments of the Clerk of the
Parliaments and the Gentleman Usher of the
Black Rod together make up the staff of the
House of Lords. Staff are not civil servants of
the Crown. The work of this permanent staff
revolves round the activity of Peers, House
committees and the parliamentary process
generally.

Responsibilities committees
Hansard
judicial business of the House
library
private bills
public bills
sittings of the House

House of Lords

Westminster, London SW1A 0PW
Tel 071-219 3000

Principal Officers and Officials

Lord Chancellor
**The Rt Hon The Lord Mackay
of Clashfern**

Chairman of Committees
The Lord Ampthill CBE

|

Secretary
B P Keith (4)
071-219 3231

|

*Principal Deputy Chairman
of Committees*
**The Lord Boston of Faversham
QC**

|

*Counsel to Chairman
of Committees*
**D Rippengal CB QC
Mrs E Denza CMG**

|

Assistant Counsel
N J Adamson CB QC (5)

Overview

Principal Officers and Officials				Department
Grade 1	*Grade 2*	*Grade 3*	*Grade 4*	

Clerk of the Parliaments

M A J Wheeler-Booth	J M Davies			Public Bill Office
		P D G Hayter		Reading Clerk
		J A Vallance White		Judicial Office
			B P Keith	Private Bill Office
			M G Pownall	Committee Office
			D J Johnson (5)	Record Office
			D L Jones (5)	Library
			Mrs M E E C Villiers (5)	Office of the Official Report
			C Preece (6/7)	Accountant's Office
			D R Beamish (5)	Establishment Office
			W G Sleath (7)	Journal and Information Office
			S P Burton (7)	Printed Paper Office
			A D O Bibbiani (SCO)	Refreshment

Gentleman Usher of the Black Rod and Serjeant-at-Arms

		Adm Sir Richard Thomas		Gentleman Usher of the Black Rod

Principal Officers and Officials

Department of the Clerk of the Parliaments

Clerk of the Parliaments
M A J Wheeler-Booth (1)

|

Principal Secretary
Ms E A Murray (HEO)
071-219 3181

|

Clerk Assistant
J M Davies (2)
(see also under Public Bills below)

|

Reading Clerk
Principal Finance Officer
P D G Hayter (3)

|

Fourth Clerk at the Table
J A Vallance White (3)
(see also under Judicial below)

|

Principal Clerk	*Principal Clerk,*	*Principal Clerk*
	Taxing Officer,	*Committee Work of the House*
	Examiner of Petitions	
J M Davies (2)	**B P Keith (4)**	**M G Pownall (4)**
071-219 3153	071-219 3231	071-219 3326
Chief Clerk		*Chief Clerks*
C A J Mitchell (5)		**Mrs F M Martin (5)**
		(European Communities)
		R H Walters (5)
		(Science and Technology)

Public Bill Office

Government and private members'
bills
Procedural advice
Assistance in drafting bills and
amendments
Preparation of acts, bills and
amendments for publishing

Private Bill Office

Bills promoted by outside
organisations
Opposed local legislation
Procedural and administrative
support to Chairman of
Committees

**Committee and Overseas
Office**

Administers select committees on
public business

Clerk of the Records

D J Johnson (5)
071-219 3074

*Principal Clerk
Judicial Taxing Officer*
J A Vallance White (3)
071-219 3111

Record Office

Accessions, lists, indexes, binds,
repairs and preserves
parliamentary and other records
of both Houses

Judicial Office

Judicial business of the House
Preparation and arrangements for
hearing of appeals
Taxation of judicial costs
Channels peerage claims

Librarian

D L Jones (5)
071-219 5242

*Editor of the Official
Report*
Mrs M E E C Villiers (5)
071-219 3031

Establishment Officer

D R Beamish (5)
071-219 3185

Library

Provides information services to
members
Supplies Appellate and Appeal
Committees with authorities
Carries out research for members
Reference information
Book lending service

Official Report of Debates

Produces verbatim report of
sittings of the house (Hansard)

Establishments

Recruitment and selection of staff
(not clerks)
Conditions of service
Employee records
Training, management and staff
relations
Promotion arrangements
Computers

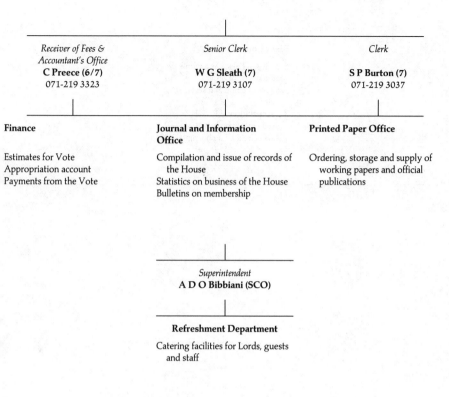

Receiver of Fees & *Accountant's Office*	*Senior Clerk*	*Clerk*
C Preece (6/7)	**W G Sleath (7)**	**S P Burton (7)**
071-219 3323	071-219 3107	071-219 3037

Finance	**Journal and Information Office**	**Printed Paper Office**
Estimates for Vote	Compilation and issue of records of	Ordering, storage and supply of
Appropriation account	the House	working papers and official
Payments from the Vote	Statistics on business of the House	publications
	Bulletins on membership	

Superintendent
A D O Bibbiani (SCO)

Refreshment Department

Catering facilities for Lords, guests
and staff

Department of Gentleman Usher of the Black Rod and Serjeant-at-Arms

*Gentleman Usher of the Black Rod
and Serjeant-at-Arms,
Secretary to the Lord Great
Chamberlain*
**Admiral Sir Richard
Thomas KCB OBE (3)**

*Yeoman Usher of the
Black Rod
Deputy Serjeant-at-Arms*
Air Cdre A C Curry OBE

Black Rod

Security of Palace as a whole
Maintenance of order
Accommodation and services for
 Lords
Administration of Royal
 Apartments on behalf of the
 Lord Great Chamberlain

National Audit Office

Founded	1866 as the Exchequer and Audit Department and reconstituted as the NAO in 1984
Status	An independent body. The head of the National Audit Office, the Comptroller and Auditor General, is an officer of the House of Commons
Responsible to	Public Accounts Committee/Commission and thence to Parliament
Responsibilities	Auditing the accounts of government departments, certain public bodies and international organisations
	Value for money audits which investigate the economy, efficiency and effectiveness with which any department, authority or other body under its jurisdiction has used its resources in discharging its functions

National Audit Office

157–159 Buckingham Palace Road, London SW1W 9SP
Tel 071-798 7000   Fax 071-828 3774

22 Melville Street, Edinburgh EH3 7NS
Tel 031-244 2736   Fax 031-244 2721

Officials

Comptroller and Auditor General
Sir John Bourn KCB (1)

|

Private Secretary
J R J Rickleton
071-798 7383

|

Deputy Comptroller and Auditor
R N Le Marechal (2)

|

Assistant Auditors General
M J Goodson (3)
D A Dewar (3)
P J C Keemer (3)
J A Higgins (3)
L H Hughes (3)

294

Overview

Officials			Department
Grade 1	*Grade 2*	*Grade 3*	
Sir John Bourn	R N Le Marechal	M J Goodson	*Unit A* Corporate Policy and Finance Office Services Human resources Certification Audit Policy and Management Value for Money Audit
		D A Dewar	*Unit B* Inland Revenue Customs and Excise Agriculture and Finance Transport and Environment Home Affairs and Courts
		P J C Keemer	*Unit C* Health Social Security Employment Scotland
		J A Higgins	*Unit D* Assets/Estate Management Central Government Services Privatisation/Regulation
		L H Hughes	*Unit E* Defence Education and Science Arts Energy Trade and Industry Welsh Affairs

Officials and Departments

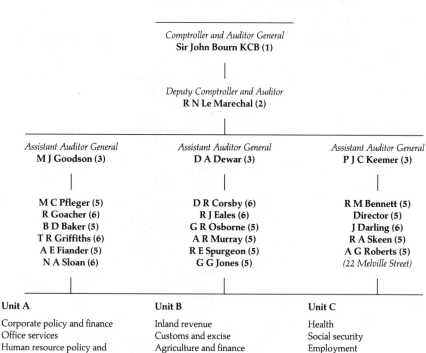

Comptroller and Auditor General
Sir John Bourn KCB (1)

Deputy Comptroller and Auditor
R N Le Marechal (2)

Assistant Auditor General	Assistant Auditor General	Assistant Auditor General
M J Goodson (3)	**D A Dewar (3)**	**P J C Keemer (3)**
M C Pfleger (5)	**D R Corsby (6)**	**R M Bennett (5)**
R Goacher (6)	**R J Eales (6)**	**Director (5)**
B D Baker (5)	**G R Osborne (5)**	**J Darling (6)**
T R Griffiths (6)	**A R Murray (5)**	**R A Skeen (5)**
A E Fiander (5)	**R E Spurgeon (5)**	**A G Roberts (5)**
N A Sloan (6)	**G G Jones (5)**	*(22 Melville Street)*

Unit A	**Unit B**	**Unit C**
Corporate policy and finance	Inland revenue	Health
Office services	Customs and excise	Social security
Human resource policy and	Agriculture and finance	Employment
management	Transport and environment	Resource management
Human resource provision	Home affairs and courts	Scotland
Certification audit policy and	Resource management	
management		
Value for Money Audit		

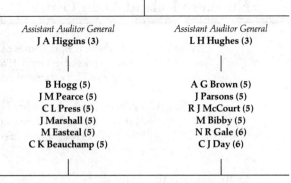

Assistant Auditor General J A Higgins (3)	*Assistant Auditor General* L H Hughes (3)
B Hogg (5) J M Pearce (5) C L Press (5) J Marshall (5) M Easteal (5) C K Beauchamp (5)	A G Brown (5) J Parsons (5) R J McCourt (5) M Bibby (5) N R Gale (6) C J Day (6)

Unit D

Assets/estate management
Overseas services
International
Privatisation/regulation
Central government services
Resource management

Unit E

Defence (organisation, manpower,
  finance, procurement, assets and
  stores)
Education and science
Trade and industry
Arts
Energy
Welsh affairs

Northern Ireland Audit Office

Founded   1987 under the provisions of the Audit
(Northern Ireland) Order 1987, and replaced
the former Exchequer and Audit Department

Status   independent body: the head of the Office, the
Comptroller and Auditor General for
Northern Ireland, is an officer of the House of
Commons

Responsible to   in the absence of an elected Northern Ireland
Assembly, the Comptroller and Auditor
General for Northern Ireland is responsible to
the Public Accounts Commission and the
Committee of Public Accounts of the House
of Commons at Westminster

Responsibilities   Controlling receipts into and issues from the
Northern Ireland Consolidated Fund

Examining the accounts of government
departments and certain public bodies in
Northern Ireland

Examinations of the economy, efficiency and
effectiveness of the use of resources by
government bodies and various other bodies
in receipt of public funds

Northern Ireland Audit Office

Rosepark House, Upper Newtownards Road, Belfast BT4 3NS
Tel 0232 484567   Fax 0232 484596

Officials

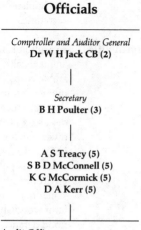

Comptroller and Auditor General
Dr W H Jack CB (2)

Secretary
B H Poulter (3)

A S Treacy (5)
S B D McConnell (5)
K G McCormick (5)
D A Kerr (5)

Audit Office

Audit of all departments and certain
  public bodies
Control of receipts into and issues
  from the Northern Ireland
  Consolidated Fund

Ministry of Agriculture, Fisheries and Food

Founded 1889 as Board of Agriculture

Ministers Minister of Agriculture, Fisheries and Food, one minister of state and two parliamentary secretaries

Responsibilities agricultural land use
animal health and welfare
arable crops
biotechnology
dairy produce quotas
disease control (animals, plants and fish)
diversification
EEC common agricultural policy and commo
fisheries policy
environmental protection (countryside and marine)
farm woodlands
flood defence
food regulation, safety and quality
food industry
fisheries
forestry
horse industry
land tenure
organic farming
pesticides
plant health
set aside
veterinary medicine
scientific, technical and professional services and advice to farmers, growers and ancillar industries

Executive Agencies Agricultural Development and Advisory Service (ADAS)*
Central Science Laboratory
Central Veterinary Laboratory
Intervention Board
Veterinary Medicines Laboratory

Joint MAFF/Welsh Office Agricultural Department agency

Ministry of Agriculture, Fisheries and Food

Whitehall Place, London SW1A 2HH
Tel 071-270 3000   Fax 071-270 8125
All personnel are based at Whitehall Place unless otherwise indicated.
For other addresses and telephone numbers see end of this section.

Ministers

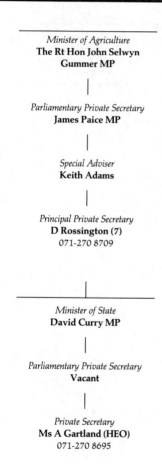

Minister of Agriculture
**The Rt Hon John Selwyn
Gummer MP**

|

Parliamentary Private Secretary
James Paice MP

|

Special Adviser
Keith Adams

|

Principal Private Secretary
D Rossington (7)
071-270 8709

Minister of State
David Curry MP

|

Parliamentary Private Secretary
Vacant

|

Private Secretary
Ms A Gartland (HEO)
071-270 8695

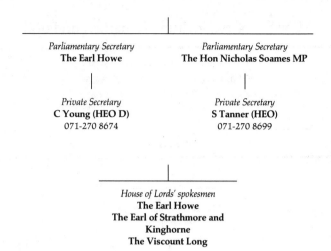

Parliamentary Secretary
The Earl Howe

Parliamentary Secretary
The Hon Nicholas Soames MP

Private Secretary
C Young (HEO D)
071-270 8674

Private Secretary
S Tanner (HEO)
071-270 8699

House of Lords' spokesmen
The Earl Howe
The Earl of Strathmore and
Kinghorne
The Viscount Long

Ministerial Responsibilities

John Gummer   overall responsibility for the department

David Curry   agricultural commodities
European Community (Common Agricultural
  Policy; Common Fisheries Policy; and
  matters falling within the areas of
  responsibility of the Parliamentary
  Secretaries)
export promotion
external trade policy
fisheries and marine environmental protection
food and drink industry including marketing
  and promotion
Intervention Board
relations with overseas countries and
  international organisations
set-aside and extensification

The Earl Howe   ADAS (Agricultural Development and
Advisory Service)
agricultural grants
agricultural land use
agricultural resources policy
departmental central services
deregulation
diversification
economics and statistics
environment and conservation
farm woodlands
flood defence
forestry
land tenure
organic farming
plant health
plant varieties and seeds
regional administration
research and development
rural affairs
structures

Nicholas Soames   animal health and medicines
animal welfare
biotechnology issues
emergency services
food safety and regulation
food science
horse industry
meat hygiene
pesticide safety

Departmental Overview

Civil Servants			Group	Minister
Grade 1	*Grade 2*	*Grade 3*		
Sir Derek Andrews	These Groups report directly to the Permanent Secretary	D H Griffiths	Establishment	Earl Howe
		A R Cruickshank	Finance	Earl Howe
		S H Dugdale (5)	Information	Earl Howe

Agricultural Commodities, Trade and Food Production

Sir Derek Andrews	R J Packer	S Wentworth	European Community Group	D Curry
		C J A Barnes	Arable Crops and Alcoholic Drinks Group	D Curry
		J W Hepburn	Food, Milk and Marketing Policy	D Curry
		Mrs E A J Attridge	Horticulture	D Curry
			Plant Protection and Agricultural Resources	Earl Howe
		G A Hollis	Livestock Products	

Food Safety

Sir Derek Andrews	C W Capstick	B H B Dickinson	Food Safety	N Soames
		P W Murphy	Pesticides, Veterinary Medicines, Emergencies and Biotechnology	N Soames
		K C Meldrum M T Haddon	Animal Health and Veterinary Group	N Soames
		I Crawford	State Veterinary Service	N Soames
		Vacant	Chief Scientist (Food)	N Soames

Countryside, Marine Environment and Fisheries

Sir Derek Andrews	C R Cann	G R Waters	Land Use, Conservation and Rural Environment	Earl Howe
		M Madden	Environment Policy Group	Earl Howe
		R E Mordue	Economics and Statistics	Earl Howe
		R J D Carden	Fisheries	D Curry

Chief Scientific Adviser and Regional Organisation

Sir Derek Andrews	Dr P J Bunyan	Dr D W F Shannon	Chief Scentific Adviser	E Howe
		D J Coates	Regional Services	E Howe

Departmental Overview

Civil Servants			Group	Minister
Grade 1	Grade 2	Grade 3		
	Legal			
Sir Derek Andrews	G J Jenkins	A E Munir	Legal	E Howe
		B T Atwood	Legal	E Howe

Civil Servants and Groups

Establishment Group, Finance, Information

Permanent Secretary
Sir Derek Andrews KCB CBE (1)

Director of Establishments	*Principal Finance Officer*	*Head of Information Division*
D H Griffiths (3)	**A R Cruickshank (3)**	**S H Dugdale (5)**
	(Woburn Place)	

Mrs A M Pickering (5)	**A G Kuyk (5)**	
(all at Victory House)	*Miss V A Smith (5)*	
J S Buchanan (5)	**D V Fisher (5)**	
(at Eastbury House)	*(all at Woburn Place)*	
P A Cocking (5)	**G Lander (5)**	
(Nobel House)	*(Ergon House)*	

Establishment	**Finance**	**Information**
Personnel	Planning	Information
Establishments (general)	Guidance	Libraries
Welfare	Purchasing and supply	Publicity
Training	Financial management	Translation
Office services	Audit	
Building and estate management	Budgeting	
Health and safety		

Agricultural Commodities, Trade and Food Protection

Permanent Secretary
Sir Derek Andrews KCB CBE (1)

Deputy Secretary
R J Packer (2)

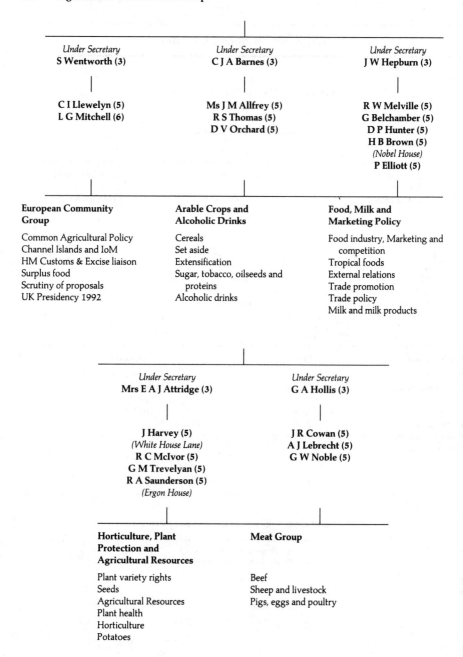

Under Secretary **S Wentworth (3)**	*Under Secretary* **C J A Barnes (3)**	*Under Secretary* **J W Hepburn (3)**
C I Llewelyn (5) **L G Mitchell (6)**	**Ms J M Allfrey (5)** **R S Thomas (5)** **D V Orchard (5)**	**R W Melville (5)** **G Belchamber (5)** **D P Hunter (5)** **H B Brown (5)** *(Nobel House)* **P Elliott (5)**

European Community Group

Common Agricultural Policy
Channel Islands and IoM
HM Customs & Excise liaison
Surplus food
Scrutiny of proposals
UK Presidency 1992

Arable Crops and Alcoholic Drinks

Cereals
Set aside
Extensification
Sugar, tobacco, oilseeds and
  proteins
Alcoholic drinks

Food, Milk and Marketing Policy

Food industry, Marketing and
  competition
Tropical foods
External relations
Trade promotion
Trade policy
Milk and milk products

Under Secretary **Mrs E A J Attridge (3)**	*Under Secretary* **G A Hollis (3)**
J Harvey (5) *(White House Lane)* **R C McIvor (5)** **G M Trevelyan (5)** **R A Saunderson (5)** *(Ergon House)*	**J R Cowan (5)** **A J Lebrecht (5)** **G W Noble (5)**

Horticulture, Plant Protection and Agricultural Resources

Plant variety rights
Seeds
Agricultural Resources
Plant health
Horticulture
Potatoes

Meat Group

Beef
Sheep and livestock
Pigs, eggs and poultry

Food Safety

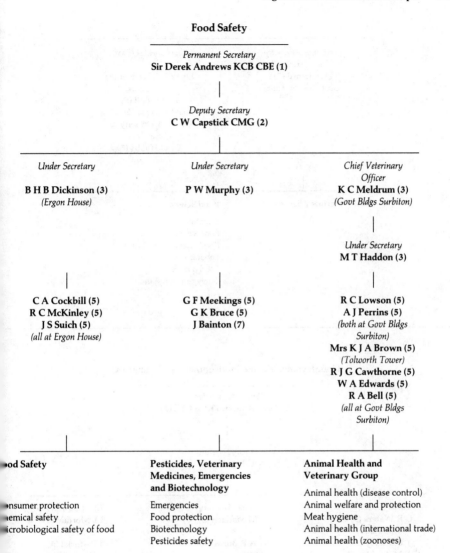

Permanent Secretary
Sir Derek Andrews KCB CBE (1)

Deputy Secretary
C W Capstick CMG (2)

Under Secretary	*Under Secretary*	*Chief Veterinary Officer*
B H B Dickinson (3)	**P W Murphy (3)**	**K C Meldrum (3)**
(Ergon House)		*(Govt Bldgs Surbiton)*

Under Secretary
M T Haddon (3)

C A Cockbill (5)	**G F Meekings (5)**	**R C Lowson (5)**
R C McKinley (5)	**G K Bruce (5)**	**A J Perrins (5)**
J S Suich (5)	**J Bainton (7)**	*(both at Govt Bldgs*
(all at Ergon House)		*Surbiton)*
		Mrs K J A Brown (5)
		(Tolworth Tower)
		R J G Cawthorne (5)
		W A Edwards (5)
		R A Bell (5)
		(all at Govt Bldgs
		Surbiton)

...od Safety	**Pesticides, Veterinary Medicines, Emergencies and Biotechnology**	**Animal Health and Veterinary Group**
...nsumer protection	Emergencies	Animal health (disease control)
...emical safety	Food protection	Animal welfare and protection
...icrobiological safety of food	Biotechnology	Meat hygiene
	Pesticides safety	Animal health (international trade)
		Animal health (zoonoses)

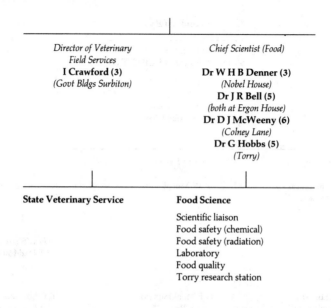

Director of Veterinary
Field Services
I Crawford (3)
(Govt Bldgs Surbiton)

Chief Scientist (Food)

Dr W H B Denner (3)
(Nobel House)
Dr J R Bell (5)
(both at Ergon House)
Dr D J McWeeny (6)
(Colney Lane)
Dr G Hobbs (5)
(Torry)

State Veterinary Service

Food Science

Scientific liaison
Food safety (chemical)
Food safety (radiation)
Laboratory
Food quality
Torry research station

Countryside, Marine Environment and Fisheries

Permanent Secretary
Sir Derek Andrews KCB CBE (1)

Deputy Secretary
C R Cann (2)

Under Secretary	*Under Secretary*	*Under Secretary*
G R Waters (3)	**M Madden (3)**	**R E Mordue (3)**
(Nobel House)		
T E D Eddy (5)	**A R Burne (5)**	**J P Muriel (5)**
G P McLachlan (5)	*(Nobel House)*	**R W Irving (5)**
C R Bodrell (5)	**Dr J R Park (5)**	**Dr A P Power (5)**
P P Nash (5)	*(Eastbury House)*	**Dr J M Slater (5)**
J Robbs (5)	**P P Nash (5)**	**Dr J P Lund (5)**
(all at Nobel House)	*(Nobel House)*	*(Ergon House)*
		D E Bradbury (5)
		(Govt Bldgs Guildford)

**Land Use, Conservation
and Rural Economy**

Rural structures and grants
Land use and tenure
Conservation policy

Environment

Environment protection
Salmon and freshwater fisheries
Whaling
Flood defence

Economics and Statistics

Farm business
International
Resource use
Food
Agricultural commodities
Census and prices

Fisheries Secretary
R J D Carden (3)
(Nobel House)

**P M Boyling (5)
Mrs A M Blackburn (5)
I C Redfern (5)
M G Jennings (6)
C J Ryder (5)**
(all at Nobel House)

*Director of Fisheries
Research*
Dr D J Garrod (4)

**Dr C E Purdom (5)
Dr J G Shepherd (5)**
*(both at
Fisheries Laboratories)*

Fisheries

Marine environmental protection
UK fishing fleet
Common Fisheries Policy
Shellfish cultivation
Fish farming
Processing and marketing
Hygiene
Law of the sea
Fisheries management
    arrangements
Sea Fisheries Inspectorate

Fisheries Laboratory

Research
Diseases

Chief Scientific Adviser and Regional Organisation

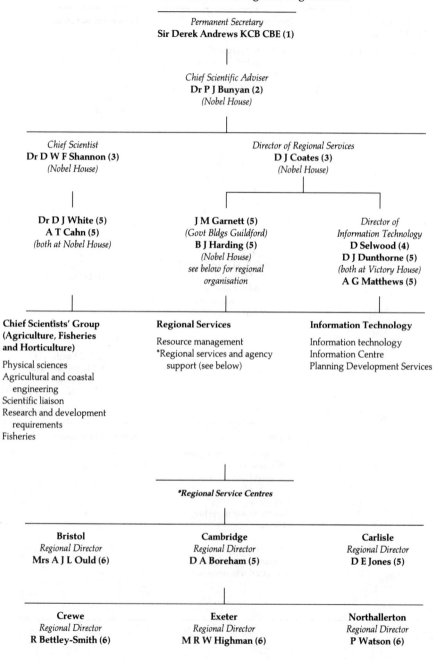

Permanent Secretary
Sir Derek Andrews KCB CBE (1)

Chief Scientific Adviser
Dr P J Bunyan (2)
(Nobel House)

Chief Scientist
Dr D W F Shannon (3)
(Nobel House)

Director of Regional Services
D J Coates (3)
(Nobel House)

Dr D J White (5)
A T Cahn (5)
(both at Nobel House)

J M Garnett (5)
(Govt Bldgs Guildford)
B J Harding (5)
(Nobel House)
see below for regional
organisation

Director of
Information Technology
D Selwood (4)
D J Dunthorne (5)
(both at Victory House)
A G Matthews (5)

**Chief Scientists' Group
(Agriculture, Fisheries
and Horticulture)**

Physical sciences
Agricultural and coastal
  engineering
Scientific liaison
Research and development
  requirements
Fisheries

Regional Services

Resource management
*Regional services and agency
  support (see below)

Information Technology

Information technology
Information Centre
Planning Development Services

***Regional Service Centres**

Bristol
Regional Director
Mrs A J L Ould (6)

Cambridge
Regional Director
D A Boreham (5)

Carlisle
Regional Director
D E Jones (5)

Crewe
Regional Director
R Bettley-Smith (6)

Exeter
Regional Director
M R W Highman (6)

Northallerton
Regional Director
P Watson (6)

Nottingham	Reading	Worcester
Regional Director	*Regional Director*	*Regional Director*
M J Finnigan (5)	R Anderson (5)	P G Gethering (6)

Legal Department

Permanent Secretary
Sir Derek Andrews KCB CBE (1)

Legal Adviser and Solicitor
G J Jenkins CB QC (2)

Principal Assistant Solicitor	*Principal Assistant Solicitor*
A E Munir (3)	B T Atwood (3)
(55 Whitehall)	*(55 Whitehall)*
P D Davis (5)	Ms C A Crisham (5)
Mrs C Davis (5)	D J Pearson (5)
M C P Thomas (5)	A I Corbett (5)
Miss E A Stephens (5)	M Parke (5)
L Gunatilleke (5)	A F N Maloney (6)
(all at 55 Whitehall)	*(all at 55 Whitehall)*

Legal

Agricultural commodities
Animal health and welfare
Plant health
Land use, drainage
Environment
Set aside
Dairy produce quotas
Fisheries
Pesticides
Common Agricultural Policy
Audit and finance
Food safety

Legal

EC litigation
Channel Islands, IoM
Civil litigation
Commercial matters
Employment
Investigation unit

Ministry of Agriculture Addresses

National addresses

Colney Lane
Norwich NR4 7UQ
Tel 0603 259350
Fax 0603 501123

Eastbury House
30–34 Albert Embankment
London SE1 7TL
Tel 071-238 3000
Fax 071-238 6616

Ergon House
17 Smith Square
London SW1P 3JR
Tel 071-238 3000
Fax 071-238 6591

Fisheries Laboratory
Pakefield Road
Lowestoft
Suffolk NR33 0HT
Tel 0502 62244
Fax 0502 513865

Government Buildings
Epsom Road
Guildford
Surrey GU1 2LD
Tel 0483 68121
Fax 0483 37396

Government Buildings
Hook Rise South
Tolworth
Surbiton
Surrey KT6 7NF
Tel 081-330 4411
Fax 081-337 3640

Nobel House
17 Smith Square
London SW1P 3JR
Tel 071-238 3000
Fax 071-238 6591

Tolworth Tower
Surbiton
Surrey KT6 7DX
Tel 081-330 4411
Fax 081-390 4425

Torry Research Station
PO Box 31
135 Abbey Road
Aberdeen AB9 8DG
Tel 0224 877071
Fax 0224 874246

Victory House
30–34 Kingsway House
London WC2B 6TU
Tel 071-405 4310
Fax 071-413 2699

White House Lane
Huntingdon Road
Cambridge CB3 0LF
Tel 0223 342382
Fax 0223 342386

55 Whitehall
London SW1A 2EY
Tel 071-270 3000
Fax 071-270 8125

19–29 Woburn Place
London WC1H 0LU
Tel 071-917 3600
Fax 071-917 3602

Regional Service Centres

Bristol
Block C Government Buildings
Burghill Road
Westbury-on-Trym
Bristol BS10 6NJ
Tel 0272 591000
Fax 0272 505392

Cambridge
Block C
Government Buildings
Brooklands Avenue
Cambridge CB2 2DR
Tel 0223 462727
Fax 0223 455911

Carlisle
Eden Bridge House
Lowther Street
Carlisle CA3 8DX
Tel 0228 23400
Fax 0228 28495

Crewe
Berkeley Towers
Crewe
Cheshire CW2 6PT
Tel 0270 69211
Fax 0270 669494

Exeter
Government Buildings
Alphington Road
Exeter EX2 8NQ
Tel 0392 77951
Fax 0392 410936

Northallerton
Government Buildings
Crosby Road
Northallerton
North Yorks DL6 1AD
Tel 0609 773751
Fax 0609 780179

Nottingham
Block 7
Chalfont Drive
Nottingham NG8 3SN
Tel 0602 291191
Fax 0602 294886

Reading
Government Buildings
Coley Park
Reading RG1 6DT
Tel 0734 581222
Fax 0734 581222 X3399

Worcester
Block C
Government Buildings
Whittington Road
Worcester WR5 2LQ
Tel 0905 763355
Fax 0905 763180

Cabinet Office (Office of Public Service and Science)

Founded In 1916 the War Cabinet and War Cabinet Secretariat were constituted from the Secretariat of the Committee for Imperial Defence (CID) which had been set up in 1904. After the war in 1920 a Cabinet Secretariat was set up on an established basis. The CID had a separate secretariat but both secretariats remained in the combined Offices of the Cabinet and CID. In 1939 a War Cabinet was again formed and the CID suspended and in 1940 the title of the Office became the Offices of the War Cabinet and the Minister of Defence. An economic section was formed and the Central Statistical Office established in 1941.

In 1947 many staff transferred to the new Ministry of Defence. In 1953 the Economic Section transferred to the Treasury. The CSO, which had become a department of the Chancellor of the Exchequer in 1989, was established as an executive agency in 1991.

Over the years the functions of the Cabinet Office (CO) have changed frequently. From 1970–83 the Central Policy Review Staff (CPRS) provided policy analysis and advice to ministers. When the CPRS disbanded, its Chief Scientist remained in the CO as Chief Scientific Adviser.

In 1983 the Management and Personnel Office (MPO) became an integral part of the CO and the Secretary of the Cabinet became Head of the Home Civil Service. In 1987 some MPO functions were transferred to the Treasury and the MPO was reconstituted as the Office of the Minister for the Civil Service (OMCS).

After the 1992 election the new Chancellor of the Duchy of Lancaster assumed responsibility for the OMCS but, because of a significant increase in the scope of the department's work, which now includes the Citizen's Charter, the Efficiency Unit, the

Market Testing Initiative, the Office of Science and Technology, and the Open Government initiative (see below for full list of responsibilities) the name has been changed to the Office of Public Service and Science (OPSS).

It has also (June 1992) taken over responsibility for the Central Office of Information, HMSO and the Chessington Computer Centre from the Treasury, which will also transfer responsibility for the Central Computer and Telecommunications Agency (CCTA) to the CO/OPSS during 1992.

Ministers   The Prime Minister, the Chancellor of the Duchy of Lancaster (Minister of Public Service and Science) and one parliamentary under secretary

Responsibilities   Support of ministers collectively in the conduct of Cabinet business
Central Computer and Telecommunications Agency (CCTA) (subject to the necessary Transfer of Functions Order, responsibility for CCTA will transfer from HM Treasury during 1992)
Citizen's Charter
Civil service personnel management issues
Efficiency and effectiveness of the civil service
Machinery of government including open government
Market testing programme
Next Steps programme
Office of the Civil Service Commissioners
Office of Science and Technology

Executive Agencies   Central Office of Information
Civil Service College
HMSO
Occupational Health Service
Recruitment and Assessment Services

Chessington Computer Centre will become an executive agency in April 1993

Cabinet Office
(Office of Public Service and Science)

70 Whitehall, London SW1A 2AS

Tel 071-270 3000

Fax *Telephone the above number and when through to the Cabinet Office ask for appropriate fax number*

All personnel are based at 70 Whitehall unless otherwise indicated.
For other addresses and telephone numbers see end of this section.

Ministers

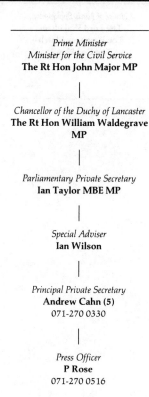

Prime Minister
Minister for the Civil Service
The Rt Hon John Major MP

Chancellor of the Duchy of Lancaster
The Rt Hon William Waldegrave MP

Parliamentary Private Secretary
Ian Taylor MBE MP

Special Adviser
Ian Wilson

Principal Private Secretary
Andrew Cahn (5)
071-270 0330

Press Officer
P Rose
071-270 0516

|

Parliamentary Under Secretary
Public Service and Science
Robert Jackson MP

|

Private Secretary
W E Jones
071-270 0410

|

House of Lords Spokesmen
The Lord Wakeham
The Baroness Blatch
The Earl Howe

Ministerial Responsibilities

William Waldegrave/
Robert Jackson

Citizen's Charter
Civil service personnel management issues
CCTA (Central Computer and
  Telecommunications Agency) (to be
  transferred from HM Treasury)
Efficiency and effectiveness of the civil
  service.
Machinery of government including open
  government
Market testing initiative
Next Steps programme
Office of the Civil Service Commissioners
Office of Science and Technology
Open government

Departmental Overview

Civil Servants			Division	Minister
Grade 1	*Grade 2*	*Grade 3*		
Sir Robin Butler (0)		J H Thompson (5)	Ceremonial	J Major
Sir Robin Butler (0)/ R Mottram (1A)		A D Whetnall (5)	Machinery of Government	J Major W Waldegrave
		R D Wright (5)	Security Division	J Major W Waldegrave

Cabinet Secretariat

Sir Robin Butler (0)	Miss L P Neville-Jones	N Bevan	Defence and Overseas	J Major
	P F Owen	T J Burr	Economic	J Major
	D Hadley	B Bender	European Affairs	J Major
		R Bird	Home and Social Affairs and Legislation	J Major

Office of Public Service and Science

R Mottram	B Hilton		Citizen's Charter Unit (Sir James Blyth, Chairman of the Advisory Panel)	J Major W Waldegrave
		D Brereton	Efficiency Unit (Sir Peter Levene, Prime Minister's Adviser)	J Major W Waldegrave
	J H Holroyd		Office of the Civil Service Commissioner	J Major W Waldegrave
R Mottram	Professor W Stewart	R Foster D A Wilkinson Dr D G Libby	Office of Science and Technology	J Major W Waldegrave
		J K Moore	Management Development Group	J Major W Waldegrave
		Miss M T Neville-Rolfe	Top Management Programme	J Major W Waldegrave
		T Perks (5)	Information Officer Management Unit *	J Major W Waldegrave
Sir Robin Butler (0)/ R Mottram		S R Davie	Establishment Officers Group	J Major W Waldegrave
		A J Merifield	Senior and Public Appointments Group	J Major W Waldegrave

* Reports to Richard Mottram on administrative matters. On professional matters reports to the Head of the Government Information Service

Civil Servants and Divisions

Secretary of the Cabinet
Head of the Home Civil Service
Sir Robin Butler GCB CVO (0)

Private Secretary
Miss S Phippard (7)
071-270 0186

Ceremonial Officer
J H Thompson CB (5)
(53 Parliament St)

Ceremonial Branch

Coordinates policy and
recommendations for the public
honours system

Secretary of the Cabinet
Head of the Home Civil Service
Sir Robin Butler GCB CVO (0)

Head of the Office of Public
Service and Science
Chief Accounting Officer
R Mottram (1A)

Senior Personal Secretary
Mrs Doreen Mayton
071-270 6451

Head of Division
A D Whetnall (5)

Head of Division
R D J Wright (5)

Machinery of Government

Organisation
Transfers of ministerial
  responsibilities
Open government
Guidance on legislative procedures
Select Committees ˙
Parliamentary Commissioner for
  Administration
Conventions on government
  publicity
Non-departmental public bodies

Security

Security and emergencies
Conduct and discipline
Acceptance of outside
  appointments by Crown
  servants

Cabinet Secretariat

Secretary of the Cabinet
Head of the Home Civil Service
Sir Robin Butler GCB CVO (0)

Head of Secretariat
Miss L P Neville-Jones (2)

Head of Secretariat
P F Owen (2)

N Bevan (3)

T J Burr (3)

J Sibson (5)

**Defence and Overseas
Secretariat**

Foreign and defence policy-making
Intelligence agencies
Northern Ireland and Anglo-Irish
  relations
Civil Contingencies Unit

Economic Secretariat

Economic policy
Industrial policy
Energy policy
Industrial relations
Inner cities policy

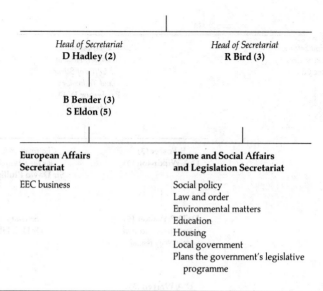

Head of Secretariat	*Head of Secretariat*
D Hadley (2)	**R Bird (3)**

B Bender (3)
S Eldon (5)

European Affairs	**Home and Social Affairs**
Secretariat	**and Legislation Secretariat**
EEC business	Social policy
	Law and order
	Environmental matters
	Education
	Housing
	Local government
	Plans the government's legislative
	programme

Office of Public Service and Science

Head of the Office of Public
Service and Science
Chief Accounting Officer
R Mottram (1A)

Chairman, PM's	*PM's Adviser on*
Citizen's Charter	*Efficiency*
Advisory Panel	**Sir Peter Levene**
Sir James Blyth	

Head of Unit	*Head of Unit*
B Hilton (2)	**D Brereton (3)**

Deputy Director	**Dr G D Coley (5)**
Mrs D A Goldsworthy	**Miss S M Scholefield (5)**
(5)	**N Cribb**
	I G Williams
	B R Ross

Citizen's Charter	**Efficiency Unit**
Unit	Improving efficiency and
Implement, develop and coordinate	effectiveness in the civil service
the Citizen's Charter initiative	Market testing initiative

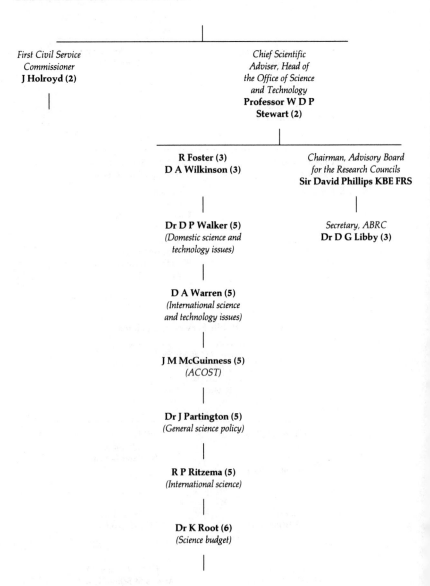

First Civil Service
Commissioner
J Holroyd (2)

Chief Scientific
Adviser, Head of
the Office of Science
and Technology
**Professor W D P
Stewart (2)**

R Foster (3)
D A Wilkinson (3)

Chairman, Advisory Board
for the Research Councils
Sir David Phillips KBE FRS

Dr D P Walker (5)
*(Domestic science and
technology issues)*

Secretary, ABRC
Dr D G Libby (3)

D A Warren (5)
*(International science
and technology issues)*

J M McGuinness (5)
(ACOST)

Dr J Partington (5)
(General science policy)

R P Ritzema (5)
(International science)

Dr K Root (6)
(Science budget)

Office of the Civil Service Commissioner	Office of Science and Technology
Responsible for senior appointments and recruitment to the fast stream	Provides the central focus for consideration for science and technology issues across government
Advising the Chancellor of the Duchy of Lancaster and the Secretary of State for Foreign Affairs on the rules for recruitment to the civil service	Responsibility for the science budget and the work of the five research councils
Monitoring the application of those rules by departments and agencies	Responsible for the Advisory Council Science and Technology (ACOST) and the Advisory Board for the Research Councils (ABRC)
Liaison with careers services of academic institutions	
Advising on nationality and character standards for entry to the Home Civil Service	

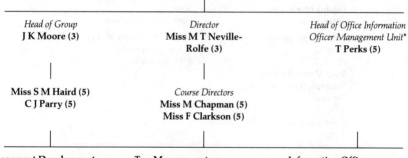

Head of Group
J K Moore (3)

Director
Miss M T Neville-Rolfe (3)

*Head of Office Information Officer Management Unit**
T Perks (5)

Miss S M Haird (5)
C J Parry (5)

Course Directors
Miss M Chapman (5)
Miss F Clarkson (5)

Management Development Group	Top Management Programme	Information Officer Management
Next Steps	The development, running and evaluation of management development programmes for senior civil servants (grade 3 level) and an equal number of top managers from other parts of the public and private sectors	Central management for members of GIS
Equal opportunities		Career advice and development
Personnel management and development		Central promotion boards
		Transfer of staff
		Secondments
		Marketing of GIS recruitment and training

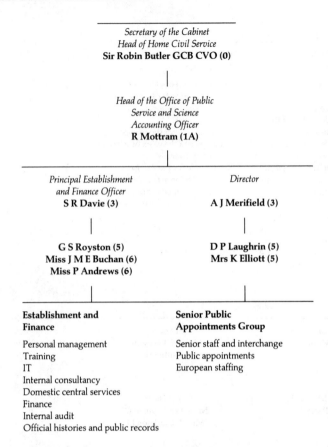

Secretary of the Cabinet
Head of Home Civil Service
Sir Robin Butler GCB CVO (0)

Head of the Office of Public
Service and Science
Accounting Officer
R Mottram (1A)

Principal Establishment
and Finance Officer
S R Davie (3)

Director

A J Merifield (3)

G S Royston (5)
Miss J M E Buchan (6)
Miss P Andrews (6)

D P Laughrin (5)
Mrs K Elliott (5)

**Establishment and
Finance**

Personal management
Training
IT
Internal consultancy
Domestic central services
Finance
Internal audit
Official histories and public records

**Senior Public
Appointments Group**

Senior staff and interchange
Public appointments
European staffing

* IOMU reports to Richard Mottram on administrative matters. On professional matters it reports to the Head of the Government Information Service.

Cabinet Committees

Main Committees

Economic and Domestic Policy (EDP)
Prime Minister *(Chairman)*
Chancellor of the Exchequer
Home Secretary
President of the Board of Trade
Leader of the House of Lords
Leader of the House of Commons
Secretary of State for the Environment
Secretary of State for Wales
Chancellor of the Duchy of Lancaster
Secretary of State for Scotland
Secretary of State for Northern Ireland
Secretary of State for Employment
Chief Secretary, Treasury

Other Ministers will be invited to attend for items in
which they have a departmental interest.

Terms of Reference: To consider strategic issues
relating to the government's economic and domestic
policies.

Defence and Overseas Policy (OPD)
Prime Minister *(Chairman)*
Foreign Secretary
Chancellor of the Exchequer
President of the Board of Trade
Secretary of State for Defence
Attorney General

The Chief of Defence Staff will attend as required, as
will the Chiefs of Staff when necessary.

Terms of Reference: To keep under review the
government's defence and overseas policy.

The Gulf (OPDG)
Prime Minister *(Chairman)*
Foreign Secretary
Secretary of State for Defence
Attorney General

Terms of Reference: To keep under review
developments in the Gulf region and to coordinate
any necessary action.

Nuclear Defence Policy (OPDN)

Prime Minister *(Chairman)*
Foreign Secretary
Chancellor of the Exchequer
Secretary of State for Defence

Terms of Reference: To keep under review the government's policy on nuclear defence.

European Security (OPDSE)

Prime Minister *(Chairman)*
Foreign Secretary
Chancellor of the Exchequer
Secretary of State for Defence

Terms of Reference: To keep under review arrangements for defence and security in Europe.

Hong Kong and Other Dependent Territories (OPDK)

Prime Minister *(Chairman)*
Foreign Secretary
Chancellor of the Exchequer
Home Secretary
President of the Board of Trade
Secretary of State for Defence
Leader of the House of Commons
Minister of State, Foreign and Commonwealth
    Office

Others, including the Attorney General, the Governor of Hong Kong, the British Ambassador in Peking, and other ministers with departmental interests, will be invited to attend as appropriate.

Terms of Reference: To keep under review the implementation of the agreement with the Chinese on the future of Hong Kong and the implications of that agreement for the government of Hong Kong and the wellbeing of its people; and to keep under review as necessary the government's policy towards other Dependent Territories.

Northern Ireland (NI)

Prime Minister *(Chairman)*
Foreign Secretary
Home Secretary
Secretary of State for Defence
Secretary of State for Northern Ireland
Chief Secretary, Treasury
Attorney General

Other ministers will be invited to attend as the
nature of the business requires.

Terms of Reference: To oversee the government's
policy on Northern Ireland issues and relations with
the Republic of Ireland on these matters.

Science and Technology (EDS)

Prime Minister *(Chairman)*
Foreign Secretary
President of the Board of Trade
Secretary of State for Transport
Secretary of State for Defence
Minister of Agriculture, Fisheries and Food
Secretary of State for the Environment
Chancellor of the Duchy of Lancaster
Secretary of State for Scotland
Secretary of State for Education
Secretary of State for Health
Chief Secretary, Treasury

The Chief Scientific Adviser is in attendance.

Terms of Reference: To review science and
technology policy.

Intelligence Services (IS)

Prime Minister *(Chairman)*
Foreign Secretary
Home Secretary
Secretary of State for Defence
Chancellor of the Duchy of Lancaster

Terms of Reference: To keep under review policy on
the security and intelligence services.

Industrial, Commercial and Consumer Affairs
(EDI)

Leader of the House of Lords *(Chairman)*
Chancellor of the Exchequer
President of the Board of Trade
Secretary of State for Transport
Leader of the House of Commons
Minister of Agriculture, Fisheries and Food
Secretary of State for the Environment
Secretary of State for Wales
Chancellor of the Duchy of Lancaster
Secretary of State for Scotland
Secretary of State for Northern Ireland
Secretary of State for Employment
Chief Secretary, Treasury

Terms of Reference: To consider industrial, commercial and consumer issues including questions of competition and deregulation.

Environment (EDE)

Leader of the House of Lords *(Chairman)*
Foreign Secretary
Chancellor of the Exchequer
President of the Board of Trade
Secretary of State for Transport
Secretary of State for the Environment
Secretary of State for Wales
Chancellor of the Duchy of Lancaster
Secretary of State for Scotland
Secretary of State for National Heritage
Secretary of State for Northern Ireland
Chief Secretary, Treasury

Terms of Reference: To consider questions of environmental policy.

Home and Social Affairs (EDH)

Leader of the House of Lords *(Chairman)*
Lord Chancellor
Home Secretary
President of the Board of Trade
Secretary of State for Transport
Leader of the House of Commons
Secretary of State for the Environment
Secretary of State for Wales
Secretary of State for Social Security
Chancellor of the Duchy of Lancaster
Secretary of State for Scotland
Secretary of State for National Heritage
Secretary of State for Northern Ireland
Secretary of State for Education
Secretary of State for Health
Secretary of State for Employment
Chief Secretary, Treasury
Chief Whip in the House of Commons

The Minister of Agriculture, Fisheries and Food, the Attorney General and the Lord Advocate also receive papers and are invited to attend as necessary.

Terms of Reference: To consider home and social policy issues.

Local Government (EDL)

Leader of the House of Lords *(Chairman)*
Chancellor of the Exchequer
Home Secretary
Secretary of State for Transport
Leader of the House of Commons
Secretary of State for the Environment
Secretary of State for Wales
Secretary of State for Social Security
Chancellor of the Duchy of Lancaster
Secretary of State for Scotland
Secretary of State for National Heritage
Secretary of State for Education
Secretary of State for Health
Chief Secretary, Treasury
Minister of State, Department of the Environment
    (Minister for Local Government).

Terms of Reference: To consider issues affecting local
government, including the annual allocation of
resources.

Queen's Speeches and Future Legislation (FLG)

Leader of the House of Commons *(Chairman)*
Lord Chancellor
Leader of the House of Lords
Chancellor of the Duchy of Lancaster
Attorney General
Lord Advocate
Chief Whip in the House of Commons
Financial Secretary, Treasury
Chief Whip in the House of Lords

The Foreign Secretary should be invited to attend or
be represented for discussion of the Queen's
speeches.

Terms of Reference: To prepare and submit to the
Cabinet drafts of the Queen's speeches to
Parliament, and proposals for the government's
legislative programme for each session of
Parliament.

Legislation (LG)

Leader of the House of Commons *(Chairman)*
Lord Chancellor
Leader of the House of Lords
Secretary of State for Wales
Secretary of State for Scotland
Attorney General
Lord Advocate
Chief Whip in the House of Commons

Minister of State, Foreign and Commonwealth
  Office
Minister of State, Home Office
Financial Secretary, Treasury
Chief Whip in the House of Lords

Terms of Reference: To examine all draft bills, to
consider the parliamentary handling of government
bills, European Community documents and private
members' business, and such other related matters as
may be necessary; and to keep under review the
government's policy in relation to issues of
parliamentary procedures.

Civil Service Pay (EDC)

Leader of the House of Commons (Chairman)
Foreign Secretary
Chancellor of the Exchequer
Home Secretary
Secretary of State for Defence
Secretary of State for the Environment
Secretary of State for Social Security
Chancellor of the Duchy of Lancaster
Secretary of State for Scotland
Secretary of State for Northern Ireland
Secretary of State for Employment
Financial Secretary, Treasury

Terms of Reference: To determine the basis of the
annual negotiations and consider other matters
concerning civil service pay.

Sub-Committees

Health Strategy (EDH[H])

Leader of the House of Commons *(Chairman)*
Minister of Agriculture, Fisheries and Food
Secretary of State for the Environment
Secretary of State for Wales
Secretary of State for Social Security
Chancellor of the Duchy of Lancaster
Secretary of State for Scotland
Secretary of State for Northern Ireland
Secretary of State for Health
Paymaster General, Treasury
Minister of State, Department of Health (Minister
    for Health)
Minister of State, Department of Employment
Parliamentary Under Secretary, Department of
    National Heritage

The Home Secretary and Secretaries of State for
Transport and Education, and the President of the
Board of Trade should receive papers and may be
invited to attend as appropriate.

Terms of Reference: To oversee the development,
implementation and monitoring of the
government's health strategy, to coordinate the
government's policies on UK-wide issues affecting
health, and report as necessary to the Cabinet
Committee on Home and Social Affairs.

Public Sector Pay (EDI[P])

Leader of the House of Lords *(Chairman)*
Chancellor of the Exchequer
Home Secretary
President of the Board of Trade
Secretary of State for Transport
Secretary of State for the Environment
Chancellor of the Duchy of Lancaster
Secretary of State for Scotland
Secretary of State for Education
Secretary of State for Health
Secretary of State for Employment
Chief Secretary, Treasury

Terms of Reference: To coordinate the handling of
pay issues in the public sector, and report as
necessary to the Cabinet Committee on Industrial,
Commercial and Consumer Affairs.

European Questions (OPD[E])
Foreign Secretary *(Chairman)*
Chancellor of the Exchequer
Home Secretary
President of the Board of Trade
Secretary of State for Transport
Leader of the House of Commons
Minister of Agriculture, Fisheries and Food
Secretary of State for the Environment
Secretary of State for Wales
Secretary of State for Scotland
Secretary of State for Northern Ireland
Secretary of State for Employment
Attorney General
Chief Whip in the House of Commons
Minister of State, Foreign and Commonwealth
    Office

Other ministers will be invited to attend as the
nature of the business requires. The UK Permanent
representative to the European Communities is also
in attendance.

Terms of Reference: To consider questions relating to
the UK's membership of the European Community
and to report as necessary to the Cabinet
Committee on Defence and Overseas Policy.

Eastern Europe (OPD[AE])
Foreign Secretary *(Chairman)*
Chancellor of the Exchequer
President of the Board of Trade
Secretary of State for Defence
Minister of Agriculture, Fisheries and Food
Secretary of State for the Environment
Secretary of State for Employment
Minister for Overseas Development
Minister of State, Foreign and Commonwealth
    Office

Other ministers may be invited to attend as the
nature of the business requires.

Terms of Reference: To consider questions relating to
Britain's policy of assisting change in the former
Soviet republics and other former Communist
countries in Europe and report as necessary to the
Cabinet Committee on Defence and Overseas
Policy.

Terrorism (OPD[T])

Home Secretary *(Chairman)*
Foreign Secretary
Secretary of State for Defence
President of the Board of Trade
Secretary of State for Transport
Secretary of State for Scotland
Secretary of State for Northern Ireland
Attorney General

Terms of Reference: To keep under review the
arrangements for countering terrorism and for
dealing with terrorist incidents and their
consequences, and to report as necessary to the
Cabinet Committee on Defence and Overseas
Policy.

London (EDL[L])

Secretary of State for the Environment *(Chairman)*
Minister of State, Home Office
Minister of State, Department of Trade and Industry
   (Minister for Industry)
Minister of State, Department of the Environment
   (Minister for Housing and Planning)
Minister of State, Department of the Environment
   (Minister for Local Government)
Minister of State, Department of Social Security
   (Minister for Social Security and Disabled People)
Minister of State, Department of Education
Minister of State, Department of Health
Minister of State, Department of Employment
Economic Secretary, Treasury
Parliamentary Under Secretary, Department of
   Transport (Minister for Transport in London)
Parliamentary Under Secretary, Department of
   National Heritage

Terms of Reference: To coordinate the government's
policies on London.

Drug Misuse (EDH[D])

Leader of the House of Commons *(Chairman)*
Solicitor General
Paymaster General, Treasury
Minister of State, Home Office
Minister of State, Ministry of Defence (Minister for
   the Armed Forces)
Minister of State, Scottish Office
Minister of State, Department of Health (Minister
   for Health)

Parliamentary Under Secretary, Foreign and
  Commonwealth Office
Parliamentary Under Secretary, Welsh Office
Parliamentary Under Secretary, Department for
  Education (PUS for Schools)

Others, including the Minister for Overseas
Development and Parliamentary Under Secretaries
from the Departments of the Environment and
Employment may be invited to attend as
appropriate and should receive papers.

Terms of Reference: To coordinate the government's
national and international policies for tackling drugs
misuse, and report as necessary to the Cabinet
Committee on Home and Social Affairs.

Coordination of Urban Policy (EDH[U])

Secretary of State for the Environment *(Chairman)*
Minister of State, Home Office
Minister of State, Northern Ireland Office
Minister of State, Department of the Environment
  (Minister for Local Government)
Economic Secretary, Treasury
Parliamentary Under Secretary, Department of
  Trade and Industry (PUS for Technology)
Parliamentary Under Secretary, Department of
  Transport
Parliamentary Under Secretary, Department of the
  Environment
Parliamentary Under Secretary, Welsh Office
Parliamentary Under Secretary, Department of
  Social Security
Parliamentary Under Secretary, Scottish Office
Parliamentary Under Secretary, Department of
  National Heritage
Parliamentary Under Secretary, Department for
  Education (PUS for Schools)
Parliamentary Secretary, Department of Health
Parliamentary Under Secretary, Department of
  Employment

City Action Team ministers will be invited to attend
for items in which they have an interest.

Terms of Reference: To monitor and coordinate
government action on inner cities and report as
necessary to the Cabinet Committee on Home and
Social Affairs.

Alcohol Abuse (EDH[A])
Chancellor of the Duchy of Lancaster *(Chairman)*
Paymaster General, Treasury
Minister of State, Scottish Office
Minister of State, Department of Health (Minister for Health)
Minister of State, Ministry of Agriculture, Fisheries and Food
Parliamentary Under Secretary, Home Office
Parliamentary Under Secretary (Department of Trade and Industry) (PUS for Consumer Affairs and Small Firms)
Parliamentary Under Secretary, Department of Transport
Parliamentary Under Secretary, Welsh Office
Parliamentary Under Secretary, Northern Ireland Office
Parliamentary Under Secretary, Department for Education (PUS for Schools)
Parliamentary Under Secretary, Department of Employment

Terms of Reference: To review and develop the government's strategy for combating the misuse of alcohol and to oversee its continuing implementation and report as necessary to the Cabinet Committee on Home and Social Affairs.

Women's Issues (EDH[W])
Secretary of State for Employment *(Chairman)*
Paymaster General, Treasury
Minister of State, Welsh Office
Minister of State, Scottish Office
Minister of State, Department for Education
Parliamentary Under Secretary, Department of Trade and Industry (PUS for Consumer Affairs and Small Firms)
Parliamentary Under Secretary, Department of Social Security
Parliamentary Under Secretary, Office of Public Services and Science
Parliamentary Under Secretary, Northern Ireland Office
Parliamentary Secretary, Department of Health
Parliamentary Under Secretary, Department of Employment

The Parliamentary Secretary, Lord Chancellor's Department and the Parliamentary Under Secretaries at the Home Office and the Department of the Environment will also receive papers and be invited to attend as necessary.

Terms of Reference: To review and develop the
government's policy and strategy on issues of
special concern to women; to oversee their
implementation; and to report as necessary to the
Cabinet Committee on Home and Social Affairs.

Cabinet Office Addresses

For fax numbers telephone the number below and ask for the appropriate fax number

Horse Guards Road
London SW1P 3AL
Tel 071-270 3000

53 Parliament Street
London SW1A 2NH
Tel 071-270 3000

The Crown Estate

Founded 1760

Status Statutory body

Responsibilities Administration of the hereditary land revenues of the Crown under the provisions of the Crown Estate Act 1961. The estate includes properties in England, Wales, Scotland, Windsor Great Park, and foreshore and seabed around the coast of the United Kingdom

The Crown Estate

16 Carlton House Terrace, London SW1Y 5AH
Tel 071-210 3000   Fax 071-930 8259/3752
All staff are based at Carlton House Terrace unless otherwise indicated.
For other addresses and telephone numbers see the end of this section.

Commissioners

Overview

Staff				Department
Chairman	**Deputy Chairman Chief Executive**	**Deputy Chief Executive**	**Senior Management Team**	
Earl of Mansfield	C K Howes	These departments report directly to Mr Howes	M L Davies	Legal
			D E G Griffiths	Accounts
			J R Mulholland	Agricultural Estates
			M J Gravestock	Scottish Estates
			A R Wiseman	Windsor Estate
		H B Clarke	C F Hynes	Urban Estates
			F G Parrish	Marine Estates
			R Wyatt	Housing Estates

Staff and Departments

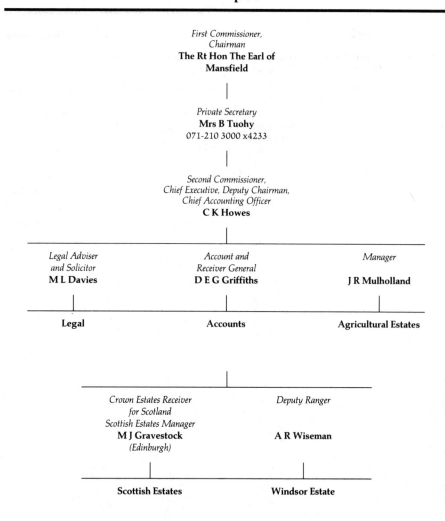

First Commissioner,
Chairman
The Rt Hon The Earl of
Mansfield

Private Secretary
Mrs B Tuohy
071-210 3000 x4233

Second Commissioner,
Chief Executive, Deputy Chairman,
Chief Accounting Officer
C K Howes

Legal Adviser	*Account and*	*Manager*
and Solicitor	*Receiver General*	
M L Davies	**D E G Griffiths**	**J R Mulholland**

Legal   **Accounts**   **Agricultural Estates**

Crown Estates Receiver   *Deputy Ranger*
for Scotland
Scottish Estates Manager
M J Gravestock   **A R Wiseman**
(Edinburgh)

Scottish Estates   **Windsor Estate**

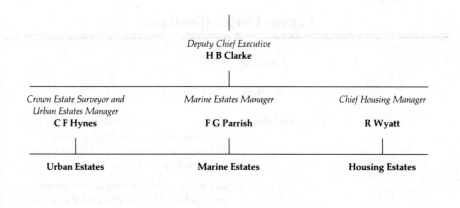

Deputy Chief Executive
H B Clarke

Crown Estate Surveyor and Urban Estates Manager	*Marine Estates Manager*	*Chief Housing Manager*
C F Hynes	**F G Parrish**	**R Wyatt**
Urban Estates	**Marine Estates**	**Housing Estates**

The Crown Estate Addresses

Crown Estate Office
10 Charlotte Square
Edinburgh EH2 4DR
Tel 031-226 7241
Fax 031-220 1366

Crown Estate Office
The Great Park
Windsor
Berks SL4 2HT
Tel 07538 60222
Fax 07538 59617

Crown Office (Scotland)

Founded   1765

Minister   Lord Advocate

Responsibilities   The public prosecution of crime in Scotland. All prosecutions in the High Court of Justiciary are conducted by Crown Counsel instructed by the Crown Office.

In the Sheriff and District Courts prosecutions are conducted by the Procurator Fiscal Service which is administered by the Crown Office

Crown Office

Regent Road, Edinburgh EH7 5BL
Tel 031-557 3800   Fax 031-556 0154

All staff are located at Regent Road unless otherwise indicated.
For other addresses and telephone numbers see end of this section.

Officials

Lord Advocate
The Rt Hon the Lord Rodger QC

|

Private Secretary
Mrs C McDivitt (EO)
031-557 3800

|

Solicitor General for Scotland
Thomas Dawson QC

|

Private Secretary
Mrs C McDivitt (EO)
031-557 3800

|

Crown Agent
J Duncan Lowe (2)

|

Deputy Crown Agent
A D Vannet (4)

|

Mrs I Guild (5)
W Gilchrist (5)
D A Brown (5)
J Watt (5)
N McFadyen (5)

Departmental Overview

Civil Servants			Department	Minister/ Solicitor General
Grade 2	*Grade 3*	*Grade 4*		
J D Lowe		A D Vannet	Crown Office	Lord Rodger T Dawson

Procurator Fiscal Service

Civil Servants			Department	Minister/ Solicitor General
J D Lowe	A C Normand	P Docherty	Glasgow and Strathkelvin	Lord Rodger T Dawson
	R F Lees		Lothian and Borders	Lord Rodger T Dawson
		S W Lockhart	Grampian, Highlands and Islands	Lord Rodger T Dawson
		B K Heywood	Tayside Central and Fife	Lord Rodger T Dawson
		J D Friel	North Strathclyde	Lord Rodger T Dawson
		W G Carmichael	South Strathclyde, Dumfries and Galloway	Lord Rodger T Dawson

Civil Servants and Departments

Crown Office

Crown Agent
J Duncan Lowe (2)

|

Deputy Crown Agent
A D Vannet (4)

|

Mrs I Guild (5)
W Gilchrist (5)
D A Brown (5)
J Watt (5)
N McFadyen (5)

|

Crown Office

Public prosecution of crime in
Scotland

Procurator Fiscal Service

Crown Agent
J Duncan Lowe (2)

|

Glasgow and Strathclyde Region	*Lothian and Borders Region*	*Grampian, Highlands and Islands Region*
Regional Procurator Fiscal	*Regional Procurator Fiscal*	*Regional Procurator Fiscal*
A C Normand (3)	**R F Lees (3)**	**S W Lockhart (4)**
(Glasgow)	*(Edinburgh)*	*(Aberdeen)*
P Docherty (4)	**K M Maciver (5)**	**I L Murray (5)**
D Spiers (5)	**J T O'Donnell (5)**	*(Aberdeen)*
Miss E C Munro (5)	*(all in Edinburgh)*	
W S Carnegie (5)		
Miss L M Ruxton (5)		
J J Miller (5)		
(all in Glasgow)		

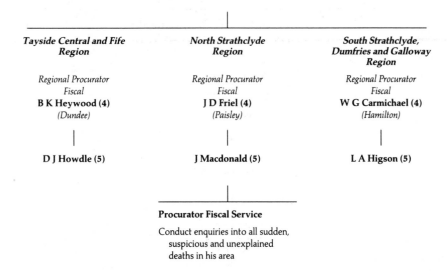

Tayside Central and Fife Region	North Strathclyde Region	South Strathclyde, Dumfries and Galloway Region
Regional Procurator Fiscal	Regional Procurator Fiscal	Regional Procurator Fiscal
B K Heywood (4)	**J D Friel (4)**	**W G Carmichael (4)**
(Dundee)	*(Paisley)*	*(Hamilton)*
D J Howdle (5)	**J Macdonald (5)**	**L A Higson (5)**

Procurator Fiscal Service

Conduct enquiries into all sudden, suspicious and unexplained deaths in his area

Crown Office Addresses

Regional Offices

Aberdeen Regional Office
Inverlair House
West North Street
Aberdeen AB9 1AL
Tel 0224 645132
Fax 0224 647005

Dundee Regional Office
15 West Bell Street
Dundee DD1 1HB
Tel 0382 27535
Fax 0382 202719

Edinburgh Regional Office
3 Queensferry Street
Edinburgh EH2 4RD
Tel 031-226 4962
Fax 031-220 4669

Glasgow Regional Office
10 Ballater Street
Glasgow G5 9PZ
Tel 041-429 5566
Fax 041-429 2066

Hamilton Regional Office
Cameronian House
3/5 Almada Street
Hamilton ML3 0HG
Tel 0698 284000
Fax 0698 422929

Paisley Regional Office
70 Inchinnan Road
Paisley PA3 2RP
Tel 041-887 5225
Fax 041-887 6172

Crown Prosecution Service

Founded   1986

Responsibilities   The independent review and conduct of criminal proceedings instituted by police forces in England and Wales (with the exception of cases conducted by the Serious Fraud Office and certain minor offences)

The Director of Public Prosecutions is the Head of the Service and is responsible for the discharge of her functions to the Attorney General

There is a headquarters office and 31 areas covering England and Wales each of which is supervised by a Chief Crown Prosecutor

Crown Prosecution Service

4–12 Queen Anne's Gate, London SW1H 9AZ
Tel 071-273 8152   Fax 071-222 0392
All staff are based at Queen Anne's Gate unless otherwise indicated.
For other addresses and telephone numbers see the end of this section.

Superintending Minister

Attorney General
The Rt Hon Sir Nicholas Lyell QC MP
(for details of his office
see Law Officers' Departments)

Officials

Director of Public Prosecutions
Mrs B J L Mills QC (1)

|

Private Secretary to the Director
Mrs T Glackin (SEO)
071-273 8100

|

Deputy Director and
Chief Executive
D S Gandy CB OBE (2)

Departmental Overview

Civil Servants			Department
rade 1	*Grade 2*	*Grade 3*	
Headquarters			
Irs B J L Iills QC	Report directly to the DPP	D J Wiblin	Establishment and Finance Group
		K R Ashken	Policy and Communications Group
	D S Gandy CB OBE	G D Etherington	Field Resources Group
		G Duff	Field Operations Group
		C Newell	Headquarters Casework Group
C P S Areas			
Irs B J L Iills QC	for names and districts see body of entry below		

Civil Servants and Departments

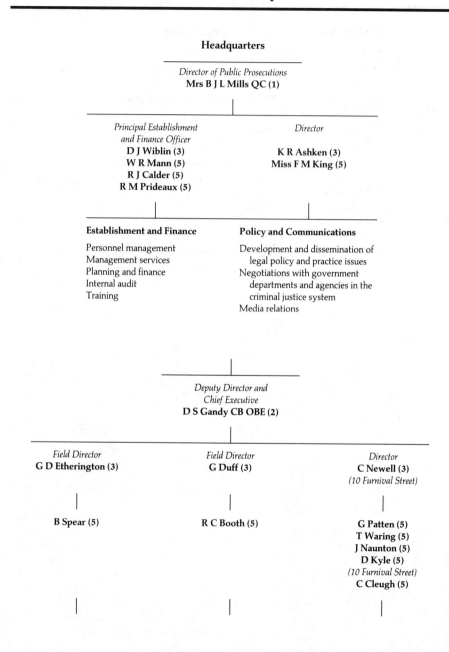

Headquarters

Director of Public Prosecutions
Mrs B J L Mills QC (1)

Principal Establishment and Finance Officer	*Director*
D J Wiblin (3)	**K R Ashken (3)**
W R Mann (5)	**Miss F M King (5)**
R J Calder (5)	
R M Prideaux (5)	

Establishment and Finance

Personnel management
Management services
Planning and finance
Internal audit
Training

Policy and Communications

Development and dissemination of
    legal policy and practice issues
Negotiations with government
    departments and agencies in the
    criminal justice system
Media relations

*Deputy Director and
Chief Executive*
D S Gandy CB OBE (2)

Field Director	*Field Director*	*Director*
G D Etherington (3)	**G Duff (3)**	**C Newell (3)**
		(10 Furnival Street)
B Spear (5)	**R C Booth (5)**	**G Patten (5)**
		T Waring (5)
		J Naunton (5)
		D Kyle (5)
		(10 Furnival Street)
		C Cleugh (5)

Field Resources	Field Operations	Headquarters Casework
Area plans	Area inspections	Fraud
Workload forecasts	Investigation of complaints	General casework
Resource allocations	Policy liaison and implementation	Special casework
Performance measures	Field systems	Police complaints
Counsel fees		
Witness expenses		

CPS Areas

Chief Crown Prosecutors	Area
C T Jones (5)	Avon/Somerset
D G Lewis (5)	Cambridgeshire/Lincolnshire
Mrs N E Hollingsworth (5)	Cheshire
D Sharp (5)	Cleveland/North Yorkshire
D R K Seddon (5)	Derbyshire
R J Green (5)	Devon/Cornwall
P Boeuf (5)	Dorset/Hampshire
J J Goodwin (5)	Essex
R A Prickett (5)	Gloucestershire/Wiltshire
A R Taylor (4)	Greater Manchester
C N Ingham (5)	Hertfordshire/Bedfordshire
L M Bell (5)	Humberside
R A Crabb (5)	Kent
J V Bates (5)	Lancashire/Cumbria
P J M Hollingworth (5)	Leicestershire/Northamptonshire
B T McArdle (4)	London (Inner)
R J Chronnell (4)	London (North)
D E J Dracup (4)	London (South and Surrey)
E C Woodcock (4)	Merseyside
M F C Harvey (5)	Norfolk/Suffolk
D A Farmer (5)	Northumbria/Durham
A S R Clarke (5)	North Wales: Dyfed/Powys
D C Beal (5)	Nottinghamshire
H G Wallace (4)	South Wales/Gwent
M J Rose (4)	South Yorkshire
D V Dickenson (5)	Staffordshire/Warwickshire
D Thompson (5)	Sussex
J Wilcox (5)	Thames Valley
D R Stott (5)	West Mercia
T M McGowran (4)	West Midlands
R Otley (4)	West Yorkshire

Crown Prosecution Service Addresses

10 Furnival Street
London EC4A 1PE
Tel 071-417 7000
Fax 071-430 0154

Avon/Somerset
1st Floor, Block A
Froomsgate House
Rupert Street
Bristol BS1 2QJ
Tel 0272 273093
Fax 0272 230697

Cambridgeshire/Lincolnshire
Justinian House
Spitfire Close
Ermine Business Park
Huntingdon
Cambridgeshire PE18 6XY
Tel 0480 432333
Fax 0480 432313

Cheshire
2nd Floor
Windsor House
Pepper Street
Chester CH1 1TD
Tel 0244 348043
Fax 0244 341355

Cleveland/North Yorkshire
6th Floor
Ryedale Building
60 Piccadilly
York YO1 1NS
Tel 0904 610726
Fax 0904 610394

Derbyshire
6th Floor
Celtic House
Heritage Gate
Friary Street
Derby DE1 1QX
Tel 0332 42956
Fax 0332 292942

Devon/Cornwall
Hawkins House
Pynes Hill
Rydon Lane
Exeter EX2 5SS
Tel 0392 422555
Fax 0392 422111

Dorset/Hampshire
1st Floor
Eastleigh House
Upper Market Street
Eastleigh
Hampshire SO5 4FD
Tel 0703 651128
Fax 0703 651613

Essex
2nd Floor
Gemini Centre
88 New London Road
Chelmsford
Essex CM2 0PD
Tel 0245 252939
Fax 0245 490476

Gloucestershire/Wiltshire
7 Avon Reach
Monkton Hill
Chippenham
Wiltshire
SN15 1EE
Tel 0249 655149
Fax 0249 660655

Greater Manchester
PO Box 377
8th Floor
Sunlight House
Quay Street
Manchester M60 3LU
Tel 061-837 7402
Fax 061-835 2663

Hertfordshire/Bedfordshire
Queens House
58 Victoria Street
St Albans AL1 3HZ
Tel 0727 44753
Fax 0727 51080

Humberside
3rd Floor
Queens House
Paragon Street
Hull HU1 3DA
Tel 0482 586611
Fax 0482 226731

Kent
Priory Gate
29 Union Street
Maidstone
Kent ME14 1PT
Tel 0622 686425
Fax 0622 685991

Lancashire/Cumbria
3rd Floor
Robert House
2 Starkie Street
Preston
Lancs PR1 3NY
Tel 0772 555030
Fax 0772 204743

Leicestershire/Northamptonshire
Princes Court
34 York Road
Leicester LE1 5TV
Tel 0533 549333
Fax 0533 550855

London (Inner)
24th Floor
Portland House
Stag Place
London SW1E 5BH
Tel 071-828 9050
Fax 071-828 8766

London (North)
3rd Floor
Solar House
1–9 Romford Road
Stratford
London E15 4LJ
Tel 081-534 6601
Fax 081-519 7037

London (South and Surrey)
17th Floor
Tolworth Tower
Surbiton
Surrey KT6 7DS
Tel 081-399 5171
Fax 081-390 9375

Merseyside
7th Floor (South)
Royal Liver Building
Pier Head
Liverpool L3 1HN
Tel 051-236 7575
Fax 051-255 0642

Norfolk/Suffolk
Saxon House
1 Cromwell Square
Ipswich
Suffolk IP1 1TS
Tel 0473 230332
Fax 0473 231377

Northumbria/Durham
3rd Floor
Benton House
136 Sandyford Road
Newcastle upon Tyne NE2 1QE
Tel 091-230 0800
Fax 091-230 0109

North Wales/Dyfed/Powys
491 Abergele Road
Old Colwyn
Colwyn Bay
Clwyd LL29 9AE
Tel 0492 512353
Fax 0492 512262

Nottinghamshire
2 King Edward Court
King Edward Street
Nottingham NG1 1EL
Tel 0602 480480
Fax 0602 586162

South Wales/Gwent
21st Floor
Pearl Assurance House
Greyfriars Road
Cardiff CF1 3PL
Tel 0222 382777
Fax 0222 373596

South Yorkshire
Belgrave House
47 Bank Street
Sheffield S1 2EH
Tel 0742 761601
Fax 0742 762468

Staffordshire/Warwickshire
Government Buildings
11a Princes Street
Stafford ST16 2EU
Tel 0785 223511
Fax 0785 223577

Sussex
Unit 3
Clifton Mews
Clifton Hill
Brighton BN1 3HR
Tel 0273 207562
Fax 0273 207849

Thames Valley
The Courtyard
Lombard Street
Abingdon
Oxon OX14 5SE
Tel 0235 555678
Fax 0235 554144

West Mercia
Orchard House
Victoria Square
Droitwich
Worcester WR9 8QT
Tel 0905 779502
Fax 0905 795896

West Midlands
6th Floor
Dale House
Dale End
Birmingham B4 7LN
Tel 021-233 3133
Fax 021-233 2499

West Yorkshire
4–5 South Parade
Wakefield WF1 1LR
Tel 0924 290620
Fax 0924 200417

Crown Solicitor's Office (Northern Ireland)

Founded	1 January 1974 replacing Chief Crown Solicitor's Office
Status	Non-ministerial department
Responsible to	Attorney General
Responsibilities	Legal services for United Kingdom and Northern Ireland government departments
	Administration of estates of people dying intestate and without known kin; dissolved companies; and failure of trustees
	The Crown Solicitor also acts as Queen's Proctor in Northern Ireland (interventions and advisory functions in matrimonial suits and cases dealing with the legitimation of children)

Crown Solicitor's Office for Northern Ireland

Royal Courts of Justice, Chichester Street, Belfast BT1 3JY
Tel 0232 235111   Fax 0232 248741

Minister

Attorney General
**The Rt Hon Nicholas
Lyell QC MP**
(for details of his office see
Law Officers' Department)

Officials

Crown Solicitor (2)

|

Private Secretary
0232 235111

|

Deputy Crown Solicitor (4)

|

8 Assistant Solicitors (5)

Her Majesty's Customs and Excise

Founded   1909 (by merger of the Boards of Customs and Excise, founded 1671 and 1683 respectively)

Minister   Chancellor of the Exchequer

Responsibilities   Collection and administration of customs and excise duties and Value Added Tax

Advice to Chancellor and Treasury Ministers on matters of customs and excise and Value Added Tax

Enforcing a range of prohibitions and restrictions on the importation of certain classes of goods, and, with other departments, on exports of certain goods

Detection and prevention of breaches of revenue laws

With other departments, control of European Community Common Agricultural Policy revenues and expenditure

Collection of trade statistics

Executive Units   While HM Customs and Excise remains a government department, it now has 30 executive units operating fully on 'Next Steps' lines. These are listed below with their directorates in brackets:

VAT Central Unit *(see VAT Control below)*
VAT Control Division C *(VAT Control)*
Tariff and Statistical Office *(Customs)*
Training Services *(Personnel)*
Information Technology *(Organisation)*
Accountant and Comptroller General's Office *(Organisation)*
Investigation Division *(Outfield)*
Internal Audit *(Internal Audit Unit)*
Solicitor's Office *(Solicitor's Office)*
Collectors (21) *(Collections)*

Her Majesty's Customs and Excise

New King's Beam House, 22 Upper Ground, London SE1 9PJ
Tel 071-620 1313   Fax 071-620 1313 x5005
All staff are based at New King's Beam House unless otherwise indicated.
For other addresses and telephone numbers see the end of this section.

Minister

The Chancellor of the Exchequer
The Rt Hon Norman Lamont MP
(for details of his office see
HM Treasury)

Officials

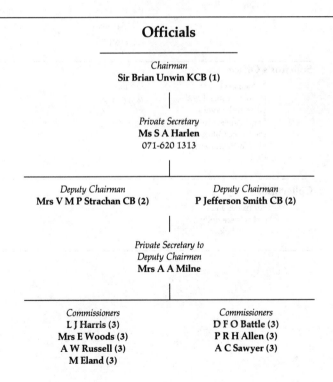

Chairman
Sir Brian Unwin KCB (1)

Private Secretary
Ms S A Harlen
071-620 1313

Deputy Chairman
Mrs V M P Strachan CB (2)

Deputy Chairman
P Jefferson Smith CB (2)

Private Secretary to
Deputy Chairmen
Mrs A A Milne

Commissioners
L J Harris (3)
Mrs E Woods (3)
A W Russell (3)
M Eland (3)

Commissioners
D F O Battle (3)
P R H Allen (3)
A C Sawyer (3)

Departmental Overview

Civil Servants			Department
Grade 1	*Grade 2*	*Grade 3*	
Internal Taxation and Customs			
Sir Brian Unwin	Mrs V M P Strachan	L J Harris	Internal Taxes
		Mrs E Woods	VAT Control
		A W Russell	Customs
		M Eland	Central Directorate
Corporate Services and Outfield			
Sir Brian Unwin	P Jefferson Smith	D F O Battle	Personnel
		P R H Allen	Organisation
		A C Sawyer	Outfield
		C Arnott (5)	Internal Audit
Solicitor's Office			
Sir Brian Unwin	M Saunders (Until October 1992 when he becomes Legal Adviser to the Home Office and the Northern Ireland Office)	G F Butt R D S Wylie	Solicitor's Office
Collections			
Sir Brian Unwin	For names and districts see body of entry below		

Civil Servants and Departments

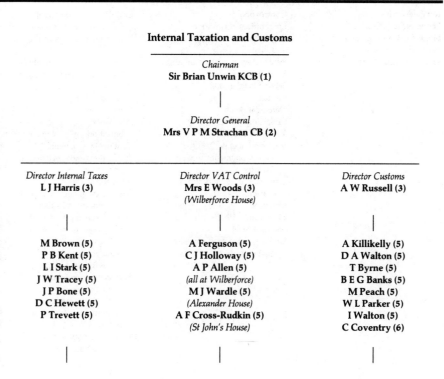

Internal Taxation and Customs

Chairman
Sir Brian Unwin KCB (1)

Director General
Mrs V P M Strachan CB (2)

Director Internal Taxes	*Director VAT Control*	*Director Customs*
L J Harris (3)	**Mrs E Woods (3)**	**A W Russell (3)**
	(Wilberforce House)	

M Brown (5)	A Ferguson (5)	A Killikelly (5)
P B Kent (5)	C J Holloway (5)	D A Walton (5)
L I Stark (5)	A P Allen (5)	T Byrne (5)
J W Tracey (5)	*(all at Wilberforce)*	B E G Banks (5)
J P Bone (5)	M J Wardle (5)	M Peach (5)
D C Hewett (5)	*(Alexander House)*	W L Parker (5)
P Trevett (5)	A F Cross-Rudkin (5)	I Walton (5)
	(St John's House)	C Coventry (6)

Internal Taxes Directorate	VAT Control Directorate	Customs Directorate
Revenue duties	Control policy	Coordination and control of
Economic regulator	Local office organisation	Customs activities related to:
Single market excise aspects	Registration and deregistration	Report and clearance of ships and
VAT administration	policy	aircraft
Excise and inland customs strategy	Retail schemes, cash accounting	Control of imported freight
	Small trader questions	Customs hours and attendance
	Second-hand goods	charges
	Car tax	Valuation of goods
	Deregulation unit	Warehousing
	Collection of VAT	Free zones
	VAT II IT project	Importations by govt departments
	VAT central unit:	Continental shelf relief
	returns, payments, repayments,	Prohibitions and restrictions on
	statistics	imports and exports
	Criminal proceedings and civil	Arms and strategic exports
	evasion	Counterfeit goods and copyright
	Insolvency	Postal imports and exports
	EC 8th and 13th directives	EC CAP and End-Use relief
	Bad debt relief	Tariff quotas and preferential
	Enforcement, default surcharges,	ceilings
	appeals	Community transit
		Customs freight systems
		Anti-smuggling policy
		Duty-free shops
		Travellers' allowances
		EC customs
		Inland control
		Registry of British ships
		Tariffs and statistics

Director
M Eland (3)

M F Knox (5)
K M Romanski (5)
A H Cowley (5)
(Portcullis House)

Central Directorate

Budget and central unit
Single Market unit
Tariffs and statistical office
Economics and statistics

Corporate Services and Outfield

Chairman
Sir Brian Unwin KCB (1)

*Principal Establishment
and Finance Officer,
Director General*
P Jefferson Smith CB (2)

Director of Personnel	*Director of Organisation*	*Director of Outfield*
D F O Battle (3)	**P R H Allen (3)**	**A C Sawyer (3)**

Ms D E Barrett (5)	**J Strachan (5)**	**F A D Rush (5)**
C R S Talbot (5)	**D P Child (5)**	**M W Summers (5)**
D L Chilvers (5)	**A G H Paynter (4)**	**F D Tweddle (5)**
J Meyler (5)	**J Campbell (5)**	*(Harmondsworth House)*
(Ralliquays)	**B G Dawbarn (5)**	
R E Kellaway (5)	**V C Whittington (5)**	
Mrs M Smith (5)	*(above 4 at Alexander House)*	
(Carby House)	**P A Blomfield ISO (5)**	
J Maclean (5)	*(Portcullis House)*	
J Tullberg (6)		
P Freeborn (6)		

Personnel Directorate	**Organisation Directorate**	**Outfield Directorate**
Human resource development Recruitment, (alternative working patterns), transfers, manpower planning Staff appraisal, promotion, succession planning, staff development, trawls, honours Pay and allowances, overtime, travelling and removal expenses, staff records Superannuation, discipline and inefficiency, data protection, absence, welfare, occupational health, health and safety, library and records, museum Accommodation policy and office services, security, personnel management, HQ training units and office facilities management, HQ relocation programme Vocational and development training Communications, industrial relations, civil emergencies, equal opportunities	Financial management Resource audit and management consultancy services IT business services IT developments IT infrastructure Personnel management unit HQ Accountant and Comptroller General's office	Organisation and management Allocation and oversight of use of resources Monitoring performance against plans Revenue cutters, drug dogs, technical equipment support Investigation of staff irregularities Investigations of prohibitions and restrictions, revenue fraud, EC fraud and smuggling, tracing proceeds of drug smuggling and other investigations under the Drug Trafficking Offences Act Standards of investigation Liaison with other enforcement agencies at home and overseas Administration, personnel

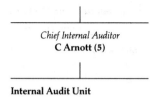

Chief Internal Auditor
C Arnott (5)

Internal Audit Unit

Solicitor's Office

Chairman
Sir Brian Unwin KCB (1)

Solicitor
M Saunders CB (2)
*(until October 1992 when he
becomes Legal Adviser to the
Home Office and the Northern
Ireland Office)*

Principal Assistant Solicitors
G F Butt (3)
R D S Wylie (3)

D J C McIntyre (5)
Miss A E Bolt (5)
M C K Gasper (5)
Miss S. G. Linton (5)
M A Cooper (5)
M Michael (5)
D N Pratt (5)
(Manchester office)
P Breuer (5)
G W M McFarlane (5)
A J Ridout (5)
J W N Tester (5)
D E T S Keefe (5)
D M North (5)
G Fotherby (5)
J A Quin (5)
I D Napper (5)
H J Flood (5)
C Allen (5)

Solicitor's Office

Preparation and conduct of penalty
proceedings in England and
Wales
Forfeitures and seizures,
prosecutions
VAT tribunals
Revenue duties
International matters
Mutual assistance, VAT question
relating to importation,
exportation and valuation
General customs matters
General, civil litigation, debt
recovery and enforcement in the
High Court and County Court
(and Civil Courts in N Ireland
and Scotland)
Insolvency and bankruptcy
Employment, Industrial Tribunal
matters and hearings
VAT liability
Zero-rating and exemptions, input
tax, partial exemption
EC questions
VAT machinery, control and
enforcement
Car tax
Prosecutions

Collections

Chairman
Sir Brian Unwin KBE (1)

Collections

England and Wales

Birmingham	*Dover*	*East Anglia*
Collector	Collector	Collector
R A Flavill (5)	**R Crossley (5)**	**R C Shepherd (5)**

East Midlands	*Leeds*	*Liverpool*
Collector	Collector	Collector
M D Patten (5)	**W J G Prollins (5)**	**C A Roberts (5)**

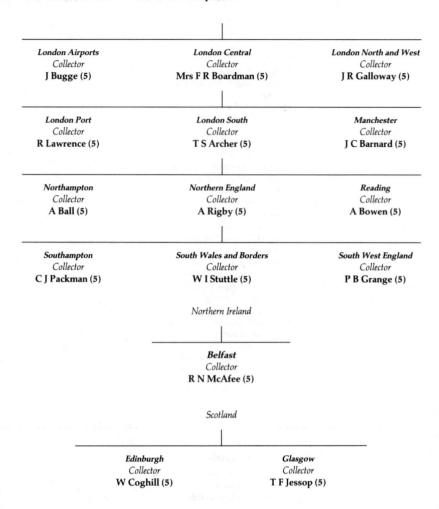

London Airports	London Central	London North and West
Collector	Collector	Collector
J Bugge (5)	Mrs F R Boardman (5)	J R Galloway (5)

London Port	London South	Manchester
Collector	Collector	Collector
R Lawrence (5)	T S Archer (5)	J C Barnard (5)

Northampton	Northern England	Reading
Collector	Collector	Collector
A Ball (5)	A Rigby (5)	A Bowen (5)

Southampton	South Wales and Borders	South West England
Collector	Collector	Collector
C J Packman (5)	W I Stuttle (5)	P B Grange (5)

Northern Ireland

Belfast
Collector
R N McAfee (5)

Scotland

Edinburgh	Glasgow
Collector	Collector
W Coghill (5)	T F Jessop (5)

HM Customs and Excise Addresses

National addresses

Alexander House
Victoria Avenue
Southend-on-Sea SS99 1AA
Tel 0702 348944

Carby House
73 Victoria Avenue
Southend-on-Sea SS2 6EB
Tel 0702 367515

Dorset House
Stamford Street
London SE1 9PS
Tel 071-620 1313

Harmsworth House
Bouverie Street
London EC4Y 8BS
Tel 071-353 1525

Portcullis House
27 Victoria Avenue
Southend-on-Sea SS2 6AL
Tel 0702 348944

Ralli Quays
3 Stanley Street
Salford M60 9LA
Tel 061-839 7839

St John's House
Merton Road
Bootle
Merseyside L20 3NN
Tel 051-922 6393

Wilberforce House
25 The Strand
Liverpool L2 7XL
Tel 051-707 1234/1453
Fax 051-707 1227

Collections addresses

England and Wales

Birmingham
Alpha Tower
Suffolk Street
Queensway
Birmingham B1 1TX
Tel 021-643 2777
Fax 021-643 9657

Dover
Burlington House
Townwall Street
Dover
Kent CT16 1SY
Tel 0304 206789
Fax 0304 224420

East Anglia
Haven House
17 Lower Brook Street
Ipswich
Suffolk IP4 1DN
Tel 0473 232388

East Midlands
Bowman House
100–102 Talbot Street
Nottingham NG1 5NF
Tel 0602 470451
Fax 0602 483487

Leeds
Royal Exchange House
Boar Lane
Leeds LS1 5TP
Tel 0532 422655
Fax 0532 421497

Liverpool
Customs House
Cunard Buildings
Liverpool L3 1DX
Tel 051-227 4343
Fax 051-236 3350

London Airports
Custom House
Nettleton Road
North Side
Heathrow Airport
Hounslow
Middlesex TW6 2LA
Tel 081-750 1515
Fax 081-750 1516

London Central, South
AMP House
Dingwall Road
Croydon CR9 1TR
Tel 081-680 1700
Fax 081-680 1063

London North and West
Dorland House
388 High Road
Wembley
Middlesex HA9 6AJ
Tel 081-930 9001
Fax 081-903 3556

London Port
Custom House
The Terrace
Gravesend DA12 2BW
Tel 0375 844121
Fax 0474 537389

Manchester
Custom House
Furness Quay
Salford M5 2XX
Tel 061-872 4282

Northampton
Britannia House
3–5 Rushmills
Northampton NN4 0XB
Tel 0604 601800

Northern England
Custom House
39 Quayside
Newcastle upon Tyne NE1 3ES
Tel 091-261 0981
Fax 091-232 9032
     091-230 3427

Reading
Eaton Court
104–112 Oxford Road
Reading RG1 7FU
Tel 0734 583921
Fax 0734 505618

Southampton
Custom House
Orchard Place
Southampton SO9 1ZD
Tel 0703 330330
Fax 0703 827088

South Wales and Borders
Portcullis House
21 Cowbridge Road East
Cardiff CF1 9SS
Tel 0222 238531
Fax 0222 387302

South West England
Froomsgate House
Rupert Street
Bristol BS1 2QP
Tel 0272 266091
Fax 0272 221723

Northern Ireland
Belfast.
Custom House
Queens Square
Belfast BT1 3EU
Tel 0232 234466
Fax 0232 232903

Scotland
Edinburgh
44 York Place
Edinburgh EH1 3JW
Tel 031-556 2433

Glasgow
Portcullis House
21 India Street
Glasgow G2 4PZ
Tel 041-221 3828
Fax 041-226 5733

Where there is no fax number shown, please phone the switchboard and ask for the fax number of the department you wish to contact

Ministry of Defence

Founded	1946 as a small coordinating department; became a ministry in 1964 with the amalgamation of the Admiralty, War Office and Air Ministry
Ministers	one secretary of state, two ministers of state and one parliamentary under secretary of state
Responsibilities	Command and administration of the armed forces
	Formulation and implementation of defence policy
	Research, development, production and purchase of weapons systems and equipment
Executive and Support Agencies	Chemical and Biological Defence Establishment
	Defence Analytical Services Agency
	Defence Operational Analysis Centre
	Defence Postal and Courier Service
	Defence Research Agency
	Directorate General of Defence Accounts
	Duke of York's Military School
	Hydrographic office
	Meteorological office
	Military survey
	Naval Aircraft Repair Organisation
	Queen Victoria School
	Royal Air Force Support Command and Maintenance Group
	Service Children's Schools (NW Europe)

Because of security considerations the Whitehall Companion has agreed to an MoD request that it should publish only the names of civil servants and members of the armed forces at grade 4/equivalent and above. Most grade 5s/equivalents and below are signified as Director (*).

The MoD is currently undergoing radical changes. Although the Whitehall Companion has provided as much up-to-date information as is available, a number of jobs within the ministry are likely to change over the next 12 months. If readers have difficulty contacting anyone listed in this section they should telephone MoD general enquiries on 071-218 9000.

Ministry of Defence

Main Building, Whitehall, London SW1A 2HB
Tel 071-218 9000
Fax *Telephone above number and ask for appropriate fax number*
All staff are based at Main Building unless otherwise indicated.
For other addresses and telephone numbers see the end of this section.

Ministers

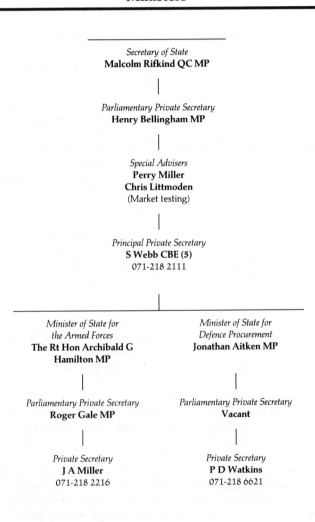

Secretary of State
Malcolm Rifkind QC MP

Parliamentary Private Secretary
Henry Bellingham MP

Special Advisers
Perry Miller
Chris Littmoden
(Market testing)

Principal Private Secretary
S Webb CBE (5)
071-218 2111

*Minister of State for
the Armed Forces*
**The Rt Hon Archibald G
Hamilton MP**

Parliamentary Private Secretary
Roger Gale MP

Private Secretary
J A Miller
071-218 2216

*Minister of State for
Defence Procurement*
Jonathan Aitken MP

Parliamentary Private Secretary
Vacant

Private Secretary
P D Watkins
071-218 6621

---

*Parliamentary Under Secretary
of State for Defence*
**The Viscount Cranborne
(The Lord Cecil)**

Private Secretary
P A Wilson
071-218 2394

House of Lords' Spokesmen
**The Viscount Cranborne
The Viscount Ullswater
The Viscount Long
The Viscount St Davids**

Ministerial Responsibilities

Malcolm Rifkind   Overall responsibility for the ministry

Archibald Hamilton   all operational matters and overseas
commitments
arms control
operational logistics
reserve forces policy
size and shape of the 3 services
strategy and general financial issues
women in the armed forces

Jonathan Aitken   defence equipment programme
defence exports
defence procurement and contracts
equipment projects
nuclear issues
quality assurance
policy for market testing and contracting out
research and development
Royal dockyards
Trident programme

Viscount Cranborne   Citizen's Charter
defence estate and service housing
environmental matters
heritage
low flying
medicine and hospitals (military)
NAAFI
"Next steps"
personnel issues
service and civilian personnel matters
works services
service and civilian personnel matters
including equal opportunities
House of Lords spokesman

List of MOD Departments in order shown

Higher Organisation of Defence

Secretary of State
Rt Hon Malcolm Rifkind QC MP

Ministers
**The Rt Hon Archibald G
Hamilton MP
Jonathan Aitken MP
The Viscount Cranborne**

*Permanent Under
Secretary of State*
**Sir Christopher France
KCB (1)**

*Chief of the
Defence Staff (CDS)*
**Field Marshal Sir
Richard Vincent
GBE KCB DSO (5*)**
*(to be replaced in December 1992
by Air Chief Marshal Sir Peter
Harding)*

*Vice Chief of
the Defence
Staff (VCDS)*
**Admiral Sir
Benjamin Bathurst
GCB (4*)**
*to be replaced in January
1993 by Admiral Jock Slater*

Defence Staff

*Chief of the
General Staff
(CGS)*
**General Sir Peter
Inge GCB (4*)**

*Chief of the
Air Staff
(CAS)*
**Air Chief Marshal
Sir Peter Harding
GCB ADC (4*)**
*to be replaced in November
1992 by Air Chief Marshal
Sir Michael Graydon*

*Chief of the
Naval Staff
(CNS)*
**Admiral Sir
Julian Oswald GCB
ADC (4*)**
*to be replaced in February
1993 by Admiral Sir Benjamin
Bathurst*

Single Service Executive Staffs

Higher Organisation of Defence

Secretary of State
Rt Hon Malcolm Rifkind QC MP

Ministers
**The Rt Hon Archibald G
Hamilton MP
Jonathan Aitken MP
The Viscount Cranbourne**

*Permanent Under Secretary
of State*
Sir Christopher France KCB (1)

*Second Permanent
Secretary of State
(2nd PUS)*
J M Stewart (1A)

*Chief Scientific
Adviser (CSA)*
Prof E R Oxburgh (1A)

*Chief Defence
Procurement
(CDP)*
Dr M K McIntosh (1)

**Office of
Management and Budget
(OMB)**

**Defence Scientific
Staff**

**Procurement
Executive**

Departmental Overview

Civil Servants and Defence Staff				Department	Minister
Grade 1/5*	Grade 1A/4*	Grade 2/3*	Grade 3/2*		
Defence Staff					
	Field Marshal Sir Richard F Vincent (to be replaced in Dec 1992 by Air Chief Mshl Sir Peter Harding)				
Defence Services Secretary					
			Majr Gen B T Pennicott	Defence Services Secretariat	M Rifkind
Defence Intelligence					
	Field Marshal Sir Richard F Vincent and Sir Christopher France	Chief of Defence Intelligence		Defence Intelligence	M Rifkind
Chiefs of Staff Secretariat					
Field Marshal Sir Richard F Vincent	Admiral Sir Benjamin Bathurst (to be replaced in January 1993 by Adm Sir Jock Slater)	Captain B Burns		Chiefs of Staff Secretariat	M Rifkind

KEY

Grade 1/5*
1 = civil service grade 1
5* = 5 star general etc

Grade 2/3*
2 = civil service grade 2
3* = 3 star general etc

(*) 1 star brigadier etc
† rank lower than (*)

Departmental Overview

Civil Servants and Defence Staff

Grade 1/5*	Grade 1A/4*	Grade 2/3*	Grade 3/2*	Department	Minister
Field Marshal Sir Richard F Vincent and Sir Christopher France		**Public Relations**	Miss G Samuel (4)	Public Relations	M Rifkind
Field Marshal Sir Richard F Vincent and Sir Christopher France	Admiral Sir Benjamin Bathurst	**Commitments** Air Mshl Sir Kenneth W Hayr	Director (*)	UK Commitments/Joint Operations	A Hamilton
			Maj Gen A G H Harley	Overseas	A Hamilton
			Air Vice Mshl D J Saunders	Logistics	A Hamilton
			W D Reeves	Commitments	A Hamilton
Field Marshal Sir Richard F Vincent and Sir Christopher France	Admiral Sir Benjamin Bathurst	**Systems** Air Mshl Sir Roger Austin	Director	Defence Systems	A Hamilton
			R Adm R F Cobbold	Sea Systems	A Hamilton
			Maj Gen S Cowan	Land Systems	A Hamilton
			Air Vice Mshl I D MacFadyen	Air Systems	A Hamilton
			R Adm R Walmsley	Command, Control, Communications Information Systems	A Hamilton

Departmental Overview

Civil Servants and Defence Staff

Grade 1/5*	Grade 1A/4*	Grade 2/3*	Grade 3/2*	Department	Minister
Field Marshal Sir Richard F Vincent and Sir Christopher France	Admiral Sir Benjamin Bathurst	Vice Adm Sir Barry N Wilson			

Programmes and Personnel

Grade 1/5*	Grade 1A/4*	Grade 2/3*	Grade 3/2*	Department	Minister
			Maj Gen The Hon T P J Boyd-Carpenter	Programmes	A Hamilton
			Director	Personnel	Vis Cranborne

Defence Medical Services (Surgeon General)

Grade 1/5*	Grade 1A/4*	Grade 2/3*	Department	Minister
Field Marshal Sir Richard F Vincent and Sir Christopher France	Admiral Sir Benjamin Bathurst	Lt Gen Sir Peter J Beale	Surgeon General	Vis Cranborne
		R Adm D A Lammiman		
		Air Vice Mshl J Brook		Vis Cranborne
				Vis Cranborne
		Maj Gen F E Ashenhurst		Vis Cranborne
		Director (*)	Defence Nursing Services	Vis Cranborne
		Director (*)	Army Medicine	Vis Cranborne
		Director (*)	Finance and Secretariat	Vis Cranborne
		Maj Gen R P Craig	Army Surgery	Vis Cranborne
		Director (*)	Army Psychiatry	Vis Cranborne
		Director (*)	Army Pathology	Vis Cranborne
		Director (*)	Army General Practice	Vis Cranborne

Departmental Overview

Civil Servants and Defence Staff

Grade 1/5*	Grade 1A/4*	Grade 2/3*	Grade 3/2*	Department	Minister
Field Marshal Sir Richard F Vincent and Sir Christopher France			Adm J R Tod	Defence Staff (Policy and Nuclear)	A Hamilton
		Policy			
		Vacant	I D Dawson	Defence (Policy)	A Hamilton

Navy Department

Assistant Chief of the Naval Staff/Commandant General, Royal Marines

Grade 1/5*	Grade 1A/4*	Grade 2/3*	Grade 3/2*	Department	Minister
Field Mshl Sir Richard F Vincent	Adm Sir Julian J R Oswald *(to be replaced in February 1993 by Adm Sir Benjamin Bathurst)*	Lt Gen Sir Henry Beverley	R Adm P C Abbott	Naval Staff	All
			Maj Gen A M Keeling	Royal Marines	

Second Sea Lord

Grade 1/5*	Grade 1A/4*	Grade 2/3*	Grade 3/2*	Department	Minister
Field Mshl Sir Richard F Vincent	Adm Sir Julian J R Oswald	Vice Adm Sir Michael Livesay	R Adm N J Wilkinson	Naval Manpower and Training	Vis Cranborne
			Director (*)	Navy Personal Services	Vis Cranborne
			R Adm C C Morgan	Naval Secretary's Office	Vis Cranborne
			J M Moss	Naval Personnel	Vis Cranborne
			Rear Admiral D A Lammiman	Naval Medical and Dental Services	Vis Cranborne
			Cmndt A C Spencer	WRNS Sea Service Implementation Team	Vis Cranborne
			The Ven M G H Henley	Naval Chaplaincy Services	Vis Cranborne

Departmental Overview

Civil Servants and Defence Staff

Grade 1/5*	Grade 1A/4*	Grade 2/3*	Grade 3/2*	Department	Minister
Field Mshl Sir Richard F Vincent	Adm Sir Julian J R Oswald				
		Chief of Fleet Support Vice Adm Sir Neville Purvis	D C R Heyhoe	Fleet Support	A Hamilton / J Aitken
			G A Allin	Ship Refitting	A Hamilton / J Aitken
			J T Baugh	Supplies and Transport (Naval)	A Hamilton / J Aitken
			R Adm G Davis	Fleet Support Policy and Services	A Hamilton / J Aitken
			R Adm R H Burn	Aircraft (Navy)	A Hamilton / J Aitken
			R Adm J A L Myres	Hydrographic Services	A Hamilton / J Aitken

Army Department

Grade 1/5*	Grade 1A/4*	Grade 2/3*	Grade 3/2*	Department	Minister
Field Mshl Sir Richard F Vincent	Gen Sir Peter Inge	**General Staff** Lt Gen Sir P R Duffell CBE MC	Maj Gen R N Wheeler	General Staff	A Hamilton
			Majr Gen S C Grant	Doctrine and Training (including Directors of Royal Armoured Corps, Royal Artillery, Infantry, Army Air Corps, Intelligence Corps)	A Hamilton
		Military Secretary Lt Gen The Hon Sir		Military Secretary	Vis Cranborne
Field Mshl Sir	Gen Sir Peter				

Departmental Overview

Civil Servants and Defence Staff

Grade 1/5*	Grade 1A/4*	Grade 2/3*	Grade 3/2*	Department	Minister
Adjutant General					
Field Mshl Sir Richard F Vincent	Gen Sir Peter Inge and Lt Gen Michael Wilkes		M L Scicluna	Adjutant General	Vis Cranborne
			Maj Gen J F J Johnston	Army Manning and Recruitment	Vis Cranborne
			Maj Gen M D Jackson	Personal Services (Army)	Vis Cranborne
			Maj Gen R D Grist	Personnel and Administrative Support	Vis Cranborne
			Director	Security Services (Army)	Vis Cranborne
			Lt Gen Sir Peter Beale	Army Medical Directorate Administration	Vis Cranborne
			Rev J Harkness	Chaplain's Services	Vis Cranborne
			Director	Military Adviser to AUS (A)	Vis Cranborne
			Director	Long-term Strategies and Studies	Vis Cranborne
Quartermaster General					
Field Mshl Sir Richard F Vincent	Gen Sir Peter Inge	Lt Gen Sir John Learmont	N Beaumont	Quartermaster	J Aitken / A Hamilton
			Maj Gen G W Field	Logistic Policy (Army)	J Aitken / A Hamilton
			Maj Gen J D MacDonald	Transport and Movements (Army)	J Aitken / A Hamilton
			Maj Gen D F E Botting	Ordnance Services	J Aitken / A Hamilton
			Maj Gen M S Heath	Equipment Support A	J Aitken / A Hamilton

Departmental Overview

Grade 1/5*	Grade 1A/4*	Grade 2/3*	Grade 3/2*	Department	Minister
Civil Servants and Defence Staff					
Air Force Department					
Field Mshl Sir Richard F Vincent	Air Chief Mshl Sir Peter R Harding *(to be replaced in November 1992 by Air Chief Mshl Sir Michael Graydon)*	**Air Staff**	Air Vice Mshl T Garden	Air Staff	All
			D J McLauchlan	National Air Traffic	Vis Cranborne
			Air Vice Mshl M Gibson	Services	
		Air Member for Personnel			
Field Mshl Sir Richard F Vincent	Air Chief Mshl Sir Roger Palin	M D Tidy		Personnel (Air)	Vis Cranborne
		Air Vice Mshl R J Honey		Air Manning and Personnel	Vis Cranborne
		Air Vice Mshl D O Crwys-Williams		RAF Personal Services	Vis Cranborne
		Air Vice Mshl J F Willis		Training (RAF)	Vis Cranborne
		Air Vice Mshl R T Dawson		Legal Services (RAF)	Vis Cranborne
		The Ven B H Lucas		Chaplaincy Services (RAF)	Vis Cranborne
		Air Vice Mshl J Brook		Medical Services (RAF)	Vis Cranborne

Departmental Overview

Civil Servants and Defence Staff

Grade 1/5*	Grade 1A/4*	Grade 2/3*	Grade 3/2*	Department	Minister
Field Mshl Sir Richard F Vincent	Air Chief Mshl Sir Peter Harding and Air Chief Mshl Sir Brendan Jackson				
		Air Member for Supply and Organisation			
			D J Gould	Supply and Organisation	A Hamilton
			Air Vice Mshl R J M Alcock	Logistic Support	A Hamilton
			Air Vice Mshl D R Hawkins	RAF Regiment Security	A Hamilton
			Director (*)	RAF Contracts	A Hamilton
			Director (*)	Supply and Organisation	A Hamilton

Scientific Staff

Grade 1/5*	Grade 1A/4*	Grade 2/3*	Grade 3/2*	Department	Minister
		Deputy Chief Scientific Adviser			
Sir Christopher France	Prof Sir Ernest Oxburgh	Dr G G Pope	J W Britton	Projects and Research	J Aitken
			H B Jordan	Capabilities	J Aitken
			Dr D Leadbeater (4)	Defence Operational Analysis Establishment	J Aitken
			Director (*)	Budgets and Finance	J Aitken
			Dr T Buckley	Research	J Aitken
			Dr G S Pearson	Chemical and Biological Defence Establishment	J Aitken
		Assistant Chief Scientific Adviser (Nuclear)			
		Dr G Pocock (4)		Nuclear Policy	J Aitken

Departmental Overview

Civil Servants and Defence Staff

Grade 1/5*	Grade 1A/4*	Grade 2/3*	Grade 3/2*	Department	Minister

Head of Strategic Defence Initiative Participation Office

			A L C Quigley	Policy and Industrial Support Technology	J Aitken

PUS of State's Organisation and Office of Management and Budget

Resources and Programmes

				Department	Minister
Sir Christopher France	J M Stewart	R T Jackling	N H Nicholls	Systems	A Hamilton
			D B Omand	Programmes	A Hamilton
			Dr M J Harte	Resources	A Hamilton

Finance

Sir Christopher France	J M Stewart	M J V Bell	T J Brack	General Finance	A Hamilton
			A J Cragg	Management Audit	A Hamilton
			M J Dymond (4)	Defence Accounts	A Hamilton

Personnel and Logistics

Sir Christopher France	J M Stewart	R L L Facer	M Gainsborough	Service Personnel	A Hamilton
			T F W B Knapp	Infrastructure and Logistics	Vis Cranborne
			B F Rule	Information Technology Systems	Vis Cranborne
			B W Stanley	Defence Works Services	Vis Cranborne

Departmental Overview

Civil Servants and Defence Staff

Grade 1/5*	Grade 1A/4*	Grade 2/3*	Grade 3/2*	Department	Minister
		Civilian Management			
Sir Christopher France	J M Stewart	J F Howe	M J Culham	Administration	Vis Cranborne
			I D Fauset	Specialists	Vis Cranborne
			A G Rucker	Security and Common Services	Vis Cranborne
			J Reddington	MOD Police	Vis Cranborne

Inter-Service and Ancillary Organisations

				Department	Minister
Field Marshal Sir Richard F Vincent		Vice Adm Sir John Coward	Maj Gen W Hicks	Royal College of Defence Studies	Vis Cranborne
			Air Vice Mshl R P O'Brien	Joint Service Defence College	Vis Cranborne
			Gp Capt I Dorrett	Defence ADP Training Centre	Vis Cranborne
			R Adm W Higgins	Defence Press and Broadcasting Committee	M Rifkind

Departmental Overview

Civil Servants and Defence Staff

Grade 1/5*	Grade 1A/4*	Grade 2/3*	Grade 3/2*	Department	Minister

Procurement Executive

Policy and Administration

	Grade 1A/4*	Grade 2/3*	Grade 3/2*	Department	Minister
	Sir Christopher France and Dr M K McIntosh	A J MacDonald	Director	Defence Procurement	J Aitken
			B Miller	Test and Evaluation	J Aitken
			J A Gulvin	International and Domestic Procurement	J Aitken
			G E Roe	Defence Contracts	J Aitken
			Maj Gen C R S Notley	Ordnance Board	J Aitken

Defence Export Services

	Grade 1A/4*	Grade 2/3*	Grade 3/2*	Department	Minister
	Sir Christopher France and Dr M K McIntosh	J A Thomas	G G Jones	International Finance Advice	J Aitken
			R Adm P B Rowe	Defence Export Services	J Aitken
			N D Paren	Marketing	J Aitken
			C T Sandars	Sales Administration	J Aitken
			Air Vice Mshl Sir William Wratten	Saudi Airforce Project	J Aitken
			Director (*)	Malaysian Project	J Aitken

Nuclear Programmes

	Grade 1A/4*	Grade 2/3*	Grade 3/2*	Department	Minister
	Sir Christopher France and Dr M K McIntosh	D M Spiers (see also Aircraft Controllerate)	G N Beavan	Nuclear Controllerate	J Aitken
		B H Richards		Atomic Weapons Establishment	J Aitken

Departmental Overview

Civil Servants and Defence Staff

Grade 1/5*	Grade 1A/4*	Grade 2/3*	Grade 3/2*	Department	Minister
Sir Christopher France and Dr M K McIntosh					
Sea Systems Controllerate					
		Vice Adm Sir Kenneth J Eaton	B R Hawtin	Material Navy	J Aitken
			R Adm D M Pulvertaft	Procurement and Support Organisation (Navy)	J Aitken
		Vice Adm Sir Robert C F Hill		Submarines	J Aitken
			Senior Director (*)	Marine Engineering	J Aitken
			D McArthur (4)	Underwater Weapons	J Aitken
			Director (*)	Naval Ship Acceptance	J Aitken
			A Phipps (4)	Navy and Nuclear Contracts	J Aitken
			H Perkins	Surface Ships	J Aitken
			Cdre F P Scourse (*)	Surface Weapons	J Aitken
			Director (*)	Technical Services (Warships)	J Aitken
			R Adm I H Pirnie	Strategic Systems	J Aitken
			Director (*)	Future Naval Projects	J Aitken
Land Systems Controllerate					
		Lt Gen A S J Blacker	Dr A M Fox	Ordnance	J Aitken
			J G H Walker (4)	Policy and Special Projects	J Aitken
			R C Harford (4)	Contracts (Ordnance)	J Aitken
			Maj Gen A C P Stone	Land Fighting Systems	J Aitken
Sir Christopher France and Dr M K McIntosh			J D Maines	Guided Weapons and Electronic Systems (Land)	J Aitken

Departmental Overview

Civil Servants and Defence Staff

Grade 1/5*	Grade 1A/4*	Grade 2/3*	Grade 3/2*	Department	Minister
Sir Christopher France and Dr M K McIntosh		**Aircraft Controllerate**			
		D M Spiers	Ms D J Seammen	Air (PE)	J Aitken
			D A Oakley (4)	Contracts (Air)	J Aitken
		Air Mshl Sir Michael Simmons	J C Mabberley	Avionics Weapons and Information Systems	J Aitken
			J A Gordon	Aircraft 1	J Aitken
			Air Vice Mshl P C Norriss	Aircraft 2	J Aitken

KEY

Grade 1/5*
1 = civil service grade 1
5* = 5 star general etc

Grade 2/3*
2 = civil service grade 2
3* = 3 star general etc

(*) 1 star brigadier etc
+ rank lower than (*)

Civil Servants and Armed Services

Defence Staff
Defence Services Secretary

Chief of the Defence Staff
**Field Marshal Sir Richard F
Vincent GBE KCB DSO (5*)**

Defence Services Secretary
Major General B T Pennicott (2*)

Defence Services Secretariat

Service interface with Royal
business
Senior appointments
Honours and awards

Defence Intelligence

Chief of the Defence Staff
**Field Marshal Sir Richard F
Vincent GBE KCB DSO (5*)**

Permanent Under Secretary of State
Sir Christopher France KCB (1)

Chief of Defence Intelligence

Defence Intelligence

All intelligence matters

Chiefs of Staff Secretariat

Chief of the Defence Staff
**Field Marshal Sir Richard F
Vincent GBE KCB DSO (5*)**

|

Vice Chief of the Defence Staff
**Admiral Sir Benjamin Bathurst
GCB (4*)**
*(to be replaced in January 1993
by Adm Sir Jock Slater)*

|

Secretary of Chiefs of Staff Committee
Capt B Burns RN (*)

|

Chiefs of Staff Secretariat

Chiefs of Staff
Corporate Business

Public Relations

Chief of the Defence Staff
**Field Marshal Sir Richard F
Vincent GBE KCB DSO (5*)**

Permanent Under Secretary of State
Sir Christopher France KCB (1)

|

Chief of Public Relations
Miss G Samuel (4)

|

*Deputy Chief of
Public Relations*
C D Verey (5) (*)

|

**Air Cdre B A E Pegnall (*)
Brig T A Glass (*)
Capt C Esplin-Jones OBE RN (*)**

|

Public Relations

PR Policy
Press Liaison
Promotions and facilities

Commitments

Chief of the Defence Staff **Field Marshal Sir Richard F** **Vincent GBE KCB DSO (5*)**	*Permanent Under Secretary of State* **Sir Christopher France KCB (1)**

Vice Chief of the Defence Staff
Admiral Sir Benjamin Bathurst
GCB (4*)

Deputy Chief of Defence
Staff (Commitments)
Air Mshl Sir Kenneth W Hayr
KCB CBE (3*)

Director *Commitments (UK)* **Director (*)**	*Assistant Chief of* *Defence Staff (Overseas)* **Maj Gen A G H Harley** **CB OBE (2*)**	*Assistant Chief of* *Defence Staff (Logistics)* **Air Vice Mshl D J** **Saunders CBE (2*)**
	Directors (*)	**Directors (*)**

UK Commitments/ **Joint Operations**	**Overseas**	**Logistics**
Policy and plans	Preparation of military advice for the Chief of the Defence Staff on policy and operational matters worldwide and on military assistance overseas	Policy and plans for deployments, exercises (movements, stores, material)

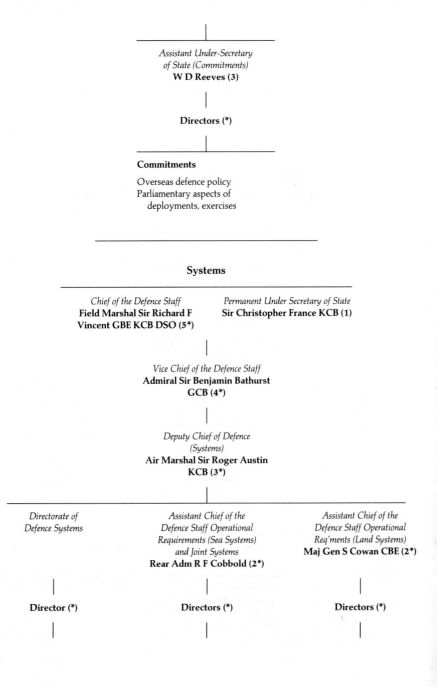

Assistant Under-Secretary
of State (Commitments)
W D Reeves (3)

Directors (*)

Commitments

Overseas defence policy
Parliamentary aspects of
deployments, exercises

Systems

Chief of the Defence Staff
**Field Marshal Sir Richard F
Vincent GBE KCB DSO (5*)**

Permanent Under Secretary of State
Sir Christopher France KCB (1)

Vice Chief of the Defence Staff
**Admiral Sir Benjamin Bathurst
GCB (4*)**

Deputy Chief of Defence
(Systems)
**Air Marshal Sir Roger Austin
KCB (3*)**

Directorate of
Defence Systems

Assistant Chief of the
Defence Staff Operational
Requirements (Sea Systems)
and Joint Systems
Rear Adm R F Cobbold (2*)

Assistant Chief of the
Defence Staff Operational
Req'ments (Land Systems)
Maj Gen S Cowan CBE (2*)

Director (*)

Directors (*)

Directors (*)

Defence Systems

Future equipment requirements
Priorities
Equipment programme

Sea Systems and Joint Service Systems

Requirements, research and specification

Land Systems Requirements

Requirements, research and specification

Assistant Chief of the Defence Staff Operational Requirements (Air Systems)

Air Vice Mshl I D MacFadyen CB, OBE (2*)

Assistant Chief of the Defence Staff (Command, Control, Communications and Information Systems)

Rear Adm R Walmsley (2*)

Directors (*)

Directors (*)

Air Systems

Operational requirements, research and specification

Command, Control, Communications and Information Systems

Policy and operational requirements
Defence Communication Network

Programmes and Personnel

Chief of the Defence Staff
Field Marshal Sir Richard F Vincent GBE KCB DSO (5*)

Permanent Under Secretary of State
Sir Christopher France KCB (1)

Vice Chief of the Defence Staff
Admiral Sir Benjamin Bathurst GCB (4*)

Deputy Chief of the Defence Staff (Programmes and Personnel)
Vice Adm Sir Barry Wilson KCB (3*)

Assistant Chief of the *Defence Staff (Programmes)* **Major Gen The Hon T P J Boyd-** **Carpenter MBE (2*)**	*Director Personnel* **Director (*)**

Directors (*)

Programmes Advice on programme matters	**Personnel** Tri-service policy on personnel including pay and joint training/education matters

Defence Medical Services Directorate (Surgeon General)
(see also single service sections)

Chief of the Defence Staff **Field Marshal Sir Richard F** **Vincent GBE KCB DSO (5*)**	*Permanent Under Secretary of State* **Sir Christopher France KCB (1)**

Vice Chief of the Defence Staff
Admiral Sir Benjamin Bathurst
GCB (4*)

Surgeon General,
Director General, Army
Medical Services
Lt Gen Sir Peter J Beale
KBE QHP (2*)
(also reports to Deputy Chief of
Defence Staff, Programmes
and Personnel)
(First Avenue House)

Deputy Surgeon General	*Deputy Surgeon General*	*Director of Defence*
(Ops and Plans)	*(Health Services)*	*Dental Services*
Medical Dir Gen (Naval)	*Dir Gen Med Svcs (RAF)*	*Dir Army Dental Services*
Surg R Adm D A Lammiman	**Air Vice Mshl J Brook**	**Maj Gen F E Ashenhurst**
LVO QHS (2*)	**QHS (2*)**	**(2*)**
(First Avenue House)	*(First Avenue House)*	*(First Avenue House)*
Directors (*)	**Directors (*)**	**Directors (*)**
(all at First Avenue House)	*(all at First Avenue House)*	*(all at First Avenue House)*

Information	Policy and planning	Policy
Systems and supply	Health services	Training and Personnel
Operations and plans	Clinical services	
	Training	
	Manpower	
	Pay	
	Conditions	

Director of Defence	*Director Army Medicine*	*Head of Medical Services*
Nursing Services	*Consultant Physician*	*(Finance and Secretariat)*
Director (*)	**Director (*)**	**Director (*)**
(First Avenue House)		*(First Avenue House)*

Defence Nursing Services	**Army Medicine**	**Medical Services (Finance**
	Directorate	**and Secretariat)**
Policy		Budget
Plans		Administration
Requirements		Briefs and visits
Training		
Personnel		
Conditions		

Director Army Surgery	*Director Army Psychiatry*
Consultant Surgeon	*and Consultant Psychiatrist*
Maj Gen R P Craig QHS	**Director (*)**
(2*)	*(First Avenue House)*
(RAMC Millbank)	

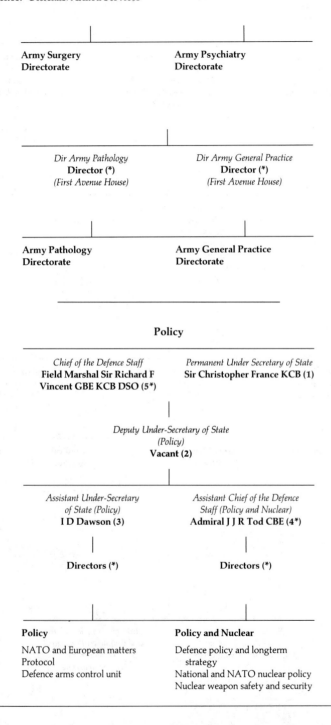

Army Surgery
Directorate

Army Psychiatry
Directorate

Dir Army Pathology
Director (*)
(First Avenue House)

Dir Army General Practice
Director (*)
(First Avenue House)

Army Pathology
Directorate

Army General Practice
Directorate

Policy

Chief of the Defence Staff
**Field Marshal Sir Richard F
Vincent GBE KCB DSO (5*)**

Permanent Under Secretary of State
Sir Christopher France KCB (1)

*Deputy Under-Secretary of State
(Policy)*
Vacant (2)

*Assistant Under-Secretary
of State (Policy)*
I D Dawson (3)

*Assistant Chief of the Defence
Staff (Policy and Nuclear)*
Admiral J J R Tod CBE (4*)

Directors (*)

Directors (*)

Policy

NATO and European matters
Protocol
Defence arms control unit

Policy and Nuclear

Defence policy and longterm
  strategy
National and NATO nuclear policy
Nuclear weapon safety and security

Navy Department
Assistant Chief of the Naval Staff and Commandant General, Royal Marines

Chief of the Defence Staff
Field Marshal Sir Richard F Vincent GBE KCB DSO (5*)

|

Chief of Naval Staff
First Sea Lord
Admiral Sir Julian J R Oswald GCB ADC (4*)
(to be replaced in February 1993 by Adm Sir Benjamin Bathurst)

|

Assistant Chief of Naval Staff **Rear Admiral P C Abbott (2*)**	*Commandant General Royal Marines* **Lt Gen Sir Henry Beverley KCB OBE RM (3*)**
	Chief of Staff Royal Marines **Maj Gen A M Keeling (2*)**
Directors (*)	**Directors (*)**
Naval Staff	**Royal Marines**
Naval security Naval warfare Operations and trade Staff duties Signals Secretariat/political aspects Coordination and briefing	Planning, operations, staff duties, training and aviation Officers' entry, promotion, appointments and records Personnel and logistics Budgets Communications

Second Sea Lord

Chief of the Defence Staff
**Field Marshal Sir Richard F
Vincent GBE KCB DSO (5*)**

*Chief of Naval Staff
First Sea Lord*
**Admiral Sir Julian J R Oswald
GCB ADC (5*)**

*Chief of Naval Personnel
Second Sea Lord*
**Vice Admiral Sir Michael
Livesay KCB (3*)**

Director General of Naval Manpower and Training	*Director Naval Personal Services*	*Naval Secretary*
Rear Adm N J Wilkinson CBE (2*)	**Senior Director (*)**	**Rear Adm C C Morgan (2*)**
(Old Admiralty Building Ripley Block)	*(Old Admiralty Building Archway South)*	*(Old Admiralty Building Ripley Block)*
Directors (*)	**Directors (*)**	**Directors (*)**

Manpower and Training	**Personal Services**	**Naval Secretary's Office**
Manpower planning	Service conditions	Officer appointments for seamen,
Manning and training for seamen, engineering, supply and secretariat, instructors	Physical training and sport Judge advocate Recruiting	engineers, supply, secretariat, WRNS and instructors
Education and training support	Job evaluation	
Foreign and commonwealth training	RN film corporation	
Naval psychologist		
Recruiting		

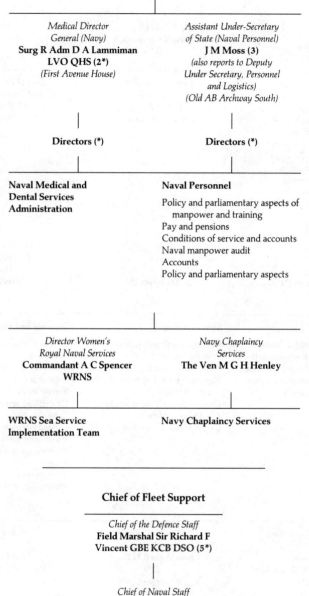

*Medical Director
General (Navy)*
**Surg R Adm D A Lammiman
LVO QHS (2*)**
(First Avenue House)

*Assistant Under-Secretary
of State (Naval Personnel)*
J M Moss (3)
*(also reports to Deputy
Under Secretary, Personnel
and Logistics)
(Old AB Archway South)*

Directors (*)

Directors (*)

**Naval Medical and
Dental Services
Administration**

Naval Personnel

Policy and parliamentary aspects of
manpower and training
Pay and pensions
Conditions of service and accounts
Naval manpower audit
Accounts
Policy and parliamentary aspects

*Director Women's
Royal Naval Services*
**Commandant A C Spencer
WRNS**

*Navy Chaplaincy
Services*
The Ven M G H Henley

**WRNS Sea Service
Implementation Team**

Navy Chaplaincy Services

Chief of Fleet Support

Chief of the Defence Staff
**Field Marshal Sir Richard F
Vincent GBE KCB DSO (5*)**

*Chief of Naval Staff
First Sea Lord*
**Admiral Sir Julian J R Oswald
GCB ADC (5*)**

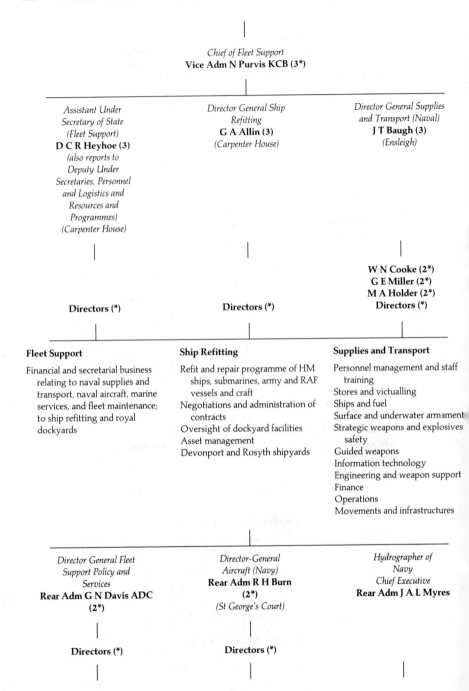

Chief of Fleet Support
Vice Adm N Purvis KCB (3*)

Assistant Under Secretary of State (Fleet Support) **D C R Heyhoe (3)** *(also reports to Deputy Under Secretaries, Personnel and Logistics and Resources and Programmes) (Carpenter House)*	*Director General Ship Refitting* **G A Allin (3)** *(Carpenter House)*	*Director General Supplies and Transport (Naval)* **J T Baugh (3)** *(Ensleigh)*

W N Cooke (2*)
G E Miller (2*)
M A Holder (2*)

Directors (*)   **Directors (*)**   **Directors (*)**

Fleet Support	**Ship Refitting**	**Supplies and Transport**
Financial and secretarial business relating to naval supplies and transport, naval aircraft, marine services, and fleet maintenance; to ship refitting and royal dockyards	Refit and repair programme of HM ships, submarines, army and RAF vessels and craft Negotiations and administration of contracts Oversight of dockyard facilities Asset management Devonport and Rosyth shipyards	Personnel management and staff training Stores and victualling Ships and fuel Surface and underwater armament Strategic weapons and explosives safety Guided weapons Information technology Engineering and weapon support Finance Operations Movements and infrastructures

Director General Fleet Support Policy and Services **Rear Adm G N Davis ADC (2*)**	*Director-General Aircraft (Navy)* **Rear Adm R H Burn (2*)** *(St George's Court)*	*Hydrographer of Navy Chief Executive* **Rear Adm J A L Myres**

Directors (*)   **Directors (*)**

Fleet Support Policy and Services	**Aircraft (Navy)**	**Hydrographic Services**
Logistic planning	Engineering and logistic supply	
Fleet supply duties	policy	
Engineering support	Tri-service helicopter and marine	
Information systems	gas turbine repair and	
OASIS	modification	
Naval shore telecoms authority	Inservice engineering management	
Marine services	Development of naval air	
Infrastructure and environment	equipment	
	Financial and material provision	
	Adviser to users of photography	

Army Department
General Staff

Chief of the Defence Staff
**Field Marshal Sir Richard F
Vincent GBE KCB DSO (5*)**

Chief of the General Staff
General Sir Peter Inge GCB (4*)

Assistant Chief of General Staff	*Inspector General Doctrine and Training*
Maj Gen R N Wheeler CBE (2*)	**Lt Gen Sir P R Duffell CBE MC (3*) (HQDT)**
	(Erskine Barracks)
Senior Directors	**Director Doctrine (*)**
Maj Gen R F L Cook (2*)	**Director CITG (*)**
Maj Gen R Wood (2*)	**Maj Gen S C Grant**
Maj Gen J A J P Barr CBE (2*)	**(2*) (DGAT)**
Directors (*)	*Arms Directors*
	Dir Royal Artillery
	Maj Gen M T Tennant (2*)
	(RA Barracks, Woolwich)

|

Dir Royal Artillery
Maj Gen M T Tennant (2*)
(RA Barracks, Woolwich)

|

Dir Royal Armoured Corps
**Maj Gen R J Hayman-Joyce
CBE (2*)**
(Bovington Camp)

|

Dir Infantry
**Maj Gen B H Dutton CBE
(2*)**
(Warminster)

|

Dir Army Air Corps
**Maj Gen S W St J Lytle
(2*)**
(Middle Wallop)

|

Intelligence Corps
Director (*)
(Ashford)

| |

General Staff

Military operations
Current commitments, force levels,
  structures
Military Survey
Staff duties
Arms control
Historical branch secretariat
Command and information systems

Doctrine and Training

Policy for doctrine training, exams
  and courses
CD, BD, TD, and NBC policy
ABCA national office
Training policy for regular and
  reserve armies
Coordination of collective training
  resources
Training assistance to other
  countries
Adventurous training
Royal Artillery
Royal Armoured Corps
Infantry
Air Corps
Intelligence Corps

Military Secretary

Chief of the Defence Staff
**Field Marshal Sir Richard F
Vincent GBE KCB DSO (5*)**

|

Chief of the General Staff
Gen Sir Peter Inge GCB (4*)

|

Military Secretary
**Lt Gen The Hon W E Rous
KCB OBE (3*)**

|

Directors (*)

|

Military Secretary's Office

Career matters for officers

Adjutant General

Chief of the Defence Staff
**Field Marshal Sir Richard F
Vincent GBE KCB DSO (5*)**

|

Chief of the General Staff
Gen Sir Peter Inge GCB (4*)

|

Adjutant-General
**Lt Gen Sir Michael
Wilkes KCB CBE (3*)**

|

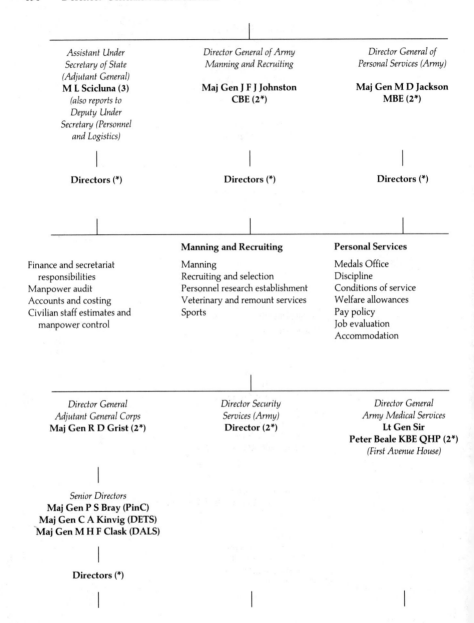

*Assistant Under
Secretary of State
(Adjutant General)*
M L Scicluna (3)
*(also reports to
Deputy Under
Secretary (Personnel
and Logistics)*

*Director General of Army
Manning and Recruiting*

**Maj Gen J F J Johnston
CBE (2*)**

*Director General of
Personal Services (Army)*

**Maj Gen M D Jackson
MBE (2*)**

Directors (*)   **Directors (*)**   **Directors (*)**

Finance and secretariat
  responsibilities
Manpower audit
Accounts and costing
Civilian staff estimates and
  manpower control

Manning and Recruiting

Manning
Recruiting and selection
Personnel research establishment
Veterinary and remount services
Sports

Personal Services

Medals Office
Discipline
Conditions of service
Welfare allowances
Pay policy
Job evaluation
Accommodation

*Director General
Adjutant General Corps*
Maj Gen R D Grist (2*)

*Director Security
Services (Army)*
Director (2*)

*Director General
Army Medical Services*
**Lt Gen Sir
Peter Beale KBE QHP (2*)**
(First Avenue House)

Senior Directors
**Maj Gen P S Bray (PinC)
Maj Gen C A Kinvig (DETS)
Maj Gen M H F Clask (DALS)**

Directors (*)

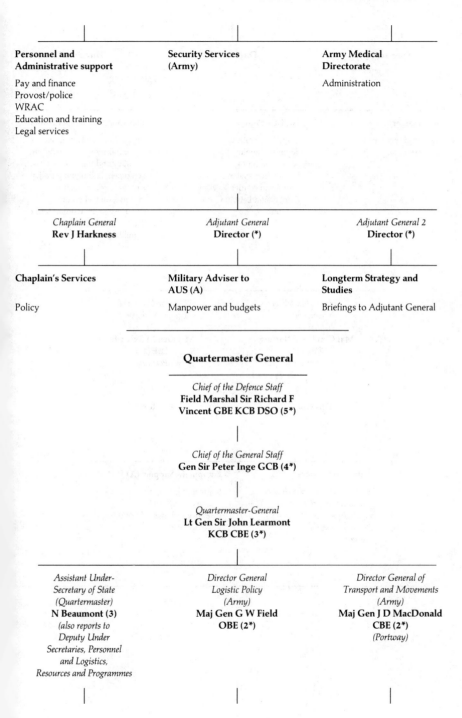

Personnel and Administrative support	Security Services (Army)	Army Medical Directorate
Pay and finance Provost/police WRAC Education and training Legal services		Administration

Chaplain General **Rev J Harkness**	*Adjutant General* **Director (*)**	*Adjutant General 2* **Director (*)**
Chaplain's Services	**Military Adviser to AUS (A)**	**Longterm Strategy and Studies**
Policy	Manpower and budgets	Briefings to Adjutant General

Quartermaster General

Chief of the Defence Staff
Field Marshal Sir Richard F Vincent GBE KCB DSO (5*)

Chief of the General Staff
Gen Sir Peter Inge GCB (4*)

Quartermaster-General
Lt Gen Sir John Learmont KCB CBE (3*)

Assistant Under-Secretary of State (Quartermaster) **N Beaumont (3)** *(also reports to Deputy Under Secretaries, Personnel and Logistics, Resources and Programmes*	*Director General Logistic Policy (Army)* **Maj Gen G W Field OBE (2*)**	*Director General of Transport and Movements (Army)* **Maj Gen J D MacDonald CBE (2*)** *(Portway)*

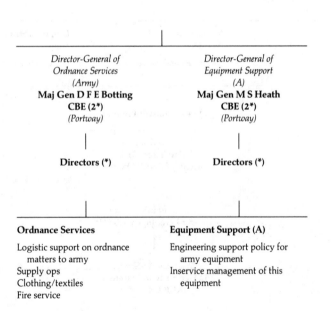

| Directors (*) | Directors (*) | Directors (*) |

Quartermaster

Financial and secretariat
  responsibilities

Logistic Policy

Logistic operations
Support planning
Army quartering
Information systems
Postal and courier services
Pioneer and Labour Corps
Catering

Transport and Movements

Royal Corps of Transport
  organisation and operations
  policy and training
Equipment and training policy
Accounting and finance
Information technology
HQ army railway organisation
Planning and coordination of all
  military movement

Director-General of
Ordnance Services
(Army)
Maj Gen D F E Botting
CBE (2*)
(Portway)

Director-General of
Equipment Support
(A)
Maj Gen M S Heath
CBE (2*)
(Portway)

Directors (*)

Directors (*)

Ordnance Services

Logistic support on ordnance
  matters to army
Supply ops
Clothing/textiles
Fire service

Equipment Support (A)

Engineering support policy for
  army equipment
Inservice management of this
  equipment

Air Force Department
Air Staff

Chief of the Defence Staff
**Field Marshal Sir Richard F
Vincent GBE KCB DSO (5*)**

|

Chief of the Air Staff
**Air Chief Marshal Sir Peter R
Harding GCB ADC (4*)**
*(to be replaced in
November 1992 by
Air Chief Mshl Sir
Michael Graydon)*

Chief Executive National	*Assistant Chief of*
Air Traffice Services	*Air Staff*
D J McLauchlan (3)	**Air Vice Mshl T Garden**
(CAA House)	**CB (2*)**

|

*Director General Policy
and Plans*
**Air Vice Mshl M J Gibson
OBE (2*)**
(CAA House)

National Air Traffic Services	**Air Staff**
UK airspace policy and planning	Briefing coordination
Financial responsibilities for	Staff duties, personnel
military air traffic services	Air offensive
NATS regulatory, policy and	Air defence
strategic planning functions	Secretariat (air staff)
Organisation, operation and	Flight safety
development of joint military	
and civil air traffic systems	

Air Member for Personnel

Chief of the Defence Staff
**Field Marshal Sir Richard F
Vincent GBE KCB DSO (5*)**

|

Chief of the Air Staff
**Air Chief Marshal Sir Peter
R Harding GCB ADC (4*)**

Air Member for Personnel
**Air Chief Marshal Sir Roger
Palin KCB CBE ADC (4*)**

Assistant Under-Secretary of State (Personnel) (Air)	*Air Secretary*	*Director General of RAF Personal Services*
M D Tidy (3) *(also reports to* **Deputy Under Secretaries, Personnel and Logistics, Resources and Programmes)** *(Adastral House)*	**Air Vice Mshl R J Honey CB CBE (2*)** *(RAF PMC Innsworth)*	**Air Vice Mshl D O Crwys-Williams CB (2*)** *(Adastral House)*
Directors (*)	**Directors (*)**	**Directors (*)**
Personnel (Air)	**Air Manning and Personnel**	**RAF Personal Services**
Secretarial assistance and advice Pay, allowances and pensions for RAF Other financial aspects Services Sound and Vision Corporation RAF museum Honours and awards Manning, terms of service Management audits and resource control reviews Civilian manpower numbers control and vote management of civilian pay and related expenditure	Manning policy, career administration and personal affairs of RAF officers and airmen Personnel information	Discipline policy, court martial reviews and petitions Royal and State visits Ceremonial and clothing Pay and allowances, job evaluation Secretarial policy WRAF, welfare RAF trusteeships and non-public funds Sports and recreation

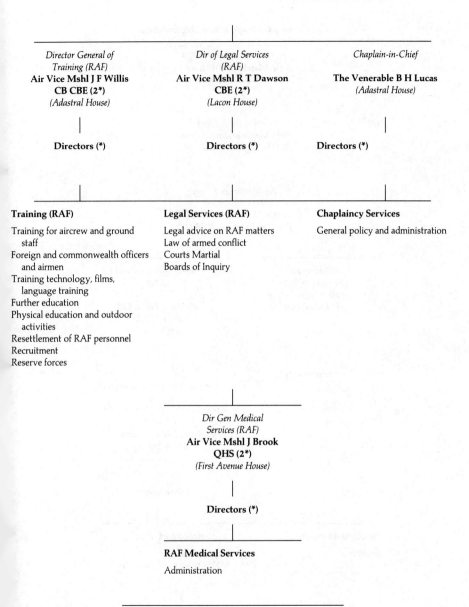

*Director General of
Training (RAF)*
**Air Vice Mshl J F Willis
CB CBE (2*)**
(Adastral House)

*Dir of Legal Services
(RAF)*
**Air Vice Mshl R T Dawson
CBE (2*)**
(Lacon House)

Chaplain-in-Chief
The Venerable B H Lucas
(Adastral House)

Directors (*)   **Directors (*)**   **Directors (*)**

Training (RAF)

Training for aircrew and ground
  staff
Foreign and commonwealth officers
  and airmen
Training technology, films,
  language training
Further education
Physical education and outdoor
  activities
Resettlement of RAF personnel
Recruitment
Reserve forces

Legal Services (RAF)

Legal advice on RAF matters
Law of armed conflict
Courts Martial
Boards of Inquiry

Chaplaincy Services

General policy and administration

*Dir Gen Medical
Services (RAF)*
**Air Vice Mshl J Brook
QHS (2*)**
(First Avenue House)

Directors (*)

RAF Medical Services

Administration

Air Member for Supply and Organisation

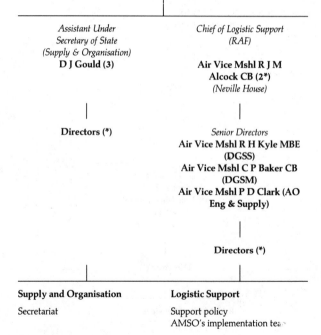

Chief of the Defence Staff
**Field Marshal Sir Richard F
Vincent GBE KCB DSO (5*)**

Chief of the Air Staff
**Air Chief Marshal Sir Peter
R Harding GCB ADC (4*)**

*Air Member for Supply
and Organisation*
**Air Chief Marshal Sir
Brendan J Jackson KCB (4*)**

*Assistant Under
Secretary of State
(Supply & Organisation)*
D J Gould (3)

*Chief of Logistic Support
(RAF)*

**Air Vice Mshl R J M
Alcock CB (2*)**
(Neville House)

Directors (*)

Senior Directors
**Air Vice Mshl R H Kyle MBE
(DGSS)
Air Vice Mshl C P Baker CB
(DGSM)
Air Vice Mshl P D Clark (AO
Eng & Supply)**

Directors (*)

Supply and Organisation

Secretariat

Logistic Support

Support policy
AMSO's implementation tea⸗

|

Works services and married
  quarters
Organisation and deployment
Management information systems
Signals
Logistic information
Logistics establishment
RAF historical records
Information and advice
Clearance of papers for publication

Management services
Transport, movements and
  petroleum
DSGM plans and budget
Defence codification authority
Catering

Engineering and Supply Directorate
HQ Strike Command

|

Comm Gen RAF Regt
Dir Gen of Security
Air Vice Mshl D R
Hawkins MBE (2*)
(Metropole Building)

Director
RAF Contracts
Director (*)

Air Member
Supply and Organisation
Director (*)

|

Directors (*)

| | |

Security

RAF provost services
Physical and personnel security
RAF Regiment
Defence Fire Services

RAF Contracts

Policy and Procurement

Supply and Organisation

Budgets
Plans

Scientific Staff
Deputy Chief Scientific Adviser

Permanent Under Secretary of State
Sir Christopher France KCB (1)

|

Chief Scientific Adviser
Professor Sir Ernest Oxburgh
KBE (1A)

|

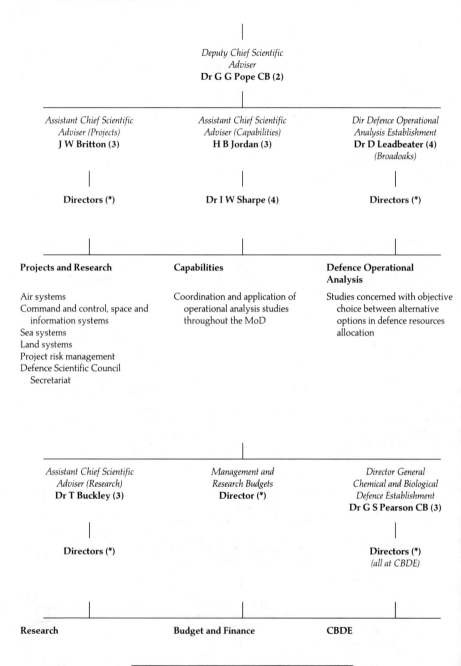

Deputy Chief Scientific
Adviser
Dr G G Pope CB (2)

Assistant Chief Scientific	Assistant Chief Scientific	Dir Defence Operational
Adviser (Projects)	Adviser (Capabilities)	Analysis Establishment
J W Britton (3)	**H B Jordan (3)**	**Dr D Leadbeater (4)**
		(Broadoaks)

Directors (*)   **Dr I W Sharpe (4)**   **Directors (*)**

Projects and Research   **Capabilities**   **Defence Operational Analysis**

Air systems   Coordination and application of   Studies concerned with objective
Command and control, space and   operational analysis studies   choice between alternative
  information systems   throughout the MoD   options in defence resources
Sea systems   allocation
Land systems
Project risk management
Defence Scientific Council
  Secretariat

Assistant Chief Scientific	Management and	Director General
Adviser (Research)	Research Budgets	Chemical and Biological
Dr T Buckley (3)	**Director (*)**	Defence Establishment
		Dr G S Pearson CB (3)

Directors (*)   **Directors (*)**
                                                             (all at CBDE)

Research   **Budget and Finance**   **CBDE**

Assistant Chief Scientific Adviser (Nuclear)

Permanent Under Secretary of State
Sir Christopher France KCB (1)

|

Chief Scientific Adviser
**Professor Sir Ernest Oxburgh
KBE (1A)**

|

*Assistant Chief Scientific Adviser
(Nuclear)*
Dr G Pocock (4)

|

Directors (*)

|

Nuclear Policy

Scientific and technical advice on
defence nuclear policy

Head of Strategic Defence Initiative Participation Office

Permanent Under Secretary of State
Sir Christopher France KCB (1)

|

Chief Scientific Adviser
**Professor Sir Ernest Oxburgh
KBE (1A)**

|

*Head of Strategic Defence
Initiative Participation
Office*
A L C Quigley (3)

|

Directors (*)

Strategic Defence Initiative
Participation Office

Policy and industrial support
Technology

PUS of State's Organisation and Office of Management and Budget
Resources and Programmes

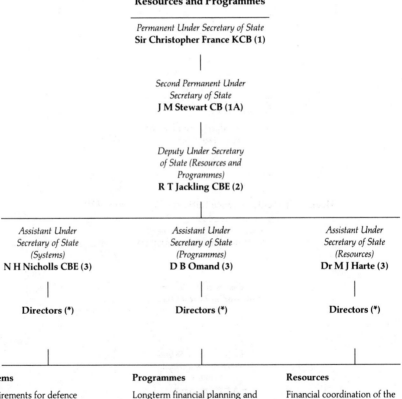

Permanent Under Secretary of State
Sir Christopher France KCB (1)

*Second Permanent Under
Secretary of State*
J M Stewart CB (1A)

*Deputy Under Secretary
of State (Resources and
Programmes)*
R T Jackling CBE (2)

Assistant Under Secretary of State (Systems) **N H Nicholls CBE (3)**	*Assistant Under Secretary of State (Programmes)* **D B Omand (3)**	*Assistant Under Secretary of State (Resources)* **Dr M J Harte (3)**
Directors (*)	Directors (*)	Directors (*)

Systems	**Programmes**	**Resources**
Requirements for defence equipment Secretariat	Longterm financial planning and resource allocation in relation to the defence programme Associated parliamentary and NATO aspects	Financial coordination of the defence programme and budget Economic advisor

Finance

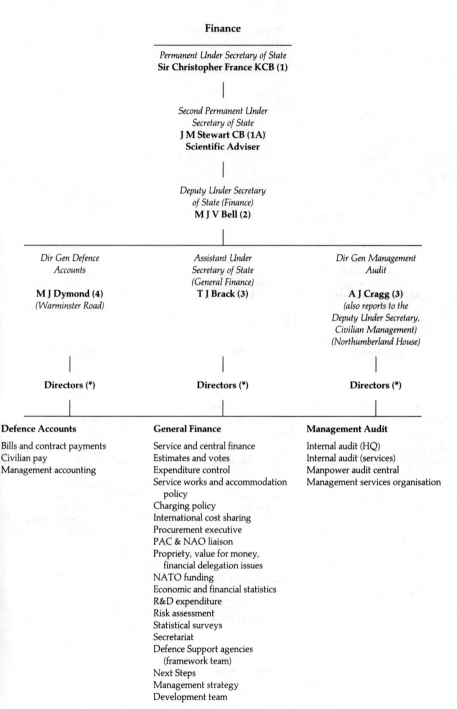

Permanent Under Secretary of State
Sir Christopher France KCB (1)

*Second Permanent Under
Secretary of State*
J M Stewart CB (1A)
Scientific Adviser

*Deputy Under Secretary
of State (Finance)*
M J V Bell (2)

Dir Gen Defence Accounts	*Assistant Under Secretary of State (General Finance)*	*Dir Gen Management Audit*
M J Dymond (4) *(Warminster Road)*	**T J Brack (3)**	**A J Cragg (3)** *(also reports to the Deputy Under Secretary, Civilian Management) (Northumberland House)*
Directors (*)	**Directors (*)**	**Directors (*)**

Defence Accounts	**General Finance**	**Management Audit**
Bills and contract payments	Service and central finance	Internal audit (HQ)
Civilian pay	Estimates and votes	Internal audit (services)
Management accounting	Expenditure control	Manpower audit central
	Service works and accommodation policy	Management services organisation
	Charging policy	
	International cost sharing	
	Procurement executive	
	PAC & NAO liaison	
	Propriety, value for money, financial delegation issues	
	NATO funding	
	Economic and financial statistics	
	R&D expenditure	
	Risk assessment	
	Statistical surveys	
	Secretariat	
	Defence Support agencies (framework team)	
	Next Steps	
	Management strategy	
	Development team	

Personnel and Logistics

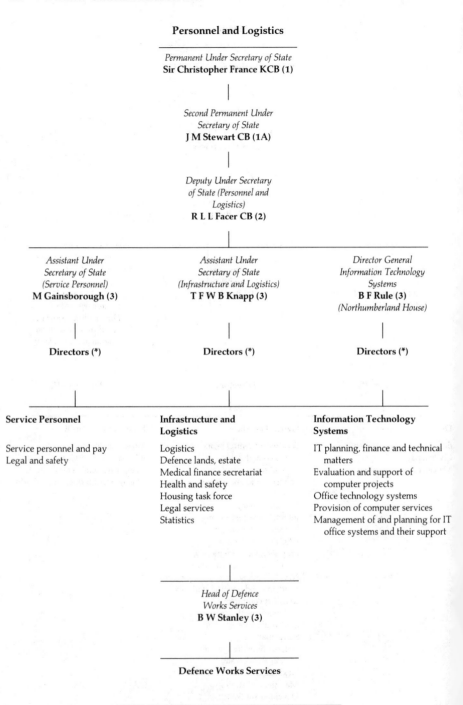

Permanent Under Secretary of State
Sir Christopher France KCB (1)

*Second Permanent Under
Secretary of State*
J M Stewart CB (1A)

*Deputy Under Secretary
of State (Personnel and
Logistics)*
R L L Facer CB (2)

Assistant Under Secretary of State (Service Personnel) **M Gainsborough (3)**	*Assistant Under Secretary of State (Infrastructure and Logistics)* **T F W B Knapp (3)**	*Director General Information Technology Systems* **B F Rule (3)** *(Northumberland House)*
Directors (*)	**Directors (*)**	**Directors (*)**

Service Personnel	**Infrastructure and Logistics**	**Information Technology Systems**
Service personnel and pay Legal and safety	Logistics Defence lands, estate Medical finance secretariat Health and safety Housing task force Legal services Statistics	IT planning, finance and technical matters Evaluation and support of computer projects Office technology systems Provision of computer services Management of and planning for IT office systems and their support

*Head of Defence
Works Services*
B W Stanley (3)

Defence Works Services

Civilian Management

Permanent Under Secretary of State
Sir Christopher France KCB (1)

|

*Second Permanent Under
Secretary of State*
J M Stewart CB (1A)

|

*Deputy Under-Secretary of State
(Civilian Management)*
J F Howe OBE (2)

Assistant Under-Secretary of State (Administrators) **M J Culham CB (3)** *(Lacon House)* **Directors (*)**	*Assistant Under-Secretary of State (Specialists)* **I D Fauset (3)** *(Pinesgate)* **Directors (*)**	*Assistant Under-Secretary of State (Security and Common Services)* **A G Rucker (3)** **Directors (*)**

Administrators

Management and career
  development
Training
Industrial relations
General conditions of service

Specialists

Personnel management
  responsibilities for MOD's
  specialist staff
Recruitment, nationality, probation,
  promotion and secondment for
  all staff employed by MOD
MOD advertising expenditure
MOD training pool

**Security and Common
Services**

Security matters affecting MOD
  HQ and Procurement Executive
Dispersal policy and planning
HQ accommodation
Office supplies and equipment
Records, archives and review
  services
Registry, messengerial transit
  services
Reprographic, editorial and printing
  services
Library services

---

*Ministry of Defence
Police Chief Constable*
J Reddington
(Empress State Bldg)

|

|

Deputy Chief Constable
N L Chapple
(Empress State Bldg)

|

W A T Aves (5)
(Empress State Bldg)

MOD Police

Information room
Secretariat

Inter Service and Ancillary Organisations

Chief of the Defence Staff
**Field Marshal Sir Richard F
Vincent GBE KCB DSO (5*)**

*Commandant Royal College
of Defence Studies*
**Vice Adm Sir John Coward
KCB (3*)**
(Empress State Building)

*Commandant Joint Service
Defence College*
**Air Vice Mshl R P O'Brien
OBE (2*)**
*(Royal Naval College,
Greenwich)*

|

**Maj Gen W Hicks CB OBE (2*)
Rear Adm J Musson (2*)
Maj Gen D P Thomson (2*)
Air Vice Mshl W McRae (2*)
J N Allen (5)**
(all at RCDS)

*Commandant Defence
ADP Training Centre*
Gp Capt I Dorrett
(Blandford Camp)

*Defence Press and
Broadcasting Committee*
**Rear Adm W Higgins CB
CBE (Rtd) (2*)**

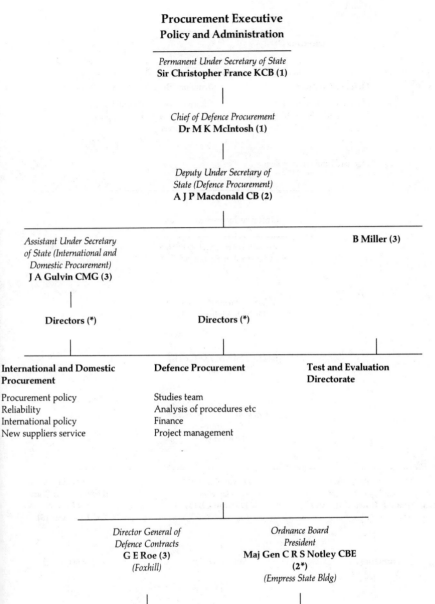

Procurement Executive
Policy and Administration

Permanent Under Secretary of State
Sir Christopher France KCB (1)

Chief of Defence Procurement
Dr M K McIntosh (1)

Deputy Under Secretary of State (Defence Procurement)
A J P Macdonald CB (2)

B Miller (3)

Assistant Under Secretary of State (International and Domestic Procurement)
J A Gulvin CMG (3)

Directors (*)

Directors (*)

International and Domestic Procurement

Procurement policy
Reliability
International policy
New suppliers service

Defence Procurement

Studies team
Analysis of procedures etc
Finance
Project management

Test and Evaluation Directorate

Director General of Defence Contracts
G E Roe (3)
(Foxhill)

Ordnance Board President
Maj Gen C R S Notley CBE (2*)
(Empress State Bldg)

Senior Directors
J V A Crawford (4) (AEPS)
E J Mansfield (4) (D/Pats)
G R Eynon (4) (DQA)

Directors (*)

Directors (*)

Defence Contracts

Contracts policy division
Accountancy, estimating and
    pricing services
Patents
Quality assurance
Standards and safety policy

Ordnance Board

Advice on safety and suitability for
    service of explosive components
    of weapons

Defence Export Services

Permanent Under Secretary of State
Sir Christopher France KCB (1)

Chief of Defence Procurement
Dr M K McIntosh (1)

Head of Defence Export Services
J A Thomas (2)

International Financial Advice
G G Jones
(Stuart House)

*Military Deputy to Head
of Defence Export Services*
**Rear Adm P B Rowe CBE LVO
(2*)**

*Director General
of Marketing*
N D Paren CB (3)

*Assistant Under Secretary
(Defence Export Policy
and Finance)*
C T Sandars (3)

Directors (*)

Directors (*)

Directors (*)

Defence Export Services	Marketing	Sales Administration
Military advice, support and training Exhibitions and inward visitors	Overseas sales Assistance to manufacturers in obtaining export orders	Sales support and disposals Political and security aspects of defence sales Financial services

Director General Saudi
Airforce Project
Air Mshl Sir William
Wratten KBE CB (3*)
(Castlewood House)

Director Malaysian
Project Office
Director (*)
(Stuart House)

Directors (*)

Saudi Airforce Project   **Malaysian Project**

Nuclear Programmes

Permanent Under Secretary of State
Sir Christopher France KCB (1)

Chief of Defence Procurement
Dr M K McIntosh (1)

Controller Aircraft
D M Spiers CB (2)
(see also Aircraft Controllerate)

Dir Atomic Weapons Est
Chief Executive
B H Richards (2)

Deputy Controller (Nuclear)
G N Beavan (3)

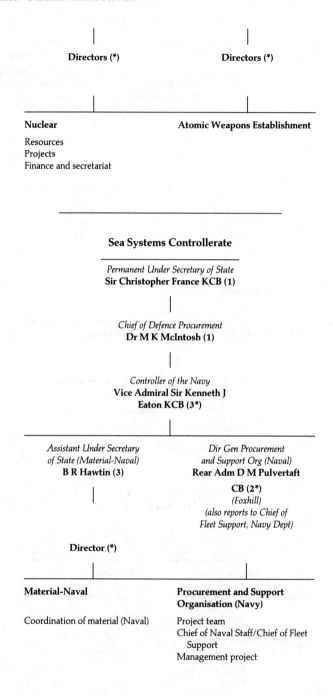

Directors (*)   Directors (*)

Nuclear   **Atomic Weapons Establishment**
Resources
Projects
Finance and secretariat

Sea Systems Controllerate

Permanent Under Secretary of State
Sir Christopher France KCB (1)

Chief of Defence Procurement
Dr M K McIntosh (1)

Controller of the Navy
**Vice Admiral Sir Kenneth J
Eaton KCB (3*)**

Assistant Under Secretary   *Dir Gen Procurement*
of State (Material-Naval)   *and Support Org (Naval)*
B R Hawtin (3)   **Rear Adm D M Pulvertaft**
                                     CB (2*)
                                     (Foxhill)
                                     (also reports to Chief of
                                     Fleet Support, Navy Dept)

Director.(*)

Material-Naval   **Procurement and Support**
                                 Organisation (Navy)

Coordination of material (Naval) Project team
                                  Chief of Naval Staff/Chief of Fleet
                                   Support
                                  Management project

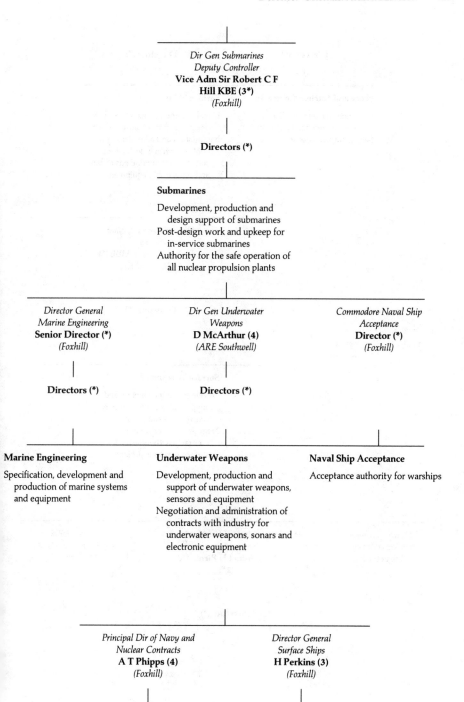

Dir Gen Submarines
Deputy Controller
Vice Adm Sir Robert C F
Hill KBE (3*)
(Foxhill)

Directors (*)

Submarines

Development, production and
design support of submarines
Post-design work and upkeep for
in-service submarines
Authority for the safe operation of
all nuclear propulsion plants

Director General	*Dir Gen Underwater*	*Commodore Naval Ship*
Marine Engineering	*Weapons*	*Acceptance*
Senior Director (*)	**D McArthur (4)**	**Director (*)**
(Foxhill)	*(ARE Southwell)*	*(Foxhill)*

Directors (*)   **Directors (*)**

Marine Engineering   **Underwater Weapons**   **Naval Ship Acceptance**

Specification, development and   Development, production and   Acceptance authority for warships
production of marine systems   support of underwater weapons,
and equipment   sensors and equipment
          Negotiation and administration of
          contracts with industry for
          underwater weapons, sonars and
          electronic equipment

Principal Dir of Navy and	*Director General*
Nuclear Contracts	*Surface Ships*
A T Phipps (4)	**H Perkins (3)**
(Foxhill)	*(Foxhill)*

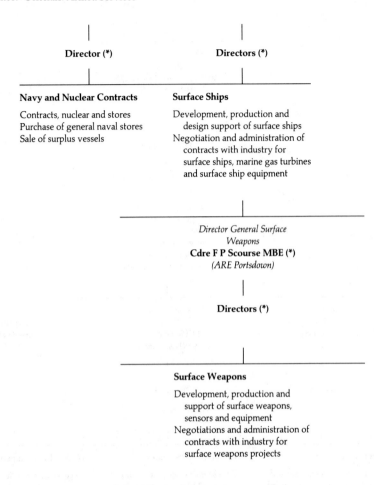

Director (*)   Directors (*)

Navy and Nuclear Contracts   **Surface Ships**

Contracts, nuclear and stores   Development, production and
Purchase of general naval stores   design support of surface ships
Sale of surplus vessels   Negotiation and administration of
                                contracts with industry for
                                surface ships, marine gas turbines
                                and surface ship equipment

*Director General Surface
Weapons*
Cdre F P Scourse MBE (*)
(ARE Portsdown)

Directors (*)

Surface Weapons

Development, production and
support of surface weapons,
sensors and equipment
Negotiations and administration of
contracts with industry for
surface weapons projects

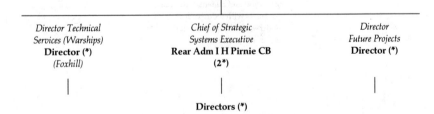

*Director Technical
Services (Warships)*
Director (*)
(Foxhill)

*Chief of Strategic
Systems Executive*
Rear Adm I H Pirnie CB
(2*)

*Director
Future Projects*
Director (*)

Directors (*)

Technical Services (Warships)	Strategic Systems	Future Navy Projects
Oversight of new construction ships and craft for MOD Provision of coordinated ship and equipment programme Maintenance of an information service for shipbuilder capacity	Procurement and in-service management of all naval strategic weapons systems Financial control	Weapons design programmes

Land Systems Controllerate

Permanent Under Secretary of State
Sir Christopher France KCB (1)

Chief of Defence Procurement
Dr M K McIntosh (1)

Master General of the Ordnance
Lt Gen Sir A S J Blacker KCB CBE (3*)

Assistant Under Secretary of State (Ordnance) **Dr A M Fox (3)** *(also reports to Deputy Under Secretary, Resources and Programmes)*	*Director General of Policy and Special Projects* **J G H Walker (4)**	*Principal Director Contracts (Ordnance)* **R C Harford (4)** *(Fleetbank House)*
Directors (*)	**Directors (*)**	**Directors (*)**

Ordnance	Policy and Special Projects	Contracts (Ordnance)
Secretariat and finance Special projects	Special responsibilities for the management of technical programmes Proof and experimental establishments Information systems	

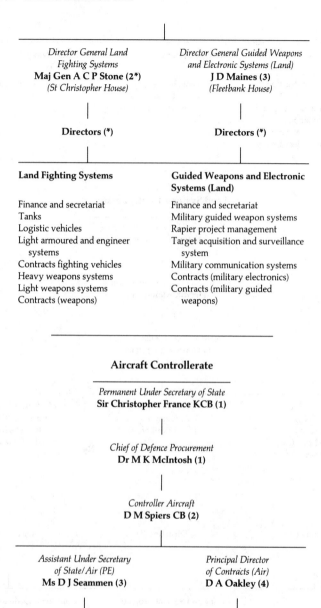

*Director General Land
Fighting Systems*
Maj Gen A C P Stone (2*)
(St Christopher House)

*Director General Guided Weapons
and Electronic Systems (Land)*
J D Maines (3)
(Fleetbank House)

Directors (*)

Directors (*)

Land Fighting Systems

Finance and secretariat
Tanks
Logistic vehicles
Light armoured and engineer
    systems
Contracts fighting vehicles
Heavy weapons systems
Light weapons systems
Contracts (weapons)

**Guided Weapons and Electronic
Systems (Land)**

Finance and secretariat
Military guided weapon systems
Rapier project management
Target acquisition and surveillance
    system
Military communication systems
Contracts (military electronics)
Contracts (military guided
    weapons)

Aircraft Controllerate

Permanent Under Secretary of State
Sir Christopher France KCB (1)

Chief of Defence Procurement
Dr M K McIntosh (1)

Controller Aircraft
D M Spiers CB (2)

*Assistant Under Secretary
of State/Air (PE)*
Ms D J Seammen (3)

*Principal Director
of Contracts (Air)*
D A Oakley (4)

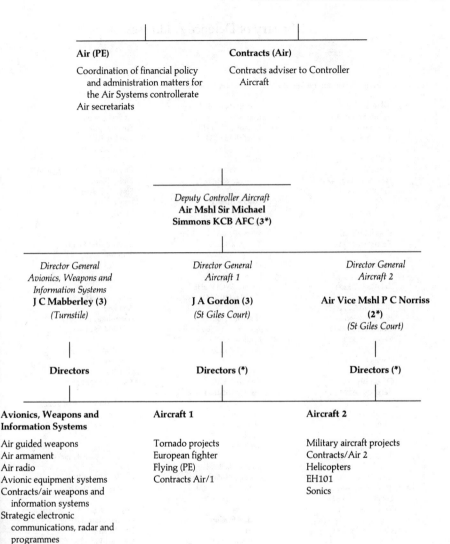

Air (PE)

Coordination of financial policy
and administration matters for
the Air Systems controllerate
Air secretariats

Contracts (Air)

Contracts adviser to Controller
Aircraft

Deputy Controller Aircraft
**Air Mshl Sir Michael
Simmons KCB AFC (3*)**

*Director General
Avionics, Weapons and
Information Systems*
J C Mabberley (3)
(Turnstile)

*Director General
Aircraft 1*

J A Gordon (3)
(St Giles Court)

*Director General
Aircraft 2*

**Air Vice Mshl P C Norriss
(2*)**
(St Giles Court)

Directors

Directors (*)

Directors (*)

**Avionics, Weapons and
Information Systems**

Air guided weapons
Air armament
Air radio
Avionic equipment systems
Contracts/air weapons and
   information systems
Strategic electronic
   communications, radar and
   programmes
Information systems
AD SANGCOM (UK)

Aircraft 1

Tornado projects
European fighter
Flying (PE)
Contracts Air/1

Aircraft 2

Military aircraft projects
Contracts/Air 2
Helicopters
EH101
Sonics

Ministry of Defence Addresses

For fax numbers telephone the number listed and ask for the appropriate fax number

Adastral House
Theobalds Road
London WC1X 8RU
Tel 071-430 5555

ARE Portsdown
Cosham
Hampshire PO6 4AA
Tel 0705 219999

ARE Southwell
Portland
Dorset DT5 2JS
Tel 0305 820381

Ashford
Kent
Tel 0233 625251

Blandford Camp
Blandford Forum
Dorset DT11 8RH
Tel 0258 52581

Bovington Camp
Wareham
Dorset BH20 6JA
Tel 0929 462721

Broadoaks
Parvis Road
West Byfleet
Surrey KT14 6LY
Tel 09323 41199

CAA House
45–49 Kingsway
London WC2B 6TE
Tel 071-379 7311

Carpenter House
Broad Quay
Bath BA1 5AB
Tel 0225 884884

Castlewood House
77–91 New Oxford Street
London WC1A 1DS
Tel 071-829 8500

Chemical Defence Establishment
Porton Down
Salisbury
Wiltshire SP4 0JG
Tel 0980 610211

Empress State Building
Lillie Road
London SW6 1TR
Tel 071-385 1244

Ensleigh
Bath BA1 5AB
Tel 0225 884884

Erskine Barracks
Wilton
Salisbury
Wilts SP2 0AG
Tel 0722 336222

First Avenue House
High Holborn
London WC1V 6HE
Tel 071-430 5555

Fleetbank House
2–6 Salisbury Square
London EC4Y 8AT
Tel 071-632 3333

Foxhill
Bath BA1 5AB
Tel 0225 884884

Lacon House
Theobalds Road
London WC1X 8RY
Tel 071-430 5555

Metropole Building
Northumberland Avenue
London WC2N 5BL
Tel 071-218 9000

Middle Wallop
Stockbridge
Hampshire SO20 8YD
Tel 0264 62121

Neville House
Page Street
London SW1P 4LS
Tel 071-218 9000

Northumberland House
Northumberland Avenue
London WC2N 5BP
Tel 071-218 9000

Old Admiralty Building (OAB)
Archway South
Spring Gardens
London SW1A 2BE
Tel 071-218 9000

Old Admiralty Building (OAB)
Ripley Block
Spring Gardens
London SW1A 2BE
Tel 071-218 9000

Pinegates
Lower Bristol Road
Bath BA1 5AB
Tel 0225 884884

Portway
Moxton Road
Andover
Hampshire SP11 8HT
Tel 0264 382111

RAF PMC Innsworth
Gloucestershire
GL3 1EZ
Tel 0452 712612

Royal Army Medical College
Millbank
London SW1P 4RJ
Tel 071-414 8206

Royal Artillery Barracks
Woolwich
London SE18 4BH
Tel 081-854 2242

Royal College of Defence Studies
Empress State Building
Lillie Road
London SW6 1TR
(until Dec 1992)
Tel 071-385 1244

Royal Naval College
Greenwich
London SE10 9NN
Tel 081-858 2154

St Christopher House
Southwark Street
London SE1 0TD
Tel 071-928 3666

St George's Court
14 New Oxford Street
London WC1A 1EJ
Tel 071-632 3333

St Giles Court
1–13 St Giles High Street
London WC2H 8LD
Tel 071-632 3333

Stuart House
Soho Square
London W1V 5FJ
Tel 071-632 3333

Turnstile House
94–99 High Holborn
London WC1V 6LL
Tel 071-430 5555

Warminster
Wiltshire BA12 0DJ
Tel 0985 214000

Warminster Road
Bath BA1 5AA
Tel 0225 884884

Department of the Director of Public Prosecutions for Northern Ireland

Founded   1972

Status   The Director of Public Prosecutions for Northern Ireland is a statutory office holder under the Crown

Responsible to   Attorney General

Responsibilities   The Director initiates and conducts on behalf of the Crown proceedings for indictable offences and for such summary offences or classes of summary offences as the Director considers should be dealt with by him

Department of the Director of Public Prosecutions for Northern Ireland

Royal Courts of Justice, Chichester Street, Belfast BT1 3NX
Tel 0232 235111   Fax 0232 240730

Statutory office holders

Director

|

Deputy Director

|

Officials

2 Senior Assistant Directors (3)

Department for Education

Founded   1899 as Board for Education. The Board became the Ministry of Education in 1945, the Department of Education and Science in 1964 and the Department for Education in 1992

Ministers   secretary of state, one minister of state and two parliamentary under secretaries

Responsibilities   admissions
adult/continuing education
Assisted Places Scheme
collective worship
CTCs and grant-maintained schools
curriculum
discipline
further education
governors
health education
higher education
independent schools
meals and milk
local management
parents' charter
play
polytechnics
primary schools
school/industry links
special education
students (including overseas) and student
    support
teachers and teacher appraisal
tests
exams, and assessment
transport
under-fives
urban programme
universities
youth service

Executive agencies   Teachers' Pension Agency

Department for Education

Sanctuary Buildings, Great Smith Street, London SW1P 3ET
Tel 071-925 5000   Fax 071-925 6000
All staff are based at Sanctuary House unless otherwise indicated.
For other addresses and telephone numbers see end of this section.

Ministers

Secretary of State
The Rt Hon John Patten MP

Parliamentary Private Secretary
Matthew Carrington MP

Special Adviser
Cliff Grantham

Private Secretary
Miss C A Bienkowska (7)
071-925 6257

Minister of State
The Baroness Blatch CBE

Parliamentary Private Secretary
David Evennett MP

Private Secretary
I Walford (HEO D)
071-925 6253

*Parliamentary Under
Secretary of State
for Schools*
Eric Forth MP

*Parliamentary Under
Secretary of State
for Further and Higher
Education*
Nigel Forman MP

Private Secretary
Miss S Wainer (HEO)
071-925 6246

Private Secretary
M S White (HEO)
071-925 6242

House of Lords' spokesmen
Baroness Blatch
The Viscount Goschen

Ministerial Responsibilities

John Patten   overall responsibility for the department
European Community
implementation of education reforms
    including the Citizens' Charter
pay
public expenditure survey

Baroness Blatch   collective worship
CTCs and grant-maintained schools
curriculum
Education Act 1980, sects 11-16
GM applications
inner cities
race relations in schools
school/industry links and careers education
school reorganisation
Section 11 grants
teachers' appraisal, training and supply
tests, assessment and exams including A/AS
    levels
under-fives
women's issues
House of Lords spokesman

Eric Forth   admissions including open enrolment
attendance
building programmes
charging
departmental purchasing
discipline
education research
energy conservation
environment
governors
independent schools including the Assisted
    Places Scheme
information technology in schools
local management
meals and milk
'Next Steps'
personal and social education
special education

teachers' misconduct
teachers' pensions
transport

Nigel Forman   adult/continuing education
departmental correspondence
further education
higher education
international (not EC)
overseas students
student support
youth service

Departmental Overview

Civil Servants			Department	Minister
Grade 1	*Grade 2*	*Grade 3*		
Schools Branches				
Sir John Caines	N W Stuart	M J Richardson	Branch 1 (Organisation and Supply)	E Forth
		B M Norbury	Branch 2 (Inner Cities, Special Educational Need and Information Technology)	Ly Blatch E Forth
		C H Saville	Branch 3 (School Curriculum Policy	Ly Blatch
		D M Forrester	Branch 4 (Grant-maintained Schools, CTCs and Independent Schools)	Ly Blatch E Forth
Further and Higher Education				
Sir John Caines	J M Vereker	C A Clark	Higher Education	N Forman
		E R Morgan	Further Education	N Forman
		N Summers	Student Support and Adult Continuing Education	N Forman
Teachers, Architects and Buildings, Information Technology and Statistics				
Sir John Caines	John Hedger	R D Horne	Teachers	Ly Blatch
		S R C Jones	International Relations, Youth and General	N Forman
		D E L Allnutt (4)	Analytical Services	
		A F Cowan (5)	Information Services	
		P Benwell (4)	Architects and Buildings	E Forth
Legal, Finance, Establishment				
Sir John Caines		R N Ricks	Legal Adviser	
		N J Sanders	Finance Branch	
		M M Capey	Establishments and Organisation Branch	
Information				
Sir John Caines		J Coe (5)	Information Branch	

Civil Servants and Departments

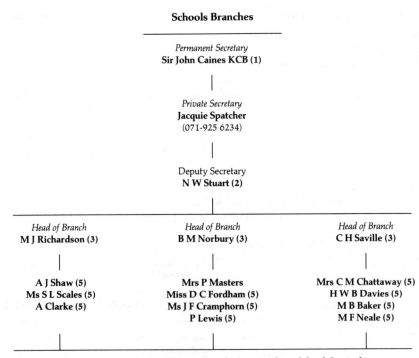

Schools Branches

Permanent Secretary
Sir John Caines KCB (1)

Private Secretary
Jacquie Spatcher
(071-925 6234)

Deputy Secretary
N W Stuart (2)

Head of Branch	*Head of Branch*	*Head of Branch*
M J Richardson (3)	**B M Norbury (3)**	**C H Saville (3)**
A J Shaw (5)	**Mrs P Masters**	**Mrs C M Chattaway (5)**
Ms S L Scales (5)	**Miss D C Fordham (5)**	**H W B Davies (5)**
A Clarke (5)	**Ms J F Cramphorn (5)**	**M B Baker (5)**
	P Lewis (5)	**M F Neale (5)**

Organisation and Supply Policy

Organisation of schools
Admissions and attendance
16-19s in schools
Capital expenditure
HMI reports
Leaving age
School government
Meals, milk, transport
Charging for school activities
Reorganisation of education in
  Inner London
Local management of schools
Parents' Charter

Inner Cities, Special Educational Need and Information Technology

Urban programme and policy for
  inner cities
Ethnic minorities
Travellers and refugees
Discipline
Attendance
Special educational needs
School health service
European Schools
School–industry liaison
Careers
Health education
Under-fives
Educational technology
Broadcasting policy
Copyright
Personal and social education

School Curriculum

Curriculum policy
Implementation
Policy on science, mathematics,
  English, history, etc
Policy on design technology,
  modern foreign languages, etc
Schools examinations, assessment
  and reporting
National Curriculum Council
Schools Examination and
  Assessment Council

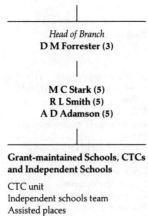

Head of Branch
D M Forrester (3)

M C Stark (5)
R L Smith (5)
A D Adamson (5)

Grant-maintained Schools, CTCs and Independent Schools

CTC unit
Independent schools team
Assisted places
Music and ballet schools
Grant-maintained schools

Further and Higher Education

Permanent Secretary
Sir John Caines KCB (1)

Deputy Secretary
J M M Vereker (2)

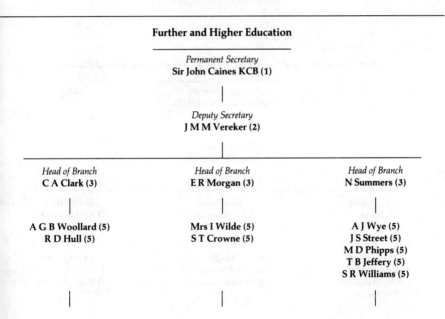

Head of Branch	*Head of Branch*	*Head of Branch*
C A Clark (3)	**E R Morgan (3)**	**N Summers (3)**
A G B Woollard (5)	**Mrs I Wilde (5)**	**A J Wye (5)**
R D Hull (5)	**S T Crowne (5)**	**J S Street (5)**
		M D Phipps (5)
		T B Jeffery (5)
		S R Williams (5)

Higher Education	Further Education	Student Support and Adult and Continuing Education
General HE policy	FE policy, management,	Adult and continuing education
Universities, polytechnics and	organisation, governance and	Open University
colleges policy and finance	funding	Student affairs
Access funds	FHE links with industry	Disabled students
Higher Education Funding Council	Education for IT micro-electronics	Careers guidance
	FE unit	Research in the humanities
	National Council for Vocational	Overseas students
	Qualifications	Student support
	Ethnic minorities	Grants
	FE staff development	Student loans
	Commercial subjects	Post-experience vocational training
	Industrial subjects	
	Arts subjects	
	Management and business	
	Modern languages	
	Further Education Funding Council	

Teachers, Architects and Buildings, Information Technology and Statistics

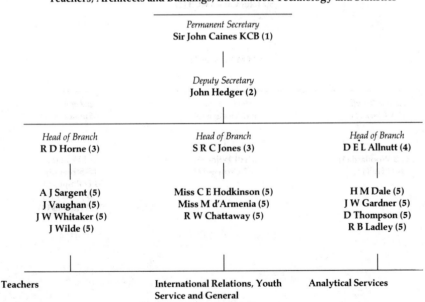

Permanent Secretary
Sir John Caines KCB (1)

Deputy Secretary
John Hedger (2)

Head of Branch	*Head of Branch*	*Head of Branch*
R D Horne (3)	**S R C Jones (3)**	**D E L Allnutt (4)**
A J Sargent (5)	**Miss C E Hodkinson (5)**	**H M Dale (5)**
J Vaughan (5)	**Miss M d'Armenia (5)**	**J W Gardner (5)**
J W Whitaker (5)	**R W Chattaway (5)**	**D Thompson (5)**
J Wilde (5)		**R B Ladley (5)**

Teachers	International Relations, Youth Service and General	Analytical Services
Pay and conditions of service	International relations	Statistics
Teachers' supply		Economic advice
Teacher training		Operational research

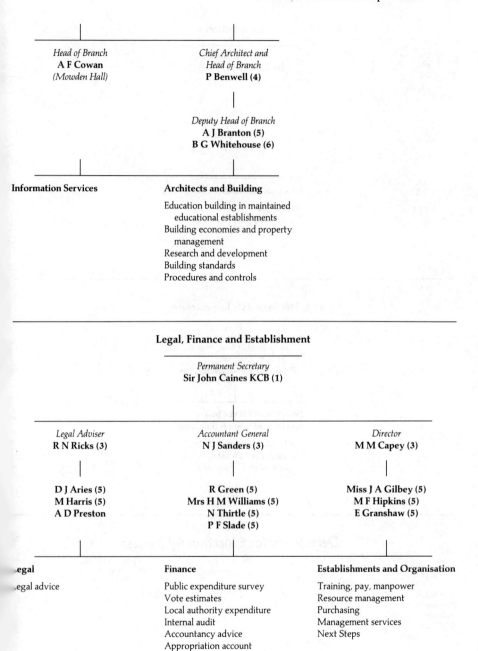

Head of Branch
A F Cowan
(Mowden Hall)

Chief Architect and
Head of Branch
P Benwell (4)

Deputy Head of Branch
A J Branton (5)
B G Whitehouse (6)

Information Services

Architects and Building

Education building in maintained
educational establishments
Building economies and property
management
Research and development
Building standards
Procedures and controls

Legal, Finance and Establishment

Permanent Secretary
Sir John Caines KCB (1)

Legal Adviser	Accountant General	Director
R N Ricks (3)	**N J Sanders (3)**	**M M Capey (3)**

D J Aries (5)	**R Green (5)**	**Miss J A Gilbey (5)**
M Harris (5)	**Mrs H M Williams (5)**	**M F Hipkins (5)**
A D Preston	**N Thirtle (5)**	**E Granshaw (5)**
	P F Slade (5)	

Legal	Finance	Establishments and Organisation
Legal advice	Public expenditure survey	Training, pay, manpower
	Vote estimates	Resource management
	Local authority expenditure	Purchasing
	Internal audit	Management services
	Accountancy advice	Next Steps
	Appropriation account	

Information

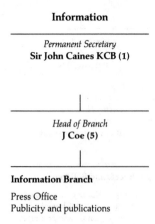

Permanent Secretary
Sir John Caines KCB (1)

Head of Branch
J Coe (5)

Information Branch

Press Office
Publicity and publications

Her Majesty's Inspectorate

*Her Majesty's Chief Inspector
Designate*
Professor Stewart Sutherland

**The Office of HM Chief
Inspector of Schools (England)**

Until HMI's location is decided
please contact via the
Department for Education

Department for Education Addresses

Mowden Hall
Staindrop Road
Darlington DL3 9BG
Tel 0325 460155
Fax 0325 392695

Employment Department Group (EDG)

The EDG comprises the department headquarters, the Employment Service, Health and Safety Commission and the Advisory Conciliation and Arbitration Service.

Founded	1916
Ministers	one secretary of state, one minister of state, two parliamentary under secretaries
Responsibilities	employee rights and involvement
	European and international employment matters
	Health and Safety Commission/Executive (liaison with)
	industrial relations
	pay and equal opportunities
	statistics
	Training and Enterprise Councils (vocational education, training and enterprise)
	women's issues
Executive Agencies	Employment Service

Employment Department Group

Caxton House, Tothill Street, London SW1H 9NF
Tel 071-273 3000   Fax 071-273 5124
All personnel are based at Caxton House unless otherwise indicated.
Other addresses and telephone numbers are listed at the end of this section.

Ministers

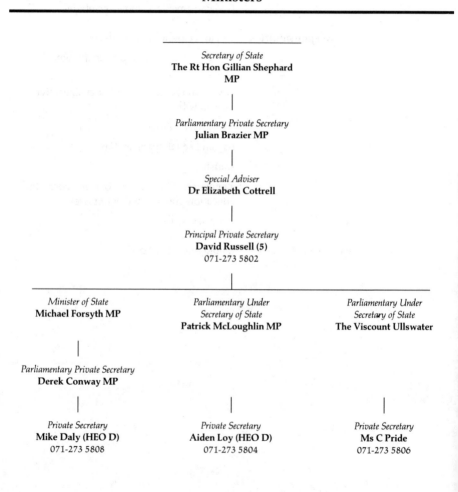

Secretary of State
**The Rt Hon Gillian Shephard
MP**

Parliamentary Private Secretary
Julian Brazier MP

Special Adviser
Dr Elizabeth Cottrell

Principal Private Secretary
David Russell (5)
071-273 5802

Minister of State **Michael Forsyth MP**	*Parliamentary Under Secretary of State* **Patrick McLoughlin MP**	*Parliamentary Under Secretary of State* **The Viscount Ullswater**
Parliamentary Private Secretary **Derek Conway MP**		
Private Secretary **Mike Daly (HEO D)** 071-273 5808	*Private Secretary* **Aiden Loy (HEO D)** 071-273 5804	*Private Secretary* **Ms C Pride** 071-273 5806

House of Lords' spokesmen
Viscount Ullswater
Baroness Denton of Wakefield
Viscount Goschen

Ministerial Responsibilities

Gillian Shephard   overall responsibility for the department

Michael Forsyth   Citizen's Charter
cross-departmental issues
European Community and international
   relations
industrial relations
offshore safety
training and education
Commons questions on people with
   disabilities

Patrick McLoughlin   ACAS
equal opportunities
industrial tribunals
inner cities
pay issues and wages councils
redundancy payments
special needs
training and education
women's issues (supports Secretary of State)
Lord Ullswater's portfolio in the Commons
   (except for people with disabilities)

Viscount Ullswater   employment agencies
Employment Service
energy conservation
local and regional employment
people with disabilities
statistics and research
work permits
departmental issues in the House of Lords

Departmental Overview

Civil Servants			Department	Minister
Grade 1	*Grade 2*	*Grade 3*		

Industrial Relations and International

Sir Geoffrey Holland KCB	G L Reid	C F Tucker	Industrial Relations 1	M Forsyth
		R Hillier	Industrial Relations 2	M Forsyth
		L Lewis	International	M Forsyth
		P J Stibbard	Statistical Services	V Ullswater

Resources and Strategy

Sir Geoffrey Holland KCB	I Johnston	P Makeham	Business Services	V Ullswater
		P Meadows	Economics, Research and Evaluation	V Ullswater
		M M Addison	Finance and Resource Management	M Forsyth
		E G Whybrew	Personnel and Development	V Ullswater
		S Normington	Strategy and Employment Policy	V Ullswater

Training, Enterprise and Education

Sir Geoffrey Holland KCB	R J Dawe	Mrs V Bayliss	Education	M Forsyth P McLoughlin
		J Lambert	Operations (North and West)	M Forsyth P McLoughlin
		J B Surr	Operations (South and East)	M Forsyth P McLoughlin
		S Loveman	Director of operations	M Forsyth P McLoughlin
		B Heatley	Training	M Forsyth P McLoughlin
		N Schofield	Quality Assurance	M Forsyth P McLoughlin
		D Grover	Training Strategy and Standards	M Forsyth P McLoughlin
		K White (4)	Training and Systems	M Forsyth P McLoughlin

Civil Servants and Departments

Industrial Relations and International Directorate

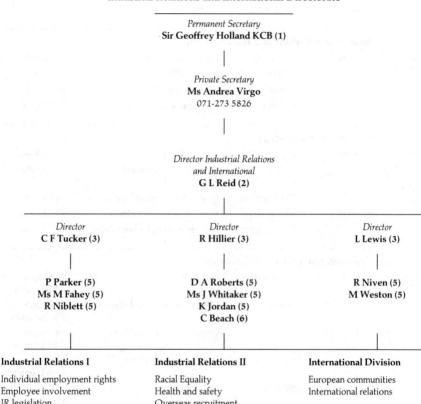

Permanent Secretary
Sir Geoffrey Holland KCB (1)

Private Secretary
Ms Andrea Virgo
071-273 5826

*Director Industrial Relations
and International*
G L Reid (2)

Director **C F Tucker (3)**	*Director* **R Hillier (3)**	*Director* **L Lewis (3)**
P Parker (5) **Ms M Fahey (5)** **R Niblett (5)**	**D A Roberts (5)** **Ms J Whitaker (5)** **K Jordan (5)** **C Beach (6)**	**R Niven (5)** **M Weston (5)**

Industrial Relations I

Individual employment rights
Employee involvement
IR legislation
Redundancy payments

Industrial Relations II

Racial Equality
Health and safety
Overseas recruitment
Disputes/pay
Wages councils
Employment agency licensing
Sex Equality

International Division

European communities
International relations

Director
P J Stibbard (3)

T Orchard (5)
D Fenwick (5)
B Werner (5)
(Runcorn office)
K R Perry (5)
Ms R Rout (5)
(Sheffield office)

Statistical Services

Earnings
Unemployment and LMS
  coordination
Labour force and small firms
Employment and business registers
Statistical services to TEED

Resources and Strategy Directorate

Permanent Secretary
Sir Geoffrey Holland KCB (1)

Director of Resources and Strategy
I Johnston (2)

Director **P Makeham (4)**	*Director* **P Meadows (3)**	*Director* **M Addison (3)**
M Pender (6) *(Sheffield)* **R Wragg (6)** **G Skinner (6)** *(Runcorn)* **K Thomson (6)** **M Allen (5)** *(Runcorn)* **R Hinchcliffe (6)** **W Styles (6)** *(Runcorn)*	**Ms Z Hornstein (5)** **Ms H Canter (5)** **J Temple (5)** *(Sheffield)* **B Wells (6)** **G S Dent (5)** **V Keddie (6)**	**N Gregory (5)** **M Davey (5)** **A Wright (5)**

Business Services	Economics, Research and Evaluation	Finance and Resource Management
Corporate services Estates Group IS strategy Information systems Management services	Employment market research unit Economic briefing Labour market analysis Social science research Economics research evaluation TEC research and evaluation Research management	Financial management Financial services Group finance policy

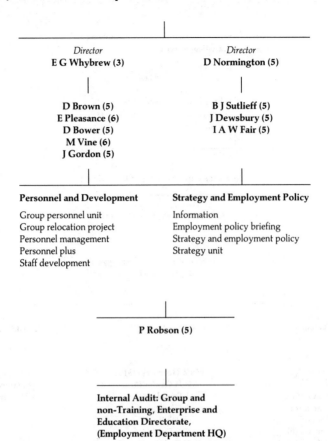

Director	*Director*
E G Whybrew (3)	D Normington (5)

D Brown (5)	B J Sutlieff (5)
E Pleasance (6)	J Dewsbury (5)
D Bower (5)	I A W Fair (5)
M Vine (6)	
J Gordon (5)	

Personnel and Development	**Strategy and Employment Policy**
Group personnel unit	Information
Group relocation project	Employment policy briefing
Personnel management	Strategy and employment policy
Personnel plus	Strategy unit
Staff development	

P Robson (5)

**Internal Audit: Group and
non-Training, Enterprise and
Education Directorate,
(Employment Department HQ)**

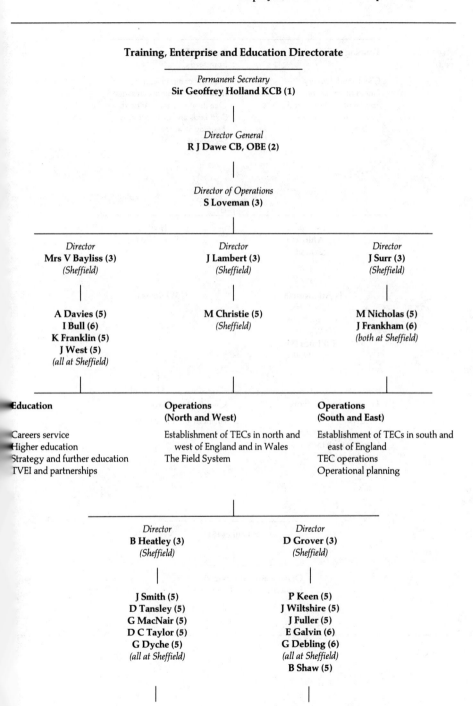

Training, Enterprise and Education Directorate

Permanent Secretary
Sir Geoffrey Holland KCB (1)

Director General
R J Dawe CB, OBE (2)

Director of Operations
S Loveman (3)

Director	*Director*	*Director*
Mrs V Bayliss (3)	**J Lambert (3)**	**J Surr (3)**
(Sheffield)	*(Sheffield)*	*(Sheffield)*

A Davies (5)	**M Christie (5)**	**M Nicholas (5)**
I Bull (6)	*(Sheffield)*	**J Frankham (6)**
K Franklin (5)		*(both at Sheffield)*
J West (5)		
(all at Sheffield)		

Education	**Operations (North and West)**	**Operations (South and East)**
Careers service	Establishment of TECs in north and	Establishment of TECs in south and
Higher education	west of England and in Wales	east of England
Strategy and further education	The Field System	TEC operations
TVEI and partnerships		Operational planning

Director	*Director*
B Heatley (3)	**D Grover (3)**
(Sheffield)	*(Sheffield)*

J Smith (5)	**P Keen (5)**
D Tansley (5)	**J Wiltshire (5)**
G MacNair (5)	**J Fuller (5)**
D C Taylor (5)	**E Galvin (6)**
G Dyche (5)	**G Debling (6)**
(all at Sheffield)	*(all at Sheffield)*
	B Shaw (5)

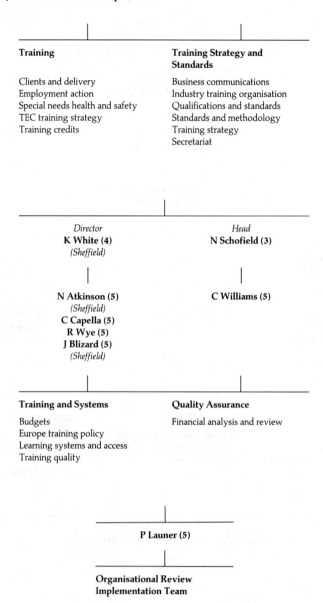

Training

Clients and delivery
Employment action
Special needs health and safety
TEC training strategy
Training credits

Training Strategy and Standards

Business communications
Industry training organisation
Qualifications and standards
Standards and methodology
Training strategy
Secretariat

Director
K White (4)
(Sheffield)

Head
N Schofield (3)

N Atkinson (5)
(Sheffield)
C Capella (5)
R Wye (5)
J Blizard (5)
(Sheffield)

C Williams (5)

Training and Systems

Budgets
Europe training policy
Learning systems and access
Training quality

Quality Assurance

Financial analysis and review

P Launer (5)

**Organisational Review
Implementation Team**

Employment Department Group Addresses

East Lane
Runcorn W7 2DN
Tel 0928 715151

Moorfoot
Sheffield S14 4PQ
Tel 0742 753275

Department of the Environment

Founded	1970 with the merger of the Ministry of Housing and Local Government and the Ministry of Building and Works
Ministers	secretary of state, three ministers of state and three parliamentary under secretaries
Responsibilities	conservation construction countryside energy efficiency environmental protection Government Car Service government civil estate management housing inner cities and inner city task forces local government London Custody Guard Service new towns Parliamentary Works Office planning PSA Services (see separate entry below) water
Executive agencies	Building Research Establishment The Queen Elizabeth Conference Centre

Department of the Environment

2 Marsham Street, London SW1P 3EB
Tel 071-276 3000
Fax *Telephone Department and ask for appropriate fax number*
All personnel are based at 2 Marsham Street unless otherwise indicated.
For other addresses and telephone numbers see end of this section.

Ministers

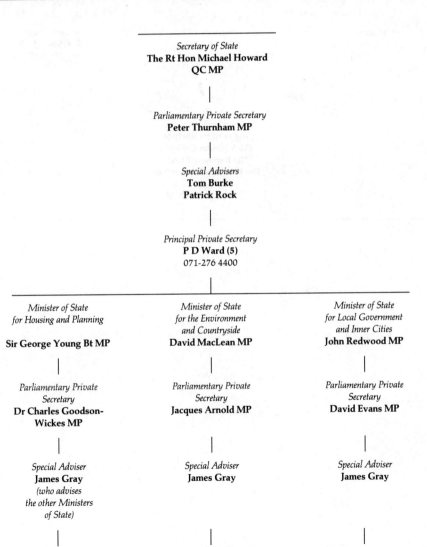

Secretary of State
**The Rt Hon Michael Howard
QC MP**

Parliamentary Private Secretary
Peter Thurnham MP

Special Advisers
**Tom Burke
Patrick Rock**

Principal Private Secretary
P D Ward (5)
071-276 4400

Minister of State for Housing and Planning	*Minister of State for the Environment and Countryside*	*Minister of State for Local Government and Inner Cities*
Sir George Young Bt MP	**David MacLean MP**	**John Redwood MP**

Parliamentary Private Secretary	*Parliamentary Private Secretary*	*Parliamentary Private Secretary*
Dr Charles Goodson-Wickes MP	**Jacques Arnold MP**	**David Evans MP**

Special Adviser	*Special Adviser*	*Special Adviser*
James Gray *(who advises the other Ministers of State)*	**James Gray**	**James Gray**

455

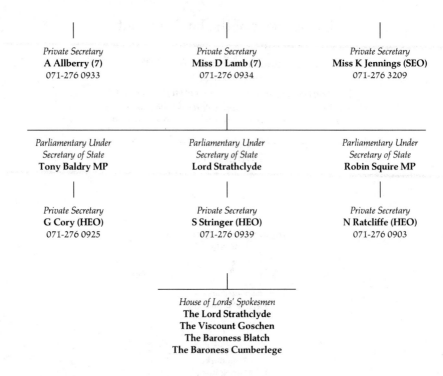

Private Secretary
A Allberry (7)
071-276 0933

Private Secretary
Miss D Lamb (7)
071-276 0934

Private Secretary
Miss K Jennings (SEO)
071-276 3209

*Parliamentary Under
Secretary of State*
Tony Baldry MP

*Parliamentary Under
Secretary of State*
Lord Strathclyde

*Parliamentary Under
Secretary of State*
Robin Squire MP

Private Secretary
G Cory (HEO)
071-276 0925

Private Secretary
S Stringer (HEO)
071-276 0939

Private Secretary
N Ratcliffe (HEO)
071-276 0903

House of Lords' Spokesmen
The Lord Strathclyde
The Viscount Goschen
The Baroness Blatch
The Baroness Cumberlege

Ministerial Responsibilities

Michael Howard	Overall responsibility for the department
Sir George Young	construction industry departmental policies affecting London housing planning Property Holdings
John Redwood	inner cities local government PSA including privatisation
David MacLean	British Waterways Board countryside environmental protection including energy efficiency water
Tony Baldry	Supports Sir George Young and reports to the Secretary of State on departmental administration
Robin Squire	Supports John Redwood and reports to the Secretary of State on regional administration
Lord Strathclyde	Supports David MacLean and is the departmental spokesman in the House of Lords and reports to the Secretary of State on the Ordnance Survey

Departmental Overview

Civil Servants			Department	Minister
Grade 1	Grade 2	Grade 3		
Richard Wilson	These departments report directly to Permanent Secretary	Mrs A Heath	Greater London	Sir G Young
		Vacant	Merseyside Task Force	J Redwood
		D A McDonald	Information	T Baldry
Environment Protection				
Richard Wilson	F A Osborn	J Hobson	Pollution Control and Waste	D MacLean
		Dr D J Fisk	Air, Climate, and Toxic Substances Chief Scientist	D MacLean
		A G Watson	Environment Policy and Analysis	D MacLean
		D H Slater	HM Inspectorate of Pollution	D MacLean
		W Rickett	Energy Efficiency Office	D MacLean
Establishments and Finance				
Richard Wilson	D J Burr	J A Owen	Personnel	T Baldry
		D A R Peel	Administrative Resources	T Baldry
		R S Dudding	Finance Central	T Baldry
Local Government				
Richard Wilson	C J S Brearley	R Green	Local Government	J Redwood
		R U Young	Local Government Review Team	J Redwood
		P Britton	Local Government Finance Policy	J Redwood
Housing and Inner Cities				
Richard Wilson	Miss E C Turton	J E Ballard	Housing Associations and Private Sector	Sir G Young
		N Glass	Housing Monitoring and Analysis	Sir G Young
		Mrs M McDonald	Public Housing Management and Resources	Sir G Young
		M B Gahagan	Inner Cities	J Redwood

Departmental Overview

Civil Servants			Department	Minister
Grade 1	*Grade 2*	*Grade 3*		
Planning, Rural Affairs and Water				
Richard Wilson	P C McQuail	P J Fletcher	Planning and Development Control	Sir G Young
		H S Crow	Chief Planning Inspector	Sir G Young
		J B Wilson (4)	Planning Services	Sir G Young
		R J A Sharp	Rural Affairs	
		N W Summerton	Water	D MacLean
		Regional Office Organisation		
		D R Ritchie	West Midlands	R Squire
		J P Henry	Yorkshire and Humberside	R Squire
		D C Renshaw	North West	R Squire
		P Shaw	Northern	R Squire
		Ms E A Hopkins	South West	R Squire
		D Morrison (4)	East Midlands	R Squire
		J W Fellows	South Eastern	R Squire
		P F Emms	Eastern	R Squire
Property Holdings, Construction and Central Support Services				
Richard Wilson	Ms D Nichols	N E Borrett	Property Holdings	Sir G Young
		A Pelling	Construction Policy	Sir G Young
		Mrs D Phillips	Government Estates	Sir G Young
Solicitor				
Richard Wilson	Mrs M Morgan	Miss S Unerman	Solicitor's Office	
		J A Catlin	Solicitor's Office	
Architecture				
Richard Wilson	J B Jefferson		Chief Architectural Adviser	Sir G Young

Civil Servants and Departments

Greater London, Merseyside Task Force, Information

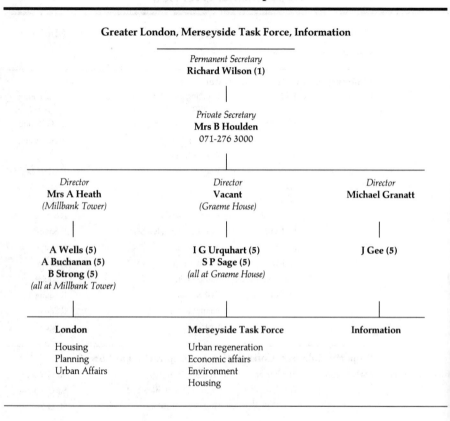

Permanent Secretary
Richard Wilson (1)

Private Secretary
Mrs B Houlden
071-276 3000

Director	*Director*	*Director*
Mrs A Heath	**Vacant**	**Michael Granatt**
(Millbank Tower)	*(Graeme House)*	

A Wells (5)	**I G Urquhart (5)**	**J Gee (5)**
A Buchanan (5)	**S P Sage (5)**	
B Strong (5)	*(all at Graeme House)*	
(all at Millbank Tower)		

London	**Merseyside Task Force**	**Information**
Housing	Urban regeneration	
Planning	Economic affairs	
Urban Affairs	Environment	
	Housing	

Environment Protection Department

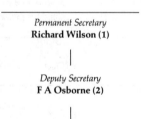

Permanent Secretary
Richard Wilson (1)

Deputy Secretary
F A Osborne (2)

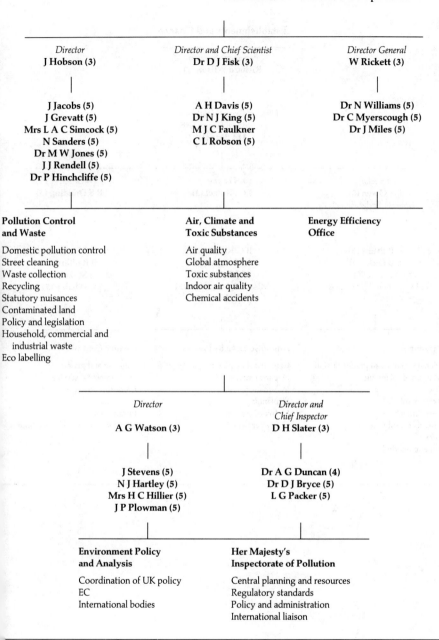

Director	*Director and Chief Scientist*	*Director General*
J Hobson (3)	Dr D J Fisk (3)	W Rickett (3)

J Jacobs (5)	A H Davis (5)	Dr N Williams (5)
J Grevatt (5)	Dr N J King (5)	Dr C Myerscough (5)
Mrs L A C Simcock (5)	M J C Faulkner	Dr J Miles (5)
N Sanders (5)	C L Robson (5)	
Dr M W Jones (5)		
J J Rendell (5)		
Dr P Hinchcliffe (5)		

Pollution Control and Waste	**Air, Climate and Toxic Substances**	**Energy Efficiency Office**
Domestic pollution control	Air quality	
Street cleaning	Global atmosphere	
Waste collection	Toxic substances	
Recycling	Indoor air quality	
Statutory nuisances	Chemical accidents	
Contaminated land		
Policy and legislation		
Household, commercial and industrial waste		
Eco labelling		

Director	*Director and Chief Inspector*
A G Watson (3)	D H Slater (3)

J Stevens (5)	Dr A G Duncan (4)
N J Hartley (5)	Dr D J Bryce (5)
Mrs H C Hillier (5)	L G Packer (5)
J P Plowman (5)	

Environment Policy and Analysis	**Her Majesty's Inspectorate of Pollution**
Coordination of UK policy	Central planning and resources
EC	Regulatory standards
International bodies	Policy and administration
	International liaison

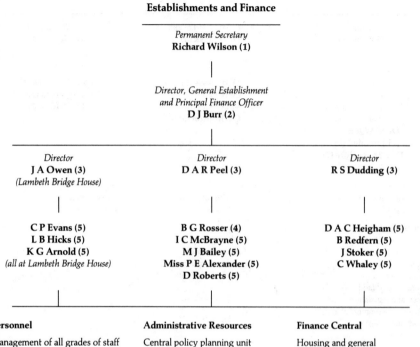

Establishments and Finance

Permanent Secretary
Richard Wilson (1)

*Director, General Establishment
and Principal Finance Officer*
D J Burr (2)

Director	*Director*	*Director*
J A Owen (3)	**D A R Peel (3)**	**R S Dudding (3)**
(Lambeth Bridge House)		

C P Evans (5)	**B G Rosser (4)**	**D A C Heigham (5)**
L B Hicks (5)	**I C McBrayne (5)**	**B Redfern (5)**
K G Arnold (5)	**M J Bailey (5)**	**J Stoker (5)**
(all at Lambeth Bridge House)	**Miss P E Alexander (5)**	**C Whaley (5)**
	D Roberts (5)	

Personnel	**Administrative Resources**	**Finance Central**
Management of all grades of staff	Central policy planning unit	Housing and general
Manpower planning	Departmental services	Environmental services
Pay	Information systems	Economic advice
Retirement	IT planning	Accounts
Recruitment	Network services	Internal audit
Travel and subsistence	Office services	Non-Departmental Public Bodies
Leave		
Superannuation		

Local Government

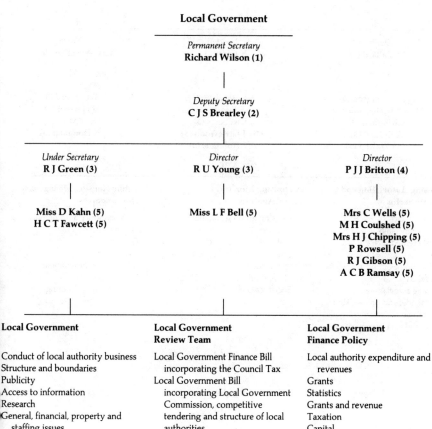

Permanent Secretary
Richard Wilson (1)

Deputy Secretary
C J S Brearley (2)

Under Secretary	*Director*	*Director*
R J Green (3)	**R U Young (3)**	**P J J Britton (4)**

Miss D Kahn (5)
H C T Fawcett (5)

Miss L F Bell (5)

Mrs C Wells (5)
M H Coulshed (5)
Mrs H J Chipping (5)
P Rowsell (5)
R J Gibson (5)
A C B Ramsay (5)

Local Government

Conduct of local authority business
Structure and boundaries
Publicity
Access to information
Research
General, financial, property and
staffing issues
Residuary bodies
EC directives
Competition
Direct labour organisations
Superannuation
Private bills
MPs' pecuniary interests

**Local Government
Review Team**

Local Government Finance Bill
incorporating the Council Tax
Local Government Bill
incorporating Local Government
Commission, competitive
tendering and structure of local
authorities

**Local Government
Finance Policy**

Local authority expenditure and
revenues
Grants
Statistics
Grants and revenue
Taxation
Capital

Housing and Inner Cities

Permanent Secretary
Richard Wilson (1)

Deputy Secretary
Miss E C Turton (2)

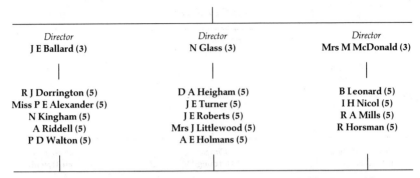

Director J E Ballard (3)	*Director* N Glass (3)	*Director* Mrs M McDonald (3)
R J Dorrington (5) Miss P E Alexander (5) N Kingham (5) A Riddell (5) P D Walton (5)	D A Heigham (5) J E Turner (5) J E Roberts (5) Mrs J Littlewood (5) A E Holmans (5)	B Leonard (5) I H Nicol (5) R A Mills (5) R Horsman (5)

Housing Association and Private Sector

Private finance
Home ownership
Private rented sector
Rent Acts
Mobile homes
Houseboats
Housing associations
Special needs accommodation
Right to buy
Home and area improvement

Housing Monitoring and Analysis

Housing group secretariat
Statistics
Building stock research
Land, planning and population
   statistics
IT applications
Social research

Public Housing Management and Resources

Local authority housing financing
Homelessness
Gipsies
New towns
Estate action programme
Housing defects
Non-traditional housing

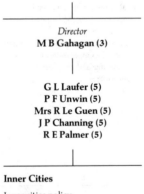

Director
M B Gahagan (3)

G L Laufer (5)
P F Unwin (5)
Mrs R Le Guen (5)
J P Channing (5)
R E Palmer (5)

Inner Cities

Inner cities policy
Private sector involvement
Finance and grants
Research and intelligence
Corporations
Enterprise zones
Task forces

Planning, Rural Affairs and Water

Permanent Secretary
Richard Wilson (1)

Deputy Secretary
P C McQuail (2)

Director	*Chief Planning Inspector*	*Director and Chief Planning Adviser*
P J Fletcher (3)	**H S Crow (3)** *(Tollgate House)*	**J B Wilson (4)**

Deputy Chief Planning Inspector
J R Mossop (4)

Director of Operations
A J M Morgan (4)

R Jones (5)	**J T Graham (5)**	**A F Richardson (5)**
C L L Braun (5)	**D F Harris (5)**	**R C Mabey (5)**
J M Leigh-Pollitt (5)	**Miss M G Pain (5)**	**J A Zetter (5)**
R G Wakeford (5)	**J Acton (5)**	
D N Donaldson (5)	**J T Dunlop (5)**	
(Tollgate House)	**M I Montague-Smith (5)**	
	R E Wilson (5)	
	D A C Marshall (5)	
	M L Brasher (5)	
	E A Simpson (5)	
	G J Lidbury (5)	
	C Jenkins (5)	
	Mrs S Bruton (5)	
	J Greenfield (5)	
	(all at Tollgate House)	

ınning and Development ıntrol	**Planning Inspectorate**	**Planning Services**
ıd for housing	Public enquiries	Research
ınning zones	Appeals on planning, housing,	Intelligence
een belts	highways, environment	International
untryside		Minerals and land reclamation
zardous development		Regional policy
lecommunications		
ecialist planning appeals		
velopment control		
ıd and property		

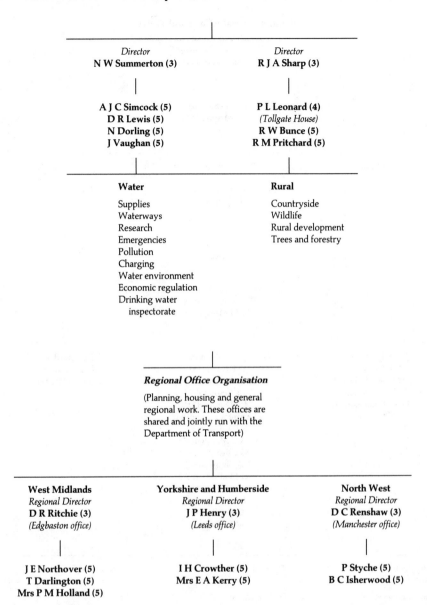

Director	*Director*
N W Summerton (3)	R J A Sharp (3)

A J C Simcock (5)	P L Leonard (4)
D R Lewis (5)	*(Tollgate House)*
N Dorling (5)	R W Bunce (5)
J Vaughan (5)	R M Pritchard (5)

Water	**Rural**
Supplies	Countryside
Waterways	Wildlife
Research	Rural development
Emergencies	Trees and forestry
Pollution	
Charging	
Water environment	
Economic regulation	
Drinking water	
inspectorate	

Regional Office Organisation

(Planning, housing and general
regional work. These offices are
shared and jointly run with the
Department of Transport)

West Midlands	**Yorkshire and Humberside**	**North West**
Regional Director	*Regional Director*	*Regional Director*
D R Ritchie (3)	J P Henry (3)	D C Renshaw (3)
(Edgbaston office)	*(Leeds office)*	*(Manchester office)*

J E Northover (5)	I H Crowther (5)	P Styche (5)
T Darlington (5)	Mrs E A Kerry (5)	B C Isherwood (5)
Mrs P M Holland (5)		

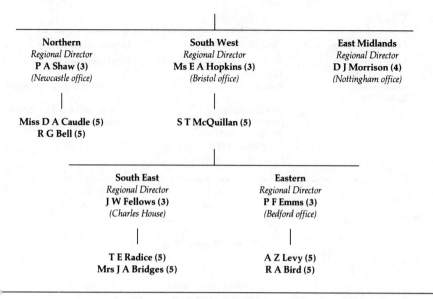

Northern
Regional Director
P A Shaw (3)
(Newcastle office)

South West
Regional Director
Ms E A Hopkins (3)
(Bristol office)

East Midlands
Regional Director
D J Morrison (4)
(Nottingham office)

Miss D A Caudle (5)
R G Bell (5)

S T McQuillan (5)

South East
Regional Director
J W Fellows (3)
(Charles House)

Eastern
Regional Director
P F Emms (3)
(Bedford office)

T E Radice (5)
Mrs J A Bridges (5)

A Z Levy (5)
R A Bird (5)

Property Holdings, Construction and Central Support Services

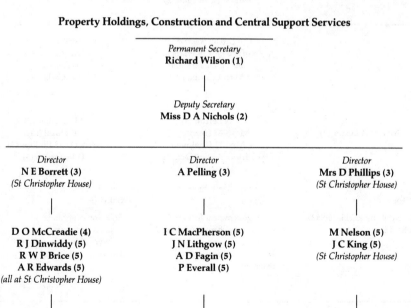

Permanent Secretary
Richard Wilson (1)

Deputy Secretary
Miss D A Nichols (2)

Director
N E Borrett (3)
(St Christopher House)

Director
A Pelling (3)

Director
Mrs D Phillips (3)
(St Christopher House)

D O McCreadie (4)
R J Dinwiddy (5)
R W P Brice (5)
A R Edwards (5)
(all at St Christopher House)

I C MacPherson (5)
J N Lithgow (5)
A D Fagin (5)
P Everall (5)

M Nelson (5)
J C King (5)
(St Christopher House)

Property Holdings	Construction Policy	Government Estates
Estate planning	Promotion of construction market	Business strategy
Central London	Technology	Common services
Central policy	Exports	Management of Property Holding
Sponsorship	EC	roles
	Quality assurance	Transport and security specialist
	Data and research	services
	Building regulations	
	Fuel procurement for Civil Estate	

Solicitor

Permanent Secretary
Richard Wilson (1)

Solicitor and Legal Adviser
Mrs M A Morgan (2)

	Deputy Solicitor (Housing, Construction and the Environment) **Ms S Unerman (3)**	*Deputy Solicitor (Local Government and Planning)* **J A Catlin (3)**
I D Day (5)	**N Lefton (5)**	**J L Comber (5)**
Miss R A Lester (5)	**Mrs S M Headley (5)**	**P J Szell (5)**
	Mrs P J Conlon (5)	**Miss D C S Phillips (5)**
	Mrs G Hedley Dent (5)	**D W Jordan (5)**

Solicitor	Solicitor	Solicitor
Commercial and establishments	Local government finance	Pollution control:
Countryside	Community charge and domestic rating	air, water, noise, international
	Local government general	Housing
	Planning	

Chief Architectural Adviser

Permanent Secretary
Richard Wilson (1)

|

Chief Architectural Adviser
in the Built Environment
J B Jefferson CB CBE (2)

|

J E Turner (5)

Department of the Environment Addresses

Main addresses

Graeme House
Derby Square
Liverpool L2 7SU
Tel 051-227 4111
Fax 051-236 1199

Lambeth Bridge House
London SE1 7SB
Tel 071-238 3000
Fax 071-238 4238

St Christopher House
Southwark Street
London SE1 0TE
Tel 071-928 3666
Fax 071-921 2294

Tollgate House
Houlton Street
Bristol BS2 9DJ
Tel 0272 218752
Fax 0272 218319

Regional addresses

Eastern
Heron House
49-51 Goldington Road
Bedford MK40 3LL
Tel 0234 63161
Fax 0234 63161 X303

London
Millbank Tower
Millbank
London SW1P 4QU
Tel 071-217 3000
Fax 071-217 4555

Midlands
Cranbrook House
Cranbrook Street
Nottingham NG1 1EY
Tel 0602 476121
Fax 0602 476560

Northern
Wellbar House
Gallowgate
Newcastle upon Tyne NE1 4TD
Tel 091-232 7575
Fax 091-261 0746

North West
Sunley Tower
Piccadilly Plaza
Manchester M1 4BE
Tel 061-832 9111
Fax 061-838 5790

South East
Charles House
375 Kensington High Street
London W14 8QH
Tel 071-605 9003
Fax 071-605 9249

South West
Tollgate House
Houlton Street
Bristol BS2 9DJ
Tel 0272 218811
Fax 0272 218319

West Midlands
Five Ways Tower
Frederick Road
Edgbaston
Birmingham B15 1SJ
Tel 021-631 4141
Fax 021-626 2404

Yorkshire and Humberside
City House
New Station Street
Leeds LS1 4JD
Tel 0532 43232
Fax 0532 444898

Export Credits Guarantee Department

Founded	1919
Responsible to	President of the Board of Trade/Secretary of State for Trade and Industry and Minister for Trade
Responsibilities	Facilitates UK exports by making available export credit insurance to British firms selling overseas
	Guarantees repayment to British banks providing finance for exports

Export Credits Guarantee Department

PO Box 2200, 2 Exchange Tower, Harbour Exchange, London E14 9GS
Tel 071-512 7000   Fax 071-512 7649

Ministers

President of the Board of Trade/
Secretary of State for Trade and
Industry
The Rt Hon Michael Heseltine
MP

|

Minister for Trade
Richard Needham MP

Officials

Chief Executive
W B Willott (2)

|

Management Board
M V Hawtin (3)
T M Jaffrey (3)
J R Weiss (3)

Departmental Overview

Civil Servants			Department	Minister
Grade 1	*Grade 2*	*Grade 3*		
	W B Willott	T M Jaffray	Resource Management Group	M Heseltine
				Richard Needham
		M V Hawtin	Underwiting Group	M Heseltine
				Richard Needham
		J R Weiss	Asset Management Group	M Heseltine
				Richard Needham

Civil Servants and Departments

Chief Executive's Division

Chief Executive
W B Willott (2)

|

Private Secretary
Valerie Gray
071-512 7003

|

Head of Division,
Secretary to the Export
Guarantees Advisory Council
(EGAC),
Secretary to the Management Board
J Croall (6)

|

Chief Executive's Division

Secretariat for the EGAC and
  ECGD management board
Publicity and public relations
Parliamentary and ministerial
  matters
Legislation

Resource Management, Underwriting and Asset Management Groups

Chief Executive
W B Willott (2)

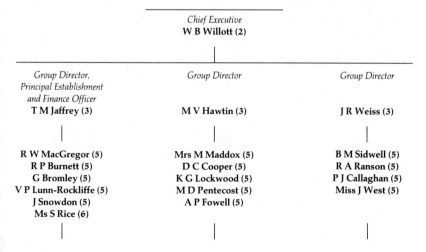

Group Director, *Principal Establishment* *and Finance Officer* **T M Jaffrey (3)**	*Group Director* **M V Hawtin (3)**	*Group Director* **J R Weiss (3)**
R W MacGregor (5)	Mrs M Maddox (5)	B M Sidwell (5)
R P Burnett (5)	D C Cooper (5)	R A Ranson (5)
G Bromley (5)	K G Lockwood (5)	P J Callaghan (5)
V P Lunn-Rockliffe (5)	M D Pentecost (5)	Miss J West (5)
J Snowdon (5)	A P Fowell (5)	
Ms S Rice (6)		

Resource Management Group

Finance
Personnel management
Management and IT services
Risk management
Planning and management
  information
Audit, investigation and review
Operational research

Underwriting Group

Policies
Financial analysis
Supplier/buyer credit:
  Australia, Far East, Asia
  Middle East, North Africa
  Europe, Israel, Sub-Saharan
  Africa
Aerospace and ships, services,
  overseas investment insurance
Arms, military aircraft, the
  Americas, South America
Bank guarantees and bond facilities

Asset Management Group

Project claims
Treasury management
International debt
International relations

Foreign and Commonwealth Office

Founded   The Diplomatic Service was established in 1965 by the merger of the former Foreign, Commonwealth and Trade Commissioner services. Subsequently it incorporated the staffs of the Colonial Office in London, which merged with the Commonwealth Relations Office in 1966 to form the Commonwealth Office. The Foreign and Commonwealth offices continued as separate departments responsible to separate secretaries of state until 1968, when they combined as the Foreign and Commonwealth Office, responsible to one secretary of state.

Ministers   Foreign Secretary, four ministers of state and one parliamentary under secretary

Responsibilities   Provides, mainly through diplomatic missions, the means of communication between the British government and other governments and international governmental organisations for the discussion and negotiation of all questions of international relations.

It is responsible for alerting the government to the implications of developments overseas; for protecting British interests overseas; for protecting British citizens abroad; for explaining British policies to, and cultivating friendly relations with, governments overseas; and for the discharge of British responsibilities to the dependent territories.

Executive Agencies   Wiston House Conference Centre (Wilton Park)
Natural Resources Institute

Foreign and Commonwealth Office

Downing Street, London SW1A 2AL
Tel 071-270 3000
Fax *Telephone the above number and when through to the FCO ask for appropriate fax number*
All staff are based at Downing Street unless otherwise indicated.
For other addresses and telephone numbers see the end of this section.

Ministers

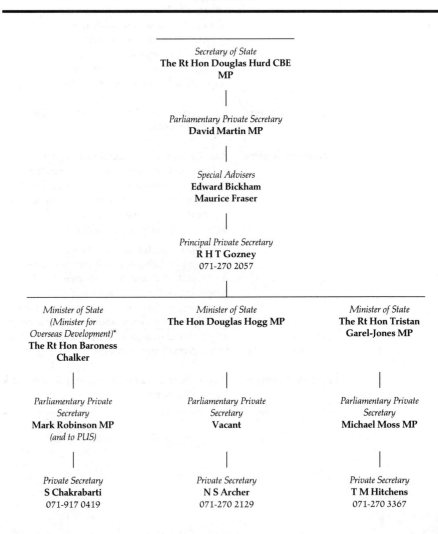

Secretary of State
**The Rt Hon Douglas Hurd CBE
MP**

Parliamentary Private Secretary
David Martin MP

Special Advisers
**Edward Bickham
Maurice Fraser**

Principal Private Secretary
R H T Gozney
071-270 2057

Minister of State *(Minister for* *Overseas Development)** **The Rt Hon Baroness** **Chalker**	*Minister of State* **The Hon Douglas Hogg MP**	*Minister of State* **The Rt Hon Tristan** **Garel-Jones MP**
Parliamentary Private *Secretary* **Mark Robinson MP** *(and to PUS)*	*Parliamentary Private* *Secretary* **Vacant**	*Parliamentary Private* *Secretary* **Michael Moss MP**
Private Secretary **S Chakrabarti** 071-917 0419	*Private Secretary* **N S Archer** 071-270 2129	*Private Secretary* **T M Hitchens** 071-270 3367

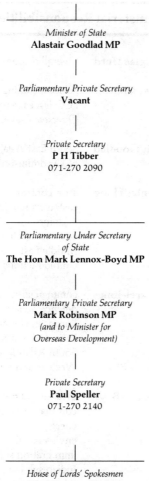

Minister of State
Alastair Goodlad MP

Parliamentary Private Secretary
Vacant

Private Secretary
P H Tibber
071-270 2090

Parliamentary Under Secretary
of State
The Hon Mark Lennox-Boyd MP

Parliamentary Private Secretary
Mark Robinson MP
(and to Minister for
Overseas Development)

Private Secretary
Paul Speller
071-270 2140

House of Lords' Spokesmen
The Baroness Chalker
The Viscount Long
The Earl of Caithness
The Baroness Trumpington

See Overseas Development Administration

Ministerial Responsibilities

Douglas Hurd Overall responsibility for the department

Baroness Chalker Africa including South Africa
FCO issues in the House of Lords
Overseas Development Administration

Alastair Goodlad South East Asia, the Far East and Australasia
FCO administration

Douglas Hogg arms control
east/west relations including former Soviet
  Union
economic policy
Middle East
United Nations

Tristan Garel-Jones commercial/trade promotion
defence policy
European Communities
Latin and South America
South Atlantic and Antarctica
Western and Southern Europe

Mark Lennox-Boyd aviation and maritime
consular questions
energy
environment
immigration and nationality
Indian sub-continent and Afghanistan
information and cultural affairs
narcotics control and AIDS
nationality treaty and claims
North America
ODA issues in the House of Commons
parliamentary liaison
protocol
science and technology
West Indies

Departmental Overview

Civil Servants			Department	Minister
Perm Under Secretary	**Deputy Under Secretary**	**Assistant Under Secretary**		

Aid Policy; Economic Advisers; Research and Analysis; Legal Advisers

Sir David Gillmore		B R Ireton (ODA)	Aid Policy*	Ly Chalker
		S H Broadbent (Head of Dept)	Economic Advisers*	As required
		B S T Eastwood (Head of Dept)	Research and Analysis	As required
	F D Berman	D H Anderson	Legal Advisers	As required

Permanent Under-Secretary's Department; International Labour Adviser; Overseas Police Adviser; Arms Control and Disarmament; Non-Proliferation and Defence; Security Policy; Ireland

Sir David Gillmore	N H R A Broomfield	I R Callan (Head of Dept)	Permanent Under Secretary's Department	D Hurd
		R B Bone	International Labour Adviser	A Goodlad
			Overseas Police Adviser	A Goodlad
		P J Goulden	Arms Control and Disarmament	D Hogg
			Non-Proliferation and Defence	D Hogg
			Security Policy	D Hogg
		J Q Greenstock	Republic of Ireland	D Hurd

Commonwealth; Africa; Middle and Near East

Sir David Gillmore	M Elliott	A M Goodenough	Commonwealth Coordination	Ly Chalker
			East Africa	Ly Chalker
			West Africa	Ly Chalker
			Central and Southern Africa	Ly Chalker
		The Hon David Gore-Booth	Middle East	D Hogg
			Near East and North Africa	D Hogg

Departmental Overview

Civil Servants			Department	Minister
Perm Under Secretary	Deputy Under Secretary	Assistant Under Secretary		

The Americas and Antarctic; Atlantic and Southern Oceans; Far East and Asia

Sir David Gillmore	Sir John Coles	A J Beamish	South Atlantic and Antarctic	T Garel-Jones
			Latin America	T Garel-Jones
			West Indian and Atlantic	T Garel-Jones
			North America	M Lennox-Boyd
		R A Burns	Far Eastern	A Goodlad
			Hong Kong	A Goodlad
			South Asian	A Goodlad
			South East Asian	A Goodlad
			South Pacific	A Goodlad

Overseas Trade Services; Aviation and Maritime; Environment, Science and Energy; Narcotics Control and AIDS; Economic Relations; European Community

Sir David Gillmore	B L Crowe	R O Miles	Overseas Trade Services**	T Garel-Jones
		R B Bone	Aviation and Maritime	M Lennox-Boyd
			Environment, Science and Energy	M Lennox-Boyd
			Narcotics Control and AIDS	M Lennox-Boyd
			Economic Relations*	T Garel-Jones
		M H Jay	European Community (Internal, External and Presidency)	T Garel-Jones

Consular; Information and News; Migration and Nationality; IT and Library; Personnel, Establishment and Security; Finance and Management; Protocol

Sir David Gillmore	A M Wood	Miss R J Spencer	Consular	M Lennox-Boyd
			Cultural Relations	M Lennox-Boyd
			Information	M Lennox-Boyd
			Migration and Visa	M Lennox-Boyd
			Nationality, Treaty and Claims	M Lennox-Boyd
			News	As required
			Parliamentary Relations	M Lennox-Boyd
		J Ling	Information Systems (Operations, Projects, Resources, Services)	M Lennox-Boyd
			Library and Records*	M Lennox-Boyd

Departmental Overview

Civil Servants			Department	Minister
Perm Under Secretary	**Deputy Under Secretary**	**Assistant Under Secretary**		
		Mrs V E Sutherland	Personnel Management, Policy and Services	A Goodlad
			Security*	A Goodlad
			Technical Security	A Goodlad
			Training	A Goodlad
			Home Estate and Services	A Goodlad
			Overseas Estate	A Goodlad
			Medical and Staff Welfare*	A Goodlad
		R J S Muir	Overseas Inspectorate*	A Goodlad
			Resource Management	A Goodlad
			Finance	A Goodlad
			Internal Audit*	A Goodlad
			Management Review*	A Goodlad
		A St J Figgis	Protocol	M Lennox-Boyd

Policy Planning; Europe; CSCE; United Nations

Civil Servants			Department	Minister
Sir David Gillmore	L V Appleyard	R F Cooper (Head of Dept)	Policy Planning	As required
		J Q Greenstock	Southern Europe	T Garel-Jones
			Western Europe	T Garel-Jones
		M L Tait	CSCE Unit	D Hogg
			Eastern European*	D Hogg
			Central European	D Hogg
		R B Bone	United Nations	D Hogg

Government Hospitality Fund

Civil Servants			Department	Minister
Sir David Gillmore		Brig A Cowen	Government Hospitality Fund	A Goodlad

*   joint FCO/ODA departments
**   joint FCO/DTI directorate

Civil Servants and Departments

Aid Policy

Permanent Under Secretary of State
Head of the Diplomatic Service
Sir David Gillmore KCMG

|

Assistant Under Secretary of State
B R Ireton (ODA)
(94 Victoria St)

|

D L Stanton (5) (ODA)
(94 Victoria St)

|

Aid Policy Department*

Size, distribution and composition
of the aid programme
Aid policy and systems
OECD
Other donors

* joint FCO/ODA department

Economic Advisers

Permanent Under Secretary of State
Head of the Diplomatic Service
Sir David Gillmore KCMG

|

Chief Economic Adviser
S H Broadbent*
(Whitehall)

|

N R Chrimes*
(Whitehall)

|

|

Economic Advisers*

Specialist advice and assistance on
economic matters

* joint FCO/ODA department

Research and Analysis

Permanent Under Secretary of State
Head of the Diplomatic Service
Sir David Gillmore KCMG

|

Director
B S T Eastwood

|

Research and Analysis

Provision of assessments and
advice based on specialist
experience

Legal Advisers

Permanent Under Secretary of State
Head of the Diplomatic Service
Sir David Gillmore KCMG

|

Legal Adviser
F D Berman CMG

|

Second Legal Adviser
D H Anderson CMG

|

Deputy Legal Advisers
M R Eaton
K J Chamberlain CMG

|

Legal Advisers

Permanent Under Secretary's Department; International Labour Adviser; Overseas Police
Adviser; Arms Control; Non-proliferation and Defence; Security; Ireland

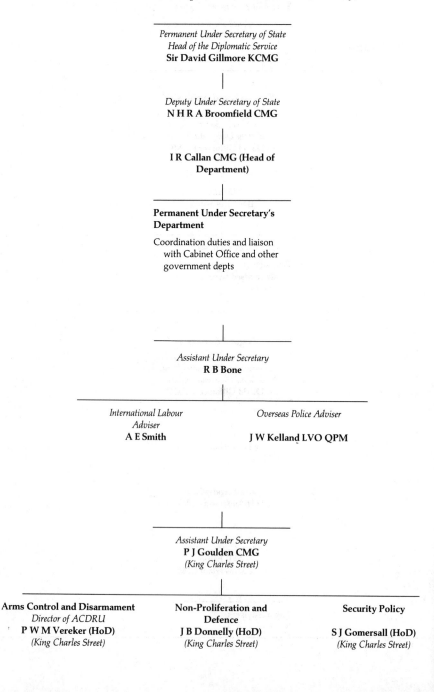

Permanent Under Secretary of State
Head of the Diplomatic Service
Sir David Gillmore KCMG

Deputy Under Secretary of State
N H R A Broomfield CMG

**I R Callan CMG (Head of
Department)**

**Permanent Under Secretary's
Department**
Coordination duties and liaison
with Cabinet Office and other
government depts

Assistant Under Secretary
R B Bone

*International Labour
Adviser*
A E Smith

Overseas Police Adviser

J W Kelland LVO QPM

Assistant Under Secretary
P J Goulden CMG
(King Charles Street)

Arms Control and Disarmament
Director of ACDRU
P W M Vereker (HoD)
(King Charles Street)

**Non-Proliferation and
Defence**
J B Donnelly (HoD)
(King Charles Street)

Security Policy

S J Gomersall (HoD)
(King Charles Street)

Assistant Under Secretary
J Q Greenstock
(Downing Street East)

G R Archer (HoD)

Republic of Ireland

Political and economic relations
N Ireland questions affecting
Republic and other foreign
countries.

Commonwealth and Africa; Middle and Near East

Permanent Under Secretary of State
Head of the Diplomatic Service
Sir David Gillmore KCMG

Deputy Under Secretary of State
M Elliott CMG

Assistant Under Secretary
of State
A M Goodenough CMG

Commonwealth Coordination	East Africa
T C S Stitt (HoD)	**T G Harris (HoD)**
(Downing Street East)	*(King Charles Street)*

West Africa	Central and Southern Africa
M E Cook (HoD)	**D R C Christopher (HoD)**
(King Charles Street)	*(King Charles Street)*

|
Assistant Under Secretary of State
The Hon David Gore-Booth
CMG

|

Middle East
P M Nixon CMG OBE (HoD)
(Downing Street West)

Near East and North Africa
S W J Fuller (HoD)
(King Charles Street and
Downing Street West)

The Americas and Antarctic; Atlantic and Southern Oceans; Far East and Asia

Permanent Under Secretary of State
Head of the Diplomatic Service
Sir David Gillmore KCMG

|

Deputy Under Secretary of State
Sir John Coles KCMG

|

Assistant Under Secretary
of State
A J Beamish CMG

|

South Atlantic and Antarctic
P M Newton (HoD)
(Whitehall)

Latin America
A R Murray (HoD)
(Whitehall)

West Indian and Atlantic
G M Baker (HoD)
(Whitehall)

|

North America
M E Pellew (HoD)
(Whitehall)

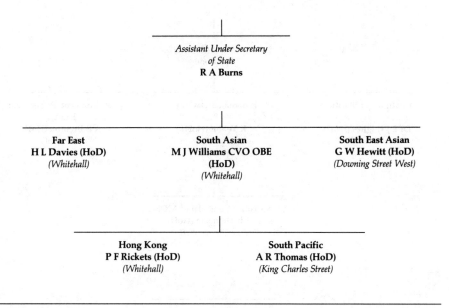

Assistant Under Secretary
of State
R A Burns

Far East	South Asian	South East Asian
H L Davies (HoD)	**M J Williams CVO OBE**	**G W Hewitt (HoD)**
(Whitehall)	**(HoD)**	*(Downing Street West)*
	(Whitehall)	

Hong Kong	South Pacific
P F Rickets (HoD)	**A R Thomas (HoD)**
(Whitehall)	*(King Charles Street)*

Overseas Trade; Aviation and Maritime; Environment, Science and Energy; Narcotics Control and AIDS; Economic Relations; European Community

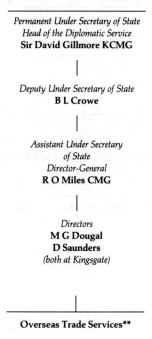

Permanent Under Secretary of State
Head of the Diplomatic Service
Sir David Gillmore KCMG

Deputy Under Secretary of State
B L Crowe

Assistant Under Secretary
of State
Director-General
R O Miles CMG

Directors
M G Dougal
D Saunders
(both at Kingsgate)

Overseas Trade Services**

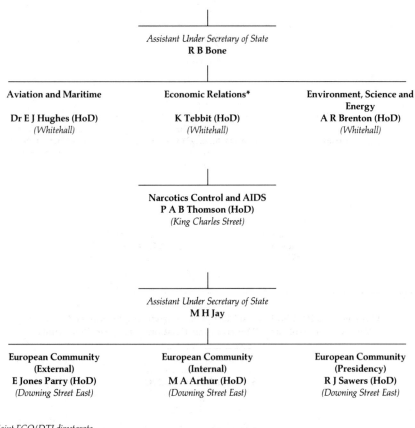

Assistant Under Secretary of State
R B Bone

Aviation and Maritime	Economic Relations*	Environment, Science and Energy
Dr E J Hughes (HoD)	K Tebbit (HoD)	A R Brenton (HoD)
(Whitehall)	*(Whitehall)*	*(Whitehall)*

Narcotics Control and AIDS
P A B Thomson (HoD)
(King Charles Street)

Assistant Under Secretary of State
M H Jay

European Community (External)	European Community (Internal)	European Community (Presidency)
E Jones Parry (HoD)	M A Arthur (HoD)	R J Sawers (HoD)
(Downing Street East)	*(Downing Street East)*	*(Downing Street East)*

** *Joint FCO/DTI directorate*
* *Joint FCO/ODA department*

Consular; Information and News; Migration and Nationality; IT and Library; Personnel; Establishment and Security; Finance and Management; Protocol

Permanent Under Secretary of State
Head of the Diplomatic Service
Sir David Gillmore KCMG

Deputy Under Secretary of State
A M Wood CMG

Assistant Under Secretary of State
Miss J R Spencer CMG

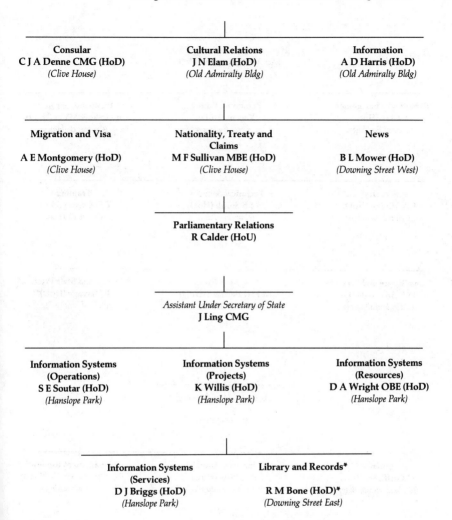

Consular	Cultural Relations	Information
C J A Denne CMG (HoD)	J N Elam (HoD)	A D Harris (HoD)
(Clive House)	*(Old Admiralty Bldg)*	*(Old Admiralty Bldg)*

Migration and Visa	Nationality, Treaty and Claims	News
A E Montgomery (HoD)	M F Sullivan MBE (HoD)	B L Mower (HoD)
(Clive House)	*(Clive House)*	*(Downing Street West)*

Parliamentary Relations
R Calder (HoU)

Assistant Under Secretary of State
J Ling CMG

Information Systems (Operations)	Information Systems (Projects)	Information Systems (Resources)
S E Soutar (HoD)	K Willis (HoD)	D A Wright OBE (HoD)
(Hanslope Park)	*(Hanslope Park)*	*(Hanslope Park)*

Information Systems (Services)	Library and Records*
D J Briggs (HoD)	R M Bone (HoD)*
(Hanslope Park)	*(Downing Street East)*

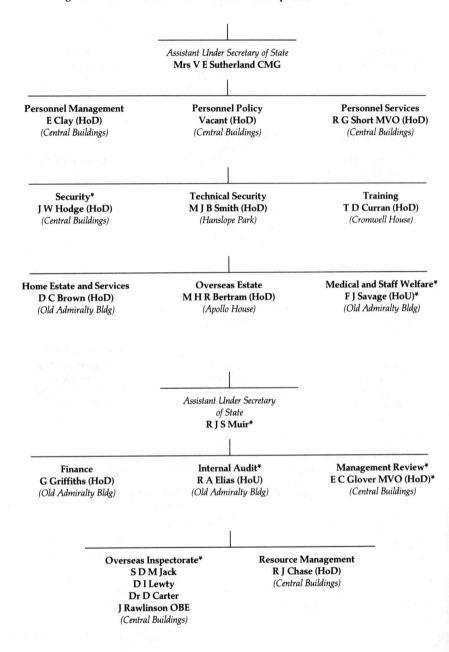

Assistant Under Secretary of State
Mrs V E Sutherland CMG

Personnel Management	**Personnel Policy**	**Personnel Services**
E Clay (HoD)	Vacant (HoD)	R G Short MVO (HoD)
(Central Buildings)	*(Central Buildings)*	*(Central Buildings)*

Security*	**Technical Security**	**Training**
J W Hodge (HoD)	M J B Smith (HoD)	T D Curran (HoD)
(Central Buildings)	*(Hanslope Park)*	*(Cromwell House)*

Home Estate and Services	**Overseas Estate**	**Medical and Staff Welfare***
D C Brown (HoD)	M H R Bertram (HoD)	F J Savage (HoU)*
(Old Admiralty Bldg)	*(Apollo House)*	*(Old Admiralty Bldg)*

*Assistant Under Secretary
of State*
R J S Muir*

Finance	**Internal Audit***	**Management Review***
G Griffiths (HoD)	R A Elias (HoU)	E C Glover MVO (HoD)*
(Old Admiralty Bldg)	*(Old Admiralty Bldg)*	*(Central Buildings)*

Overseas Inspectorate*	**Resource Management**
S D M Jack	R J Chase (HoD)
D I Lewty	*(Central Buildings)*
Dr D Carter	
J Rawlinson OBE	
(Central Buildings)	

Assistant Under Secretary of State
A St J H Figgis

Protocol
D C B Beaumont (HoD)
S W F Martin LVO
(Old Admiralty Bldg)

* joint FCO/ODA department

Europe; United Nations

Permanent Under Secretary of State
Head of the Diplomatic Service
Sir David Gillmore KCMG

Deputy Under Secretary of State
L V Appleyard
R F Cooper MVO

Policy Planning Staff

Planning only (Sir David Gillmore)
Coordination only (L V Appleyard)
Contacts with unofficial opinion on
   policy problems
Speech writing

Assistant Under Secretary of State
J Q Greenstock CMG

Southern Europe	**Western Europe**
D C A Madden ((HoD)	**Miss M MacGlashan (HoD)**
(King Charles Street)	*(Downing Street West)*

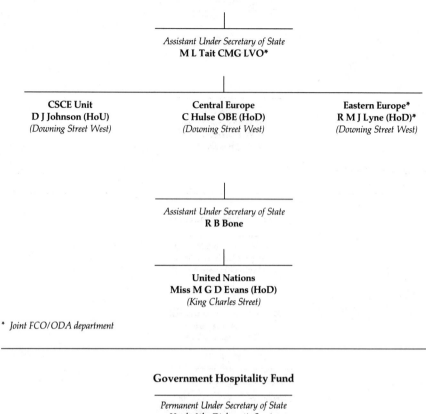

Assistant Under Secretary of State
M L Tait CMG LVO*

CSCE Unit **D J Johnson (HoU)** *(Downing Street West)*	**Central Europe** **C Hulse OBE (HoD)** *(Downing Street West)*	**Eastern Europe*** **R M J Lyne (HoD)*** *(Downing Street West)*

Assistant Under Secretary of State
R B Bone

United Nations
Miss M G D Evans (HoD)
(King Charles Street)

* *Joint FCO/ODA department*

Government Hospitality Fund

Permanent Under Secretary of State
Head of the Diplomatic Service
Sir David Gillmore KCMG

Secretary of the Fund
Brig A Cowan CBE (5)
(8 Cleveland Row)

Government Hospitality Fund
Official hospitality for overseas
ministerial visitors

Foreign and Commonwealth Office Addresses

For all fax numbers telephone the office concerned and ask for appropriate fax number

Apollo House
36 Wellesley Road
Croydon CR9 3RR
Tel 081-686 5622

2/3/4 Central Buildings
Matthew Parker Street
London SW1H 9NL
Tel 071-210 3000

Century House
Westminster Bridge Road
London SE1 7XF
Tel 071-928 5600

Clive House
Petty France
London SW1H 9HD
Tel 071-270 3000

Cornwall House
Stamford Street
London SE1 9NS
Tel 071-211 3000

Cromwell House
Dean Stanley Street
London SW1P 3JG
Tel 071-276 7676

FCO Whitehall
London SW1A 2AP
Tel 071-270 3000

Hanslope Park
Hanslope
Milton Keynes MK19 7BH
Tel 0908 510444

King Charles Street
London SW1A 2AL
Tel 071-270 3000

Kingsgate House
66–74 Victoria Street
London SW1E 6SW
Tel 071-215 5000

Old Admiralty Building
Whitehall
London SW1A 2AF
Tel 071-210 3000

94 Victoria Street
London SW1E 5JL
Tel 071-917 7000

Forestry Commission

Founded   1919

Ministers   Secretary of State for Scotland
                  Minister of Agriculture, Fisheries and Food
                  Secretary of State for Wales

Responsibilities   Administration of the woodland grant system
                       forestry research

                       Management of the Commission's forest
                       estate

                       Regulation and monitoring standards in all
                       forestry including the Forestry Enterprise

Forestry Commission

231 Corstorphine Road, Edinburgh EH12 7AT
Tel 031-334 0303   Fax 031-334 3047, 031-316 4891
All staff are based at Corstorphine Road unless otherwise indicated.
For other addresses and telephone numbers see the end of this section.

Ministers

Secretary of State for Scotland	Minister of Agriculture, Fisheries and Food	Secretary of State for Wales
The Rt Hon Ian Lang MP	**The Rt Hon John Selwyn Gummer MP**	**The Rt Hon David Hunt MP**
(for details of his office see Scottish Office)	(for details of his office see MAFF)	(for details of his office see Welsh Office)

Officials

Chairman
Raymond Johnstone

|

Private Secretary
Ms Anne Stohlner
031-334 0303

|

Director General
T R Cutler (3)

Departmental Overview

Civil Servants			Department	Minister
Grade 1	Grade 2	Grade 3		
Chairman Johnstone	T R Cutler	R T Bradley	Forestry Authority	All
		D L Foot	Forest Enterprise	All
		D S Grundy	Policy and Resources	All

Civil Servants and Departments

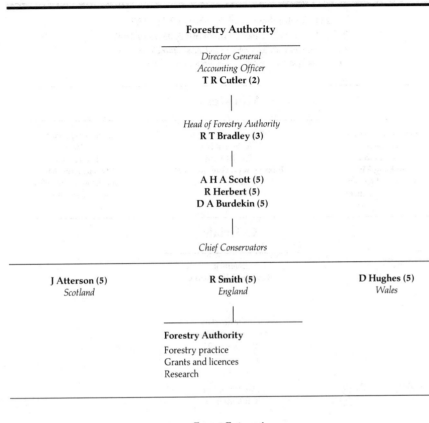

Forestry Authority

Director General
Accounting Officer
T R Cutler (2)

Head of Forestry Authority
R T Bradley (3)

A H A Scott (5)
R Herbert (5)
D A Burdekin (5)

Chief Conservators

| **J Atterson (5)** | **R Smith (5)** | **D Hughes (5)** |
| *Scotland* | *England* | *Wales* |

Forestry Authority
Forestry practice
Grants and licences
Research

Forest Enterprise

Director General and
Accounting Officer
T R Cutler (2)

Chief Executive
D L Foot (3)

S E Quigley (5)
J Dewar (6)
P Ranken (5)
C T Spillane (5)
R M Hay (5)

Regional Directors

G Hamilton (5)	**G M Cowie (5)**	**G Hatfield (5)**
North Scotland	*South Scotland*	*North and East England*

R J N Busby (5)   **J F Morgan (5)**
South and West England   *Wales*

Forest Enterprise

Business enterprise
Forest management
Estate management
Finance
Engineering

Policy and Resources

Director General and
Accounting Officer
T R Cutler (2)

Commissioner
D S Grundy (3)

P J Clarke (4)
J McGough (5)
W Prest (5)
Dr S Harding (5)
J McSorley (7)
J F Lindsay (PI0)
E K Arthurs (5)

Policy and Resources

Secretariat
Personnel
Parliamentary accounts
Policy services
Internal audit
Public information
Business systems

Forestry Commission Addresses

Research

Alice Holt Lodge
Wrecclesham
Farnham
Surrey GU10 4LH
Tel 0420 22255
Fax 0420 23653

Northern Research Station
Roslin
Midlothian EH25 9SY
Tel 031-445 2176
Fax 031-445 5124

Forest Enterprise Regional Offices

South and West England Office
Avon Fields House
Somerdale
Keynsham
Bristol BS18 2BD
Tel 0272 869481
Fax 0272 861981

North Scotland Office
21 Church Street
Inverness IV1 1EL
Tel 0463 232811
Fax 0463 243846

South Scotland Office
55/57 Moffat Road
Dumfries DG1 1NP
Tel 0387 69171
Fax 0387 51491

North and East England Office
1a Grosvenor Terrace
York YO3 7BD
Tel 0904 620221
Fax 0904 610664

Wales Office
Victoria House
Victoria Terrace
Aberystwyth
Dyfed SY23 2DQ
Tel 0970 612367
Fax 0970 625282

Forest Authority National Offices

England Office
Great Eastern House
Tenison Road
Cambridge CB1 2DU
Tel 0223 314546
Fax 0223 460699

Scotland Office
Portcullis House
21 India Street
Glasgow G2 4PL
Tel 041-248 3931
Fax 041-226 5007

Wales Office
North Road
Aberystwyth
Dyfed SY23 2EF
Tel 0970 625866
Fax 0970 626177

Government Actuary's Department

Founded   1919

Status   Established by Treasury Minute; for management purposes GAD is one of the departments for which the Chancellor of the Exchequer is responsible to Parliament. Ministerial responsibility currently rests with the Economic Secretary to the Treasury.

Responsibilities   Consultancy service to government departments, the public sector and overseas governments

Advice on social security and superannuation schemes, population and other studies

Advice on supervision of insurance companies and friendly societies and any actuarial matter

Government Actuary's Department

22 Kingsway, London WC2B 6LE
Tel 071-242 6828   Fax 071-831 6653

Minister

Economic Secretary
Anthony Nelson MP
(for details of his office
see HM Treasury)

Officials

Government Actuary
C D Daykin (2)

|

Private Secretary
Mrs M Eskrick
071-242 6828

Departmental Overview

Civil Servants		Department	Minister
Grade 2	*Grade 3*		
C D Daykin	D G Ballantine	Superannuation Advice	A Nelson*
	M A Pickford	Insurance Companies & Friendly Societies	A Nelson
	D H Loades	Social Security and Research	A Nelson
	A C Beer (6)	Establishment and Accounts	A Nelson

* Currently the minister responsible to Parliament but the Department gives advice to any minister of home or overseas department

Civil Servants and Departments

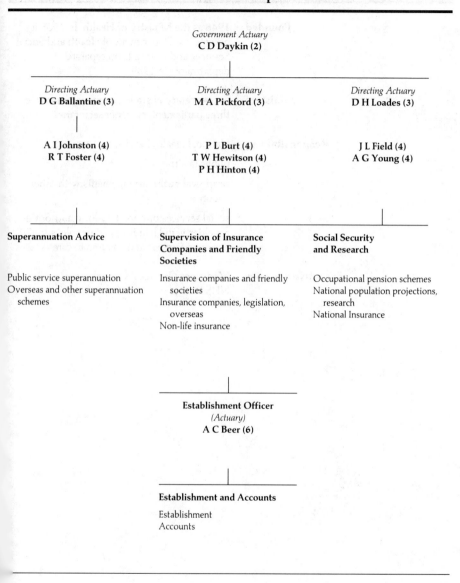

Government Actuary
C D Daykin (2)

Directing Actuary	*Directing Actuary*	*Directing Actuary*
D G Ballantine (3)	**M A Pickford (3)**	**D H Loades (3)**

A I Johnston (4)	P L Burt (4)	J L Field (4)
R T Foster (4)	T W Hewitson (4)	A G Young (4)
	P H Hinton (4)	

Superannuation Advice	**Supervision of Insurance Companies and Friendly Societies**	**Social Security and Research**
Public service superannuation	Insurance companies and friendly	Occupational pension schemes
Overseas and other superannuation	societies	National population projections,
schemes	Insurance companies, legislation,	research
	overseas	National Insurance
	Non-life insurance	

Establishment Officer
(Actuary)
A C Beer (6)

Establishment and Accounts

Establishment
Accounts

Department of Health

Founded 1948 as the Ministry of Health. In 1968 it became the Department of Health and Social Services and split to form separate departments in 1989

Ministers one secretary of state, one minister of state, three parliamentary under secretaries

Responsibilities National Health Service

public health

reciprocal health arrangements with other countries

social services provided by local authorities for elderly and handicapped people, socially deprived families and children in care

Executive agencies Medicines Control Agency
NHS Estates

Department of Health

Richmond House, 79 Whitehall, London SW1A 2NS
Tel 071-210 3000   Fax 071-210 5523
All staff are based at Richmond House unless otherwise indicated.
For other addresses and telephone numbers see the end of this section.

Ministers

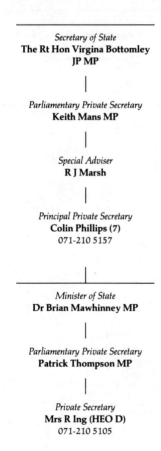

Secretary of State
**The Rt Hon Virgina Bottomley
JP MP**

Parliamentary Private Secretary
Keith Mans MP

Special Adviser
R J Marsh

Principal Private Secretary
Colin Phillips (7)
071-210 5157

Minister of State
Dr Brian Mawhinney MP

Parliamentary Private Secretary
Patrick Thompson MP

Private Secretary
Mrs R Ing (HEO D)
071-210 5105

|

Parliamentary Under	*Parliamentary Under*	*Parliamentary Under*
Secretary of State	*Secretary of State*	*Secretary of State*
The Hon Thomas Sackville MP	**Tim Yeo MP**	**Baroness Cumberlege CBE**

Private Secretary	*Private Secretary*	*Private Secretary*
R▪Armstrong (SEO)	**Ms H White (HEO)**	**Miss A Burnett (HEO)**
071-210 5113	071-210 5564	071-210 5879

House of Lords' spokesmen
Baroness Cumberlege CBE
Lord Henley
Baroness Trumpington

Ministers' Responsibilities

Virgina Bottomley   NHS Review
Office of Population Censuses and Surveys
overall responsibility for the department

Dr Brian Mawhinney   alcohol
community care overview
drugs
European Community and international affairs
general dental services
general medical services
general ophthalmic services
health education and promotion
health exports
London
medical and dental manpower and education
NHS appointments
NHS management
NHS pay and personnel
NHS reforms overview
pharmaceutical services
pharmaceuticals
primary care services
public health (including health strategy)
research
smoking
special health authorities
supplies

Tim Yeo   children's services/YTS
community care
all services for:
elderly
mentally ill
mentally handicapped
disabled (including sensorily disabled)
homelessness
personal social services
special hospitals

Thomas Sackville   abortion
acute services
ambulances
blood
capital loans
civil defence
complaints
confidentiality
crown immunity
deregulation
DH management (including Next Steps)
disciplinary cases
family planning
income generation
laboratories
NHS estates
NHS information technology
OPCS
Patients' Charter
private sector
superannuation
transplantation
unconventional finance
value for money/competitive tendering
voluntary sector
waiting lists
Warnock

Baroness Cumberlege   AIDS
alternative therapies
environmental health
ethnic issues
food hygiene
green issues
hospices
hospital chaplaincy
hospital security
infectious diseases
inner cities
nursing
nutrition
Opportunity 2000
vaccine damage
women's health (including maternity services
and breast and cervical cancer and related
screening services)

Departatmental Overview

Civil Servants			Department	Minister
Grade 1	*Grade 2*	*Grade 3*		
Departmental Resources and Services				
G Hart	Mrs A Bowtell	Ms M E Stuart	Finance Division	T Sackville
		M G Lillywhite	Departmental Management Division	T Sackville
		C Smee	Economics and Operational Research Division	T Sackville
		Mrs R J Butler	Statistics and Management Information	T Sackville
		Dr A Holt (4)	Information Systems Division	T Sackville
	Reports directly to Mr Hart	Ms R Christopherson (4)	Information Division	T Sackville
Health and Social Services Group				
G Hart	T S Heppell	N M Hale	Health Promotion	B Mawhinney
		C H Wilson	Health Care	T Sackville
		Miss R D Pease	Health Aspects of Environment and Food	T Sackville
		B Bridges	P Division	B Mawhinney
		R B Mouatt	Dental Division	B Mawhinney
		T Luce	Community Services	T Yeo
		W H Laming*	Social Services Inspectorate	T Yeo
G Hart	Dr J Metters	G Podger (4)	International Relations Unit	B Mawhinney
Dr K Calman (1A)	Dr J Metters	Dr E Rubery	Health Promotion (Medical)	B Mawhinney
		Dr J Reed	Health Community (Medical)	T Yeo
		Dr J H Steadman	Health Environment and Food Safety (Medical)	Baroness Cumberlege
		A Barton	Medical Devices Directorate	B Mawhinney

Departmental Overview

Civil Servants			Department	Minister
Grade 1	*Grade 2*	*Grade 3*		
NHS Management Executive				
D K Nichol*	Dr D Walford**	J H Barnes	Health Care Directorate	B Mawhinney
		Dr P Bourdillon	Medical Manpower and Education	B Mawhinney
		Dr Lakhani	Public Health	B Mawhinney Baroness Cumberlege
	M Malone-Lee	R Rogers	Corporate Affairs Directorate/ Information Management Group	T Sackville
	A Foster*	J Shaw	Performance Management Directorate	T Sackville
	G Greenshields*	Mrs J Firth	Finance and Corporate Information	T Sackville
	E Caines	R W D Venning	NHS Personnel	B Mawhinney
D K Nichol* G Hart	Prof M Peckham	P M Johnson Dr W Burroughs	Research and Development	B Mawhinney
		Mrs Y Moores**	Nursing	Baroness Cumberlege

Solicitor's Office (part of Department of Social Security)

G Hart	P K J Thompson	A D Roberts	Solicitor's Office	

*   *On secondment from outside the Civil Service so do not have grades.*
** *Also responsible to Chief Medical Officer.*

Civil Servants and Departments

Departmental Resources and Services

Permanent Secretary
Graham Hart CB (1)

|

Private Secretary
Ms C Wright
071-210 5310

|

*Principal Establishment
and Finance Officer*
Mrs A Bowtell (2)

Head of Department	*Principal Establishment Officer (London)*	*Chief Economic Adviser*
Ms M E Stuart (3) *(Friars House)*	**M G Lillywhite (3)**	**C Smee (3)** *(Millbank Tower)*

Miss A Mithani (5)	Ms R Derbyshire (5)	J W Hurst (5)
K J Guinness (5)	M Brown (5)	M A Parsonage (5)
J M Brownlee (5)	Mrs S M Hughes (5)	Dr G H D Royston (5)
(Friars House)	Ms P Stewart (5)	A P G Hare (5)
		(all above at Millbank Tower)

Finance Division	**Departmental Management Division (London)**	**Economics and Operational Research Division**
Supply estimates and appropriation accounts (HPSS) Family health services Centrally financed services Departmental administrations' expenditure, investment, appraisals, personal social services Local authority expenditure Internal audit and accountancy services	Personnel management Corporate and manpower planning Staff development Departmental management and communications Facilities management Next Steps and Citizen's Charter Office services	Economic support and operational research studies

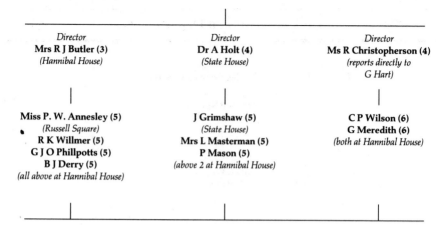

Director	Director	Director
Mrs R J Butler (3)	**Dr A Holt (4)**	**Ms R Christopherson (4)**
(Hannibal House)	*(State House)*	*(reports directly to G Hart)*

Miss P. W. Annesley (5)	**J Grimshaw (5)**	**C P Wilson (6)**
(Russell Square)	*(State House)*	**G Meredith (6)**
R K Willmer (5)	**Mrs L Masterman (5)**	*(both at Hannibal House)*
G J O Phillpotts (5)	**P Mason (5)**	
B J Derry (5)	*(above 2 at Hannibal House)*	
(all above at Hannibal House)		

Statistics Division

Statistical analysis of:
   manpower and remuneration
   prescriptions
   health service activities
   preventative and environmental
      health
   mental health
   population
   personal social services
Production of performance
   indicators
Statistical publications
Social surveys

Information Systems Division

Information systems
Library services
Information development centre
Telecommunications and office
   systems services

Information Division

Liaison with press, radio and
   television
Production and distribution of
   publicity material, promotion of
   publicity campaigns

Health and Social Services Group

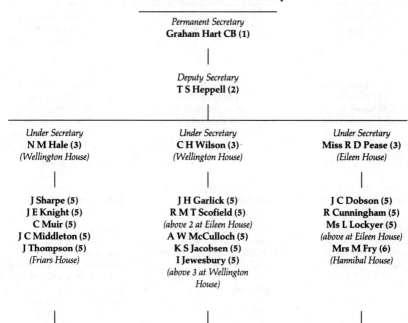

Permanent Secretary
Graham Hart CB (1)

Deputy Secretary
T S Heppell (2)

Under Secretary **N M Hale (3)** *(Wellington House)*	*Under Secretary* **C H Wilson (3)** *(Wellington House)*	*Under Secretary* **Miss R D Pease (3)** *(Eileen House)*
J Sharpe (5) **J E Knight (5)** **C Muir (5)** **J C Middleton (5)** **J Thompson (5)** *(Friars House)*	**J H Garlick (5)** **R M T Scofield (5)** *(above 2 at Eileen House)* **A W McCulloch (5)** **K S Jacobsen (5)** **I Jewesbury (5)** *(above 3 at Wellington House)*	**J C Dobson (5)** **R Cunningham (5)** **Ms L Lockyer (5)** *(above at Eileen House)* **Mrs M Fry (6)** *(Hannibal House)*

Health Promotion/Education

Health strategy
Substance abuse and misuse
Battered women
Abortion, family planning,
 infertility, maternity and
 neo-natal services
AIDS unit
Sexually transmitted diseases
Education
Liaison with health education
 authority
Child health services
Ethnic minorities
Development of NH survey work
Cancer education

Health Care

Policies on services for people with
 learning disabilities, those who
 are mentally ill, and who have
 physical disabilities or sensory
 impairments
Forensic psychiatry
Miscellaneous health service issues
Most hospital acute services

**Health Aspects of
Environment and Food**

Radiation
Medicines policy
Environmental health issues
Food legislation
Water quality and diseases
Food safety and hygiene
Nutrition
Linen and laundry services
Pest control
Transport and radio
 communications

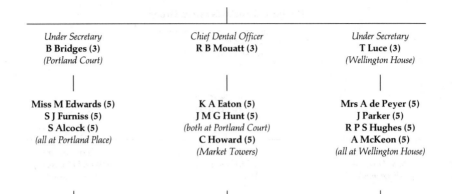

Under Secretary **B Bridges (3)** *(Portland Court)*	*Chief Dental Officer* **R B Mouatt (3)**	*Under Secretary* **T Luce (3)** *(Wellington House)*
Miss M Edwards (5) **S J Furniss (5)** **S Alcock (5)** *(all at Portland Place)*	**K A Eaton (5)** **J M G Hunt (5)** *(both at Portland Court)* **C Howard (5)** *(Market Towers)*	**Mrs A de Peyer (5)** **J Parker (5)** **R P S Hughes (5)** **A McKeon (5)** *(all at Wellington House)*

P Division

Dentists and dental services
General ophthalmic services
NHS pharmaceutical services
Pharmaceutical price regulation
  scheme

Dental Division

General dental services
Community dental services
Hospital dental services
Scientific services
Dental medicines
Preventative dentistry
Child health

Community Services

Local authority social services
Voluntary sector
Juvenile delinquents
Community homes
Children – fostering, boarding out,
  employment and performances
Care and protection of children
Community care policies

Chief Inspector
W H Laming CBE (3)
(Wellington House)

D C Brand (4)
Miss C M Hey (4)
Miss J Baraclough (5)
Mrs W Rose (5)
J G Smith (5)
S Mitchell (5)
J Kennedy (5)
(all at Wellington House)

Social Services Inspectorate

Social work and social service
  aspects of the services for which
  the Dept is responsible
Regional organisation of Social
  Services Inspectorate

Permanent Secretary
Graham Hart CB (1)

Chief Medical Officer
Dr K Calman OBE (1A)

Deputy Secretary
T S Heppell CB (2)

Deputy Chief Medical Officer
Dr J Metters (2)

Head of Unit
G Podger (4)
(Hannibal House)

**Dr P Hyzler (4)
P Allen (5)
Dr C Collier (5)**
(all at Hannibal House)

International Relations Unit

International relations (health)
Relations with European
   Community, World Health
   Organisation and other
   international agencies
Bilateral health agreements
Advice on vaccination to travellers

Chief Medical Officer
Dr K Calman (1A)

Deputy Chief Medical Officer
Dr J Metters (2)

*Senior Principal Medical
Officer*
Dr E Rubery (3)

*Senior Principal Medical
Officer*
Dr J Reed
(Wellington House)

*Senior Principal Medical
Officer*
Dr J H Steadman (3)
(Hannibal House)

Dr J Bellamy (4)
Dr G Lewis (4)
Dr D McInnes (4)
Dr D Milner (5)
Dr S Shepherd (5)
Dr D Ernaelsteen (5)
Dr F Harvey (5)
Dr W J Modle (5)
Dr H L J Markowe (5)
Dr I A F Lister Cheese (5)
Dr K Binysh (5)
Dr J Hilton (5)
Dr D M Salisbury (5)
Dr H Williams (5)
Dr S Lader (5)
Dr P Exon (5)
Dr M McGovern (5)
Dr S Gupta (5)
Dr J Leese (5)
Dr M Guy (5)
Dr E Tebbs (5)
Dr R Stanwell-Smith (5)

Dr R Jenkins (4)
Dr S Munday (5)
Prof S Ebrahim (5)
Dr A Rawson (5)
Dr D Brooksbank (5)
Dr D Jones (5)
Dr D Kingdon (5)
Dr E Miller (5)
(above at Wellington Hse)
Dr J Shanks (4)
Dr H Hangartner (4)
Dr J Ashwell (5)
Dr D Rothman (5)
Dr N Halliday (5)
Dr P Furnell (5)
Dr N Melia (5)
Dr E Clissold (5)
Dr A Rejman (5)
Dr H Sutton (5)
Dr E Hills (5)
(all at Eileen House)

Dr R Skinner (4)
Dr E Smales (4)
Dr G E Diggle (4)
Dr R L Maynard (5)
Dr T J Meredith (5)
Dr T C Marrs (5)
Dr N Lazarus (5)
Dr R B Singh (5)
Dr M Waring (5)
Dr A Bolman (5)
(above at Hannibal House)
Dr P Clarke (5)
Dr M J Wiseman (5)
(both at Wellington Hse)
Dr C Swinson (5)
Dr A Dawson (5)
Dr L Robinson (5)
Dr A Wright (5)
(above at Eileen House)

Health Promotion (Medical)

Health and social services for
  children
Preventive medicine
Prevention of coronary heart
  disease and smoking-related
  diseases
Maternity, gynaecology, infertility
  and genetic services
Abortion and family planning
Vaccination and immunisation
Alcohol and drugs misuse
Publications

Health Care (Medical)

Pathology services
Services for the disabled
Medical and surgical specialities
Clinical complaints procedure
Mental health and handicap
Psychiatry
Special hospitals
Services for the elderly

**Health Aspects of
Environment and Food
(Medical)**

Microbiology of food and the
  environment
Hazards to human health from
  environment radiation and from
  chemicals in food, consumer
  products and the environment

Director
A B Barton (4)
(Russell Square House)

Miss M N Duncan (5)
D C Potter (5)
(both at Russell Square House)

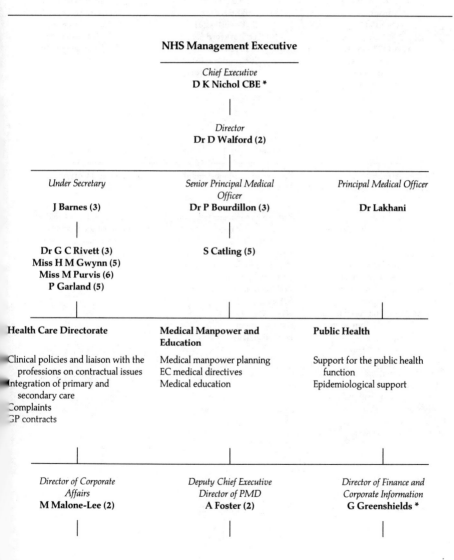

Medical Devices Directorate
Scientific and technical services for
the regulation of medical devices
Quality and safety assessment
Product evaluation

NHS Management Executive

Chief Executive
D K Nichol CBE *

Director
Dr D Walford (2)

Under Secretary	*Senior Principal Medical Officer*	*Principal Medical Officer*
J Barnes (3)	**Dr P Bourdillon (3)**	**Dr Lakhani**

Dr G C Rivett (3)	**S Catling (5)**	
Miss H M Gwynn (5)		
Miss M Purvis (6)		
P Garland (5)		

Health Care Directorate

Clinical policies and liaison with the
professions on contractual issues
Integration of primary and
secondary care
Complaints
GP contracts

**Medical Manpower and
Education**

Medical manpower planning
EC medical directives
Medical education

Public Health

Support for the public health
function
Epidemiological support

Director of Corporate Affairs	*Deputy Chief Executive Director of PMD*	*Director of Finance and Corporate Information*
M Malone-Lee (2)	**A Foster (2)**	**G Greenshields ***

Director of Information Management Group
R T Rogers (3)

Deputy Director
J Shaw (3)

Deputy Director Finance
Mrs J Firth (3)

Ms K James (5)
J Caslake (5)
Miss N Fenton (5)
Vacant (4)
I Smith (5)
(above 2 at Market Towers)
M A O'Flynn (5)
(Hannibal House)
J W Hurst (5)
A Hare (5)
A Bacon (5)
(above 3 at Millbank Tower)

Miss S O'Toole (5)
Miss I Nisbet (5)
J Rogers (4)
B Slater (5)
N Beverley (4)
D Stockford (5)
D Hewlett (6)
R Creighton (6)
J Stopes-Roe (6)

J Rushforth (5)
C P Kendall (5)
M A Harris (5)
Mrs E Hunter Johnston (5)
Miss A Simkins (5)
B J Derry (5)
J Tomlinson (5)

Corporate Affairs Directorate/Information Management Group

NHS ME secretariat
Communications within the NHS ME
Quality of care
Development of strategic plans
Conduct of development projects
Implementation of information systems for the NHS
Implementation and coordination of NHS review information system requirements
Production of health service indicators
Patients' Charter
Intelligence unit
Economics and operational research divisions
ME policy unit
Personnel and resources in ME

Performance Management Directorate

Performance management issues in the different regions
National priorities
Systems development
Health authority mergers
Task force programme
Waiting times initiative
Reforms group
NHS trusts unit
Purchasing unit
London enquiry

Finance and Corporate Information

Public expenditure health and personal social services
Resource management
Value for money
Financial management

Director
E Caines (2)

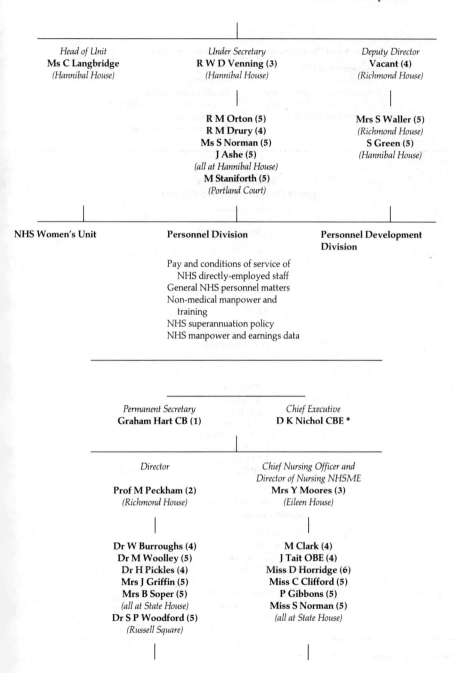

Head of Unit	*Under Secretary*	*Deputy Director*
Ms C Langbridge	**R W D Venning (3)**	**Vacant (4)**
(Hannibal House)	*(Hannibal House)*	*(Richmond House)*

R M Orton (5)
R M Drury (4)
Ms S Norman (5)
J Ashe (5)
(all at Hannibal House)
M Staniforth (5)
(Portland Court)

Mrs S Waller (5)
(Richmond House)
S Green (5)
(Hannibal House)

NHS Women's Unit

Personnel Division

Pay and conditions of service of
    NHS directly-employed staff
General NHS personnel matters
Non-medical manpower and
    training
NHS superannuation policy
NHS manpower and earnings data

**Personnel Development
Division**

Permanent Secretary
Graham Hart CB (1)

Chief Executive
D K Nichol CBE *

Director

Prof M Peckham (2)
(Richmond House)

*Chief Nursing Officer and
Director of Nursing NHSME*
Mrs Y Moores (3)
(Eileen House)

Dr W Burroughs (4)
Dr M Woolley (5)
Dr H Pickles (4)
Mrs J Griffin (5)
Mrs B Soper (5)
(all at State House)
Dr S P Woodford (5)
(Russell Square)

M Clark (4)
J Tait OBE (4)
Miss D Horridge (6)
Miss C Clifford (5)
P Gibbons (5)
Miss S Norman (5)
(all at State House)

Research and Development

Development of NHS research and
development strategy
Responsibility for research and
development in health and
personal social services

Nursing Directorate

Nursing
Midwifery
Health visiting services
Monitor scale and provision of
nursing services
Nurse training and education

Solicitor's Office
(part of Department of Social Security)

Permanent Secretary
Graham Hart CB (1)

|

Solicitor
P K J Thompson (2)

|

Principal Assistant Solicitor
A D Roberts (3)

|

D Curtis (5)
R Powell (5)
C G Blake (5)
P Milledge (5)
Miss A Brett-Holt (5)
R G S Aitken (5)
J F McCleary (5)
J P Canlin (5)

Solicitor's Office

Criminal proceedings
Staffing matters and departmental
and NHS contracts
Litigation relating to departments
of health and social security
All other legal matters to do with
health and personal social
services

* on secondment from outside the Civil Service

Department of Health Addresses

For fax numbers, please phone the
switchboard and ask for the relevant fax
number

Eileen House
80–94 Newington Causeway
London SE1 6EF
Tel 071-972 2000

Market Towers
1 Nine Elms Lane
London SW8 5NQ
Tel 071-720 2188

Russell Square House
14 Russell Square
London WC1B 5EP
Tel 071-636 6811

Friars House
157–168 Blackfriars Road
London SE1 8EU
Tel 071-972 2000

Millbank Tower
21–24 Millbank
London SW1P 4QU
Tel 071-972 8505

State House
High Holborn
London WC1R 4SX
Tel 071-972 2000

Hannibal House
Elephant & Castle
London SE1 6TE
Tel 071-972 2000

Portland Court
158–176 Great Portland Street
London W1N 5TB
Tel 071-972 2000

Wellington House
133–135 Waterloo Road
London SE1 8UG
Tel 071-972 2000

Home Office

Founded	1782
Ministers	Home Secretary, three ministers of state and one parliamentary under secretary of state
Responsibilities	animal welfare
	civil defence
	community relations and inner cities
	cremations and burials
	criminal injuries compensation scheme
	criminal law
	criminal policy
	data protection
	drugs
	electoral matters
	exhumations
	extradition
	fire safety in theatres and cinemas
	fire services
	firearms
	gaming and lotteries
	immigration
	liquor licensing
	local legislation/byelaws
	marriage
	nationality
	passports
	police
	prisons
	probation and aftercare
	race relations
	refugees resettlement
	Royal matters
	shops
	voluntary organisations
Executive Agencies	Forensic Science Service
	UK Passport Agency
	Fire Service College

Home Office

50 Queen Anne's Gate, London SW1H 9AT

Tel 071-273 3000   Fax 071-273 2190

All personnel are based at 50 Queen Anne's Gate unless otherwise indicated.
For other addresses and telephone numbers see end of Home·Office section.

Ministers

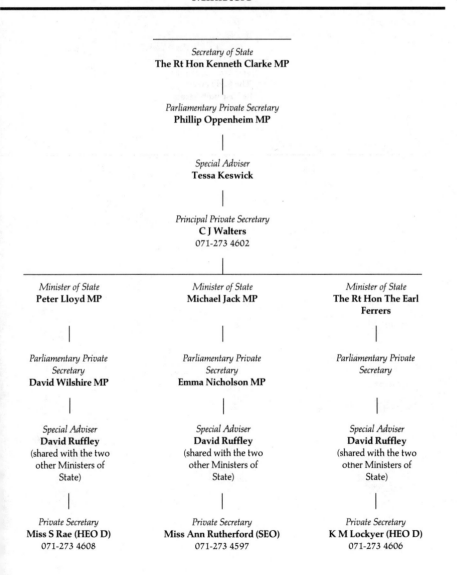

Secretary of State
The Rt Hon Kenneth Clarke MP

Parliamentary Private Secretary
Phillip Oppenheim MP

Special Adviser
Tessa Keswick

Principal Private Secretary
C J Walters
071-273 4602

Minister of State	*Minister of State*	*Minister of State*
Peter Lloyd MP	**Michael Jack MP**	**The Rt Hon The Earl Ferrers**
Parliamentary Private Secretary	*Parliamentary Private Secretary*	*Parliamentary Private Secretary*
David Wilshire MP	**Emma Nicholson MP**	
Special Adviser	*Special Adviser*	*Special Adviser*
David Ruffley (shared with the two other Ministers of State)	**David Ruffley** (shared with the two other Ministers of State)	**David Ruffley** (shared with the two other Ministers of State)
Private Secretary	*Private Secretary*	*Private Secretary*
Miss S Rae (HEO D) 071-273 4608	**Miss Ann Rutherford (SEO)** 071-273 4597	**K M Lockyer (HEO D)** 071-273 4606

|

*Parliamentary Under Secretary of
State*
Charles Wardle MP

|

Private Secretary
Miss J E Hutheon
071-273 4604

|

House of Lords' Spokesmen
The Earl Ferrers
The Viscount Astor
Baroness Cumberlege

Ministerial Responsibilities

Kenneth Clarke   Overall responsibility for department
Deals personally with:
Emergencies
Establishment
Finance and manpower
Legal adviser's branch
Royal matters
Security

Peter Lloyd   Community relations and inner cities
Data Protection and privacy
Electoral matters
Gambling
Prisons
Shops
Summer time
House of Commons business on fire and civil
defence

Michael Jack   Coordination on European matters
Crime prevention
Criminal justice casework
Criminal policy and criminal justice
Drugs
Extradition
Juvenile offenders
Mentally disordered offenders
Probation and after-care
Voluntary sector
House of Commons business on charities law,
cults, Channel Islands/Isle of Man

The Earl Ferrers   Channel Islands/Isle of Man
Charities law
Civil defence
Cults
Fire service
Police
Departmental business in the Lords

Charles Wardle   Animal welfare
Coroners
Electoral licensing
Immigration and nationality
Liquor licensing
Local legislation/bye-laws
Passports
Refugee resettlement
House of Commons business on police

Departmental Overview

Civil Servants			Department	Minister
Grade 1	*Grade 2*	*Grade 3*		
Criminal, Research and Statistics Department and Constitutional Division				
Sir Clive Whitmore	J F Halliday	A P Wilson	Criminal Policy	M Jack
		R M Morris	Criminal Justice and Constitutional	M Jack
		C P Nuttall	Research and Statistics	
Prisons				
Sir Clive Whitmore	J G Pilling	Miss P Drew	Custody	P Lloyd
		I Dunbar	Inmate Administration	P Lloyd
		B A Emes	Inmate Programmes	P Lloyd
		Dr R J Wool	Prison Medical Services	P Lloyd
		Mrs J E Reisz	Buildings and Services	P Lloyd
		A J Butler	Personnel and Finance	P Lloyd
Fire and Emergency Planning				
Sir Clive Whitmore	T C Platt	W J A Innes	Fire and Emergency Planning	Earl Ferrers
Establishment, Finance and Manpower				
	T C Platt	C L Scoble	Establishment	K Clarke
		S G Norris	Finance and Manpower	K Clarke
Police				
Sir Clive Whitmore	I M Burns	Miss C Sinclair	Police	Earl Ferrers
		Ms M A Clayton	Police	Earl Ferrers
		G J Wasserman	Science and Technology	Earl Ferrers
		Sir John Woodcock	HM Inspectorate of Constabulary	Earl Ferrers

Departmental Overview

Civil Servants			Department	Minister
Grade 1	Grade 2	Grade 3		
Legal Adviser's Branch				
Sir Clive Whitmore	A H Hammond (until October 1992 when he is replaced by Michael Saunders CB)	Ms P A Edwards	Principal Assistant Legal Adviser	K Clarke
		D Bentley	Principal Assistant Legal Adviser	K Clarke
Equal Opportunities and General, Immigration and Nationality				
Sir Clive Whitmore	A J Langdon	M E Head	Equal Opportunities and General	C Wardle
		A R Rawsthorne	Immigration and Nationality	C Wardle
		W Jeffrey	Immigration and Nationality	C Wardle

Civil Servants and Departments

Criminal and Research and Statistics Departments and Constitutional Division

Permanent Under Secretary of State
Sir Clive Whitmore GCB CVO (1)

Private Secretary
Ms A Blackshaw
071-273 2199

Deputy Under Secretary of State
J F Halliday (2)

Assistant Under Secretary of State Head of Dept **A P Wilson (3)**	*Assistant Under Secretary of State Head of Dept* **R M Morris (3)**	*Assistant Under Secretary of State Head of Dept* **C P Nuttall (3)**
Miss J MacNaughton (5) **R J Baxter (5)** **Miss C J Stewart (5)** **Miss L Pallett (5)** **A Norbury (6)** **A Harding (5)** **Miss S Marshall (5)**	**Miss P C Drew (5)** **C H Thomas OBE (5)** **P J Honour (5)**	**R Tarling (5)** **C G Lewis (5)** **P W Ward (5)** *(Abell House)* **J Walker (5)**
Criminal Policy Department Criminal policy Criminal law Drugs Central drug prevention Victims Criminal injuries compensation scheme International cooperation Criminal justice conferences	**Criminal Justice and Constitutional Department** Probation service HM Inspectorate of Probation Constitutional issues	**Research and Statistics Department** Research Statistics

Prisons

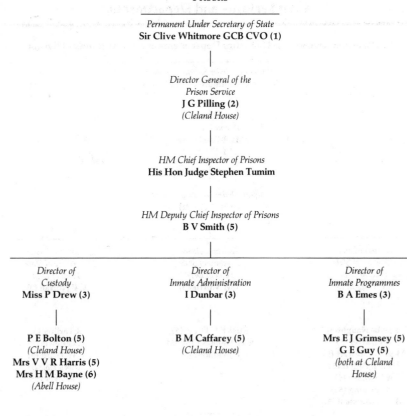

Permanent Under Secretary of State
Sir Clive Whitmore GCB CVO (1)

*Director General of the
Prison Service*
J G Pilling (2)
(Cleland House)

HM Chief Inspector of Prisons
His Hon Judge Stephen Tumim

HM Deputy Chief Inspector of Prisons
B V Smith (5)

Director of *Custody* **Miss P Drew (3)**	*Director of* *Inmate Administration* **I Dunbar (3)**	*Director of* *Inmate Programmes* **B A Emes (3)**
P E Bolton (5) *(Cleland House)* **Mrs V V R Harris (5)** **Mrs H M Bayne (6)** *(Abell House)*	**B M Caffarey (5)** *(Cleland House)*	**Mrs E J Grimsey (5)** **G E Guy (5)** *(both at Cleland* *House)*

Directorate of **Custody**	**Directorate of** **Inmate Administration**	**Directorate of** **Inmate Programmes**
Security and incident control Tactical management Category A and life sentence prisoners Parole Life sentence review	Adjudications Grievance procedures Visits and home links Race relations Boards of visitors Suicide prevention	Inmate regime policy Throughcare Education Physical education Chaplaincy

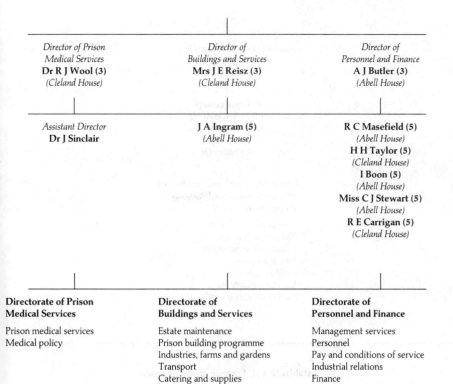

Director of Prison *Medical Services* **Dr R J Wool (3)** *(Cleland House)*	*Director of* *Buildings and Services* **Mrs J E Reisz (3)** *(Cleland House)*	*Director of* *Personnel and Finance* **A J Butler (3)** *(Abell House)*
Assistant Director **Dr J Sinclair**	**J A Ingram (5)** *(Abell House)*	**R C Masefield (5)** *(Abell House)* **H H Taylor (5)** *(Cleland House)* **I Boon (5)** *(Abell House)* **Miss C J Stewart (5)** *(Abell House)* **R E Carrigan (5)** *(Cleland House)*
Directorate of Prison **Medical Services** Prison medical services Medical policy	**Directorate of** **Buildings and Services** Estate maintenance Prison building programme Industries, farms and gardens Transport Catering and supplies	**Directorate of** **Personnel and Finance** Management services Personnel Pay and conditions of service Industrial relations Finance Info tech

Fire and Emergency Planning

Permanent Under Secretary of State
Sir Clive Whitmore GCB CVO (1)

Deputy Under Secretary of State
T C Platt (2)

HM Chief Inspector, Fire Service
Inspectorate
Sir Reginald Doyle CBE

|

Assistant Under Secretary of State
W J A Innes (3)

|

P G Spurgeon (5)
J R K de Quidt (5)
Dr D M Peace (5)
E Soden (5)
R J Miles (5)

|

Fire and Emergency Planning
Department

Fire service
Fire prevention
Fire service inspectorate
Fire service college
Civil defence
Emergency planning
Safety of sports grounds

Establishment, Finance and Manpower

Permanent Under Secretary of State
Sir Clive Whitmore GCB CVO
(1)

|

Deputy Under Secretary of State
T C Platt (2)

|

Assistant Under Secretary
of State
Head of Department
C L Scoble (3)
(Grenadier House)

|

Assistant Under Secretary
of State
Principal Finance Officer
S G Norris (3)

|

P Canovan (5)
R M Whalley (5)
Mrs C L Crawford (5)
Mrs E I France (5)
(St John's House)
B W Buck (5)
(Clive House)
A E Moorey (4)

B O Bubbear (5)
G C Robertson (5)
M P Bolt (5)
A K Holman (6)
D W Diamond (6)
D Mullarkey (7)

Establishment

Accommodation and common
 services
Staff development
Personnel management
Information systems
Information technology
Public relations

Finance and Manpower

Procurement
Planning and control of
 expenditure
Local government
Management services
Accounts
Internal audit

Police

Permanent Under Secretary of State
Sir Clive Whitmore GCB CVO
(1)

Deputy Under Secretary of State
I M Burns (2)

Assistant Under
Secretary of State
Miss C Sinclair (3)

Assistant Under
Secretary of State
Miss M A Clayton (3)

Assistant Under
Secretary of State
Head of Science and
Technology Group
G J Wasserman (3)
(Horseferry House)

R A Harrington (5)
J L Goddard (5)
J Le Vay (5)

Miss A M Edwards (5)
K H Heal (5)
Mrs P G W Catto (5)
M Cunliffe 95)

J W Cane (5)
N F K Finlayson (5)
A Holt (5)
C B J Sutton (5)
(all at Horseferry House)
Dr P Young (5)
(Sandridge)

Police Department	Police Department	Police Department
Metropolitan police	Police powers	Scientific and technical support to
Public order	Complaints	police forces
Value for money	Crime prevention	Telecommunications
	Training	Police national computer
	Recruitment	Police requirements support unit
		Police scientific development

Chief Inspector of Constabulary
**Sir John Woodcock, CBE, QPM,
CBIM**

**HM Inspectorate of
Constabulary**

Inspections
Professional policing matters
Promoting policy efficiency and
effectiveness

Legal Adviser's Branch

Permanent Under Secretary of State
**Sir Clive Whitmore GCB CVO
(1)**

*Deputy Under Secretary of State
Legal Adviser*
A H Hammond CB (2)
(until October 1992
when he is replaced by
Michael Saunders CB)

**Miss P A Edwards (3)
D Bentley (3)**

Legal Adviser's Branch

Advice on legal matters
Preparation of bills
Drafting of statutory instruments
etc

Equal Opportunities and General; Immigration and Nationality

Permanent Under Secretary of State
Sir Clive Whitmore GCB CVO
(1)

|

Deputy Under Secretary of State
A J Langdon (2)

Assistant Under	*Assistant Under*	*Assistant Under Secretary*
Secretary of State	*Secretary of State*	*of State*
Head of Department	**A R Rawsthorne (3)**	**W A Jeffrey (3)**
M E Head CVO (3)	*(Lunar House)*	*Lunar House*

| | | |

N M Johnson (5)	**Miss V M Dews (5)**	**N C Sanderson (5)**
J Sibson (5)	**R G Yates (5)**	**Vacant (5)**
Mrs B H Fair (5)	**N R Varney (5)**	**E B Nicholls (5)**
P R C Storr (5)	**A Walmsley (6)**	**Ms K Collins** *(Ports)*
Dr R M Watt (4)	*(Liverpool)*	**C Manchip** *(Enforcement)*

| | | |

Equal Opportunities	**Policy and**	**Immigration and Nationality**
and General	**Nationality**	**Operations and Resources**
Race relations	Immigration policy	Immigration service
Sex discrimination	Refugees and asylum	After entry casework
Electoral matters	European business	Appeals and enforcement
Gambling	Nationality	Finance and management services
Voluntary sector		Information technology
Charities		
Refugee resettlement		
Data protection and privacy		
Coroners		
Local legislation		
Animals		

Home Office Addresses

Abell House
John Islip Street
London SW1P 4LH
Tel 071-217 3000
Fax 071-828 7643

Calthorpe House
P O Box 2078
Edgbaston
Birmingham B16 8QZ
Tel 021-455 9855
Fax 021-454 6738

Cleland House
Page Street
London SW1P 4LN
Tel 071-217 3000
Fax 071-217 6635

Clive House
Petty France
London SW1H 9HD
Tel 071-271 3000
Fax 071-271 8553

Crown House
52 Elizabeth House
Corby
Northants NN17 1PJ
Tel 0536 202101
Fax 0536 68557

Grenadier House
99/105 Horseferry Road
London SW1P 2DD
Tel 071-217 3000
Fax 071-217 0002

Horseferry House
Dean Ryle Street
London SW1P 2AW
Tel 071-217 3000
Fax 071-217 8619

James Wolfe Road
Cowley
Oxford OX4 2PT
Tel 0865 776005
Fax 0865 747671

Liverpool Nationality Office
India Buildings
Water Street
Liverpool LZ 0QN
Tel 051-227 3939
Fax 051-255 1160

Lunar House
40 Wellesley Road
Croydon CR9 2BY
Tel 081-686 0688
Fax 081-760 1181

St John's House
Merton Road
Bootle
Merseyside L20 3QE
Tel 051-934 7209
Fax 051-933 6340

Whittington House
19/30 Alfred Place
London WC1E 7LU
Tel 071-636 9501
Fax 071-436 0804

Board of Inland Revenue

Founded	1849
Ministers	Chancellor of the Exchequer and Financial Secretary to the Treasury
Responsibilities	Administers and collects direct taxes, mainly income tax, corporation tax, capital gains tax, stamp duty – and advises the Chancellor of the Exchequer on policy questions
Executive Agencies	Valuation Office
Executive Offices	The department is organised into a series of accountable management units under the Next Steps programme. The day-to-day operations in assessing and collecting tax and in providing internal support services are carried out by 34 executive offices. These are listed below and, where relevant, their directorates/divisions in brackets:

Regional Executive Offices (14)
(Directorate Operations 1)

Capital Taxes Office (Scotland)
(Capital Valuation)

Foreign Dividends
(International)

Claims
(Savings and Investments)

Information Technology Office
(Information Technology)

Corporate Communications Office

Internal Audit Office
(Finance Division)

Enforcement Office
(Directorate Operations 1)

Oil Taxation Office
(Company Tax)

Accounts Office (Cumbernauld)
(Directorate Operations 1)

Financial and Management Accounts
System (FAMAS) Office
(Finance Division)

Pensions Schemes Office
(Savings and Investment)

Accounts Office (Shipley)
(Directorate Operations 1)

Financial Services Office
(Finance Division)

Solicitor's Office (Scotland)

Special Compliance Office
(Directorate Operations 2)

Stamp Office
(Savings and Investment)

Statistics Office
(Statistics)

Training Office
(Manpower and Support Services)

Solicitor's Office

Capital Taxes Office (England, Wales, NI)
(Capital and Valuation)

Board of Inland Revenue

Somerset House, Strand, London WC2R 1LB
Tel 071-438 6622
Fax *Telephone the above number and ask for the appropriate fax number*
All staff are based at Somerset House unless otherwise indicated.
For other addresses and telephone numbers see the end of this section.

Ministers

Chancellor of the Exchequer
The Rt Hon Norman Lamont MP
(for details of his office see
HM Treasury section)

Financial Secretary to the Treasury
Stephen Dorrell MP
(for details see HM Treasury
section)

The Board

Chairman
Sir Anthony Battishill KCB (1)

|

Private Secretary
G Lloyd
071-438 6615

|

Deputy Chairmen
T J Painter CB (2)
L J H Beighton CB (2)

|

Directors General
S C T Matheson (2)
C W Corlett (2)

Departmental Overview

Civil Servants			Department
Grade 1	*Grade 2*	*Grade 3*	
Sir Anthony Battishill	These divisions report directly to the Chairman	J M Crawley (see also under Manpower and Support Services below)	Finance
		K V Deacon	Directorate, Operations 1
		J H Roberts	Directorate, Operations 2

Personal Tax; Capital and Valuation; Savings and Investment; Statistics Office

Sir Anthony Battishill	T J Painter	E McGivern	Personal Tax
		M F Cayley	Capital and Valuation
		B A Mace	Savings and Investment
		J R Calder	Statistics Office

International; Business Profits; Company Tax; Financial Institutions

Sir Anthony Battishill	L J H Beighton	I R Spence	International
		E J Gribbon	Business profits
		P Lewis	Company Tax
		M Templeman	Financial Institutions

Personnel Directorate; Manpower and Support Services Division; Information Technology Office

Sir Anthony Battishill	S C T Matheson	P B G Jones	Personnel Directorate
		J M Crawley	Manpower and Support Services
		G H Bush	Information Technology Office

Manning

Sir Anthony Battishill	C W Corlett	M A Johns	Central
		J Yard (4)	Change Management Group

Departmental Overview

Civil Servants			Department
Grade 1	*Grade 2*	*Grade 3*	

Solicitor's Office

Sir Anthony Battishill	B E Cleave	J G H Bates	Taxation of Profits, Capital Gains Tax, Avoidance Schemes, Criminal Prosecutions
		J D H Johnston	Legislation, Inheritance Tax, Stamp Duties, Charities
		P L Ridd	Personal Taxation, Rating, Recovery and Enforcement, International, Double Taxation, Oil

Solicitor for Scotland

Sir Anthony Battishill		T H Scott (4)	

Corporate Communications Office

Sir Anthony Battishill		Mrs S Cullum (5)	Corporate Communications Office

Regional Executive Offices

Sir Anthony Battishill		M J Hodgson (4)	East Inland Revenue
		T L Hope (4)	Greater Manchester
			London
		R A Jones (4)	East London
		J F Carling (4)	North and West London
		R E German (4)	South London
		J A Robson (4)	Midlands
		R I Ford (4)	North
		J I White (4)	North West
		D L S Bean (4)	South East
		D S Aldridge (4)	South West
		A C Sleeman (4)	South Yorkshire
		R S T Ewing (5)	Northern Ireland
		O J D Clarke (4)	Scotland
		M W Kirk (4)	Wales

Civil Servants and Departments

Finance; Directorate Operations 1 and 2

Chairman
Sir Anthony Battishill KCB (1)

|

Principal Finance Officer
J M Crawley (3)

|

N R Buckley (5)
(GKN House)
J H Reed (5)
J R Cavell (5)
R R Martin (5)

|

Finance Division

Financial planning
Internal audit
Management planning
Financial services
Financial and management accounts
Central Purchasing

|

Director   *Director*
K V Deacon (3)   **J H Roberts (3)**

| |

J Gant (4)
D W Muir (4)
T R Evans (5)
J M Thomas (5)
J Calder (5)
S J McManus (5)
J P Gilbody (5)
Dr E A Harrison (5)
(all above at SW Wing
Bush House)
E C Jones (5)
(Apsley House)
M G Oakley (5)
(Matheson House)

J Mawson (5)
D F Parrett (5)
Miss K C S H Linnell (5)
J T Cawdron (5)
(above 4 at Angel Court)
F B Dunbar (6)
J M L Davenport (4)
(SW Wing Bush House)
F J Brannigan (4)

Directorate Operations 1

Network management group
Customer service quality
Collection
Audit and enforcement procedures
District
Collection and regional
  organisation
Accounts offices
Training
Technical standards
Penalties
CI pay and file and compliance
  projects
Operational policy
Operational strategy
Business systems
Computer projects
Special projects

Directorate Operations 2

Compliance, criminal proceedings
Information powers
Collection industry
Interest on unpaid/overpaid tax
Special investigations
Enquiries
Insolvency
Construction industry

Personal Tax; Capital and Valuation; Savings and Investment; Statistics

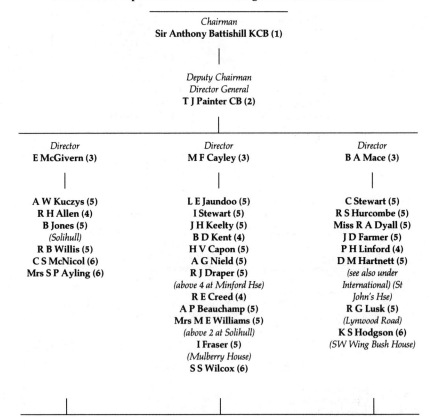

Chairman
Sir Anthony Battishill KCB (1)

Deputy Chairman
Director General
T J Painter CB (2)

Director **E McGivern (3)**	*Director* **M F Cayley (3)**	*Director* **B A Mace (3)**
A W Kuczys (5) R H Allen (4) B Jones (5) *(Solihull)* R B Willis (5) C S McNicol (6) Mrs S P Ayling (6)	L E Jaundoo (5) I Stewart (5) J H Keelty (5) B D Kent (4) H V Capon (5) A G Nield (5) R J Draper (5) *(above 4 at Minford Hse)* R E Creed (4) A P Beauchamp (5) Mrs M E Williams (5) *(above 2 at Solihull)* I Fraser (5) *(Mulberry House)* S S Wilcox (6)	C Stewart (5) R S Hurcombe (5) Miss R A Dyall (5) J D Farmer (5) P H Linford (4) D M Hartnett (5) *(see also under* *International) (St* *John's Hse)* R G Lusk (5) *(Lynwood Road)* K S Hodgson (6) *(SW Wing Bush House)*

Personal Tax	**Capital and Valuation**	**Savings and Investment**

Income tax rates and allowances
Independent taxation
Schedule E
Benefits in kind and expenses
Foreign earnings
Lump sums
Employment/self-employment
Social security benefits
PAYE
Personal taxation
	Inheritance tax
	Capital transfer tax
	Capital gains tax
	Death duties
	Inheritance tax
	Development land tax
	IR affidavits and accounts
	Assessment of duty and tax
	Shares valuation
	Enforcement
	Special cases
	Relief for designated property
	Settled property
	Gifts
	Affidavits
	Capital taxes (Scotland)
		Charities
		Stamp duty
		Provision for retirement and
		  pensions
		Taxation on savings including PEPs
		  and TESSAs
		Trusts, settlements and
		  administration of estates
		Covenants, maintenance and
		  alimony
		Adjudication
		Stamp Office
		TOBBI
		MIRAs
		Employee share schemes and
		  financial participation schemes,
		  profit-related pay

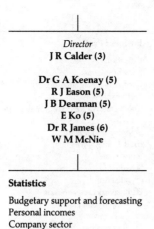

Director
J R Calder (3)

Dr G A Keenay (5)
R J Eason (5)
J B Dearman (5)
E Ko (5)
Dr R James (6)
W M McNie

Statistics

Budgetary support and forecasting
Personal incomes
Company sector
Capital and wealth
Information technology
Economic advice

International; Business Profits; Company Tax; Financial Institutions

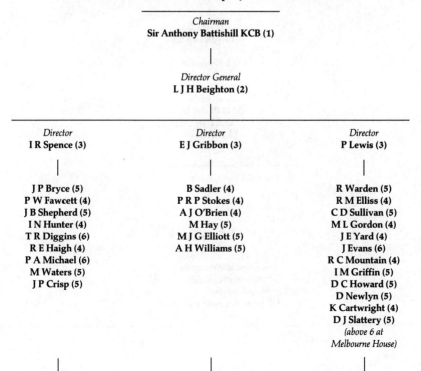

Chairman
Sir Anthony Battishill KCB (1)

Director General
L J H Beighton (2)

Director **I R Spence (3)**	*Director* **E J Gribbon (3)**	*Director* **P Lewis (3)**
J P Bryce (5)	**B Sadler (4)**	**R Warden (5)**
P W Fawcett (4)	**P R P Stokes (4)**	**R M Elliss (4)**
J B Shepherd (5)	**A J O'Brien (4)**	**C D Sullivan (5)**
I N Hunter (4)	**M Hay (5)**	**M L Gordon (4)**
T R Diggins (6)	**M J G Elliott (5)**	**J E Yard (4)**
R E Haigh (4)	**A H Williams (5)**	**J Evans (6)**
P A Michael (6)		**R C Mountain (4)**
M Waters (5)		**I M Griffin (5)**
J P Crisp (5)		**D C Howard (5)**
		D Newlyn (5)
		K Cartwright (4)
		D J Slattery (5)
		(above 6 at Melbourne House)

International	Business Profits	Company Tax
OECD	Cessations	Corporation tax
Individual residence and domicile	New businesses	Business expansion scheme
Non-resident trusts	Company amalgamations	Purchase of own shares
International business	Partnerships	Close companies
Double taxation agreements	Capital allowance (except mines, oil	Demergers
Paying agents	wells)	Industrial and provident societies
Diplomatic privilege	Shipping and leasing	Trade unions
International organisations	Land, farming, forestry	Cooperatives
Overseas tax comparisons	Stock relief	Capital allowances (mines and oil
Company residence and migration	Schedule D	wells)
Offshore funds	Privatisation	Group relief and losses
Foreign partnerships	EC business tax proposals	Housing Associations
Thin capitalisation	Self-employed persons	North Sea fiscal regimes
Foreign companies and traders	Property income	Oil Taxation Office
International avoidance problems	Trading profits	Petroleum Revenue Tax
Foreign dividends claims branch	Trade Protection Associations	
Liaison with EC	Literary and artistic profits	
	Copyright royalties	
	Building and contracting	
	Particular trades	

Director
M Templeman (3)

M D E Newstead (4)
M T Evans (5)
R N Page (4)
M Keith (4)
M D Phelps (5)
M O R Haigh (5)
J E Morris (5)

Financial Institutions

Banks
Financial concerns
Lloyds
Stock Exchange
Building societies
Unit and investment trusts
New financial instruments
Taxation of interest received, relief
    for interest paid
Life assurance, general assurance

Personnel Directorate; Manpower and Support Services Division; Information Technology Office

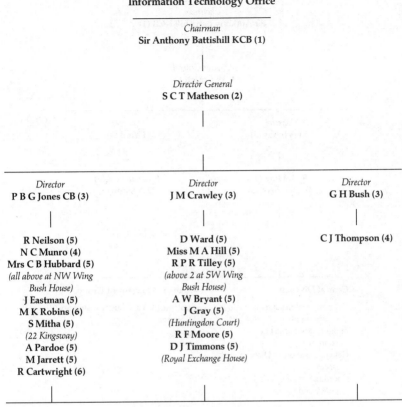

Chairman
Sir Anthony Battishill KCB (1)

Director General
S C T Matheson (2)

Director	*Director*	*Director*
P B G Jones CB (3)	**J M Crawley (3)**	**G H Bush (3)**

R Neilson (5)	**D Ward (5)**	**C J Thompson (4)**
N C Munro (4)	**Miss M A Hill (5)**	
Mrs C B Hubbard (5)	**R P R Tilley (5)**	
(all above at NW Wing	*(above 2 at SW Wing*	
Bush House)	*Bush House)*	
J Eastman (5)	**A W Bryant (5)**	
M K Robins (6)	**J Gray (5)**	
S Mitha (5)	*(Huntingdon Court)*	
(22 Kingsway)	**R F Moore (5)**	
A Pardoe (5)	**D J Timmons (5)**	
M Jarrett (5)	*(Royal Exchange House)*	
R Cartwright (6)		

Personnel (M1)	**Manpower and Support Services (M2)**	**Information Technology Office**
Taxes and collection	Pay policy and superannuation	Secretariat
Administration	Accommodation	Human resources
Personnel policy and planning	Manpower	Business support
Confidentiality	Estimates	Communications strategy
Industrial relations	Complementing	Standards
Training, conduct and discipline	Operational research	Computer services
Office services	Management services	System development
Library	O&M	Office and management support
Recruitment	Forms and stationery	systems
	Communications	Network systems
	Training Office	

Manning

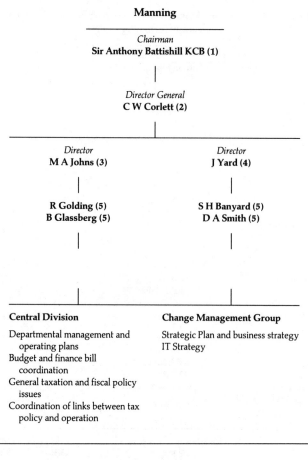

Chairman
Sir Anthony Battishill KCB (1)

Director General
C W Corlett (2)

Director
M A Johns (3)

Director
J Yard (4)

R Golding (5)
B Glassberg (5)

S H Banyard (5)
D A Smith (5)

Central Division

Departmental management and
operating plans
Budget and finance bill
coordination
General taxation and fiscal policy
issues
Coordination of links between tax
policy and operation

Change Management Group

Strategic Plan and business strategy
IT Strategy

Solicitor's Office

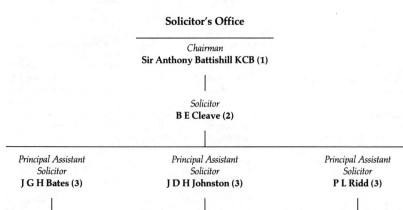

Chairman
Sir Anthony Battishill KCB (1)

Solicitor
B E Cleave (2)

*Principal Assistant
Solicitor*
J G H Bates (3)

*Principal Assistant
Solicitor*
J D H Johnston (3)

*Principal Assistant
Solicitor*
P L Ridd (3)

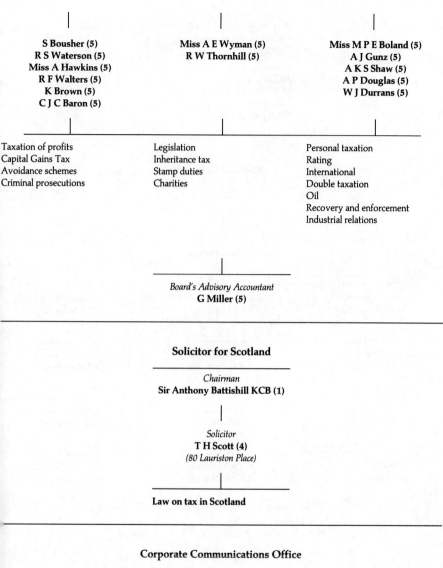

S Bousher (5)
R S Waterson (5)
Miss A Hawkins (5)
R F Walters (5)
K Brown (5)
C J C Baron (5)

Miss A E Wyman (5)
R W Thornhill (5)

Miss M P E Boland (5)
A J Gunz (5)
A K S Shaw (5)
A P Douglas (5)
W J Durrans (5)

Taxation of profits
Capital Gains Tax
Avoidance schemes
Criminal prosecutions

Legislation
Inheritance tax
Stamp duties
Charities

Personal taxation
Rating
International
Double taxation
Oil
Recovery and enforcement
Industrial relations

Board's Advisory Accountant
G Miller (5)

Solicitor for Scotland

Chairman
Sir Anthony Battishill KCB (1)

Solicitor
T H Scott (4)
(80 Lauriston Place)

Law on tax in Scotland

Corporate Communications Office

Chairman
Sir Anthony Battishill KCB (1)

Controller
Mrs S Cullum (5)
(GKN House)

Corporate Communications Office

Press office
Publications
Mobile enquiry centres
Exhibitions
Video production

Regional Offices

Chairman
Sir Anthony Battishill KCB (1)

Regional Offices

East Midlands	Greater Manchester	London/East
M Hodgson (4)	T L Hope (4)	R A Jones (4)

London/North West	London/South	Midlands
J F Carling (4)	R E German (4)	J A Robson (4)

North	North West	South East
R I Ford (4)	J I White (4)	D L S Bean (4)

South West	South Yorkshire	Northern Ireland
D S Aldridge (4)	A C Sleeman (4)	R S T Ewing (5)

Scotland	Wales
O J D Clarke (4)	M W Kirk (4)

Board of Inland Revenue Addresses

For fax numbers telephone the office concerned and ask for the appropriate fax number

80 Lauriston Place
Edinburgh EH3 9SL
Tel 031-229 9344 ext 3635

Alexandra House
Kingsway
Tel 071-438 6875

Angel Court
199 Borough High Street
London SE1 1HZ
Tel 071-234 3716

Apsley House
Wellington Road North
Stockport SK4 1EY
Tel 061-480 6009

GKN House
22 Kingsway
London WC2B 6NR
Tel 071-405 7622

Lodden House
Basing View
Basingstoke
Hants RG21 2JT
Tel 0256 842200

Lynwood Road
Thames Ditton
Surrey KT7 0DP
Tel 081-398 4242

Matheson House
Telford Development Centre
Grange Central
Telford
Shropshire TF3 4ER
Tel 0952 290044/294896

Melbourne House
Aldwych
London WC2B 4LL
Tel 071-438 6622

Minford House
Rockley Road
London W14 0DF
Tel 071-603 4622

Mulberry House
16 Picardy Place
Edinburgh EH1 3NB
Tel 031-556 8511

North West Wing
Bush House
Aldwych
London WC2B 7239
Tel 071-438 6622

Queens House
55–56 Lincoln's Inns Fields
London WC2A 3LJ
Tel 071-438 7090/7212

Royal Exchange House
Boar Lane
Leeds LS1 5PG
Tel 0532 425577

St John's House
Merton Road
Bootle
Merseyside L69 9BB
Tel 051-922 6363

Sapphire House
550 Streetsbrooke Road
Solihull
West Midlands B91 1QU
Tel 021-711 3232

South West Wing
Bush House
Strand
London WC2B 4QN
Tel 071-438 6622

Worthing Development Centre
Barrington Road
Worthing
West Sussex BN12 4XL
Tel 0903 700222

Regional Offices

East
Midgate House
Peterborough PE1 1TD
Tel 0733 63241

Greater Manchester
Apsley House
Wellington Road North
Stockport SK4 1EY
Tel 061-480 6009

East London
New Court
Carey Street
London WC2A 2JE
Tel 071-324 1232

North and West London
New Court
Carey Street
London WC2A 2JE
Tel 071-324 1229

South London
New Court
Carey Street
London WC2A 2JE
Tel 071-324 1255

Midlands
Chadwick House
Blenheim Court
Solihull
West Midlands B91 2AA
Tel 021-711 1144

North
Corporation House
73 Albert Road
Middlesborough
Cleveland TS1 2RZ
Tel 0642 241144

North West
The Triad
Stanley Road
Bootle
Merseyside L20 3PD
Tel 051-922 4055

South East
Albion House
Chertsey Road
Woking GU21 1BT
Tel 048-62 76133

South West
Finance House
Barnfield Road
Exeter EX1 1QX
Tel 0392 77801

South Yorkshire
Sovereign House
40 Silver Street
Sheffield S1 2EN
Tel 0742 739099

Northern Ireland
Windsor House
9–15 Bedford Street
Belfast BT2 7EL
Tel 0232 245123

Scotland
80 Lauriston Place
Edinburgh EH3 9SL
Tel 031-229 9344

Wales
Brunel House
2 Fitzalan Road
Cardiff CF2 1SE
Tel 0222 471818

Law Officers' Department (Legal Secretariat)

Founded	1893
Ministers	Attorney General Solicitor General
Responsibilities	All major international and domestic legislation involving the government
	Enforcement of the criminal law
	Principal legal adviser to the government
	Questions referred to the Law Officers by MPs
	Work of the: Treasury Solicitor's Department Crown Prosecution Service Serious Fraud Office Legal Secretariat/Law Officers
	The Director of Public Prosecutions for Northern Ireland is also responsible to the Attorney General

Law Officers' Department (Legal Secretariat)

Attorney General's Chambers, 9 Buckingham Gate, London SW1E 6JP
Tel 071-828 7155   Fax 071-828 0593

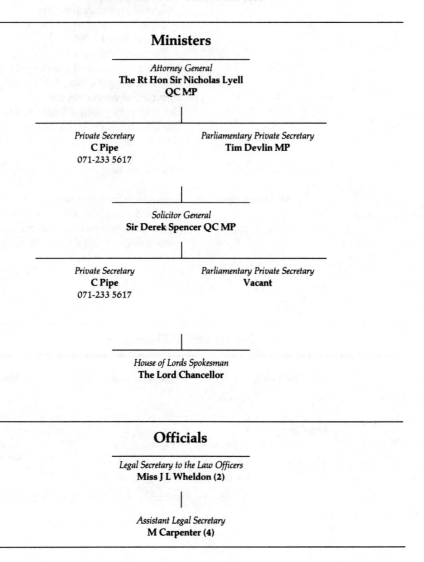

Ministers

Attorney General
**The Rt Hon Sir Nicholas Lyell
QC MP**

Private Secretary
C Pipe
071-233 5617

Parliamentary Private Secretary
Tim Devlin MP

Solicitor General
Sir Derek Spencer QC MP

Private Secretary
C Pipe
071-233 5617

Parliamentary Private Secretary
Vacant

House of Lords Spokesman
The Lord Chancellor

Officials

Legal Secretary to the Law Officers
Miss J L Wheldon (2)

Assistant Legal Secretary
M Carpenter (4)

Ministerial Responsibilities

Sir Nicholas Lyell   Overall responsibility for the work of the
Crown Prosecution Service
Legal Secretariat to the Law Officers
Serious Fraud Office
Treasury Solicitor's Department
All major international and domestic litigation
involving the government
Enforcement of criminal law
Government's principal legal adviser
The Director of Public Prosecutions for
Northern Ireland is also superintended by the
Attorney General
Head of the Bar

Sir Derek Spencer   Responsible for such matters as the Attorney
General delegates to him
Shares with Attorney General the handling of
matters referred to the Law Officers by MPs

Departmental Overview

Civil Servants			Department	Minister
Grade 2	*Grade 4*	*Grade 5*		
Legal Secretariat				
Miss J L Wheldon	M C L Carpenter	T J Middleton	Legal Secretariat	Attorney General
	S J Wooler	R Alderman		
		R Jeffreys		

Civil Servants and Departments

Legal Secretariat

Attorney General
**The Rt Hon Sir Nicholas Lyell
QC MP**

|

Solicitor General
**The Rt Hon Sir Derek Spencer
QC MP**

|

*Legal Secretary
Head of Department*
Miss J L Wheldon (2)

|

*Assistant Legal Secretary
Deputy Head of Department*
M C L Carpenter (4)

|

Assistant Legal Secretary
S J Wooler (4)

|

Legal Advisers
**T J Middleton (5)
R Alderman (5)
R Jeffreys (5)**

|

Legal Secretariat

Supports the Law Officers in their
ministerial and parliamentary
functions

Lord Advocate's Department

Founded The Office of the Lord Advocate was founded in the 15th century. The department in its present form was created in 1925

Ministers The Lord Advocate
Solicitor General for Scotland
(who are the Law Officers of the Crown for Scotland and chief legal advisers to the government on Scottish questions)

Responsibilities The department assists the Law Officers on Scottish questions and acts as the legal adviser on Scottish matters to certain government departments

As Scottish parliamentary counsel, staff draft government legislation relating exclusively to Scotland and are responsible for the adaptation to Scotland of other legislation

All judicial work for the Lord Advocate's Department is carried out by the Crown Office, Scotland

Lord Advocate's Department

Fielden House, 10 Great College Street, London SW1P 3SL
Tel 071-276 3000   Fax 071-276 6834

Ministers and Officials

Lord Advocate
The Rt Hon The Lord Rodger QC

|

Private Secretary
A G Maxwell
071-276 6819

|

Solicitor General for Scotland
Thomas C Dawson QC

|

Private Secretary
A G Maxwell
071-276 6819

|

Legal Secretary and First
Scottish Parliamentary Counsel
J C McCluskie (2)

|

Private Secretary
Mrs G M Bryan
081-276 6835

|

Assistant Legal Secretary and
Scottish Parliamentary Counsel
G M Clark (3)
G Kowalski (3)
P J Layden TD (3)

|

Assistant Legal Secretaries and
Depute Parliamentary Counsel
J D Harkness (5)
D C Macrae (5)
C A M Wilson (5)

Lord Chancellor's Department

Founded 1885 (and assumed its present form and responsibilities in 1972 following the Courts Act 1971)

Ministers The Lord Chancellor

Responsibilities courts: procedure of the civil courts and administration of the appeal, high, crown and county courts, and, from April 1992, responsibility for the locally-administered magistrates' courts
Great Seal of the Realm (custodian of)
immigration appellate authorities
judges (advice on the appointment of)
Lands Tribunal
land reform
legal aid
magistrates, masters and district judges of the High Court and county court district judges (appointment of)
Pensions Appeal Tribunal
Social Security Commissioners
Special Commissioners of Income Tax
VAT Tribunals

Executive Agencies HM Land Registry
Public Record Office

Lord Chancellor's Department

House of Lords, London SW1A 0PW
Tel 071-210 8500   Fax 071-210 8549
All staff are based at House of Lords unless otherwise indicated.
For other addresses and telephone numbers see the end of this section.

Officers and Officials

Lord Chancellor
The Rt Hon the Lord Mackay of Clashfern

|

Private Secretary to the Lord Chancellor
Miss J Rowe (7)
071-219 3232

|

Assistant Private Secretaries
Miss F Sandell
Mrs N Seath

|

Parliamentary Secretary
John Taylor MP
(Trevelyan House)

|

Private Secretary
Ms J Morgan (HEO D)
071-210 8640

Ministerial Responsibilities

Lord Mackay of Clashfern   Administration of the appeal, high, crown and
county courts in England and Wales, and,
from April 1992, magistrates courts (locally
administered)
Appointment of masters and district judges of
the high court, county court district judges
and magistrates
Advice to Crown on appointment of judges
and other officers
Great Seal of the Realm (custodian thereof)
Immigration Appellate authorities
Lands Tribunal
Northern Ireland Court Service (separate
department; see under that name)
Pensions Appeal Tribunal
Procedure of the civil courts
Promotion of general reforms in civil law
Social Security Commissioners
Special Commissioners of Income Tax
VAT tribunals

John Taylor   Budget and resource issues
Development of legal services
Energy efficiency
Equal opportunities and women's issues
HM Land Registry
Legal aid
Public Record Office
Spokesman in the House of Commons

Departmental Overview

Civil Servants			Department	Minister
Grade 1	Grade 2	Grade 3		

Judicial Appointments Group, Establishment and Finance Group

Thomas Legg	These report directly to Mr Legg	R E K Holmes	Judicial Appointments	Lord Chancellor
		B H Cousins	Establishment and Finance Group	J Taylor

Law and Policy Group

Thomas Legg	M Huebner	R White	Legal and Law Reform	Lord Chancellor
		C W V Everett	Policy and Legal Services	J Taylor
		P L Jacob (5)	Central Unit	J Taylor

Court Service

Thomas Legg	R Potter	J F Brindley (4)	Court Service Management Group	Lord Chancellor
		P G Harris (5)	Court Service Secretariat	Lord Chancellor
		Circuits		Lord Chancellor
		L C Oates	Midland and Oxford	Lord Chancellor
		S W L James	North Eastern	Lord Chancellor
		P M Harris	Northern	Lord Chancellor
		B Cooke	South Eastern	Lord Chancellor
		D Howe (4)	Wales and Chester	Lord Chancellor
		G Jones (4)	Western	Lord Chancellor

		H D S Venables	Official Solicitor's Department	

These are offices associated with the Lord Chancellor's Department

			Office of the Lord Chancellor's Visitors	Lord Chancellor
		P J Farmer (4)	Public Trust Office	Lord Chancellor
		Mrs A B Macfarlane	Court of Protection	Lord Chancellor
		Judge Waley	Judge Advocate of the Fleet	
		J Stuart-Smith	Judge Advocate General of the Forces	Lord Chancellor
		J R Catford	Ecclesiastical Patronage	Prime Minister/ Lord Chancellor

Civil Servants and Departments

Crown Office

Permanent Secretary,
Clerk of the Crown in Chancery
Thomas Legg CB QC (1)

Private Secretary
N Chibnall (HEO D)
071-219 6080

Deputy Clerk of the Crown
in Chancery
R Potter CB (2)

Clerk of the Chamber
Miss J L Waine (SEO)

Judicial Appointments Group, Establishment and Finance Group

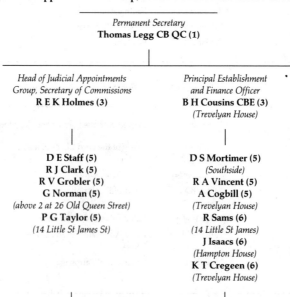

Permanent Secretary
Thomas Legg CB QC (1)

Head of Judicial Appointments *Group, Secretary of Commissions* **R E K Holmes (3)**	*Principal Establishment* *and Finance Officer* **B H Cousins CBE (3)** *(Trevelyan House)*
D E Staff (5) **R J Clark (5)** **R V Grobler (5)** **G Norman (5)** *(above 2 at 26 Old Queen Street)* **P G Taylor (5)** *(14 Little St James St)*	**D S Mortimer (5)** *(Southside)* **R A Vincent (5)** **A Cogbill (5)** *(Trevelyan House)* **R Sams (6)** *(14 Little St James)* **J Isaacs (6)** *(Hampton House)* **K T Cregeen (6)** *(Trevelyan House)*

Judicial Appointments Group	**Establishment and Finance**
Circuit bench	Court buildings and estate
District bench and tribunals	management
Magistrates (appointments)	Personnel management
Magistrates (training)	Resources
Judicial Studies Board	Training
	Internal audit
	Procurement services

Law and Policy Group

Permanent Secretary
Thomas Legg CB QC (1)

Deputy Secretary
M Huebner (2)
(Trevelyan House)

Head of Legal and Law Reform Group	*Head of Policy and Legal Services Group*	*Head of Unit*
R White (3)	**C W V Everett (3)**	**P L Jacob (5)**
(26 Old Queen Street)	*(Trevelyan House)*	*(Trevelyan House)*
R A Venne (5)	**Mrs N A Oppenheimer (5)**	
J A C Watherston (5)	**M Kron (5)**	
R H H White (5)	*(Trevelyan House)*	
(all at 26 Old Queen St)	**M W Sayers (5)**	
J M Gibson (5)	*(America House)*	
(America House)		

Legal and Law Reform	**Policy and Legal Services**	**Central Unit**
Legal advice and law reform	Legal services and agencies	Secretariat
Procedure and property law	Legal aid	Next steps
International	Family law	Information systems
Statutory publications		Press Office

Court Service

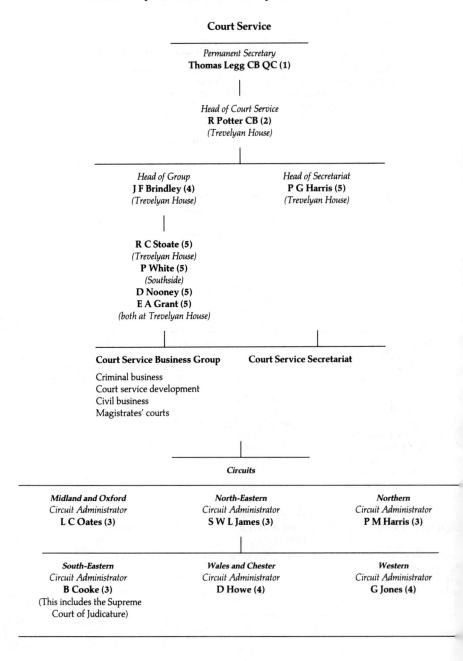

Permanent Secretary
Thomas Legg CB QC (1)

Head of Court Service
R Potter CB (2)
(Trevelyan House)

Head of Group
J F Brindley (4)
(Trevelyan House)

Head of Secretariat
P G Harris (5)
(Trevelyan House)

R C Stoate (5)
(Trevelyan House)
P White (5)
(Southside)
D Nooney (5)
E A Grant (5)
(both at Trevelyan House)

Court Service Business Group

Criminal business
Court service development
Civil business
Magistrates' courts

Court Service Secretariat

Circuits

Midland and Oxford	**North-Eastern**	**Northern**
Circuit Administrator	*Circuit Administrator*	*Circuit Administrator*
L C Oates (3)	**S W L James (3)**	**P M Harris (3)**

South-Eastern	**Wales and Chester**	**Western**
Circuit Administrator	*Circuit Administrator*	*Circuit Administrator*
B Cooke (3)	**D Howe (4)**	**G Jones (4)**
(This includes the Supreme Court of Judicature)		

Official Solicitor's Department

Official Solicitor
H D S Venables (3)
(81 Chancery Lane)

|

Official Solicitor's Department
Confidential adviser to the Court
Representation of minors, persons
of unsound mind, and persons
committed for contempt of court
Judicial and other trusteeships
Administration of deceased estates

The following groups are independent offices associated with the Lord Chancellor's Department

Legal Visitor	*Public Trustee and Accountant General*	*Master*
M H Fauvelle	**P J Farmer (4)**	**Mrs A B Macfarlane**
(Trevelyan House)	*(Stewart House)*	*(Stewart House)*

|

Medical Visitors
Dr A G Fullerton
Dr K Khan
Dr F E Kenyon
Dr R J Kerry
Dr P A Morris
Dr D Parr
Dr J Roberts
(Trevelyan House)

H N de V Mather (5)
(Stewart House)

Office of the Lord Chancellor's Visitors

Special inspection powers for
appeals

Public Trust Office

Client services
Internal services
Investments
Property

Court of Protection

Protection of property of patients
under Mental Health Act

Judge Advocate of the Fleet	*Judge Advocate General of the Forces*	*Secretary for Ecclesiastical Patronage*
His Honour Judge Waley QC	**J Stuart-Smith CB QC**	**J R Catford CBE**
(Law Courts, Maidstone)	*(22 Kingsway)*	*(10 Downing St)*

Judge Advocate of the Fleet	**Judge Advocate General of the Forces**	**Ecclesiastical Patronage**
Naval ϲourts martial and disciplinary courts Naval Discipline Act Assist Admiralty Board	Provision of Judge Advocates at courts martial and military courts in the UK and abroad Post-trial legal advice to the army, RAF and MOD	

Lord Chancellor's Department Addresses

America House
Spring Gardens
London SW1A 2BP
Tel 071-389 3200
Fax 071-389 7490

81 Chancery Lane
London WC2A 1DD
Tel 071-911 7127
Fax 071-911 7105

10 Downing Street
London SW1
Tel 071-930 4433
Fax 071-270 3000

Hampton House
20 Albert Embankment
London SE1 7JT
Tel 071-238 5050
Fax 071-238 5057

7th Floor
22 Kingsway
London WC2B 6LE
Tel 071-430 5335
Fax 071-430 5744

Law Courts
Barker Road
Maidstone
Kent ME16 8EQ
Tel 0622 754966
Fax 0622 687349

14 Little St James' Street
London SW1A 1DP
Tel 071-925 0185
Fax 071-321 0142

26–28 Old Queen Street
London SW1H 9HP
Tel 071-210 3508
Fax 071-210 3460

Stewart House
24 Kingsway
London WC2B 6JX
Tel 071-269 7000
Fax 071-831 0060

Trevelyan House
30 Great Peter Street
London SW1P 2BY
Tel 071-210 8873
Fax 071-210 8549

4th Floor Southside
105 Victoria Street
London SW1
Tel 071-210 2050
Fax 071-210 2059

Circuit offices

Northern
2nd Floor
Aldine House
New Bailey Street
Salford
Manchester M3 5EU
Tel 061-832 9571
Fax 061-832 8596

Western
Bridge House
Clifton Down
Bristol BS8 4BN
Tel 0272 743763
Fax 0272 744133

Wales and Chester
3rd Floor
Churchill House
Churchill Way
Cardiff CF1 4HH
Tel 0222 396925
Fax 0222 373882

South-Eastern
New Cavendish House
18 Maltravers Street
London WC2R 3EU
Tel 071-936 6000
Fax 071-936 7230

Midland and Oxford
2 Newton Street
Birmingham B4 7LU
Tel 021-200 1234
Fax 021-212 1359

North-Eastern
17th Floor
West Riding House
Albion Street
Leeds LS1 5AA
Tel 0532 441841
Fax 0532 438737

Department of National Heritage

Founded	1992, when it took over the functions of the old Office of Arts and Libraries and a number of other responsibilities (broadcasting, films, heritage, royal parks, sport and tourism) from other departments
Ministers	one secretary of state and one parliamentary under secretary of state
Responsibilities	arts policy broadcasting films historic buildings and ancient monuments libraries National Heritage Memorial Fund national lottery (when established) royal parks sport tourism
Executive Agencies	Historic Royal Palaces

Department of National Heritage

Horse Guards Road, London SW1P 3AL
Tel 071-270 3000   Fax 071-270 5776

Ministers

Secretary of State
**The Rt Hon David Mellor QC
MP**

Parliamentary Private Secretary
Anthony Coombs MP

Special Advisers
**Chris Hopson
Lady Cobham**
(Heritage and Tourism)

Private Secretary
Nick Holgate
071-270 5925

*Parliamentary Under Secretary of
State*
Robert Key MP

Private Secretary
Keith Parker
071-270 5790

House of Lords' Spokesmen
**Viscount Astor
Baroness Trumpington**

Ministerial Responsibilities

David Mellor/Robert Key   arts policy (Arts Council and other arts
bodies)
broadcasting
films
Government Art Collection
historic buildings and ancient monuments
(including Historic Royal Palaces Agency)
libraries (including British Library)
museums and galleries
National Heritage Memorial Fund
national lottery (when established)
royal parks
sport (including safety of sports grounds)
tourism

Departmental Overview

Civil Servants			Groups	Minister
Grade 1	Grade 3	Grade 5		
Hayden Phillips (1A)	Reports directly to Permanent Secretary	Andrea MacLean	Information	
Arts				
Hayden Phillips (1A)	Miss M O'Mara	Miss S E Brown	Arts Policy	D Mellor/ R Key
		Vacant	Museums and Galleries	D Mellor/ R Key
		C C Leamy	Libraries	D Mellor/ R Key
		J R W Pardey	British Library Project	D Mellor/ R Key
		Miss C R Morrison (6)	Works of Art	D Mellor/ R Key
		Dr W Baron (6)	Government Art Collection	D Mellor/ R Key
Broadcasting Films and Sport				
Hayden Phillips (1A)	P Wright	Miss J M Goose	Broadcasting Policy	D Mellor/ R Key
		P C Edwards	Broadcasting, Films and Press	D Mellor/ R Key
		Miss A Stewart	Sports and Recreation	D Mellor/ R Key
Heritage and Tourism				
Hayden Phillips (1A)	J A L Gunn	A H Corner	Heritage	D Mellor/ R Key
		C P Douglas	Royal Estates	D Mellor/ R Key
		D Welch	Royal Parks	D Mellor/ R Key
		P Gregory	Tourism	D Mellor/ R Key

Departmental Overview

Civil Servants			Groups	Minister
Grade 1	*Grade 3*	*Grade 5*		
Resources and Services				
Hayden Phillips (1A)	N Pittman (4)	Miss S Booth	Finance and Corporate Planning	D Mellor/ R Key
		Dr K Gray	Implementation and Review	D Mellor/ R Key
		Vacant (6)	Personnel Management and Policy	D Mellor/ R Key

Civil Servants and Groups

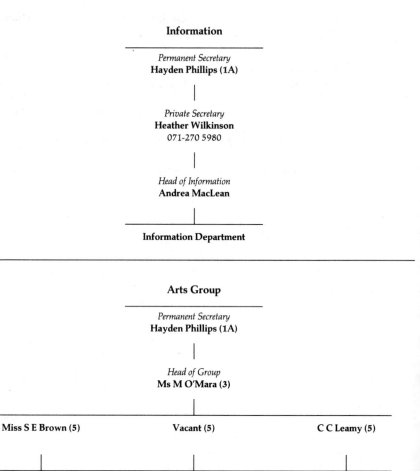

Information

Permanent Secretary
Hayden Phillips (1A)

Private Secretary
Heather Wilkinson
071-270 5980

Head of Information
Andrea MacLean

Information Department

Arts Group

Permanent Secretary
Hayden Phillips (1A)

Head of Group
Ms M O'Mara (3)

Miss S E Brown (5)   **Vacant (5)**   **C C Leamy (5)**

Arts Policy

Arts Council and other performing
  arts matters
Crafts
International relations
Arts taxation matters
Business sponsorship of the arts

Museums and Galleries

National and local museums and
  galleries in England

Libraries

Libraries and information services
British Library
Public libraries in England

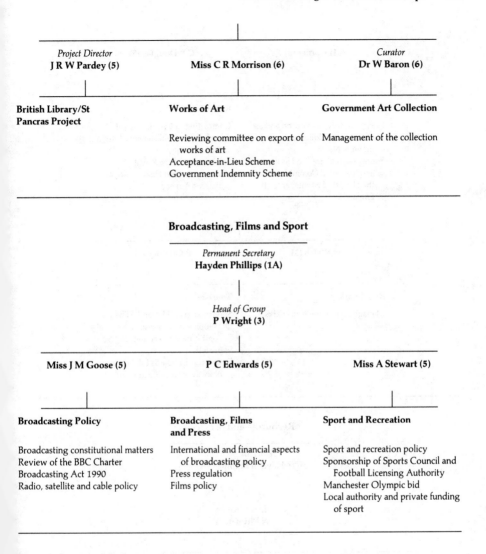

| *Project Director*
J R W Pardey (5) | Miss C R Morrison (6) | *Curator*
Dr W Baron (6) |

| British Library/St
Pancras Project | Works of Art | Government Art Collection |
| | Reviewing committee on export of works of art
Acceptance-in-Lieu Scheme
Government Indemnity Scheme | Management of the collection |

Broadcasting, Films and Sport

Permanent Secretary
Hayden Phillips (1A)

Head of Group
P Wright (3)

| **Miss J M Goose (5)** | **P C Edwards (5)** | **Miss A Stewart (5)** |

| **Broadcasting Policy** | **Broadcasting, Films and Press** | **Sport and Recreation** |
| Broadcasting constitutional matters
Review of the BBC Charter
Broadcasting Act 1990
Radio, satellite and cable policy | International and financial aspects of broadcasting policy
Press regulation
Films policy | Sport and recreation policy
Sponsorship of Sports Council and Football Licensing Authority
Manchester Olympic bid
Local authority and private funding of sport |

Heritage and Tourism

Permanent Secretary
Hayden Phillips (1A)

Head of Group
J A L Gunn (3)

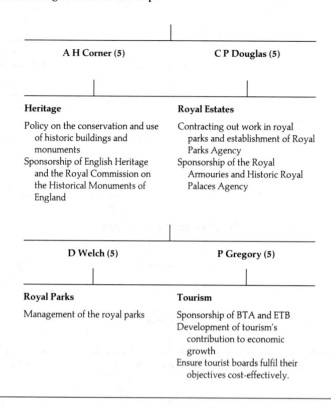

A H Corner (5)   C P Douglas (5)

Heritage   **Royal Estates**

Policy on the conservation and use   Contracting out work in royal
  of historic buildings and   parks and establishment of Royal
  monuments   Parks Agency
Sponsorship of English Heritage   Sponsorship of the Royal
  and the Royal Commission on   Armouries and Historic Royal
  the Historical Monuments of   Palaces Agency
  England

D Welch (5)   P Gregory (5)

Royal Parks   **Tourism**

Management of the royal parks   Sponsorship of BTA and ETB
                                     Development of tourism's
                                       contribution to economic
                                       growth
                                     Ensure tourist boards fulfil their
                                       objectives cost-effectively.

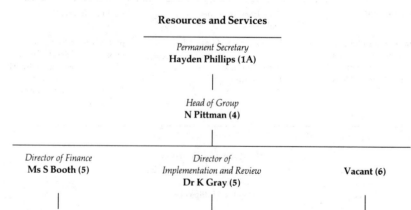

Resources and Services

Permanent Secretary
Hayden Phillips (1A)

Head of Group
N Pittman (4)

Director of Finance   *Director of*
Ms S Booth (5)   *Implementation and Review*   **Vacant (6)**
                              Dr K Gray (5)

Finance and Corporate Planning	Implementation and Review	Personnel Management and Policy
Financial management	Establishment of accommodation	Personnel management
Accounting systems	and services for new department	Equal opportunities
Estimates	Management of change and project	Welfare
Public Expenditure Survey forecasts	management	Pay
		Superannuation
		Conditions of service

Department for National Savings

Founded   1861

Responsible to   Economic Secretary, HM Treasury

Responsibilities   The Department is the goverment's savings
organisation and its products include:
savings certificates
income bonds
premium bonds
savings bank ordinary and investment
   accounts
capital bonds
children's bonus bonds
yearly plan

Department for National Savings

Charles House, 375 Kensington High Street, London W14 8SD
Tel 071-605 9300   Fax 071-605 9438
All staff are based at Charles House unless otherwise indicated.
For other addresses and telephone numbers see the end of this section.

Minister

Economic Secretary
Anthony Nelson MP
(for details of his office
see HM Treasury section)

Officials

Director
C D Butler (2)

|

Private Secretary
Miss E Dziadulewicz
071-605 9463

|

Deputy Director
D Howard (3)

Departmental Overview

Civil Servants			Department
Grade 2	*Grade 3*	*Grade 5*	
C D Butler	D Howard	P N S Hickman Robertson	Planning and Product Policy Division
		D S Speedie	.Establishment
		C Ward	Finance
		Miss A Nash	Marketing and Information
		D W Kellaway (6)	Procedures, Legal and Agency
C D Butler	These divisions report directly to the Director	D Monaghan	National Savings, Glasgow
		E B Senior	National Savings, Durham
		A S McGill	National Savings, Lytham

Civil Servants and Departments

Director
C D Butler (2)

|

Deputy Director
D Howard (3)

|

Head of Planning and Product Policy Division	*Establishment Officer*	*Finance Officer*
P N S Hickman Robertson (5)	**D S Speedie (5)**	**C Ward (5)**

Controller of Marketing Information Division	*Head of Procedures, Legal and Agency*
Miss A Nash (5)	**D W Kellaway (6)**

National Savings, Glasgow

Director
C D Butler (2)

|

Controller
D H Monaghan (5)
(Boydstone Road)

|

Bank Operations

Administration of Capital Bonds,
National Savings Bank
Investment, Ordinary Accounts,
Children's Bonus Bonds

National Savings, Durham

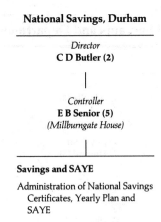

Director
C D Butler (2)

Controller
E B Senior (5)
(Millburngate House)

Savings and SAYE

Administration of National Savings
Certificates, Yearly Plan and
SAYE

National Savings, Lytham

Director
C D Butler (2)

Controller
A S McGill (5)
(Govt Bldgs, Heyhouses Lane)

Premium Bonds

Department for National Savings Addresses

Boydstone Road
Cowglen
Glasgow G58 1SB
Tel 041-649 4555
Fax 041-649 3998

Government Buildings
Heyhouses Lane
Lytham St Annes
Lancs FY0 1YN
Tel 0253 66151
Fax 0253 715667

Millburngate House
Durham DH99 1NS
Tel 091-386 4900
Fax 091-374 5495

Northern Ireland Court Service

Founded 1979

Status A unified and distinct civil service of the Crown

Minister The Lord Chancellor

Responsibilities To facilitate the conduct of the business of the Supreme Court, county courts, magistrates' courts, coroners' courts, office of the Social Security Commissioner for Northern Ireland and the Enforcement of Judgments Office

Administrative responsibility for the Office of the Social Security Commissioner transferred during the 1980s to the Court Service

The officers and other staff are appointed by the Lord Chancellor

Northern Ireland Court Service

Windsor House, Bedford Street, Belfast BT2 7LT
Tel 0232 328594   Fax 0232 439110

Ministers

Lord Chancellor
**The Rt Hon The Lord
Mackay of Clashfern**
(for details of his office
see Lord Chancellor's Department)

Officials

Director (3)

|

Personal Secretary
0232 328594 x244

Civil Servants and Departments

Northern Ireland Court Service

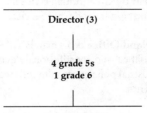

Director (3)

4 grade 5s
1 grade 6

Northern Ireland Court Service

Court business
Press liaison
Legal aid
Policy evaluation
Judicial appointments
Judicial studies
Personnel
Finance
Training
Customer service
Communication
Enforcement of judgments
Management information systems
Accommodation and office services
Information technology
Internal audit
Legal advisers

Northern Ireland

The administration of the Province is carried out by the Northern Ireland Office (NIO) and the Northern Ireland departments. The NIO is staffed in part by Great Britain civil servants and in part by members of the Northern Ireland Civil Service.

The **Northern Ireland Office** deals mainly with security, law and order issues and political and constitutional developments. Social, economic and industrial policies are administered by the **Northern Ireland departments**.

For security reasons the names of most civil servants have been omitted.

Northern Ireland Office

Founded 1972 as a separate UK government department under the provisions of the Northern Ireland (Temporary Provisions) Act 1972, when the executive and legislative powers of the Northern Ireland Government and Parliament were transferred to the Secretary of State for Northern Ireland and the Parliament of the United Kingdom respectively

Ministers secretary of state, two ministers of state and two parliamentary under secretaries of state

Responsibilities To combat terrorism and to seek to establish stable political institutions in Northern Ireland

The NIO is staffed by about 200 civil servants from the Home Civil Service and 1350 from the Northern Ireland Civil Service in London and Belfast, and is organised into the following divisions:

Constitutional and Political
Criminal Justice
Economic and Social
Finance and Personnel
Forensic Science
Police
Political Affairs
Prisons
Probation and Training Schools
Security and International
Security Policy and Operations

Executive Agency Compensation Agency (NI)

Northern Ireland Office

Stormont Castle, Belfast NT4 3ST
Tel 0232 763255   Fax 0232 768938
Whitehall, London SW1A 2AZ
Tel 071-210 3000   Fax 071-210 6549
For other addresses and telephone numbers see the end of this section.

Ministers

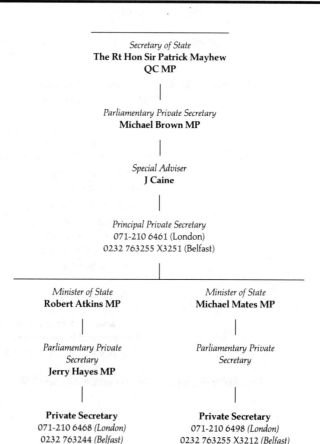

Secretary of State
**The Rt Hon Sir Patrick Mayhew
QC MP**

Parliamentary Private Secretary
Michael Brown MP

Special Adviser
J Caine

Principal Private Secretary
071-210 6461 (London)
0232 763255 X3251 (Belfast)

Minister of State
Robert Atkins MP

Minister of State
Michael Mates MP

*Parliamentary Private
Secretary*
Jerry Hayes MP

*Parliamentary Private
Secretary*

Private Secretary
071-210 6468 *(London)*
0232 763244 *(Belfast)*
0232 760338 *(Belfast)*

Private Secretary
071-210 6498 *(London)*
0232 763255 X3212 *(Belfast)*

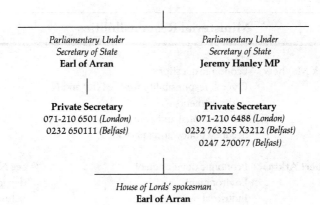

*Parliamentary Under
Secretary of State*
Earl of Arran

*Parliamentary Under
Secretary of State*
Jeremy Hanley MP

Private Secretary
071-210 6501 *(London)*
0232 650111 *(Belfast)*

Private Secretary
071-210 6488 *(London)*
0232 763255 X3212 *(Belfast)*
0247 270077 *(Belfast)*

House of Lords' spokesman
Earl of Arran

Ministerial Responsibilities

Sir Patrick Mayhew   Economic questions
Overall responsibility for the NIO and NI
    departments
Constitutional and political
Security policy and operations

Robert Atkins   Economic development   see NICS
Environment   departments
Industrial development   below
Roads   departments
Training and employment
Transport
Urban renewal
Water

Michael Mates   Information services   see NICS
Finance and personnel   departments
Law and order   below

Jeremy Hanley   Community relations   see NICS
Education   departments
Political development   below

Earl of Arran   Agriculture   see NICS
Health and social services   departments
House of Lords spokesman on all   below
    NI matters

Departmental Overview

Civil Servants			Department	Ministers
John Chilcot	Reports directly to the PUS	Grade 3	Establishment and Finance	M Mates
			Security	M Mates

Control and Coordination (London)

John Chilcot	Grade 2	Grade 3	Security and International	M Mates
			Constitutional and Political	M Mates/ J Hanley
			Economic and Social	M Mates
		Grade 3	Political Affairs	M Mates/ J Hanley
			Inter-Governmental Secretariat	M Mates
		Grade 4	Information Services	M Mates

Control and Coordination (Belfast)

John Chilcot	Grade 2	Grade 3	Security Policy and Operations	M Mates
			Forensic Science	M Mates
		Grade 3	Criminal Justice	M Mates
			Police	M Mates
			Probation and Training Schools	M Mates
			Compensation Agency	M Mates
		Grade 3	Prisons	M Mates

Civil Servants and Departments

Establishment and Finance

Permanent Under Secretary of State
John A Chilcot CB (1)

Private Secretary
071-210 6456 *(London)*
0232 763255 X3362 *(Belfast)*

*Second Permanent Under
Secretary of State and
Head of Northern Ireland Civil Service*
David Fell CB (1A)

Private Secretary
0232 763255 X3283 *(Belfast)*

Under Secretary (3)
(Belfast)

Grade 5
(London)
Grade 5
Grade 5
(both in Belfast)

Establishment

Personnel, accounts and general
   administration
Resources control
Services

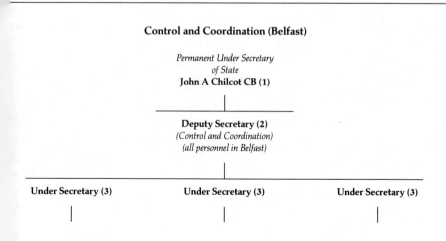

Control and Coordination (London)

*Permanent Under Secretary
of State*
John A Chilcot CB (1)

Deputy Secretary (2)
*(Control and Coordination
London)*

| **Under Secretary (3)** | **Under Secretary (3)** | **Grade 4** |
| *(London)* | *(Belfast)* | *(London and Belfast)* |

Grade 5	**Grade 5**	**Grade 5**
Grade 5	**Grade 5**	*(Belfast)*
Grade 5	*(both in Belfast)*	**Grade 6**
(all in London)		*(London)*

Security and International	**Political Affairs**	**Information Services**
Liaison on law and order matters	Inter-governmental secretariat	
Constitutional and Political		
Economic and Social		

Control and Coordination (Belfast)

*Permanent Under Secretary
of State*
John A Chilcot CB (1)

Deputy Secretary (2)
(Control and Coordination)
(all personnel in Belfast)

| **Under Secretary (3)** | **Under Secretary (3)** | **Under Secretary (3)** |

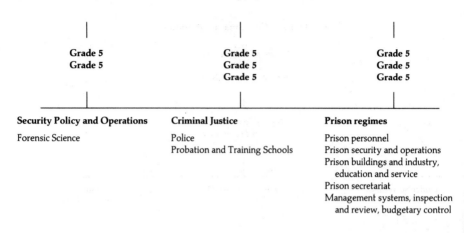

Grade 5	Grade 5	Grade 5
Grade 5	Grade 5	Grade 5
	Grade 5	Grade 5

Security Policy and Operations

Forensic Science

Criminal Justice

Police
Probation and Training Schools

Prison regimes

Prison personnel
Prison security and operations
Prison buildings and industry,
 education and service
Prison secretariat
Management systems, inspection
 and review, budgetary control

Northern Ireland Civil Service Departments

Department of Agriculture for Northern Ireland
Department of Economic Development Northern Ireland
Department of Education for Northern Ireland
Department of the Environment for Northern Ireland
Department of Finance and Personnel (including NI Civil Service)
Department of Health and Social Services, Northern Ireland

Department of Agriculture for Northern Ireland

Founded	1974
Minister	parliamentary under secretary of state, Northern Ireland Office
Responsibilities	Development of the agricultural, forestry and fishing industries in Northern Ireland
	Provision of an advisory service for farmers, agricultural research and education
	Agent of the Ministry of Agriculture, Fisheries and Food in the administration of Northern Ireland of schemes affecting the whole of the United Kingdom
	Involvement with the application to Northern Ireland of the agricultural policy of the EC
	Promotion of community-led regeneration in areas of rural deprivation
Executive Agencies	None

Department of Agriculture for Northern Ireland

Dundonald House, Upper Newtownards Road, Belfast BT4 3ST
Tel 0232 650111   Fax 0232 659856

Minister

*Parliamentary Under
Secretary of State*
The Earl of Arran

|

Private Secretary
071-210 6500 (London)
0232 650111 X611 (Belfast)

Departmental Overview

Civil Servants		Division	Minister
Grade 2	Grade 3	Personnel and Finance	E of Arran
	Grade 3	Commodities	E of Arran
	Grade 3	Lands	E of Arran
	Grade 3	Agricultural Service	E of Arran
	Grade 3	Agricultural Research	E of Arran
	Grade 3	Veterinary Inspectorate	E of Arran

Civil Servants and Divisions

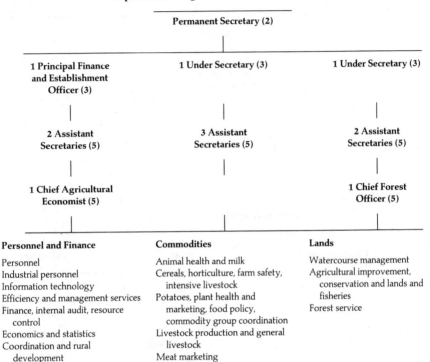

Department of Agriculture for Northern Ireland

Permanent Secretary (2)

| 1 Principal Finance and Establishment Officer (3) | 1 Under Secretary (3) | 1 Under Secretary (3) |

| 2 Assistant Secretaries (5) | 3 Assistant Secretaries (5) | 2 Assistant Secretaries (5) |

1 Chief Agricultural Economist (5)   1 Chief Forest Officer (5)

Personnel and Finance

Personnel
Industrial personnel
Information technology
Efficiency and management services
Finance, internal audit, resource
  control
Economics and statistics
Coordination and rural
  development

Commodities

Animal health and milk
Cereals, horticulture, farm safety,
  intensive livestock
Potatoes, plant health and
  marketing, food policy,
  commodity group coordination
Livestock production and general
  livestock
Meat marketing

Lands

Watercourse management
Agricultural improvement,
  conservation and lands and
  fisheries
Forest service

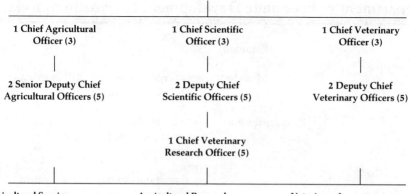

1 Chief Agricultural Officer (3)	1 Chief Scientific Officer (3)	1 Chief Veterinary Officer (3)
2 Senior Deputy Chief Agricultural Officers (5)	2 Deputy Chief Scientific Officers (5)	2 Deputy Chief Veterinary Officers (5)
	1 Chief Veterinary Research Officer (5)	

Agricultural Service	Agricultural Research	Veterinary Inspectorate
Food industry and marketing	Food microbiology	Technical services
Farm and countryside	Food and agricultural chemistry	Disease control
Education, training and technology	Agricultural zoology	Import, export and quarantine
Agricultural business service	Animal and crop husbandry	controls
Central planning unit	Biometrics	Artificial insemination
	Agricultural botany	Animal welfare
	Aquatic sciences	Animal health schemes and surveys
	Plant pathology	Meat inspection and hygiene
	Veterinary research	control
	Aquatic sciences research	Licensing at meat plants
		Veterinary education
		General advice

Department of Economic Development for Northern Ireland

Founded	1982
Minister	parliamentary under secretary of state, Northern Ireland Office
Responsibilities	company affairs consumer protection electricity energy equality of opportunity in employment health and safety at work industrial development policy industrial relations mineral development promotion of small businesses through the Local Enterprise Development Unit science and technology tourism
	The Industrial Development Board for Northern Ireland is responsible for attracting new investment to Northern Ireland, and for the development and maintenance of existing industry
Executive Agencies	Training and Employment Agency (NI)

Department of Economic Development for Northern Ireland

Netherleith, Massey Avenue, Belfast BT4 2JP
Tel 0232 763244   Fax 0232 761430

Minister

*Parliamentary Under
Secretary of State*
Robert Atkins MP

|

Private Secretary
071-210 6501 (London)
0232 763244 x2209 (Belfast)

Departmental Overview

Civil Servants		Divisions	Minister
Grade 2	Grade 3	Resources Group	R Atkins
	Grade 3	Regulatory Services Group	R Atkins
	Grade 3	Science and Technology Group	R Atkins
Industrial Development Board			
Chairman Grade 2	Grade 3	Inward Investment Group	R Atkins
	Grade 3	Home Industry Group	R Atkins
	Grade 3	Corporate Services Group	R Atkins

Civil Servants and Divisions

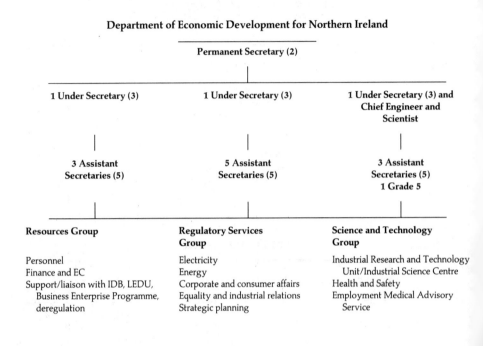

Department of Economic Development for Northern Ireland

Permanent Secretary (2)

1 Under Secretary (3)	1 Under Secretary (3)	1 Under Secretary (3) and Chief Engineer and Scientist
3 Assistant Secretaries (5)	5 Assistant Secretaries (5)	3 Assistant Secretaries (5) 1 Grade 5

Resources Group	Regulatory Services Group	Science and Technology Group
Personnel	Electricity	Industrial Research and Technology
Finance and EC	Energy	Unit/Industrial Science Centre
Support/liaison with IDB, LEDU,	Corporate and consumer affairs	Health and Safety
Business Enterprise Programme,	Equality and industrial relations	Employment Medical Advisory
deregulation	Strategic planning	Service

Industrial Development Board for Northern Ireland (IDB)
(Department of Economic Development)
IDB House, 64 Chichester Street, Belfast BT1 4JX
Tel 0232 233233   Fax 0232 231328

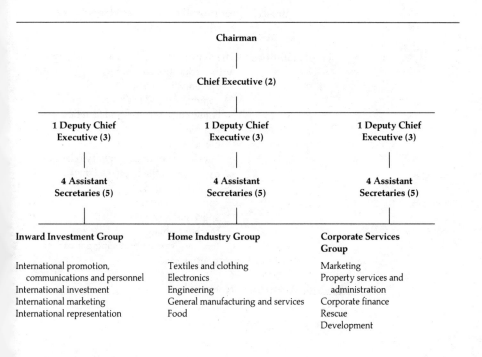

Chairman

|

Chief Executive (2)

|

1 Deputy Chief Executive (3)	1 Deputy Chief Executive (3)	1 Deputy Chief Executive (3)
4 Assistant Secretaries (5)	4 Assistant Secretaries (5)	4 Assistant Secretaries (5)

Inward Investment Group	Home Industry Group	Corporate Services Group
International promotion, communications and personnel	Textiles and clothing	Marketing
International investment	Electronics	Property services and administration
International marketing	Engineering	Corporate finance
International representation	General manufacturing and services	Rescue
	Food	Development

Department of Education for Northern Ireland

Founded 1973

Minister parliamentary under secretary of state,
Northern Ireland Office

Responsibilities The development of primary, secondary and
further education, including:
arts and libraries
community and adult education
community services and facilities
examinations
higher education
improvement of community relations
oversight of the five area Education and
  Library Boards
special education
sport and recreation
teacher training
teachers' salaries and superannuation
youth services

Executive Agencies None

Department of Education for Northern Ireland

Rathgael House, Balloo Road, Bangor, Co Down BT19 2PR
Tel 0247 270077   Fax 0247 456451

Minister

Parliamentary Under
Secretary of State
Jeremy Hanley MP

|

Private Secretary
071-210 6488 (London)
0232 763255 x3212 (Belfast)

Departmental Overview

Civil Servants		Divisions	Minister
Grade 2			
	Grade 3	Educational Services	J Hanley
	Grade 3	Establishment and Finance	J Hanley
	Grade 3	Education and and Training Inspectorate	J Hanley

Civil Servants and Divisions

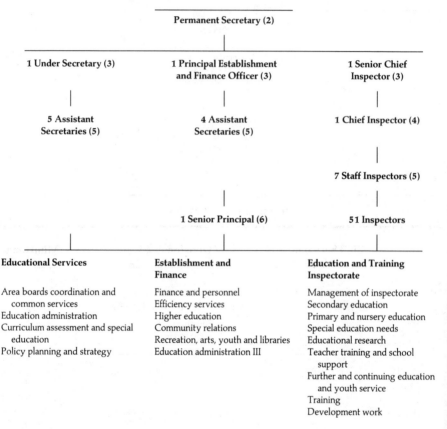

Department of Education for Northern Ireland

Permanent Secretary (2)

| 1 Under Secretary (3) | 1 Principal Establishment and Finance Officer (3) | 1 Senior Chief Inspector (3) |

| 5 Assistant Secretaries (5) | 4 Assistant Secretaries (5) | 1 Chief Inspector (4) |

7 Staff Inspectors (5)

1 Senior Principal (6)   51 Inspectors

Educational Services	Establishment and Finance	Education and Training Inspectorate
Area boards coordination and common services	Finance and personnel	Management of inspectorate
Education administration	Efficiency services	Secondary education
Curriculum assessment and special education	Higher education	Primary and nursery education
Policy planning and strategy	Community relations	Special education needs
	Recreation, arts, youth and libraries	Educational research
	Education administration III	Teacher training and school support
		Further and continuing education and youth service
		Training
		Development work

Department of the Environment for Northern Ireland

Founded 1976

Minister parliamentary under secretary of state,
Northern Ireland Office

Responsibilities archaeological survey
conservation and safekeeping of the records
of government departments, local
authorities etc
creation and management of country parks
and the designation of nature reserves and
areas of outstanding natural beauty
disposal and management of department's
land and property holdings
environmental protection
fire services
housing policies
listing and preservation of historic buildings
and ancient monuments
planning
registration of title of land and registration of
deeds
roads
transport policies
urban regeneration
water
works services

Executive Agencies Driver and Vehicle Testing Agency (NI)
Ordnance Survey (NI)
Rate Collection Agency (NI)

Department of the Environment for Northern Ireland

Stormont, Belfast BT4 3SS
Tel 0232 763210   Fax 0232 761425

Minister

Minister of State
Robert Atkins MP

|

Private Secretary
071-210 6501 (London)
0232 763255 x2211 (Belfast)

Departmental Overview

Civil Servants		Division	Minister
Grade 2	Grade 3	Personnel, Central Management, Finance, Solicitors and Central Claims	R Atkins
	Grade 3	Planning, Urban Affairs, Lands Service, Comprehensive Development	R Atkins
	Grade 3	Roads Service, Public Records Office and Works Service	R Atkins
	Grade 3	Housing, Local Government, Environment Service	R Atkins
	Grade 3	Water Service, Ordnance Survey, Land Registry, Transport, Fire Service, Road Casualty	R Atkins

Civil Servants and Divisions

Department of the Environment for Northern Ireland

Permanent Secretary (2)

1 Under Secretary (3)	1 Under Secretary (3)	1 Under Secretary (3)
5 Assistant Secretaries (5)	1 Grade 4	2 Grade 4s
	5 Grade 5s	8 Grade 5s

Personnel etc

Personnel management
Management and IT services
Central management
Central claims
Solicitor's division
Finance

Planning and Urban Affairs

Planning service
Urban development office
Lands service

Roads, Public Record Office and Works

Roads service
Public record office
Works service
New works
Estate maintenance and civil
   engineering
Advisory services
Administration

1 Under Secretary (3)	1 Under Secretary (3)
1 Grade 4	1 Grade 4
7 Grade 5s	6 Grade 5s

Housing etc

Housing
Local government
Countryside and wildlife
Historic monuments and buildings
Environment service

Water Service etc

Water service
Ordnance survey
Land registry
Registry of deeds
Transport

Department of Finance and Personnel, Northern Ireland

Founded 1982

Minister minister of state, Northern Ireland Office

Responsibilities Northern Ireland Civil Service (equal
opportunities policy, management and
training consultancy and information
technology service)
charities
economic and social planning and research
expenditure of NI departments
Government Purchasing Service (NI)
liaison with HM Treasury and NIO on
financial matters
personnel management
provision of staff for the Civil Service
Commission
Ulster Savings
Valuation and Lands Service (NI)

Executive Agencies None

Department of Finance and Personnel, Northern Ireland

Parliament Buildings, Stormont, Belfast BT4 3SW
Tel 0232 763210   Fax 0232 763716
Rosepark House, Upper Newtownards Road, Belfast BT4 3NR
Tel 0232 484567   Fax 0232 485711

Minister

Minister of State
Michael Mates MP

|

Parliamentary Private Secretary
Vacant

|

Private Secretary
071-210 6498/9 (London)
0232 763255 x3350/3351/3352
(Belfast)

Departmental Overview

Civil Servants	Divisions	Minister
Northern Ireland Civil Service		
D Fell (1A)	Grade 3	Central Secretariat	M Mates
Head of the	Grade 3	Legal Services	M Mates
Civil Service	Grade 3	Office of the Legislative Counsel	M Mates
Grade 2	Grade 3	Supply Group	M Mates
	Grade 3	Resources Control and Professional Services	M Mates
	Grade 4	Establishment, Finance and Consultancy	M Mates
	Grade 3	Central Personnel Group	M Mates
	Grade 3	Valuation and Lands Office	M Mates
	Grade 3	Government Purchasing Service	M Mates
	Grade 5	International Fund	M Mates
	Grade 5	Law Reform	M Mates

Civil Servants and Divisions

Northern Ireland Civil Service

Head of Northern Ireland Civil Service
David Fell (1A)

|

Under Secretary (3)

|

3 Assistant Secretaries (5)

|

Central secretariat

Protocol issues
Central appointments unit
Cross-border economic
    co-operation
NI legislative programme
Public Records Scrutiny
Central Community Relations Unit
Central Unit for 'Making Belfast
    Work' programme

|

1 Head of Legal Services (3)   **1 1st Legislative Draftsman (2)**

|

8 Assistant Solicitors (5)   **1 2nd Legislative Draftsman (3)**

2 Assistant Solicitors (5)

Legal Services   **Office of the Legislative
                        Counsel**

Provides legal advice and services   Drafting of primary legislation
    to NI government departments   (Orders in Council) for NI

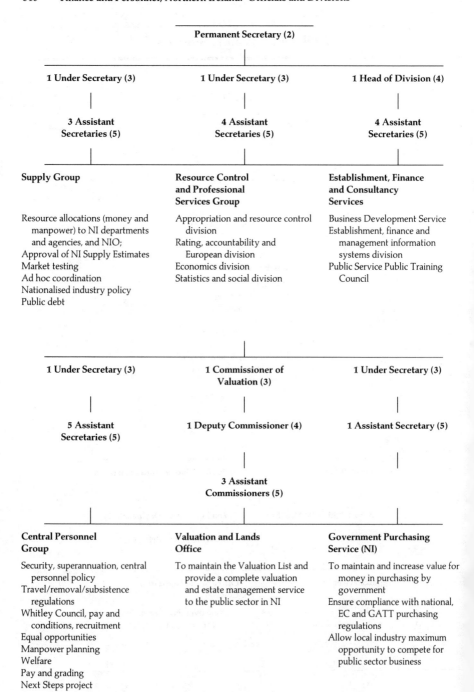

Permanent Secretary (2)

1 Under Secretary (3)	1 Under Secretary (3)	1 Head of Division (4)
3 Assistant Secretaries (5)	4 Assistant Secretaries (5)	4 Assistant Secretaries (5)

Supply Group

Resource allocations (money and manpower) to NI departments and agencies, and NIO; Approval of NI Supply Estimates Market testing Ad hoc coordination Nationalised industry policy Public debt

Resource Control and Professional Services Group

Appropriation and resource control division Rating, accountability and European division Economics division Statistics and social division

Establishment, Finance and Consultancy Services

Business Development Service Establishment, finance and management information systems division Public Service Public Training Council

1 Under Secretary (3)	1 Commissioner of Valuation (3)	1 Under Secretary (3)
5 Assistant Secretaries (5)	1 Deputy Commissioner (4)	1 Assistant Secretary (5)
	3 Assistant Commissioners (5)	

Central Personnel Group

Security, superannuation, central personnel policy Travel/removal/subsistence regulations Whitley Council, pay and conditions, recruitment Equal opportunities Manpower planning Welfare Pay and grading Next Steps project

Valuation and Lands Office

To maintain the Valuation List and provide a complete valuation and estate management service to the public sector in NI

Government Purchasing Service (NI)

To maintain and increase value for money in purchasing by government Ensure compliance with national, EC and GATT purchasing regulations Allow local industry maximum opportunity to compete for public sector business

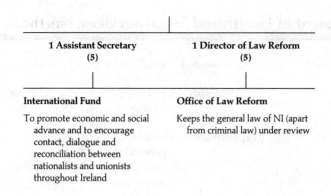

1 Assistant Secretary (5)	**1 Director of Law Reform** (5)

International Fund

To promote economic and social advance and to encourage contact, dialogue and reconciliation between nationalists and unionists throughout Ireland

Office of Law Reform

Keeps the general law of NI (apart from criminal law) under review

Department of Health and Social Services, Northern Ireland

Founded 1965

Minister parliamentary under secretary of state,
Northern Ireland Office

Responsibilities health
personal social services
social legislation and administration
social security

Executive Agencies Social Security Agency (NI)
Child Support Agency (NI) 1993

Department of Health and Social Services, Northern Ireland

Dundonald House, Upper Newtownards Road, Belfast BT4 3SF
Tel 0232 650111   Fax 0232 484858

Minister

Parliamentary Under
Secretary of State
The Earl of Arran

|

Private Secretary
071-210 6488 (London)
0232 650111 X375 (Belfast)

Departmental Overview

	Civil Servants	Divisions	Minister
Grade 2	Grade 3	Health and Personal Social Services Management Executive	E of Arran
	Grade 3	Health and Personal Social Services Policy and Strategy Command	E of Arran
	Grade 4	Social Services Inspectorate	E of Arran
	Grade 4	Nursing and Midwifery Advisory Group	E of Arran
Chief Medical Officer (2a)	Grade 3	Medical and Allied Services	E of Arran
Reports to the Grade 2	Grade 4	Dental Services	E of Arran
	Grade 5	Pharmaceutical Advice and Services	E of Arran
	Grade 3	Social Security Policy and Strategy Command	E of Arran

Civil Servants and Divisions

Department of Health and Social Security, Northern Ireland

Permanent Secretary (2)

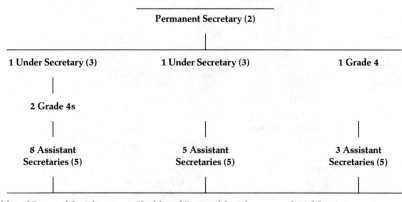

1 Under Secretary (3)	1 Under Secretary (3)	1 Grade 4

2 Grade 4s

8 Assistant Secretaries (5)	5 Assistant Secretaries (5)	3 Assistant Secretaries (5)

Health and Personal Social Services Management	**Health and Personal Social Services Policy and Strategy Command**	**Social Services Inspectorate**
Operations directorate	Health policy division	Family and child care programmes
Office of the Chief Executive	Child care and social policy	Belfast Action Team overview
Financial management directorate	Client groups division	Physical handicap programme
Management and personnel directorate	Social legislation division	Mental health and substance abuse programme
HPSS review directorate	Strategy and intelligence group	Elderly care programme
Directorate of information systems		Training schools and probation service
Estates and property division		
Design and consultancy services division		
Project planning and procurement division		

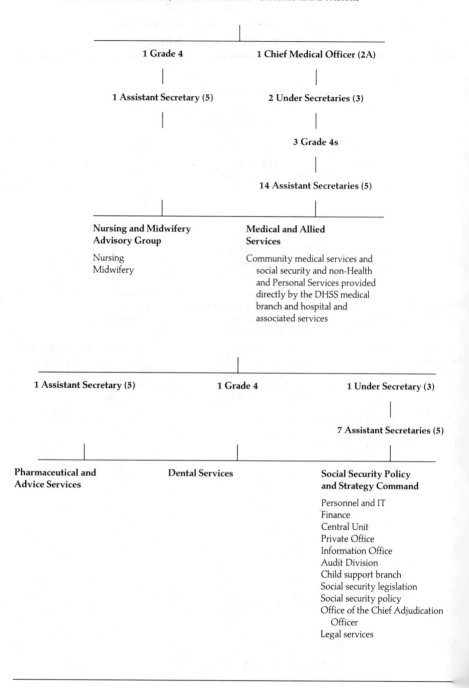

1 Grade 4   1 Chief Medical Officer (2A)

1 Assistant Secretary (5)   2 Under Secretaries (3)

                                              3 Grade 4s

                                              14 Assistant Secretaries (5)

Nursing and Midwifery   Medical and Allied
Advisory Group   Services

Nursing   Community medical services and
Midwifery   social security and non-Health
                                     and Personal Services provided
                                     directly by the DHSS medical
                                     branch and hospital and
                                     associated services

1 Assistant Secretary (5)   1 Grade 4   1 Under Secretary (3)

                                                          7 Assistant Secretaries (5)

Pharmaceutical and   Dental Services   Social Security Policy
Advice Services   and Strategy Command

                                                        Personnel and IT
                                                        Finance
                                                        Central Unit
                                                        Private Office
                                                        Information Office
                                                        Audit Division
                                                        Child support branch
                                                        Social security legislation
                                                        Social security policy
                                                        Office of the Chief Adjudication
                                                            Officer
                                                        Legal services

Office of Population, Censuses and Surveys

Founded   1970 when the General Register Office, established in 1837, merged with the Government Social Survey which started in 1941

Responsibilities   Analysis of vital, medical and demographic statistics and publication of reports

Census of the population

Registration of births marriages and deaths in England and Wales

Regulation of civil marriages

Research

Executive Agencies   None

Office of Population Censuses and Surveys

Head Office, St Catherine's House, 10 Kingsway, London WC2B 6JP
Tel 071-242 0262   Fax 071-242 0262 X2176

Minister

Secretary of State for Health
The Hon Tom Sackville MP
(for details of his office
see Department of Health)

Officials

Director and Registrar General
P J Wormald CB

|

Private Secretary
Mrs C Daniel
071-242 0262 X2139

Civil Servants and Departments

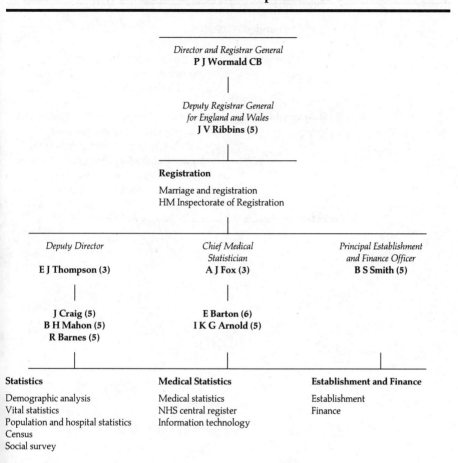

Director and Registrar General
P J Wormald CB

*Deputy Registrar General
for England and Wales*
J V Ribbins (5)

Registration

Marriage and registration
HM Inspectorate of Registration

Deputy Director	*Chief Medical Statistician*	*Principal Establishment and Finance Officer*
E J Thompson (3)	**A J Fox (3)**	**B S Smith (5)**

J Craig (5)	**E Barton (6)**	
B H Mahon (5)	**I K G Arnold (5)**	
R Barnes (5)		

Statistics	**Medical Statistics**	**Establishment and Finance**
Demographic analysis	Medical statistics	Establishment
Vital statistics	NHS central register	Finance
Population and hospital statistics	Information technology	
Census		
Social survey		

Overseas Development Administration

Founded   1964

Ministers   Secretary of State for Foreign and
Commonwealth Affairs and Minister for
Overseas Development

Responsibilities   British aid to overseas countries. This includes
capital aid on concessionary terms and
technical cooperation provided directly to
developing countries or through multilateral
aid organisations, including the United
Nations and its specialised agencies

Executive Agencies   Natural Resources Institute

Overseas Development Administration

94 Victoria Street, London SW1E 5JL
Tel 071-917 7000   Fax 071-917 0016/0019
All personnel are based at 94 Victoria Street unless otherwise indicated.
For other addresses and telephone numbers see the end of this section.

Ministers

Secretary of State for Foreign
and Commonwealth Affairs
The Rt Hon Douglas Hurd CBE
MP

|

Minister of State for Foreign
and Commonwealth Affairs,
Minister for Overseas Development
The Rt Hon Baroness Chalker*

|

Parliamentary Private Secretary
Mark Robinson MP

|

Private Secretary
S Chakrabarti
071-917 0419

*For details of Lady Chalker's responsibilities see under Foreign and Commonwealth Office

Departtmental Overview

Civil Servants			Department	Minister
Grade 1A	Grade 2	Grade 3		
Timothy Lankester	These divisions report directly to the Permanent Secretary	B R Ireton	Aid Policy and Finance	Ly Chalker
		J V Kerby	Establishment, Information, Emergency Aid, Management Review Staff, Medical and Staff Welfare	Ly Chalker
		J B Wilmshurst	Economic and Social	Ly Chalker
Timothy Lankester	R M Ainscow	J V Kerby	Overseas Manpower and Pensions, Latin America and the Caribbean	Ly Chalker
		J A L Faint	Eastern Europe	Ly Chalker
		N B Hudson	Africa	Ly Chalker
		R G M Manning	Asia	Ly Chalker
		P D M Freeman	International	Ly Chalker
		Dr R O Iredale (5)	Education	Ly Chalker
		T D Pike (5)	Engineering	Ly Chalker
		Dr D Nabarro (5)	Health and Population	Ly Chalker
		A J Bennett	Natural Resources and Environment	Ly Chalker

Civil Servants and Departments

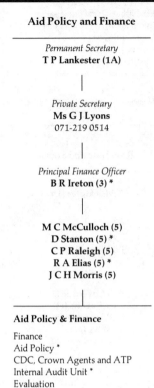

Aid Policy and Finance

Permanent Secretary
T P Lankester (1A)

Private Secretary
Ms G J Lyons
071-219 0514

Principal Finance Officer
B R Ireton (3) *

M C McCulloch (5)
D Stanton (5) *
C P Raleigh (5)
R A Elias (5) *
J C H Morris (5)

Aid Policy & Finance

Finance
Aid Policy *
CDC, Crown Agents and ATP
Internal Audit Unit *
Evaluation

* *Staff and divisions are part of a joint ODA/FCO department*

Establishment and Information

Permanent Secretary
T P Lankester (1A)

Establishment Officer
J V Kerby (3) *

G M Steggman (5)
B W Hammond (6)
P A Bearpark (5)

|

Establishment and Information

Establishment and organisation
Information Technology unit
Information
Library *
Medical and staff welfare *
Management review staff *

* *Staff and divisions are part of a joint ODA/FCO department*

Economic and Social

Permanent Secretary
T P Lankester (1A)

|

Head of Division
J B Wilmshurst (3)

|

A G Coverdale (5)
J T Roberts (5)
B P Thomson (5)
M Foster (5)
K L Sparkhall (5)

|

Economic and Social

Asia, Caribbean and Pacific group
Africa and Middle East group
Multilateral agencies and research
    group
Aid and social policy group
Finance and management advisory
    group
Social development group

Overseas Manpower and Pensions, Latin America, Caribbean and Atlantic

Permanent Secretary
T P Lankester (1A)

|

Deputy Secretary
R M Ainscow (2)

|

Under Secretary
J V Kerby (3)

|

W Hobman (5)
J Hodges (5)
D S Fish (5)
(above at East Kilbride)

|

Overseas Manpower

Latin America and the Caribbean
Overseas appointments and
  contracts
Personnel services
Recruitment and consultancies
Pensions

Eastern Europe

Permanent Secretary
T P Lankester (1A)

|

Deputy Secretary
R M Ainscow (2)

|

Head of Division
J A L Faint (3) *

|

M A Powers (5)
L B Smith (5) *

|

|

Eastern Europe

Eastern Europe and former Soviet
Union *
European Bank for Reconstruction
and Development

* *Staff and divisions are part of a joint ODA/FCO department*

Africa

Permanent Secretary
T P Lankester (1A)

|

Deputy Secretary
R M Ainscow (2)

|

Head of Division
N B Hudson (3)

|

Ms B M Kelly (5)
C I Myhill (5)
J H S Chard (5)
D Sands-Smith (5)
(Kenya)
Ms S E Unsworth (5)
(Malawi)

|

Africa

Eastern Africa
Central and Southern Africa
West and North Africa and the
Mediterranean
British development division in
East Africa
British development division in
Southern Africa

Asia

Permanent Secretary
T P Lankester (1A)

Deputy Secretary
R M Ainscow (2)

Head of Division
R G M Manning (3)

V J McClean (5)
M G Bawden (5)
(Barbados)
Mrs P M Wilkinson (5)
R J Wilson (5)
Ms A M Archbold (5)
M J Dinham (5)
(Bangkok)

Asia

East Asia
British development division in the
  Caribbean (Barbados)
Pacific department
South Asia I
South Asia II
South East Asia development
  division

International

Permanent Secretary
T P Lankester (1A)

Deputy Secretary
R M Ainscow (2)

Head of Division
P D M Freeman (3)

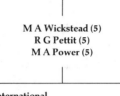

M A Wickstead (5)
R G Pettit (5)
M A Power (5)

International

European Community and Food
Aid
United Nations and
Commonwealth
International Financial Institutions

Education

Permanent Secretary
T P Lankester (1A)

Deputy Secretary
R M Ainscow (2)

Dr R O Iredale (5)

Education

Education aid policy
Functional programmes of
assistance
Technical cooperation programmes
British Council
Commonwealth Scholarship
Commission

Engineering

Permanent Secretary
T P Lankester (1A)

Deputy Secretary
R M Ainscow (2)

T D Pike (5)

Engineering

Research on new and renewable
sources of energy
Engineering, geological and
building research projects
Relations with Building Research
Establishment, Hydraulics
Research Station, Institute of
Hydrology, Transport and Road
Research Laboratory

Health and Population

Permanent Secretary
T P Lankester (1A)

|

Deputy Secretary
R M Ainscow (2)

|

Dr D Nabarro (5)

Health and Population

World Health Organisation
Medical and nutrition research
projects
Population policy and family
planning

Natural Resources and Environment

Permanent Secretary
T P Lankester (1A)

|

Deputy Secretary
R M Ainscow (2)

|

Chief Natural Resources Adviser
A J Bennett (3)

|

Dr J C Davies OBE (5)
J M Scott (5)
D P Turner (5)

Natural Resources

Policy on agricultural and rural
development, cooperatives and
institutions
Support for international research
Renewable natural resources
research
Contract research
Relations with ODA scientific
units, Overseas Surveys
Directorate of Ordnance Survey
Relations with ODA core-funded
associated bodies
Science and technology for
development

Overseas Development Administration Addresses

Abercrombie House
Eaglesham Road
East Kilbride
Glasgow G75 8EA
Tel 035584 4000
Fax 035584 4097

PO Box 167
Bridgetown
Barbados
Tel Barbados 426 2190
Fax Barbados 426 2194

Central Avenue
Chatham Maritime
Chatham
Kent ME4 4TB
Tel 0634 880088
Fax 0634 880066/77

PO Box 30465
Bruce House
Standard Street
Nairobi
Kenya
Tel Nairobi 335944
Fax Nairobi 340260

PO Box 30059
Lilongwe 3
Malawi
Tel Lilongwe 731 544
Fax Lilongwe 731 4163/31200

c/o British Embassy
Bangkok
Thailand
Tel Bangkok 252 7161
Fax Bangkok 252 37124

Parliamentary Counsel Office

Founded   1869

Status   Part of the Cabinet Office

Responsible to   The Lord Privy Seal and the Lord President of the Council in respect of professional matters; and the Chancellor of the Duchy of Lancaster in respect of administrative matters

Responsibilities   Drafting of government bills (except for those relating exclusively to Scotland); drafting of amendments to, and motions etc. relating to, bills; advice on parliamentary procedure

Parliamentary Counsel Office

36 Whitehall, London SW1A 2AY
Tel 071-210 6633   Fax 071-210 6632

Ministers

The Lord Privy Seal
The Rt Hon the Lord Wakeham

The Lord President of the Council
The Rt Hon Antony Newton MP

in respect of professional matters

The Chancellor of the Duchy of Lancaster
The Rt Hon William Waldegrave MP

in respect of administrative matters

Counsel

First Parliamentary Counsel
Peter Graham CB QC

|

Private Secretary
P J Moore MBE (7)
071-210 6629

|

Second Parliamentary Counsel
J C Jenkins CB

|

Parliamentary Counsel
J S Mason CB
D W Saunders CB
E G Caldwell CB
E G Bowman CB
G B Sellers CB
E R Sutherland
P F A Knowles
S C Laws
R S Parker

|

Deputy Parliamentary Counsel
Miss C E Johnston
P J Davies
J M Sellers
J R Jones

Senior Assistant Parliamentary
Counsel
A J Hogarth
Dr Helen J Beynon
D J Ramsay
Miss C T Balfour Davies

Assistant Parliamentary Counsel
Miss L A Nodder
P R de Val
Mrs E A F Gardiner
R N Cory
D J Cook
Ms K A Cooper
D I Greenberg
Mrs D S Jones
Miss B A Waplington
Miss J M Piesse
Ms A L Brice

Prime Minister's Office

10 Downing Street, London SW1A 2AA
Tel 071-270 3000
Fax *Telephone the above number and ask for appropriate fax number*

70 Whitehall, London SW1A 2AS
Tel 071-270 0260/0435   Fax 071-930 1419

Prime Minister and
First Lord of the Treasury and
Minister for the Civil Service
The Rt Hon John Major MP

|

Principal Private Secretary
to the Prime Minister
Alex Allan (3)
071-930 4433

Overview

Civil Servants and Other Staff

Private Office

The Rt Hon John Major	Alex Allan (3)	*Private Secretaries*
	S Wall (5)	Overseas Affairs
	B Potter (5)	Economic Affairs
	W Chapman (7)	Parliamentary Affairs
	M Adams (7)	Home Affairs and Diary
	J R Catford (5)	Secretary for Appointments
	Miss L Wilkinson (SEO)	Honours Secretary

Foreign Affairs Adviser

The Rt Hon John Major	Sir Rodric Braithwaite (1A)	Foreign Affairs Adviser

Political Office

The Rt Hon John Major	Jonathan Hill	Political Secretary
	Graham Bright MP	Parliamentary Private Secretary

No 10 Policy Unit

The Rt Hon John Major	Mrs S Hogg (1A)	*Special Advisers*
	Nicholas True	
	Alan Rosling	
	David Poole	
	Lucy Neville-Rolfe	
	Katharine Ramsay	
	Damian Green	
	Jill Rutter	

Press Office

The Rt Hon John Major	G O'Donnell (3)	Chief Press Secretary

Efficiency Unit*

The Rt Hon John Major	Sir Peter Levene	Prime Minister's Adviser on Efficiency
	D Brereton (3)	Head of Unit

* Under the general jurisdiction of the Chancellor of the Duchy of Lancaster

Civil Servants, Other Staff and Departments

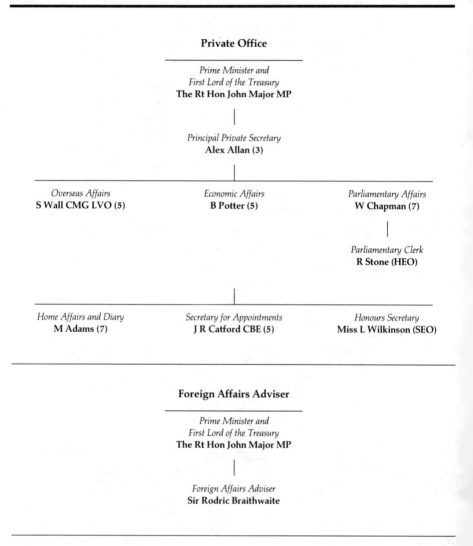

Private Office

*Prime Minister and
First Lord of the Treasury*
The Rt Hon John Major MP

Principal Private Secretary
Alex Allan (3)

| *Overseas Affairs* | *Economic Affairs* | *Parliamentary Affairs* |
| **S Wall CMG LVO (5)** | **B Potter (5)** | **W Chapman (7)** |

Parliamentary Clerk
R Stone (HEO)

| *Home Affairs and Diary* | *Secretary for Appointments* | *Honours Secretary* |
| **M Adams (7)** | **J R Catford CBE (5)** | **Miss L Wilkinson (SEO)** |

Foreign Affairs Adviser

*Prime Minister and
First Lord of the Treasury*
The Rt Hon John Major MP

Foreign Affairs Adviser
Sir Rodric Braithwaite

Political Office

Prime Minister and
First Lord of the Treasury
The Rt Hon John Major MP

Political Secretary	*Parliamentary Private Secretary*
Jonathan Hill	**Graham Bright MP**

No 10 Policy Unit

Prime Minister and
First Lord of the Treasury
The Rt Hon John Major MP

No 10 Policy Unit

Head of Unit **Sarah Hogg**	Economic and European issues
Deputy Head of Unit **Nicholas True**	Education, Social security, Sport, Charities
Alan Rosling	Defence, Transport, Science, Employment, Scotland, N Ireland
David Poole	Industry, Energy, the City, Financial services, Utilities
Lucy Neville-Rolfe	Citizen's Charter, Civil service, Home Office, Agriculture, EC issues
Katharine Ramsay	Speech writing
Damian Green	Housing, Inner cities, Broadcasting, Heritage, Lottery, Wales, London
Jill Rutter	Health, Social services, Local government, Environment, Women's issues

Press Office

Prime Minister and
First Lord of the Treasury
The Rt Hon John Major MP

|

Chief Press Secretary
G O'Donnell (3)

|

Deputy Chief Press Secretary
J Haslam (5)

Efficiency Unit*

Prime Minister and
First Lord of the Treasury
The Rt Hon John Major MP

|

The Prime Minister's Adviser
on Efficiency
Sir Peter Levene
(70 Whitehall)

|

Head of Unit
D Brereton (3)
(70 Whitehall)

|

Deputy Head
Dr G D Coley (5)

|

N Cribb (5)
Dr I V Howell (5)
B R Ross (5)
(all above at 70 Whitehall)

* *see also Cabinet Office*

Privy Council Office

Founded	During the 13th and 14th centuries
Responsible to	Lord President of the Council (since 1940 most often the Leader of the House of Commons or the House of Lords and usually a senior member of the Cabinet) and thence the sovereign

Responsibilities:

Lord President of the Council

Administering the appointments of Privy Counsellors (of whom there are about 400)

Royal proclamations and Orders in Council

Granting of royal charters

Approval of bye-laws and statutes of chartered bodies

Approval of regulations and rules made by the governing bodies of the medical and certain allied professions

Appointment of high sheriffs and many Crown and Privy Council appointments to government bodies

Administration of the judicial committee of the Privy Council (the final court of appeal for Commonwealth citizens), which is composed of all Privy Counsellors who hold or have held high judicial office

Leader of the Commons

Arranging government business

Procedural matters

Supervision of the government's legislative programme

Upholding the rights and privileges of the House as a whole

There are no longer any responsibilities or functions of any kind attaching to the office of Lord Privy Seal (currently The Rt Hon Lord Wakeham, Leader of the House of Lords) as such. This office is currently based in the Privy Council Office as a matter of convenience.

Privy Council Office

68 Whitehall, London SW1A 2AT
Tel 071-270 3000

Ministers

*Lord President of the Council and
Leader of the House of Commons*
**The Rt Hon Anthony Newton
OBE MP**

|

Parliamentary Private Secretary
John Marshall MP

|

Special Adviser
Ian Stewart

|

Principal Private Secretary
T M Sutton

|

Private Secretary
Mrs H Paxman
071-270 0480

*The Lord Privy Seal and
Leader of the House of Lords*
The Rt Hon The Lord Wakeham

|

Private Secretary
Miss G M Kirton
071-270 0501

Officials

Clerk of the Council
G I de Deney CVO (3)

*Deputy Clerk of the Council
and Establishment Officer*
R P Bulling (6)

*Registrar of the Judicial
Committee of the Privy Council*
D H O Owen (5)

**Assistance to the Clerk in all his
functions**

**Organisation of the work of the
Judicial Committee**

Ministerial Responsibilities

Anthony Newton *as Lord President*	Responsible for the work of the Privy Council Office: royal proclamations and Orders in Council granting of royal charters administers appointments of Privy Counsellors approval of statutes and byelaws of chartered bodies; rules and regulations of certain professions various Crown and Privy Council appointments administration of judicial committee
as Leader of the Commons	Advice on procedural matters and upholding the rights and privileges of the House Arrangement of government business in the House including legislation

PSA Services

Founded	The Property Services Agency was created as part of the Department of the Environment in 1972 and became PSA Services in 1989.
	It is split into three main businesses: **PSA Projects** to be offered for sale in 1992/3; **PSA Building Management**, divided into five regionally based organisations which will be offered for sale as separate businesses later; and **PSA International** which will remain in the public sector until its closure in late 1993.
Responsibilities	Provides and maintains central government property and now operates commercially in competition with the private sector.

PSA Services

2 Marsham Street, London SW1P 3EB
Tel 071-276 3000   Fax 071-276 0818

Minister

Minister of State,
Department of the Environment
John Redwood MP

(for details of his office see
Department of the Environment)

Officials

Chief Executive and
Permanent Secretary
Sir Geoffrey Chipperfield KCB (1)

|

Managing Director,
PSA Building Management
J A Anderson (2)

|

Chairman, PSA Projects
J B Jefferson CB CBE (2)

|

Managing Director
PSA Projects
J P G Rowcliffe (2)

|

Managing Director
PSA International
R G S Johnston (3)

Departmental Overview

Civil Servants			Department	Minister
Grade 1	*Grade 2*	*Grade 3*		
PSA Services				
Sir Geoffrey Chipperfield	These divisions report directly to the Permanent Secretary	Mrs J M Williams	Privatisation and Strategy	J Redwood
		P S Draper	PSA Group Personnel	J Redwood
		A Marson	PSA Finance	J Redwood
	J Anderson	P J M Butter	PSA Building Management	J Redwood
	J B Jefferson	R Gray	PSA Projects	J Redwood
	J P G Rowcliffe	A S Gosling		
		S G D Duiguid		
		A S Kennedy		
		R G S Johnston	PSA International	J Redwood

Civil Servants and Departments

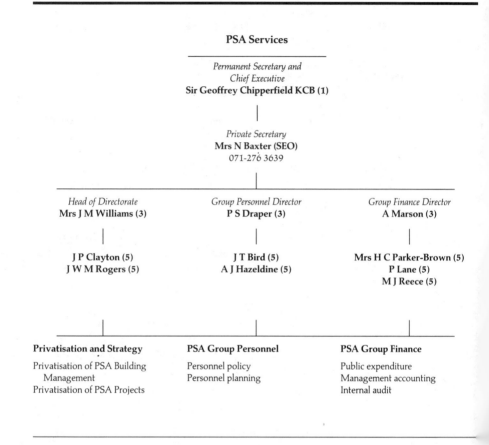

PSA Services

Permanent Secretary and
Chief Executive
Sir Geoffrey Chipperfield KCB (1)

Private Secretary
Mrs N Baxter (SEO)
071-276 3639

Head of Directorate	*Group Personnel Director*	*Group Finance Director*
Mrs J M Williams (3)	**P S Draper (3)**	**A Marson (3)**
J P Clayton (5)	J T Bird (5)	Mrs H C Parker-Brown (5)
J W M Rogers (5)	A J Hazeldine (5)	P Lane (5)
		M J Reece (5)

Privatisation and Strategy	**PSA Group Personnel**	**PSA Group Finance**
Privatisation of PSA Building Management	Personnel policy	Public expenditure
Privatisation of PSA Projects	Personnel planning	Management accounting
		Internal audit

PSA Building Management, Whitgift Centre

Permanent Secretary and
Chief Executive
Sir Geoffrey Chipperfield KCB (1)

|

Managing Director
J Anderson (2)

|

P J M Butter (3)
J E Bridgeman (4)
D G A Cheal (5)
Dr M S Barrett (5)

BM Regional Offices

Scotland	*South East*	*North East*
Managing Director	*Managing Director*	*Managing Director*
B A Taylor (4)	**P M Livesey (4)**	**A J B Staveley (4)**
H Love (5)	**J N Mutch (5)**	
	J Forster (5)	
	R Service (5)	

Manchester	*South and West*
Managing Director	*Managing Director*
M M Harrison (4)	**S P Todd (4)**
D A R Reeson (5)	**J Lawless (5)**
R Williams [5]	

PSA Projects, Whitgift Centre

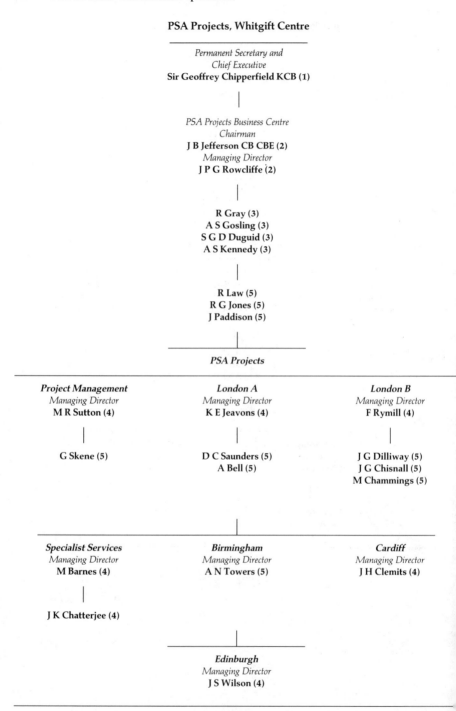

Permanent Secretary and
Chief Executive
Sir Geoffrey Chipperfield KCB (1)

PSA Projects Business Centre
Chairman
J B Jefferson CB CBE (2)
Managing Director
J P G Rowcliffe (2)

R Gray (3)
A S Gosling (3)
S G D Duguid (3)
A S Kennedy (3)

R Law (5)
R G Jones (5)
J Paddison (5)

PSA Projects

Project Management	*London A*	*London B*
Managing Director	*Managing Director*	*Managing Director*
M R Sutton (4)	**K E Jeavons (4)**	**F Rymill (4)**
G Skene (5)	**D C Saunders (5)**	**J G Dilliway (5)**
	A Bell (5)	**J G Chisnall (5)**
		M Chammings (5)

Specialist Services	*Birmingham*	*Cardiff*
Managing Director	*Managing Director*	*Managing Director*
M Barnes (4)	**A N Towers (5)**	**J H Clemits (4)**
J K Chatterjee (4)		

Edinburgh
Managing Director
J S Wilson (4)

PSA International, Whitgift Centre

*Permanent Secretary and
Chief Executive*
Sir Geoffrey Chipperfield KCB (1)

|

Managing Director
R G S Johnston (3)

|

M J Reynolds (5)
Ms R Doidge (5)
A Sannia (5)
R B Perry (4)
P Birkett (6)
W E K Mesquitta (6)
T Baker (6)

PSA Addresses

Whitgift Centre
Wellesley Road
Croydon CR9 3LY
Tel 081-760 4377
Fax 081-760 4160

Building Management Regional Offices

Manchester
Ashburner House
Seymour Grove
Manchester M16 0JL
Tel 061-954 6000
Fax 061-954 6400

North East
Lawnswood
Otley Road
Leeds LS16 5PX
Tel 0223 455369
Fax 0223 455476

Scotland
Argyle House
3 Lady Lawson Street
Edinburgh EH3 9SD
Tel 031-222 6007
Fax 031-222 6690

South East
St Christopher House
Southwark Street
London SE1 0TE
Tel 071-921 4929
Fax 071-921 3928

South and West
Burghill Road
Westbury-on-Trym
Bristol BS10 6DZ
Tel 0272 764000
Fax 0272 764999

PSA Projects Addresses

Birmingham
Five Ways House
Islington Row
Middle Way
Birmingham BL5 1SL
Tel 021-626 2000
Fax 021-626 2339

Cardiff
PSA Projects
St Agnes Road
Gabalfa
Cardiff CF4 4YT
Tel 0222 693131
Fax 0222 520665

Edinburgh
30/31 Queen Street
Edinburgh EH2 1LZ
Tel 031-529 2000
Fax 031-529 20001

Registry of Friendly Societies

Founded	RFS: 1875
	Building Societies Commission: 1986
Status	non-ministerial department serving two statutory bodies: the Building Societies Commission and the Central Office of the Registry of Friendly Societies
Responsible to	Economic Secretary, HM Treasury
Responsibilities	Advice to ministers on friendly societies and building societies

The Building Societies Commission:
exercises prudential supervision over building societies in the interests of investors. It administers the system of regulation and promotes the financial stability of the building society industry generally

The Central Office of the Registry of Friendly Societies:
exercises prudential supervision over friendly societies and credit unions

Provides a public registry of mutual organisations registered under the Building Societies Act 1986, Friendly Societies Act 1974, and the Industrial and Provident Societies Act 1965.

Registry of Friendly Societies

15 Great Marlborough Street, London W1V 2AX
Tel 071-437 9992   Fax 071-437 1612

58 Frederick Street, Edinburgh EH2 1AB
Tel 031-225 3224   Fax 031-225 5687

Minister

Economic Secretary, HM Treasury
Anthony Nelson MP

Officials

*Chairman, Registry of Friendly
Societies
Chairman and First Commissioner,
Building Societies Commission*
Mrs R E J Gilmore (2)

|

Private Secretary
C J Forster
071-494 6641

|

Deputy Chairman
H G Walsh (3)

Departmental Overview

Civil Servants			Department	Minister
Grade 2	Grade 3	Grade 4		
Mrs R E J Gilmore	H G Walsh	T F Mathews	Building Societies Commission	A Nelson
Mrs R E J Gilmore		A Wilson D W Lee (5) A J Perrett (5) J L J Craig (5)	Central Office	A Nelson

Civil Servants and Departments

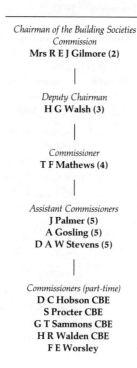

*Chairman of the Building Societies
Commission*
Mrs R E J Gilmore (2)

Deputy Chairman
H G Walsh (3)

Commissioner
T F Mathews (4)

Assistant Commissioners
J Palmer (5)
A Gosling (5)
D A W Stevens (5)

Commissioners (part-time)
D C Hobson CBE
S Procter CBE
G T Sammons CBE
H R Walden CBE
F E Worsley

*Chief Registrar of Friendly Societies,
Industrial Assurance Commissioner*
Mrs R E J Gilmore (2)

Assistant Registrars
A Wilson (4)
D W Lee (5)
A J Perrett (5)

*Registry of Friendly Society (Scotland)
Assistant Registrar*
J L J Craig (5)
(58 Frederick Street)

Scottish Courts Administration

Founded   1971

Ministers   The Lord Advocate
Secretary of State for Scotland

Responsibilities   *Secretary of State*
Organisation, administration and staffing of the court offices (except the district courts)

Lord Advocate
The jurisdiction and procedure of Scottish courts in civil proceedings

Framing the law relating to the enforcement of the judgements of Scottish courts in civil matters and the recognition and enforcement of judgements of foreign courts, other than orders for the payment of maintenance

Framing the law relating to arbitration and fatal accident inquiries

Framing the law relating to tribunals and in some cases responsibility for their conduct and administration

Scottish Courts Administration

26/27 Royal Terrace, Edinburgh EH7 5AH
Tel 031-556 0755   Fax 031-556 3604

Ministers

Secretary of State for Scotland
The Rt Hon Ian Lang MP

The Lord Advocate
The Rt Hon The Lord Rodger QC

Civil Servants

Director
G Murray (3)

|

Deputy Directors
Court Organisation and Management
M Ewart (5)

|

Court Procedures, Jurisdiction and
Legislation; Law Reform
P Beaton
Assistant Solicitor

Scottish Office

Founded	1885
Ministers	secretary of state, one minister of state, three parliamentary under secretaries of state
Responsibilities	a number of statutory functions administered by five main departments: Scottish Office Agriculture and Fisheries Department Scottish Office Education Department Scottish Office Environment Department Scottish Office Home and Health Department Scottish Office Industry Department Other departments for which the Secretary of State has some degree of responsibility are: Forestry Commission General Register Office for Scotland Scottish Courts Administration Scottish Record Office
Executive Agencies	Historic Scotland Registers of Scotland Scottish Agricultural Science Agency Scottish Fisheries Protection Agency

Scottish Office

St Andrew's House, Regent Road, Edinburgh EH1 3DG
Tel 031-556 8400   Fax 031-244 2683
Dover House, Whitehall, London SW1A 2AU
Tel 071-270 3000   Fax 071-270 6719
All staff are based at St Andrew's House unless otherwise indicated.
For other addresses and telephone numbers see the end of this section.

Ministers

Secretary of State
The Rt Hon Ian Lang MP

|

Parliamentary Private Secretary
Vacant

|

Special Advisers
Alan Young
Gregor MacKay

|

Principal Private Secretary
A W Fraser (5)
031-244 4011

|

Minister of State
The Rt Hon Lord Fraser
of Carmyllie QC

|

Private Secretary
I D Kernohan (HEO)
031-244 4017

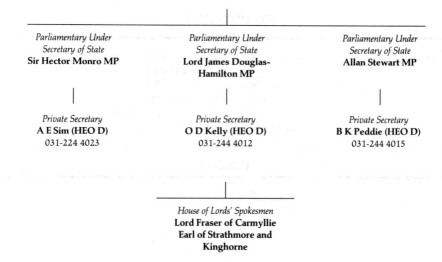

*Parliamentary Under
Secretary of State*
Sir Hector Monro MP

*Parliamentary Under
Secretary of State*
**Lord James Douglas-
Hamilton MP**

*Parliamentary Under
Secretary of State*
Allan Stewart MP

Private Secretary
A E Sim (HEO D)
031-224 4023

Private Secretary
O D Kelly (HEO D)
031-244 4012

Private Secretary
B K Peddie (HEO D)
031-244 4015

House of Lords' Spokesmen
**Lord Fraser of Carmyllie
Earl of Strathmore and
Kinghorne**

Ministerial Responsibilities

Ian Lang   overall responsibility for the Scottish Office
Forestry Commission
General Register Office (Scotland)
life prisoners
Registers of Scotland
royal prerogative of mercy
Scottish Courts Administration
Scottish Record Office

Lord Fraser of Carmyllie   health and social work
home affairs including women's issues and
    constitutional matters
Scottish business in the House of Lords

Sir Hector Monro   agriculture
arts
co-ordination of rural affairs
environment
fisheries
forestry
heritage
sport and recreation

Allan Stewart   energy
industry
local government including finance and
    planning
new towns
Commons spokesman on health and social
    work

Lord James Douglas-Hamilton   building control
education
Highlands and Islands
housing
roads and transport
tourism
urban policy
Commons spokesman on home affairs

Departmental Overview

Civil Servants			Department	Minister
Grade 1	*Grade 2*	*Grade 3*		

Agricultural and Fisheries

Sir Russell Hillhouse	K J MacKenzie	E C Davison (5)	Division A	Sir H Monro
		K W Moore (5)	Division C	Sir H Monro
		Dr T W Hegerty (5)	Scientific Adviser's Unit	Sir H Monro
		T A Cameron	Commodities and Land Groups	Sir H Monro
		G Robson	Fisheries	Sir H Monro
		J F Hutcheson (4)	Agricultural staff	Sir H Monro

Central Services

Sir Russell Hillhouse	G R Wilson	C C MacDonald	Personnel Management and Organisation	
		Ms E A Mackay	Finance	
		E W Ferguson (5)	Liaison Division (London)	
		R S B Gordon (4)	Administrative Services	
		Miss E S D Drummond (5)	Scottish Office Information Directorate	
		D A Stewart (7)	Management Group Support	
	R Brodie	N W Boe	Solicitor's Office	

Education

Sir Russell Hillhouse	G R Wilson	H Robertson	Schools	Ld J D Hamilton
		W A P Weatherston	Formal post-Schools Education; Arts and Sport	Ld J D Hamilton
		T N Gallacher	HM Inspectorate of Schools	Ld J D Hamilton

Departmental Overview

Civil Servants			Department	Minister
Grade 1	*Grade 2*	*Grade 3*		
Environment				
Sir Russell Hillhouse	H H Mills	J F Laing	Rural Affairs and Environmental Protection	Sir H Monro
		A M Russell	Housing	Ld J D Hamilton
		J S Graham	Development Planning and Local Government	A Stewart
		J E Gibbons	Building Directorate	Ld J D Hamilton
		A C Paton	Civil Engineering, Water Services and Environmental Protection	Sir H Monro
		A G Bell	Inquiry Reporters	A Stewart
		A MacKenzie (4)	Planning Services	A Stewart
		Dr J R Cuthbert (5)	Statistical Services	
Home and Health				
Sir Russell Hillhouse	J Hamill	D J Essery	Police, Fire, Home Defence, Emergency, Law and General	Ld Fraser
		Mrs G M Stewart	Criminal Justice, Licensing, Parole and Life Imprisonment	Ld Fraser
		E W Frizell	Scottish Prison Service	Ld Fraser
		D G Cruickshank	Chief Executive for NHS Scotland	Ld Fraser
		D J Belfall	Health Service (Policy, Strategic Planning and Primary Care)	Ld Fraser
		N G Campbell	Social Work Services	Ld Fraser
		Dr C Levein (5)	Research	Ld Fraser
		N Colquhoun (4)	Dental Services	Ld Fraser
		Miss A Jarvie	Nursing Services	Ld Fraser
		A Winton (4)	Fire Services	Ld Fraser
	C Sampson		HM Constabulary	Ld Fraser
		A H Bishop (5)	HM Inspectorate of Prisons	Ld Fraser
		J E Fraser (6)	Commissions	Ld Fraser
	Dr R E Kendell	Dr A B Young	Medical Services	Ld Fraser

Departmental Overview

Civil Servants			Department	Minister
Grade 1	*Grade 2*	*Grade 3*		
Industry Department				
Sir Russell Hillhouse	P Mackay	E J Weeple	Urban Policy, European Funds, New Towns, Economics and Statistics	Ld J D Hamilton A Stewart
		A D F Findlay	Electricity, Employment and Energy, Highland and Tourism, Transport and Local Roads	A Stewart Ld J D Hamilton
		H Morison	Industrial Expansion, Steel and Shipbuilding	A Stewart
		J A L Dawson	Roads Directorate	Ld J D Hamilton

Civil Servants and Departments

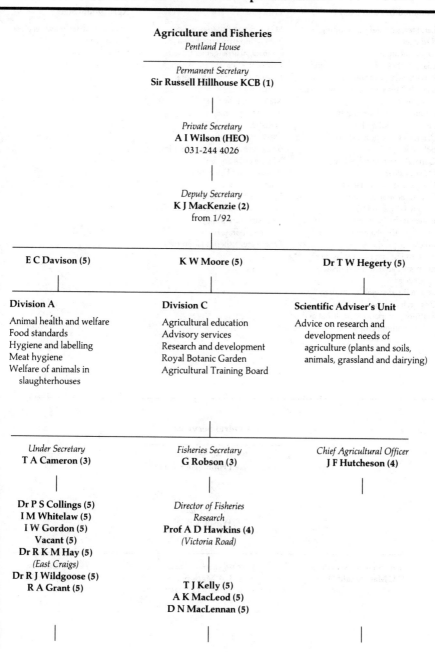

Agriculture and Fisheries
Pentland House

Permanent Secretary
Sir Russell Hillhouse KCB (1)

Private Secretary
A I Wilson (HEO)
031-244 4026

Deputy Secretary
K J MacKenzie (2)
from 1/92

E C Davison (5)	**K W Moore (5)**	**Dr T W Hegerty (5)**

Division A

Animal health and welfare
Food standards
Hygiene and labelling
Meat hygiene
Welfare of animals in
  slaughterhouses

Division C

Agricultural education
Advisory services
Research and development
Royal Botanic Garden
Agricultural Training Board

Scientific Adviser's Unit

Advice on research and
  development needs of
  agriculture (plants and soils,
  animals, grassland and dairying)

Under Secretary
T A Cameron (3)

Fisheries Secretary
G Robson (3)

Chief Agricultural Officer
J F Hutcheson (4)

Dr P S Collings (5)
I M Whitelaw (5)
I W Gordon (5)
Vacant (5)
Dr R K M Hay (5)
(East Craigs)
Dr R J Wildgoose (5)
R A Grant (5)

*Director of Fisheries
Research*
Prof A D Hawkins (4)
(Victoria Road)

T J Kelly (5)
A K MacLeod (5)
D N MacLennan (5)

Commodities and Land	Fisheries	Agricultural Staff
Land tenure, land use, crofting	EC Common fisheries policy	Professional/technical services
Red deer	Fishing industry structure and	Estate management
Extensification	financial arrangements	Surveying services
Classification of agricultural land	Law of the Sea	
Rural policy affecting agriculture	Pelagic and whitefish quota	
Cereals, horticulture, seed and plant	management	
varieties	Marketing policy	
Potatoes and plant health	International trade	
Environmental pollution	Statistics	
Pesticides and pest control	Diseases and cultivation	
Set aside	Salmon and freshwater fisheries	
General agricultural policy	Marine environment	
EC coordination	Research and Development	
Cooperation and marketing	Seals	
Structural support for both	Fisheries protection	
agriculture and fisheries	Liaison with offshore oil industry	
Fish and shellfish farming policy	Fleet structure policy	
Emergencies planning	Marine laboratory	
Livestock products	Freshwater fisheries laboratory	
Hillfarming and other subsidies		
Economic advice and statistical		
services		
Agricultural scientific services		
Research and development		
Statutory work on agricultural and		
horticultural crops		

Central Services

Permanent Secretary
Sir Russell Hillhouse KCB (1)

Deputy Secretary
G R Wilson CB (2)

Principal Establishment Officer	*Principal Finance Officer*	*Head of Division*
C C MacDonald (3)	**Miss E A Mackay (3)**	**E W Ferguson (5)**
(16 Waterloo Place)	*(New St Andrew's House)*	*(Dover House)*

G D Calder (5) *(16 Waterloo Place)* **J A Rennie (5)** **Mrs V MacNiven (5)** *(James Craig Walk)*	**S F Hampson (5)** **L Mosco (5)** **B Naylor (5)** **A J Rushworth (5)** **Vacant (6)** *(all at New St Andrew's House)* **W T Tait (5)** *(St Margaret's House)*	

Personnel Management and Organisation

Personnel management
Personnel development
Management, organisation and industrial relations
Machinery of government of Scotland
Next Steps initiative
Industrial relations
Efficiency unit
Pay, leave and superannuation

Finance

Public expenditure
Accountancy services
Scottish Office Audit Unit
Purchase and supply unit
Finance information systems
Finance services to all Scottish departments

Liaison Division (London)

Liaison between Scottish departments and Whitehall

Director **R S B Gordon (4)** *(James Craig Walk)*	*Director* **Miss E S D Drummond (5)** *(New St Andrew's House)*	*Principal* **D A Stewart (7)**

J Duffy (5)
(Broomhouse Drive)
D Stevenson (5)
R I K White (6)
B V Surridge (6)
(all 3 at James Craig Walk)
A F Harrison (6)

Administrative Services

Scottish Office Computer Services
Telecommunications
Office management
Library services
Travel and subsistence
Management of Scottish Office Estate
Development of accommodation strategy
Physical security matters
Property investment management and disposal
Graphics

Scottish Information Office

Information to the media
Publicity campaigns
Press arrangements for Royal and state visits
Agent for COI in Scotland

Management Group Support

Honours, public appointments
Royal and state visits
Government hospitality
Parliamentary Commissioner for Administration
Women's issues

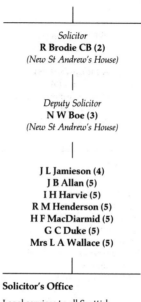

Solicitor
R Brodie CB (2)
(New St Andrew's House)

Deputy Solicitor
N W Boe (3)
(New St Andrew's House)

J L Jamieson (4)
J B Allan (5)
I H Harvie (5)
R M Henderson (5)
H F MacDiarmid (5)
G C Duke (5)
Mrs L A Wallace (5)

Solicitor's Office

Legal services to all Scottish
departments and to certain other
Government departments

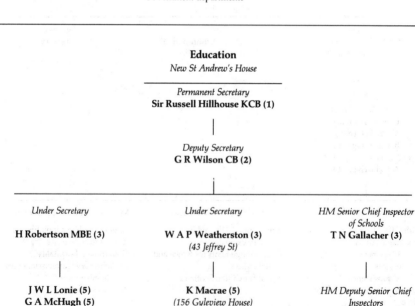

Education
New St Andrew's House

Permanent Secretary
Sir Russell Hillhouse KCB (1)

Deputy Secretary
G R Wilson CB (2)

Under Secretary	*Under Secretary*	*HM Senior Chief Inspector of Schools*
H Robertson MBE (3)	**W A P Weatherston (3)** *(43 Jeffrey St)*	**T N Gallacher (3)**
J W L Lonie (5) **G A McHugh (5)** **D S Henderson (5)**	**K Macrae (5)** *(156 Gyleview House)* **R D Jackson (5)** **Miss M Maclean (5)** *(43 Jeffrey Street)*	*HM Deputy Senior Chief Inspectors* **D W Mack (4) till 4/92** **W T Beveridge (4)**

|

HM Chief Inspectors
W F L Bigwood (5)
H M Stalker (5)
(231 Corstophine Road)
G P D Gordon (5)
(Corunna House)
G H C Donaldson (5)
(Greyfriars House)
D A Osler (5)
J J McDonald (5)
J Howgego (5)
J T Donaldson (5)
A S McGlynn (5)
(above 6 at New St Andrew's House)
A M Rankin (5)

|

Chief Statistician
D Salmond (5)
(43 Jeffrey Street)

Schools	**Formal Post-Schools Education, Arts and Sport**	**HM Inspectorate of Schools**
Schools	Vocational education	Inspection of schools, colleges and other educational institutions
Schools curriculum and examinations	Higher education	Educational needs
Teachers	Further education	National development
	Student awards	Education research and technology
	Education statistics	Educational statistics
	Arts	Management of education and resources
	Broadcasting	
	Sport	
	Heritage matters	
	Gaelic	

Environment

Permanent Secretary
Sir Russell Hillhouse KCB (1)

|

Deputy Secretary
H H Mills (2)

|

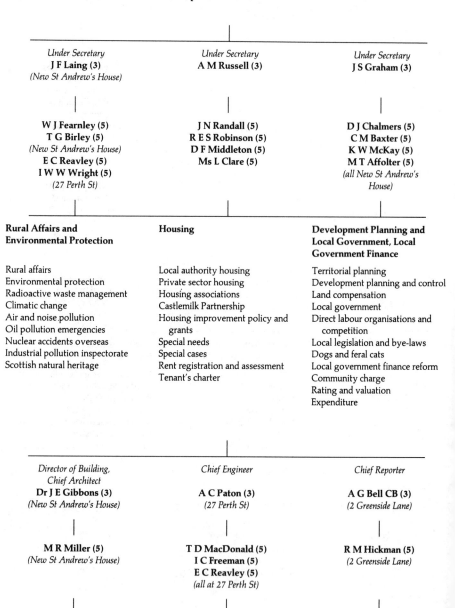

Under Secretary **J F Laing (3)** *(New St Andrew's House)*	*Under Secretary* **A M Russell (3)**	*Under Secretary* **J S Graham (3)**

W J Fearnley (5) **T G Birley (5)** *(New St Andrew's House)* **E C Reavley (5)** **I W W Wright (5)** *(27 Perth St)*	**J N Randall (5)** **R E S Robinson (5)** **D F Middleton (5)** **Ms L Clare (5)**	**D J Chalmers (5)** **C M Baxter (5)** **K W McKay (5)** **M T Affolter (5)** *(all New St Andrew's* *House)*

Rural Affairs and Environmental Protection	**Housing**	**Development Planning and Local Government, Local Government Finance**

Rural affairs
Environmental protection
Radioactive waste management
Climatic change
Air and noise pollution
Oil pollution emergencies
Nuclear accidents overseas
Industrial pollution inspectorate
Scottish natural heritage
	Local authority housing
	Private sector housing
	Housing associations
	Castlemilk Partnership
	Housing improvement policy and
	  grants
	Special needs
	Special cases
	Rent registration and assessment
	Tenant's charter
		Territorial planning
		Development planning and control
		Land compensation
		Local government
		Direct labour organisations and
		  competition
		Local legislation and bye-laws
		Dogs and feral cats
		Local government finance reform
		Community charge
		Rating and valuation
		Expenditure

Director of Building, *Chief Architect* **Dr J E Gibbons (3)** *(New St Andrew's House)*	*Chief Engineer* **A C Paton (3)** *(27 Perth St)*	*Chief Reporter* **A G Bell CB (3)** *(2 Greenside Lane)*

M R Miller (5) *(New St Andrew's House)*	**T D MacDonald (5)** **I C Freeman (5)** **E C Reavley (5)** *(all at 27 Perth St)*	**R M Hickman (5)** *(2 Greenside Lane)*

Building Directorate	**Civil Engineering, Water Services and Environmental Protection**	**Inquiry Reporters**
Education and social work and building	Engineering advice and design of buildings	Conduct of all land use related public local inquiries in Scotland
Building control	Water pollution control, supply and quality	Operation of planning appeals system
Construction industry and procurement policy	Hazardous waste	
Housing	Water engineering	
Police and fire building	Environmental protection	
	Water policy	
	Litter	
	Solid waste policy and legislation	
	Post consumer recycling	

Chief Planner
A Mackenzie (4)
(New St Andrew's House)

Chief Statistician
Dr J R Cuthbert (5)
(New St Andrew's House)

D R Dare (5)
(New St Andrew's House)

Planning Services

Physical planning advice
Whitfield partnership team

Statistical Services

Development of statistical
framework
Career development for
statisticians within the SO
Liaison with CSO

Home and Health

Permanent Secretary
Sir Russell Hillhouse KCB (1)

Deputy Secretary
J Hamill (2)

Under Secretary
D J Essery (3)

Under Secretary
Mrs G M Stewart (3)

Chief Executive
E W Frizell (3)

R H Scott (5)	Mrs M H Brannon (5)	A R Walker (4)
P M Russell (5)	C M A Lugton (5)	J W H Irvine (5)
A M Burnside (5)		J D Gallagher (5)
		N Harvey (6)
		D D Sutherland (6)
		C M Reeves (5)
		L McBain (5)
		(all at Calton House)

Police, Fire, Emergency, Law and General	Criminal Justice, Licensing, Parole and Life Imprisonment	Prison Service
Legal aid	Criminal justice and licensing	Administrative planning and development
Police service	Statistics unit	Operations
Fire service	Criminological research	Personnel
Emergency planning	Parole and life imprisonment	Regime services and supplies
Legal profession		Estates and buildings
Law and general		Research and statistics
Land tenure		Finance and information systems
Electoral and ceremonial matters		Training, planning and development

Chief Executive NHS in Scotland	*Under Secretary*	*Under Secretary*
D G Cruickshank (3)	**D J Belfall (3)**	**N G Campbell (3)**
		(43 Jeffrey St)

Director of Strategic Management	*Chief Scientist*	A Skinner (4)
G A Anderson (4)	**Prof I A D Bouchier CBE (2)**	M J P Cunliffe (5)
		D Wishart (5)
		J W Sinclair (5)

Dr D R Steel (5)	W J Farquhar (5)
M Collier (5)	G Calder (5)
C B Knox (5)	C K McIntosh (5)
(2 Redheughs Rigg)	J T Brown (5)
A J Matheson (5)	N Macleod (5)
H R McCallum (6?)	
W Moyes (5)	
G W Tucker (5)	
G M D Thomson (5)	
Miss I Low (5)	
C J Hickinbotham (5)	
W J Farquar (5)	

NHS in Scotland

Health boards, capital buildings,
   service provision
State hospitals
Health building
Estate surveys
Disposal of NHS land
Supplies and common services
Competitive tendering
Primary health care
Quality of service, service
   committee appeals
Emergency planning
Appointments
Financial management
Manpower and cost monitoring
Economic advice
Information technology services
Personnel
NHS review implementation
Clinical resources and audit

**Health Policy and
Public Health**

Specific diseases, acute services,
   maternity and family planning
   services
Child health
Private health care
Mental health services
Services for disabled
AIDS – education and prevention
Drug and alcohol misuse
Scottish Health Service Advisory
   Council
Pharmaceutical services
Medical and operational research
Superannuation: NHS, teachers,
   local government, fire, police and
   other minor schemes

Social Work Services

Manpower and education
Planning service and practice
   development
Capital programme for local
   authorities
Analysis research and statistics
Oversight recruitment
Deployment of professional staff
Offenders and addictions
Community care
Child care

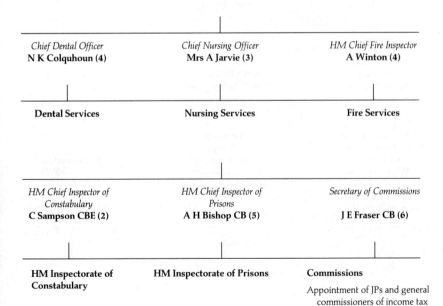

Chief Dental Officer
N K Colquhoun (4)

Chief Nursing Officer
Mrs A Jarvie (3)

HM Chief Fire Inspector
A Winton (4)

Dental Services

Nursing Services

Fire Services

*HM Chief Inspector of
Constabulary*
C Sampson CBE (2)

*HM Chief Inspector of
Prisons*
A H Bishop CB (5)

Secretary of Commissions

J E Fraser CB (6)

**HM Inspectorate of
Constabulary**

HM Inspectorate of Prisons

Commissions

Appointment of JPs and general
   commissioners of income tax
Lieutenancy matters

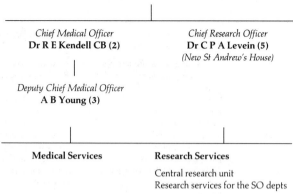

Chief Medical Officer
Dr R E Kendell CB (2)

Chief Research Officer
Dr C P A Levein (5)
(New St Andrew's House)

Deputy Chief Medical Officer
A B Young (3)

Medical Services

Research Services

Central research unit
Research services for the SO depts

Industry

Permanent Secretary
Sir Russell Hillhouse KCB (1)

Deputy Secretary
P Mackay (2)
(New St Andrew's House)

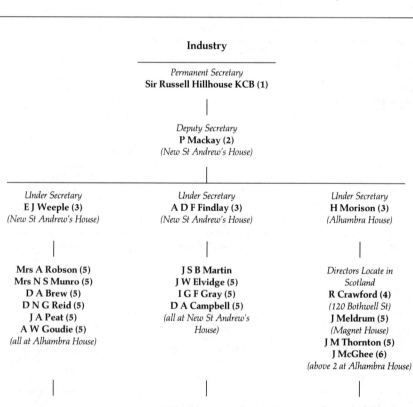

Under Secretary
E J Weeple (3)
(New St Andrew's House)

Under Secretary
A D F Findlay (3)
(New St Andrew's House)

Under Secretary
H Morison (3)
(Alhambra House)

Mrs A Robson (5)
Mrs N S Munro (5)
D A Brew (5)
D N G Reid (5)
J A Peat (5)
A W Goudie (5)
(all at Alhambra House)

J S B Martin
J W Elvidge (5)
I G F Gray (5)
D A Campbell (5)
*(all at New St Andrew's
House)*

*Directors Locate in
Scotland*
R Crawford (4)
(120 Bothwell St)
J Meldrum (5)
(Magnet House)
J M Thornton (5)
J McGhee (6)
(above 2 at Alhambra House)

Urban Policy, European Funds, New Towns, Economics and Statistics	**Electricity, Employment and Energy, Highland and Tourism, Transport and Local Roads**	**Industrial Expansion, Steel and Shipbuilding**
New towns	Electricity, energy, North Sea oil,	Regional policy, enterprise,
Urban policy and programme	and gas, coal, nuclear energy,	development grants
European funds	energy efficiency	Industrial policy and technology
Economics and statistics	Scottish enterprise, training and	Steel and shipbuilding
	employment	Export promotion, monitoring and
	Highlands and Islands and tourism	common services
	Transport: bus, ferry, ports and	Locate in Scotland
	waterways, airports, rail, roads,	Regional enterprise grants for
	freight	innovation

Director of Roads,
Chief Road Engineer
J A L Dawson (3)

G S Marshall (5)
J Innes (5)
R S T MacEwan (5)
(all at New St Andrew's House)

Roads Directorate

Trunk roads policy and
   programme, legislation, traffic
   regulations, local roads, road
   safety
Schemes and territorial
Motorway and trunk road design
   and construction
Maintenance, minor works and
   speed limits
Planning application
Engineering and procurement
Technical standards, contracts,
   planning applications, bridges,
   traffic signs, lighting,
   landscaping

Scottish Office Addresses

Alhambra House
45 Waterloo Street
Glasgow G2 6AT
Tel 041-248 4774
Fax 041-248 5404

120 Bothwell Street
Glasgow G2 7BT
Tel 041-248 2700
Fax 041-221 3217

Broomhouse Drive
Edinburgh EH11 3XD
Tel 031-244 8119
Fax 031-244 8176

Calton House
5 Redheughs Rigg
Edinburgh EH12 9HW
Tel 031-244 8745
Fax 031-244 8774

231 Corstophine Road
Edinburgh EH12 0PQ
Tel 031-316 4639
Fax 031-334 3047

Corunna House
29 Cadogan Street
Glasgow G2 7LP
Tel 041-204 1220
Fax 041-248 5736

East Craigs
Edinburgh EH12 8NJ
Tel 031-244 8843
Fax 031-244 8940

Greyfriars House
Gallowgate
Aberdeen AB9 1UE
Tel 0224 642544
Fax 0224 625370

156 Gyleview House
3 Redheughs Rigg
South Gyle
Edinburgh EH12 9HH
Tel 031-244 5819
Fax 031-244 5887

James Craig Walk
Edinburgh EH1 3BA
Tel 031-556 8400
Fax 031-244 3891

43 Jeffrey Street
Edinburgh EH1 1DN
Tel 031-556 8400
Fax 031-244 5387

New St Andrew's House
Edinburgh EH1 3SY
Tel 031-556 8400
Fax 031-244 4785

Pentland House
47 Robb's Loan
Edinburgh EH14 1TW
Tel 031-556 8400
Fax 031-244 6001/2/3

27 Perth Street
Edinburgh EH3 5RB
Tel 031-556 8400
Fax 031-244 2903

Robert Stevenson House
2 Greenside Place
Edinburgh EH1 3AH
Tel 031-556 8400
Fax 031-244 5680

St Margaret's House
Edinburgh EH8 7TG
Tel 031-556 8400
Fax 031-244 3334

PO Box 101
Victoria Road
Aberdeen AB9 8DB
Tel 0224 876544
Fax 0224 879156

Serious Fraud Office

Founded	1987
Status	Non-ministerial department
Responsible to	Attorney General
Responsibilities	Investigation and prosecution of cases involving serious and complex fraud in England, Wales and Northern Ireland

Serious Fraud Office

Elm House, 10–16 Elm Street, London WC1X 0BJ
Tel 071-239 7272   Fax 071-837 1689

Minister

Attorney General
**The Rt Hon Sir Nicholas
Lyell QC MP**
(for details of his office
see Law Officers' Department)

Officials

Director of the Serious Fraud Office
G W Staple (2)

|

Personal Secretary
Mrs A Wright
071-239 7272

|

*Deputy Director of the Serious Fraud
Office*
J A Knox (3)

Departmental Overview

Civil Servants		Department	Minister
Grade 2	**Grade 3**		
G W Staple	J A Knox	Lawyers and Accountants	Attorney General
	J Graham (5)	Establishment and Finance	Attorney General

Civil Servants and Departments

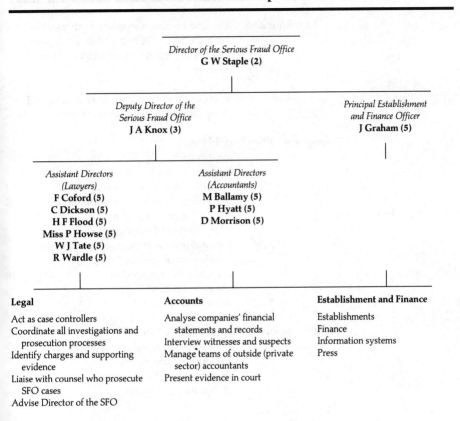

Director of the Serious Fraud Office
G W Staple (2)

Deputy Director of the
Serious Fraud Office
J A Knox (3)

Principal Establishment
and Finance Officer
J Graham (5)

Assistant Directors
(Lawyers)
**F Coford (5)
C Dickson (5)
H F Flood (5)
Miss P Howse (5)
W J Tate (5)
R Wardle (5)**

Assistant Directors
(Accountants)
**M Ballamy (5)
P Hyatt (5)
D Morrison (5)**

Legal

Act as case controllers
Coordinate all investigations and
  prosecution processes
Identify charges and supporting
  evidence
Liaise with counsel who prosecute
  SFO cases
Advise Director of the SFO

Accounts

Analyse companies' financial
  statements and records
Interview witnesses and suspects
Manage teams of outside (private
  sector) accountants
Present evidence in court

Establishment and Finance

Establishments
Finance
Information systems
Press

Department of Social Security

Founded	The DSS became a separate department in 1988. Between 1968 and 1988 it had been part of the Department of Health and Social Security
Ministers	secretary of state, one minister of state and three parliamentary under secretaries of state
Responsibilities	child benefit family credit income support industrial injuries scheme (payment of benefits, collection of contributions) legal aid (assessment of means) lone parents and maintenance National Insurance (payment of benefits, collection of contributions) non-contributory benefits one parent benefit social fund
Executive agencies	Social Security Benefits Agency SS Child Support Agency (1993) SS Contributions Agency SS Information Technology Services Agency SS Resettlement Agency

Department of Social Security

Richmond House, 79 Whitehall, London SW1A 2NS
Tel 071-210 5664   Fax 071-210 5523
All staff are based at Richmond House unless otherwise indicated.
For other addresses and telephone numbers see the end of this section.

Ministers

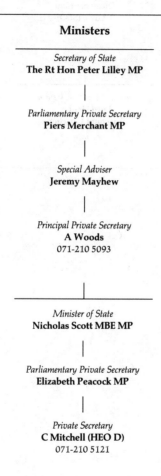

Secretary of State
The Rt Hon Peter Lilley MP

Parliamentary Private Secretary
Piers Merchant MP

Special Adviser
Jeremy Mayhew

Principal Private Secretary
A Woods
071-210 5093

Minister of State
Nicholas Scott MBE MP

Parliamentary Private Secretary
Elizabeth Peacock MP

Private Secretary
C Mitchell (HEO D)
071-210 5121

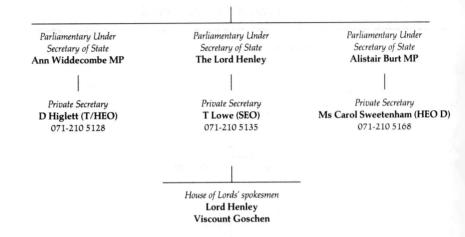

Parliamentary Under Secretary of State **Ann Widdecombe MP**	Parliamentary Under Secretary of State **The Lord Henley**	Parliamentary Under Secretary of State **Alistair Burt MP**
Private Secretary **D Higlett (T/HEO)** 071-210 5128	Private Secretary **T Lowe (SEO)** 071-210 5135	Private Secretary **Ms Carol Sweetenham (HEO D)** 071-210 5168

House of Lords' spokesmen
Lord Henley
Viscount Goschen

Ministerial Responsibilities

Peter Lilley   overall responsibility for the department

Nicholas Scott   disability
disablement benefits
Independent Living Fund
industrial injuries benefit
Social Fund
social security policy

Ann Widdecombe   equal treatment
ministerial group voluntary sector
National Insurance
pensions
Resettlement Agency
widows benefits

The Lord Henley   Citizen's Charter
Contributions Agency
departmental purchasing/value for money
deregulation
fraud and overpayment
'green' issues and energy efficiency
incapacity benefits (including sickness
    benefits)
inner cities
IT Services Agency
maternity benefits
methods of payment
ministerial group on crime prevention
unemployment benefit
vaccine damage
war pensions
departmental business in the House of Lords

Alistair Burt   adjudication
Benefits Agency
child benefit
Child Support Agency
community charge/council tax benefit
equal opportunities in the department
family credit
housing benefit
income support
low incomes
ministerial group on women's issues

Departptmental Overview

Civil Servants			Department	Minister
Grade 1	*Grade 2*	*Grade 3*		
Sir Michael Partridge		S Reardon (5)	Information Division	

Social Security Policy Group

Sir Michael Partridge	R A Birch	B Walmsley	Division A (Sick/Disabled/ Maternity Benefits	N Scott Ld Henley
		Miss M Pierson	Division B (Unemployment Benefit/ Lone Parents and Maintenance)	Ld Henley A Burt
		D J Clark	Division C (National Insurance, Pensions	A Widdecombe
		B J Ellis	Division D (Income Support, Housing Benefit)	A Burt

Resource Management Policy

Sir Michael Partridge	B Gilmore	Miss A Perkins	Personnel and Management Services	
		J Tross	Finance Division	
		R B Brown	Corporate Management Division	
		D Stanton	Analytical Services Division	

Solicitor's Office

Sir Michael Partridge	P K J Thompson	Mrs G S Kerrigan	Division A	
		P C Nilsson	Division B	
		A D Roberts	Division C	

Civil Servants and Departments

Permanent Secretary
Sir Michael Partridge KCB (1)

Private Secretary
Mrs V E Andrews (HEO)
Tel 071-210 5545

Head of Information
S Reardon (5)

Information Division

Media liaison
Publicity material
Publicity campaigns
Design and language of forms, draft
    letters and circulars

Social Security Policy Group

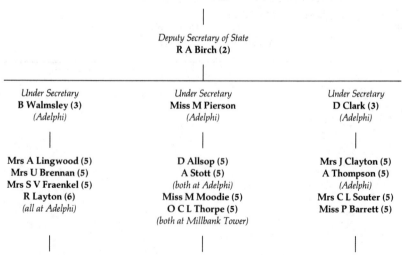

Permanent Secretary
Sir Michael Partridge KCB (1)

Deputy Secretary of State
R A Birch (2)

Under Secretary **B Walmsley (3)** *(Adelphi)*	*Under Secretary* **Miss M Pierson** *(Adelphi)*	*Under Secretary* **D Clark (3)** *(Adelphi)*
Mrs A Lingwood (5) **Mrs U Brennan (5)** **Mrs S V Fraenkel (5)** **R Layton (6)** *(all at Adelphi)*	**D Allsop (5)** **A Stott (5)** *(both at Adelphi)* **Miss M Moodie (5)** **O C L Thorpe (5)** *(both at Millbank Tower)*	**Mrs J Clayton (5)** **A Thompson (5)** *(Adelphi)* **Mrs C L Souter (5)** **Miss P Barrett (5)**

Division A (Sick/Disabled/Maternity Benefits)	Division B (Unemployment Benefit)	Division C (National Insurance, Pensions)
Cash benefits for sick and disabled people includes: war pensions industrial injuries sickness benefit invalidity benefit maternity attendance and mobility vaccine damage invalid care statutory sick pay disability allowance disability employment credit SS policy on claims and payments, duplication of payments, over-payments, disclosure of information Social fund	Family credits Incentives to work/earn more Unemployment and poverty traps Family support issues Tax/benefit interaction Free welfare foods Help with NHS charges and hospital fares SS reforms Child benefit Guardian's allowance Lone parents Residual issues of single payments Direct payments of benefit for fuel costs International aspects of SS Maintenance Adjudication appeals Sanction for non-cooperation IT development Personnel issues Telecommunications	National insurance contributions Retirement pensions Concessions for elderly people Widows' benefits Christmas bonus Uprating Liaison and focal point equal treatment issues Occupational pensions Personal pensions Contracting-out Equal treatment

Under Secretary
B Ellis (3)
(Adelphi)

P Tansley (5)
M E Street (5)
I Williams (5)
A Herscovitch (5)
(all at the Adelphi)

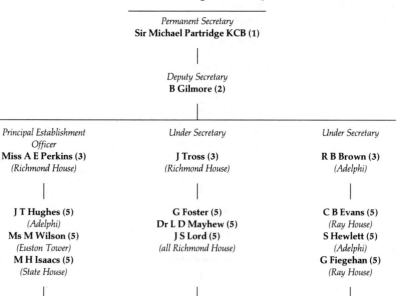

**Division D
(Income Support, Housing
Benefit)**

Income support on:
  education
  people from abroad
  21-HR rule
Dependency
Children and young persons
  residential care
Nursing homes and hostels
Housing costs
Housing benefit
Residential care
Local government finance

Resource Management Policy

Permanent Secretary
Sir Michael Partridge KCB (1)

Deputy Secretary
B Gilmore (2)

Principal Establishment Officer **Miss A E Perkins (3)** *(Richmond House)*	*Under Secretary* **J Tross (3)** *(Richmond House)*	*Under Secretary* **R B Brown (3)** *(Adelphi)*
J T Hughes (5) *(Adelphi)* **Ms M Wilson (5)** *(Euston Tower)* **M H Isaacs (5)** *(State House)*	**G Foster (5)** **Dr L D Mayhew (5)** **J S Lord (5)** *(all Richmond House)*	**C B Evans (5)** *(Ray House)* **S Hewlett (5)** *(Adelphi)* **G Fiegehan (5)** *(Ray House)*

Personnel and Management	Finance Division	Corporate Management Division
Manpower planning	Financial aspects of SS benefit	Agency implementation in DSS
Personnel management	Liaison with HM Treasury and	Manpower planning
Strategic management	Government Actuary's Dept	Liaison with agencies
HQ running costs, budgets and	Investment appraisal	Corporate planning
management accounts	Financial aspects of departmental	Information systems strategy
Efficiency issues	administration policy	Administrative resource
Industrial relations	Estimates, vote and fund accounts	management systems
Whitley matters	Budgetary control	Accommodation policy
Pay and allowance policy	Internal audit	Purchasing and supply
Misconduct and discipline		O & M
Health matters		Staff inspection
Retirement policy		Efficiencies scrutinies
Establishment procedures		Consultancies
Assaults on staff		Staff suggestions
Staff welfare		Distribution services
Security		Travel section
Emergency and home defence		Review of DSS, HQ role, functions
planning		and organisation
Parliamentary Commissioner for		
Administration		
Honours		

Director
D Stanton (3)
(Adelphi)

G C Jones (5)
(Newcastle Central Office)
Dr L D Mayhew (5)
J M Ball (5)
G Harris (5)
(all at Adelphi)

Analytical Services Division

Economic advice
Operational research
Social security research
Statistics

Solicitor's Office

Permanent Secretary
Sir Michael Partridge KCB (1)

Solicitor
P K J Thompson (2)
(Richmond House)

Principal Assistant Solicitor	*Proceedings Operational Director*	*Principal Assistant Solicitor*
Mrs G S Kerrigan (3)	**P C Nilsson (3)**	**A D Roberts (3)**
(New Court)	*(New Court)*	*(New Court)*
Mrs G Massiah (5)	**J F McCleary (5)**	**Miss A Brett-Holt (5)**
Mrs M Astbury (5)	**D Curtis (5)**	**P Milledge (5)**
J H Swainson (5)	**R S Powell (5)**	**Miss A Windsor (5)**
D P Dunleavy (5)	**G G Blake (5)**	**R G S Aitken (5)**
(all at New Court)	*(all at New Court)*	**J P Canlin (5)**
		(all at New Court)

Division A	**Division B**	**Division C**
Advice and services on SS policy	Civil and criminal proceedings	Health and personal social services
War pensions	Industrial relations	EC and international matters
Occupational and personal pensions	Establishment matters	
	Legal services to Chief Adjudication Officer	

Department of Social Security Addresses

For fax numbers, contact the switchboard at the relevant location

Adelphi
1–11 John Adam Street
London WC2N 6HT
Tel 071-962 8000

Euston Tower
286 Euston Road
London NW1 3DN
Tel 071-388 1188

Friars House
157–168 Blackfriars Road
London SE1 8EU
Tel 071-972 2000

Millbank Tower
21–24 Millbank
London SW1P 4QU
Tel 071-217 3000

Newcastle Central Office
Newcastle upon Tyne NE9B 1YX
Tel 091-213 5000

New Court
48 Carey Street
London WC2 2LS
Tel 071-831 6111

Portland Court
158–176 Great Portland Street
London W1N 5TB
Tel 071-872 9302

Ray House
6 St Andrew Street
London EC4A 3AD
Tel 071-353 2090

State House
High Holborn
London WC1R 4SX
Tel 071-831 2525

Department of Trade and Industry

Founded	As the Board of Trade in 1786, as Department of Trade and Industry in 1970, split in 1974 and reconstituted in 1983
Ministers	President of the Board of Trade/secretary of state; three ministers of state and three parliamentary under secretaries
Responsibilities	company legislation competition policy consumer protection (including relations with the Office of Fair Trading, the Monopolies and Mergers Commission and OFTEL) deregulation policy energy industrial competitiveness industry and commerce policy information and manufacturing technology international trade policy promotion of UK exports regional development and inward investment regulation of insurance industry science and technology research and development policy small firms sponsorship role for sectors where DTI has governmental responsibility
Executive agencies	Accounts Services Agency Companies House Insolvency Service Laboratory of the Government Chemist National Engineering Laboratory National Physical Laboratory National Weights and Measures Laboratory Patent Office Radiocommunications Agency Warren Spring Laboratory

The DTI is still completing its recent reorganisation and, as the Whitehall Companion goes to press, some structures, functions, staff and locations are still unclear. Although we have provided as much up-to-date information as is available we suggest that where location etc unclear, enquirers contact the main Ashdown House telephone number and address in the first instance (see over page)

Department of Trade and Industry

Ashdown House, 123 Victoria Street, London SW1E 6RB
Tel 071-215 5000   Fax 071-828 3258
All personnel are based at Ashdown House unless otherwise indicated.
For other addresses and telephone numbers see the end of this section.

Ministers

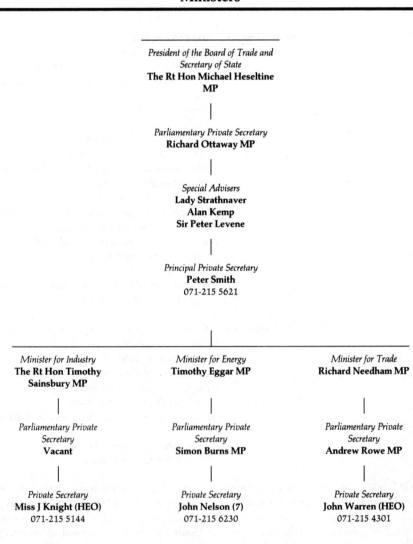

*President of the Board of Trade and
Secretary of State*
**The Rt Hon Michael Heseltine
MP**

Parliamentary Private Secretary
Richard Ottaway MP

Special Advisers
**Lady Strathnaver
Alan Kemp
Sir Peter Levene**

Principal Private Secretary
Peter Smith
071-215 5621

Minister for Industry **The Rt Hon Timothy Sainsbury MP**	*Minister for Energy* **Timothy Eggar MP**	*Minister for Trade* **Richard Needham MP**
Parliamentary Private Secretary **Vacant**	*Parliamentary Private Secretary* **Simon Burns MP**	*Parliamentary Private Secretary* **Andrew Rowe MP**
Private Secretary **Miss J Knight (HEO)** 071-215 5144	*Private Secretary* **John Nelson (7)** 071-215 6230	*Private Secretary* **John Warren (HEO)** 071-215 4301

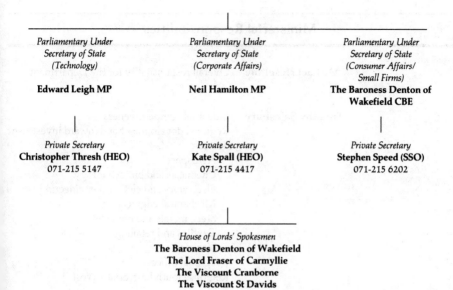

Parliamentary Under	*Parliamentary Under*	*Parliamentary Under*
Secretary of State	*Secretary of State*	*Secretary of State*
(Technology)	*(Corporate Affairs)*	*(Consumer Affairs/*
		Small Firms)
Edward Leigh MP	**Neil Hamilton MP**	**The Baroness Denton of**
		Wakefield CBE

Private Secretary	*Private Secretary*	*Private Secretary*
Christopher Thresh (HEO)	**Kate Spall (HEO)**	**Stephen Speed (SSO)**
071-215 5147	071-215 4417	071-215 6202

House of Lords' Spokesmen
The Baroness Denton of Wakefield
The Lord Fraser of Carmyllie
The Viscount Cranborne
The Viscount St Davids

Ministerial Responsibilities

Michael Heseltine   Overall responsibility for the Department

Timothy Sainsbury   Industrial competitiveness
Regional development and inward investment
Sectors:
   Aerospace
   Chemicals and biotechnology
   Electronics and electrical engineering
   Mechanical engineering
   Steel, metals and minerals
   Textiles and retailing
   Vehicles
8 regional offices
Regions: South East, South West

Timothy Eggar   Atomic energy
Coal
Electricity
Environment
International energy unit
Offshore supplies industry
Oil and gas
Common services
Region: North East

Richard Needham   Europe
Export Credits Guarantee Department
International trade policy
Joint Directorate
Overseas trade
Projects and exports policy
Region: West Midlands

Edward Leigh   British National Space Centre
Industrial research establishments
Information and manufacturing technology
Patent Office
Radiocommunications Agency
Research and technology policy
Telecommunications and posts
Supports Mr Needham on trade with tropical
Africa, Indian sub-continent and South
America
Departmental spokesman in Commons on
matters for which Baroness Denton is
responsible
Regions: East, East Midlands

Neil Hamilton   Companies
Companies House Agency
Competition policy
Deregulation unit
Insolvency Service Agency
Insurance
Investigations
National Weights and Measures Laboratory
Solicitors
Region: North West

The Baroness Denton of   Consumer affairs
Wakefield   Enterprise initiative
Public appointments
Small firms policy
Supports Mr Sainsbury on regional
development and inward investment
Departmental spokesman in the House of
Lords
Region: Yorkshire and Humberside

Departmental Overview

Civil Servants			Department	Minister
Grade 1	*Grade 2*	*Grade 3*		

Trade Policy and Export Promotion

Sir Peter Gregson	C W Roberts	R O Miles*	Joint Directorate*	R Needham
		D T Hall	Projects and Exports Policy	R Needham
		R J Meadway	Overseas Trade 2	R Needham
		P G F Bryant	Overseas Trade 3	R Needham
		M M Baker	Overseas Trade 4	R Needham
		N R Thornton	Europe	R Needham
		J Cooke	International Trade Policy	R Needham

Corporate and Consumer Affairs

Sir Peter Gregson	C Henderson	Dr J P Spencer	Insurance	N Hamilton
		A C Russell	Companies	N Hamilton
		Dr Catherine Bell	Competition Policy	N Hamilton
		Dr Catherine Bell	Deregulation Unit	N Hamilton
		C S Kerse	Consumer Affairs	Lady Denton

Science and Technology

Sir Peter Gregson	Dr G Robinson	Dr C Hicks	Research and Technology Policy	E Leigh
		Dr K C Shotton	Information and Manufacturing Technology	E Leigh
		A Pryor	British National Space Centre	E Leigh
		Dr W D Evans	Environment	T Eggar

Departmental Overview

Civil Servants			Department	Minister
Grade 1	*Grade 2*	*Grade 3*		

Regional and Small Firms

Sir Peter Gregson	R Williams	P M S Corley	Regional Development and Inward Investment	T Sainsbury
		Mrs S E Brown	Enterprise Initiative	Lady Denton
		Mrs S E Brown	Small Firms	Lady Denton
		Regional Organisation		
		Mrs P A Denham	North East	T Sainsbury
		J H Pownall	North West	T Sainsbury
		E Wright	Yorkshire and Humberside	T Sainsbury
		R M Anderson (5)	East Midlands	T Sainsbury
		S G Linstead	West Midlands	T Sainsbury
		J Bowder (5)	South West	T Sainsbury
		I M Jones (5)	South East	T Sainsbury
		W J Hall (5)	East	T Sainsbury

Industry 1

Sir Peter Gregson	A J Lane	T Muir	Textiles and Retailing	T Sainsbury
		P S Salvidge	Telecommunications and Posts	E Leigh

Industry 2

Sir Peter Gregson	Alastair Macdonald	E Finer	Chemicals and Biotechnology	T Sainsbury
		R Simpson	Steels, Metals and Minerals	T Sainsbury
		M Stanley	Vehicles	T Sainsbury
		A Nieduszynski	Aerospace	T Sainsbury
		R M Rumbelow	Electronics and Electrical Engineering	T Sainsbury
		R M Rumbelow	Mechanical Engineering	T Sainsbury

Industrial Competitiveness

Sir Peter Gregson		Dr R Dobbie	Industrial Competitiveness	T Sainsbury

Departmental Overview

Civil Servants			Department	Minister
Grade 1	*Grade 2*	*Grade 3*		

Establishment and Finance

Sir Peter Gregson	A C Hutton	M K O'Shea	Finance and Resource Management	T Eggar
		Miss J M Caines (4)	Information Division	
		A Elkington (5)	Internal Audit	
		A Titchener	Personnel	T Eggar
		Dr F R Heath-coate	Services Management	T Eggar
		D Coates	Economics and Statistics	T Eggar

Solicitors' Office

Sir Peter Gregson	G A Hosker (until October 1992 then A H Hammond)	H V B Brown	Investigations Division	N Hamilton
		J R Woolman	Solicitors Division B	
		J M Stanley	Solicitors Division C	
		P H Bovey	Solicitors Division D	
		D E J Nissen	Solicitors Division E	

Energy

Sir Peter Gregson	R J Priddle	Dr T E H Walker	Atomic Energy	T Eggar
		W I MacIntyre	Coal	T Eggar
		C C Wilcock	Electricity	T Eggar
		D R Davis	Oil and Gas	T Eggar
		J E d'Ancona	Offshore Supplies	T Eggar
		S W Fremantle (4)	International Energy Unit	T Eggar
	Professor Sir Richard Norman		Chief Scientific Adviser	T Eggar

* a joint DTI/FCO Department

Civil Servants and Departments

Joint Directorate, Kingsgate House

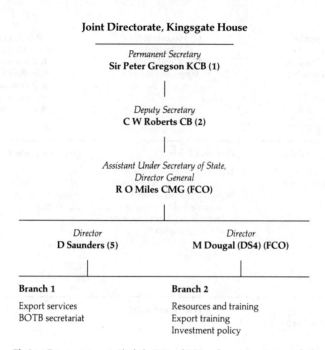

Permanent Secretary
Sir Peter Gregson KCB (1)

Deputy Secretary
C W Roberts CB (2)

*Assistant Under Secretary of State,
Director General*
R O Miles CMG (FCO)

| *Director*
D Saunders (5) | *Director*
M Dougal (DS4) (FCO) |

Branch 1

Export services
BOTB secretariat

Branch 2

Resources and training
Export training
Investment policy

The Joint Directorate is part of both the DTI and FCO and reports to ministers in both

Trade Policy and Export Promotion

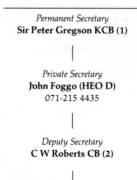

Permanent Secretary
Sir Peter Gregson KCB (1)

Private Secretary
John Foggo (HEO D)
071-215 4435

Deputy Secretary
C W Roberts CB (2)

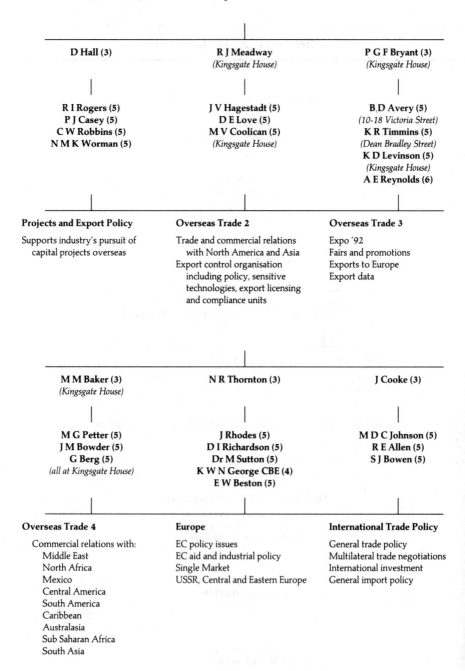

D Hall (3)	R J Meadway	P G F Bryant (3)
	(Kingsgate House)	*(Kingsgate House)*

R I Rogers (5)	J V Hagestadt (5)	B D Avery (5)
P J Casey (5)	D E Love (5)	*(10-18 Victoria Street)*
C W Robbins (5)	M V Coolican (5)	K R Timmins (5)
N M K Worman (5)	*(Kingsgate House)*	*(Dean Bradley Street)*
		K D Levinson (5)
		(Kingsgate House)
		A E Reynolds (6)

Projects and Export Policy	**Overseas Trade 2**	**Overseas Trade 3**
Supports industry's pursuit of capital projects overseas	Trade and commercial relations with North America and Asia Export control organisation including policy, sensitive technologies, export licensing and compliance units	Expo '92 Fairs and promotions Exports to Europe Export data

M M Baker (3)	N R Thornton (3)	J Cooke (3)
(Kingsgate House)		

M G Petter (5)	J Rhodes (5)	M D C Johnson (5)
J M Bowder (5)	D I Richardson (5)	R E Allen (5)
G Berg (5)	Dr M Sutton (5)	S J Bowen (5)
(all at Kingsgate House)	K W N George CBE (4)	
	E W Beston (5)	

Overseas Trade 4	**Europe**	**International Trade Policy**
Commercial relations with: Middle East North Africa Mexico Central America South America Caribbean Australasia Sub Saharan Africa South Asia	EC policy issues EC aid and industrial policy Single Market USSR, Central and Eastern Europe	General trade policy Multilateral trade negotiations International investment General import policy

Corporate and Consumer Affairs

Permanent Secretary
Sir Peter Gregson KCB (1)

Deputy Secretary
C Henderson (2)*

J P Spencer (3)

A C Russell (3)**
(10-18 Victoria Street)

Ms S Seymour (5)
M G Roberts (5)
Miss A Lambert (5)
Miss V Evans (5)

C W Johnston (5)
M J C Butcher (5)
J M Healey (5)
F C Jenkins (5)
(all at 10-18 Victoria Street)

Insurance

Insurance companies
Lloyds
Life and specialist re-insurance
Annual returns regulations
Divisional training
EC insurance
International bodies
Financial Services Act
General policy
Public complaints and enquiries
Divisional administration

Companies

Boards and directors
Company legislation
European laws
Barriers to takeovers
Company accounting and
  disclosures
Accounting standards

Dr Catherine Bell (3)

Dr Catherine Bell (3)

C S Kerse (3)
(10-18 Victoria Street)

J H M Alty (5)
G C Riggs (5)
C Bridge(5)
Mrs M Bloom (5)

Mrs G Allitson (5)
R Watson (5)

M D Oldham (5)
M A R Lunn (5)
D W Hellings (5)
D Jones (5)
(all at 10-18 Victoria Street)

Competitive Policy	Deregulation Unit	Consumer Affairs
Mergers control	New and existing requirements	Trading standards administration
Monopolies		Consumer credit and hire
Restrictive trade practices		Estate agency
International and EC policy		Weights and measures
Privatisation		Consumer bodies
Competition		Trade Descriptions Act 1968
Energy and water		Advertising standards
Pricing		Hallmarking standards
Citizen's Charter		Consumers' interests
Competition and Service (Utilities)		International consumer protection
Bill		Safety

*Mr Henderson chairs Steering Board for the Insolvency Agency Service
**Mr Russell chairs Steering Board for the Companies House Agency

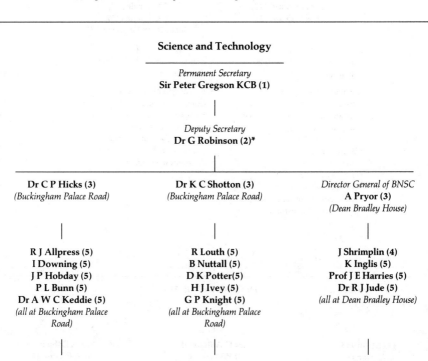

Science and Technology

Permanent Secretary
Sir Peter Gregson KCB (1)

Deputy Secretary
Dr G Robinson (2)*

Dr C P Hicks (3)	**Dr K C Shotton (3)**	*Director General of BNSC*
(Buckingham Palace Road)	*(Buckingham Palace Road)*	**A Pryor (3)**
		(Dean Bradley House)

R J Allpress (5)	**R Louth (5)**	**J Shrimplin (4)**
I Downing (5)	**B Nuttall (5)**	**K Inglis (5)**
J P Hobday (5)	**D K Potter(5)**	**Prof J E Harries (5)**
P L Bunn (5)	**H J Ivey (5)**	**Dr R J Jude (5)**
Dr A W C Keddie (5)	**G P Knight (5)**	*(all at Dean Bradley House)*
(all at Buckingham Palace Road)	*(all at Buckingham Palace Road)*	

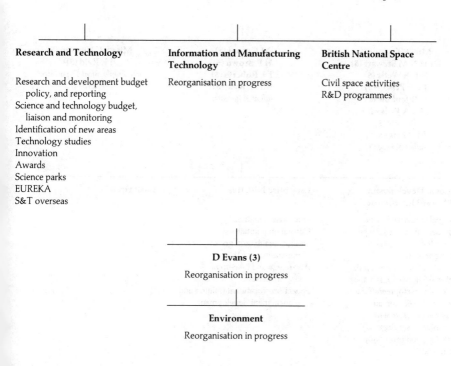

Research and Technology

Research and development budget
  policy, and reporting
Science and technology budget,
  liaison and monitoring
Identification of new areas
Technology studies
Innovation
Awards
Science parks
EUREKA
S&T overseas

**Information and Manufacturing
Technology**

Reorganisation in progress

**British National Space
Centre**

Civil space activities
R&D programmes

D Evans (3)

Reorganisation in progress

Environment

Reorganisation in progress

*Dr Robinson chairs Steering Board for the Patent Office

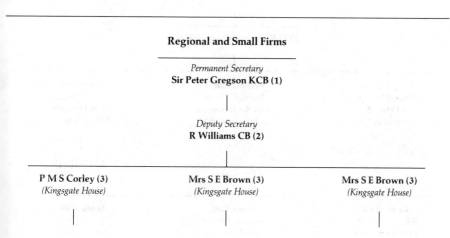

Regional and Small Firms

Permanent Secretary
Sir Peter Gregson KCB (1)

Deputy Secretary
R Williams CB (2)

P M S Corley (3)
(Kingsgate House)

Mrs S E Brown (3)
(Kingsgate House)

Mrs S E Brown (3)
(Kingsgate House)

Mrs A Taylor (5)
Dr H N M Stewart (5)
R H S Wells (5)
J C S Prison (5)
C R Jenkins (3)
Mrs A Wilks (5)
K Holt (5)
M P Briggs (6)
(all at Kingsgate)

M Garrod (5)
H P Brown (5)
T L Roberts (5)
Mrs E Ryle (5)
(all at Kingsgate)

Miss S C Newton (5)
J R Reid (5)
*(c/o Employment Department
Moorfoot)*

**Regional Development
and Inward Investment**

Regional industrial policy
Regional Enterprise Grants
English Industrial Estates
  Corporation
EC regional policy and funds
Regional Selective Assistance
Regional Development Grants
Invest in Britain Bureau
Industrial development
Accountancy services
Marketing and promotion of
  England

Enterprise Initiative

Enterprise Initiatives
Consultancy Initiatives
Design, quality and good
  purchasing practice
Awareness and take-up of
  opportunities
Education, vocational training and
  management development

Small Firms

DTI Regional Organisation

East
Regional Director
W J Hall (5)
(Cambridge office)

East Midlands
Regional Director
R M Anderson (5)
(Nottingham office)

North East
Regional Director
Mrs P A Denham (3)
(Newcastle office)

A W Dell (5)

North West
Regional Director
J H Pownall (3)
(Manchester office)

South East
Regional Director
I M Jones (5)
(Bridge Place)

South West
Regional Director
J Bowder (5)
(Bristol office)

J K Chapman (5)
(Liverpool office)

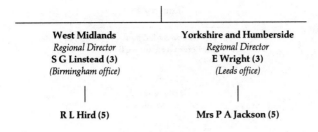

West Midlands	Yorkshire and Humberside
Regional Director	*Regional Director*
S G Linstead (3)	**E Wright (3)**
(Birmingham office)	*(Leeds office)*

R L Hird (5)	**Mrs P A Jackson (5)**

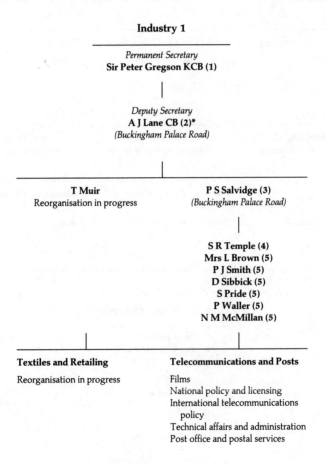

Industry 1

Permanent Secretary
Sir Peter Gregson KCB (1)

Deputy Secretary
A J Lane CB (2)*
(Buckingham Palace Road)

T Muir	**P S Salvidge (3)**
Reorganisation in progress	*(Buckingham Palace Road)*

S R Temple (4)
Mrs L Brown (5)
P J Smith (5)
D Sibbick (5)
S Pride (5)
P Waller (5)
N M McMillan (5)

Textiles and Retailing	**Telecommunications and Posts**
Reorganisation in progress	Films
	National policy and licensing
	International telecommunications policy
	Technical affairs and administration
	Post office and postal services

*Mr Lane chairs Steering Board for the National Physical Laboratory, Warren Spring Laboratory, Laboratory of the Government Chemist, National Engineering Laboratory, National Weights and Measures Laboratory and the Radiocommunications Agency

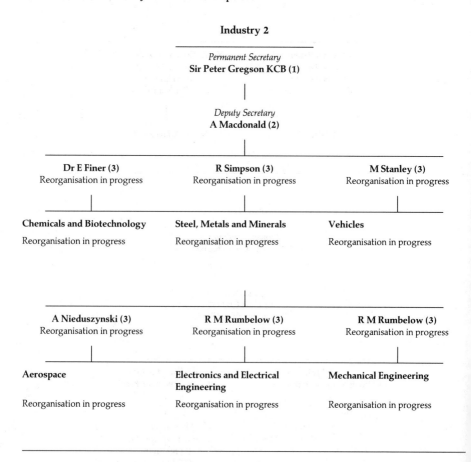

Industry 2

Permanent Secretary
Sir Peter Gregson KCB (1)

Deputy Secretary
A Macdonald (2)

| **Dr E Finer (3)** | **R Simpson (3)** | **M Stanley (3)** |
| Reorganisation in progress | Reorganisation in progress | Reorganisation in progress |

Chemicals and Biotechnology | **Steel, Metals and Minerals** | **Vehicles**

Reorganisation in progress | Reorganisation in progress | Reorganisation in progress

| **A Nieduszynski (3)** | **R M Rumbelow (3)** | **R M Rumbelow (3)** |
| Reorganisation in progress | Reorganisation in progress | Reorganisation in progress |

Aerospace | **Electronics and Electrical Engineering** | **Mechanical Engineering**

Reorganisation in progress | Reorganisation in progress | Reorganisation in progress

Industrial Competitiveness

Permanent Secretary
Sir Peter Gregson KCB (1)

Dr R Dobbie (3)

M Gibson (5)
G Dart (5)
(three above at Buckingham Palace Road)

Industrial Competitiveness

Responsible for ensuring that
government policies, both of the
DTI and other departments, are
designed and implemented with
full regard to the importance of
making UK industry more
competitive at home and abroad
Briefs ministers on general
industrial policies and on the
policies of other government
departments
Maintains a dialogue with national
organisations on these issues

Establishment and Finance

Permanent Secretary
Sir Peter Gregson KCB (1)

*Principal Establishment and
Finance Officer*
A C Hutton (2)

| **M K O'Shea (3)*** | *Director of Information*
Miss J Caines (4)
S Lyle-Smythe (5) | *Head of Internal Audit*
A C Elkington (5)
(Buckingham Palace Road) |

W Stow (5)
D Smith (5)

| inance and Resource
Management | Information | **Internal Audit** |

inancial management
accounts

Press
Promotions
Publicity
Publications
Literature
Single Market Campaign

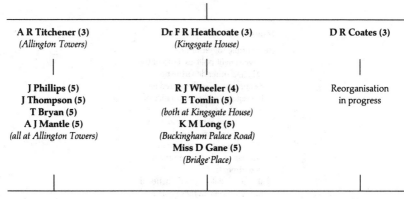

| A R Titchener (3) | Dr F R Heathcoate (3) | D R Coates (3) |
| (Allington Towers) | (Kingsgate House) | |

J Phillips (5)	R J Wheeler (4)	Reorganisation
J Thompson (5)	E Tomlin (5)	in progress
T Bryan (5)	(both at Kingsgate House)	
A J Mantle (5)	K M Long (5)	
(all at Allington Towers)	(Buckingham Palace Road)	
	Miss D Gane (5)	
	(Bridge'Place)	

Personnel	**Services Management**	**Economics and Statistics**
Policy	IT Services	Reorganisation in progress
Queen's Award office	Industrial relations	
Honours' secretariat	Procurement	
Training	Building management	
Promotion, recruitment	Information management services	
Trawling units	Office services	

*Mr O'Shea chairs the Steering Board for the Accounts Services Agency

Solicitors' Office

Permanent Secretary
Sir Peter Gregson KCB (1)

The Solicitor
G A Hosker CB QC (2)
(until October 1992)

A H Hammond (2)
(from October 1992)
(10-18 Victoria Street)

Head of Management Support Unit
R Nicklen (5)
(10-18 Victoria Street)

Head of Division	*Head of Division*	*Head of Division*
H V B Brown (3)	**J R Woolman (3)**	**J M Stanley (3)**
	(10-18 Victoria Street)	*(10-18 Victoria Street)*

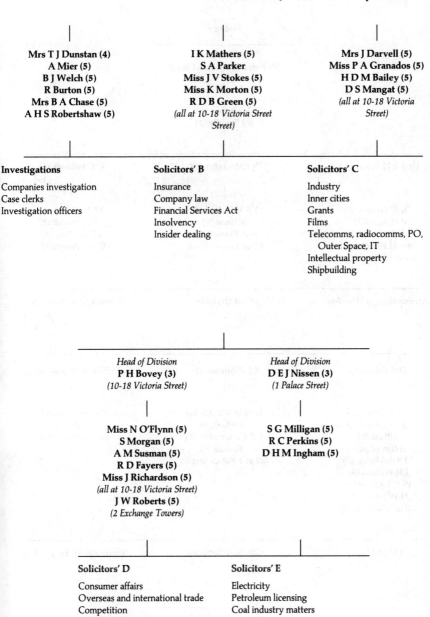

Mrs T J Dunstan (4)
A Mier (5)
B J Welch (5)
R Burton (5)
Mrs B A Chase (5)
A H S Robertshaw (5)

I K Mathers (5)
S A Parker
Miss J V Stokes (5)
Miss K Morton (5)
R D B Green (5)
*(all at 10-18 Victoria Street
Street)*

Mrs J Darvell (5)
Miss P A Granados (5)
H D M Bailey (5)
D S Mangat (5)
*(all at 10-18 Victoria
Street)*

Investigations

Companies investigation
Case clerks
Investigation officers

Solicitors' B

Insurance
Company law
Financial Services Act
Insolvency
Insider dealing

Solicitors' C

Industry
Inner cities
Grants
Films
Telecomms, radiocomms, PO,
    Outer Space, IT
Intellectual property
Shipbuilding

Head of Division
P H Bovey (3)
(10-18 Victoria Street)

Head of Division
D E J Nissen (3)
(1 Palace Street)

Miss N O'Flynn (5)
S Morgan (5)
A M Susman (5)
R D Fayers (5)
Miss J Richardson (5)
(all at 10-18 Victoria Street)
J W Roberts (5)
(2 Exchange Towers)

S G Milligan (5)
R C Perkins (5)
D H M Ingham (5)

Solicitors' D

Consumer affairs
Overseas and international trade
Competition
Weights and measures etc
Exports, imports, trade sanctions
Exports Credits Guarantee Branch

Solicitors' E

Electricity
Petroleum licensing
Coal industry matters

Energy

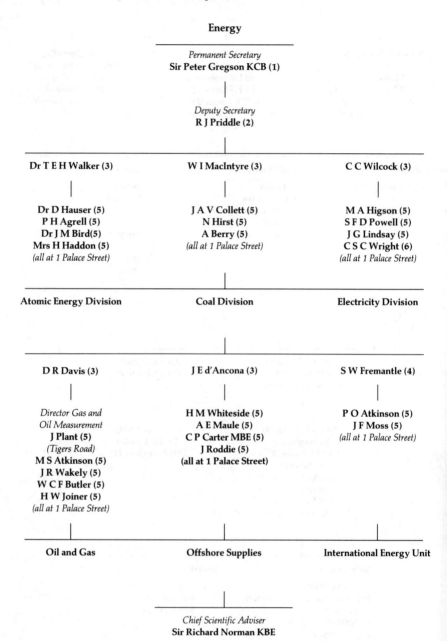

Permanent Secretary
Sir Peter Gregson KCB (1)

Deputy Secretary
R J Priddle (2)

Dr T E H Walker (3)   **W I MacIntyre (3)**   **C C Wilcock (3)**

Dr D Hauser (5)   **J A V Collett (5)**   **M A Higson (5)**
P H Agrell (5)   **N Hirst (5)**   **S F D Powell (5)**
Dr J M Bird(5)   **A Berry (5)**   **J G Lindsay (5)**
Mrs H Haddon (5)   *(all at 1 Palace Street)*   **C S C Wright (6)**
(all at 1 Palace Street)   *(all at 1 Palace Street)*

Atomic Energy Division   **Coal Division**   **Electricity Division**

D R Davis (3)   **J E d'Ancona (3)**   **S W Fremantle (4)**

Director Gas and   **H M Whiteside (5)**   **P O Atkinson (5)**
Oil Measurement   **A E Maule (5)**   **J F Moss (5)**
J Plant (5)   **C P Carter MBE (5)** *(all at 1 Palace Street)*
(Tigers Road)   **J Roddie (5)**
M S Atkinson (5)   **(all at 1 Palace Street)**
J R Wakely (5)
W C F Butler (5)
H W Joiner (5)
(all at 1 Palace Street)

Oil and Gas   **Offshore Supplies**   **International Energy Unit**

Chief Scientific Adviser
Sir Richard Norman KBE

Department of Trade and Industry Addresses

Allington Towers
19 Allington Street
London SW1E 5EB
Tel 071-215 5000
Fax 071-215 0323

29 Bressenden Place
London SW1E 5DT
Tel 071-215 3941
Fax 071-215 3656

Bridge Place
88-89 Eccleston Square
London SW1V 1DT
Tel 071-215 5000
Fax (tel the no above and
ask for relevant fax no)

151 Buckingham Palace Road
London SW1 9SS
Tel 071-215 5000
Fax 071 215 2909

Dean Bradley House
52 Horseferry Road
London SW1P 2AG
Tel 071-276 3000
Fax: 071-222 4707

East Kilbride
Glasgow G75 0QU
Tel 03552 20222
Fax 03552 36930

Export Credits Guarantee Dept
2 Exchange Towers
Harbour Exchange Square
London E14 9GS
Tel 071-512 7000
Fax 071-512 7649

Kingsgate House
66-74 Victoria Street
London SW1E 6SW
Tel 071-215 5000
Fax 071-931 0397

1 Palace Street
London SW1E 5HE
Tel 071-215 5000
Fax 071-834 3771

3 Tigers Road
(off Saffron Road)
Wigston
Leicestershire LE18 4UX
Tel 0533 785354
Fax 0533 770027

10-18 Victoria Street
London SW1H 0NN
Tel 071-215 5000
Fax 071-222 9280

DTI Regional Offices

East
Building A
Westbrook Centre
Milton Road
Cambridge CB4 1YG
Tel 0223 461939
Fax 0223 461941

East Midlands
Severns House
20 Middle Pavement
Nottingham NG1 7DW
Tel 0602 506181
Fax 0602 587074

North East
Stangate House
2 Groat Street
Newcastle upon Tyne NE1 1YN
Tel 091-232 4722
Fax 091-232 6742

North West
Sunley Tower
Piccadilly Plaza
Manchester M1 4BA
Tel 061-236 2171
Fax 061-228 3740

South East
Bridge Place
88-89 Eccleston Square
London SW1V 1PT
Tel 071-215 5000
Fax 071-828 1105

South West
The Pithay
Bristol BS1 2PB
Tel 0272 272666
Fax 0272 299494

West Midlands
77 Paradise Circus
Queensway
Birmingham B1 2DT
Tel 021-212 5000
Fax 021-212 1010

Yorkshire and Humberside
25 Queen Street
Leeds LS1 2TW
Tel 0532 443171
Fax 0532 338301/2

Department of Transport

Founded	1919
Ministers	secretary of state, two ministers of state and two parliamentary under secretaries
Responsibilities	airports Bus and road freight licensing bus industry, sponsorship of civil aviation, domestic and international driver testing and licensing HM Coastguard local authorities, oversight of transport planning marine pollution shipping and ports motorways and trunk roads rail industry, sponsorship of road safety taxis and private hire cars, regulation of vehicle standards, registration and licensing
Executive agencies	Driver and Vehicle Licensing Agency Driving Standards Agency DVOIT Agency Transport and Road Research Laboratory Vehicle Certification Agency Vehicle Inspectorate

Department of Transport

2 Marsham Street, London SW1P 3EB
Tel 071-276 3000   Fax 071-276 0818
All personnel are based at 2 Marsham Street unless otherwise indicated.
For other addresses and telephone numbers see end of section.

Ministers

Secretary of State
**The Rt Hon John MacGregor
OBE MP**

|

Parliamentary Private Secretary
Graham Riddick MP

|

Special Adviser
**Mrs Eleanor Laing
Sir Christopher Foster**
(BR privatisation)

|

Principal Private Secretary
S C Whiteley (5)
071-276 0804

| | |

*Minister of State
for Public Transport*
Roger Freeman MP

*Minister of State
for Aviation and Shipping*
**The Rt Hon The Earl of
Caithness**

| |

*Parliamentary
Private Secretary*
Bowen Wells MP

*Parliamentary
Private Secretary*
Bowen Wells MP

| |

**Private Secretary
Ms S Watkin (7)**
071-276 0823

**Private Secretary
A N Bowmer (HEO D)**
071-276 0815

Parliamentary Under Secretary
of State for Roads and Traffic
Kenneth Carlisle MP

Parliamentary Under Secretary
of State for Transport in London
Steven Norris MP

Private Secretary
Mrs C L Spink
071-276 0811

Private Secretary
P J Downie
071-276 0827

House of Lords' Spokesman
The Earl of Caithness

Ministerial Responsibilities

John MacGregor   overall responsibility for the work of the
                        department and for financial planning and
                        environmental aspects of transport

Roger Freeman   Channel Tunnel rail link
                        disabled people
                        financial planning
                        opening up British Rail to private sector
                        promotion of private sector finance of all
                            modes of transport
                        public transport outside London

Lord Caithness   airlines
                        airports
                        departmental administration
                        marine and shipping matters including the
                            coastguard and ports
                        spokesman in House of Lords

Kenneth Carlisle   driver and vehicle licensing
                        driver testing and training
                        inner cities policy outside London
                        local roads and traffic outside London
                        motorways and trunk road programme
                            outside London
                        research outside London
                        road freight
                        road safety and traffic law
                        road taxation
                        vehicle testing and safety

Steve Norris   aviation matters in the House of Commons
                        London Underground
                        roads and traffic in London
                        transport coordination in London including
                            Docklands

Departmental Overview

Civil Servants			Department	Minister
Grade 1	*Grade 2*	*Grade 3*		
A P Brown	Vacant	Information		

Public Transport

A P Brown	N L J Montagu	D J Rowlands	Railways 1	R Freeman
		P Wood	Railways 2	R Freeman
		H M G Stevens	Public Transport	R Freeman S Norris
		J R Coates	Urban and General	R Freeman

Central Services

A P Brown	E B C Osmotherly	R A Allan	Personnel	J MacGregor
		C R Grimsey	Finance	J MacGregor
		M J Spackman	Economics (Transport)	J MacGregor
		D W Flaxen	Statistics	J MacGregor
		Dr D Metz (4)	Chief Scientist's Unit	K Carlisle

Highways Safety and Traffic

A P Brown	J W S Dempster	T A Rochester	Engineering Policy	K Carlisle
		B J Billington	Network Management and Maintenance	K Carlisle
		D J Lyness	Highways Policy and Resources	K Carlisle
		A Whitfield	Road Programme	K Carlisle S Norris
		Miss S Lambert	Road and Vehicle Safety	K Carlisle
		I Yass	London Region	S Norris

Departmental Overview

Civil Servants			Department	Minister
Grade 1	*Grade 2*	*Grade 3*		

Regional Organisation

A P Brown		D R Ritchie	West Midlands	K Carlisle
		J P Henry	Yorkshire and Humberside	K Carlisle
		D C Renshaw	North West	K Carlisle
		P A Shaw	Northern	K Carlisle
		Ms E A Hopkins	South West	K Carlisle
		D Morrison (4)	East Midlands	K Carlisle
		J W Fellows	South East	K Carlisle
		P F Emms	Eastern	K Carlisle

Aviation, Shipping and International

A P Brown	G R Sunderland	A J Goldman	Civil Aviation Policy	Ld Caithness
		D C Moss	International Aviation	Ld Caithness
		K P R Smart (4)	Air Accidents	Ld Caithness
		J D Henes	International and Freight	R Freeman
		R E Clarke	Shipping Policy, Emergencies and Security	Ld Caithness
		H B Wenban-Smith	Marine	Ld Caithness
		A B Martin	Channel Tunnel Safety Unit	R Freeman
		Capt P Marriott (5)	Marine Accidents	Ld Caithness

Civil Servants and Departments

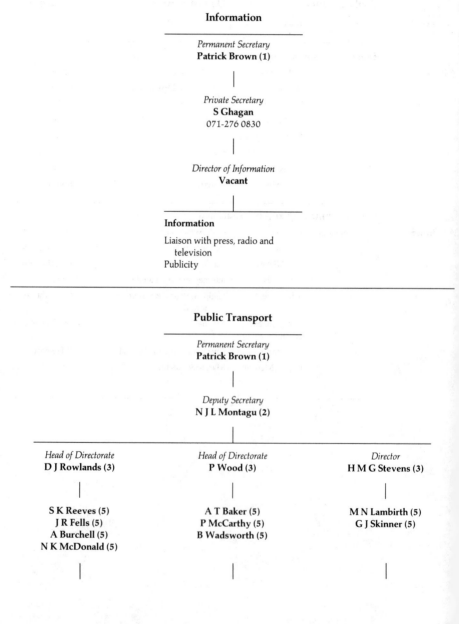

Information

Permanent Secretary
Patrick Brown (1)

Private Secretary
S Ghagan
071-276 0830

Director of Information
Vacant

Information

Liaison with press, radio and
television
Publicity

Public Transport

Permanent Secretary
Patrick Brown (1)

Deputy Secretary
N J L Montagu (2)

Head of Directorate
D J Rowlands (3)

Head of Directorate
P Wood (3)

Director
H M G Stevens (3)

S K Reeves (5)
J R Fells (5)
A Burchell (5)
N K McDonald (5)

A T Baker (5)
P McCarthy (5)
B Wadsworth (5)

M N Lambirth (5)
G J Skinner (5)

Railways 1 Directorate

Government/BR board
Board appointments and salaries
Channel Tunnel
Inter City
Regional railways
Royal Train
Passenger service obligation
EEC
Pay and industrial relations
Network South East
Fares
Quality of Service
Procurement
International
Noise
Transport Police
Property and Land

Railways 2 Directorate

Privatisation
Liberalisation
Freight and parcels

Public Transport Directorate

London transport
Board appointments and salaries
Pay and industrial relations
Rail strategy for London
London underground
London buses
Deregulation and privatisation
Quality of service
Fares
Crime prevention/passenger
    security
Riverbus
Coach terminals in London
Public transport for disabled people

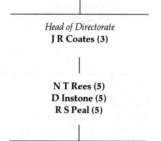

Head of Directorate
J R Coates (3)

N T Rees (5)
D Instone (5)
R S Peal (5)

Urban and General

Public transport outside London
Taxis
PTAs and PTEs
The bus industry
Concessionary travel schemes
Light rail projects
Inner cities
Bus priority measures
Traffic management
Pedestrians and cyclists
Parking policy
Planning guidance
Tourism
Inter-modal questions
Environment
Legislation on transport works
Light rail orders

Principal Establishment and Finance Group

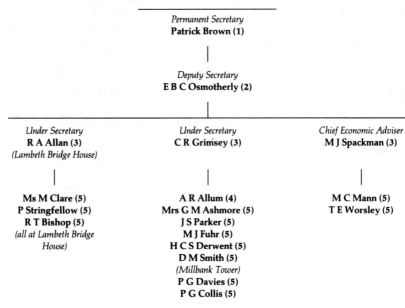

Permanent Secretary
Patrick Brown (1)

Deputy Secretary
E B C Osmotherly (2)

Under Secretary	*Under Secretary*	*Chief Economic Adviser*
R A Allan (3)	**C R Grimsey (3)**	**M J Spackman (3)**
(Lambeth Bridge House)		

Ms M Clare (5)	**A R Allum (4)**	**M C Mann (5)**
P Stringfellow (5)	**Mrs G M Ashmore (5)**	**T E Worsley (5)**
R T Bishop (5)	**J S Parker (5)**	
(all at Lambeth Bridge	**M J Fuhr (5)**	
House)	**H C S Derwent (5)**	
	D M Smith (5)	
	(Millbank Tower)	
	P G Davies (5)	
	P G Collis (5)	

Personnel	**Finance**	**Economics**
Personnel management	Accounts	Aviation
Personnel policy	Public expenditure	Shipping
Secondments	Public appointments	Marine
Training	Grants	Local transport
Pay and superannuation	Executive agencies	General
Accommodation	Internal audit	
Office services	Management support services	
Welfare service	Contracts and procurement	
	Citizen's Charter	

Director of Statistics	*Chief Scientist*
D W Flaxen (3)	**Dr D Metz (4)**
(Romney House)	
Miss B J Wood (5)	
H Collings (5)	
G R Emes (5)	
R P Donachie (5)	
(all at Romney House)	

Statistics

National and London traffic
Roads and road vehicles
Buses and coaches
Domestic and international road
    haulage
London and urban transport
Road accidents
Ports
Shipping and sea passengers
Aviation
National Travel Survey

Chief Scientist's Unit

Research and development
Science and technology issues

Highways Safety and Traffic

Permanent Secretary
Patrick Brown (1)

Deputy Secretary
J W S Dempster (2)

Chief Highway Engineer	*Director*	*Under Secretary*
T A Rochester (3)	**B J Billington (3)**	**D J Lyness (3)**
(St Christopher House)	*(Monck Street)*	
J A Kerman (5)	**A S D Whybrow (5)**	**P E Pickering (5)**
N S Organ (5)	**P R Smith (5)**	**P J Coby (5)**
P H Dawe (5)	*(both at Monck Street)*	**D J Kershaw (5)**
(all at St Christopher	**R S Wilson (5)**	**J B W Robins (5)**
House)	*(Bristol office)*	**R W Linnard (5)**
	Dr R M Kimber (5)	

ngineering Policy

licy and programme
ghways
idges and tunnels

**Network Management
and Maintenance**

Network management
Public utilities
Maintenance
Trunk roads and motorways
Local authority roads
Motorway service areas
Development control
Third party claims
Comunications
Driver information
Signs and signals

**Highway Policy and
Resources**

Highway policy
Local roads
Private finance
Resource management
Computing
Financial control
Toll roads and crossings

Road Programme Director **A Whitfield (3)**	*Under Secretary* **Miss S Lambert (3)**	*Under Secretary* **I Yass (3)**
D A Holland (4) **Ms A M Munro (5)** **M R Nevard (5)** *(St Christopher House)* **Miss P Williams (5)** *(Monck Street)* **Dr J H Denning (4)** **N E Firkins (5)** *(above 2 at Friars House)* (see Regional Construction Programme Divisions below)	**Dr P H Martin (5)** **I R Jordan (5)** **E Dunn (4)** **Dr J F Taylor (4)** **J Winder (6)**	**P R Smethurst (4)** **P E Butler (5)** **R M C Edridge (4)** **Dr S Chatterjee (5)** **D J C Miles (5)** **Vacant (5)** **R J Mance (5)**

Road Programme Directorate	**Road and Vehicle Safety**	**London Regional Directorate**

Highways programme support
Environmental appraisal
Engineering
Contracts and lands
Motorway widening
Network management and
    construction
	Legislation and enforcement
	Education and publicity
	Vehicle safety
	Environmental standards
	Vehicle testing
	Mechanical engineering
	Medical adviser
	Traffic area coordination
		London traffic and transportation
		    unit
		Parking
		London regional office:
		    Construction programme
		    Network management
		London docklands
		Central services

Regional Construction Programme Divisions

Programme Director
A Whitfield (3)

East Midlands **S Rose (5)** *(Cranbrook House)*	*Northern* **D Ward (5)** *(Wellbar House)*	*Eastern* **A J Homer (4)** **J P Boud (5)** *(Heron House)*
North West **G E Hancock (4)** **E A Sherwin (5)** *(Sunley Tower)*	*South East* **B A Sperring (4)** **M G Quinn (5)** *(Federated House)*	*South West* **W E Gallagher (4)** **G D Rowe (5)** *(Tollgate House)*

West Midlands **P E Nutt (4)** **J P Bradley (5)** *(5 Broadway)*	*Yorkshire and Humberside* **D York (5)** *(Jefferson House)*

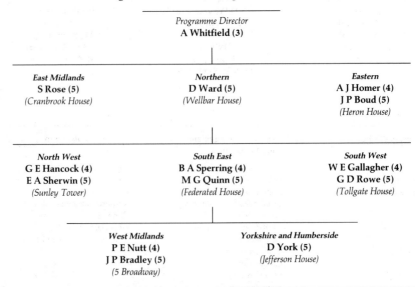

Regional Organisation

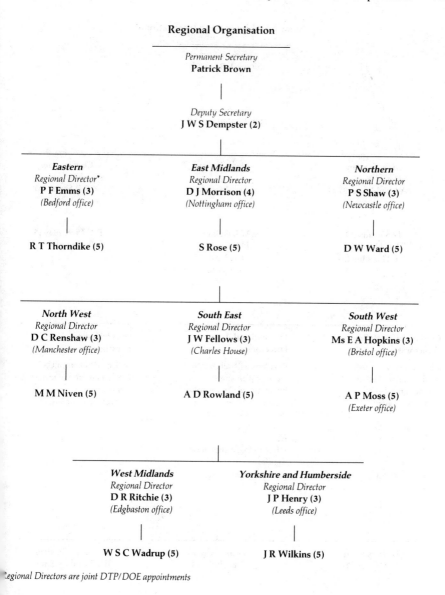

Permanent Secretary
Patrick Brown

Deputy Secretary
J W S Dempster (2)

Eastern	*East Midlands*	*Northern*
*Regional Director**	*Regional Director*	*Regional Director*
P F Emms (3)	**D J Morrison (4)**	**P S Shaw (3)**
(Bedford office)	*(Nottingham office)*	*(Newcastle office)*
R T Thorndike (5)	**S Rose (5)**	**D W Ward (5)**

North West	*South East*	*South West*
Regional Director	*Regional Director*	*Regional Director*
D C Renshaw (3)	**J W Fellows (3)**	**Ms E A Hopkins (3)**
(Manchester office)	*(Charles House)*	*(Bristol office)*
M M Niven (5)	**A D Rowland (5)**	**A P Moss (5)**
		(Exeter office)

West Midlands	*Yorkshire and Humberside*
Regional Director	*Regional Director*
D R Ritchie (3)	**J P Henry (3)**
(Edgbaston office)	*(Leeds office)*
W S C Wadrup (5)	**J R Wilkins (5)**

Regional Directors are joint DTP/DOE appointments

Aviation, Shipping and International

Permanent Secretary
Patrick Brown (1)

|

Deputy Secretary
G R Sunderland CB (2)

|

Under Secretary	*Under Secretary*	*Chief Inspector of Accidents*
A J Goldman (3)	**D C Moss (3)**	**K P R Smart (4)**
|	|	|
D S Evans (5)	**M L Fielder (5)**	**R C McKinlay (5)**
E C Neve (5)	**D B Cooke (5)**	*(both at Farnborough)*
A F Thorning (5)	**F A Neal (5)**	
	(Quebec)	

Civil Aviation Policy Directorate	**International Aviation Directorate**	**Air Accidents Investigation**
Airport policy	Relations with all countries	Civil air accidents in UK
Civil Aviation Authority	Defence planning	British registered or manufactured
Airline competition	International Civil Aviation	aircraft
Airspace capacity	Organisation	Investigations for MOD (Air)
Safety	European Civil Aviation	
Search and rescue	Conference	
Environment and noise	EC	
	International competition	
	Tariffs	
	Concorde routes	

Under Secretary	*Under Secretary*	*Under Secretary*
J D Henes (3)	**R E Clarke (3)**	**H B Wenban-Smith (3)**
		(Sunley House office)
|	|	|

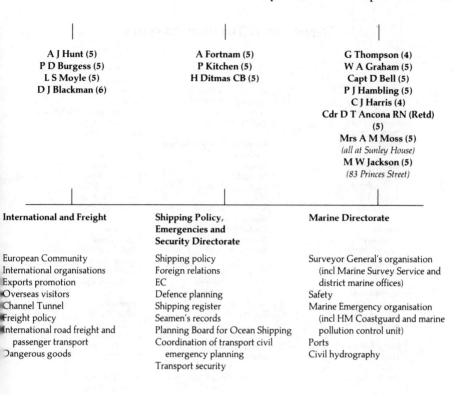

A J Hunt (5)
P D Burgess (5)
L S Moyle (5)
D J Blackman (6)

A Fortnam (5)
P Kitchen (5)
H Ditmas CB (5)

G Thompson (4)
W A Graham (5)
Capt D Bell (5)
P J Hambling (5)
C J Harris (4)
Cdr D T Ancona RN (Retd) (5)
Mrs A M Moss (5)
(all at Sunley House)
M W Jackson (5)
(83 Princes Street)

International and Freight

European Community
International organisations
Exports promotion
Overseas visitors
Channel Tunnel
Freight policy
International road freight and
    passenger transport
Dangerous goods

**Shipping Policy,
Emergencies and
Security Directorate**

Shipping policy
Foreign relations
EC
Defence planning
Shipping register
Seamen's records
Planning Board for Ocean Shipping
Coordination of transport civil
    emergency planning
Transport security

Marine Directorate

Surveyor General's organisation
    (incl Marine Survey Service and
    district marine offices)
Safety
Marine Emergency organisation
    (incl HM Coastguard and marine
    pollution control unit)
Ports
Civil hydrography

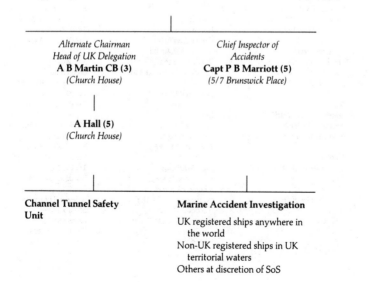

*Alternate Chairman
Head of UK Delegation*
A B Martin CB (3)
(Church House)

*Chief Inspector of
Accidents*
Capt P B Marriott (5)
(5/7 Brunswick Place)

A Hall (5)
(Church House)

**Channel Tunnel Safety
Unit**

Marine Accident Investigation

UK registered ships anywhere in
    the world
Non-UK registered ships in UK
    territorial waters
Others at discretion of SoS

Department of Transport Addresses

National addresses

5/7 Brunswick Place
Southampton
Hants SO1 2AN
Tel 0703 232424
Fax 0703 232459

Church House
Great Smith Street
London SW1P 3BL
Tel 071-276 2014
Fax 071-276 2078

Crowthorne
Berkshire RG11 6AU
Tel 0344 773131
Fax 0344 770356

Friars House
Warwick Road
Coventry CV1 2TN
Tel 0203 535101
Fax 0203 535330

Lambeth Bridge House
London SE1 7SB
Tel 071-238 4449
Fax 071-238 5215

Millbank Tower
London SW1P 4QU
Tel 071-217 4479
Fax 071-217 4399

2 Monck Street
London SW1 2BQ
Tel 071-276 2820
Fax 071-276 2770

83 Princes Street
Edinburgh EH2 2HH
Tel 031-225 5567
Fax 031-220 4066

Suite 928
1000 Sherbrook Street West
Montreal
Quebec
Canada H3A 3G4
Tel 285 8302
Fax 285 8001

Romney House
43 Marsham Street
London SW1P 3EB
Tel 071-276 3000
Fax 071-276 8355

Royal Aerospace Establishment
Farnborough
Hants GU14 6TD
Tel 0252 510300
Fax 0252 540535

St Christopher House
Southwark Street
London SE1 0TE
Tel 071-921 4571
Fax 071-921 4745

Sunley House
90–93 High Holborn
London WC1V 6LP
Tel 071-405 6911
Fax 071-831 2508

Tollgate House
Houlton Street
Bristol BS2 9DJ
Tel 0272 218283
Fax 0272 218264

Regional Offices

Eastern
Heron House
Goldington Road
Bedford MK40 3LL
Tel 0234 63161
Fax 0234 63161 Ext 300

Federated House
London Road
Dorking
Surrey RH4 1SZ
Tel 0306 885922
Fax 0306 741648

East Midlands
Cranbrook House
Cranbrook Street
Nottingham NG1 1EY
Tel 0602 476121
Fax 0602 476121 Ext 560

Northern
Wellbar House
Gallowgate
Newcastle upon Tyne NE1 4TD
Tel 091-232 7575
Fax 091-261 0746

North West
Sunley Tower
Piccadilly Plaza
Manchester M1 4BE
Tel 061-832 9111
Fax 061-838 5790

South East
Charles House
375 Kensington High Street
London W14 4QH
Tel 071-605 9003
Fax 071-605 9248

South West
Tollgate House
Houlton Street
Bristol BS2 9DJ
Tel 0272 218811
Fax 0272 218264

West Midlands
Five Ways Tower
Frederick Road
Edgbaston
Birmingham B15 1SJ
Tel 021-626 2000
Fax 021-626 2404

5 Broadway
Broad Street
Birmingham B15 1BL
Tel 021-631 8234
Fax 021-631 8186

Yorkshire and Humberside
City House
New Station Street
Leeds LS1 4JD
Tel 0532 438232
Fax 0532 444898

Jefferson House
27 Park Place
Leeds LS1 2SZ
Tel 0532 541293
Fax 0532 541002

HM Treasury

The Prime Minister (who is also First Lord of Treasury), the government whips in both Houses and the Leader of the House of Lords are all officially part of HM Treasury. They do not, however, play a part in the day-to-day life of the departmental Treasury which is headed by the Chancellor of the Exchequer

---

Departmental Treasury

Founded Eleventh century

Ministers Chancellor of the Exchequer, Chief Secretary, Financial Secretary, Paymaster General, Economic Secretary

Responsibilities To formulate and put into effect the government's financial and economic policy

To plan public expenditure and see that it conforms to the approved plans

Central oversight of civil service pay and personnel management

Financial services and institutions

Overseas financial relations, including international monetary affairs

Privatisation and wider share ownership

Procurement policy

Taxation

Executive Agencies None

HM Treasury

Parliament Street, London SW1P 3AG
Tel 071-270 3000   Fax 071-270 5653 071-839 2082
All personnel are based at Parliament Street unless otherwise indicated.
For other addresses and telephone numbers see end of Treasury section.

Ministers

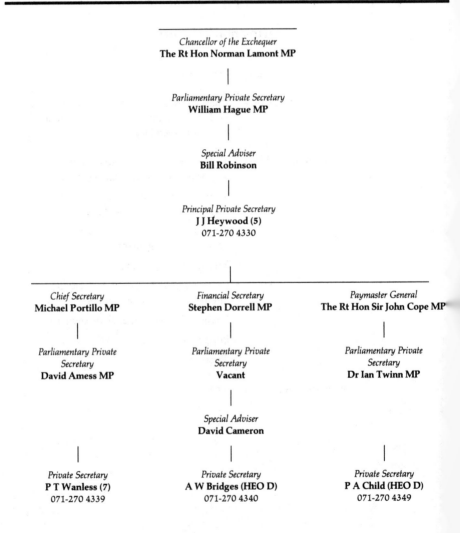

Chancellor of the Exchequer
The Rt Hon Norman Lamont MP

|

Parliamentary Private Secretary
William Hague MP

|

Special Adviser
Bill Robinson

|

Principal Private Secretary
J J Heywood (5)
071-270 4330

Chief Secretary	*Financial Secretary*	*Paymaster General*
Michael Portillo MP	**Stephen Dorrell MP**	**The Rt Hon Sir John Cope MP**

Parliamentary Private Secretary
David Amess MP

Parliamentary Private Secretary
Vacant

Parliamentary Private Secretary
Dr Ian Twinn MP

Special Adviser
David Cameron

Private Secretary
P T Wanless (7)
071-270 4339

Private Secretary
A W Bridges (HEO D)
071-270 4340

Private Secretary
P A Child (HEO D)
071-270 4349

Economic Secretary
Anthony Nelson MP

Private Secretary
M R Buckler (HEO)
071-270 4350

House of Lords' Spokesmen
The Viscount Long
The Viscount Astor
The Viscount Goschen
The Rt Hon the Baroness
Trumpington

Ministerial Responsibilities

Norman Lamont   ministerial head of the Treasury
overall responsibility for
- the economy
- fiscal policy
- finance and monetary policy
- civil service management and pay

Michael Portillo   public expenditure planning control
value for money in the public services
including Next Steps agencies

Stephen Dorrell   Civil Service pay, personnel management,
industrial relations and relocation
competition and deregulation policy
Inland Revenue taxes
legislative programme
oversight of Inland Revenue, excluding
Valuation Office
parliamentary financial business
privatisation and wider share ownership
policy

Sir John Cope   charities
Customs and Excise duties and taxes
environment, including energy efficiency
EC budget and future financing
ministerial correspondence
oversight of Customs and Excise
Paymaster General's office
Treasury interest in general accounting issues
women's issues

Anthony Nelson   Central Statistical Office
Department for National Savings
economic and monetary union
financial systems, including banks, building
    societies and friendly societies and other
    financial institutions; and financial services
FORWARD (CISCO)
Government Actuary's Department
international financial issues and institutions
monetary policy
National Investment and Loans Office
public expenditure casework
Royal Mint
stamp duties
Treasury Bulletin and Economic Briefing
Valuation Office

Departmental Overview

Civil Servants				Division	Minister
Grade 1	*Grade 1A*	*Grade 2*	*Grade 3*		
Sir Terence Burns	These divisions report directly to the Permanent Secretary	Sir Alan Hardcastle (ungraded)	B Fox	Establishment and Organisation Group	A Nelson
			M C Mercer (5)	Economic Briefing	A Nelson
			R B Saunders (5)	Information	
			J S Beastall	Treasury Officer of Accounts	Sir J Cope
				Accountancy Advice	

Public Expenditure

		Industry			
Sir Terence Burns	N J Monck	R Mountfield	G W Monger	Industry, Agriculture and Employment Group	M Portillo
			S A Robson	Public Enterprise Group	M Portillo
			M Whippman	Home, Education and Arts Group	M Portillo

Public Services

	N J Monck	A J C Edwards	I P Wilson	CCTA (Central Computer and Telecommunications Agency)*	A Nelson
			Vacant	Social Services	M Portillo
			R I G Allen	Local Government Group	M Portillo
			P Forshaw	Central Unit on Purchasing	M Portillo
					S Dorrell

Departmental Overview

	Civil Servants		Division		Minister
Grade 1	Grade 1A		Grade 2	Grade 3	
General Expenditure Policy, Defence Policy					
	N J Monck		These divisions report directly to the Second Permanent Secretary	C W Kelly — General Expenditure Policy Group	M Portillo
				D J L Moore — Defence Policy Manpower and Materiel Group	M Portillo
Economic Service					
Sir Terence Burns	A Budd			C J Riley — Medium Term and Policy Analysis	
				Dr J H Rickard — Public Expenditure Economics Group	M Portillo
				C J Mowl — Economic Assessment and Public Sector Finance	
Finance					
Public Finance					
Sir Terence Burns	N L Wicks		A Turnbull	R P Culpin — Fiscal Policy Division	S Dorrell / Sir J Cope
				P R C Gray — Monetary Group	A Nelson
Financial Institutions and Markets					
Sir Terence Burns	N L Wicks		Mrs J R Lomax	E J W Gieve — Banking Group	A Nelson
				A Whiting — Securities and Investment Services Group	A Nelson

Departmental Overview

Civil Servants	Division			Minister
Grade 1	**Grade 1A**	**Grade 2**	**Grade 3**	
	N L Wicks			
		Overseas Finance		
		H P Evans	J E Mortimer	Aid and Export Finance Group	A Nelson
			D J Bostock	European Community	Sir J Cope / A Nelson
			P N Sedgwick	International Finance	A Nelson
		Civil Service Management and Pay		
Sir Terence Burns		M C Scholar	Mrs A F Case	Pay Division	S Dorrell
			B A E Taylor	Personnel Policy group	S Dorrell
			S Boys Smith	Management Policy and Running Costs	M Portillo
			R V C Wheeler (4)	FORWARD (Civil Service Catering)	A Nelson

This division reports directly to the Permanent Secretary

*transferring to Cabinet Office/OPSS later this year

Civil Servants and Divisions

Establishment and Finance; Economic Briefing; Information

Permanent Secretary to the Treasury
Sir Terence Burns (1)

Private Secretary
Mrs J W Henser
071-270 4360

Principal Establishment and Finance Officer	*Economic Briefing Assistant Secretary*	*Press Secretary and Head of Information*
B Fox (3)	**M C Mercer (5)**	**R B Saunders (5)**

A J T MacAuslan (5)
D Todd (5)
E I Cooper (5)
J Gilhooly (5)
D N Walters (6)
P Tickner (6)
J W Stevens (6)

Establishment and Organisation	**Economic Briefing**	**Information Division**
Personnel management (senior staff)	Advice on UK economy	Information
Whitley Council	Briefing on Treasury interest	Press liaison
Office services	Policy coordination	Treasury Bulletin
Finance	Relations with Select Committees	Economic Briefing

Accountancy

Permanent Secretary to the Treasury
Sir Terence Burns (1)

Treasury Officer of Accounts
J Beastall (3)

I S Thomson (5)

*Chief Accountancy Adviser
to the Treasury,*

*Head of the Government
Accountancy Service*
Sir Alan Hardcastle

*Deputy Chief Accountancy Adviser,
Head of the Government Accountancy
Service Management Unit*
D T Cooke (4)
D Jamieson (5)
G Dixon (6)
C Butler (6)

Treasury Officer of Accounts

Relations between Parliament and
executive in financial matters
Government accounting issues
Form of government accounts
Accounting officers' functions and
responsibilities
Relations with Public Accounts
Committee and National Audit
Office
Fees and charges policy
Departmental banking
arrangements

Accountancy Advice

Support for the Head of the
Government Accountancy
Service
Personnel management of
accountants
Internal audit development

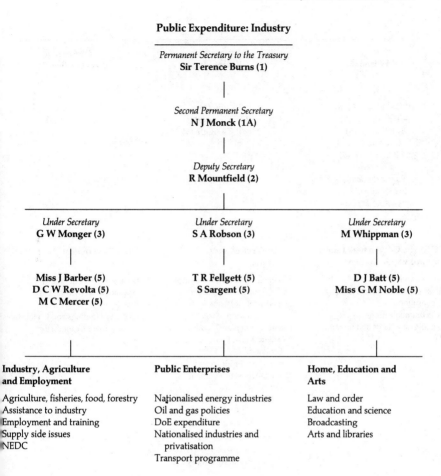

Public Expenditure: Industry

Permanent Secretary to the Treasury
Sir Terence Burns (1)

|

Second Permanent Secretary
N J Monck (1A)

|

Deputy Secretary
R Mountfield (2)

|

| *Under Secretary* | *Under Secretary* | *Under Secretary* |
| **G W Monger (3)** | **S A Robson (3)** | **M Whippman (3)** |

Miss J Barber (5)	**T R Fellgett (5)**	**D J Batt (5)**
D C W Revolta (5)	**S Sargent (5)**	**Miss G M Noble (5)**
M C Mercer (5)		

Industry, Agriculture and Employment

Agriculture, fisheries, food, forestry
Assistance to industry
Employment and training
Supply side issues
NEDC

Public Enterprises

Nationalised energy industries
Oil and gas policies
DoE expenditure
Nationalised industries and
   privatisation
Transport programme

Home, Education and Arts

Law and order
Education and science
Broadcasting
Arts and libraries

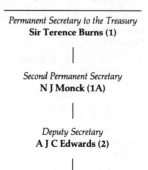

Public Expenditure: Public Services

Permanent Secretary to the Treasury
Sir Terence Burns (1)

|

Second Permanent Secretary
N J Monck (1A)

|

Deputy Secretary
A J C Edwards (2)

|

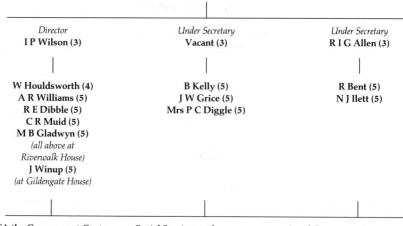

Director **I P Wilson (3)**	*Under Secretary* **Vacant (3)**	*Under Secretary* **R I G Allen (3)**

W Houldsworth (4)
A R Williams (5)
R E Dibble (5)
C R Muid (5)
M B Gladwyn (5)
*(all above at
Riverwalk House)*
J Winup (5)
(at Gildengate House)

B Kelly (5)
J W Grice (5)
Mrs P C Diggle (5)

R Bent (5)
N J Ilett (5)

CCTA the Government Centre for Information Systems*

IS strategies
IT procurement services and
 consultancies
Telecommunications
IS issues, standards and methods

Social Services and Territorial

SS benefits and NI contributions
DSS manpower and resources
Department of Health
 administration
Health and personal social services
Northern Ireland, Wales and
 Scotland
National Audit Office
Miscellaneous government
 departments

Local Government

Local government finance
Housing and environment
PSA Services
Property Holdings and Civil Estates
Crown Estate Commission

Director
P Forshaw CB (3)

M J Hoare (5)
J R Colling (5)

Central Unit on Purchasing

Advice to government departments
 on purchasing
Monitor purchasing practice
Promotion of market testing
Advice on works projects
Promotion of standards and quality
Public purchasing policy including
 international obligations
 (EC/GATT)

*transfering to Cabinet Office/OPSS later this year

Public Expenditure: General Expenditure Policy, Defence Policy

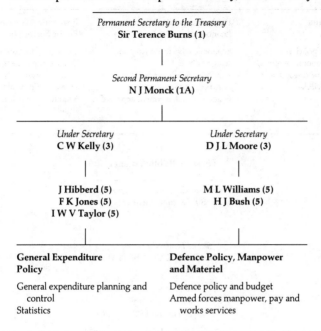

Permanent Secretary to the Treasury
Sir Terence Burns (1)

Second Permanent Secretary
N J Monck (1A)

Under Secretary	*Under Secretary*
C W Kelly (3)	**D J L Moore (3)**

J Hibberd (5)	M L Williams (5)
F K Jones (5)	H J Bush (5)
I W V Taylor (5)	

General Expenditure Policy

General expenditure planning and control
Statistics

Defence Policy, Manpower and Materiel

Defence policy and budget
Armed forces manpower, pay and works services

Economic Service

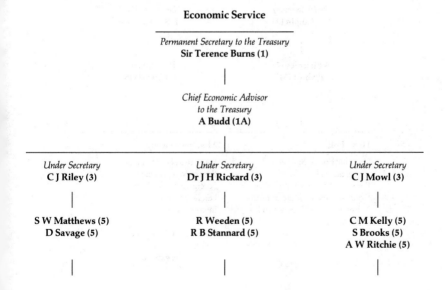

Permanent Secretary to the Treasury
Sir Terence Burns (1)

Chief Economic Advisor to the Treasury
A Budd (1A)

Under Secretary	*Under Secretary*	*Under Secretary*
C J Riley (3)	**Dr J H Rickard (3)**	**C J Mowl (3)**

S W Matthews (5)	R Weeden (5)	C M Kelly (5)
D Savage (5)	R B Stannard (5)	S Brooks (5)
		A W Ritchie (5)

Medium Term and Policy Analysis	Public Expenditure Economics	Economic Assessment and Public Sector Finance
Macro-economic policies Medium term economic analysis, macro-economic research and the Treasury Model	Economic advice: industry and agriculture Advice to public services expenditure groups Guidance on investment appraisal	Domestic forecasting and analysis Balance of payments forecasting and analysis Domestic financial forecasts Monitoring and forecasting public sector finance

Finance: Public Finance

Permanent Secretary to the Treasury
Sir Terence Burns (1)

Second Permanent Secretary
N L Wicks CVO CBE (1A)

Deputy Secretary
A Turnbull (2)

Under Secretary **R P Culpin (3)**	*Under Secretary* **P R C Gray (3)**
A Sharples (5) **P Short (5)**	**J P McIntyre (5)** **S J Davies (5)**

Fiscal Policy	Monetary Group
Coordination of Budget and Finance Bill Direct/indirect taxation policies Control of expenditure in Inland Revenue and Customs and Excise	Forex markets and rates Reserves management Foreign currency borrowing Funding policy Interest rates Gilts National Savings policy CTDs DNS public expenditure

Finance: Financial Institutions and Markets

Permanent Secretary to the Treasury
Sir Terence Burns (1)

|

Second Permanent Secretary
N L Wicks CVO CBE (1A)

|

Deputy Secretary
Mrs J R Lomax (2)

|

| *Under Secretary* | *Under Secretary* |
| E J W Gieve (3) | A Whiting (3) |

L Watts (4)	**Dr J P Compton (5)**
C Farthing (5)	**Miss R Thompson (5)**
J M G Taylor (5)	**P Loughead (5)**
	(all above at
	10–18 Victoria Street)

Banking Group

Banking laws
Building, friendly and other
  societies
Money laundering
National Loan Fund policy
Bank of England, Royal Mint,
  currency and coinage
Local authority borrowing and
  creditworthiness
City competitiveness
Equity and bond markets
Securities futures
Wider share ownership
Tax matters affecting financial
  services
Fraud, leasing, consumer credit
Trustee Investment Act

**Securities and Investment
Services Group**

Policy, legislation and over-seeing
  regulation in investment
  business collective investment
  schemes, the issue of securities to
  the public, and investor
  protection
Responsibility for the regulatory
  system under the Financial
  Services Act 1986 and oversight
  of the Securities and Investment
  Board
Regulation of the Company
  Securities (Insider Dealing) Act
  1985 and Pt VII (financial
  markets and insolvency) and Pt
  IX (Taurus) of the Companies
  Act 1989

Central accounts
Civil List
Judicial salaries and pensions
Election expenses Westminster and
   European
CGBR Forecast
	EC directives in the financial
	   services sector
	Arrangements with overseas
	   regulators for exchanging
	   information
	Encouraging international
	   liberalisation in financial services
	   through GATT and OECD
	Pursuing international regulatory
	   standards in the securities and
	   investment services sectors
	   through IOSCO
	Pursuing market access for UK
	   firms in third countries
	Litigation to recover the
	   government's ex gratia
	   payments scheme to Barlow
	   Clowes investors

Finance: Overseas Finance

Permanent Secretary to the Treasury
Sir Terence Burns (1)

|

Second Permanent Secretary
N L Wicks CVO CBE (1A)

|

Deputy Secretary
H P Evans (2)

|

Under Secretary **J E Mortimer (3)**	*Under Secretary* **D J Bostock (3)**	*Under Secretary* **P N Sedgwick (3)**
Mrs S D Brown (5) **S N Wood (5)**	**R C Pratt (5)** **N J Kroll (5)** **M E Corcoran (5)**	**C R Pickering (5)** **D E W Owen (5)** **Ms E Young (5)**

Aid and Export Finance	European Community	International Finance
Developing countries	EC involvement in financial and	International financial institutions
FCO expenditure	economic policy including EMU	International debt
Commonwealth Development	Single market issues	World economy
Corporation	EC finance ministers meeting	OECD
Export finance and credit policy	preparation	Economic advice on international
International debt re-scheduling	International trade policy	economic issues, trade policy,
Financial relations with other	European Investment Bank	international monetary systems
countries	EC budget	and the EC
Overseas aid	EC financial matters affecting UK	Eastern Europe and the former
Crown Agents	expenditure	Soviet Union
	UK payments to EC institutions	
	EC budget revenue	

Civil Service Management and Pay

Permanent Secretary to the Treasury
Sir Terence Burns (1)

|

Second Permanent Secretary
M C Scholar (2)

|

Under Secretary
Mrs A F Case (3)ʃ

Under Secretary
B A E Taylor (3)

| |

R J Evans (5)
J S Cunliffe (5)
J Strachan (5)

N M Hansford (5)
J Dixon (5)
S Kingaby (5)
D Rayson (5)
D Pain (5)

Pay

Civil service pay
Public and private sector pay

Personnel Policy

Strategic personnel management
  issues
Recruitment
Structure
Personnel management
Staff transfers
Allowances (UK and overseas)
Superannuation
Personnel statistics
Industrial relations policy and
  procedures
Non-financial conditions of service

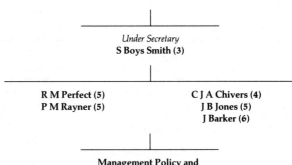

Under Secretary
S Boys Smith (3)

R M Perfect (5)	**C J A Chivers (4)**
P M Rayner (5)	**J B Jones (5)**
	J Barker (6)

Management Policy and Running Costs

Financial management in
   government departments
Control of running costs
Consultancy
Inspection services
Value for money
Management systems
Operational research
Implementation of Next Steps

Chief Executive
R V C Wheeler (4)
(Grosvenor House)

FORWARD (Civil Service Catering)

Development of commercial terms
   of business
Provision of operational and client
   services including hygiene
   inspections
Planning, design and independent
   consultancy services

HM Treasury Addresses

Gildengate House
Upper Green Lane
Norwich NR3 1DW
Tel 0603 694620
Fax 0603 694817

Grosvenor House
Basing View
Basingstoke
Hants RG21 2EH
Tel 0256 29171
Fax 0256 29171 X406

Riverwalk House
157–161 Millbank
London SW1P 4RT
Tel 071-217 3000/3338
Fax 071-217 3449

The Securities and Investment Services
Group, now under HM Treasury
jurisdiction, will be based at the DTI at
10–18 Victoria Street until later this year
when it will move into the main
Treasury building:

10–18 Victoria Street
London SW1H 0NN
Tel 071-215 5000
Fax 071-222 9280

Treasury Solicitor's Department

Founded 17th century

Status Non-ministerial department

Responsible to Attorney General

Responsibilities Litigation and conveyancing services for most government departments and some other public bodies and legal advice for those which do not have their own lawyers

Administration of estates of people dying intestate and without known kin; dissolved companies; and failure of trustees

Provision of legal advice on European Community law; conduct of litigation before the European Court of Justice

The Treasury Solicitor is also the Queen's Proctor (interventions and advisory functions in matrimonial suits and legitimation cases)

Treasury Solicitor's Department

Queen Anne's Chambers, 28 Broadway, London SW1H 9JS
Tel 071-210 3000   Fax 071-222 6006

Minister

Attorney General
**The Rt Hon Sir Nicholas
Lyell QC MP**
(for details of his office see
Law Officers Department)

Officials

*HM Procurator General and
Treasury Solicitor*
Sir James Nursaw KCB QC (1)
(until October 1992)
Gerald Hosker CB QC (1)
(from October 1992)

|

Deputy Treasury Solicitor
T J G Pratt (2)

|

Private Office
Mrs M S Powell
Tel 071-210 3012

|

Mrs K Minall
Tel 071-210 3031

Departmental Overview

Civil Servants			Department
Grade 1	*Grade 2*	*Grade 3*	
Sir James Nursaw	T J G Pratt	M A Blythe	Central Advisory Division
(Gerald Hosker from October 1992)		J E G Vaux	European Division
		A D Osborne	Property Division
		D A Hogg	Litigation Division
		H R L Purse	Department of Employment Division
		D F W Pickup	Ministry of Defence Division
		R N Ricks	Department of Education and Science Division
		D E J Nissen	Department of Energy Division
		G H Beetham	Department of Transport Division
		Mrs M Harrop (5)	Lawyers' Management Unit
		A J E Hollis (6)	Establishments, Finance and General Services Division
		I Hood (5) reports directly to Sir James Nursaw	Queen's Proctor

Civil Servants and Departments

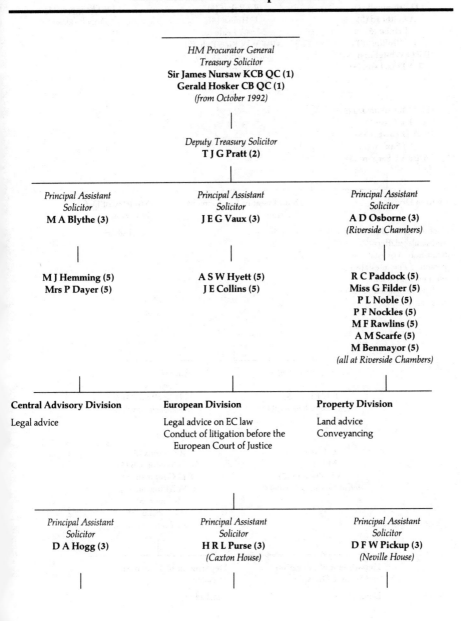

HM Procurator General
Treasury Solicitor
Sir James Nursaw KCB QC (1)
Gerald Hosker CB QC (1)
(from October 1992)

Deputy Treasury Solicitor
T J G Pratt (2)

Principal Assistant Solicitor	Principal Assistant Solicitor	Principal Assistant Solicitor
M A Blythe (3)	**J E G Vaux (3)**	**A D Osborne (3)** *(Riverside Chambers)*

M J Hemming (5) **Mrs P Dayer (5)**	**A S W Hyett (5)** **J E Collins (5)**	**R C Paddock (5)** **Miss G Filder (5)** **P L Noble (5)** **P F Nockles (5)** **M F Rawlins (5)** **A M Scarfe (5)** **M Benmayor (5)** *(all at Riverside Chambers)*

Central Advisory Division	**European Division**	**Property Division**
Legal advice	Legal advice on EC law Conduct of litigation before the European Court of Justice	Land advice Conveyancing

Principal Assistant Solicitor	Principal Assistant Solicitor	Principal Assistant Solicitor
D A Hogg (3)	**H R L Purse (3)** *(Caxton House)*	**D F W Pickup (3)** *(Neville House)*

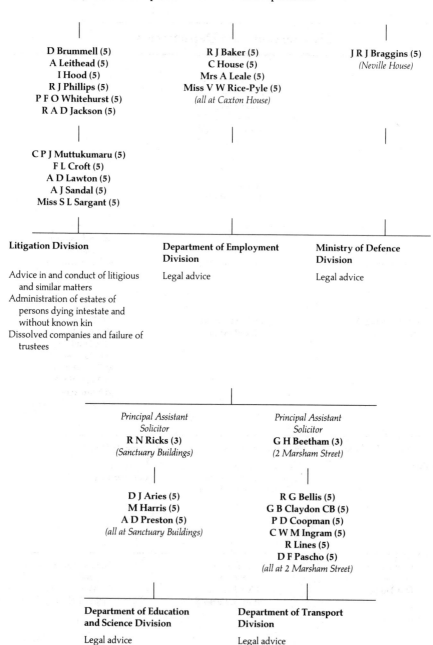

D Brummell (5)
A Leithead (5)
I Hood (5)
R J Phillips (5)
P F O Whitehurst (5)
R A D Jackson (5)

R J Baker (5)
C House (5)
Mrs A Leale (5)
Miss V W Rice-Pyle (5)
(all at Caxton House)

J R J Braggins (5)
(Neville House)

C P J Muttukumaru (5)
F L Croft (5)
A D Lawton (5)
A J Sandal (5)
Miss S L Sargant (5)

Litigation Division

Advice in and conduct of litigious
and similar matters
Administration of estates of
persons dying intestate and
without known kin
Dissolved companies and failure of
trustees

**Department of Employment
Division**

Legal advice

**Ministry of Defence
Division**

Legal advice

*Principal Assistant
Solicitor*
R N Ricks (3)
(Sanctuary Buildings)

*Principal Assistant
Solicitor*
G H Beetham (3)
(2 Marsham Street)

D J Aries (5)
M Harris (5)
A D Preston (5)
(all at Sanctuary Buildings)

R G Bellis (5)
G B Claydon CB (5)
P D Coopman (5)
C W M Ingram (5)
R Lines (5)
D F Pascho (5)
(all at 2 Marsham Street)

**Department of Education
and Science Division**

Legal advice

**Department of Transport
Division**

Legal advice

Head of Unit	*Establishment, Finance and Security Officer*
Mrs M Harrop (5)	**A J E Hollis (6)**

Lawyers' Management Unit	**Establishments, Finance and General Services**
Central management unit for members of Government Legal Service	Establishment matters
	Personnel
Career advice and development	Security
Recruitment	Accounts
Training	Legal costs
Organisation of legal trainee scheme	

Queen's Proctor

Queen's Proctor
Sir James Nursaw KCB QC (1)
Gerald Hosker CB QC (1)
(from October 1992)

Assistant Queen's Proctor
I Hood (5)

Queen's Proctor

Interventions and advisory
   functions in matrimonial suits
Legitimation cases

Treasury Solicitor's Department Addresses

Caxton House
Tothill Street
London SW1H 9NF
Tel 071-273 3000
Fax 071-273 5605

2 Marsham Street
London SW1P 3EB
Tel 071-276 3000
Fax 071-276 3330

Neville House
Page Street
London SW1P 4LS
Tel 071-218 4691
Fax 071-218 0844

1 Palace Street
London SW1E 5HE
Tel 071-238 3000
Fax 071-834 3771

Riverside Chambers
Tangier
Taunton
Somerset TA1 4AP
Tel 0823 345200
Fax 0823 345202

Sanctuary Buildings
Great Smith Street
London SW1P 3BT
Tel 071-925 6174
Fax 071-925 6992

Welsh Office

Founded	1964
Ministers	secretary of state, one minister of state and one parliamentary under secretary of state
Responsibilities	agriculture and fisheries ancient monuments and historic buildings civil emergencies economic affairs and regional planning (oversight) education environmental protection European Regional Development Fund forestry health housing industry (financial assistance) land use including planning local government personal social services roads sport tourism training water and sewerage Welsh language and culture countryside and nature conservation non-departmental public bodies
Executive agencies	CADW (Welsh Historic Monuments)

Welsh Office

New Crown Building, Cathays Park, Cardiff CF1 3NQ
Tel 0222 825111   Fax 0222 823036
Gwydyr House, Whitehall, London SW1A 2ER
Tel 071-270 3000   Fax 071-270 0568
All staff are based at Cathays Park unless otherwise indicated.
For other addresses and telephone numbers see the end of this section.

Ministers

Secretary of State
The Rt Hon David Hunt MBE MP

|

Parliamentary Private Secretary
John Bowis OBE MP

|

Special Adviser
Michael McManus

|

Principal Private Secretary
Miss J C Simpson
071-270 0549 (London)
0222 823200 (Cardiff)

|

Minister of State
The Rt Hon Sir Wyn Roberts MP

|

Parliamentary Private Secretary
David Tredinnick MP

|

Private Secretary
Dr H O Jones
071-270 0559 (London)
0222 825448 (Cardiff)

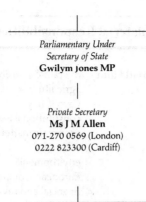

*Parliamentary Under
Secretary of State*
Gwilym Jones MP

Private Secretary
Ms J M Allen
071-270 0569 (London)
0222 823300 (Cardiff)

House of Lords' Spokesman
Viscount St Davids

Ministerial Responsibilities

David Hunt   overall responsibility for the department
agriculture
Cardiff Bay
constitutional issues
economic matters including Welsh Economic
   Council
environment
European Community
financial and revenue support grant
industry
programme for valleys
regional policy
rural initiative
security policy and operations
sport
Welsh Development Agency and
   Development Board for Rural Wales

Sir Wyn Roberts   arts and culture
broadcasting
conservation
Countryside Council for Wales
education, enterprise and training
forestry
historic buildings and ancient monuments
National Library
National Museum of Wales
national parks
public appointments
public libraries
rural affairs
small businesses
tourism
transport and highways
Welsh language
Welsh Tourist Board
women's issues

Gwilym Jones   Citizen's Charter
community care and personal social services
energy
enterprise zones
environmental protection
fisheries
health
housing
land use planning
local government
NHS trusts
urban affairs
water

Departmental Overview

Civil Servants			Department	Minister
Grade 1	Grade 2	Grade 3		

Legal, Information, Establishment, Finance, Health Professional Group, NHS Directorate

Sir Richard Lloyd Jones		D G Lambert	Legal Division	D Hunt
		H G Roberts (5)	Information	D Hunt
		G C G Craig	Establishment Group	D Hunt
		R A Wallace	Finance Group	D Hunt
		Dr D J Hine	Health Professional Group	G Jones
		J W Owen	NHS Directorate in Wales	G Jones

Agriculture, Economic and Regional Policy, Industry

Sir Richard Lloyd Jones	J F Craig	O Rees	Agriculture	D Hunt
		M J A Cochlin	Economic and Regional Policy	D Hunt
		C D Stevens	Industry	D Hunt

Education, Health and Social Work, Housing, Water and Environmental Protection, Transport, Highways and Planning

Sir Richard Lloyd Jones	J W Lloyd	R H Jones	Education	Sir W Roberts
		R L James (4)	HM Inspectorate	Sir W Roberts
		R W Jarman	Housing, Health and Social Services	G Jones
		P R Gregory	Transport, Planning Environment	Sir W Roberts D Hunt

Civil Servants and Departments

Legal, Information, Establishment,
Finance, Health Professional Group,
NHS Directorate

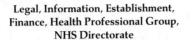

Permanent Secretary
Sir Richard Lloyd Jones KCB (1)
(Whitehall and Cardiff)

Private Secretary
P J Higgins
071-270 0539
0222 823289

Solicitor and Legal Adviser	*Director of Information*	*Principal Establishment Officer*
D G Lambert (3)	**H G Roberts (5)**	**G C G Craig (3)**
P J Murrin (5) **J H Turnbull (5)**		**R M Abel (5)** **G A Thomas (5)** **Mrs H F O Thomas (5)** **O T Hooker (5)** **Dr M P G Pepper (5)**

Legal	**Information**	**Establishment**
Advice to all divisions on legal matters	Liaison with media Production and distribution of publicity material Press arrangement for royal visits	Personnel management Central and management services Emergencies Economic and statistical services

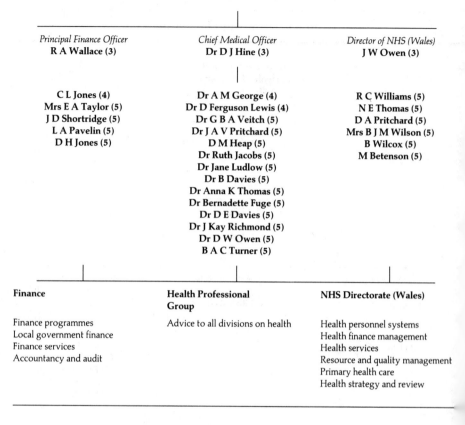

Principal Finance Officer	Chief Medical Officer	Director of NHS (Wales)
R A Wallace (3)	Dr D J Hine (3)	J W Owen (3)
C L Jones (4)	Dr A M George (4)	R C Williams (5)
Mrs E A Taylor (5)	Dr D Ferguson Lewis (4)	N E Thomas (5)
J D Shortridge (5)	Dr G B A Veitch (5)	D A Pritchard (5)
L A Pavelin (5)	Dr J A V Pritchard (5)	Mrs B J M Wilson (5)
D H Jones (5)	D M Heap (5)	B Wilcox (5)
	Dr Ruth Jacobs (5)	M Betenson (5)
	Dr Jane Ludlow (5)	
	Dr B Davies (5)	
	Dr Anna K Thomas (5)	
	Dr Bernadette Fuge (5)	
	Dr D E Davies (5)	
	Dr J Kay Richmond (5)	
	Dr D W Owen (5)	
	B A C Turner (5)	

Finance	Health Professional Group	NHS Directorate (Wales)
Finance programmes	Advice to all divisions on health	Health personnel systems
Local government finance		Health finance management
Finance services		Health services
Accountancy and audit		Resource and quality management
		Primary health care
		Health strategy and review

Agriculture, Economic and Regional Policy, Industry

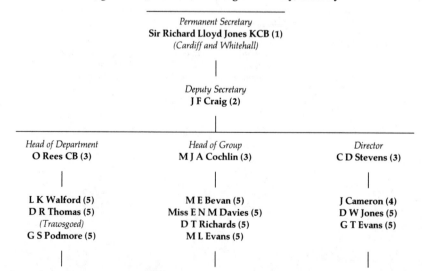

Permanent Secretary
Sir Richard Lloyd Jones KCB (1)
(Cardiff and Whitehall)

Deputy Secretary
J F Craig (2)

Head of Department	Head of Group	Director
O Rees CB (3)	M J A Cochlin (3)	C D Stevens (3)
L K Walford (5)	M E Bevan (5)	J Cameron (4)
D R Thomas (5)	Miss E N M Davies (5)	D W Jones (5)
(Trawsgoed)	D T Richards (5)	G T Evans (5)
G S Podmore (5)	M L Evans (5)	

Agriculture	Economic and Regional Policy	Industry
Commodities, structure and general policy	Economic and regional policy	Industrial policy
Animal health welfare, fisheries and R&D	Employment and training	Exports
Land agricultural subsidies and grants	Enterprise and small businesses	R&D
	European affairs	Energy efficiency
	Steel	Industrial development
	Energy	
	Telecommunications	
	Countryside and nature conservation	
	National parks	
	Development Board	
	Tourism	
	Urban affairs	

Education, Health and Social Work, Housing, Water and Environmental Protection, Transport, Highways and Planning

Permanent Secretary
Sir Richard Lloyd Jones KCB (1)
(Cardiff and Whitehall)

Deputy Secretary
J W Lloyd CB (2)

Head of Department **R H Jones (3)** *(Government Bldgs)*	*Chief Inspector* **R L James (4)**	*Head of Group* **R H Jarman (3)**
H Evans (5) B J Mitchell (5) W G Davies (5) R C Simpson (5) *(Government Bldgs)*	M J F Wynn (5) P Thomas (5) W R Jenkins (5) T E Parry (5) S J Adams (5) G Thomas (5)	R J Davies (5) S H Martin (5) A G Thornton (5) Dr D Adams (5) D G Evans (5) Miss M P Bull (5)

Education

Schools curriculum
Schools administration
Further and higher education
Education services

HM Inspectorate

Assessment of education process in
all institutions except
universities
Advice to teachers and local
education authorities

Housing, Health and Social Services Policy Group

Public health and family
Community care
Health policy and resources
Social services inspectorate
Housing
Architects and surveyors
Nursing

Head of Group
P R Gregory (3)

K J Thomas (4)
H R Bollington (5)
D I Westlake (5)
A H H Jones (5)

Transport, Planning and Environment Group

Local government
Environment
Planning
Planning services
Estates
Transport policy
Highways
Roads administration
Roads engineering
Roads construction

Welsh Office Addresses

Trawsgoed
Aberystwyth
Dyfed SY23 1NG
Tel 09743 301
Fax 09743 259

Brunel House
2 Fitzalan House
Cardiff CF2 1UY
Tel 0222 465511
Fax 0222 465511 X218

Government Buildings
Tyglass Road
Llanishen
Cardiff CF4 5PL
Tel 0222 761456
Fax 0222 747901

'Next Steps' Executive Agencies

Next Steps is the name given to the civil service reforms under which agencies are being set up to deliver government services, the main aims of which are to improve civil service management and thereby the delivery of services. They were launched in February 1988 following the main recommendations of the Efficiency Unit report "Improving Management in Government: the Next Steps". The report recommended that, to the greatest extent practical, the executive functions of government should be carried out by units designated as agencies headed by chief executives.

Since then, 75 agencies have been established and about 291,000 civil servants, half the total, are now working in agencies and other organisations operating on Next Steps lines.

Another 26 candidates have been announced covering over 66,000 more civil servants, and many more areas are under consideration. The candidates for agency status include HM Prison Service, the Youth Treatment Service, and the Pesticide Safety Directorate. A list of these candidates will be found below, after the list of those already established.

The role of the chief executive

Next Steps agencies are headed by a chief executive to whom management of the agency has been delegated by the responsible minister within the terms of the agency's published framework document.

The minister, in consultation with the Treasury, sets the policy framework for the agency, delegates authority to carry out the specified task and allocates the agency's budget. He sets key performance targets for the agency and approves its corporate plan and annual business plan. He then monitors the agency's performance, measures its success against its targets and is accountable to Parliament for its activities. These arrangements are set out in each agency's framework document.

The chief executive manages the day-to-day operation and is accountable to the minister for the use of the resources provided, the performance of the agency and for ensuring that the agreed targets are met. Often, an element of the chief executive's salary is linked to the achievement of these targets. The chief executive will also be the accounting officer accountable to Parliament for the proper handling of the resources for which he or she is responsible.

Chief executives are civil servants, although many of them may be directly recruited from outside the civil service for a contract period. Their 'grading' in civil service terms is that appropriate to the job to be done; currently there are chief executives graded from 1A (second permanent secretary) to 6 (senior principal).

Next Steps Executive Agencies

(as at 1 July 1992)

Accounts Services Agency   ASA
ADAS   ADAS
Building Research Establishment   BRE
The Buying Agency   BA
CADW (Welsh Historic Monuments)   CADW
Central Office of Information   COI
Central Science Laboratory   CSL
Central Statistical Office   CSO
Central Veterinary Laboratory   CVL
Chemical and Biological Defence Establishment   CBDE
Child Support Unit (becomes an Agency in April 1993)   CSU
Civil Service College   CSC
Companies House   CH
Compensation Agency (NI)   CA(NI)
Defence Analytical Services Agency   DASA
Defence Operation Analysis Centre   DOAC
Defence Postal and Courier Service   DPCS
Defence Research Agency   DRA
Directorate General of Defence Accounts   DGDA
Driver and Vehicle Licensing Agency   DVLA
Driver and Vehicle Testing Agency (NI)   DVTA(NI)
Driving Standards Agency   DSA
Duke of York's Royal Military School   DYRMS
DVOIT   DVOIT
Employment Service   ES
Fire Service College   FSC
Forensic Science Service   FSS
Historic Royal Palaces   HRP
Historic Scotland   HS
HMSO   HMSO
Hydrographic Office   HyO
Insolvency Service   IS
Intervention Board   IB
Laboratory of the Government Chemist   LGC
HM Land Registry   HMLR
Medicines Control Agency   MCA
Meteorological Office   MO
Military Survey   MS
National Engineering Laboratory   NEL
National Physical Laboratory   NPL
National Weights and Measures Laboratory   NWML
Natural Resources Institute   NRI
Naval Aircraft Repair Organisation   NARO
NHS Estates   NHSE
Occupational Health Service   OHS
Ordnance Survey   OS
Ordnance Survey (NI)   OS(NI)
UK Passport Agency   UKPA

Patent Office   PO
Planning Inspectorate Agency   PIA
Public Record Office   PRO
Queen Elizabeth II Conference Centre   QECC
Queen Victoria School   QVS
Radiocommunications Agency   RA
RAF Support Command Maintenance Group   RAFSCMG
Rate Collection Agency (NI)   RCA(NI)
Recruitment and Assessment Services Agency   RASA
Registers of Scotland   RS
Royal Mint   RM
Scottish Agricultural Science Agency   SASA
Scottish Fisheries Protection Agency   SFPA
Service Children's Schools (NW Europe)   SCS(NWE)
Social Security Agency (NI)   SSA(NI)
Social Security Benefits Agency   SSBA
Social Security Contributions Agency   SSCA
Social Security Information Technology Services Agency   SSITSA
Social Security Resettlement Agency   SSRA
Teachers' Pensions Agency   TPA
Training and Employment Agency (NI)   TEA(NI)
Transport Research Laboratory   TRL
Valuation Office Agency   VOA
Vehicle Certification Agency   VCA
Vehicle Inspectorate   VI
Veterinary Medicines Directorate   VMD
Warren Spring Laboratory   WSL
Wilton Park Conference Centre   WPCC

Customs and Excise (30 Executive Units)*
Inland Revenue (34 Executive Units)*

*See under Government Departments Section

Candidates for Agency Status (26)

Army Logistics	Defence
Chessington Computer Centre	Cabinet Office/OPSS
Child Support Agency	N Ireland
Common Services Division	Defence
Defence Animal Centre	Defence
Directorate Information Technology Bureau Services	Defence
Driver and Vehicle Licencing Agency	N Ireland
Equipment Test and Evaluation	Defence
Fuel Suppliers Branch	Environment
HM Prison Service	Home Office
Human Factors Research	Defence

Meat Hygiene Service	Agriculture
MoD Police	Defence
Naval Training	Defence
NHS Superannuation Branch	Health
Office of Population Censuses and Surveys	Health
Pesticide Safety Directorate	Agriculture
Property Division	Treasury Solicitor
Property Holdings Portfolio Management	Environment
RAF Training	Defence
Royal Parks	National Heritage
Scottish Office Superannuation	Scottish Office
Scottish Prison Service	Scottish Office
Social Security Child Support Agency*	Social Security
Valuation and Lands Office	N Ireland
Youth Treatment Service	Health

*See under Child Support Unit in the Executive Agencies section

Accounts Services Agency

Government Buildings, Cardiff Road, Newport, Gwent NP9 1ZA
Tel 0633 810636   Fax 0633 810660

Staff	*Director and*
	Chief Executive
	D Michael Hoddinot (5)
	Assistant Directors
	Mrs Mary Hoppis (7)
	Graham Price (7)
Responsibilities	To provide financial and management accounting services to the DTI and other government departments
Department	Trade and Industry
Launched	1 October 1991

ADAS

Nobel House, 17 Smith Square, London SW1P 2JR
Tel 071-238 5619/5631   Fax 071-238 5633/5732

Staff	*Chief Executive* **Dr Julia M Walsh (2)** *Director of Operations* **Phillip Needham** *Director of Research* **Dr David Hughes** *Director of Marketing* **Vacant** *Director of Finance* **Chris Herring** *Director of Personnel* **Ms Sarah Nason** *Director, Wales* **Cyril Davies** *Non Executive Directors* **Charles Bystram** (Chairman) **Paul Christensen** **Kenneth Fraser** *Consultancy Centres* (see next page)
Responsibilities	ADAS, formerly known as the Agricultural Development and Advisory Service, provides a comprehensive range of consultancy services to the food, farming, land and leisure industries. In addition, ADAS carries out research in these same areas; performs certain statutory functions; and provides advice on policy for MAFF and the Welsh Office.
Department	Agriculture, Fisheries and Food
Launched	1 April 1992

ADAS Consultancy Centre Addresses

Bury St Edmunds
Southgate Street
Bury St Edmunds
Suffolk IP33 2BD
Tel 0283 753271
Fax 0284 732025

Cardiff
St Agnes Road
Gabalfa
Cardiff CF4 4YH
Tel 0222 586000
Fax 0222 586228

Guildford
Block B, Government Bldgs
Epsom Road
Guildford GU1 2LD
Tel 0483 62881
Fax 0483 65356

Huntingdon
Government Buildings
Chequers Court
Huntingdon
Cambs PE18 6LT
Tel 0480 52161
Fax 0480 412049

Leeds
Block 2 Government Bldgs
Otley Road
Lawnswood
Leeds LS16 5PY
Tel 0532 611222
Fax 0532 300174

Lincoln
Ceres House
2 Searby Road
Lincoln LN2 4DW
Tel 0522 29951
Fax 0522 513694

Maidstone
Crown House
Sittingbourne Road
Maidstone
Kent ME14 5TY
Tel 0622 754300
Fax 0622 675929

Newcastle
Government Buildings
Kenton Bar
Newcastle upon Tyne
NE1 1YA
Tel 091-286 9811
Fax 091-286 2362

Oxford
Government Buildings
Marston Road
New Marston
Oxford OX3 0TP
Tel 0865 244891
Fax 0865 794175

Preston
Government Buildings
Cop Lane
Penwortham
Preston
Lancs PR1 0SP
Tel 0772 744123
Fax 0772 745311

Ruthin
Station Road
Ruthin
Clwyd LL15 1BP
Tel 08242 2611
Fax 08242 7163

Starcross
Staplake Mount
Starcross
Exeter
Devon EX6 8PE
Tel 0626 890481
Fax 0626 891259

Taunton
Quantock House
Paul Street
Taunton TA1 3NX
Tel 0823 337922
Fax 0823 253284

Wolverhampton
Woodthorne
Wergs Road
Wolverhampton WV6 8TQ
Tel 0902 754190
Fax 0902 743602

Worcester
Block C Government Bldgs
Whittingdon Road
Worcester WR5 2LQ
Tel 0905 763355
Fax 0905 763180

Building Research Establishment

Garston, Watford WD2 7JR
Tel 0923 894040   Fax 0923 664010

Staff	*Chief Executive* **Roger Courtney (3)**
	Deputy Chief Executive *Director (Materials)* **N O Milbank (4)**
	Director (Planning and Resources) **C R Durham (5)**
	Director (Construction and Application) **B O Hall (5)**
	Director (Geotechnics and Structures) **Dr N J Cook (5)**
	Director (Fire Research Station **Dr W D Woolley (5)**
	Director (Environment and Energy) **Dr V H C Crisp (5)**
Responsibilities	To support the Secretary of State for the Environment and other departments in their policy and executive responsibilities relating to construction and the health and safety of people in and around buildings
	To carry out research and provide guidance on the design, construction and performance of built works, the prevention and control of fire and the protection of the environment
	To provide research and consultancy services to non-government customers
	To make available its research findings and knowledge through seminars and publications
Department	Environment
Launched	2 April 1990

The Buying Agency

Royal Liver Building, Pier Head, Liverpool L3 1PE
Tel 051-227 4262   Fax 051-227 3315

Staff

Chief Executive
R H Powell (5)

Finance Director
G Aldridge (6)

Operations Director
C Hancock (6)

Secretariat
P McCallum (7)

Responsibilities   To provide a professional purchasing service to central government departments, the NHS and other public sector bodies. TBA's core business encompasses mechanical, electrical, engineering, building and domestic products and accommodation services

Department   Environment

Launched   31 October 1991

CADW (Welsh Historic Monuments)

Brunel House, 2 Fitzalan Road, Cardiff CF2 1UY
Tel 0222 465511   Fax 0222 450859

Staff	*Chief Executive* **John Carr (5)** *Directors* **R W Hughes (6)** **J H Pavitt (6)**
Responsibilities	To support directly and indirectly the preservation, conservation, appreciation and enjoyment of the built heritage in Wales through advice, education, example, persuasion and, where appropriate, intervention and financial support
Department	Welsh Office
Launched	2 April 1991

Central Office of Information

Hercules Road, London SE1 7DU
Tel 071-928 2345   Fax 071-261 0942

Staff

Chief Executive
Mike Devereau

Private Secretary
Mrs J Shinn
071-261 8211

Deputy Chief Executive
J Bolitho

Press Officer
Miss L Justice

Campaigns Group
Group Director
R Windsor

Films, Television and Radio
Director
M Nisbet

Publications, Press and Exhibitions
Group Director
D A Low

Regional Services and Emergency Planning
Group Director
P T Brazier

Training and Total Quality Management
Director
R Smith

Client Services and Marketing
Group Director
R N Hooper

Finance and Management Services
Group Director and
Principal Finance Officer
K E Williamson

Responsibilities   To supply information and publicity services and give advice in all media for government departments, agencies and other public sector clients, on a repayment basis

Department   The COI is a department in its own right. The Chief Executive was accountable to
                               Treasury ministers until June 1992. He is now accountable to the Cabinet Office
                               (Office of Public Service and Science)

Launched   5 April 1990

Central Science Laboratory

London Road, Slough, Berks SL3 7JH
Tel 0753 534626   Fax 0753 824058

Staff

Chief Executive
Dr Peter Stanley (3)

Research Director
Dr A R Hardy (5)

Resource Director
J Stubbs (6)

Finance Director
B Simmons (6)

Commercial Director
Dr M Tas (6)

Head Plant Health Group
Dr S Hill (6)

Head Infestation Risk Evaluation Group
D Rowlands (6)

Head Pest Management Strategies Group
Dr N Price (6)

Head Pesticides and Contaminants Group
Dr M Wilson (6)

*Head Conservation and Environment
Protection Group*
Dr P Greig-Smith (6)

Responsibilities

To provide commissioned research and development and scientific and technical advice to meet both the statutory and policy objectives of MAFF. In addition CSL offers R&D and advice to other government departments and to public and private sector organisations both nationally and internationally on a commercial basis. Main areas are:

To maintain plant health and exclude non-indigenous plant pests and diseases

To assess the impact of agricultural practices on the environment and the consumer

To develop safe, effective, humane and environmentally friendly pest management techniques

To carry out the humane control of vertebrate pests

Department   Agriculture, Fisheries and Food

Launched   1 April 1992

Central Statistical Office

Government Offices, Great George Street, London SW1P 3AQ
Tel 071-270 3000   Fax 071-270 5866

Millbank Tower, Millbank, London SW1P 4QU
Tel 071-217 3000   Fax 071-217 4338

Government Buildings, Cardiff Road, Newport NP9 1XG
Tel 0633 815696   Fax 0633 812863

Staff

*Director and Head of the
Government Statistical
Service*
William McLennan (1A)

*Deputy Director
Director of National Accounts*
D Wroe (2)

Board Members
**William McLennan
David Wroe (2)
Reg Ward (3)
Neil Harvey (3)
John Kidgell (3)
Frank Martin (4)
Mrs Mary Berg
Paul Thornton**

*Division 1
Head of Division*
R G Ward (3)

**D C K Stirling (5)
T J Griffin (5)
D J Sellwood (5)**
(all at Millbank)
R J Scott (5)
(Newport)
**Miss S P Carter (5)
P B Kenny (5)**

*Division 2
Head of Division*
N Harvey (3)

K Francombe (5)
C J Spiller (5)
R M Norton (5)
R G Lynch (5)
(all at Newport)
K Mansell (5)

Division 3
Head of Division
J E Kidgell (3)

G Jenkinson (5)
B J Buckingham (5)
(Newport)
Mrs P G Walker (5)
(Millbank)
P Turnbull (5)

Division 4
Head of Division
F Martin (4)

Dr J H Ludley (5)
J B Wright (5)
D R Lewis (5)
(Newport)

Responsibilities	The CSO is responsible for compiling and publishing the key statistics needed for central economic management. CSO liaises with the EC and other international statistical institutions on domestic and international statistics. The CSO is also responsible for central management of the government statistical service.
	It also publishes press notices on macro-economic statistics and a range of publications on specific industries and activities
Department	The CSO is a department in its own right. The Chief Executive is accountable to the Chancellor of the Exchequer
Launched	19 November 1991

Central Veterinary Laboratory

New Haw, Addlestone, Surrey KT15 3NB
Tel 0932 341111   Fax 0932 347046

Staff

Chief Executive
and Director
Dr T W A Little

Director of Research
Dr B J Shreeve

Director of Operations
R W Saunders

Director of Business
Dr J A Morris

Responsibilities

To provide consultancy, research, services and products to promote animal health and welfare, and to minimise hazards from animals to public health and the environment

Department

Agriculture, Fisheries and Food

Launched

2 April 1990

Chemical and Biological Defence Establishment

Porton Down, Salisbury, Wilts SP4 0JQ
Tel 0980 613000   Fax 0980 611777

Staff

Chief Executive
Director General
Dr Graham S Pearson CB (3)

Director (Life
Sciences)
Dr L Leadbeater (5)

Director (Physical
Sciences)
Dr R J Powell CBE (5)

Establishment Secretary
G Wright (6)

Responsibilities   To carry out research so that its principal customers, the armed forces, are
provided with effective protective measures against threats from chemical and
biological weapons

To give advice and support to the MOD, FCO, Home Office and other
departments on chemical and biological warfare and defence matters

Department   Defence

Launched   1 April 1991

Child Support Unit
(Agency from April 1993)

Millbank Tower, 21-24 Millbank, London SW1 4QU
Tel 071-217 4789   Fax 071-217 4824

Staff	*Chief Executive* **Ros Hepplewhite (4)** *Project Director* **Owen Thorpe (5)** *Resources Director* **Derek Rutherford (5)** *Business Development Director* **John Hughes (5)**
Responsibilities	When the Unit becomes an Agency in April 1993 it will provide a service for the assessment, collection and enforcement of child maintenance
Department	Social Security
Launched	April 1993

Civil Service College

Sunningdale Park, Ascot, Berks SL5 0QE
Tel 0344 634000   Fax 0344 842491

11 Belgrave Road, London SW1V 1RB
Tel 071-834 6644   Fax 071-630 6888

Staff

Chief Executive
Miss M T Neville-Rolfe (3)

Director of Studies
Dr R J Smith (5)

*Director of Services
and Resources*
I Cameron (5)

Secretary
Miss M A Wood (6)

Business Group Directors
Ms C M Bentley (5)
Ms E Chennels (6)
P A Daffern (6)
J G Fuller (6)
P J C O'Connell (6)
P G Tebby (6)
Miss J A Topham (6)

Responsibilities   To help develop the managerial and professional skills of civil servants especially those at or aspiring to relatively senior levels, and to promote good practice in government in management and key professional areas

Department   Cabinet Office (Office of Public Service and Science)

Launched   6 June 1989

Companies House

Crown Way, Maindy, Cardiff CF4 3UZ
Tel 0222 388588   Fax 0222 380900

Staff

Chief Executive
Registrar of Companies
for England and Wales
David Durham (4)

Operations and Marketing
Director
Derek Marsh (5)

Information Systems
Director
David Garnett (5)

Finance and Planning
Director
Peter Lawrence (5)

Personnel Director
Miss Elizabeth Rees (6)

Legal Director
Herbert Hart (6)

Responsibilities   To incorporate companies, register documents which companies are obliged to file, and provide company information

It also exercises certain statutory powers on behalf of the Secretary of State for Trade and Industry, eg the registrar can authorise a change of company name

Department   Trade and Industry

Launched   3 October 1988. It became a trading on 1 October 1991

782 Next Steps Executive Agencies

Compensation Agency (NI)

Royston House, 34 Upper Queen Street, Belfast BT1 6FD
Tel 0232 249944   Fax 0232 246956

Staff	**Chief Executive (5)**
Responsibilities	To administer statutory criminal injuries and criminal damage schemes in Northern Ireland
Department	Northern Ireland Office
Launched	1 April 1992

Defence Analytical Services Agency

MoD, First Avenue House, High Holborn, London WC1V 6HE
Tel 071-530 5420

Staff	*Chief Executive* **P P Altobell**
Responsibilities	Provides services, including compilation of manpower, financial and logistical statistics and a manpower planning and forecasting service to the Armed Services. It also provides project-based statistical services to ministers and senior officials
Department	Defence
Launched	1 July 1992

Defence Operational Analysis Centre

MoD, Broadoaks, Parvis Road, West Byfleet, Surrey KT14 6LY
Tel 0252 3405030

Staff	*Chief Executive* **Dr D Leadbetter**
Responsibilities	Provides policy advice, based on operational analysis and field studies, to ministers, senior officials and officers, on various topics and particularly on equipment procurement
Department	Defence
Launched	1 July 1992

Defence Postal and Courier Service

MoD, Inglis Barracks, Mill Hill, London NW7 1PY
Tel 081-346 2611 x3300

Staff	*Chief Executive* **Brig M A Browne**
Responsibilities	Provides a world-wide mail and secure courier service for service personnel and the MoD. It also supports forces post offices and provides a transit system for the MoD in the UK
Department	Defence
Launched	1 July 1992

Defence Research Agency

Meudon Avenue, Farnborough, Hants GU14 7TU
Tel 0252 244614   Fax 0252 375930

Staff

Chief Executive
and Director
John A R Chisholm (2)

Managing Director
Military and Aeronautics
Group
Dr R H Warren (3)

Managing Director
Command and Maritime
Systems Group
P D Ewins (3)

Finance Director
G Love (3)

Rationalisation
Director
Dr D C Tyte (3)

Group Services Director
Dr D J L Smith

Commercial Director
Dr M Goodfellow (3)

Technical and
Quality Director
Dr A L Mears (3)

Quality Assurance
Technical Services
Director
Dr J P Catchpole (4)

Company Secretary
Mrs E Peace (5)

Group Services

Director
Dr D J L Smith (3)

Head of Site Services
P Fitzgibbon (5)

Head of Engineering Services
S Calvard (5)

Head of Personnel
R C Hack (5)

Head of Information Systems
P Webb (6)

Military and Aeronautics Business Group

Managing Director
Dr R H Warren (3)

Director Programmes
Dr A F J Cox (5)

Director Fighting Vehicles
and Systems
D Kimberley (5)

Director Aircraft Systems
R E Jones (4)

Director Weapons Systems
J M Flood (3)

Director Operational Studies
R J Sherwell (4)

Director Chemical and Electronics
R Seaney (5)

Command and Maritime Systems Business Group

Managing Director
P D Ewins (3)

Director Programmes
C D Fallows (5)

Director Command and
Information Systems
Dr J M Hinsley (5)

Director Electronics
Dr V G Roper (5)

Director Space
B Atkinson (5)

Director Underwater Systems
P M Sutcliffe (3)

Director Above-Water Systems
C R Stonehouse (5)

Responsibilities	Provides non-nuclear research for the MoD, other government departments and the private sector
Department	Defence
Launched	1 April 1991

Directorate General of Defence Accounts

Ministry of Defence, Warminster Road, Bath BA1 5AA
Tel 0225 828474   Fax 0225 828176

Mersey House, Drury Lane, Liverpool L2 7PK
Tel 051-242 2234   Fax 051-242 2470

Staff

Chief Executive
and Director
Michael J Dymond (4)

Director of Accounts
(Civil Pay)
P J Trevelyan (5)

Director of Financial
and Management Accounting
Services
D D Morrison (5)

Director of Accounts
(Bills)
M A Rowe (5)
(Liverpool)

Responsibilities

To provide a central accounting function for the MOD, comprising:
  production of the appropriate accounts
  payment of bills and claims
  recovery of monies due
  audit of MOD equipments held by contractors
  payment of civilian salaries and wages
  awarding of civilian superannuation benefits

To provide accounting and other information for the management of the MOD

To define and promulgate MOD accounting policies and regulations

To provide civilian pay and pensions services to other government departments
on a repayment basis

Department   Defence

Launched   1 April 1991

Driving Standards Agency

Stanley House, 56 Talbot Street, Nottingham NG1 5GU
Tel 0602 474222   Fax 0602 485734

Staff

Chief Executive
Dr Chris M Woodman (5)

Deputy Chief Executive
G J B Donaldson (6)

Finance Director
G A Lobo (6)

*Registrar of Approved
Driving Instructors*
B G Austin (7)

Property Manager
D Anderson (7)

*Policy and External
Relations Manager*
P Butler (7)

*Customer Service
Manager*
W J Wilson (7)

Personnel Manager
A E Evans (7)

Planning Manager
G C Morgan (7)

Chief Driving Examiner
D Norris

Responsibilities   To test drivers of cars, lorries, buses and motor cycles and approve driving
instructors

Department   Transport

Launched   2 April 1990

Driver and Vehicle Licensing Agency

Longview Road, Morriston, Swansea SA6 7JL
Tel 0792 782363   Fax 0792 783003

Staff	*Chief Executive* **Stephen R Curtis (3)**
	Heads of Division *Driver Licensing* **R J Verge (5)**
	Vehicle Registration *Licensing and Taxation* **T J Horton (5)**
	Management Services **I Heawood (5)**
Responsibilities	The registration and licensing of drivers and vehicles in Great Britain and collection of excise duty. It also runs the scheme to sell attractive registration marks.
	It provides a wide range of services for the Department of Transport and other government departments, the police and the general public including answering queries; supplying information to the police, the courts, insurance companies and the public; and helping road safety
Department	Transport
Launched	1 April 1990

Driver and Vehicle Testing Agency (NI)

Headquarters, Balmoral Road, Belfast BT12 6QL
Tel 0232 681831   Fax 0232 665520

Staff   Chief Executive (6)

Responsibilities To promote and improve road safety in Northern Ireland through the
                      advancement of driving standards and implementation of the government's
                      policies for improving the mechanical standards of vehicles

Department   Department of the Environment for Northern Ireland

Launched   1 April 1992

Duke of York's Royal Military School

Dover, Kent CT15 5EQ
Tel 0303 249541 X5025   Fax 0303 249541 X55019

Staff	*Chief Executive* **Lt Col Gordon H Wilson**
Responsibilities	To provide boarding school education primarily for the dependents, aged between 11 and 18 years, of service personnel
Department	Defence
Launched	1 April 1992

DVOIT

Oldway Centre, 36 Orchard Street, Swansea SA99 5AX
Tel 0792 304050   Fax 0792 304190

Staff

Chief Executive
David Evans (4)

Directors

Marketing
J K Griffiths (5)

Application Delivery
G D J Wilks (6)

Finance
J Gibbings (6)

Operational Services
K I Wood (6)

Responsibilities

To provide a full range of IT services to the Department of Transport, its agencies and others. These services include:

strategic planning and consultancy
project planning and management
systems analysis and design
data management
computer security
software development
computer operations
facilities management
printing and document handling
training
procurement, installation and management of computing and
  telecommunications equipment and facilities

Department

Transport

Launched

1 April 1992

Employment Service

St Vincent House, 30 Orange Street, London WC2H 7HT
Tel 071-839 5600   Fax 071-389 1373

Staff

Chief Executive
M E G Fogden (3)

*Corporate Development
and Secretariat*
J Cowper (6)

Deputy Chief Executive
J Turner
(Sheffield)

Field Services Directorate
Director
J W Cooper (4)

*Network Implementation
Branch*
Miss R Threw (5)

*Business Consultancy
Service*
D Benham (6)

Pay Strategy Project
H Tollyfield (6)
(Above 3 in Sheffield)

Directorate of Human Resources
Director
D B Price (4)

Personnel
Mrs C Thompson (5)

Deputy Head of Personnel
Mrs S Keyse (6)

Training and Development
P Benzies (6)

Psychology
Dr M Killcross (5)

Estates
J Davies (6)
(all in Sheffield)

Business Development Directorate
Director
M Emmott (4)

Business Strategy
Mrs L Ammon (6)

Research and Evaluation
J S Child (5)

Job Broking
R Lasko (5)

Claimant Advice
M Groves (5)

Benefit Management
R Halstead (5)

Disability Services
J A Robertson (5)

Deputy Head of
Disability Services
C Turner (6)
(all in Sheffield)

Finance and Resources Directorate
Director
A G Johnson (4)

Internal Audit
Ms S Orr (6)
(Sheffield)

Finance, Resource and
Planning
K Tolladay (6)

Financial Management
Services
J B Stewart (5)
J Davitt (6)

Information Technology
D Wood (5)
G Dodsworth (6)
J Charlton (6)
R Harris (6)

Regional Organisation
Regional Directors
London and South East
M Horsman (4)

Office for Scotland
A R Brown (5)

Northern
K M Pascoe (5)

North West
R M Philips (4)

Yorkshire & Humberside
R Parr (5)

West Midlands
M Raff (5)

East Midlands and Eastern
Mrs A Le Sage (5)

Office for Wales
E B Pearce (5)

South West
Ms J Henderson (5)

Responsibilities	To help unemployed people get back into work and to pay benefits to those entitled to them. In addition it runs a number of special programmes for the unemployed and for people with disabilities
Department	Employment
Launched	2 April 1990

Employment Service Addresses

Rockingham House
123 West Street
Sheffield S1 4ER
Tel 0742 596243
Fax 0742 724528

Regional addresses
London and South East
236 Gray's Inn Road
London WC1X 8HL
Tel 071-278 0363

Office for Scotland
9 St Andrew's Square
Edinburgh EH2 2QX
Tel 031-225 8500

Northern
Broadacre House
Market Street
Newcastle upon Tyne
NE1 6HH
Tel 091-236 6181

North West
Ontario House
2 Furnace Quay
Salford M5 2XZ
Tel 061-873 1000

Yorkshire and Humberside
Jubilee House
33–41 Park Place
Leeds LS1 2RE
Tel 0532 446299

West Midlands
2 Duchess Place
Hagley Road
Birmingham B16 8NS
Tel 021-456 2548

East Midlands and Eastern
Newton House
Maid Marion Way
Nottingham NG1 6GG
Tel 0602 483308

Office for Wales
Companies House
Crown Way
Maindy
Cardiff CF4 3UW
Tel 0222 388588

South West
The Pithay
Bristol BS1 2NQ
Tel 0272 273710

Fire Service College

Moreton-in-Marsh, Gloucestershire GL56 0RH
Tel 0608 50831   Fax 0608 51788

Staff	*Commandant Chief Executive* **Brian Fuller CBE**
Responsibilities	To provide command, leadership and management training for the UK Fire Service through a progressive system of training, and also to provide training in finance and specialist fire-related subjects
	To provide training for commerce and industry, and for students from overseas fire brigades
Department	Home Office
Launched	1 April 1992 with Trading Fund status

Forensic Science Service

Horseferry House, Dean Ryle Road, London SW1P 2AW
Tel 071-217 8344   Fax 071-976 5131
Priory House, Gooch Street North, Birmingham B5 6QQ
Tel 021-666 6606   Fax 021-622 3536

Staff

Chief Executive
Dr Janet Thompson (3)

Head of Business Organisation
P W Ward (5) (London)

Head of Business Development
Dr P D B Clarke (5)

Head of Finance
R G Rogers (5)

Chief Scientist
Dr A W Scaplehorn (5)

Head of Operations
Dr D J Werrett (6)

Head of Scientific Support
Mr V J Emerson (5)

Responsibilities   To provide scientific support in the investigation of crime and expert evidence to the courts. Its customers include the police, the Crown Prosecution Service and the defence.

Department   Home Office

Launched   1 April 1991

Historic Royal Palaces

Hampton Court Palace, East Molesey, Surrey KT8 9AU
Tel 081-977 7222   Fax 081-977 9714

Staff

Chief Executive
David C Beeton

Director of Finance and Resources
Ms S A Booth (5)

Marketing Director
P D Hammond (6)

Curator
Dr S J Thurley (6)

Surveyor of the Fabric
S Bond (5)

Director (Hampton Court and Kew)
D J C Macdonald (5)

Resident Governor (Tower of London)
Maj Gen C Tyler CB (5)
071-488 5695

Director (Kensington Palace)
N J Arch (7)
071-937 9561

Manager (Banqueting House)
Ms L M Kennedy (HEO)
071-930 4179

Responsibilities   To manage the five Historic Royal Palaces (Tower, Hampton Court, The Banqueting House, Kensington and Kew Palaces)

Department   National Heritage

Launched   1 October 1989

Historic Scotland

20 Brandon Street, Edinburgh EH3 5RA
Tel 031-244 3144   Fax 031-244 3030

Staff

Chief Executive
Graeme N Munro (3)

Deputy Directors

*Conservation and
Historic Buildings*
F J Lawrie (5)

*Corporate Planning and
Resources*
S Rosie (6)

Monuments
D Macniven (5)

*Works and Professional
Services, Assistant Director*
I Maxwell (6)

Responsibilities   To protect and promote public understanding and enjoyment of Scotland's ancient
monuments and archaeological sites and landscapes, historic buildings, parks,
gardens and designed landscapes

Department   Scottish Office Environment Department

Launched   2 April 1991

HMSO

St Crispins, Duke Street, Norwich NR3 1DN
Tel 0603 622211   Fax 0603 695582

Staff

*Controller and Chief
Executive*
Dr Paul I Freeman (2)

Deputy Chief Executive
M D Lynn (4)

Business Supplies Director
C N Southgate (5)

Print Procurement Director
B Ekers (5)

Publications Director
C J Penn (5)

Production Director
D G Forbes (5)
(Sovereign House)

*Director General,
Corporate Services*
P J MacDonald (4)

*Marketing and Corporate
Development Director*
V G Bell (5)

Personnel Services Director
A J Davies (5)
(Sovereign House)

*Information Technology
Director*
D C Kerry (5)
(Sovereign House)

*Industrial Personnel
Director*
A Mackie (5)
(Sovereign House)

Finance Director
A M Cole (5)

Quality and Innovation
Director
J R Eveson (6)

Engineering and Estates
Director
W E Scott (6)
(Sovereign House)

HMSO Scotland Director
G W Bedford (7)
(Edinburgh)

HMSO Northern Ireland
Director
Miss V J Wilson OBE (7)
(Belfast)

Responsibilities	The purchase of general office supplies (including office machinery, stationery and furniture), the procurement of print, and the provision of publishing, printing and reprographic services to Parliament, government departments and publicly funded bodies
Department	HMSO is a department in its own right and a Trading Fund. The Chief Executive was accountable to the Economic Secretary at the Treasury until June 1992. He is now accountable to the Cabinet Office (Office of Public Service and Science)
Launched	14 December 1988

HMSO Addresses

Sovereign House	HMSO Scotland	HMSO Northern Ireland
Botolph Street	Bankhead Avenue	IDB House
Norwich NR3 1DN	Edinburgh EH11 4AB	64 Chichester Street
Tel 0603 622211	Tel 031-479 3991	Belfast BT1 4PS
Fax 0603 695179	Fax 031-479 3400	Tel 0232 238451
		Fax 0232 230782

Hydrographic Office

Taunton, Somerset TA1 2DN
Tel 0823 337900   Fax 0823 284077

Lacon House, Theobalds Road, London WC1X 8RY
Tel 071-430 6371   Fax 071-430 6919

Staff

*Hydrographer of the Navy
and Chief Executive*
Rear Admiral J A L Myres (2*)†

*Director (Hydrographic
Charting and Sciences)*
Mrs B A Bond (5)

*Director (Hydrographic
Requirements and Services)*
Capt R A Cotton RN

*Director (Hydrographic
Finance and Marketing)*
B J Amor (6)

*Director (Surveying
Services Policy)*
Capt P D Barton RN (*)
(Lacon House)

*Director (Naval Oceanography
and Meteorology)*
Capt P Nicholas RN (*)
(Lacon House)

Responsibilities   To produce charts and navigational publications for the Royal Navy and other
customers at home and abroad

Department   Defence

Launched   1 April 1990

† 2*, * = armed forces ranking equivalent to Civil Service grades 3 and 5 respectively

Insolvency Service

Bridge Place, 88/89 Eccleston Square, London SW1V 1PT
Tel 071-215 5000   Fax 071-215 0752

Staff

Inspector General and
Chief Executive
Peter Joyce(3)

Deputy Inspectors General
HQ Operations
D J Flynn (4)

Official Receiver
Operations
J R Donnison ISO (4)

Head of Policy and
Planning
Ms R J R Anderson (5)

Responsibilities

To administer and investigate the affairs of individuals in bankruptcy and companies wound up by the courts

To report criminal offences in those failures and take proceedings for the disqualification of directors in all corporate failures

To regulate, directly or through professional bodies, private sector insolvency practitioners

To provide banking and investment services for bankruptcy and liquidation funds (funds from the realisation of assets are required to be paid by trustees and liquidators into the Insolvency Services account and may be invested in government securities)

To provide advice to ministers on insolvency policy issues

Department

Trade and Industry

Launched

21 March 1990

Intervention Board

Fountain House, Queen's Walk, Reading RG1 7QW
Tel 0734 583626   Fax 0734 566735

Staff

Chief Executive
Guy Stapleton (3)

Chairman
A J Ellis CBE

Secretary
S P Briggs (SEO)

Director (Finance)
J N Diserens (5)

*Director (External
Trade)*
G N Dixon (5)

*Director (Livestock
Products)*
M J Griffiths (5)

Director (Crops)
H MacKinnon (5)

*Director (Corporate
Services)*
J W M Peffers (5)

Responsibilities   To implement the UK's obligations under the EC's Common Agricultural Policy
by operating some 70 separate schemes to support the market in farm and food
products

Department   The Intervention Board is a department in its own right. The Chief Executive is
accountable to the Secretaries of State for Scotland, Wales and Northern Ireland
and the Minister of Agriculture, Fisheries and Food

Launched   1 April 1990

Laboratory of the Government Chemist

Queens Road, Teddington, Middlesex TW11 0LY
Tel 081-943 7000   Fax 081-943 2767

Staff

Chief Executive
and Government Chemist
Dr R D Worswick (3)

Deputy Directors
Resources
J Reynolds (5)

Government Analyst
Dr B King (5)

Biosciences and
Innovation
Dr R Dietz (5)

Heads of Division
Forensic and Customs
Dr T A Gough (6)

Planning, Marketing and
Services
R Lees ISO (6)

Food and Biosciences
Dr P B Baker (6)

Analytical Quality
Dr M Sargent (6)

Environmental Services
J Day (6)

Business Development
J Lisle (6)

Accounting and Finance
A Wilson (6)

Training and Personnel
T G L Alliston (6)

Responsibilities   To provide customers in both the public and private sectors with authoritative, independent and impartial consultancy and support on analytical chemistry, biotechnology and biomaterials and related sciences

It also plays an important role in the enforcement of law, the maintenance of public health, the protection of government duty revenue, the consumer and the environment

Its customers include government departments, the European Community, local authorities, law enforcement agencies, and private industry

Department   Trade and Industry

Launched   30 October 1991

HM Land Registry

Lincoln's Inn Fields, London WC2A 3PH
Tel 071-405 3488   Fax 071-242 0825

Staff

Chief Land Registrar,
Chief Executive
J J Manthorpe (2)

Solicitor
C J West (3)

Senior Land Registrar
Mrs J G Totty (5)

Director (Personnel and
Corporate Services)
E G Beardsall (5)

Director (Operations)
G N French (5)

Director (Information
Technology)
R J Fenn (5)

Director (Finance)
Miss H M Jackson (5)

Controller (Management
Services)
P J Smith (6)

Land Registrar
M L Wood (5)

District Land Registrars

Birkenhead	*Gloucester*	*Lytham*
M G Garwood (5)	**W W Budden (5)**	**J G Cooper (5)**
Coventry	*Harrow*	*Nottingham*
S P Kelway (5)	**J V Timothy (5)**	**P J Timothy (5)**
Croydon	*Kingston upon Hull*	*Peterborough*
D M J Moss (5)	**S R G Coveney (5)**	**M Avens (5)**
Durham	*Leicester*	*Plymouth*
C W Martin (5)	**L M Pope (6)**	**A J Pain (5)**

Portsmouth	*Swansea*	*Tunbridge*
S R Sehrawat (6)	G A Hughes (5)	G R Tooke (5)
Stevenage	*Telford*	*Weymouth*
D M T Mullett (5)	M A Roche (5)	Mrs P M Reeson (5)

Responsibilities   To keep and maintain a register of title to freehold and leasehold land in England and Wales

To deliver land registration services

Department   HM Land Registry is a department in its own right. The Chief Executive is directly accountable to the Lord Chancellor

Launched   2 July 1990

District Land Registrars Addresses

Birkenhead
Old Market House
Hamilton Street
Birkenhead L41 5FL
Tel 051-647 2377

Coventry
Greyfriars Business Centre
2 Eaton Road
Coventry CV1 2SD
Tel 0203 632442

Croydon
Sunley House
Bedford Park
Croydon CR9 3LE
Tel 081-781 9100

Durham
Southfield House
Southfield Way
Durham DH1 5TR
Tel 091-386 6151

Gloucester
Twyver House
Bruton Way
Gloucester GL1 1DQ
Tel 0452 511111

Harrow
Lyon House
Lyon Road
Harrow HA1 2EU
Tel 081-427 8811

Kingston upon Hull
Earle House
Portland Street
Hull HU2 8JN
Tel 0482 223244

Leicester
Thames Tower
99 Burleys Way
Leicester LE1 3UB
Tel 0533 510010

Lytham
Birkenhead House
East Beach
Lytham St Annes
Lancashire FY8 5AB
Tel 0253 735999

Nottingham
Chalfont Drive
Nottingham NG8 3RN
Tel 0602 291166

Peterborough
Touthill Close
City Road
Peterborough
Northants PE1 1XN
Tel 0733 288288

Plymouth
Plumer House
Tailyour Road
Crownhill
Plymouth PL6 5HY
Tel 0752 701234

Portsmouth
St Andrew's Court
St Michael's Road
Portsmouth
Hants PO1 2JH
Tel 0705 865022

Stevenage
Brickdale House
Swingate
Stevenage
Herts SG1 1XG
Tel 0438 313003

Swansea
Ty Bryn Glas
High Street
Swansea SA1 1PW
Tel 0792 458877

Telford
Parkside Court
Hall Park Way
Telford TF3 4LR
Tel 0952 290355

Tunbridge
Curtis House
Tunbridge Wells
Kent TN2 5AQ
Tel 0892 510015

Weymouth
1 Cumberland Drive
Weymouth
Dorset DT4 9TT
Tel 0305 776161

Medicines Control Agency

Market Towers, 1 Nine Elms Lane, London SW8 5NQ
Tel 071-720 2188   Fax 071-720 1595

Staff	*Chief Executive* **Dr Keith Jones (3)** *Business Managers* **Dr D Jeffreys (4)** **D Hagger (4)** **Dr Susan Wood (4)** **B H Hartley (4)** **R K Alder (4)** *Finance Director* **M R Read (5)**
Responsibilities	To safeguard public health by controlling medicines, through a system of licensing, monitoring, inspection and enforcement which ensures that medicines marketed in the UK are safe, efficacious and of good quality
Department	Health
Launched	11 July 1991

Meteorological Office

London Road, Bracknell, Berks RG12 2SZ
Tel 0344 854600   Fax 0344 856909

Staff

Chief Executive
Professor Julian C R Hunt (2)

Director (Operations)
Dr P Ryder (3)

Deputy Directors
C R Flood (5)
F Singleton (5)
Dr R L Wiley (5)
Dr S J Caughey (5)

Director (Research)
Dr P Mason (4)

Deputy Directors
Dr P W White (5)
Dr M J P Cullen (5)
Dr D J Carson (5)

Director (Commercial Services)
B L Herdan (5)

Director (Finance and Administration)
M H Bowack (5)

Responsibilities   To provide an effective, modern and efficient national meteorological service for United Kingdom military and civil users

Department   Defence

Launched   2 April 1990

Military Survey

Elmwood Avenue, Feltham, Middlesex TW13 7AE
Tel 081-890 3622   Fax 081-890 3622 x4148

Staff

Chief Executive
Major General Roy Wood (2*)†

Directors
Brigadier J P Elder (*)
Brigadier M P B G Wilson (*)
B R Candy

Responsibilities

To provide maps, air charts and other geographical data (including computer-readable data) to ensure the armed forces can plan, train and fight

To undertake surveys to determine position and orientation of weapon systems, and provide technical services and advice on any geographic matter that affects military questions

Department

Defence

Launched

1 April 1991

† 2*, * = armed forces equivalent of Civil Service grades 3 and 5 respectively

National Engineering Laboratory

East Kilbride, Glasgow G75 0QU
Tel 03552 20222   Fax 03552 36930

Staff

Chief Executive
William Edgar (3)

Operations Director
W Paton (5)

*Sales and Marketing
Director*
C Patten (5)

*Finance and
Administration Director*
G M MacDonald (5)

Manager, Flow Centre
Dr F C Kinghorn (5)

*Manager, Energy and
Environment Centre*
Dr T J S Brain (5)

Responsibilities   To provide comprehensive engineering technology services and consultancy to the government and the private sector in the fields of energy, process engineering, defence and transport

Department   Trade and Industry

Launched   5 October 1990

National Physical Laboratory

Queens Road, Teddington, Middlesex TW11 0LW
Tel 081-977 3222   Fax 081-943 2155

Staff

Chief Executive
and Director
Dr Peter Clapham (3)

Deputy Director
Dr A J Wallard (4)

Secretary
J M Whitlock (5)

Heads of Division
Electrical Science
Dr T G Blaney (5)

IT and Computing
A J Marks (5)

Materials Metrology
Dr M K Hossain (5)

Mechanical and Optical
Metrology
Dr A R Colclough (5)

Quantum Metrology
Dr J R Gott (5)

Radiation Science and
Acoustics
Dr A R Cox (5)

National Measurement
Accreditation Service
W T K Henderson (5)

Responsibilities

To develop and maintain national standards for measuring physical quantities

To provide calibration services essential to UK industry

To undertake research on standards for engineering materials and for information technology

To ensure that accurate measurement standards, compatible with those of Britain' major trading partners, are available to UK organisations

To provide the base for the National Measurement Accreditation Service (NMA which accredits public and private sector calibration and testing laboratories

Department   Trade and Industry

Launched   3 July 1990

National Weights and Measures Laboratory

Stanton Avenue, Teddington, Middlesex TW11 0JZ
Tel 081-943 7272   Fax 081-943 7270

Staff	*Chief Executive and Director* **Dr Seton Bennett (5)**
Responsibilities	To administer weights and measures legislation, especially regulation and certification of equipment for use in shops etc
Department	Trade and Industry
Launched	18 April 1989

Natural Resources Institute

Central Avenue, Chatham Maritime, Chatham, Kent ME4 4TB
Tel 0634 880088   Fax 0634 880066/77

Staff	*Chief Executive* **G Anthony Beattie (3)** *Deputy Directors* **Dr J Nabney (5)** **T J Perfect (5)** **Dr R D Cooke (5)**
Responsibilities	To collaborate with developing countries to increase the sustainable productivity of their natural resources – farming, forestry and fisheries – through the application of science and technology
Department	Overseas Development Administration
Launched	2 April 1990

Naval Aircraft Repair Organisation

RN Aircraft Yard, Fleetlands, Gosport PO13 0AW
Tel 0705 822351   Fax 0329 823043/2

Staff	*Chief Executive* **Capt David Symonds RN**
Responsibilities	To provide repair, modification, overhaul and storage services for the tri-service helicopter fleet, their engines and selected components and for marine gas turbine engines and their components
Department	Defence (Defence Support Agency)
Launched	1 April 1992

NHS Estates

286 Euston Road, London NW1 3DN
Tel 071-388 1188   Fax 071-388 3213

Staff

Chief Executive
John C Locke (3)

Director (Estate Policy)
G G Mayers (5)

Director (Estate Management/
Chief Architect)
P L Ward (5)

Director (Resources)
L J Wardle (5)

Head of Policy and
Administration
T Whitely (5)

Chief Surveyor
D Eastwood (6)

Chief Engineer
L W M Arrowsmith (5)

Head of Consultancy
Services
C Davies (5)

Responsibilities

To act as property advisers and consultants to the NHS and the healthcare industry at home and abroad

To provide advice and support over the complete range of health care estate functions including monitoring services for the NHS

To provide cost effective services to help customers deliver health care in a well managed environment

Its customers include the NHS Management Executive, health authorities, NHS trusts, government departments and others including substantial overseas interests

Department

Health

Launched

1 April 1991

Occupational Health Service

18–20 Hill Street, Edinburgh EH2 3NB
Tel 031-220 4177   Fax 031-220 4183

Murray House, Vandon Street, London SW1 0AL
Tel 071-273 6310   Fax 071-273 6362

Staff	*Chief Executive* **Dr George S Sorrie**
	Deputy Medical Adviser **Dr P M Brown (4)**
Responsibilities	To improve health and safety at work in government departments, agencies and public bodies
	To provide statutory and non-statutory health surveillance, health and safety audits, advice and rehabilitation of the disabled, clinical services for the staff and their families working overseas and a full range of health care services
Department	Cabinet Office (Office of Public Service and Science)
Launched	2 April 1990

Ordnance Survey

Romsey Road, Maybush, Southampton SO9 4DH
Tel 0703 792559   Fax 0703 792888

Staff	*Director General* **Professor D W Rhind (3)** *Director (Marketing,* *Planning and Development)* **J P Leonard (5)** *Director (Surveys and* *Production)* **A S Macdonald (5)** *Director (Establishment* *and Finance)* **I G Lock (5)**
Responsibilities	The official topographic surveying and mapping of Great Britain
Department	Ordnance Survey is a department in its own right. The Director General is accountable to the Secretary of State for the Environment
Launched	1 May 1990

Ordnance Survey of Northern Ireland

Colby House, Stranmillis Court, Belfast BT9 5BJ
Tel 0232 661244   Fax 0232 683211

Staff	**Chief Executive (5)**
Responsibilities	To maintain a topographical information archive for Northern Ireland
	To provide information from the archive to customers in forms most approprate to their needs
	To undertake special surveys, aerial photography, cartographic and reprographic services and technical assistance to government departments and others at home and abroad
Department	Department of the Environment, Northern Ireland
Launched	1 April 1992

UK Passport Agency

Clive House, Petty France, London SW1H 9HD
Tel 071-271 3000   Fax 071-271 8645

Staff	*Chief Executive* **John Hayzelden (5)**
	Deputy Chief Executive *Director (Operations)* **Miss A Smith (6)**
	Director (Planning and *Resources)* **N S Benger (6)**
	Director (Systems) **T L Lonsdale (6)**
Responsibilities	To issue passports to British nationals in the United Kingdom
Department	Home Office
Launched	2 April 1991

Patent Office

Concept House, Cardiff Road, Newport, Gwent NP9 1RH
Tel 0633 814000   Fax 0633 814504

Staff   *Comptroller General*
                            Paul R S Hartnack (3)

                            Assistant Comptrollers
                            Industrial Property and
                            Copyright
                            A Sugden (4)

                            Patents and Designs
                            T W Sage (4)

                            Assistant Registrar
                            J M Mayall (4)

                            Secretary
                            T Cassidy (5)

Responsibilities   To grant patents and trade marks, register designs, and formulate policy on
                            intellectual property

Department   Trade and Industry

Launched   1 March 1990

Planning Inspectorate Agency

Tollgate House, Holton Street, Bristol BS2 3NQ
Tel 0272 218950   Fax 0272 218769
Cathays Park, Cardiff CF1 3NQ
Tel 0222 823892   Fax 0222 825622

Staff

Chief Planning Inspector,
Chief Executive
Stephen Crow (3)

Deputy Chief Planning Inspector
J R Mossop (4)

Director of Planning Appeals
A J M Morgan (4)

Assistant Chief Planning Inspectors
J T Graham (5)
R E Wilson (5)
J T Dunlop (5)
Miss G P Pain (5)
G J Lidbury (5)
D F Harris (5)
Mrs S Bruton (5)
C A Jenkins (5)
J Greenfield (5)
J Acton (5)
E A Simpson (5)
M Montague-Smith (5)

Head of Planning Appeals Administration
D A C Marshall (5)

Director of Finance and Management Services
M Brasher (5)

Head of Agency Support Group
M T Davey (6)

Information Systems
P Millard (6)

Responsibilities   To carry out appeals and other casework involving planning, housing, environmental, highways and allied legislation

Department   Environment and Wales

Launched   1 April 1992

Public Record Office

Ruskin Avenue, Kew, Richmond, Surrey TW9 4DU
Tel 081-876 3444   Fax 081-876 8905

Chancery Lane, London WC2A 1LR
Tel 081-876 3444   Fax 081-878 7231

Staff	*Keeper of Public Records* **Mrs S J Tyacke (3)**
	Director of Public Services **C D Chalmers (5)**
	Director of Government Services **N G Cox (5)**
	Director of Corporate Services **W Arnold (5)**
Responsibilities	Under the general direction of the Lord Chancellor the Public Record Office is responsible for the records of central government and the courts dating from the 11th century onwards.
	It coordinates arrangements for the selection and disposal of public records, their safekeeping and their use by the public.
	Records selected for preservation are normally transferred to the Public Record Office and made available for public inspection when they are thirty years old.
Department	Lord Chancellor's Department
Launched	1 April 1992

Queen Elizabeth II Conference Centre

Broad Sanctuary, London SW1P 9AU
Tel 071-798 4060   Fax 071-798 4200

Staff

Chief Executive
M C Buck (5)

Business Manager
Miss G Price (6)

Financial Controller
D G Remington (7)

Presentation Facilities
Manager
A Curtis (7)

Security Manager
Group Captain D Reilly (7)

Engineering Manager
D J Coles (7)

Responsibilities   To provide and manage secure conference and banqueting facilities for national and international government meetings and to market the centre commercially for both private sector and government use

Department   Environment

Launched   6 July 1989

Queen Victoria School

Dunblane, Perthshire FK15 0JY
Tel 0786 822288   Fax 031-310 2519

Staff	*Chief Executive and* *Head Master* **Julian Hankinson**
Responsibilities	To provide continuity of Scottish education in a stable boarding environment for the (10–18-year-old) sons of Scottish sailors, soldiers and airmen
	To prepare them for entry to university, other higher or further education institutions, the armed services, professions, business or industry
Department	Defence
Launched	1 April 1992

Radiocommunications Agency

Waterloo Bridge House, Waterloo Road, London SE1 8UA
Tel 071-215 5000   Fax 071-928 4309

Staff	*Chief Executive* **M John Michell (3)** *Heads of Branches* **M Goddard (5)** **S Spivey (5)** **R A Bedford (5)** **A D I Reed (5)** **B A Maxwell (6)** **R M Skiffins (5)**
Responsibilities	Most civil radio matters other than those concerned with telecommunications broadcasting policy and the radio equipment market To ensure that the radio spectrum is used as efficiently as possible and that the maximum amount of spectrum is available for civil use To ensure compliance by radio users with the Wireless Telegraphy Acts and other relevant legislation
Department	Trade and Industry
Launched	2 April 1990

RAF Support Command Maintenance Group

RAF Support Command, RAF Brampton, Huntingdon, Cambs PE18 8QL
Tel 0480 52151   Fax 0480 451511

Staff	*Chief Executive* **Air Vice Marshal David R French (2*)†**
	Air Cdre J S Jones (*) **Air Cdre N T Carter (*)**
Responsibilities	To provide maintenance support to RAF fixed wing aircraft and the other Services
	To provide a comprehensive spares and materials storage and distribution system
	To provide and maintain a major part of the defence communications network
	To provide specialist logistic services for the RAF's Support Command
Department	Defence
Launched	1 April 1991

† 2*, * = armed forces ranking equivalent to Civil Service grades 3 and 5 respectively

Rate Collection Agency (Northern Ireland)

Oxford House, 40/55 Chichester Street, Belfast BT1 4HH
Tel 0232 235211   Fax 0232 231936

Staff	**Chief Executive (6)**
Responsibilities	To collect district rates on behalf of Northern Ireland's 26 district councils and the regional rate for the NI Department of Finance and Personnel
	To administer the housing benefit scheme for those ratepayers who are owner-occupiers
Department	Department of the Environment for Northern Ireland
Launched	2 April 1991

Recruitment and Assessment Services Agency

Alencon Link, Basingstoke RG21 1JB
Tel 0256 29222   Fax 0256 846315

24 Whitehall, London SW1A 2ED
Tel 071-210 6666

Staff	*Chief Executive* **Michael Geddes (3)**
	Director of Civil *Service Selection Board* *Schemes* **A A Carter (5)**
	Director of Professional *and Specialist* *Recruitment* **K N Bastin (6)**
	Director of Business *Development Unit* **P Cook (6)**
	Director of Consultancy *and Research* **F D Bedford (6)**
	Director of Finance and *Administration* **Miss E M Goodison (6)**
Responsibilities	To provide a full range of professional recruitment and related services for government departments and agencies and the wider public sector
Department	Cabinet Office (Office of Public Service and Science)
Launched	2 April 1991

Registers of Scotland

Meadowbank House, 153 London Road, Edinburgh EH8 7AU
Tel 031-659 6111   Fax 031-459 1221

Staff

*Chief Executive
and Keeper*
James W Barron (4)

Senior Director
R C Brown (5)

*Director Central
Services*
A W Ramage (6)

Responsibilities

To maintain the public registers provided for the registration in Scotland of legal documents, in particular those deeds relating to rights in land, but also covering a wide range of deeds relating to succession, trusts, family agreements, state appointments and others

Department

Scottish Office

Launched

6 April 1990

Royal Mint

Llantrisant, Pontyclun, Mid Glam CF7 8YT
Tel 0443 222111   Fax 0443 2288799

7 Grosvenor Gardens, London SW1W 0BH
Tel 071-828 8724   Fax 071-630 6592

Staff

Master of the Mint
The Chancellor of the Exchequer

Deputy Master and
Chief Executive
Anthony Garrett (3)

Finance Director
D C Snell (4)

Sales Director
A R Lotherington (5)

Marketing Director
B D Williams (6)

Director of Operations
R D Burchill (5)

Director of Human
Resources and
Establishment Officer
C J J Boyle (6)

Responsibilities   The manufacture and distribution of UK and overseas circulating and commemorative coinage, medals and seals

Department   The Royal Mint is a department in its own right. The Chief Executive is accountable to the Chancellor of the Exchequer

Launched   2 April 1990

Scottish Agricultural Science Agency

East Craigs, Edinburgh EH12 8NJ
Tel 031-224 8890   Fax 031-244 8940

Staff	*Director* **Dr R K M Hay (5)**
	Heads of Divisions
	Plant varieties and seeds **S R Cooper** (Deputy Director)
	Pesticides and zoology **A D Ruthven**
	Potato and plant health **M J Richardson**
Responsibilities	To provide scientific information and advice on agricultural and horticultural crops and the environment. It also has statutory and regulatory functions in relation to plant health, bee health, plant variety registration and crop improvement, genetically manipulated organisms, and the protection of crops, food and the environment.
Department	Scottish Office Agriculture and Fisheries Department
Launched	1 April 1992

Scottish Fisheries Protection Agency

Pentland House, 47 Robb's Loan, Edinburgh EH14 1TW
Tel 031-556 8400   Fax 031-244 6001

Staff   *Chief Executive*
                     A K MacLeod (5)

                     Director of Policy and
                     Resources
                     J B Roddin (6)

                     Chief Inspector of Sea
                     Fisheries
                     J F Fenton (6)

                     Marine Superintendent
                     Captain R Mill Irving (6)

Responsibilities   Enforces UK, EC and international fisheries law and regulations in Scottish waters
                     and ports to secure the conservation of fish stocks

Department   Scottish Office

Launched   2 April 1991

Service Children's Schools (North West Europe)

HQ BAOR, BFPO 140
Tel 010 49 2161 472-3296   Fax 010 49 2161 472-3487

Staff	*Chief Executive* **Ian S Mitchelson (4)** **Ian Duncan (6 equivalent)** **R Peter Gaskell (7 equivalent)** **Peter W Taylor (SEO)** **Richard S Beetham (SEO)**
Responsibilities	To provide an education service for the dependant children living with MOD personnel in North West Europe
Department	Defence
Launched	1 April 1991

Social Security Agency (Northern Ireland)

Castle Buildings, Stormont, Belfast BT4 3SJ
Tel 0232 763939   Fax 0232 761053

Staff	**Chief Executive (3)**
	Planning and Support Director (5)
	Finance Director (5)
	Personnel Director (5)
	Central Operations Director (5)
	Local Operations Director (5)
Responsibilities	To administer the payment of social security benefits, and the collection of national insurance contributions
	To provide processing services for the Benefits Agency in Great Britain and to audit and store encashed social security payment orders
Department	Department of Health and Social Services for Northern Ireland
Launched	1 July 1991

Social Security Benefits Agency

Quarry House, Quarry Hill, Leeds LS2 7UA
Tel 0532 324000   Fax telephone the SSBA for fax number

*All personnel based at Quarry House unless otherwise indicated. For other addresses
and telephone numbers see end of Benefits Agency section.*

Staff

Chief Executive
Michael Bichard (2)

Personnel Director
George Bardwell (4)

Managers
P Murphy (5)
J Parker (6)
P Farr (6)

Finance Director
David Riggs (3)

Managers
J Simpson CBE (5)
C Leivers (5)
J Mason (5)
D H Evans (6)
R Langford (6)
T Skidmore (6)

*Policy and Planning
Director*
Mrs M Ann Robinson (3)

Managers
E Hazlewood (5)
S Hickey (5)
K Beech (6)
M Rose (6)
M Coyne (6)
I Watson (6)

Territorial Directors:

Wales and Central England
Terry Green (4)
(Five Ways Tower)
Southern Territory

Ian Magee (4)
(Olympic House)
*Scotland and Northern
England*

Tony Laurance (4)
(Sandyford House)

Area Directors:

Benefits Agency Central Office
I Stewart (5)
S Godfrey (6)
G Goulding (6)
C Percy (6)
J Hewlett (6)
(all at Longbenton)

Fylde Benefits and War Pensions Directorate
P Dalby (5)
K Eckersley (6)
M Walker (6)
E Boyd (6)
Mrs S Shepherd (6)
Mrs P Rogers (6)
(all at Norcross)

Chief Medical Adviser, Director of Medical Services
Dr Peter Castaldi (3)

Principal Medical Officer
Dr David Findlay (4)
(both the above at Friars House)

Responsibilities	To administer claims for and payments of social security benefits and war pensions
Department	Social Security
Launched	2 April 1991

Social Security Benefits Agency Addresses

Five Ways Tower
Frederick Road
Edgbaston
Birmingham B15 1ST
Tel 021-626 2000
Fax 021-626 3000

DSS
Friars House
157-68 Blackfriars Road
London SE1 8EU
Tel 071-972 2000
Fax call above tel no and ask for relevant
fax no

DSS Longbenton
Newcastle upon Tyne NE98 1YX
Tel 091-213 5000
Fax call above tel no and ask for relevant
fax no

DSS Norcross
Blackpool
Lancashire FY5 3TA
Tel 0253 856123
Fax call above tel no and ask for relevant
fax no

Olympic House
Olympic Way
Wembley
Middlesex HA9 0DL
Tel 081-902 8822
Fax 081-902 9523

Sandyford House
Archbold Terrace
Newcastle upon Tyne NE2 1AA
Tel 091-225 6249
Fax 091-225 6384

Social Security Contributions Agency

Longbenton, Newcastle upon Tyne NE98 1YX
Tel 091-213 5000   Fax 091-225 7380

Staff	*Chief Executive* **Miss Ann Chant (4)**
	Deputy Chief Executive **George Bertram (5)**
	Director (Planning) **R D Bruce (6)**
	Director (Finance, *Management Information* *Services and* *Government Contracts)* **S Heminsley (6)**
	Director (Personnel) **K Wilson (6)**
	Director (Central *Operations)* **R J K Roberts (6)**
	Non-Executive Director **Roy Brimblecombe**
Responsibilities	To collect and record National Insurance contributions
	To maintain individual NI records
	To provide an advisory service to the DSS, other government departments, the business community, members of the public and employers and contributors
Department	Social Security
Launched	2 April 1991

Social Security Information Technology Services Agency

Euston Tower, 286 Euston Road, London NW1 3DN
Tel 071-383 3884   Fax 071-387 6826

Staff

Chief Executive
John Kenworthy (3)

Deputy Chief Executive
Philip Dunn (4)

Finance Director
Alan Smith (5)

Personnel Director
Steven Williams (5)

*Infrastructure Services
Director*
George McCorkell (5)

*Benefits Systems
Director*
Kevin Caldwell (5)

*Management Systems
Director*
Alexis Cleveland (5)

*Service Delivery
Director*
Norman Haighton (5)

*Management Services
Director*
Ian Marshall (5)

Non-Executive Directors
Martin Bankier CBE
Gordon Beaven

Responsibilities   To develop and run computing and communications technology systems required
by the DSS and its agencies, and to provide services to other customers within
government

Department   Social Security

Launched   2 April 1990

Social Security Resettlement Agency

Euston Tower, 286 Euston Road, London NW1 3DN
Tel 071-388 1188   Fax 071-383 7199

Staff	*Chief Executive* **Tony Ward (6)**
Responsibilities	To run efficiently and effectively resettlement units (hostels) to provide unsettled single homeless men and women with the first step towards resettlement in the community. The agency attempts to recover some of the costs of the hostels through board and lodging charges.
	To arrange and fund facilities to be run by local authorities and voluntary organisations which will replace gradually the old Department of Social Security hostels
Department	Social Security
Launched	24 May 1989

Teachers' Pensions Agency (TPA)

Mowden Hall, Standrop Road, Darlington DL3 9EE
Tel 0325 392929   Fax 0325 392216

Staff

Chief Executive
Mrs D Metcalfe (5)

Responsibilities

To administer the teachers' superannuation scheme (a contributory pension scheme for full and part-time teachers employed in England and Wales)

Department   Education

Launched   1 April 1992

Training and Employment Agency (Northern Ireland)

Clarendon House, 9–21 Adelaide Street, Belfast BT2 8DJ
Tel 0232 239944   Fax 0232 234417

Staff	Chairman
	Chief Executive (3)
	Deputy Chief Executive, Director Training Operations (4)
	Director Policy Research and Central Services (5)
	Director, Management Development (5)
	Director, Training Programmes (5)
	Director, Employment Services (5)
Responsibilities	To provide employment and training services in Northern Ireland
Department	Department of Economic Development for Northern Ireland
Launched	2 April 1990

Transport Research Laboratory

Old Wokingham Road, Crowthorne, Berkshire RG11 6AU
Tel 0344 773131   Fax 0344 770356

Staff

Chief Executive
Professor John Wootton (3)

Deputy Director
Dr R S Hinsley (4)

Highways Group
J Porter (5)

Structure Group
Dr P G Tilly (5)

Road User Group
G Maycock (5)

Traffic Group
P B Hunt (5)

Vehicles Group
Dr P H Bly (5)

Technology Transfer Unit
C S Downing (6)

Overseas Unit
J S Yerrell (6)

Responsibilities   To conduct and manage the Department of Transport's transport research and provide advice on scientific, technical and other matters in the transport field

Department   Transport

Launched   1 April 1992

Valuation Office Agency

New Court, Carey Street, London WC2A 2JE
Tel 071-324 1158   Fax 071-324 1190

Staff

Chief Executive
Rex Shutler (2)

Deputy Chief Executives
A J Langford (3)
R J Pawley (3)

Chief Valuer, Scotland
J A Sutherland (4)

Management Division

Director (Operations)
P Upton (4)

Communications and IT
B G Jones (5)

Finance and Planning
D K Park (5)

Customer Services
M J Loveridge (5)

Personnel and Training
J H Ebdon (5)

Technical Divisions

Taxation and Land Services
R A Dales (4)

Superintending Valuers
W J Reed (5)
P Crease (5)
A B Prior (5)
D N Huckle (5)
A Dixon (5)

Crown Property Unit, Valuer-in-Charge
C J Brooks (6)

Responsibilities	To provide land and buildings valuation services to government departments, other public bodies and a number of local authorities
Department	Inland Revenue
Launched	30 September 1991

Vehicle Certification Agency

1 Eastgate Office Centre, Eastgate Road, Bristol BS5 6XX
Tel 0272 515151   Fax 0272 524103

Staff	*Chief Executive* **Derek W Harvey (5)** *Deputy Chief Executive* **P F Nicholl (6)** *Head of Compliance* *Systems* **D Porritt (7)** *Head of Finance and* *Business Support* **L W Andrews (7)** *Head of Planning and* *Management Systems* **E P Williams (7)** *Head of Test Operations* **A W Stenning (7)**
Responsibilities	To test and certificate vehicles (and vehicle parts) to UK and international standards
Department	Transport
Launched	2 April 1990

Vehicle Inspectorate

Berkeley House, Croydon Street, Bristol BS5 0DA
Tel 0272 543274   Fax 0272 543212

Staff

Chief Executive
Ron Oliver (4)

*Deputy Chief Executive
and Operations Director*
J A T David (5)

*Personnel and Training
Director*
K N Walton (6)

*Customer Liaison and
Business Development
Director*
H G Edwards (6)

*Finance and Information
Director*
J A Belt (6)

Responsibilities

To carry out annual testing and inspection of heavy goods vehicles, public service vehicles and light goods vehicles

To administer and supervise the MOT testing scheme for motorcycles, cars and light goods vehicles

To carry out operator licensing and enforcement including checks on vehicle weights and drivers' hours

To investigate serious accidents and vehicle defects and oversee vehicle recall campaigns

Department

Transport

Launched

1 August 1988

Veterinary Medicines Directorate

Woodham Road, New Haw, Addlestone, Surrey KT15 3NB
Tel 0932 336911   Fax 0932 336618

Staff   *Chief Executive*
                           and Director of
                           Veterinary Medicines
                           Dr J Michael Rutter (4)

                           Director (Policy and
                           Finance)
                           C J Lawson (5)

                           Director (Licensing)
                           D K N Woodward (5)

Responsibilities   To license and control the manufacture and marketing of animal medicines

                           To provide post licensing surveillance of suspected adverse reactions and
                           veterinary residues in meat

                           To provide policy advice on these matters to the Agriculture and Health ministers
                           in the UK

Department   Agriculture, Fisheries and Food

Launched   2 April 1990

Warren Spring Laboratory

Gunnels Wood Road, Stevenage, Herts SG1 2BX
Tel 0438 741122   Fax 0438 360858

Staff

*Chief Executive
and Director*
Dr D Cormack (3)

Deputy Director
Dr L Goldstone (5)

Secretary
K Hills (6)

Marketing Manager
Dr M Kibblewhite (6)

Resource Manager
M Webb (6)

Heads of Research Divisions

Air Pollution
Dr M L Williams (6)

*Biological Treatment
and Marine Pollution*
N Hurford (6)

Materials Recovery
J R Barton (6)

Pollution Abatement
Dr C Schofield (6)

Responsibilities   To manage research and development programmes, and technical services in the environmental science and technology field, for national and local governments, international government agencies and other funding bodies, and the private sector, with the requirement to cover full costs in the open market

Department   Trade and Industry

Launched   20 April 1989

Wilton Park Conference Centre

Wiston House, Steyning, Sussex BN44 3DZ
Tel 0903 815020   Fax 0903 815931

Staff	*Chief Executive* **Geoffrey Denton** *Manager* **John Melser**
Responsibilities	To organise conferences on international affairs for politicians, officials, academics and others from around the world It is also hired out on commercial terms to government departments, business and other users
Department	Foreign and Commonwealth Office
Launched	1 September 1991

Regulatory Organisations and Public Bodies

This section includes over 80 regulatory organisations and other public bodies ranging from OFTEL and the National Rivers Authority to the Boundary Commissions and parliamentary and other ombudsmen. The full list is given below.

Accounting Standards Board *see* Financial Reporting Council
Advertising Standards Authority   ASA
Advisory, Conciliation and Arbitration Service   ACAS
Audit Commission for Local Authorities and the NHS in England and Wales   AC
Bank of England   BE
Boundary Commission for England   BCE
Boundary Commission for Northern Ireland   BCNI
Boundary Commission for Scotland   BCS
Boundary Commission for Wales   BCW
Broadcasting Complaints Commission   BCC
Broadcasting Standards Council   BSC
Building Society Ombudsman   BSO
Charity Commission   CC
Civil Aviation Authority   CAA
Commission for Local Administration in England   CLAE
Commissioner for Local Administration in Scotland   CLAS
Commission for Local Administration in Wales   CLAW
Commission for Racial Equality   CRE
Committee on Safety of Medicines *see* Medicines Commission
Council on Tribunals   CT
Criminal Injuries Compensation Board   CICB
Economic and Social Research Council   ESRC
Equal Opportunities Commission   EOC
Financial Reporting Council   FRC
    Accounting Standards Board   FRC: ASB
    Financial Reporting Review Panel   FRC: FRRP
Financial Reporting Review Panel *see* Financial Reporting Council
Gaming Board for Great Britain   GB
General Register Office (Scotland)   GRO(S)
Health Education Authority   HEA
Health and Safety Commission   HSC
    including Health and Safety Executive   HSE
Higher Education Funding Council for England   HEFCE
Highlands and Islands Enterprise   HIE
Horserace Betting Levy Board   HBLB
Immigration Appeals, the Appellate Authorities   IA
Independent Television Commission   ITC
Independent Tribunal Service   ITS
Insurance Ombudsman Bureau   IOB
Joint Nature Conservation Committee   JNCC
Law Commission   LC
Medical Research Council   MRC
Medicines Commission   MC
    including Committee on Safety of Medicines   CSM

Monopolies and Mergers Commission   MMC
National Consumer Council   NCC
National Criminal Intelligence Service   NCIS
National Economical Development Council   NEDC
National Radiological Protection Board   NRPB
National Rivers Authority   NRA
Natural Environment Research Council   NERC
Occupational Pensions Board   OPB
Office of the Banking Ombudsman   OBO
Office of the Data Protection Registrar   ODPR
Office of Electricity Regulation   OFFER
Office of Fair Trading   OFT
Office of Gas Supply   OFGAS
Office of the Legal Services Ombudsman   OLSO
Office of Manpower Economics   OME
Office of the NI Commissioner for Complaints (Ombudsman)   O(NI)CC
Office of the NI Parliamentary Commissioner for Administration (Ombudsman)   O(NI)PCA
Office of the Parliamentary Commissioner for Administration and Health Service Commissioners
    (Ombudsman)   OPCA/HSC
Office of Telecommunications   OFTEL
Office of Water Services   OFWAT
Panel on Takeovers and Mergers   PTM
Parole Board for England and Wales   PB(EW)
Parole Board for Scotland   PB(S)
Pensions Ombudsman   (PO)
Police Authority for NI   PA(NI)
Police Complaints Authority   PCA
Political Honours Scrutiny Committee   PHSC
Polytechnics and Colleges Funding Council   PCFC
Press Complaints Commission   PCC
Radio Authority   RA
Scottish Consumer Council   SCC
Scottish Enterprise   SE
Scottish Law Commission   SLC
Scottish Legal Services Ombudsman   SLSO
Scottish Record Office   SRO
Securities and Investments Board   SIB
Security Commission   SC
Security Service Tribunal   SST
Standing Advisory Commission for Human Rights   SACHR
UK Atomic Energy Authority   UKAEA
Universities Funding Council   UFC
Welsh Consumer Council   WCC
Welsh Development Agency   WDA

Advertising Standards Authority

Brook House, 2-16 Torrington Place, London WC1E 7HN
Tel 071-580 5555   Fax 071-631 3051

Officials

Chairman
The Rt Hon TImothy Raison

Director General
Matti Alderson

Press Officer
Caroline Crawford

Responsibilities   To regulate the content of advertising in non-broadcast media in the United Kingdom

Founded   1962

Advisory, Conciliation and Arbitration Service

27 Wilton Street, London SW1X 7AZ
Tel 071-210 3000   Fax 071-210 3708

Officials

Chairman of Council
Sir Douglas Smith CB

Personal Secretary
Miss J Simmons
071-210 3670

Chief Conciliation Officer
J D Evans (4)

Directors
E Norcross (5)
D Russell (5)
F Noonan (5)

Responsibilities

A general duty to promote the improvement of industrial relations

To prevent and resolve disputes by fostering constructive relationships between employers, employees and trade unions; and by providing conciliation, arbitration and mediation

To help ensure that statutory protections, rights and ȯbligations of individual employees are assured fairly and effectively; and to promote the settlement of complaints by conciliation

To provide information and advice on industrial relations and employment policies

Founded

1974 and then under the provisions of the Employment Protection Act 1975

Audit Commission for Local Authorities and the NHS in England and Wales

1 Vincent Square, London SW1P 2PN
Tel 071-828 1212   Fax 071-976 6187
Nicholson House, Lime Kiln Close, Stoke Gifford, Bristol BS12 6SU
Tel 0272 236757   Fax 0272 794100

Officials

Chairman
D J Cooksey

Deputy Chairman
M Stuart

Commissioners
Sir Peter Bowness
Alan Brown
Tony Christopher
John Clout
Lawrence Eilbeck
Jennifer Hunt
Dr Donald Irvine
Jeremy Orme
Clive Thompson
Tony Travers
Sir Robert Wall
Chris West
Clive Wilkinson
Peter Wood

Controller (Temporary)
D P Brokenshire

Director, Accounting Practice
H R Wilkinson

Director, Legal Services
A A Child

Director, Health Studies
C E R Tristem

Director of Audit
B H Skinner

Director, Local Government Studies
R Chilton

Responsibilities   To appoint auditors to local authorities and health authorities and to help
authorities to bring about improvements in efficiency, directly through the
auditing process and through the 'value for money' studies which the Commission
carries out.

The auditors appointed may be the District Audit Service or private firms of
accountants

The Commission members include senior people from industry, local government,
the accounting profession and the trade unions

Founded   1983 under the provisions of the Local Government Finance Act 1982

Bank of England

Threadneedle Street, London EC2R 8AH
Tel 071-601 4444   Fax 071-601 4471

Officials

Governor
The Rt Hon Robin Leigh-Pemberton

Deputy Governor
E A J George

Secretary
G A Croughton

Responsibilities

As the central bank of the UK, the Bank of England has three main objectives:

To maintain the value of the nation's money, mainly through policies and market operations agreed with the government

To ensure the soundness of the financial system, including direct supervision of banks and participants in some city financial markets

To promote the efficiency and competitiveness of the financial system, notably in the field of domestic and international payment and settlement systems

The Bank offers a range of services to its customers (the government, the clearing banks, other central banks and members of the staff) such as cheques, accounts, foreign exchange transactions, gold bullion deposits, and in the case of staff members, normal banking services

It is also responsible for:
The design, production and issue of banknotes in England and Wales

Government borrowing (in the form of Treasury bills, gilts and foreign currency borrowing)

Advising on the terms of new debt, and managing the stock of existing debt

Founded

1694 by Act of Parliament and Royal Charter. It was nationalised in 1964 and a new Royal Charter granted.

It is governed by a Court of Directors, all of whom are appointed by the Crown

Boundary Commission for England

St Catherine's House, 10 Kingsway, London WC2B 6JP
Tel 071-242 0262   Fax 071-242 0262 X2253

Officials

Chairman
The Speaker of the House of Commons

Deputy Chairman
The Hon Mr Justice Knox

Commission Members
Miss S C Cameron
D D Macklin

Joint Secretaries
R McLeod (6)
Mrs J S Morris (7)

Responsibilities   To review parliamentary constituencies and European parliamentary constituencies in England

Founded   1944 under the provisions of the House of Commons (Redistribution of Seats) Act 1944. Currently constituted under the Parliamentary Constituencies Act 1986

Boundary Commission for Northern Ireland

Old Admiralty Building, Whitehall, London SW1A 2AZ
Tel 071-210 6569   Fax 071-210 6549

Officials

Chairman
The Speaker of the House of Commons

Deputy Chairman
The Hon Mr Justice Higgins

Secretary
J R Fisher (7)

Commission Members
D J Clement
P G Duffy

Responsibilities

To review parliamentary constituencies in Northern Ireland and report on the number of members to be returned by each constituency to any future Northern Ireland Assembly

Founded

1944 under the provisions of the House of Commons (Redistribution of Seats) Act 1944. Currently constituted under the Parliamentary Constituencies Act 1986

Boundary Commission for Scotland

St Andrew's House, Edinburgh EH1 3DE
Tel 031-244 2196   Fax 031-244 2683

Officials	*Chairman* **The Speaker of the House of Commons**
	Deputy Chairman **The Hon Lord Davidson**
	Secretary **D K C Jeffrey (7)**
	Commission Members **A R Napier** **Professor U A Wannop**
Responsibilities	To review parliamentary constituencies and European parliamentary constituencies in Scotland
Founded	1944 under the provisions of the House of Commons (Redistribution of Seats) Act 1944. Currently constituted under the Parliamentary Constituencies Act 1986

Boundary Commission for Wales

St Catherine's House, 10 Kingsway, London WC2B 6JP
Tel 071-242 0262   Fax 071-242 0262 X2253

Officials	*Chairman* **The Speaker of the House of Commons** *Deputy Chairman* **The Hon Mr Justice Evans** *Commission Members* **W P Davey** **M A McLaggan** *Joint Secretaries* **R McLeod (6)** **Mrs J S Morris (7)**
Responsibilities	To review parliamentary constituencies and European parliamentary constituencies in Wales
Founded	1944 under the provisions of the House of Commons (Redistribution of Seats) Act 1944. Currently constituted under the Parliamentary Constituencies Act 1986

Broadcasting Complaints Commission

Grosvenor Gardens House, 35-37 Grosvenor Gardens, London SW1W 0BS
Tel 071-630 1966   Fax 071-828 7316

Members   *Chairman of Commission*
                         The Reverend Canon Peter Pilkington

                         Members
                         Donald Allen CMG
                         David Holmes
                         Tony Christopher CBE
                         Mrs Brigid Wells

Officials   *Secretary*
                         Richard Hewlett

Responsibilities   To consider and adjudicate upon complaints of
                         − unjust or unfair treatment in sound or television programmes
                         − unwarranted infringement of privacy in, or in connection with the obtaining of
                           material included in, such programmes

Founded   1981 under the provisions of the Broadcasting Act 1980. Now operates under the
                         provisions of the Broadcasting Act of 1990

Broadcasting Standards Council

5-8 The Sanctuary, London SW1P 3JS
Tel 071-233 0544   Fax 071-233 0397

Council Members	*Chairman* **The Lord Rees-Mogg**
	Deputy Chairman **Dame Jocelyn Barrow**
	Members **Richard Baker OBE** **Dr Jean Curtis-Raleigh** **The Rt Rev William J Westwood,** **Bishop of Peterborough** **The Rev Charles Robertson** **Rhiannon Bevan** **Alf Dubs**
Officials	*Director* **Colin Shaw**
	Deputy Director **Trevor Cobley**
	Research Director **Andrea Millwood Hargrave**
	Press and Programmes Officer **Katherine Lannon**
Responsibilities	To consider the portrayal of violence, sexual conduct and matters of taste and decency in television and radio programmes and broadcast advertisements To consider and make findings on complaints, to monitor programmes, to undertake relevant research, to draw up a Code of Practice, and consult on developments in Europe concerning the future regulation of transfrontier broadcasting
Founded	Established as a non-statutory body in 1988; became a statutory body in 1991 under the provisions of the Broadcasting Act 1990

Building Societies Ombudsman

Grosvenor Gardens House, 35-37 Grosvenor Gardens, London SW1X 7AW
Tel 071-931 0044   Fax 071-931 8485

Officials	*Chairman of the Council* **Lord Barnett**
	Registrar to the Council **Kevin Shears**
	Ombudsmen **Stephen Edell** **Mrs Jane Woodhead** **Brian Murphy**
	Office Manager **Mrs Barbara Cheney**
Responsibilities	To settle complaints by customers against building societies
Founded	1987 under the provisions of the Housing Act 1986

Charity Commission

St Alban's House, 57-60 Haymarket, London SW1Y 4QX
Tel 071-210 3000   Fax 071-930 9173

Officials

Chief Commissioner
R J Fries (3)

Secretary, Executive Director
E Shaw (4)
071-210 4419

Commissioner, Head of Legal Staff
R M C Venables (3)

Commissioners
J Farquarson (4)
Mrs D H Yeo (4)
M Webber (4)

Official Custodian
Mrs S E Gillingham (6)

Controller of Operations
V F Mitchell (5)

Deputy Commissioners
J F Claricoat (5)
K M Dibble (5)
G S Goodchild (5)
J Dutton (5)
S Slack (5)

Responsibilities

To hold investments and land for charities in the name of the Official Custodian for Charities

To maintain a register of charities in England and Wales

To encourage the development of better administration

To investigate and check abuses

Founded

1853 under the provisions of the Charitable Trusts Act 1853

Civil Aviation Authority

CAA House, 45/59 Kingsway, London WC2B 6TE
Tel 071-379 7311   Fax 071-240 1153

Officials   *Chairman*
                         The Rt Hon Christopher Chataway

                         Managing Director
                         Tom Murphy CBE

                         Secretary and Legal Adviser
                         Miss G M E White

                         Members
                         R Ashford
                         C Paice
                         D J McLaughlan
                         R Crawford
                         F Chorley
                         C Saunders
                         R Stunt
                         Sir Peter Lazurus KCB
                         B Trubshaw CBE MVO
                         R A Smith
                         L W Priestley
                         Miss E Gloster QC
                         F Vibert

Responsibilities   The economic, safety and technical regulation of British civil aviation

                         Operation of the National Air Traffic Services jointly with the Ministry of Defence

Founded   1972 under the provisions of the Civil Aviation Act 1971

Commission for Local Administration in England (Local Government Ombudsman)

21 Queen Anne's Gate, London SW1H 9BU
Tel 071-222 5622   Fax 071-233 0396

Officials

Chairman
Dr D C M Yardley
(Local Government Ombudsman for London,
Kent, Surrey, East and West Sussex)

Vice-Chairman
F G Laws
(Local Government Ombudsman for South West,
South, West and most of Central England)

Members
Mrs P A Thomas
(Local Government Ombudsman for East Midlands
and North of England)

Parliamentary Commissioner
W K Reid CB *(ex officio)*

Secretary
G D Adams

Responsibilities   To investigate complaints of injustice arising from maladministration by local authorities and certain other bodies

Founded   1974 under the provisions of the Local Government Act 1974

Commission for Local Administration in Scotland (Local Government Ombudsman)

23 Walker Street, Edinburgh EH3 7HX
Tel 031-225 5300   Fax 031-225 9495

Officials	*Commissioner* R G E Peggie CBE *Deputy Commissioner, Secretary* Janice H Renton
Responsibilities	To investigate complaints from members of the public of injustice attributed to maladministration in local government
Founded	1975 under the provisions of the Local Government Scotland Act 1975

Commission for Local Administration in Wales (Local Government Ombudsman)

Derwen House, Court Road, Bridgend, Mid Glamorgan CF31 1BN
Tel 0656 661325   Fax 0656 658317

Officials

Local Commissioner
E R Moseley

Parliamentary Commissioner
W K Reid CB *(ex officio)*

Secretary to the Commission
D Bowen

Responsibilities   To consider complaints of maladministration made against local authorities in Wales

Founded   1974 under the provisions of the Local Government Act 1974

Commission for Racial Equality

Elliot House, 10-12 Allington Street, London SW1E 5EH
Tel 071-828 7022   Fax 071-630 7605

Officials

Chairman
Michael Day OBE

Deputy Chairmen
Joe Abrams OBE
Ramindar Singh

Commissioners
Rev E A Brown
Dr M C K Chan MBE
R Kent
T A Khan
D A C Lambert
Dr D Ray
A Rose OBE
Mrs S Sadeque
Miss P Scotland QC
M D Skillicorn
R Sondhi
A Ward

Chief Executive
Dr P Sanders

Responsibilities   To promote equality of opportunity and good relations between different racial groups

To work towards elimination of discrimination

Founded   1977 under the provisions of the Race Relations Act 1976

Council on Tribunals

22 Kingsway, London WC2B 6LE
Tel 071-936 7045   Fax 071-936 7044

Council Members

Chairmen
Sir Cecil Clothier KCB QC

T N Biggart CBE *(Chairman, Scottish Committee)*
Mrs A Anderson
G A Anderson
M B Dempsey
Professor D L Foulkes JP
T R H Godden CB
B Hill CBE
Professor M J Hill
W N Hyde
Mrs J U Kellock JP
L F Read QC
W K Reid CB *(Parliamentary Commissioner
for Administration)*

Officials

Secretary
C W Dyment (5)

Secretary (Scottish Committee)
Ms L Wilkie (SEO)

Responsibilities

Tribunals cover a variety of subjects, including agriculture, immigration, employment, pensions, road traffic, social security, taxation and the allocation of school places. Examples include industrial tribunals which deal with alleged unfair dismissals and social security appeal tribunals which deal with disputes regarding benefits

The Council's main functions are:

To keep under review the constitution and working of some 60 tribunals which have been placed under its general supervision

To consider and report on administrative procedures relating to statutory inquiries, ie those set up as a result of situations specified in acts of parliament as needing such inquiries

To advise government departments on proposals for legislation affecting tribunals and inquiries, and on proposals where the need for an appeal procedure may arise

Members of the Council are appointed by the Lord Chancellor and the Lord Advocate

Founded

1958 and now operates under the provisions of the Tribunals and Inquiries Acts 1971 and 1992

Criminal Injuries Compensation Board

Whittington House, 19 Alfred Place, London WC1E 7LG
Tel 071-355 6800   Fax 071-436 0804

Blythswood House, 200 West Regent Street, Glasgow G2 4SW
Tel 041-221 0945   Fax 041-221 0928

Officials	*Chairman* **Lord Carlisle of Bucklow QC** *Director* **Mrs L Pallett (5)** *Secretary and Solicitor* **Vacant** *Operations Manager* **J S Lawson (7)**
Responsibilities	The Criminal Injuries Compensation Board administers a scheme for financially compensating victims of crimes of violence and people injured while arresting an offender or preventing an offence
Founded	1964 by the Home Secretary and Secretary of State for Scotland under the prerogative powers of the crown

Economic and Social Research Council

Polaris House, North Star Avenue, Swindon SN2 1UJ
Tel 0793 413000   Fax 0793 413001

Officials

Chairman
Professor H Newby

Secretary
W Solesbury (5)

Responsibilities

To make grants to students for postrgraduate study and training in economic and social research

Provide advice and information about the social sciences

Support and encourage research in the social sciences

Founded

1965 by Royal Charter

Equal Opportunities Commission

Overseas House, Quay Street, Manchester M3 3HN
Tel 061-833 9244   Fax 061-835 1657

Officials	*Chair* **Joanna Foster**
	Deputy Chair **June Bridgeman**
	Commissioners **Noreen Bray** **Lady Brittan** **Anne Gibson** **Amina Hasan** **Mrs Barbara Kelly** **Clive Mather** **Margaret Monk** **Margaret Prosser** **Janet Trotter** **Bernadette Hillon** **Anne Watts** **Cecilia Wells**
	Chief Executive **Valerie Amos**
	Legal Adviser **Alan Lakin**
Responsibilities	To keep under review the working of the Sex Discrimination Act and the Equal Pay Act To promote the quality of opportunity between men and women To work towards the elimination of discrimination
Founded	1976 under the provisions of the Sex Discrimination Act 1975

Financial Reporting Council

Holborn Hall, 100 Gray's Inn Road, London WC1X 8AL
Tel 071-404 8818   Fax 071-404 4497

Members	*Chairman* **Sir Ronald Dearing CB** *Deputy Chairmen* **Sir Trevor Holdsworth** **Sir Andrew Hugh Smith** **Ian Plaistowe** There are 26 other members and observers
Officials	*Secretary* **Sydney Treadgold**
Responsibilities	To promote good financial reporting The FRC is the overarching and facilitating body for making appointments to, and providing guidance and support for, its operational bodies: the **Accounting Standards Board** (see below) and the **Financial Reporting Review Panel** (see below) These three bodies are not government controlled but have its strong support. The Chairman and the three deputy chairmen of the FRC are appointed by the Secretary of State for Trade and Industry and the Governor of the Bank of England
Founded	1990 following the report of the Review Committee on the Making of Accounting Standards. Related provisions were introduced into company law by the Companies Act 1989

Financial Reporting Council:
Accounting Standards Board

Holborn Hall, 100 Gray's Inn Road, London WC1X 8AL
Tel 071-404 8818   Fax 071-404 4497

Board Members

Chairman
David Tweedie

Vice-Chairman
Vacant

Robert Bradfield
Sir Bryan Carsberg
Elwyn Eilledge
Michael Garner
Donald Main
Roger Munson
Graham Stacy

Technical Director
Allan Cook

Officials

Academic Adviser
Professor Geoffrey Whittington

Legal Adviser
Professor Robert Jack

Secretary
Sydney Treadgold

Responsibilities

To make, amend and withdraw accounting standards

Prescribed by Statutory Instrument 1990 No 1667 for this purpose

Founded

1990, taking over from the Accounting Standards Committee. One of the Financial Reporting Council's operational bodies. See FRC above

Financial Reporting Council:
Financial Reporting Review Panel

Holborn Hall, 100 Gray's Inn Road, London WC1X 8AL
Tel 071-404 8818   Fax 071-404 4497

Panel Members	*Chairman* **Edwin Glasgow QC** *Deputy Chairman* **Michael Renshall CBE** There are 20 other panel members
Officials	*Secretary* **Sydney Treadgold**
Responsibilities	Authorised by the Secretary of State for Trade and Industry to examine departures from the accounting requirements of the Companies Act by large companies and where appropriate to seek to persuade the company to take corrective action. Failing that it will seek a remedy from the court
Founded	1991. One of the Financial Reporting Council's operational bodies. See FRC above

Gaming Board for Great Britain

Berkshire House, 168-173 High Holborn, London WC1V 7AA
Tel 071-240 0821   Fax 071-497 2481

Officials	*Chairman* **Lady Littler** *Secretary* **T Kavanagh** *Members* **Sir Richard Barratt CBE QPM** **M H Hogan** **Lady Trethowan JP** **W B Kirkpatrick JP**
Responsibilities	To keep under review the extent and character of gaming in Great Britain To keep criminals out of gaming and lotteries To ensure gaming is run fairly and in accordance with the law To advise the Home Secretary of developments in gambling so that the law can respond to change
Founded	1968 under the provisions of the Gaming Act 1968. The Board also has responsibilities in relation to lotteries under the Lotteries and Amusements Act 1976

General Register Office (Scotland)

New Register House, Edinburgh EH1 3YT
Tel 031-334 0380   Fax 031-314 4400

Ministers and Officials	**Minister of State, Scottish Office** (for details of his office see Scottish Office)
	Registrar General **Dr C M Glennie (4)**
	Deputy Registrar General **B V Philp (5)**
	Census Manager **D A Orr (6)**
Responsibilities	To administer the law on marriage
	To maintain the NHS Central Register
	To produce and supply a wide range of population and vital statistics
	To register births, marriages and deaths
	To take censuses of population
Founded	1855

Health Education Authority

Hamilton House, Mabledon Place, London WC1H 9TX
Tel 071-383 3833   Fax 071-387 0550

Officials	*Chairman* **Sir Donald Maitland GCMG OBE**
	Chief Executive **Dr S Hagard**
Responsibilities	To advise the Secretary of State on matters relating to health education
	To undertake health education activity
	To plan and carry out programmes of other activities in cooperation with health authorities, Family Health Services Authorities, local authorities, local education authorities, voluntary organisations and other persons or bodies concerned with health education
	To sponsor research and evaluation
	To assist the provision of appropriate training
	To prepare, publish or distribute material
	To provide a national centre of information and advice
Founded	1987 after taking over the responsibilities in England of the Health Education Council. The HEA is a special health authority of the National Health Service

Health and Safety Commission

Baynards House, 1 Chepstow Place, London W2 4TF
Tel 071-243 6630   Fax 071-727 2254
All staff are based at Baynards House unless otherwise indicated.
For other addresses and telephone numbers see the end of this section.

Officials

Chairman
Sir John Cullen

Members
Rex Symons
Peter Jacques
Dr Colin Shannon
Alan Tuffin
Dame Rachel Waterhouse
John C Marvin
Paul Gallagher
Edward Carrick
Nigel Pitcher

Secretary
J L Grubb

Responsibilities

To reform health and safety law

To propose new regulations

To promote the protection of people at work and the public from hazards arising from industrial (including commercial) activity including major industrial accidents and the transportation of hazardous materials

The Commission guides and is advised by the Health and Safety Executive (see below for details)

Liaison with the Employment Department Group

Founded

1974 under the provisions of the Health and Safety at Work Act

See Health and Safety Executive over page

Health and Safety Executive

Baynards House, 1 Chepstow Place, London W2 4TF
Tel 071-243 6630   Fax 071-727 2254

Officials

Director General
J D Rimington CB (2)

Deputy Directors General
Ms J H Bacon (2)
D C T Eves (2)

Responsibilities

The HSE is a statutory body consisting of the Director General and two other people appointed by the Health and Safety Commission to which the HSE gives advice. HSE staff are the primary instrument for carrying out the Commission's policies which they do as necessary in liaison with other regulatory bodies.

The HSE has a special responsibility to ensure that the Health and Safety at Work Act and other law on health and safety is observed. This is achieved through HSE's field force who operate through a network of 21 area offices throughout the UK and HSE inspectors systematically visit and review a wide range of work activities.

Founded

1974 under the provisions of the Health and Safety at Work Act

Organisational Overview

Civil Servants			Department
Grade 1	*Grade 2*	*Grade 3*	

Health and Safety Executive

J D Rimington (2)	These divisions report directly to the Director General	D J Hodgkins B J Ecclestone (4) Dr J T McQuaid	Resources and Planning Solicitor's Office Strategy and General

Operations

J D Rimington (2)	D C T Eves	Dr A F Roberts (4)	Research and Laboratory Services
		Dr A F Ellis	Technology and Health Sciences Division
		K L Twist	Mines Inspectorate
		R J Seymour	Railways Inspectorate
		Dr J T Carter	Field Operations Division

Policy

J D Rimington (2)	Ms J H Bacon	R S Allison	Safety Policy Division
		Dr S Harbison	Nuclear Safety Division
		A W Brown	Health Policy Division
		A C Barrell	Offshore Safety Division

Civil Servants and Departments

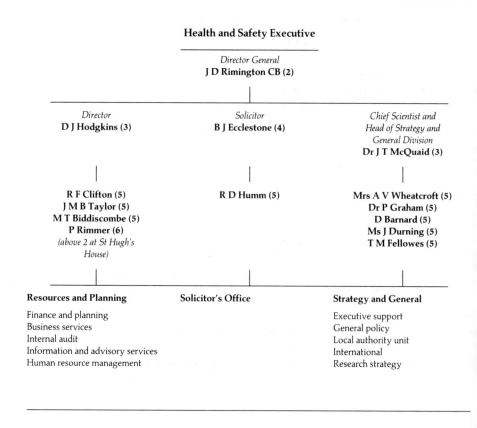

Health and Safety Executive

Director General
J D Rimington CB (2)

Director **D J Hodgkins (3)**	*Solicitor* **B J Ecclestone (4)**	*Chief Scientist and* *Head of Strategy and* *General Division* **Dr J T McQuaid (3)**
R F Clifton (5) **J M B Taylor (5)** **M T Biddiscombe (5)** **P Rimmer (6)** *(above 2 at St Hugh's* *House)*	**R D Humm (5)**	**Mrs A V Wheatcroft (5)** **Dr P Graham (5)** **D Barnard (5)** **Ms J Durning (5)** **T M Fellowes (5)**
Resources and Planning Finance and planning Business services Internal audit Information and advisory services Human resource management	**Solicitor's Office**	**Strategy and General** Executive support General policy Local authority unit International Research strategy

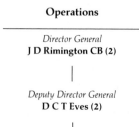

Operations

Director General
J D Rimington CB (2)

Deputy Director General
D C T Eves (2)

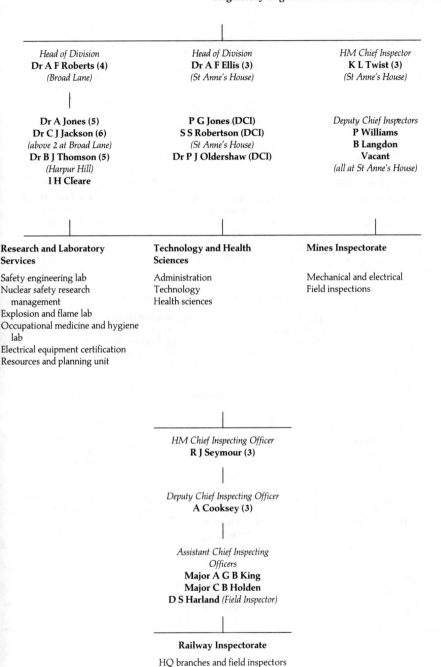

Head of Division
Dr A F Roberts (4)
(Broad Lane)

Head of Division
Dr A F Ellis (3)
(St Anne's House)

HM Chief Inspector
K L Twist (3)
(St Anne's House)

Dr A Jones (5)
Dr C J Jackson (6)
(above 2 at Broad Lane)
Dr B J Thomson (5)
(Harpur Hill)
I H Cleare

P G Jones (DCI)
S S Robertson (DCI)
(St Anne's House)
Dr P J Oldershaw (DCI)

Deputy Chief Inspectors
P Williams
B Langdon
Vacant
(all at St Anne's House)

Research and Laboratory Services

Safety engineering lab
Nuclear safety research
  management
Explosion and flame lab
Occupational medicine and hygiene
  lab
Electrical equipment certification
Resources and planning unit

Technology and Health Sciences

Administration
Technology
Health sciences

Mines Inspectorate

Mechanical and electrical
Field inspections

HM Chief Inspecting Officer
R J Seymour (3)

Deputy Chief Inspecting Officer
A Cooksey (3)

Assistant Chief Inspecting Officers
Major A G B King
Major C B Holden
D S Harland *(Field Inspector)*

Railway Inspectorate

HQ branches and field inspectors

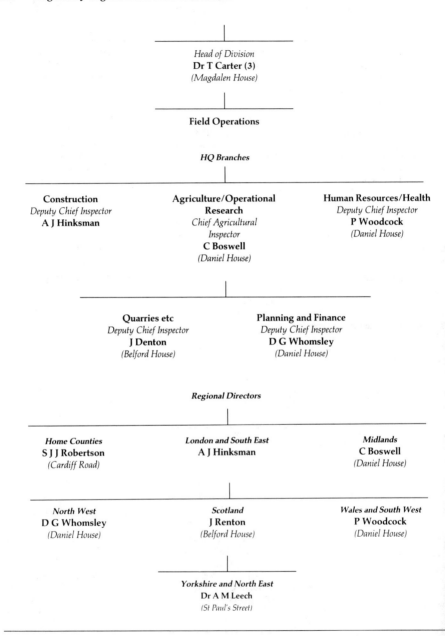

Head of Division
Dr T Carter (3)
(Magdalen House)

Field Operations

HQ Branches

Construction
Deputy Chief Inspector
A J Hinksman

**Agriculture/Operational
Research**
*Chief Agricultural
Inspector*
C Boswell
(Daniel House)

Human Resources/Health
Deputy Chief Inspector
P Woodcock
(Daniel House)

Quarries etc
Deputy Chief Inspector
J Denton
(Belford House)

Planning and Finance
Deputy Chief Inspector
D G Whomsley
(Daniel House)

Regional Directors

Home Counties
S J J Robertson
(Cardiff Road)

London and South East
A J Hinksman

Midlands
C Boswell
(Daniel House)

North West
D G Whomsley
(Daniel House)

Scotland
J Renton
(Belford House)

Wales and South West
P Woodcock
(Daniel House)

Yorkshire and North East
Dr A M Leech
(St Paul's Street)

Policy

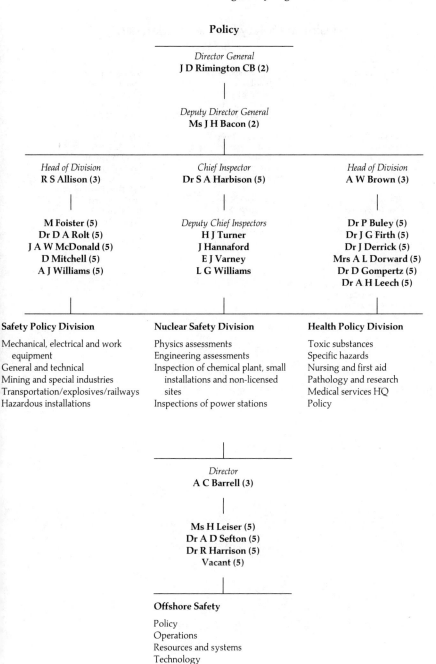

Director General
J D Rimington CB (2)

Deputy Director General
Ms J H Bacon (2)

Head of Division	*Chief Inspector*	*Head of Division*
R S Allison (3)	**Dr S A Harbison (5)**	**A W Brown (3)**

	Deputy Chief Inspectors	**Dr P Buley (5)**
M Foister (5)	**H J Turner**	**Dr J G Firth (5)**
Dr D A Rolt (5)	**J Hannaford**	**Dr J Derrick (5)**
J A W McDonald (5)	**E J Varney**	**Mrs A L Dorward (5)**
D Mitchell (5)	**L G Williams**	**Dr D Gompertz (5)**
A J Williams (5)		**Dr A H Leech (5)**

Safety Policy Division	**Nuclear Safety Division**	**Health Policy Division**
Mechanical, electrical and work equipment	Physics assessments	Toxic substances
General and technical	Engineering assessments	Specific hazards
Mining and special industries	Inspection of chemical plant, small	Nursing and first aid
Transportation/explosives/railways	installations and non-licensed	Pathology and research
Hazardous installations	sites	Medical services HQ
	Inspections of power stations	Policy

Director
A C Barrell (3)

Ms H Leiser (5)
Dr A D Sefton (5)
Dr R Harrison (5)
Vacant (5)

Offshore Safety

Policy
Operations
Resources and systems
Technology

Health and Safety Executive Addresses

Belford House
59 Belford Road
Edinburgh EH4 3UE
Tel 031-225 1313
Fax 031-225 6783

14 Cardiff Road
Luton
Beds LU1 1PP
Tel 0582 34121
Fax 0582 459775

Daniel House
Stanley Precinct
Bootle L20 7HE
Tel 051-951 4000
Fax 051-951 3827

Harpur Hill
Buxton
Derbyshire SK17 9JN
Tel 0298 26211
Fax 0298 79514

Information Centre
Broad Lane
Sheffield S3 7HQ
Tel 0742 892345
Fax 0742 892333

Magdalen House
Stanley Precinct
Bootle L20 3QZ
Tel 051-951 4000
Fax 051-922 7918

St Anne's House
Stanley Precinct
Bootle L20 3RA
Tel 051-951 4000
Fax 051-951 4232

St Hugh's House
Stanley Precinct
Bootle L20 3QY
Tel 051-951 4000
Fax 051-922 5394

8 St Paul's Street
Leeds LS1 2LE
Tel 0532 446191
Fax 0532 450626

St Peter's House
Stanley Precinct
Bootle L20 3LZ
Tel 051-951 4000
Fax 051-922 5980

Higher Education Funding Council for England

Northavon House, Coldharbour Lane, Bristol BS16 1QD
Tel 0272 317317   Fax 0272 317173

Officials

Chairman
Sir Ron Dearing CB

Chief Executive
Professor Graeme Davies

Secretary
Finlay M Scott TD

Responsibilities

The Higher Education Funding Council for England (HEFCE) will be responsible under the Further and Higher Education Act 1992 for the distribution of funds made available by the Secretary of State for Education for the provision of education and the undertaking of research by institutions of higher education in England.

Founded

6 May 1992 and will assume its full responsibilities, in succession to the Universities' Funding Council and Polytechnics' and Colleges' Funding Council, on 1 April 1993.

Highlands and Islands Enterprise

Bridge House, 20 Bridge Street, Inverness IV1 1QR
Tel 0463 234171   Fax 0463 244469

Officials	*Chairman* **Fraser Morrison** *Chief Executive* **Iain Robertson** *Secretary* **Anne Maclean**
Responsibilities	HIE has the statutory functions of stimulating economic and social development; enhancing skills and capacities relevant to employment and promoting self-employment; and improving the environment of the Highlands and Islands In support of these functions HIE's principal activities are: To encourage startup and growth of companies in their area To ensure that such companies are provided with appropriate assistance, advice and information To promote the Highlands and Islands as a location for investment To reduce the amount of derelict land and return it to use To help young people and the longterm unemployed to gain the skills required for employment To exercise its social remit in a way which helps sustain population and thus creates and maintains viable and self-sustaining local economies There are ten Local Enterprise Companies (LECs) which are free-standing private companies carrying out programmes of activities agreed with HIE. These activities differ according to the needs of their area.
Founded	1991 under the provisions of the Enterprise and New Towns (Scotland) Act 1990. It took over the functions of the Highlands and Islands Development Board

Horserace Betting Levy Board

52 Grosvenor Gardens, London SW1V 0AU
Tel 071-333 0043   Fax 071-333 0041

Board Members	*Chairman* **Sir John Sparrow** *Deputy Chairman* **Sir Patrick Meany** *Members* **Mrs A A McCurley** **C H Sporborg** **C J M Haines** **Sir Nevil McCready Bt CBE** **A Bruce** **The Lord Wyatt of Weeford**
Officials	*Chief Executive* **R T Ricketts** *Deputy Chief Executive* **R L Brack** *Projects Development Executive* **D M Stewart** *Scientific Liaison Executive* **Ms E K Archer**
Responsibilities	To collect a levy on the turnover of bookmakers and the Horserace Totalisator Board, and apply it for the improvement of breeds, veterinary science and education, and the improvement of horseracing To provide on all racecourses through Racecourse Technical Services the technical facilities required to maintain the integrity of racing To provide through the Horseracing Forensic Laboratory a research-backed drugscreening service for both the Jockey Club and commercial clients Ownership of Epsom, Kempton Park and Sandown Park racecourses, managed by United Racecourses To supervise the National Stud at Newmarket
Founded	1961 under the provisions of the Betting Levy Act 1961

Immigration Appeals, the Appellate Authorities

Thanet House, 231 Strand, London WC2R 1DA
Tel 071-353 8060   Fax 071-583 1976

Immigration Appeal Tribunal	*President* **G W Farmer**
	Vice-President **Professor D C Jackson**
Adjudicators	*Chief Adjudicator* **M Patey MBE**
	Secretary **Mrs L Heddon (7)**
Responsibilities	To hear and determine appeals in the UK against immigration decisions
Founded	1971 under the provisions of the Immigration Act 1971

Independent Television Commission

70 Brompton Road, London SW1 1EV
Tel 071-584 7011   Fax 071-589 5533

Officials	*Chairman* **Sir George Russell CBE**
	Deputy Chairman **Jocelyn Stevens**
	Chief Executive **David Glencross**
	Secretary **Ken Blyth**
Responsibilities	To licence and regulate all commercially funded UK television services including cable and satellite service as well as terrestial UHF services
Founded	1991 under the provisions of the Broadcasting Act 1990
	The Independent Television Commission and the Radio Authority (see this section) replaced the Independent Broadcasting Authority

Independent Tribunal Service

(formerly Office of the President of Social Security Appeal Tribunals, Medical Appeal Tribunals and Vaccine Damage Tribunals)

Clements House, Gresham Street, London EC2V 7DN
Tel 071-606 2106   Fax 071-606 5129

Officials	*President* **His Hon Judge Derek Holden** *Chief Administrator* **J Read (7)**
Responsibilities	To exercise judicial and administrative control over social security appeal tribunals, medical appeal tribunals, vaccine damage tribunals, disability appeal tribunals and child support appeal tribunals
Founded	1983 under the provisions of the Health and Social Services and Social Security Adjudications Act 1983

Insurance Ombudsman Bureau

City Gate One, 135 Park Street, London SE1 9EA
Tel 071-928 4488   Fax 071-401 8700

Officials

Chairman of the Council
Ms Barbara Saunders

Insurance Ombudsman
Dr Julian Farrand

Deputy Ombudsman
Laurie Slade

Bureau Manager and Clerk to the Council
Christopher Hamer

Responsibilities

To provide a dispute resolution service for personal insurance policy holders and holders of unit trusts

The IOB has an agreement with the Pensions Ombudsman that it will process disputes relating to personal pension policies where the company involved is a member of the IOB scheme

Founded

1981

Joint Nature Conservation Committee

Monkstone House, City Road, Peterborough PE1 1JY
Tel 0733 62626   Fax 0733 555948

Officials	*Chairman* **The Earl of Selborne OBE** *Chief Officer* **Dr F B O'Connor** *Director, Life Science Division* **Dr M W Pienkowski (6)**
Responsibilities	Advising ministers on the development and implementation of policies for, or affecting, nature conservation in Great Britain as a whole, or nature conservation outside Great Britain Establishment of common scientific standards for monitoring and research into nature conservation, and the analysis of resulting information Provision of advice and the dissemination of knowledge about nature conservation Provision of advice to the country councils (see below) for nature conservation Undertaking and commissioning of research
Founded	1990 under the provisions of the Environmental Protection Act 1990. JNCC and its three country councils (English Nature, Scottish Natural Heritage and the Countryside Council for Wales) carry forward duties previously undertaken by the Nature Conservancy Council (NCC)

Law Commission

Conquest House, 37-38 John Street, Theobald's Road, London WC1N 2BQ
Tel 071-411 1220   Fax 071-411 1297

Commissioners	*Chairman* **The Hon Mr Justice Peter Gibson** **Trevor M Aldridge** (property law) **Jack Beatson** (common law and administrative law) **Richard J Buxton QC** (criminal law) **Professor Brenda M Hoggett QC** (family law)
Officials	*Secretary* **M H Collon (4)** *Head of Statute Law Revision* **R H Streeten CBE (5)** *Parliamentary Draftsmen* **J S Mason CB** **G B Sellers CB** **A J Hogarth** **Sir Henry de Waal KCB QC**
Responsibilities	Reform of the law with a view to its systematic development and its simplification and modernisation To revise and consolidate statute law and repeal obsolete and unnecessary laws
Founded	1965 under the provisions of the Law Commissions Act 1965

Medical Research Council

20 Park Crescent, London W1N 4AL
Tel 071-636 5422   Fax 071-436 6179

Officials

Chairman
Sir David Plastow

*Deputy Chairman and
Secretary of the Council*
Dr D A Rees

Members
N H Winterton (5)
Dr J A Alwen (5)
Dr M B Davies (5)
Dr K Levy (4)
Dr D R Dunstan (5)
B C Dodd (5)
Dr D L Smith (5)
Dr D A A Owen (5)
Vacant (5)

Second Secretary
Dr D C Evered

Administrative Secretary
Mrs Norma Morris (3)

Responsibilities

To advance knowledge that will lead to improved health care

To promote the balanced development of medical and related biological research

To provide grants to enable individual scientists who are not members of its own staff to undertake research programmes and projects

Founded

1920 when it succeeded the Medical Research Committee established in 1913. Under the Science and Technology Act 1965 it was responsible to the Secretary of State for Education and Science and from 1992 to the Office of Public Service and Science, Cabinet Office

Medicines Commission

Market Towers, 1 Nine Elms Lane, London SW8 5NQ
Tel 071-273 0392   Fax 071-273 0387

Officials

Chairman
Professor Dame Rosalinde Hurley

Secretary
Miss A Field

Principal Assessor
Dr K Jones

Pharmaceutical Assessor
Miss D Hepburn

Responsibilities

To advise the UK Health and Agriculture Ministers on broad issues of policy in relation to the Ministers' functions under the Medicines Acts 1968 and 1971

Founded

1969 under the provisions of the Medicines Act 1968

Committees set up under Section 4 of the Medicines Act 1968

Committee on Safety of Medicines
Market Towers, 1 Nine Elms Lane, London SW8 5NQ
Tel 071-273 0451   Fax 071-273 0453

Officials

Chairman
Professor Sir William Asscher (Professor M D Rawlins from 1/1/93)

Secretary
L Whitbread

Assessor (New Drugs)
Dr D Jeffreys

Assessor (Adverse Reactions)
Dr Susan Wood

Assessor (Abridged Licencing)
Miss D Hepburn

Responsibilities   To advise UK Health ministers on the safety, efficacy and quality of medicinal products

To collect and investigate reports of adverse reactions to medicinal products

Founded   1970

Other: Committee on Dental and Surgical Materials and Veterinary Products Committee

Monopolies and Mergers Commission

New Court, 48 Carey Street, London WC2A 2JT
Tel 071-324 1467   Fax 071-324 1400

**Commission
Members**

Chairman
Sir Sydney Lipworth

Deputy Chairmen
P H Dean
D G Goyder
H H Liesner CB

Members
A G Armstrong
C C Baillieu
I S Barter
Professor M E Beesley CBE
Mrs C M Blight
F E Bonner CBE
P Brenan
J S Bridgeman
K S Carmichael CBE
R O Davies
Professor S Eilon
J Evans
A Ferry MBE
M R Hoffman
J D Keir QC
A L Kingshott
Miss P K R Mann
G C S Mather
N F Matthews
Prof J S Metcalfe
Mrs D Miller MBE
Professor A P L Minford
J D Montgomery
Dr D J Morris
B C Owens
Professor J F Pickering
L Priestley
Lady Scott
Alister Sutherland
D P Thompson
C A Unwin MBE
Professor G Whittington
R Young

Staff

Secretary
S N Burbridge CB

Team Managers
J A Banfield (5)
A O H Blair (5)
G M Field (5)
Mrs G D J Steel (5)
Ms A U Willcocks (5)

Senior Legal Adviser
N D Ing (4)

Chief Industrial Adviser
M F Shutler (4)

Accountant Adviser
L Brown (5)

Senior Economic Advisers
G P Sumner (5)
D A Miner (5)

Press and Information Adviser
G Segal
071-324 1407

Responsibilities

To investigate and report on monopoly and merger situations, newspaper mergers, certain general questions, anti-competitive practices and questions of efficiency, costs and possible abuse of monopoly positions in the public sector

To conduct inquiries under the provisions of certain acts designed to effect the privatisation of undertakings formerly in the private sector

The Commission has no power to initiate its own investigations. References are made to it either by the Secretary of State for Trade and Industry, the Director General of Fair Trading or, in the case of the privatised industries, by the appropriate regulator. Completed reports are submitted to the Secretary of State for Trade and Industry or, in the case of the privatised industries, to the appropriate regulator

Founded

1948 as the Monopolies and Restrictive Practices Commission. Became the Monopolies and Mergers Commission under the provisions of the Fair Trading Act 1973. It also operates under the provisions of the Competition Act 1980

National Consumer Council

20 Grosvenor Gardens, London SW1W 0DH
Tel 071-730 3469   Fax 071-730 0191

Members	*Chairman* **Lady Wilcox**
	Vice-Chairman **Ann Scully**
	Members **Professor Kumar Bhattacharyya** **Anthony Burton OBE** **Philip Circus** **Professor Paul Fairest** **Jennifer Francis** **John Hughes** **George Jones** **Mary McAnally** **Lady McCollum** **John Mitchell** **Jill Moore OBE** **John Nelson-Jones** **Jean Varnam** **Alan White** **Martin Wolf**
	Chairman, Scottish Consumer Council **Deirdre Hutton**
	Chairman, Welsh Consumer Council **Beata Brookes**
Officials	*Director (Chief Executive)* **Ruth Evans**
	Head of Public Affairs **Diana Whitworth**
Responsibilities	To ensure that the consumer viewpoint is fully taken into account in the formation of economic, social and public service policies, and to persuade the suppliers of goods and services – both public and private – to be more responsive to consumers' needs and more caring in dealing with the problems of individual consumers
Founded	1975 as a result of a government White Paper

National Criminal Intelligence Service

Box 8000, Spring Gardens, London SE11 5EH
Tel 071-238 8000

Officials	*Director General* **Anthony Mullett** *Director of Intelligence* **Simon Crawshaw**
Responsibilities	To provide a quality service in the gathering, collation, evaluation, analysis and development of relevant information and intelligence about serious crime (excluding terrorism) and major criminals of regional, national and international interest To facilitate the bringing to justice of offenders through the dissemination of this information and intelligence to the country's police forces and regional crime squads Existing units which have become part of NCIS include: seven regional criminal intelligence offices the National Drugs Intelligence Unit the National Football Intelligence Unit Metropolitan Police Specialist Operations Department units such as the National Office on Counterfeit Currency, Public Sector Corruption Index, Paedophile Index, the UK Branch of Interpol, Production Contamination, Kidnap and Extortion Index and part of the Research Unit of the Stolen Vehicle Squad
Founded	1992 as a result of the work of a tripartite steering group set up by the Home Office, which included representatives of the Association of Metropolitan Authorities, the Association of County Councils, the Association of Chief Police Officers and HM Customs and Excise.

National Economic Development Council*

Millbank Tower, Millbank, London SW1P 4QX
Tel 071-217 4000   Fax 071-821 1099

Officials	*Chairman* **The Chancellor of the Exchequer** *Director General, NEDO* **Dr Walter Eltis** *Industrial Director, NEDO* **Douglas Fraser** *Economic Director, NEDO* **Professor Martin Ricketts** *Secretary to the Council* **Martin Couchman**
Responsibilities	A national forum set up to examine the United Kingdom's economic performance, to consider what can be done to improve efficiency, and to seek agreement between the government, management, and the unions upon ways of improving the competitiveness of industry and the rate of sound growth The National Economic Development Office (NEDO) provides administrative and research support for the work of the National Economic Development Council and its sector groups and working parties. It also works independently to assist the improvement of economic performance in UK companies and the macroeconomy. It acts as the United Kingdom equivalent of the national level Economic and Social Councils in other European Community countries
Founded	1962

To close down at the end of 1992

National Radiological Protection Board

Chilton, Didcot, Oxon OX11 0RQ
Tel 0235 831600   Fax 0235 833891

Officials	*Chairman* **Sir Richard Southwood**
	Director **Dr R H Clarke**
	Secretary **G A M Webb**
	Assistant Directors **Miss F A Fry** **Dr Barbara H MacGibbon CB** (Medical) **Dr J W Stather**
Responsibilities	To advance by research the acquisition of knowledge about the protection of mankind from radiation hazards
	To provide advice to the government on the acceptability to the UK of standards recommended or proposed by international bodies, and on their application
	To provide information and advice to those with responsibilities in the UK in relation to the protection from radiation hazards, either of the community as a whole, or particular sections of it
	To specify Emergency Reference Levels for use following an accident at a nuclear installation
Founded	1970 under the provisions of the Radiological Protection Act 1970

National Rivers Authority

30-34 Albert Embankment, London SE1 7TL
Tel 071-820 0101   Fax 071-820 1603

Rivers House, Waterside, Aztec West, Almondsbury, Bristol BS12 4UD
Tel 0454 624400   Fax 0454 624409

Officials

Chairman
The Rt Hon The Lord Crickhowell

Chief Executive
Edward Gallagher

Director, Chief Executive's Office
Mrs M Evans

Director of Operations
Dr K Bond

Chief Scientist
Dr R J Pentreath

Technical Director
Dr C Swinnerton

Personnel Director
P Humphreys

Finance Director
N Reader

Responsibilities

An independent body with statutory responsibilities for water resources, pollution control, flood defence, fisheries, recreation, conservation and navigation in England and Wales

It also has substantial responsibilities for the marine environment around the coast of England and Wales:

— for pollution control and salmonid fisheries purposes it has duties and powers to distances of three nautical miles out respectively

— for flood defence it is responsible for a large number of sea defences (but not coastal protection which falls within the remit of local authorities)

Founded

1989 under the provisions of the Water Act 1989, now consolidated under the Water Resources Act 1991

Natural Environment Research Council

Polaris House, North Star Avenue, Swindon SN2 1EU
Tel 0793 411500   Fax 0793 411501

Officials	*Chairman of the Council* **Professor J L Knill**
	Secretary to Council **Dr Eileen Buttle**
	Director of Earth Sciences **Professor J C Briden (3)**
	Director of Terrestrial and *Freshwater Sciences* **Dr P B H Tinker (3)**
	Director of Marine and *Atmospheric Sciences* **Dr J D Woods (3)**
	Director, NERC Scientific Services **B J Hinde (5)**
	Establishment Officer **D V Griffiths (5)**
	Finance Officer **C M Read (5)**
Responsibilities	To encourage, plan and execute research in the physical and biological sciences which relate to man's natural environment and its resources
Founded	1965 by Royal Charter under the provisions of the Science and Technology Act 1965

Occupational Pensions Board

PO Box 2EE, Newcastle on Tyne NE99 2EE
Tel 091-225 6414   Fax 091-225 6283
PO Box 1NN, Newcastle on Tyne NE99 1NN
Tel 091-225 66237   Fax 091-225 6390

Officials

Chairman
Sir Jeremy Rowe CBE

Deputy Chairman
Miss Harriet Dawes

Secretary to the Board and
General Manager of the
Executive Office
A Scaife

Members
R J Amy
Mrs R Brown
Miss C H Dawes
R Ellison
R J Hebblethwaite
A V Lyburn
R Neale
A Pickering
W M R Ramsay
K R Thomas
Baroness Turner of Camden

Responsibilities

To report to the Secretary of State for Social Services on regulations relating to occupational pension schemes and to advise as required on particular matters relating to such schemes

To ensure compliance with the requirements for preservation of scheme benefits and for equal access to membership by men and women

To supervise arrangements for contracting-out of the state scheme to final salary schemes, money purchase and appropriate personnel pension schemes

To order the modification or winding up of an occupational pension scheme

To ensure that occupational pension schemes comply with the requirements for disclosure of information by giving advice to scheme administrators and, where appropriate, determining whether scheme rules conform with the requirements

To act as Registrar of Occupational and Personal Pension Schemes and to operate a tracing service to enable individuals to trace past preserved pension rights

To make grants to appropriate bodies providing advice or assistance in connection with occupational or personal pensions

Founded

1973 under the Social Security Act 1973

Office of the Banking Ombudsman

Citadel House, 5-11 Fetter Lane, London EC4 1BR
Tel 071-583 1395   Fax 071-583 5873

Officials	*Ombudsman* **Laurence Shurman**
	Deputy Ombudsman **C J Eadie**
	Office Manager **C W Bigland**
	Chairman of the Council **Dame Mary Donaldson GBE**
	Clerk to the Council **Brendon Sewill CBE**
Responsibilities	To settle complaints by individuals against any member bank, or designated associate of a member
Founded	1986

Office of the Data Protection Registrar

Wycliffe House, Water Lane, Wilmslow, Cheshire SK9 5AF
Tel 0625 535711   Fax 0625 524510

Officials

Data Protection Registrar
E J Howe CBE (2)

Deputy Registrar
F G B Aldhouse (5)

Legal Adviser to the Registrar
Mrs R P Jay (5)

Responsibilities

To give information and advice on the operation of the Data Protection Act 1984

To promote the observance of the Data Protection Principles

To consider complaints that the Data Protection Principles or the Act have been contravened and take appropriate action

To encourage the preparation and dissemination of codes of practice for guidance in complying with the Data Protection Principles

To underpin compliance with the Act through prosecution for offences or via enforcement action for contraventions of the Data Protection Principles

To compile, maintain and publish a register of data users and computer bureaux

To give advice and support to other countries which have ratified the Council of Europe Convention and act as the United Kingdom authority

Founded

1984 under the provisions of the Data Protection Act 1984

Office of Electricity Regulation (OFFER)

Hagley House, Hagley Road, Birmingham B16 8QG
Tel 021-456 2100   Fax 021-456 4664

48 St Vincent Street, Glasgow G2 5TS
Tel 041-248 5917   Fax 041-248 5915

Officials

Director General
Professor S C Littlechild

Deputy Director General
Miss P A Boys (3)

Deputy Director General (Scotland)
R N Irvine (5)

Legal Adviser
M Brocklehurst (5)

Directors Regulation and Business Affairs
Dr Eileen Marshall (5)
G Horton (5)

Director Administration
D Smith (6)

Director Public Affairs
Miss J D Luke (6)

Technical Director
Dr B Wharmby (5)

Chief Meter Examiner
J Cooper (6)

Responsibilities

To ensure that all reasonable demands for electricity are satisfied

To promote competition in the generation and supply of electricity

To protect consumers' interests on prices, security of supply and quality of services as well as to promote energy efficiency

Founded

1989 under the provisions of the Electricity Act 1989

Office of Fair Trading

Field House, Bream's Buildings, London EC4A 1PR
Tel 071-242 2858   071-269 8800

Chancery House, Chancery Lane, London WC2A 1SP
Tel 071-242 2858   Fax 071-269 8773

Officials

Director General of Fair Trading
Sir Bryan Carsberg

Deputy Director General
J W Preston CB (2)

Director, Consumer Affairs
J Mills

Director, Competition Policy
Dr M Howe (3)

Director, Legal Department
A Inglese (3)

Senior Economics Adviser
D Elliott (5)
(Chancery House)

Establishments and Finance Officer
Miss C Banks (5)
(Chancery House)

Responsibilities

To keep watch on commercial activities and trading practices in the United Kingdom

To assess monopolies, mergers and trade practices that may be restrictive or anti-competitive and, where necessary refer cases to the Monopolies and Mergers Commission or the Restrictive Practices Court, or offer advice to the Secretary of State for Trade and Industry

As a United Kingdom 'competent authority', to assist the European Commission enforce Community competition law

To propose and promote changes in law and practice if the interests of consumers are being harmed

To take legal action against businesses that persistently cause problems for consumers

To equip customers with the information and advice they need

To licence traders offering credit or hire facilities

Founded   1973 under the provisions of the Fair Trading Act 1973, with additional
responsibilities under the Consumer Credit Act 1974, the Restrictive Trade
Practices Act 1976, the Estate Agents Act 1979 and the Competition Act 1980

Office of Gas Supply (OFGAS)

Southside, 105 Victoria Street, London SW1E 6QT
Tel 071-828 0898   Fax 071-630 8164

Officials

Director General of Gas Supply
Sir James McKinnon

Deputy Director General
A J Dorken (4)

Director, Consumer Affairs
W Macleod (5)

Legal Adviser
D R M Long (5)

Director, Competition and Tariffs
G McGregor (5)

Responsibilities

To grant authorisations to other suppliers of gas through pipes

To fix and publish maximum charges for reselling gas

To investigate complaints where enforcement powers may be exercisable

To publish information and advice for the benefit of tariff customers

To settle the terms on which other suppliers have access to British Gas pipelines in the event of disagreement

Founded

1986 under the provisions of the Gas Act 1986

Office of the Legal Services Ombudsman

22 Oxford Court, Oxford Street, Manchester M2 3WQ
Tel 061-236 9532   Fax 061-236 2651

Officials	Ombudsman
	Michael Barnes
	Secretary
	Kevin Fox

Responsibilities   To oversee the handling of complaints against solicitors, barristers and licensed conveyancers. In particular, to investigate allegations about the manner in which complaints have been dealt with by the relevant professional body. The Ombudsman may also investigate the matter to which a complaint relates

Founded   1991 under the provisions of the Courts and Legal Services Act 1990

Office of Manpower Economics

22 Kingsway, London WC2B 6JY
Tel 071-405 5944   Fax 071-405 5148

Officials	*Director* **D G Talintyre (3)**
	Chief Statistician **Dr M E McDowell (5)**
	Assistant Secretaries **P J H Edwards (5)** **H E Miller (5)** **P Thorpe (5)**
Responsibilities	To service independent review bodies which advise on the pay of various public sector groups: School Teachers' Review Body, the Top Salaries Review Body, the Armed Forces Review Body, the Doctors' and Dentists' Review Body and the Review Body for Nurses and other NHS professions. The Office also provides services for the Pharmacists Review Panel, the Police Negotiating Board and the Civil Service Arbitration Tribunal. To undertake research into pay and associated matters as requested by Government
Founded	1971

Office of the Northern Ireland Commissioner for Complaints (Ombudsman)

33 Wellington Place, Belfast BT1 6HN
Tel 0232 233821   Fax 0232 234912

Officials	*Commissioner for Complaints* **Mrs J McIvor**
	Senior Director (5)
Responsibilities	To investigate complaints by people claiming to have sustained injustice in consequence of maladministration in connection with the administrative actions of local authorities and certain public bodies
Founded	1969 under the provisions of the Commissioner for Complaints Act (NI) 1969

Office of the Northern Ireland Parliamentary Commissioner for Administration (Ombudsman)

33 Wellington Place, Belfast BT1 6HN
Tel 0232 233821   Fax 0232 234912

Officials	*Parliamentary Commissioner* *for Administration* **Mrs J McIvor**
	Senior Director (5)
Responsibilities	To investigate complaints by people claiming to have sustained injustice in consequence of maladministration arising from action taken by one of the various Northern Ireland government departments and local authorities
Founded	1969 under the provisions of the Parliamentary Commissioner Act (NI) 1969

Office of the Parliamentary Commissioner for Administration and Health Service Commissioners (Ombudsman)

Church House, Great Smith Street, London SW1P 3BW
Tel 071-276 2130 (PCA)   071-276 2035 (HSC)   Fax 071-276 2104

Commissioner	*Parliamentary Commissioner (Ombudsman)* **W K Reid CB (1)**
Officials	*Deputy Parliamentary Commissioner* **J E Avery (3)**
	Deputy Health Service Commissioner **R A Oswald (3)**
	Parliamentary Commissioners **Mrs J M Fowler (5)** **M D Randall (5)** **M P Cornwell-Kelly (5)**
	Health Service Commissioners **M A Johnson (5)** **J C Bateman (5)** **P J Belsham (5)**
Responsibilities	***Parliamentary Commissioner's Office*** To investigate complaints referred to him by MPs from members of the public who claim to have suffered injustice through maladministration by government departments and certain non-departmental bodies
	Health Service Commissioners for England, Scotland and Wales To investigate complaints from members of the public against the administrative actions of the National Health Service Authorities
Founded	PCA: 1967 under the provisions of the Parliamentary Commissioner Act 1967
	HSC: established by statute in 1973, the Commissioners' powers are now set out primarily in the National Health Service Act 1977 and National Health (Scotland) Act 1978

Office of Telecommunications (OFTEL)

Export House, 50 Ludgate Hill, London EC4M 7JJ
Tel 071-822 1600   Fax 071-822 1643

Officials

Acting Director General
W R B Wigglesworth

Deputy Director General
W R B Wigglesworth (3)

Director, Competition
Mrs A Walker (5)

Director, PTO (Public Telecommunication Officer) Licensing
Mrs P Sellers (5)

Director, International and Consumer Affairs
D Hyde (5)

Director, Legal Affairs
A Woods (5)

Senior Economic Adviser
A R Bell (5)

Technical Director
A G Orbell (5)

Responsibilities

To advise the Secretary of State for Trade and Industry on licensing and other telecommunications issues

To approve apparatus

To enforce telecommunications licences

To initiate licence amendments

To investigate complaints

To maintain and promote effective competition in telecommunications and the international effectiveness of the UK telecommunications industry

To maintain public registers of various documents including copies of licences

To promote the interests of consumers, purchasers and other users in respect of prices, quality and variety

Founded

1984 under the provisions of the Telecommunications Act 1984

Office of Water Services (OFWAT)

Centre City Tower, 7 Hill Street, Birmingham B5 4UA
Tel 021-625 1300   Fax 021-625 1400

Officials

Director General of Water Services
I C R Byatt

Deputy Director General
G A Booker (3)

Head of Charges Control
C W Bolt (5)

Head of Administration
M Toulmin (5)

Head of Engineering Intelligence
Dr W Emery (5)

Head of Legal Division
A Merry (5)

Head of Consumer Affairs
M Saunders (5)

Head of Information
Ms D Plant (6)

Responsibilities

To monitor the water and sewerage industry in England and Wales

To regulate charges

To promote economy and efficiency

To protect customers with regard to pricing and standards of service

To facilitate competition

To compare the performance of water companies

To adjudicate complaints about companies

Ten regional Customer Services Committees represent consumer views and investigate complaints about companies. The chairman and members are appointed by the Director General

Founded

1989 under the provisions of the Water Act 1989

Panel on Takeovers and Mergers

226 Stock Exchange Building, London EC2P 2JX
Tel 071-382 9026   Fax 071-638 1554

Officials

Chairman
Sir David Calcutt QC

Deputy Chairmen
John F C Hull
John F Goble

Members
Dennis Stevenson
Sir Adrian Cadbury
Robert B Jack
Ian L Rushton
Paul V S Manduca
Sir Nicholas Goodison
Robin D Broadley
Mark A Smith
Martin G Taylor
W Ian D Plaistowe
Charles K R Nunneley
Sir Andrew Hugh Smith
Angus W Matheson
The Hon Christopher J Shaprles
Barry R J Bateman

Director-General
Mrs Frances Heaton

Responsibilities

The Panel was set up as a non-statutory body following a proposal by the Governor of the Bank of England and the Chairman of the Stock Exchange, in response to concerns about practices unfair to shareholders at the time of take-overs.

The Panel, which continues to have the support of the Bank of England, draws its members from major UK financial and business institutions. The day-to-day work is carried out through its Executive, headed by the Director General.

The principal objective of the Panel is to ensure fair conduct of a takeover bid from the point of view of shareholders.

The Panel requires those whom it regulates to adhere to the principles and rules set out in the City Code on Takeovers and Mergers and the rules governing substantial acquisitions of shares.

Founded   1968

Parole Board for England and Wales

Abell House, John Islip Street, London SW1P 4LH
Tel 071-217 5329   Fax 071-217 5223

Officials	*Chairman* **The Viscount Colville of Culross QC** *Vice-Chairman* **The Hon Mr Justice Schiemann** *Secretary* **T E Russell**
Responsibilities	To advise the Home Secretary on the release of prisoners under licence, on the conditions of such licences, the revocation of licences, and allied matters in England and Wales
Founded	1967 under the provisions of the Criminal Justice Act 1967

Parole Board for Scotland

Calton House, 5 Redheughs Rigg, Edinburgh EH12 9HW
Tel 031-244 8528   Fax 031-244 8774

Officials	*Chairman* **Mrs J D O Morris CBE** *Vice-Chairman* **J M Scott** *Secretary* **Miss W M Doonan (7)**
Responsibilities	To advise the Secretary of State for Scotland on the release of prisoners under licence, on the conditions of such licences, the revocation of such licences and allied matters in Scotland
Founded	1968 under the provisions of the Criminal Justice Act 1967

The Pensions Ombudsman

11 Belgrave Road, London SW1V 1RB
Tel 071-834 9144   Fax 071-821 0065

Officials	*Ombudsman* **Michael Platt**
	Legal Adviser **Alan Edwards**
	Office Manager **John Coles**
Responsibilities	To investigate complaints or resolve disputes about occupational pensions. They also deal with complaints and disputes about some personal pension schemes. (See also the Insurance Ombudsman Bureau.)
Founded	1991 under the provisions of the Social Security Act 1990

Police Authority for Northern Ireland

River House, 48 High Street, Belfast BT1 2DR
Tel 0232 230111   Fax 0232 245098

Officials	*Chairman* **T Rainey**
	Secretary **R Armstrong (3)**
	Assistant Secretary, Establishment (5)
	Assistant Secretary, Support Services (5)
Responsibilities	To advise the Secretary of State for Northern Ireland on general questions affecting the police force in Northern Ireland
Founded	1970 under the provisions of the Police Act (NI) 1970

Police Complaints Authority

10 Great George Street, London SW1P 3AE
Tel 071-273 6450   Fax 071-273 6401

Officials

Chairman
His Honour Judge Francis Petre

Deputy Chairmen
Brigadier J Pownall (Investigations)
P W Moorhouse (Discipline)

Members
Mrs L Cawsey
M Chapman
J Crawford
G V Marsh
W McCall
K Singh
Captain N Taylor
Brigadier A Vivian
Miss B Wallis
E Wignall
Mrs R Wolff

Responsibilities   The independent body to oversee public complaints against police officers in England and Wales

Founded   1985 under the provisions of the Police and Criminal Evidence Act 1984

Political Honours Scrutiny Committee

53 Parliament Street, London SW1A 2NH
Tel 071-210 5059

Officials

Chairman
The Rt Hon Lord Shackleton KG OBE

Members
The Rt Hon the Lord Pym MC DL
The Rt Hon the Lord Grimond TD

Secretary
J H Thompson CB

Responsibilities   To report to the Prime Minister on the suitability of people put forward for appointment to an honour for political services

Founded   1923

Polytechnics and Colleges Funding Council

Northavon House, Coldharbour Lane, Bristol BS16 1QD
Tel 0272 317317   Fax 0272 317100

Officials	*Chairman* **Sir Ron Dearing**
	Secretary **Finlay Scott**
	Chief Executive **Professor Graeme Davies**
	Director of Finance **Nigel Brown**
	Director of Programmes **F Alan Hibbert**
Responsibilities	To allocate funds between polytechnics and colleges and prescribed courses in local education authority colleges
	To advise the Secretary of State on its financial appraisal of the financing of the polytechnics and colleges sector, and on other matters on which the Secretary of State invites, or the Council wishes to offer advice
Founded	1988 under the provisions of the Education Reform Act 1988, replacing the National Advisory Body for Public Sector Higher Education (NAB). It will be replaced by the Higher Education Council for England on 1 April 1993. See entry for HEFCE.

Press Complaints Commission

1 Salisbury Square, London EC4Y 8AE
Tel 071-353 1248   Fax 071-353 8355

Officials	*Chairman* **The Lord McGregor of Durris** *Members* **William Anderson CBE** **Lady Elizabeth Cavendish LVO JP** **Patricia Chapman** **David Chipp** **Michael Clayton** **The Rt Hon the Lord Colnbrook KCMG** **Dame Mary Donaldson GBE** **Sir Richard Francis KCMG** **Max Hastings** **Brian Hitchen CBE** **Andrew Hughes** **Sir Edward Pickering** **Professor Robert Pinker** **Professor Lesley Rees** **Robert Ridley** *Director* **Mark Bolland**
Responsibilities	To deal with complaints from the public about the contents and conduct of newspapers and magazines, enforcing a Code of Practice agreed by the press
Founded	1991 replacing the Press Council, following the recommendations of the Calcutt Committee on Privacy and Related Matters

Radio Authority

Holbrook House, 14 Great Queen Street, London WC2 5DP
Tel 071-430 2724   Fax 071-405 7062

Officials	*Chairman* **The Rt Hon the Lord Chalfont OBE MC**
	Deputy Chairman **Jill McIvor**
	Chief Executive **Peter Baldwin**
	Deputy Chairman **Paul Brown**
	Secretary **John Norrington**
Responsibilities	To plan frequencies, award licences, regulate programming and radio advertising (where necessary)
	To play an active role in the discussion and formulation of policies which affect the independent radio industry and its listeners
Founded	1991 under the provisions of the Broadcasting Act 1990
	The Radio Authority and the Independent Television Commission (see this section) replaced the Independent Broadcasting Authority

Scottish Consumer Council

314 St Vincent Street. Glasgow G3 8XW
Tel 041-226 5261   Fax 041-221 0731

Members

Chairman
Deirdre Hutton

Members
Ms Joan Aitken
Mrs Pat Cooper
Ms Kim Donald
Peter Edmondson OBE
Cowan Ervine
Bernard Forteath
Ken Gilbert
Mrs Winifred Sherry JP
Gordon Smith
Mark Steiner
Mrs May Kidd
Ms Yvonne Osman
Ralph Palmer

Officials

Director
Ann Foster

Information Officer
Katie Carr

Responsibilities

To represent the interests of Scottish consumers and to ensure that a consumer viewpoint is expressed wherever possible, when public and private services are under consideration

Founded

1975 as a result of a government White Paper

Scottish Enterprise

120 Bothwell Street, Glasgow G2 7JP
Tel 041-248 2700   Fax 041-221 3217

Officials	*Chairman* **Sir David Nickson KBE DL**
	Deputy Chairman **Ronald Garrick**
	Chief Executive **Crawford Beveridge**
Responsibilities	To help develop a high output, high income and low unemployment economy in Scotland which provides a high quality of life and is sustainable both in economic and environmental terms
	Through "Locate in Scotland", to diversify and develop the economy by attracting and assisting inward investors
	Scottish Enterprise's 13 Local Enterprise Companies work in partnership with all sections of the community to develop the local economy, improve the environment and provide training at all levels
Founded	1991 when it took over the economic development and environmental improvement functions of the Scottish Development Agency and the training functions of the Training Agency in Lowlands Scotland

Scottish Law Commission

140 Causewayside, Edinburgh EH9 1PR
Tel 031-668 2131   Fax 031-662 4900

Members	*Chairman* **The Hon Lord Davidson**
	Commissioners **Dr E M Clive** **Sheriff I D MacPhail QC** **Professor P N Love CBE** **W A Nimmo Smith QC**
Officials	*Secretary* **K F Barclay**
	Parliamentary Draftsmen **J F Wallace QC** **G S Douglas QC** **W C Galbraith QC**
	Assistant Solicitors **N R Whitty** **R Bland**
Responsibilities	To keep under review with a view to its systematic development and reform, the law of Scotland
Founded	1965 under the provisions of the Law Commissions Act 1965

Scottish Legal Services Ombudsman

2 Greenside Lane, Edinburgh EH1 3AH
Tel 031-556 5574

Officials	*Scottish Legal Services Ombudsman* **D W J Morrell**
Responsibilities	To oversee the handling of complaints against legal practitioners. Members of the public first approach the relevant professional organisation such as the Law Society of Scotland or the Faculty of Advocates. Complainers who are not satisfied that they have had a full and fair hearing may then raise the matter with the Ombudsman
Founded	1991 under the provisions of the Law Reform (Miscellaneous Provisions) (Scotland) Act 1990. The Ombudsman replaced the Lay Observer

Scottish Record Office

HM General Register House, Edinburgh EH1 3YY
Tel 031-556 6585   Fax 031-557 9569

Officials	*Keeper of the Records of Scotland* **P M Cadell (5)** *Deputy Keeper Modern Records* **A M Broom** *Deputy Keeper Historical Records* **J D Galbraith** *Secretary, National Register of* *Archives (Scotland)* **Dr I D Grant**
Responsibilities	The Scottish Record Office is responsible for preserving the public records of Scotland and other records (including Church records and private archives) which have been transmitted to the Keeper of the Records of Scotland and for making them available for public inspection The Office assists government departments and other public bodies and courts of law in Scotland with review of non-current records and advises local authorities over their records The National Register of Archives (Scotland) surveys archives in private hands
Founded	Before 1286

Securities and Investments Board

Gavrelle House, 2-14 Bunhill Row, London EC1Y 8RA
Tel 071-638 1240   Fax 071-382 5900

Board	*Chairman* **Andrew Large** *Deputy Chairmen* **R N Quartano CBE** **Viscount Runciman CBE** *Members* **Denis Child CBE** **John Craven** **Roy Croft CB** **John Gardiner** **Norman Lessels** **John Manser** **Joe Palmer CBE** **Graham Ross Russell** **Lady Scott CBE** **Leonard Warwick** **Dame Rachel Waterhouse DBE** **Brian Williamson CBE**
Officials	*Group Directors* **M C Blair** **Miss C Bowe** **J D Orme** **M J Vile** *Chief Operating Officer* **Roy H F Croft CB**
Responsibilities	The regulation of the financial services industry. Regulatory activity is then delegated to and exercised by recognised Self-Regulating Organisations (see below) and the Recognised Professional Bodies of the legal, accounting and insurance professions SIB set up a Formation Committee in April to establish a new SRO which will regulate investment business done with, or directly for, the private investor. The new body is likely to include all the current activities regulated by LAUTRO and FIMBRA, and some activities currently regulated by IMRO and, to a much lesser extent, by SFA. The new SRO, probably to be known as the Personal Investment Authority (PIA), should be operational by April 1993 SIB presents an annual report to Parliament
Founded	1987 under the provisions of the Financial Services Act 1986

Self-Regulating Organisations

Financial Intermediaries, Managers and Brokers Regulatory Association (FIMBRA)
Hertsmere House
Hertsmere Road
London E14 4AB
Tel 071-538 8860
Fax 071-895 8579

Investment Management Regulatory Organisation (IMRO)
Broadwalk House
5 Appold Street
London EC2A 2LL
Tel 071-628 6022
Fax 071-920 9285

Life Assurance and Unit Trust Regulatory Organisation (LAUTRO)
Centre Point
103 New Oxford Street
London WC1A 1QH
Tel 071-379 0444
Fax 071-379 4121

Securities and Futures Association (SFA)
Stock Exchange Building
Old Broad Street
London EC2N 1EQ
Tel 071-256 9000
Fax 071-628 5799

Security Commission

c/o Cabinet Office, Whitehall, London SW1A 2AS
Tel 071-270 0170

Officials

Chairman
The Rt Hon Lord Justice Lloyd QC

Members
Sir Alan Cottrell
The Rt Hon Sir Michael Palliser GCMG
Sir John Blelloch KCB
Lt General Sir Derek Boorman KCB
Sir Christopher Curwen KCMG

Secretary
R D J Wright

Responsibilities

On the Prime Minister's request, to investigate and report on the circumstances in which a breach of security has occurred in the public service, and on any related failure of departmental security arrangements or neglect of duty.

In the light of any such investigation, advise whether any change in the security arrangements is necessary or desirable

Founded

1964

Security Service Tribunal

PO Box 18, London SE1 0TZ
Tel 071-273 4096

Officials	*Commissioner* **The Rt Hon Lord Justice Stuart-Smith**
	President **Justice Simon Brown**
	Vice-President **Sheriff John McInnes QC**
	Member **Sir Richard Gaskell**
Responsibilities	To investigate public complaints against the security service
Founded	1989

Standing Advisory Commission on Human Rights

55 Royal Avenue, Belfast BT1 1TA
Tel 0232 243987   Fax 0232 247844

Officials	*Chairman* **Charles Hill QC**
	Secretary **E D Carson (7)**
Responsibilities	To provide the Secretary of State for Northern Ireland with independent advice on the adequacy and effectiveness of the law as regards religious and political discrimination in Northern Ireland
Founded	1973 under the provisions of the Northern Ireland Constitution Act 1973

UK Atomic Energy Authority (AEA Technology)

Harwell Laboratory, Didcot, Oxfordshire OX11 0RA
Tel 0235 821111   Fax 0235 832591

Members

Chairman
J N Maltby CBE

Chief Executive and Deputy Chairman
Dr B L Eyre CBE
J Bullock
Professor Sir Roger Elliott
J A Gardiner
Professor Sir Peter Hirsch
R Sanderson OBE

Officials

Managing Director, Sites and Personnel
A W Hills

Managing Director, Industrial Business Group
Dr R S Nelson

Managing Director, Nuclear Business Group
Dr D Pooley

Secretary
J R Bretherton

Chief Press Officer
A Munn

Responsibilities

AEA Technology is the trading name of the United Kingdom Atomic Energy Authority (UKAEA), which was set up in 1954 to develop the UK nuclear power programme. Since 1965 it has progressively widened its fields of application and customer base and now serves many markets – aerospace, defence, oil and gas, chemicals and pharmaceuticals, transport and public utilities, environment and safety – as well as the nuclear industry

AEA Technology is based at six research and engineering centres in the United Kingdom: Culham and Harwell (Oxfordshire), Culcheth and Risley (Cheshire), Dounreay (Caithness) and Winfrith (Dorset). It operates principally through nine separate business divisions

AEA Technology's products and services include nuclear fuels production and reprocessing; radioactive waste management and plant decommissioning services; consultancy, technical services and R&D for nuclear power station operators, designers and regulatory bodies; oil reservoir engineering and offshore inspection instrumentation; safety and reliability studies; and environment hazard assessments and support services

Founded   1954 under the provisions of the Atomic Energy Authority Act 1954, amended by the Atomic Energy Authority Acts of 1959 and 1971; UKAEA's functions were extended by the Science and Technology Act 1965. The Atomic Energy Act 1986 put the Authority's finances on a trading fund basis. Since 1989 it has traded under the name AEA Technology

Universities Funding Council

Northavon House, Coldharbour Road, Bristol BS16 1QD
Tel 0272 317317   Fax 0272 317173

Officials	*Chairman* **Sir Ronald Dearing CB** *Chief Executive* **Professor Graeme Davies** *Secretary* **Finlay M Scott**
Responsibilities	To administer funds made available to the Council by the Secretary of State for Education for the purpose of providing financial support for the provision of education and the undertaking of research by universities
Founded	1988 under the provisions of the 1988 Education Reform Act, replacing the University Grants Committee. It will be replaced by the Higher Education Funding Council for England on 1 April 1993. See entry for HEFCE

Welsh Consumer Council/Cyngor Defnyddwyr Cymru

Castle Buildings, Womanby Street, Cardiff CF1 2BN
Tel 0222 396056   Fax 0222 238360

Members	*Chairman* **Beata Brookes** *Members* **Nerys Biddulph** **R Ian Edge** **J Arwel Edwards** **Jane Lloyd Hughes** **Gareth Morgan** **Elinor Patchell** **Mair Stephens** **Ian Thomson** **Roderick Thurman** **Mary Watkins**
Officials	*Director* **Katherine Hughes** *Press and Public Affairs Officer* **Rwth Williams**
Responsibilities	To ensure that Welsh consumers are represented in central and local government decision-making, as well as commerce and industry, with particular attention being given to the disadvantaged
Founded	1975 as a result of a government White Paper

Welsh Development Agency

Pearl House, Greyfriars Road, Cardiff CF1 3XX
Tel 0222 222666   Fax 0222 390752

Officials

Chairman
Dr Gwyn Jones

Deputy Chairman
Sir Donald Walters

Chief Executive
Philip Head

Responsibilities

To further the regeneration of the economy and improve the environment of Wales

To help boost the growth, profitability and competitiveness of indigenous Welsh business

To build speculative and bespoke premises for industry and encourage private sector investment in property development

To fund land reclamation and environmental improvement throughout the Principality

To stimulate urban and rural regeneration and development

To promote Wales as a location for inward investment

Founded

1976 under the provisions of the Welsh Development Agency Act 1975

Abbreviations

A

AC	Audit Commission for Local Authorities and the NHS in England and Wales
ACA	Associate, Institute of Chartered Accountants
ACAS	Advisory, Conciliation and Arbitration Service
ACGI	Associate, City and Guilds of London Institute
ACIArb	Associate, Chartered Institute of Arbitrators
ACIS	Associate, Chartered Institute of Secretaries
ACS	Assistant Chief Scientist
AD	Assistant Director; Allied Dunbar
ADAS	Agricultural Development and Advisory Service
ADC Gen	Aide-de-Camp General
ADC	Aide-de-Camp
ADS	Army Dental Service
AE	Agricultural Economist
AFC	Air Force Cross
AFSA	Associate, Faculty of Secretaries and Administrators
AHSM	Associate, Institute of Health Services Management
AKC	Associate, Kings College, London
ALA	Assistant Legal Adviser
AM	Master of Arts (United States of America)
AO	Actuarial Officer; Agricultural Officer
AOR	Assistant Official Receiver
AP	Assistant Principal
APC	Assistant Parliamentary Counsel
APS	Assistant Private Secretary
ARCS	Associate, Royal College of Science
ARCST	Associate, Royal College of Science and Technology, Glasgow
ARIBA	Associate, Royal Institute of British Architects
ARIC	Associate, Royal Institute of Chemistry
ARICS	Associate, Royal Institution of Chartered Surveyors
ARSM	Associate, Royal School of Mines
AS	Assistant Secretary; Assistant Solicitor
ASA	Advertising Standards Authority; Accounts Services Agency
ASWE	Admiralty Surface Weapons Establishment
ATS	Assistant Treasury Solicitor
AUS	Assistant Under Secretary

B

BA	Bachelor of Arts; The Buying Agency
BAOR	British Army of the Rhine
BBC	British Broadcasting Corporation
BCC	Broadcasting Complaints Commission
BCE	Boundary Commission for England
BCh or BChir	Bachelor of Surgery
BCL	Bachelor of Civil Law
BCNI	Boundary Commission for Northern Ireland
BCom	Bachelor of Commerce
BCS	Boundary Commission for Scotland
BCW	Boundary Commission for Wales
BDS	Bachelor of Dental Surgery
BE	Bank of England
BL	Bachelor of Law
BM	Bachelor of Medicine
BP	British Petroleum
BPharm	Bachelor of Pharmacy
BPhil	Bachelor of Philosophy
BRE	Building Research Establishment
BRPB	British Rail Property Board
BS	Bachelor of Surgery; Bachelor of Science
BSc	Bachelor of Science
BSC	Broadcasting Standards Council
BScAgric	Bachelor of Science, Agriculture

BScEcon	Bachelor of Science, Economics	CLAW	Commission for Local Administration in Wales
BScEng	Bachelor of Science, Engineering	CMG	Companion, Order of St Michael and St George
BScMet	Bachelor of Science, Metallurgy	CMO	Chief Medical Officer
BSO	Building Society Ombudsman	CNO	Chief Nursing Officer
BSocSc	Bachelor of Social Science	CO	Cabinet Office; (Office of Public Service and Science); Commanding Officer
BUPA	British United Provident Association		
BVMS	Bachelor of Veterinary Medicine and Surgery	COI	Central Office of Information
BVSc	Bachelor of Veterinary Science	CPA	Chartered Patent Agent
		CPMG	Committee on Proprietary Medicinal Products
		CPS	Crown Prosecution Service
		CQSW	Certificate of Qualification in Social Work

C

		CRE	Commission for Racial Equality
C&E	Customs and Excise	CrO(S)	Crown Office, Scotland
CA	Chartered Accountant; Chartered Accountant (Scotland)	CS	Chief Statistician
		CSC	Civil Service College
		CSD	Civil Service Department
CAA	Civil Aviation Authority	CSF	Civil Service Fellow
CADW	Welsh Historic Monuments	CSL	Central Science Laboratory
CA(NI)	Compensation Agency (NI)	CSM	Medicines Commission, Committee on Safety of Medicines
CB	Companion, Order of the Bath		
CBC	County Borough Council	CSO	Central Statistical Office
CBDE	Chemical and Biological Defence Establishment	CSolO(NI)	Crown Solicitor's Office (Northern Ireland)
CBE	Commander, Order of the British Empire	CSU	Child Support Unit
		CT	Council on Tribunals
CBIM	Companion, British Institute of Management	CTO	Capital Taxes Office, Inland Revenue
CC	County Council; Chief Constable; Charity Commission	CVL	Central Veterinary Laboratory
		CVO	Companion, Victoria Order
CChem	Chartered Chemist		
CDEP	Central Directorate of Environmental Pollution		

D

CDipAF	Certified Diploma in Accounting and Finance	DA	Diploma in Anaesthesia
CEng	Chartered Engineer	DAFS	Department of Agriculture and Fisheries for Scotland
CEO	Chief Executive Officer		
CertEd	Certificate of Education	DANI	Department of Agriculture for Northern Ireland
CEst	Crown Estate		
CFE	College of Further Education	DAQMG	Deputy Assistant Quartermaster General
ChB	Bachelor of Surgery		
CH	Companies House	DASA	Defence Analytical Services Agency
CICB	Criminal Injuries Compensation Board		
		DBE	Dame Commander, Order of the British Empire
CinC	Commander in Chief		
CLAE	Commission for Local Administration in England	DC	Deputy Chairman
		DCL	Doctor of Civil Law
CLAS	Commission for Local Administration in Scotland	DEA	Department of Economic Affairs

DEDNI	Department of Economic Development for Northern Ireland	DoEnvNI	Department of the Environment for Northern Ireland
DEmp	Department of Employment	DoH	Department of Health
DENI	Department of Education for Northern Ireland	DPCS	Defence Postal and Courier Service
DES	Department of Education and Science (now Department for Education [DfE])	DPH	Diploma in Public Health
		DPP	Director of Public Prosecutions
DfE	Department for Education	DPP(NI)	Department of the Director
DFPNI	Department of Finance and Personnel, Northern Ireland		of Public Prosecutions (Northern Ireland)
		Dr	Doctor
DG	Director General	DRA	Defence Research Agency
DGDA	Directorate General of Defence Accounts	DSA	Driving Standards Agency
		DS	Deputy Secretary
DHSS	Department of Health and Social Security	DSc	Doctor of Science
		DSO	Companion of the
DHSSNI	Department of Health and Social Security Northern Ireland		Distinguished Service Order
DI	District Inspector	DSS	Department of Social Security; Director of Social
DIC	Diploma of the Imperial College		Services
		DTI	Department of Trade and
DIH	Diploma in Industrial Health		Industry; District Tax
DipArch	Diploma in Architecture		Inspector
DipBact	Diploma in Bacteriology	DTp	Department of Transport
DipCrim	Diploma in Criminology	DUniv	Doctor of the University
DipEcon	Diploma in Economics	DVLA	Driver and Vehicle Licensing
DipEd	Diploma in Education		Agency
DipHSM	Diploma in Health Service Management	DVOIT	DVOIT
		DVSM	Diploma in Veterinary State
DipPE	Diploma in Physical Education		Medicine
DipSocSci	Diploma in Social Science	DVTA(NI)	Driver and Vehicle Testing Agency (NI)
DipStat	Diploma in Statistics	DYRMS	Duke of York's Royal
DipTP	Diploma in Town Planning		Military School
DL	Deputy Lieutenant		
DLitt	Doctor of Literature; Doctor of Letters		
DNH	Department of National Heritage		**E**
DNS	Department for National Savings	EA	Economic Adviser
DO	Dental Officer	EAD	Exchequer and Audit
DOAC	Defence Operational Analysis Centre		Department (now National Audit Office)
DObstRCOG	Diploma of the Royal College of Obstetricians and Gynaecologists	EC	European Commission
		ECGD	Export Credits Guarantee Department
DoE	Department of the Environment	Econ	Economics
		ED	Education Department, Scottish Office
DoEDNI	Department of Economic Development for Northern Ireland	EDG	Employment Department Group
DoENI	Department for Education in Northern Ireland	EEB	European Environmental Bureau

EEC	European Economic Community	FIDPM	Fellow, Institute of Data Processing Management
Eng	Engineering	FIEE	Fellow, Institution of Electrical Engineers
EOC	Equal Opportunities Commission	FIGeol	Fellow, Institution of Geologists
ES	Employment Service		
ESRC	Economic and Social Research Council	FIHT	Fellow, Institution of Highways and Transportation
		FIMechE	Fellow, Institution of Mechanical Engineers

F

		FInstPS	Fellow, Institute of Purchasing and Supply
FAPS	Fellow, American Physical Society	FIWEM	Fellow, Institution of Water and Environmental Management
FBCS	Fellow, British Computer Society	FO	Flag Officer
FBIM	Fellow, British Institute of Management	FRAeS	Fellow, Royal Aeronautical Society
FC	Forestry Commission	FRC	Financial Reporting Council
FCA	Fellow, Institute of Chartered Accountants	FRC:ASB	Financial Reporting Council, Accounting Standards Board
FCAA	Fellow, Chartered Association of Accountants	FRC:FRRP	Financial Reporting Council, Financial Reporting Review Panel
FCCA	Fellow, Chartered Association of Certified Accountants	FRCGP	Fellow, Royal College of General Practitioners
FCIA	Fellow, Chartered Institute of Arbitrators	FRCP	Fellow, Royal College of Physicians, London
FCIBS	Fellow, Chartered Institution of Building Services	FRCPEd	Fellow, Royal College of Physicians, Edinburgh
FCIS	Fellow, Institute of Chartered Secretaries and Administrators	FRCPGlas	Fellow, Royal College of Physicians and Surgeons of Glasgow
FCO	Foreign and Commonwealth Office	FRCPsych	Fellow, Royal College of Psychiatrists
FD	Finance Director	FREconS	Fellow, Royal Economic Society
FFA	Fellow, Faculty of Actuaries		
FFARCS	Fellow, Faculty of Anaesthetists, Royal College of Surgeons of England	FRGS	Fellow, Royal Geographical Society
		FRIC	Fellow, Royal Institute of Chemistry (now see FRSC)
FFOM	Fellow, Faculty of Occupational Medicine	FRICS	Fellow, Royal Institution of Chartered Surveyors
FFPHM	Fellow, Faculty of Public Health Medicine	FRPharmS	Fellow, Royal Pharmaceutical Society
FFPM	Fellow, Faculty of Pharmaceutical Medicine	FRS	Fellow, Royal Society
		FRSA	Fellow, Royal Society of Arts
FIA	Fellow, Institute of Actuaries	FRSC	Fellow, Royal Society of Chemistry
FIBiol	Fellow, Institute of Biology		
FICE	Fellow, Institution of Civil Engineers	FRSE	Fellow, Royal Society of Edinburgh
FIChemE	Fellow, Institution of Chemical Engineers	FRSS	Fellow, Royal Statistical Society
FICMA	Fellow, Institute of Cost and Management Accountants	FS	First Secretary
		FSC	Fire Service College

FSRP	Fellow, Society for Radiological Protection	**IB**	Intervention Board
FSS	Forensic Science Service	**IBRD**	International Bank for Reconstruction and Development (World Bank)

G

		ICA	Institute of Chartered Accountants
GAD	Government Actuary's Department	**ICR**	Institute of Cancer Research
GB	Gaming Board for Great Britain	**IHQP**	Insolvency Headquarters, Policy
GBE	Knight or Dame Grand Cross, Order of the British Empire	**IND**	Immigration and Nationality Department, Home Office
GCB	Knight or Dame Grand Cross, Order of the Bath	**INSEAD**	Institut Europeen d'Administration des Affaires
GRO(S)	General Register Office (Scotland)	**IOB**	Insurance Ombudsman Bureau
		IR	Inland Revenue
		IRRV	Institute of Rating Revenues and Valuation

H

		IS	Insolvency Service
		ISO	Imperial Service Order
HA	Health Authority	**IT**	Information Technology
HBLB	Horserace Betting Levy Board	**ITC**	Independent Television Commission
HC	House of Commons	**ITS**	Independent Tribunal Service
HD	Health District		
HEA	Health Education Authority		
HEFCE	Higher Education Funding Council for England		
HIE	Highlands and Islands Enterprise		

J

HL	House of Lords	**JNCC**	Joint Nature Conservation Committee
HMLR	HM Land Registry		
HMS	Her Majesty's Ship	**JP**	Justice of the Peace
HMSO	Her Majesty's Stationery Office	**jssc**	completed course at Joint Services Staff College
HMT	Her Majesty's Treasury		
HMY	Her Majesty's Yacht		
HNC	Higher National Certificate		
HO	Home Office		

K

HQ	Headquarters		
HRP	Historic Royal Palaces	**KBE**	Knight Commander, Order of the British Empire
HS	Historic Scotland		
HSC	Health and Safety Commission	**KCB**	Knight Commander, Order of the Bath
HSE	Health and Safety Commission: Health and Safety Executive	**KCMG**	Knight Commander, Order of St Michael and St George
HyO	Hydrographic Office	**KCVO**	Knight Commander, Royal Victorian Order
		KG	Knight, Order of the Garter
		KSG	Knight, Order of St Gregory the Great

I

		KStJ	Knight, Most Venerable Order of the Hospital of St John of Jerusalem
IA	Immigration Appeals, The Appellate Authorities; Inspector of Accidents	**Kt**	Knight

L

LA	Legal Assistant
LAD	Lord Advocate's Department
LBS	London Business School
LC	Law Commission; Lancashire Constabulary
LCD	Lord Chancellor's Department
LGC	Laboratory of the Government Chemist
LGF	Local Government Finance
LLB	Bachelor of Laws
LLM	Master of Laws
LOD	Law Officers' Department
LRCP	Licentiate, Royal College of Physicians, London
LSE	London School of Economics
LVO	Lieutenant, Royal Victorian Order

M

MA	Master of Arts; Ministry of Aviation
MAEcon	Master of Arts, Economics
MAFF	Ministry of Agriculture, Fisheries and Food
MB	Bachelor of Medicine
MBA	Master of Business Administration
MBCS	Member of the British Computer Society
MBE	Member, Order of the British Empire
MBIM	Member, British Institute of Management
MC	Medicines Commission; Military Cross
MCA	Medicines Control Agency
MCC	Marylebone Cricket Club
MCIBSE	Member, Chartered Institution of Building Services Engineers
MCIT	Member, Chartered Institute of Transport
MD	Managing Director; Doctor of Medicine
MEng	Master of Engineering
Met	Metallurgy
MFCM	Member, Faculty of Community Medicine
MFOM	Member, Faculty of Occupational Medicine

MGDS RCS	Member in General Dental Surgery, Royal College of Surgeons
MHSM	Member, Institute of Health Services Management
MICE	Member, Institution of Civil Engineers
MIEE	Member, Institution of Electrical Engineers
MIMarE	Member, Institute of Marine Engineers
MIMechE	Member, Institution of Mechanical Engineers
MIProdE	Member, Institution of Production Engineers (*now see* MIEE)
MIPM	Member, Institute of Personnel Management
MIPS	Member, Institute of Purchasing and Supply
MIS	Member, Institute of Statistics
MIWEM	Member, Institution of Water and Environmental Management
MMC	Monopolies and Mergers Commission
MO	Meteorological Office; Medical Officer
MoD	Ministry of Defence
MoH	Ministry of Health
MoT	Ministry of Transport
MP	Member of Parliament
MPA	Master of Public Administration
MPhil	Master of Philosophy
MPNI	Ministry of Pensions and National Insurance
MRC	Medical Research Council
MRCGP	Member, Royal College of General Practitioners
MRCP	Member, Royal College of Physicians, London
MRCPsych	Member, Royal College of Psychiatrists
MRCS	Member, Royal College of Surgeons of England
MRCVS	Member, Royal College of Veterinary Science
MRTPI	Member, Royal Town Planning Institute
MS	Master of Science (US); Military Survey
MSC	Manpower Services Commission
MSc	Master of Science
MScEcon	Master of Science, Economics

N

NAA	North Atlantic Assembly
NAB	National Assistance Board
NAO	National Audit Office
NARO	Naval Aircraft Repair Organisation
NATO	North Atlantic Treaty Organisation
NCC	National Consumer Council
NCIS	National Criminal Intelligence Service
ndc	National Defence College; NATO Defence College
NEDC	National Economic Development Council
NEL	National Engineering Laboratory
NERC	Natural Environment Research Council
NHS	National Health Service
NHSE	NHS Estates
NIAO	Northern Ireland Audit Office
NICS	Northern Ireland Court Service
NID	Northern Ireland Departments
NIO	Northern Ireland Office
NPL	National Physical Laboratory
NRA	National Rivers Authority
NRI	Natural Resources Institute
NRPB	National Radiological Protection Board
NWML	National Weights and Measures Laboratory

O

OBE	Officer, Order of the British Empire
OBO	Office of the Banking Ombudsman
OC	Officer Commanding
ODA	Overseas Development Administration
ODC(US)	Overseas Defence College (United States)
ODM	Ministry of Overseas Development
ODPR	Office of the Data Protection Registrar
OFFER	Office of Electricity Regulation
OFGAS	Office of Gas Supply
OFT	Office of Fair Trading

OFTEL	Office of Telecommunications
OFWAT	Office of Water Services
OHS	Occupational Health Service
OLSO	Office of the Legal Services Ombudsman
OMCS	Office for the Minister for the Civil Service
OME	Office of Manpower Economics
O(NI)CC	Office of the NI Commissioner for Complaints (Ombudsman)
O(NI)PCA	Office of the NI Parliamentary Commissioner for Administration (Ombudsman)
OPB	Occupational Pensions Board
OPCA/HSC	Office of the Parliamentary Commissioner for Administration and Health Service Commissioners (Ombudsman)
OPCS	Office of Population Censuses and Surveys
OPSS	Office of Public Service and Science
OR	Operations Research
OS	Ordnance Survey
OS(NI)	Ordnance Survey (NI)
OSO	Office of Offshore Supplies
OStJ	Most Venerable Order of the Hospital of St John of Jerusalem
OUP	Oxford University Press

P

PA(NI)	Police Authority for NI
PB(EW)	Parole Board for England and Wales
PB(S)	Parole Board for Scotland
PC	Parliamentary Counsel; Privy Counsellor
PCA	Police Complaints Authority
PCC	Press Complaints Commission
PCFC	Polytechnics and Colleges Funding Council
PCO	Privy Council Office
PE	Principal Engineer Procurement Executive; Principal Examiner
PEFO	Principal Establishment and Finance Officer

PF	Procurator Fiscal	RCA(NI)	Rate Collection Agency (NI)
PGCE	Postgraduate Certificate in Education	rcds	completed a course, or served for a year on the staff of Royal College of Defence Studies
PhB	Bachelor of Philosophy		
PhD	Doctor of Philosophy		
PHSC	Political Honours Scrutiny Committee	RCOG	Royal College of Obstetricians and Gynaecologists
PI	Planning Inspector		
PIA	Planning Inspectorate Agency	RCP	Royal College of Physicians, London
PMO	Principal Medical Officer; Prime Minister's Office	RCPEdinburgh	Royal College of Physicians, Edinburgh
PM	Prime Minister	RFS	Registry of Friendly Societies
PO	Patent Office(r); Probation Officer; Pensions Ombudsman	RHA	Regional Health Authority
		RIBA	Royal Institute of British Architects
PPS	Principal Private Secretary; Parliamentary Private Secretary	RICS	Royal Institution of Chartered Surveyors
		RM	Royal Mint
PRO	Public Record Office	RMA	Royal Military Academy
PS	Private Secretary	RMCS	Royal Military College of Science
PSA	Property Services Agency; PSA Services	RN	Royal Navy
psc	Graduate of Staff College († indicates Graduate of Senior Wing Staff College)	RNAS	Royal Naval Air Service
		RNH	Royal Naval Hospital
		RS	Registers of Scotland
psc(N)	Graduate of Staff College (Navy)		
PS	Private Secretary		
PTM	Panel on Takeovers and Mergers		

S

		SACHR	Standing Advisory Commission for Human Rights

Q

		SASA	Scottish Agricultural Science Agency
QC	Queen's Counsel	SC	Security Commission
QECC	Queen Elizabeth II Conference Centre	SCA	Scottish Courts Administration
QHDS	Queen's Honorary Dental Surgeon	SCC	Scottish Consumer Council
		ScD	Doctor of Science
QHP	Queen's Honorary Physician	SCS(NWE)	Service Children's Schools (NW Europe)
QHS	Queen's Honorary Surgeon		
QVS	Queen Victoria School	SDD	Scottish Development Department
		SE	Scottish Enterprise
		SED	Scottish Education Department

R

		SFO	Serious Fraud Office
RA	Radio Authority; Radiocommunications Agency; Royal Artillery	SFPA	Scottish Fisheries Protection Agency
		SHHD	Scottish Home and Health Department
RADC	Royal Army Dental College		
RAF	Royal Air Force	SIB	Securities and Investments Board (inc FIMBRA, LAUTRO, IMRO and SFA)
RAFSCMG	RAF Support Command Maintenance Group		
RASA	Recruitment and Assessment Services Agency	SJD	Doctor of Juristic Science

SLC	Scottish Law Commission
SLSO	Scottish Legal Services Ombudsman
SO	Scientific Officer; Scottish Office; Staff Officer
SoS	Secretary of State
SPO	Senior Patent Officer
SRM	State Registered Midwife
SRN	State Registered Nurse
SRO	Scottish Record Office
SS	Second Secretary, Steamship; Security Service
SSA(NI)	Social Security Agency (NI)
SSBA	Social Security Benefits Agency
SSC	Sea Systems Controllerate
SSCA	Social Security Contributions Agency
SSITSA	Social Security Information Technology Services Agency
SSRA	Social Security Resettlement Agency
SST	Security Service Tribunal

T

TA	Territorial Army
TD	Territorial Efficiency Decoration
TEA(NI)	Training and Employment Agency(NI)
TI	Tax Inspector
TPA	Teachers' Pension Agency
TRL	Transport Research Laboratory
TS	Third Secretary
TSD	Treasury Solicitor's Department
tt	Tank Technology Course

U

UCLA	University of California, Los Angeles
UFC	Universities Funding Council
UK	United Kingdom
UK Perm Rep	UK Permament Representation, Brussels
UKAEA	UK Atomic Energy Authority
UKPA	UK Passport Agency
UN	United Nations
US	Under Secretary
USA	United States of America

V

VAT	Value Added Tax
VCA	Vehicle Certification Agency
VI	Vehicle Inspectorate
VMD	Veterinary Medicines Directorate
VO	Veterinary Officer
VOA	Valuation Office Agency
VRD	Royal Naval Volunteer Reserve Officers' Decoration
VSO	Voluntary Service Overseas

W

WCC	Welsh Consumer Council
WDA	Welsh Development Agency
WO	Welsh Office
WPCC	Wilton Park Conference Centre
WSL	Warren Spring Laboratory

Name Index

An alphabetical list of people whose names appear in *The Whitehall Companion*. See *Abbreviations* for full names of departments and other organisations.

Index